Fodor's

BEST OF ITALY

WELCOME TO ITALY

Timelessly elegant, Italy's great cities are some of the most magical places in Europe. Rome, Florence, and Venice are home to awe-inspiring art and architecture, iconic museums, and stunning historical ruins—as well as some of the world's best food, wine, and shopping. Also beckoning are the sun-kissed olive groves and vineyards, charming hill towns, and atmospheric castles, monastaries, and farmhouses of the Tuscan and Umbrian countryside. Once you've been to Italy, it's easy to undertand why travelers return again and again.

TOP REASONS TO GO

★ **Food:** Italy is a pasta lover's paradise, but don't forget the pizza and the gelato.

★ **Romance:** Whether you're strolling atmospheric Venice or sipping wine, Italy enchants.

★ **History:** The ruins of ancient Rome and the leaning tower of Pisa breathe antiquity.

★ **Art:** The big hitters—Botticelli, Michelangelo, Raphael, Caravaggio, and more.

★ **Shopping:** Few things say quality or style like "made in Italy."

★ **Stunning landscapes:** Tuscany, Umbria, the Cinque Terre, to name just a few.

Fodor's BEST OF ITALY

Editorial: Douglas Stallings, *Editorial Director*; Salwa Jabado and Margaret Kelly, *Senior Editors*; Alexis Kelly, Jacinta O'Halloran, and Amanda Sadlowski, *Editors*; Teddy Minford, *Associate Editor*; Rachael Roth, *Content Manager*

Design: Tina Malaney, *Art Director*

Photography: Jennifer Arnow, *Senior Photo Editor*

Maps: Rebecca Baer, *Senior Map Editor*; David Lindroth, Mark Stroud (Moon Street Cartography), *Cartographers*

Production: Jennifer DePrima, *Editorial Production Manager*; Carrie Parker, *Senior Production Editor*; Elyse Rozelle, *Production Editor*; David Satz, *Director of Content Production*

Business & Operations: Chuck Hoover, *Chief Marketing Officer*; Joy Lai, *Vice President and General Manager*; Stephen Horowitz, *Head of Business Development and Partnerships*

Public Relations: Joe Ewaskiw, *Manager*

Writers: Ariston Anderson, Nicole Arriaga, Peter Blackman, Agnes Crawford, Liz Humphreys, Fergal Kavnagh, Bruce Leimsidor, Megan MacCaffrey-Guerrera, Maria Pasquale, Patricia Rucidlo

Editor: Amanda Sadlowski

Production Editor: Carrie Parker

Production Design: Liliana Guia

1st Edition

ISBN 978-0-14-754715-6

ISSN 2476-0951

PRINTED IN THE UNITED STATES OF AMERICA

10 9 8 7 6 5 4 3 2 1

CONTENTS

Fodor's Features

MAPS

ABOUT THIS GUIDE

Fodor's Recommendations

Everything in this guide is worth doing—we don't cover what isn't—but exceptional sights, hotels, and restaurants are recognized with additional accolades. Fodor'sChoice★ indicates our top recommendations. Care to nominate a new place? Visit Fodors.com/contact-us.

Trip Costs

We list prices wherever possible to help you budget well. Hotel and restaurant price categories from $ to $$$$ are noted alongside each recommendation. For hotels, we include the lowest cost of a standard double room in high season. For restaurants, we cite the average cost of a meal. The meal includes three courses: *primo* (usually pasta or an appetizer), *secondo* (meat or fish main course), and *dolce* (dessert). For attractions, we always list adult admission fees; discounts are usually available for children, students, and senior citizens.

Hotels

Our local writers vet every hotel to recommend the best overnights in each price category, from budget to expensive. Unless otherwise specified, you can expect private bath, phone, and TV in your room. For expanded hotel reviews visit Fodors.com.

Top Picks	Hotels &
★ Fodor'sChoice	Restaurants
	☒ Hotel
Listings	⤵ Number of
⊠ Address	rooms
⊠ Branch address	⑂ Meal plans
☎ Telephone	✕ Restaurant
🖷 Fax	⌣ Reservations
⊕ Website	🏛 Dress code
✑ E-mail	▭ No credit cards
🎫 Admission fee	⑃ Price
☉ Open/closed	
times	**Other**
Ⓜ Subway	⇨ See also
✛ Directions or	☞ Take note
Map coordinates	⚐ Golf facilities

Restaurants

Unless we state otherwise, restaurants are open for lunch and dinner daily. We mention dress code only when there's a specific requirement and reservations only when they're essential or not accepted.

Credit Cards

The hotels and restaurants in this guide typically accept credit cards. If not, we'll say so.

EUGENE FODOR

Hungarian-born Eugene Fodor (1905–91) began his travel career as an interpreter on a French cruise ship. The experience inspired him to write *On the Continent* (1936), the first guidebook to receive annual updates and discuss a country's way of life as well as its sights. Fodor later joined the U.S. Army and worked for the OSS in World War II. After the war, he kept up his intelligence work while expanding his guidebook series. During the Cold War, many guides were written by fellow agents who understood the value of insider information. Today's guides continue Fodor's legacy by providing travelers with timely coverage, insider tips, and cultural context.

EXPERIENCE ITALY

1

WHAT'S WHERE

Numbers correspond to the book's chapter numbers.

2 Rome. Italy's capital is one of the greatest cities in Europe. It's a large, busy metropolis that lives in the here and now, yet there's no other place on earth where you'll encounter such powerful evocations of a storied and spectacular past, from the Colosseum to St. Peter's.

3 Venice. One of the world's most unusual—and most beautiful—cities, Venice has canals instead of streets, along with an atmosphere of faded splendor. It's also a major international cultural center.

4 Northern Italy. In the **Veneto** region of Italy, the green plains stretching west of Venice hold three of northern Italy's most artistically significant midsize cities: **Padua, Vicenza,** and **Verona.** To the west is **Milan,** Italy's second-largest city and its business capital. It holds Italy's most renowned opera house, and as the hub of Italian fashion and design, it's a shopper's paradise. Northern Italy's attractive coastline runs along the Italian Riviera and includes **Cinque Terre** and its famous hiking trails and villages. Many of Italy's signature foods come from the **Emilia-Romagna** region, where **Bologna** is a significant

cultural center and the mosaics of **Ravenna** are glittering Byzantine treasures.

5 Florence. In the 15th century, Florence was at the center of an artistic revolution, later labeled the Renaissance, which changed the way people saw the world. Five hundred years later the Renaissance remains the reason people visit Florence—the abundance of treasures found here is mind-boggling.

6 Tuscany and Umbria. Outside of Florence, the town of **Lucca** is laid-back yet elegant while **Pisa** is still famous for its leaning tower and other impressive buildings. The hills spreading south of Florence make up **Chianti,** a region of sublime wine and fabulous views. South of Chianti, hillside towns like **Arezzo** and **Cortona** offer stunning architecture and gorgeous views of the countryside. In Tuscany, **Siena,** once Florence's main rival, remains one of Italy's most appealing medieval towns. **Umbria,** north of Rome, is a region of beautiful rolling hills topped by attractive old towns full of history, like **Orvieto, Spoleto, Perugia,** and **Assisi,** the birthplace of Saint Francis.

Elevation	
15,577	4,748
10,825	3,300
9,840	3,000
8,860	2,700
7,875	2,400
6,900	2,100
5,900	1,800
4,920	1,500
3,940	1,200
2,920	900
1,970	600
980	300
490	150
250	75
100	30
feet	meters

NEED TO KNOW

ITALY
Rome
SARDINIA
SICILY
Mediterranean Sea

AT A GLANCE

Capital: Rome

Population: 60,920,000

Currency: Euro

Money: ATMs are common; cash is more common than credit.

Language: Italian

Country Code: 29

Emergencies: 112

Driving: On the right

Electricity: 200v/50 cycles; electrical plugs have two round prongs.

Time: Six hours ahead of New York

Documents: Up to 90 days with valid passport; Schengen rules apply.

Mobile Phones: GSM (900 and 1800 bands)

Major Mobile Companies: Vodafone, TIM, Wind, Tre

WEBSITES

Italy: ⊕ www.italia.it

Farm stays:
⊕ www.agriturismo.it

Culture:
⊕ www.beniculturali.it

GETTING AROUND

✈ **Air Travel:** The major airports are Rome, Milan, Bergamo, and Venice.

🚌 **Bus Travel:** Good for smaller towns and the best way to travel the Amalfi Coast.

🚗 **Car Travel:** Rent a car to explore at your own pace, but never to use in the cities themselves (including Rome and Florence). Always rent a GPS along with the car, as Italy's roads can be confounding. Gas is very expensive.

🚆 **Train Travel:** Excellent and fast between major cities. Slower regional trains connect many smaller towns, as well.

PLAN YOUR BUDGET

	HOTEL ROOM	MEAL	ATTRACTIONS
Low Budget	€140	€25	Visiting Florence's Duomo, free
Mid Budget	€290	€45	Ticket to the Vatican and the Sistine Chapel, €16
High Budget	€350	€60	Evening gondola ride in Venice, €150

WAYS TO SAVE

Stay at an *agriturismo*. Farm stays are Italy's best-kept secret. In beautiful settings, they sometimes include meals and are often for half the price of a hotel.

Drink from the free fountains. No need to buy bottled water; fill up at the free public fountains, especially in Rome.

Book rail tickets in advance. Book online (⊕ www.trenitalia.com) at least a week in advance for half the price.

Enjoy aperitivo. This northern Italian tradition entails a drink and a buffet (light or heavy) for about €8–€10.

PLAN YOUR TIME

Hassle Factor	Low. Flights to Rome, Milan, and Venice are frequent, and Italy has great transport elsewhere.
3 days	You can see some of the magic of Rome and perhaps take a day trip to Pompeii or Florence.
1 week	Spend time in Rome with a day trip to Pompeii, Umbria, or the Amalfi coast, as well as an additional day or two in Florence. Alternatively, tour the main cities with three days in Rome, two in Florence, and one in Venice.
2 weeks	You have time to move around and for the highlights, including stops in Rome, Florence, and Venice, excursions to Pompeii, Naples, and the Amalfi coast, and a trip to beautiful Tuscany or Umbria.

WHEN TO GO

High Season: June through September is expensive and busy. In August, most Italians take their own summer holidays; cities are less crowded, but many shops and restaurants close. July and August can be uncomfortably hot.

Low Season: Unless you are skiing, winter offers the least appealing weather, though it's the best time for airfare and hotel deals and to escape the crowds. Temperatures are still mild, especially in the south.

Value Season: By late September, temperate weather, saner airfares, and more cultural events can make for a happier trip. October is also great, but November is often rainy and (hence) quiet. From late April to early May, the masses have not yet arrived but cafés are already abuzz. March and early April can be changeable and wet.

BIG EVENTS

February: Carnival kicks off across Venice and around Italy. ⊕ www.carnevaleitaliano.it

April: Religious processions commemorate Easter. On Pasquetta (Easter Monday), most Italians picnic.

June: The Festa della Repubblica commemorates Italy's 1946 vote for the republic. ⊕ www.festadellarepubblica.it

October: Alba's Fiera del Tartufo is devoted to the area's white truffles. ⊕ www.fieradeltartufo.org

READ THIS

■ *Delizia! The Epic History of the Italians and Their Food,* John Dickie. A history of Italian flavors.

■ *Under the Tuscan Sun,* Frances Mayes. The memoir that launched a thousand Tuscan trips.

■ *Neapolitan Novels,* Elena Ferrante. A four-volume series focusing on two best friends growing up in Naples.

WATCH THIS

■ *Roman Holiday.* The 1953 classic starring Audrey Hepburn—and, of course, Rome.

■ *La Dolce Vita.* Fellini's famous study of glitzy 1950s Italy.

■ *Il Postino.* Romance in an Italian fishing village.

EAT THIS

■ *Mozzarella di bufala*: a specialty of Campania and the south.

■ *Prosciutto crudo*: tender, dry-cured ham, especially from Parma and San Daniele.

■ *Pasta carbonara*: a Roman dish of eggs, guanciale, cheese, and pepper.

■ *Wine*: from Barolo to Chianti.

■ *Sfogliatelle*: a layered and filled southern Italian pastry.

WHAT'S NEW

Steeped in history and tradition, and bearing a lustrous patina of antiquity, Italy luxuriates in the illusion that change comes slowly—or maybe not at all—in the *bel paese*. Despite the ravages of war and urban renewal, Italians have skillfully retained so much of the past that it seems the historical centers of many Italian cities would be easily recognizable to residents of 350 years ago. The present and the past merge seamlessly. Tiny cars and whining scooters in Italian cities and towns maneuver without missing a beat through narrow cobblestone streets designed for horses and carriages.

Modern Design

The pervasiveness of the past also makes us forget that Italy, not by breaking with tradition but rather by continuing it, has been in the forefront of producing major monuments of contemporary style. By creating everything from skyscrapers to sports cars, raincoats to coffeepots, today's Italian designers and architects have infused beauty into the everyday lives of people around the world. In so doing, they have proved themselves to be true sons and daughters of the Renaissance, heirs to Brunelleschi and Leonardo da Vinci, who combined beauty and functionality to create marvelous works of art.

Despite Italy's ties to the past, "modern" and "Italian design" have become almost synonymous. Perhaps because Italy (or more exactly, Milan) has become the epicenter of the fashion and design world, Italians seem to be more obsessed with fashion and the "new" than other Europeans are. While you'll easily be able to buy your choice of a classic suit or dress for business wear, for casual wear you'll have to look hard for a sweater or shirt that's not in the very latest season's color or cut. And be forewarned: there's zero tolerance for anything even slightly worn or frayed.

Politics

Visitors also tend to forget that Italy is one of Western Europe's newest countries, having been unified only in 1861. Before that, Italy was divided into myriad states, some at times independent and glorious, but, since the Renaissance, mainly under the domination of Spain, France, Austria, or the Papal States. To this day, most Italians identify more strongly with their region or city than with the Italian nation, and local cultural and even linguistic differences are still valued.

The variety and contrast between Italian regions, an inheritance from its centuries-long division, while making Italy a fascinating place to visit, has hindered its development as a modern nation-state. Many Italians thought new man Silvio Berlusconi would usher in reform. Others thought progress would come from submitting to an ever-stronger guiding hand from the European Union. Then Berlusconi embarrassed himself out of power, just as the 2008 financial crisis left Italy's economy reeling.

By insisting on austerity at all costs, even the EU has lost favor with most Italians. Young prime minister Matteo Renzi had support when he first gained power in 2014, but the recent tide of populism spreading through Europe reached Italy in late 2016, when a constitutional referendum to amend parts of the Italian Constitution was overwhelmingly defeated by voters and Renzi stepped down in response to what he saw as a vote against his government. President Sergio Mattarella instated Paolo Gentiloni as prime minister in December 2016, keeping with the center left policies of Renzi, but many believe the president will still be calling for an election to find a permanent replacement.

Immigration

Italians long enjoyed a reputation for being friendly and hospitable to those down on their luck, but lately this has changed. Although Italy has received more migrants and refugees than it has exported since the 1970s, this trend has grown to alarming proportions over the last two decades. This increased immigration has had no effect either on crime or the unemployment rate. Nevertheless, xenophobes and opportunists fanned the flames of fear and promoted policies that brought Italy under the scrutiny of European human rights monitors. Italian friendliness and hospitality, however, haven't entirely disappeared; even those who complain about immigrants will then contribute generously to charities assisting them, and incidents of violence against immigrants remain less frequent in Italy than in neighboring countries, where recently governments have also been bolting their doors, as the financial situation in Europe and the Syrian refugee crisis remains precarious.

Religion

Rome is still the spiritual home of the world's 1.1 billion Catholics, but, as in other European countries, church attendance in Italy has been eroding since the 1950s, and today fewer than one in five Italians attend church regularly. The April 2013 papal election of the Argentinean cardinal Jorge Mario Bergoglio, who took the name of Francis, appears to have burnished the image of the church, even in the eyes of many non-Catholics.

Meanwhile, the Conference of Bishops still wields considerable political influence and is not expected to alter its conservative stance on birth control, same-sex relationships, and a greater participation of women in the Church any time soon.

And although the Italian Constitution (1948) proclaims that Italy is a secular state, a crucifix still adorns all courts and schoolrooms, and if you're unlucky enough to land in jail, a statue of the Madonna is likely to greet you as you enter. The Italian courts have ruled crucifixes can stay where they are, reasoning that they are merely innocuous symbols of Italy's cultural heritage, and not symbols of religious allegiance.

Transportation

Romans are still patiently awaiting the completion of the new Metro C subway line (started in 2007), which will cut through the city center with stops at Piazza Venezia and link with both the A and the B lines at Ottaviano for St. Peter's and the Colosseum, respectively. Expected to considerably ease surface-traffic congestion, the new line progresses slowly, because every time a shaft is sunk in Roman ground, some important archaeological site comes to light and all work halts while it is investigated. The planned station at Piazza Torre Argentina, in fact, had to be canceled due to the wealth of material uncovered. In November 2014, the surface rail part out to Monte Compatri and a few underground stations to the still relatively peripheral Parco di Centocelle were opened. The section through central Rome, with connection to the other lines is still a ways off, however.

BEST OF ITALY
TOP ATTRACTIONS

The Vatican, Rome

(A) The home of the Roman Catholic Church, Vatican City, a tiny independent state tucked within central Rome, holds some of the city's most spectacular sights, including St. Peter's Basilica, the Vatican Museums, and Michelangelo's Sistine Chapel ceiling.

Ancient Rome

(B) The Colosseum and the Roman Forum are remarkable ruins from Rome's ancient past. Sitting above it all is the Campidoglio, with a piazza designed by Michelangelo and museums containing one of the world's finest collections of ancient art.

Galleria Borghese, Rome

Only the best could satisfy the aesthetic taste of Cardinal Scipione Borghese, whose holdings evoke the essence of Baroque Rome. Spectacularly painted ceilings and colored marble frame great Bernini sculptures and paintings by Caravaggio, Titian, and Raphael, among others.

Basilica di San Francesco, Assisi

(C) The giant basilica—made up of two churches, one built on top of the other— honors St. Francis with its remarkable fresco cycles.

Piazza del Campo, Siena, Tuscany

(D) Siena is Tuscany's classic medieval hill town, and its heart is the Piazza del Campo, the beautiful, one-of-a-kind town square.

Galleria degli Uffizi, Florence

The Uffizi—Renaissance art's hall of fame—contains masterpieces by Leonardo, Michelangelo, Raphael, Botticelli, Caravaggio, and dozens of other luminaries.

Duomo, Florence

(E) The massive dome of Florence's Cathedral of Santa Maria del Fiore (aka the Duomo) is one of the world's greatest feats of engineering.

Ravenna's Mosaics, Emilia-Romagna

This town off the Adriatic Sea, once the capital of the Western Roman Empire and seat of the Byzantine Empire in the West, is home to 5th- and 6th-century mosaics that rank among the greatest art treasures in Italy.

Giotto's Frescoes in the Scrovegni Chapel, Padua

(F) A contemporary of Dante, Giotto decorated this chapel with an eloquent and beautiful fresco cycle. Its convincing human dimension helped to change the course of Western art.

Palladio's Villas and Palazzi, Northern Italy

(G) The 16th-century genius Andrea Palladio is one of the most influential figures in the history of architecture. You can visit his creations in his hometown of Vicenza, in and around Venice, and outside Treviso.

Piazza San Marco, Venice

The centerpiece of Venice's main square is the Basilica di San Marco, arguably the most beautiful Byzantine church in the West, with not only its shimmering Byzantine Romanesque facade, but also its jewel-like mosaic-encrusted interior.

The Grand Canal, Venice

(H) A trip down Venice's "Main Street," whether by water bus or gondola, is a signature Italian experience.

ITALY'S TOP EXPERIENCES

Relaxing Like an Italian

Il dolce far niente, or "the sweetness of doing nothing," has long been an art form in Italy. This is a country in which life's pleasures are warmly celebrated, not guiltily indulged.

Of course, doing "nothing" doesn't really mean nothing. It means doing things differently: lingering over a glass of wine for the better part of an evening as you watch the sun slowly set; savoring a slow and flirtatious evening *passeggiata* (stroll) along the main street of a little town; and making a commitment—however temporary—to thinking that there's nowhere that you have to be next, and no other time but the magical present.

Driving the Back Roads

If you associate Italian roads with unruly motorists and endless traffic snarls, you're only partly right. Along the rural back roads, things are more relaxed. You might stop on a lark to take a picture of a crumbling farmhouse, have a coffee in a time-stood-still hill town, or enjoy an epic lunch at a rustic *agriturismo* inaccessible to public transportation. Driving, in short, is the best way to see Italy.

Hiking in the Footsteps of Saint Francis

Umbria, which bills itself as "Italy's Green Heart," is fantastic hiking country. Among the many options are two with a Franciscan twist: from the town of Cannara, 16 km (10 miles) south of Assisi, an easy half-hour walk leads to the fields of Pian d'Arca, where St. Francis delivered his sermon to the birds. For slightly more demanding walks, you can follow the saint's path from Assisi to the Ermeo delle Carceri (Hermitage of Prisons), where Francis and his followers went to "imprison" themselves in prayer,

and from here continue along the trails that crisscross Monte Subasio.

Wine-Tasting in Chianti

The gorgeous hills of the Chianti region, between Florence and Siena, produce exceptional wines, and they never taste better than when sampled on their home turf. Many Chianti vineyards are visitor-friendly, but the logistics of a visit are different from what you may have experienced in other wine regions. If you just drop in, you're likely to get a tasting, but for a tour you usually need to make an appointment several days ahead of time. The upside is that your tour may end up being a half day of full immersion—including extended conversation with the winemakers and even a meal.

Eating in Bologna

Italians recognize Emilia as the star of its culinary culture and Bologna as its epicenter. Many dishes native to Bologna, such as the slow-cooked meat-and-tomato sauce sugo alla Bolognese, have become so famous that they're widely available throughout Italy and abroad. But you owe it to yourself to try them in the city where they were born, and where they remain a subject of local pride. Take note, however: in Bologna, a sugo is never served with spaghetti, but rather with tagliatelle, lasagna, or tortellini.

Visiting a Church

Few images are more identifiable with Italy than the country's great churches, amazing works of architecture that often took centuries to build. The name "Duomo" (derived from the Latin *domus,* or house) is used to refer to the principal church of a town or city. Generally speaking, the bigger the city, the more splendid its Duomo.

Still, impressive churches inhabit some unlikely places—in the Umbrian hill towns of **Assisi** and **Orvieto,** for example. In Venice the Byzantine-influenced **Basilica di San Marco** is a testament to the city's East-meets-West character. **Milan's Duomo** is the largest, most imposing Gothic cathedral in Italy. The spectacular dome of **Florence's Duomo** is a work of engineering genius. The **Basilica di San Pietro** in Rome has all the grandeur you'd expect from the seat of the Roman Catholic Church.

Discovering the Cinque Terre

Along the Italian Riviera east of Genoa are five fishing villages known collectively as the Cinque Terre. The beauty of the landscape—with vine-covered hills pushing against an azure sea—and the charm of the villages have turned the area into one of Italy's top destinations. The number one activity is hiking the trails that link the villages—the views are once-in-a-lifetime gorgeous—but if hiking isn't your thing, you can still have fun lounging about in cafés, admiring the water, and wandering through the medieval streets.

Shopping in Milan

Italian clothing and furniture design are world famous, and the center of the Italian design industry is Milan. The best way to see what's happening in the world of fashion is to browse the showrooms and boutiques of the fabled quadrilatero della moda, along and around Via Montenapoleone. The main event in the world of furniture design is Milan's annual Salone Internazionale del Mobile, held at the Milan fairgrounds for a week in April. Admission is generally restricted to the trade, but the Salone is open to the general public for one day, generally on a Sunday, during the week of the show.

Celebrating the Festivals of Venice

Few people love a good party as much as the Venetians. The biggest is, of course, **Carnevale,** culminating on Fat Tuesday, but with revelry beginning about 10 days earlier. Hundreds of thousands of visitors from the world over come to enjoy a period of institutionalized fantasy, dressing in exquisitely elaborate costumes. The program changes each year and includes public, mostly free cultural events in all districts of the city.

The **Redentore,** on the third weekend in July, is a festival essentially for Venetians, but in recent years more and more guests have come to view the festivities and now actually outnumber the locals. The Venetians pack a picnic dinner and eat in boats decorated with paper lanterns in the Bacino di San Marco or on tables set up for private parties along the canals. Just before midnight, there's a magnificent fireworks display. After the fireworks, young people head for the Lido, where there is dancing on the beach until dawn. The next day (Sunday), everyone crosses a temporary bridge spanning the Canale della Giudecca to Palladio's Redentore church to light a candle.

Venice Biennale is a cutting-edge international art exposition held in odd-numbered years from June to November in exhibition halls in the Venice Public Gardens (Giardini) and in the 14th-century industrial complex (Le Corderie) in the Arsenale. It's the most important exhibition of contemporary art in Italy and one of the three most important in Europe. In even-numbered years the Biennale devotes itself to architecture, and the Biennale di Architettura has become a must for those interested in contemporary architecture.

QUINTESSENTIAL ITALY

Il Caffè (Coffee)

The Italian day begins and ends with coffee, and more cups of coffee punctuate the time in between. To live like the Italians do, drink as they drink, standing at the counter or sitting at an outdoor table of the corner bar. (In Italy, a "bar" is a coffee bar.) A primer: *caffè* means coffee, and Italian standard issue is what Americans call espresso—short and strong. *Cappuccino* is a foamy half-and-half of espresso and steamed milk; cocoa powder (*cacao*) on top is acceptable, and sometimes cinnamon, too.

If you're thinking of having a cappuccino for dessert, think again—some Italians drink only caffè or caffè *macchiato* (with a spot of steamed milk) after lunchtime. However, if that's what you want, by all means order it: many Italians do, too. Confused? Homesick? Order caffè *americano* for a reasonable facsimile of good-old filtered joe. Note that you usually pay for your coffee first, then take your receipt to the counter and order.

Il Calcio (Soccer)

Imagine the most rabid American football fans—the ones who paint their faces on game day and sleep in pajamas emblazoned with the logo of their favorite team. Throw in a dose of melodrama along the lines of a tear-jerking soap opera. Ratchet up the intensity by a factor of 10, and you'll start to get a sense of how Italians feel about their national game, soccer—known in the mother tongue as *calcio*. On Sunday afternoons during the long September-to-May season, stadiums are packed throughout Italy.

Those who don't get to games in person tend to congregate around televisions in restaurants and bars, rooting for the home team with a passion that feels like a last vestige of the days when the country was a series of warring medieval city-states. How calcio mania affects your stay in

If you want to get a sense of contemporary Italian culture and indulge in some of its pleasures, start by familiarizing yourself with the rituals of daily life. These are a few highlights—things you can take part in with relative ease.

Italy depends on how eager you are to get involved. At the very least, you may notice an eerie Sunday-afternoon quiet on the city streets, or erratic restaurant service around the same time, accompanied by cheers and groans from a neighboring room. If you want a memorable, truly Italian experience, attend a game yourself. Availability of tickets may depend on the current fortunes of the local team, but they often can be acquired with help from your hotel concierge.

Il Gelato (Ice Cream)

During warmer months, *gelato*—the Italian equivalent of ice cream—is a national obsession. Although it's often on restaurant menus, it's usually considered more a snack than a dessert, bought at stands and shops in piazzas and on street corners, and consumed on foot, usually at a leisurely stroll. Gelato is softer, less creamy, more intensely flavored, and less sugary than its American counterpart.

It comes in simple flavors that capture the essence of the main ingredient. Pick from conventional choices like pistachio, *nocciola* (hazelnut), caffè, and numerous fresh-fruit varieties, or try new flavors, such as Chianti gelato in Florence. Quality varies; the surest sign that you've hit on a good spot is a line at the counter.

La Passeggiata (Strolling)

A favorite Italian pastime is *la passeggiata* (literally, "the promenade"). In the late afternoon and early evening, especially on weekends, couples, families, and packs of teenagers stroll the main streets and piazzas of Italy's towns. It's a ritual of exchanged news and gossip, window-shopping and flirting that adds up to a uniquely Italian experience. To join in, simply hit the streets for a bit of wandering. You may feel more like an observer than a participant, until you realize that observation is what la passeggiata is all about.

GREAT ITINERARIES

VENICE, FLORENCE, ROME, AND HIGHLIGHTS IN BETWEEN

This itinerary is designed for maximum impact. Think of it as a rough draft for you to revise according to your own interests and time constraints.

Day 1: Venice

Arrive in Venice's Marco Polo Airport (there are direct flights from the United States), hop on the bus into the main bus station in Venice, then check into your hotel, get out, and get lost in the back canals for a couple of hours before dinner. If you enjoy fish, you should indulge yourself at a traditional Venetian restaurant. There's no better place for sweet, delicate Adriatic seafood.

Logistics: At the airport, avoid the Alilaguna boat into Venice on arrival. It's expensive, slow, and singularly unromantic. The bus is quick and cheap—save the romance for later. When you get to the main station, transfer to the most delightful main-street "bus" in the world: the *vaporetto* ferry. Enjoy your first ride up the Grand Canal, and make sure you're paying attention to the *fermata* (or stop) where you need to get off. As for water taxis from the airport to the city, they're very expensive, although they'll take you directly to your hotel.

Day 2: Venice

Begin by skipping the coffee at your hotel and have a real Italian coffee at a real Italian coffee shop. Spend the day at Venice's top sights, including the Basilica di San Marco, Palazzo Ducale, and Galleria dell'Accademia; don't forget Piazza San Marco, which is probably the densest concentration of major artistic and cultural monuments in the world. The

TIPS

■ The itinerary can also be completed by car on the modern *autostrade* (four-lane highway system), although you'll run into dicey traffic in Florence and Rome. For obvious reasons, you're best off waiting to pick up your car until Day 3, when you leave Venice.

■ When it comes to trains, aim for the reservations-only Eurostar Italia or the relative newcomer to the scene, Italo.

■ The sights along this route are highly touristed; you'll have a better time if you make the trip outside the busy months of June, July, and August.

intense anticipation as you near the giant square through a maze of tiny shop-lined alleys and streets climaxes in the stunning view of the piazza (return at 7 am the next morning to see it *senza popolo* [without people], when it will look like a Canaletto painting come alive). Stop for lunch, perhaps sampling Venice's traditional specialty, *sarde in saor* (sardines in a mouthwatering sweet-and-sour preparation that includes onions and raisins), and be sure to check out the fish market at the foot of the Rialto Bridge; then sunset at the Zattere before dinner. Later, stop at one of the bars around the Campo San Luca or Campo Santa Margarita, where you can toast to being free of automobiles.

Logistics: Venice is best seen by wandering. The day's activities can be done on foot, with the occasional vaporetto ride if you feel the urge to be on the water. Never leave your lodgings without a city map: Venice is very easy to get totally lost in.

Day 3: Ferrara/Bologna

Get an early start and leave Venice on a Bologna-bound train. The ride to Ferrara, your first stop in Emilia-Romagna, is about an hour and a half. Visit the Castello Estense and Duomo before grabbing lunch. A panino and a beer at one of Ferrara's cafés should fit the bill. Wander Ferrara's cobblestone streets, then hop on the train to Bologna (a ride of less than an hour). Once you've arrived, check into your hotel and walk around Piazza Maggiore before dinner. Later you can check out some of northern Italy's best nightlife.

Logistics: In Ferrara, the train station lies a bit outside the city center, so you may want to take a taxi or a less-expensive city bus into town (though the distance is easily walkable, too). Going out, there's a taxi stand near the back of the castle, toward Corso Ercole I d'Este. In Bologna the walk into town from the station is more manageable, particularly if you're staying along Via dell'Indipendenza.

Day 4: Bologna/Florence

After breakfast, check out some of Bologna's churches and piazzas, including a climb up the leaning Torre degli Asinelli for a red-rooftop-studded panorama. After lunch, head back to the train station and take the short ride to Florence. You'll arrive in time for an afternoon siesta and an evening passeggiata.

Logistics: Florence's Santa Maria Novella train station is within easy access to some hotels, and farther from others. Florence's traffic is legendary, but taxis at the station are plentiful. (The taxi stand is just outside the station.)

Day 5: Florence

This is your day to see the sights of Florence. Start with the Uffizi Gallery (reserve your tickets in advance), where you'll see Botticelli's *Primavera* and *Birth of Venus*. Next, walk to Piazza del Duomo, the site of Brunelleschi's spectacular dome, which you can climb for an equally spectacular view. By the time you descend, you'll be more than ready for a simple trattoria lunch. Depending on your preferences, either devote the afternoon to art or hike up to Piazzale Michelangelo, overlooking the city. Either way, finish the evening in style with a traditional *bistecca alla fiorentina* (grilled T-bone steak with olive oil).

Day 6: Lucca/Pisa

After breakfast, board a train for Lucca. It's an easy 1½-hour trip to see this walled medieval city. Don't miss the Romanesque Duomo, or a walk along the city's ramparts. Have lunch at a trattoria before continuing on to Pisa, where you'll spend an afternoon seeing—what else?—the Leaning Tower, along with the equally impressive Duomo and Battistero. Walk down to the banks of the Arno River, contemplate the majestic views at sunset, and have dinner at one of the many inexpensive local restaurants in the real city center—a bit removed from the most touristy spots.

Logistics: Lucca's train station lies just outside the walled city—it's a very easy walk. Pisa's train station isn't far from the city center, although it is on the other side of town from the Campo dei Miracoli (site of the Leaning Tower). Since Lucca and Pisa are only 15 minutes apart by train, you may want to return from Pisa to spend the night in more-charming Lucca.

Day 7: Orvieto/Rome
Three hours south of Pisa is Orvieto, one of the prettiest and most characteristic towns of the Umbria region, conveniently situated right on the Florence–Rome train line. Check out the memorable cathedral before a light lunch accompanied by one of Orvieto's famous white wines. Get back on a train bound for Rome, and in a little more than an hour you'll arrive in the Eternal City in time to make your way to your hotel and relax for a bit before you head out for the evening. When you do, check out Piazza Navona, Campo de' Fiori, and the Trevi Fountain—it's best in the evening—and have a stand-up *aperitivo* (Campari and soda is a classic) at an unpretentious local bar before dinner. It's finally pizza time; you can't go wrong at any of Rome's popular local pizzerias.

Logistics: To get from Pisa to Orvieto, you'll first catch a train to Florence and then get on a Rome-bound train from here. Be careful at Rome's Termini train station, a breeding ground for pickpockets. Keep your possessions close, and only get into a licensed taxi.

Day 8: Rome
Rome took millennia to build, but on this whirlwind trip you'll only have a day and a half to see it. In the morning, head to the Vatican Museums to see Michelangelo's glorious frescoes at the Sistine Chapel. See St. Peter's Basilica and Square before heading back into Rome proper for lunch around the Pantheon, followed by a coffee from one of Rome's famous coffee shops. Next, visit ancient Rome: first see the magnificent Pantheon, and then head across to the Colosseum, stopping along the way along Via dei Fori Imperiali to check out the Roman Forum from above. From the Colosseum, walk or take a taxi to Piazza di Spagna, a good place to see the sunset and shop at stylish boutiques. Taxi to Piazza Trilussa at the entrance of Trastevere, a beautiful old working-class neighborhood where you'll have a relaxing dinner.

Day 9: Rome/Departure
Head by taxi to Termini station and catch the train to the Fiumicino airport.

Logistics: The train from Termini station to the airport is fast, and easy—for most people, it's preferable to an exorbitantly priced taxi ride that, in bad traffic, can take twice as long and cost much, much more.

ROME

WELCOME TO ROME

TOP REASONS TO GO

★ **Roman Forum:** This fabled labyrinth of ruins variously served as a political playground, a center of commerce, and a place where justice was dispensed during the days of the Roman Republic and Empire (500 BC–AD 500).

★ **St. Peter's Square and Basilica:** The primary church of the Catholic faith is truly awe-inspiring.

★ **Campo de' Fiori:** The city comes alive in this bustling market square.

★ **The Colosseum:** One of the Seven Wonders of the World, the mammoth amphitheater was begun by Emperor Vespasian and inaugurated by Titus in the year AD 80.

★ **The Pantheon:** Constructed to honor all pagan gods, this best-preserved temple of ancient Rome was rebuilt in the 2nd century AD by Emperor Hadrian, and has survived intact because it was consecrated as a Christian church. Its dome is still considered an architectural marvel.

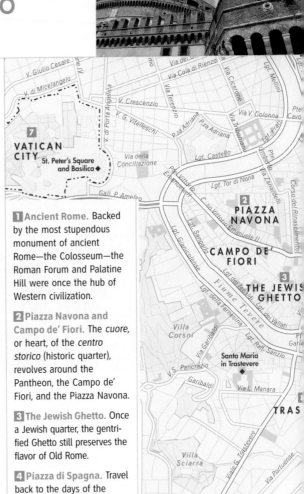

1 Ancient Rome. Backed by the most stupendous monument of ancient Rome—the Colosseum—the Roman Forum and Palatine Hill were once the hub of Western civilization.

2 Piazza Navona and Campo de' Fiori. The *cuore*, or heart, of the *centro storico* (historic quarter), revolves around the Pantheon, the Campo de' Fiori, and the Piazza Navona.

3 The Jewish Ghetto. Once a Jewish quarter, the gentrified Ghetto still preserves the flavor of Old Rome.

4 Piazza di Spagna. Travel back to the days of the Grand Tour in this glamorous area. After people-watching at the Spanish Steps, shop along Via dei Condotti, then be sure to throw a coin in the Trevi Fountain.

5 Repubblica and Quirinale. These areas bustle with government offices during the day, but are also home to several churches and sights, including the Bernini's Baroque Sant'Andrea al Quirinale.

6 Villa Borghese and Piazza del Popolo. Rome's most famous park is home to playful fountains, sculptured gardens, and the treasure-packed Galleria Borghese. Piazza del Popolo—a

2

GETTING ORIENTED

Rome is a sprawling city, but you'll likely spend most of your time in and around the historic center. The area is split by the River Tiber (*Tevere* in Italian). To its west are the Vatican and the Trastevere neighborhood. To its east is everything else you've come to see: the Colosseum, the Spanish Steps, and scores of other exceptional sights, not to mention piazzas, fountains, shops, and restaurants. This is one of the most culturally rich plots of land in the world.

10 Monti, Celio, Esquilino, and San Lorenzo. Near Termini station, these are some of Rome's least touristy neighborhoods, with plenty of ancient sights and spectacular churches, as well as Monti's artisanal shops, restaurants, bars, and high-end boutiques.

11 Aventino and Testaccio. These neighborhoods are off the usual tourist track but have all the vibrancy of true Rome. Aventino is a posh residential area; Testaccio is more working class and has a happening nightlife scene.

beautiful place to watch the world go by—lies south.

7 The Vatican. The Vatican draws millions of pilgrims and art lovers to St. Peter's Basilica, the Vatican Museums, and the Sistine Chapel.

8 Trastevere. Rome's left bank has kept its authentic roots thanks to mom-and-pop trattorias, medieval alleyways, and Santa Maria in Trastevere, stunningly spotlighted at night.

9 Via Appia Antica. Follow in the footsteps of St. Peter to this district, home to the spirit-warm catacombs and the Tomb of Cecilia Metella.

EAT LIKE A LOCAL IN ROME

In Rome, tradition is the dominant feature of the cuisine, with a focus on freshness and simplicity, so when Romans continue ordering the standbys, it's easy to understand why. That said, Rome is the capital of Italy, and the influx of residents from other regions of the country has yielded many variations on the staples.

ARTICHOKES

There are two well-known preparations of *carciofo*, or artichoke, in Rome. Carciofi *alla romana* are stuffed with wild mint, garlic, and pecorino, then braised in olive oil, white wine, and water. Carciofi *alla giudia* (Jewish-style) are whole artichokes, deep-fried twice, so that they open like a flower, the outer leaves crisp and golden brown, while the heart remains tender. When artichokes are in season—late winter through the spring—they're served everywhere.

BUCATINI ALL'AMATRICIANA

It might look like spaghetti with red sauce, but there's much more to *bucatini all'amatriciana*. It's a spicy, rich, and complex dish that owes its flavor to *guanciale*, or cured pork jowl, as well as tomatoes and crushed red pepper flakes. It's often served over *bucatini*, a hollow, spaghetti-like pasta, and topped with grated pecorino Romano.

CODA ALLA VACCINARA

Rome's largest slaughterhouse in the 1800s was in the Testaccio neighborhood and that's where you'll find dishes like *coda alla vaccinara,* or "oxtail in the style of the cattle butcher." This dish is made from ox or veal tails stewed with tomatoes, carrots, celery, and wine, and it's usually seasoned with cinnamon. It's simmered for hours and then finished with raisins and pine nuts or bittersweet chocolate.

GELATO

For many travelers, their first taste of gelato is revelatory. Its consistency is often said to be a cross between regular American ice cream and soft-serve. The best versions of gelato are extremely flavorful, and almost always made fresh daily. When choosing a *gelateria*, watch for signs that say *gelato artigianale* (artisan- or homemade): otherwise, keep an eye out for the real deal by avoiding gelato that looks too bright or fluffy.

PIZZA

There are two kinds of Roman pizza: *al taglio* (by the slice) and *tonda* (round pizza). The former has a thicker, focaccia-like crust and is cut into squares; these are sold by weight and generally available all day. The typical Roman pizza tonda has a very thin crust and is served almost charred—it's cooked in wood-burning ovens that reach extremely high temperatures. Because they're so hot, the ovens are usually fired up only in the evening, which is why Roman pizzerie tend to open for dinner only.

CACIO E PEPE

The name means "cheese and pepper" and it's a simple pasta dish from the

cucina povera, or rustic cooking, tradition. It's a favorite Roman primo, usually made with *tonnarelli* (fresh egg pasta a bit thicker than spaghetti), which is coated with a pecorino-cheese sauce and lots of freshly ground black pepper. Some restaurants serve the dish in an edible bowl of paper-thin baked cheese, for added delicious effect.

FRITTI

The classic Roman starter in a trattoria and especially at the pizzeria, is *fritti*: an assortment of fried treats, usually crumbed or in batter. Often, before ordering a pizza, locals will order their fritti: a *filetti di baccala* (salt cod in batter), *fiori di zucca* (zucchini flowers, usually stuffed with anchovy and mozzarella), *supplì* (rice balls stuffed with mozzarella and other ingredients), or *olive ascolane* (stuffed olives). Fritti can also be found at many pizza al taglio joints or at *tavole calde* (snackbar). They make a great quick snack.

LA GRICIA

This dish is often referred to as a "white amatriciana," because it's precisely that: pasta (usually spaghetti or rigatoni) served with pecorino cheese and guanciale—thus amatriciana without the tomato sauce. It's a lighter alternative to *carbonara* in that it doesn't contain egg, and its origins date back further than the amatriciana.

Updated by Ariston Anderson, Nicole Arriaga, Agnes Crawford, and Maria Pasquale

The timeless city to which all roads lead, Mamma Roma, enthralls visitors today as she has since time immemorial. Here the ancient Romans made us heirs-in-law to what we call Western Civilization; where centuries later Michelangelo painted the Sistine Chapel; and where Gian Lorenzo Bernini's Baroque nymphs and naiads still dance in their marble fountains.

Today the city remains a veritable Grand Canyon of culture. Ancient Rome rubs shoulders with the medieval, the modern runs into the Renaissance, and the result is like nothing so much as an open-air museum.

But always remember: "*Quando a Roma vai, fai come vedrai*" (When in Rome, do as the Romans do). Don't feel intimidated by the press of art and culture. Instead, contemplate the grandeur from a table at a sun-drenched café on Piazza della Rotonda; let Rome's colorful life flow around you without feeling guilty because you haven't seen everything. It can't be done, anyway. There's just so much here that you'll have to come back, so be sure to throw a coin in the Trevi Fountain.

PLANNER

WHEN TO GO

Spring and fall are the best times to visit, with mild temperatures and many sunny days. Summers are often sweltering so come in July and August if you like, but we advise doing as the Romans do—get up and out early, seek refuge from the afternoon heat, resume activities in early evening, and stay up late to enjoy the nighttime breeze.

Most attractions are closed on major holidays. Come August, many shops and restaurants close as locals head out for vacation. Remember that air-conditioning is still relatively rare in this city, so carrying a small paper fan in your bag can work wonders. Roman winters are relatively mild, with persistent rainy spells.

GETTING HERE AND AROUND

AIR TRAVEL

Rome's principal airport is Leonardo da Vinci Airport (☎ 06/65951 ⊕ www.adr.it), commonly known by the name of its location, Fiumicino (FCO). It's 30 km (19 miles) southwest of the city but has a direct train link with downtown Rome. Rome's other airport, with no direct train link, is Ciampino (CIA ☎ 06/65951 ⊕ www.adr.it), 15 km (9 miles) south of downtown and used mostly by low-cost airlines.

Two trains link downtown Rome with Fiumicino. Inquire at the PIT counter in the International Arrivals hall (Terminal 2) or at the train information counter near the tracks to determine which takes you closest to your destination in Rome. The 30-minute nonstop Airport–Termini line (the "Leonardo Express") goes directly to Termini Station, Rome's main train station; tickets cost €14. The FM1 train stops in Trastevere and Ostiense. Always stamp your tickets in the little machines near the track before you board. As for Ciampino, COTRAL buses connect to trains that go to the city and Terravision (☎ 06/97610632 ⊕ www.terravision.eu) buses link the airport to Termini Station for €4 each way. Taxi transport to and from Fiumicino carries a flat fee of €48; to and from Ciampino is €30. The price includes all luggage.

BUS TRAVEL

Bus lines cover Rome's surrounding Lazio region and are operated by the Consorzio Trasporti Lazio, or COTRAL (☎ 800/174471 ⊕ www.cotralspa.it). These bus routes terminate either near Tiburtina Station or at outlying Metro stops, such as Laurentina and Ponte Mammolo (Line B) and Anagnina (Line A). COTRAL buses are good options for short day trips from Rome, such as those that leave daily from Rome's Ponte Mammolo Metro station (Line B) for the town of Tivoli, where Hadrian's villa and Villa D'Este await.

ATAC city buses and trams are orange, gray and red, or blue and orange. Remember to board at the front or rear and to exit at the middle; in most cases, you must buy your ticket before boarding, and always stamp it in a machine as soon as you enter. The ticket is good for a single Metro ride and unlimited buses and trams within the next 100 minutes.

ATAC has a website (⊕ www.atac.roma.it) that will help you calculate the number of stops and bus routes needed.

CAR TRAVEL

The main access route from the north is the A1 (Autostrada del Sole) from Milan and Florence. The same A1 continues south to Naples and beyond. All roads in and out of the city connect with the Grande Raccordo Anulare (GRA) ring road, which channels traffic into the city center. For driving directions, check out ⊕ www.autostrade.it and ⊕ www.tuttocitta.it. Note: parking in Rome can be a nightmare—private cars are not allowed access to the centro storico weekdays 6:30 am–8 pm and Saturday 2–6 pm, except for residents. Contact your hotel to ask about parking facilities.

PUBLIC TRANSIT TRAVEL

Rome's integrated transportation system is ATAC (☎ *06/57003, 06/46951, or 800/431784* ⊕ *www.atac.roma.it*), which includes the Metropolitana subway, city buses, and municipal trams. A ticket (BIT) valid for 100 minutes on any combination of buses and trams and one entrance to the Metro costs €1.50. Day-long *giornaliero* passes are €6, three-day passes are €16.50, and weekly passes are €24.

The Metropolitana (or Metro) is the easiest and fastest way to get around Rome. Street entrances are marked with red and white "M" signs.

The Metro Line A, known as the *linea rossa,* will take you to a chunk of the main attractions in Rome: Piazza di Spagna (Spagna stop), Piazza del Popolo (Flaminio), St. Peter's Square (Ottaviano–San Pietro), the Vatican Museums (both Ottaviano and Cipro–Musei Vaticani), and the Trevi Fountain (Barberini).

Line B (*linea blu*) will take you to the Colosseum (Colosseo stop), Circus Maximus and Aventino (Circo Massimo stop), the Pyramid (Piramide stop for Testaccio, Ostiense Station, and trains for Ostia Antica), and Basilica di San Paolo Fuori le Mura (San Paolo stop). The two lines intersect at Rome's main station, Termini.

Tickets (singly or in quantity—it's a good idea to keep a few tickets handy so you don't have to hunt for a vendor) are sold at tobacconists, newsstands, some coffee bars, ticket machines in Metro stations, some bus stops, and ATAC ticket booths. Some buses also have ticket machines onboard.

Time-stamp tickets at Metro turnstiles and in little yellow machines on buses and trams when boarding the first vehicle. The expiration date and time will be printed on the reverse side of the ticket.

TAXI TRAVEL

Taxis in Rome do not cruise, but if free they'll stop if you flag them down. They wait at stands, but can also be called by phone (☎ *0609, 06/5551, 06/6645, 06/3570, 06/4994, or 06/0609*). You will be asked to give an address when you phone. If you are on the street, give the street number of the nearest building.

Always ask for a receipt (*ricevuta*) to make sure the driver charges you the correct amount, and ensure the driver is running the meter (unless you're coming from the airport, when it's the flat fare). Use only licensed cabs with a plaque next to the license plate reading "*Servizio Pubblico.*"

TRAIN TRAVEL

State-owned Trenitalia (☎ *892021 in Italy, 06/68475475 abroad* ⊕ *www. trenitalia.it*) trains also serve some destinations on side trips outside Rome. The main Trenitalia stations in Rome are Termini, Tiburtina, Ostiense, and Trastevere. On long-distance routes (to Florence and Naples, for instance) you can either travel on the cheap but slow *regionali* trains, or on the fast but more expensive Intercity, Eurostar Alta Velocità. The state railways' website is user-friendly. The privately run Italo high-speed train (⊕ *www.italotreno.it*) has two lines serving Rome. The Turin–Salerno line stops in Bologna, Florence, Rome, Naples, and Salerno, and the Venice–Napoli line serves Padua, Bologna, Florence, and Rome.

MAKING THE MOST OF YOUR TIME

There's so much to do in Rome that it's hard to fit it all in, no matter how much time you have. If you're a first-time visitor, the Vatican Museums and the remains of ancient Rome are must-sees, but both require at least half a day, so if you only have one day, you're best-off picking one or the other. Save time and skip lines by purchasing tickets for the Vatican Museums and the Colosseum (with the Roman Forum and Palatine Hill) online beforehand. If you have more than one day, do one on one morning and the other on the next. If you're planning to visit the Galleria Borghese, tickets can sell out days (or weeks) in advance during high season, so make sure to book early.

ADDRESSES IN ROME

In the centro storico, most street names are posted on ceramic-like plaques on the side of buildings, which can make them hard to see. Addresses are fairly straightforward: the street name is followed by the street number, but it's worth noting that Roman street numbering, even in the newer outskirts of town, can be erratic. Usually numbers are even on one side of the street and odd on the other, but sometimes numbers are in ascending consecutive order on one side of the street and descending order on the other side.

ETIQUETTE

Although you may find Rome much more informal then many other European cities, Romans will nevertheless appreciate attempts to abide by local etiquette. When entering an establishment, the key words to know are: *buongiorno* (good morning), *buona sera* (good evening), and *buon pomeriggio* (good afternoon). These words can also double as a goodbye upon exit. Remember to avoid short hemlines and sleeveless or low-cut tops in churches. It is common practice (but not obligatory) to leave a tip in a restaurant: usually 5%–10% will be appreciated, or just round up. Taxi drivers don't expect tips, but if you round up the tab they will be grateful. Even in bars, leave a small coin for your cappuccino.

STREET SMARTS

As in most big cities, use common sense with your valuables. If you carry a purse, keep a firm grip on it, and don't leave it unattended or on the back of a chair, and be especially aware of pickpockets at major tourist sights and train stations. It's never a bad idea to look at menu prices before ordering and check your bill when leaving. Be careful when crossing streets, as Roman motorists have a rather carefree attitude toward traffic lights.

HOW TO SAVE MONEY

In addition to single- and multiday transit passes, a three-day Roma Pass (€36 ⊕ *www.romapass.it*) covers unlimited use of buses, trams, and the Metro, plus free admission to two museums or archaeological sites of your choice and discounted entrance to others. A two-day pass is €28 and includes one museum.

HOP-ON, HOP-OFF

Rome has multiple hop-on, hop-off sightseeing-bus tours, with competing operators aggressively trying to lure you with flyers, though City Sightseeing runs the ones you'll see most frequently. Note that Rome is actually not ideally served by bus tours, as most of the main sights are close together and on small streets not accessible by bus.

City Sightseeing. Hop-on, hop-off buses leave every 15–20 minutes daily, beginning at 9 am from Via Marsala (beside Termini station), on a 100-minute loop, which passes the Colosseum and St. Peter's, and makes stops close to the Trevi Fountain and Piazza Navona. ⊕ *www.city-sightseeing.com* ✉ *From €25.*

ROMAN HOURS

On Sunday, Rome virtually shuts down, and on Monday, most state museums and exhibition halls, plus many restaurants are closed. Daily food shop hours generally run 10 am–1 pm and 4 pm–7:30 pm or 8 pm; but other stores in the center usually observe continuous opening hours. Pharmacies tend to close for a lunch break and keep night hours (*ora rio notturno*) in rotation. As for churches, most open at 8 or 9 in the morning, close noon–3 or 4, then reopen until 6:30 or 7. St. Peter's, however, has continuous hours 7 am–7 pm (until 6 pm in the fall and winter); and the Vatican Museums are open Monday but closed Sunday (except for the last Sunday of the month).

VISITOR INFORMATION

The Department of Tourism in Rome, called Roma Capitale, staffs green information kiosks (with multilingual personnel) near important sights, as well as at Termini station and Leonardo da Vinci Airport.

EXPLORING ROME

Most visitors to Rome begin by discovering the grandeur that was Rome: the Colosseum, the Forum, and the Pantheon. Then many move on to the Vatican, the closest thing to heaven on Earth for some.

The historical pageant continues with the 1,001 splendors of the Baroque era: glittering palaces, jewel-studded churches, and Caravaggio masterpieces. Arrive refreshed—with the help of a shot of espresso—at the foot of the Spanish Steps, where the picturesque world of the classic Grand Tour (peopled by such spirits as John Keats and Tosca) awaits you.

Thankfully, Rome provides delightful ways to catch your historic breath along the way: a walk through the cobblestone valleys of Trastevere or an hour stolen alongside a splashing Bernini fountain. Keep in mind that an uncharted ramble through the heart of the old city can be just as satisfying as the contemplation of a chapel or a trek through marbled museum corridors. No matter which aspect of Rome you end up enjoying the most, a visit to the Eternal City will never be forgotten.

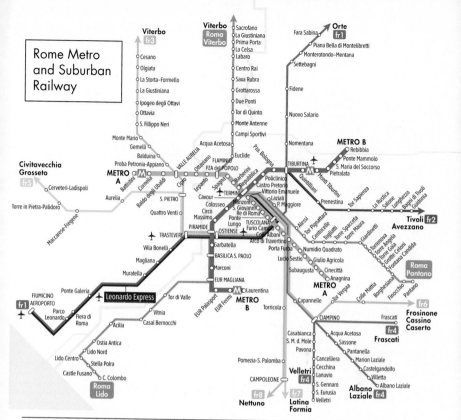

Rome Metro and Suburban Railway

ANCIENT ROME

Time has reduced ancient Rome to fields of silent ruins, but the powerful impact of what happened here, of the genius and power that made Rome the center of the Western world, echoes across the millennia. In this one compact area of the city, you can step back into the Rome of Cicero, Julius Caesar, and Virgil. You can walk along the streets they knew, cool off in the shade of the Colosseum that loomed over the city, and see the sculptures poised over their piazzas. Today, this part of Rome, more than any other, is a perfect example of the layering of historic eras, the overlapping of ages, of religions, of a past that is very much a part of the present.

GETTING HERE AND AROUND

The Colosseo Metro station is right across from the Colosseum and a short walk from both the Roman and Imperial forums, as well as the Palatine Hill. Walking from the very heart of the historic center will take about 20 minutes, much of it along the wide Via dei Fori Imperiali. The little electric Bus No. 117 from the center or No. 175 from Termini will also deliver you to the Colosseum's doorstep. Any of the following buses will take you to or near the Roman Forum: Nos. 60, 75, 85, 95, and 175.

For more information on Ancient Rome sights, see the highlighted feature in this chapter.

Continued on page 46

Map Labels

V. d. Plebiscito

Piazza Venezia

Piazza M. di Loreto

Piazza S. Marco

V.S. Marco

Foro di Traiano

V. Panisperna

V. S. Agata d. Goti

V. d. Serpenti

V. d. Boschetto

MERCATI DI TRAIANO

V. Alessandrina

Sal del Grillo

ALTARE DELLA PATRIA

FORO DI CESARE

V. Baccina

Via dei Monti

S. MARIA IN ARACOELI

PAL. NUOVO

Fori Imperiali

V. dei Fori

V. Cavour

V. d. Cardello

Frangipane

P.za Campitelli

di Marcello

Pza. del Campidoglio

SS. LUCA & MARTINO

Via Salara Vecchia

i **Tourist Info Office**

V. d. Colosseo

V. d. Carine

V. d. Annibald

Musei Capitolini

PAL. SENATORIO

Exit

CURIA

BAS. EMILIA

Entrance

Imperiali

V. del Teatro

CAMPIDOGLIO

PAL. DEI CONSERVATORI

TEMPIO DI VESPASIANO

ARCO DI S. SEVERO

BAS. DI MASSENZIO

Musei Capitolini Café

BASILICA GIULIA

FORO ROMANO

V. d. Consolazione

TEMPIO DI VESTA

Foro Romano

TEMP. D. VENUS & ROME

COLOSSEO Ⓜ

Vico Jugario

P.za d. Consolazione

V. d. Foraggi

V. di S. Teodoro

ARCO DI TITO

Colosseo Entrance

ADMISSION

ADMISSION	
Arco di Constantino	Free
Circo Massimo	Free
Mercato di Traiano	€15
Colosseo, Colle Palatino & Foro Romano	€12
Musei Capitolini	€14
Piazza del Campidoglio	Free
Santa Maria d'Aracoeli	Free
Terme di Caracalla	€6

ORTI FARNESIANI

Foro Romano Exit

Arco di Constantino

V. di S. Gregorio

V. Celio

Tevere

COLLE PALATINO

HOUSE OF AUGUSTUS

PAL. DEI FLAVI

Entrance

V.S. Maria in Cosmedin

V. d. Greca

DOMUS AUGUSTO

MONTE AVENTINO

0   100 yards
0   100 meters

V. dei Cerchi

Circo Massimo

Terme di Caracalla

CAPITOLINE HILL: The ancient Romans built their most important temples here, and it's been the seat of city government since the Middle Ages. It now holds the Capitoline Museums, chock-full of the treasures of antiquity.

ROMAN FORUM: Downtown Ancient Rome. People from all corners of the empire crowded into the Forum to do business, to hear the latest news, and to worship.

PALATINE HILL: Home of the empire's rich and famous. Luxurious villas lined Palatine Hill; emperors held court on its heights and vied with their predecessors for lasting renown.

CAMPIDOGLIO   FORO ROMANO   COLLE PALATINO

ANCIENT ROME
GLORIES OF
THE CAESARS

Time has reduced ancient Rome to fields of silent ruins, but the powerful impact of what happened here, of the genius and power that made Rome the center of the Western world, echoes across the millennia.

In this one compact area of the city, you can step back into the Rome of Cicero, Julius Caesar, and Virgil. Walk along the streets they knew, cool off in the shade of the Colosseum that loomed over the city, and see the sculptures poised above their piazzas. At the end of a day of exploring, climb one of the famous hills and watch the sun set over what was once the heart of the civilized world.

Today, this part of Rome, more than any other, is a perfect example of that layering of historic eras, the overlapping of ages, of religions, of a past that is very much a part of the present. Christian churches rise from the foundations of ancient pagan temples. An immense marble monument to a 19th-century king shares a square with a Renaissance palace built by a pope. Still, the history and memory of ancient Rome dominate the area. It's fitting that in the aftermath of centuries of such pageantry Percy Bysshe Shelley and Edward Gibbon reflected here on the meaning of *sic transit gloria mundi* (so passes away the glory of the world).

COLOSSEUM: Gladiators fought for the chance to live another day on the floor of the Colosseum, iconic symbol of ancient Rome.

KEY

☕ *Cafe / Restaurant*

The Capitoline Museums are closed on Monday. Late evening is an option for this area. Though the Santa Maria d'Aracoeli church is closed, the museums are open until 8 pm, and the views of the city lights and the illuminated Altare della Patria (aka the Victor Emmanuel II monument) and the Foro Romano are striking.

CLIMB MICHELANGELO'S DRAMATIC RAMP TO THE SUMMIT of one of Rome's famous hills, the Campidoglio (also known as Capitoline Hill), for views across the rooftops of modern Rome in one direction and across the ruins of ancient Rome in the other. Check out the stellar Musei Capitolini, crammed with a collection of masterpieces rivaled only by the Vatican museums.

★ **Piazza del Campidoglio.** In Michelangelo's piazza at the top of the Campidoglio stands a bronze equestrian statue of Marcus Aurelius (AD 121–180). A legend foretells that some day the statue's original gold surface will return, heralding the end of the world. Pending the arrival of that day, the original 2nd century statue was moved inside the Musei Capitolini; a copy sits on the piazza. Stand with your back to it to survey central Rome.

The Campidoglio, the site of the Roman Republic's first and holiest temples, had fallen into ruin by the Middle Ages and was called *Monte Caprino* (Goat Hill). In 1536 Pope Paul III (1468–1549) decided to restore its grandeur for the triumphal entry into the city of Charles V (1500–1558), the Holy Roman Emperor. He called upon Michelangelo to create the staircase ramp, the buildings and facades

on the square, the pavement decoration, and the pedestal for the bronze statue.

The two buildings that make up the **Musei Capitolini** are on the piazza, flanking the **Palazzo Senatorio**. The Campidoglio has long been the seat of Rome's government; its Latin name is the root for the word capitol. Today, Rome's city hall occupies the Palazzo Senatorio. Head to the vantage points in the belvederes on the sides of the palazzo for great views of the ruins of ancient Rome.

★ **Musei Capitolini** (Capitoline Museums). Housed in the twin Palazzo dei Conservatori and Palazzo Nuovo buildings, this is a greatest hits collection of Roman art through the ages, from the ancients to the baroque.

Lining the courtyard of the **Palazzo dei Conservatori** are the colossal fragments

AN EMPEROR CHEAT SHEET

OCTAVIAN/AUGUSTUS (27 BC–AD 14)

After the death of Julius Caesar, Octavian gained control of Rome following a decade-long civil war that ended with the defeat of Antony and Cleopatra at Actium. Later known as Caesar Augustus, he was Rome's first emperor. His rule began a 200-year period of peace known as the Pax Romana.

Colle Palatino

CALIGULA (AD 37–41)

Caligula was tremendously popular when he came to power at the age of 25, but he very soon became infamous for his excessive cruelty, immorality, and erratic behavior. His contemporaries universally considered him to be insane. He was murdered by his own guard within four years.

of a head, leg, foot, and hand—all that remains of the famous statue of the emperor Constantine. These immense effigies were much in vogue throughout the Roman Empire. The renowned symbol of Rome, the *Capitoline Wolf*, a medieval bronze (long thought to be Etruscan), holds a place of honor in the museum; the suckling twins were added during the Renaissance to adapt the statue to the legend of Romulus and Remus.

The Palazzo also contains some of baroque painting's great masterpieces, including Caravaggio's *La Buona Ventura* (1595) and *San Giovanni Battista* (1602), Peter Paul Rubens's *Romulus and Remus* (1615), and Pietro da Cortona's sumptuous portrait of Pope Urban VIII (1627). When museum fatigue sets in, enjoy the view and refreshments on a large open terrace in the Palazzo dei Conservatoria.

The **Palazzo Nuovo** contains hundreds of Roman busts of philosophers and emperors—a fascinating Who's Who of the ancient world. A dozen Roman emperors are represented. Unlike the Greeks, whose portraits are idealized, the Romans preferred a more realistic representation.

Other notable sculptures include the poignant *Dying Gaul* and the regal *Capitoline Venus*. In the Capitolino courtyard is a gigantic, reclining sculpture of Oceanus, found in the Roman Forum and later dubbed *Marforio*. This was one of Rome's "talking statues" to which citizens from the 1500s to the 1900s affixed anonymous satirical verses and notes of political protest. ☎ *06/0608* ⊕ *www.museicapitolini.org* ⊙ *Tues.–Sun. 9–8.* €14

Santa Maria in Aracoeli. Seemingly endless, steep stairs climb from Piazza Venezia to the church of Santa Maria. There are 15th-century frescoes by Pinturicchio (1454–1513) in the first chapel on the right. ✉ *Scala dell'Arce Capitolina 14* ⊙ *May–Sept., daily, 9–12:30 and 3–6:30; Oct.–Apr., daily 7–12:30 and 3–6:30.*

NERO (AD 54–68)

Nero is infamous as a violent persecutor of Christians. He also murdered his wife, his mother, and countless others. Although it's certain he didn't actually fiddle as Rome burned in AD 64, he was well known as a singer and a composer of music.

Domus Aurea

DOMITIAN (AD 81–96)

The first emperor to declare himself "Dominus et Deus" (Lord and God), he stripped away power from the Senate. After his death, the Senate retaliated by declaring him "Damnatio Memoriae" (his name and image were erased from all public records).

Colle Palatino

FORO ROMANO

It takes about an hour to explore the Roman Forum. There are entrances on the Via dei Fori Imperiali and from the Palatine Hill. A 30-minute walk will cover the Imperial Fora. You can reserve tickets online or by phone—operators speak English. If you are buying tickets in person, remember there are shorter lines here than at the Colosseum and the ticket is good for both sights.

EXPERIENCE THE ENDURING ROMANCE OF THE FORUM. Wander among its lonely columns and great, broken fragments of sculpted marble and stone—once temples, law courts, and shops crowded with people from all corners of the known world. This was the heart of ancient Rome and a symbol of the values that inspired Rome's conquest of an empire.

★ **Foro Romano** (Roman Forum). Built in a marshy valley between the Capitoline and Palatine hills, the Forum was the civic core of Republican Rome, the austere era that preceded the hedonism of the emperors. The Forum was the political, commercial, and religious center of Roman life. Hundreds of years of plunder and the tendency of later Romans to carry off what was left of the better building materials reduced it to the series of ruins you see today. Archaeological digs continue to uncover more about the sight; bear in mind that what you see are the ruins not of one period but of almost 900 years, from about 500 BC to AD 400.

The **Basilica Giulia**, which owes its name to Julius Caesar who had it built, was where the Centumviri, the hundred-or-so judges forming the civil court, met to hear cases. The open space before it was the core of the forum proper and prototype of Italy's famous piazzas. Let your imagination dwell on Mark Antony (circa 83 BC–30 BC), who delivered the funeral address in Julius Caesar's honor from the rostrum left of the **Arco di Settimio Severo**. This arch, one of the grandest of all antiquity, was built several hundred years later in AD 203 to celebrate the victory of the emperor Severus (AD 145–211) over the Parthians, and was topped by a bronze equestrian statuary group with four horses. You can explore the reconstruction of the large brick senate hall, the **Curia**; three Corinthian columns (a favorite of 19th-century poets) are all that remains of the **Tempio di Vespasiano el Tito**. In the **Tempio di Vesta**, six highly privileged vestal virgins kept the sacred fire, a tradition that dated back to the very earliest days of Rome. Their luxurious villa beside the temple was opened to the public in 2011. The cleaned

AN EMPEROR CHEAT SHEET

TRAJAN (AD 98–117)

Trajan, from Southern Spain, was the first Roman emperor not born in Italy. He enlarged the empire's boundaries to include modern-day Romania, Armenia, and Upper Mesopotamia.

Colonna di Traiano, Foro di Traiano, Mercati di Traiano

HADRIAN (AD 117–138)

He expanded the empire in Asia and the Middle East. He's best known for rebuilding the Pantheon, constructing a majestic villa at Tivoli, and initiating myriad other constructions across the empire, including the famed wall across Britain.

and restored **Arco di Tito**, which stands in a slightly elevated position on a spur of the Palatine Hill, was erected in AD 81 to honor the recently dead Emperor Titus. It depicts the sacking of Jerusalem 10 years earlier, after the great Jewish revolt. A famous relief shows the captured contents of Herod's Temple—including its huge seven-branched menorah—being carried in triumph down Rome's Via Sacra. The temple of Venus and Roma sits between the arch and the Colosseum. Making sense of the ruins isn't always easy; consider renting an audio guide (€4) or buying a booklet that superimposes an image of the Forum in its heyday over a picture of it today. ☎ 06/39967700 ⊕ *www. pierreci.it* ⊗ *Daily, Jan.–Feb. 15 and last Sun. in Oct.–Dec., 8:30–4:30; Feb. 16–Mar. 15, 8:30–5; Mar. 16–last Sat. in Mar., 8:30–5:30; last Sun. in Mar.–Aug., 8:30–7:15; Sept., 8:30–7; Oct.1–last Sat. in Oct., 8:30–6:30. €12*

THE OTHER FORA

Fori Imperiali (Imperial Fora). These five grandly conceived squares flanked with columnades and temples were built by Caesar, Augustus, Vespasian, Nerva, and Trajan. The original Roman Forum, built up over 500 years of Republican Rome, had grown crowded, and Julius Caesar was the first to attempt to rival it. He built the **Foro di Cesare** (Forum of Caesar), including a temple dedicated to the goddess Venus. Four emperors followed his lead, creating their own fora. The grandest was the **Foro di Traiano** (Forum of Trajan) a veritable city unto itself built by Trajan (AD 53–117). Here you find the 100-ft Colonna di Traiano (Trajan's Column, AD 110), carved with 2,600 figures in relief. In the 20th century, Benito Mussolini built the Via dei Fori Imperiali directly through the Imperial Fora area. Marble and limestone maps on the wall along the avenue portray the extent of the Roman Republic and Empire, and many of the remains of the Imperial Fora lay buried beneath its surface.

Mercati di Traiano (Trajan's Markets). This huge multilevel brick complex of 120 offices was one of the marvels of the ancient world. It provides a glimpse into Roman daily life and offers a stellar view from the belvedere at its top. ☎ 06/0608 ⊕ *www. mercatiditraiano.it* ⊗ *Daily 9–7. €15*

MARCUS AURELIUS (AD 161–180)

Remembered as a humanitarian emperor, Marcus Aurelius was a Stoic philosopher and his *Meditations* are still read today. Nonetheless, he was an aggressive leader devoted to expanding the empire.

Piazza del Campidoglio

CONSTANTINE I (AD 306–337)

Constantine changed the course of history by legalizing Christianity. He legitimized the once-banned religion and paved the way for the papacy in Rome. Constantine also established Constantinople as an Imperial capital in the East.

Arco di Constantino

COLLE PALATINO

A stroll on the Palatino, with a visit to the Museo Palatino, takes about two hours. The hill was once home to several major imperial palaces. Domitian's 1st-century AD palace is the best preserved. The Colle Palatino entrances are from the Roman Forum and at Via S. Gregorio 30.

IT ALL BEGAN HERE. ACCORDING TO LEGEND, ROMULUS, THE FOUNDER OF ROME, lived on the Colle Palatino (Palatine Hill). It was an exclusive address in ancient Rome, where emperors built palaces upon the slopes. Tour the Palatine's hidden corners and shady lanes, take a welcome break from the heat in its peaceful gardens, and enjoy a view of the Circo Massimo fit for an emperor.

★ **Colle Palatino** (Palatine Hill). A lane known as the Clivus Palatinus, paved with worn stones that were once trod by emperors and their slaves, climbs from the Forum area to a site that historians identify as one of Rome's earliest settlements. The legend goes that the infant twins Romulus and Remus were nursed by a she-wolf on the banks of the Tiber and adopted by a shepherd. Encouraged by the gods to build a city, Romulus chose this site in 753 BC. Remus preferred the Aventine. The argument that ensued left Remus dead and Romulus Rome's first king.

During the Republican era the hill was an important religious center, housing the Temple of Cybele and the Temple of Victory, as well as an exclusive residential area. Cicero, Catiline, Crassus, and Agrippa all had homes here. Augustus was born on the hill, and as he rose in power, he built libraries, halls, and temples here; the **House of Augustus,** opened in 2008, preserves exquisite 1st-century BC frescoes. Emperor Tiberius was the next to build a palace here; others followed. The structures most visible today date back to the late 1st century AD, when the Palatine experienced an extensive remodeling under Emperor Domitian. During the Renaissance, the powerful Farnese family built gardens in the area overlooking the ruins of the Forum. Known as the **Orti Farnesiani,** they were Europe's first botanical gardens. The **Museo Palatino** charts the history of the hill. Splendid sculptures, frescoes, and mosaic intarsia from various imperial buildings are on display. ☎ *06/39967700* ⊕ *www.pierreci.it* ⊙ *Daily, Jan.–Feb. 15 and last Sun. in Oct.–Dec., 8:30–4:30; Feb. 16–Mar. 15, 8:30–5; Mar. 16–last*

THE RISE AND FALL OF ANCIENT ROME

218 BC

ca. 800 BC	Rise of Etruscan city-states.
509–510	Foundation of the Roman republic; expulsion of Etruscans from Roman territory.
343	Roman conquest of Greek colonies in Campania.
264–241	First Punic War (with Carthage): increased naval power helps Rome gain control of southern Italy and then Sicily.
212–202	Second Punic War: Hannibal's attempted conquest of Italy, using elephants, is eventually crushed.

Sat. in Mar., 8:30–5:30; last Sun. in Mar.–Aug., 8:30–7:15; Sept., 8:30–7; Oct.1–last Sat. in Oct., 8:30–6:30.

NEAR THE COLLE PALATINO

Circo Massimo (Circus Maximus). Ancient Rome's oldest and largest racetrack lies in the natural hollow between the Palatine and Aventine hills. From the imperial box in the palace on Palatine Hill, emperors could look out over the oval course. Stretching about 660 yards from end to end, the Circus Maximus could hold more than 200,000 spectators. On certain occasions there were as many as 100 chariot races a day, and competitions could last for 15 days. The central ridge was framed by two Egyptian obelisks. Check out the panoramic views of the Circus Maximus from the Palatine Hill's Belvedere. You can also see the green slopes of the Aventine and Celian hills, as well as the bell tower of Santa Maria in Cosmedin.

Terme di Caracalla (Baths of Caracalla). For the Romans, public baths were much more than places to wash. The baths also had recital halls, art galleries, libraries, massage rooms, sports grounds, and gardens. Even the smallest public baths had at least some of these amenities, and in the capital of the Roman Empire, they were provided on a lavish scale. Ancient Rome's most beautiful and luxurious public baths were opened by the emperor Caracalla in AD 217 and were used until the 6th century.

Taking a bath was a long process, and a social activity first and foremost. You began by sweating in the *sudatoria*, small rooms resembling saunas. From these you moved on to the *calidarium* for the actual business of washing, using an olive-oil-and-sand exfoliant, then removing it with a *strigil* (scraper). Next was the *tepidarium*, where you gradually cooled down. Finally, you splashed around in the *frigidarium*, in essence a cold–water swimming pool. There was a nominal admission fee, often waived by officials and emperors wishing to curry favor with the plebeians. The baths' functioning depended on the slaves who cared for the clients and stoked the fires that heated the water. ☎06/39967700 ⊕ *www.pierreci.it* ⊙ *Tues.–Sun., 9-4.30 (6.30 in summer). All Mondays, 9–1.* €6

150 BC	Roman Forum begins to take shape as the principal civic center in Italy.
149–146	Third Punic War: Rome razes city of Carthage and emerges as the dominant Mediterranean force.
133	Rome rules entire Mediterranean Basin except Egypt.
58–52	Julius Caesar conquers Gaul.
44	Julius Caesar is assassinated.
27	Rome's Imperial Age begins; Octavian (now named Augustus) becomes the first emperor and is later deified. The Augustan Age is celebrated in the works of Virgil (70–19 BC), Ovid (43 BC–AD 17), Livy (59 BC–AD 17), and Horace (65–8 BC).

44 BC

COLOSSEO

You can give the Colosseum a cursory look in about 30 minutes, but it deserves at least an hour. Make reservations by phone (there are English-speaking operators) or online at least a day in advance to avoid long lines. Or buy your ticket at the Roman Forum or Palatine Hill, where the lines are usually shorter.

LEGEND HAS IT THAT AS LONG AS THE COLOSSEUM STANDS, ROME WILL STAND; and when Rome falls, so will the world. No visit to Rome is complete without a trip to the obstinate oval that has been the iconic symbol of the city for centuries.

★ **Colosseo.** A program of games and shows lasting 100 days celebrated the opening of the massive and majestic Colosseum in AD 80. On the opening day Romans claimed that 5,000 wild beasts perished. More than 50,000 spectators could sit within the arena's 596-yard circumference, which had limestone facing, hundreds of statues for decoration, and a *velarium*—an ingenious system of sail-like awnings rigged on ropes manned by imperial sailors—to protect the audience from the sun and rain. Before the imperial box, gladiators would salute the emperor and cry, "*Ave, imperator, morituri te salutant*" ("Hail, emperor, men soon to die salute you"); it is said that when one day they heard the emperor Claudius respond, "Or maybe not," they were so offended that they called a strike.

Originally known as the Flavian Amphitheater, it took the name Colosseum after a truly colossal gilt bronze statue of Nero that stood nearby. Gladiator combat ended by the 5th century and staged animal hunts by the 6th. The arena later served as a quarry from which materials were looted to build Renaissance churches and palaces, including St. Peter's Basilica. Finally, it was declared sacred by the Vatican in memory of the many Christians believed martyred here. (Scholars now maintain that Christians met their death elsewhere.) During the 19th century, romantic poets lauded the glories of the ruins when viewed by moonlight. Now its arches glow at night with mellow golden spotlights.

Expect long lines at the entrance and actors dressed as gladiators who charge a hefty fee to pose for pictures. (Agree on a price in advance if you want a photo.) Once inside you can walk around about half of the outer ring of the structure and look down into the exposed passages under what was once the arena floor, now represented by a small stage at one end. Climb the steep stairs for

THE RISE AND FALL OF ANCIENT ROME

AD 116

58 AD	Rome invades Britain.
50	Rome is the largest city in the world, with a population of possibly as much as a million.
64–68	Emperor Nero begins the persecution of Christians in the Empire; Saints Peter and Paul are executed.
72–80	Vespasian begins the Colosseum; Titus completes it.
98–117	Trajan's military successes are celebrated with his Baths (98), Forum (110), and Column (113); the Roman Empire reaches its apogee.

panoramic views in the Colosseum and out to the Palatine and Arch of Constantine. A museum space on the second floor holds temporary archaeological exhibits. ☎ 06/39967700 ⊕ *www.pierreci.it* ⊙ *Daily, 9–sunset. €12, includes Forum.*

Arco di Costantino. The largest (69 feet high, 85 feet long, 23 feet wide) and the best preserved of Rome's triumphal arches was erected in AD 315 to celebrate the victory of the emperor Constantine (280–337) over co-emperor Maxentius (died 312). According to legend, it was just before this battle that Constantine, the emperor who legalized Christianity, had a vision of a cross in the heavens and heard the words "In this sign, thou shalt conquer."

NEAR THE COLOSSEO

Domus Aurea. The site gives a good sense of the excesses of Imperial Rome. After fire destroyed much of the city in AD 64, Nero took advantage of the resulting open space to construct a lavish palace so large that it spread over a third of the city. It had a facade of marble, seawater piped into the baths, gilded vaults, decorations of mother-of-pearl, and vast gardens. Not much of this ornamentation has survived; a good portion of the building and grounds was buried under the public works with which subsequent emperors sought to make reparation to the Roman people for Nero's phenomenal greed. As a result, the site of the Domus Aurea itself remained unknown for many centuries. A few of Nero's original halls were discovered underground at the end of the 15th century. Raphael (1483–1520) was one of the artists who had themselves lowered into the rubble-filled rooms, which resembled grottoes. The artists copied the original painted Roman decorations, barely visible by torchlight, and scratched their names on the ceilings. Raphael later used these models—known as *grotesques* because they were found in the so-called grottoes—in his decorative motifs for the Loggia of Julius II in the Vatican. The palace remains impressive in scale, even if a lot of imagination is required to envision the original. ⊠ *Via della Domus Aurea* ☎ *06/39967700* ⊕ *www.pierreci.it.*

238 AD	The first wave of Germanic invasions penetrates Italy.
293	Diocletian reorganizes the Empire into West and East.
330	Constantine founds a new Imperial capital (Constantinople) in the East.
410	Rome is sacked by Visigoths.
476	The last Roman emperor, Romulus Augustus, is deposed. The western Roman empire falls.

PIAZZA NAVONA AND CAMPO DE' FIORI

Set between Via del Corso and the Tiber bend, these time-burnished districts are some of the city's most beautiful. They're filled with airy piazzas, half-hidden courtyards, and narrow streets bearing curious names. Some of Rome's most coveted residential addresses are nestled here. So, too, are the ancient Pantheon and the Renaissance square of Campo de' Fiori, but the spectacular, over-the-top Baroque monuments of the 16th and 17th centuries predominate.

The hub of the district is the queen of squares, Piazza Navona—a cityscape adorned with the most jaw-dropping fountain by Gian Lorenzo Bernini, father of the Baroque. Streets running off the square lead to many historic must-sees, including noble churches by Borromini and Caravaggio's greatest paintings at San Luigi dei Francesi. This district has been an integral part of the city since ancient times, and its position between the Vatican and Lateran palaces, both seats of papal rule, put it in the mainstream of Rome's development from the Middle Ages onward. Craftsmen, shopkeepers, and famed artists toiled in the shadow of the huge palaces built to consolidate the power of leading figures in the papal court. Artisans and artists still live here, but their numbers are diminishing as the district becomes increasingly posh and—so critics say—"Disneyfied." But three of the liveliest piazzas in Rome—Piazza Navona, Piazza della Rotonda (home to the Pantheon), and Campo de' Fiori—are lodestars in a constellation of some of Rome's finest cafés, stores, and wine bars.

GETTING HERE AND AROUND

The Piazza Navona and Campo de' Fiori are an easy walk from the Vatican or Trastevere, or a half-hour stroll from the Spanish Steps. From Termini or the Vatican, take Bus No. 40 Express or No. 64 to Largo Torre Argentina; then walk 10 minutes to either piazza. Bus No. 116 winds from Via Veneto past the Spanish Steps to Campo de' Fiori.

TOP ATTRACTIONS

Campo de' Fiori. A bustling marketplace in the morning (Monday–Saturday 8–2) and a trendy meeting place the rest of the day and night, this piazza has plenty of earthy charm. Just after lunchtime, all the fruit and vegetable vendors disappear, and this so-called *piazza trasformista* takes on another identity, becoming a circus of bars particularly favored by study-abroads, tourists, and young expats. Brooding over the piazza is a hooded statue of the philosopher Giordano Bruno, who was burned at the stake here in 1600 for heresy, one of many victims of the Roman Inquisition. ⊠ *Intersection of Via dei Baullari, Via Giubbonari, Via del Pellegrino, and Piazza della Cancelleria, Campo de' Fiori.*

Fodor'sChoice
★
Il Gesù. The mother church of the Jesuits in Rome is the prototype of all Counter-Reformation churches. Considered the first fully Baroque church, it has a spectacular interior that tells a great deal about an era of religious triumph and turmoil. Its architecture influenced ecclesiastical buildings in Rome for more than a century (the overall design was by Vignola, the facade by della Porta) and was exported by the Jesuits throughout the rest of Europe. Though consecrated as early as 1584, the interior of the church wasn't decorated for another 100 years. It

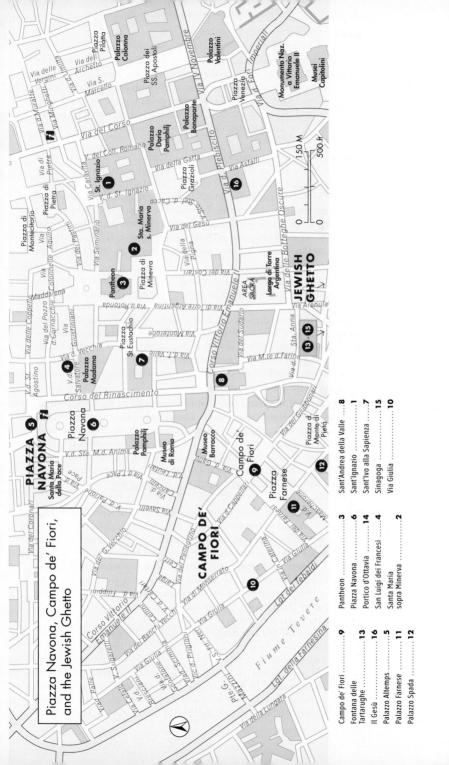

Piazza Navona, Campo de' Fiori, and the Jewish Ghetto

was originally intended that the interior be left plain to the point of austerity—but, when it was finally embellished, the mood had changed and no expense was spared. Its interior drips with gold and lapis lazuli, gold and precious marbles, gold and more gold, all covered by a fantastically painted ceiling by Baciccia. Unfortunately, the church is also one of Rome's most crepuscular, so its visual magnificence is considerably dulled by lack of light.

The architectural significance of Il Gesù extends far beyond the splendid interior. As the first of the great Counter-Reformation churches, it was put up after the Council of Trent (1545–63) had signaled the determination of the Roman Catholic Church to fight back against the Reformed Protestant heretics of northern Europe. The church decided to do so through the use of overwhelming pomp and majesty, in an effort to woo believers. As a harbinger of ecclesiastical spectacle, Il Gesù spawned imitations throughout Italy and the other Catholic countries of Europe as well as the Americas.

The most striking element is the ceiling, which is covered with frescoes that swirl down from on high to merge with painted stucco figures at the base, the illusion of space in the two-dimensional painting becoming the reality of three dimensions in the sculpted figures. Baciccia, their painter, achieved extraordinary effects in these frescoes, especially in the *Triumph of the Holy Name of Jesus,* over the nave. Here, the figures representing evil cast out of heaven and seem to be hurtling down onto the observer. To appreciate in detail, the spectacle is best viewed through a specially tilted mirror in the nave.

The founder of the Jesuit order himself is buried in the Chapel of St. Ignatius, in the left-hand transept. This is surely the most sumptuous Baroque altar in Rome; as is typical, the enormous globe of lapis lazuli that crowns it is really only a shell of lapis over a stucco base—after all, Baroque decoration prides itself on achieving stunning effects and illusions. The heavy, bronze altar rail by architect Carlo Fontana is in keeping with the surrounding opulence. ✉ *Piazza del Ges, off Via del Plebiscito, Campo de' Fiori* ☎ *06/697001* ⊕ *www.chiesadelgesu.org.*

Fodor's Choice ★ **Palazzo Altemps.** Containing some of the finest ancient Roman statues in the world, Palazzo Altemps is part of the Museo Nazionale Romano. The palace's sober exterior belies a magnificence that appears as soon as you walk into the majestic courtyard, studded with statues and covered in part by a retractable awning. The restored interior hints at the Roman lifestyle of the 16th–18th centuries while showcasing the most illustrious pieces from the Museo Nazionale, including the collection of the Ludovisi noble family. In the frescoed salons you can see the Galata Suicida, a poignant work portraying a barbarian warrior who chooses death for himself and his wife, rather than humiliation by the enemy. Another highlight is the large Ludovisi sarcophagus, magnificently carved from marble. In a place of honor is the Ludovisi Throne, which shows a goddess emerging from the sea and being helped by her acolytes. For centuries this was heralded as one of the most sublime Greek sculptures, but, today, at least one authoritative art historian considers it a colossally overrated fake.

2

Look for the framed explanations of the exhibits that detail (in English) how and exactly where Renaissance sculptors, Bernini among them, added missing pieces to the classical works. In the lavishly frescoed Loggia stand busts of the Caesars. In the wing once occupied by early-20th-century poet Gabriele d'Annunzio (who married into the Altemps family), three rooms host the museum's Egyptian collection. ⊠ *Piazza Sant'Apollinare 46, Piazza Navona* ☎ *06/39967700* ⊕ *www. coopculture.it* 🖾 *€7, includes 3 other Museo Nazionale Romano sites (Crypta Balbi, Palazzo Massimo alle Terme, Museo delle Terme di Diocleziano); €10 if any one of them has a special exhibit* ⊘ *Closed Mon.* Ⓜ *Bus Nos. 70, 81, 87, 116T, 186, 492, and 628.*

Fodor's Choice
★

Palazzo Farnese. The most beautiful Renaissance palace in Rome, the Palazzo Farnese is fabled for the Galleria Carracci, whose ceiling is to the Baroque age what the Sistine Chapel ceiling is to the Renaissance. The Farnese family rose to great power and wealth during the Renaissance, in part because of the favor Pope Alexander VI showed to the beautiful Giulia Farnese. The massive palace was begun when, with Alexander's aid, Giulia's brother became cardinal; it was further enlarged on his election as Pope Paul III in 1534. The uppermost frieze decorations and main window overlooking the piazza are the work of Michelangelo, who also designed part of the courtyard, as well as the graceful arch over Via Giulia at the back. The facade on Piazza Farnese has geometrical brick configurations that have long been thought to hold some occult meaning. When looking up at the palace, try to catch a glimpse of the splendid frescoed ceilings, including the **Galleria Carracci** vault painted by Annibale Carracci between 1597 and 1604. The Carracci gallery depicts the loves of the gods, a supremely pagan theme that the artist painted in a swirling style that announced the birth of the Baroque. Other opulent salons are among the largest in Rome, including the Salon of Hercules, which has an overpowering replica of the ancient *Farnese Hercules,* front and center. The French Embassy, which occupies the palace, offers tours (in English) on Wednesday; book at least eight days in advance through the website, and bring photo ID. ⊠ *French Embassy, Servizio Culturale, Piazza Farnese 67, Campo de' Fiori* ☎ *06/686011* ⊕ *www.inventerrome.com* 🖾 *€9.*

Palazzo Spada. In this neighborhood of huge, austere palaces, Palazzo Spada strikes an almost frivolous note, with its pretty ornament-encrusted courtyard and its upper stories covered with stuccoes and statues. While the palazzo houses an impressive collection of old-master paintings, it's most famous for its trompe-l'oeil garden gallery, a delightful example of the sort of architectural games rich Romans of the 17th century found irresistible. Even if you don't go into the gallery, step into the courtyard and look through the glass window of the library to the colonnaded corridor in the adjacent courtyard. See—or seem to see—an 8-meter-long gallery quadrupled in depth, a sort of optical telescope taking the Renaissance's art of perspective to another level, as it stretches out for a great distance with a large statue at the end. In fact the distance is an illusion: the corridor grows progressively narrower and the columns progressively smaller as they near the statue, which is just two feet tall. The Baroque period is known for special effects, and this is rightly one of the most famous. It was long thought that Borromini was responsible for this ruse; it's now known that it was designed by an Augustinian priest, Giovanni Maria da Bitonto. Upstairs is a seignorial picture gallery with the paintings shown as they would have been, piled on top of each other clear to the ceiling. Outstanding works include Brueghel's *Landscape with Windmills,* Titian's *Musician,* and Andrea del Sarto's *Visitation.* Look for the fact-sheets that have descriptive notes about the objects in each room. ⊠ *Piazza Capo di Ferro 13, Campo de' Fiori* ☎ *06/6861158* ⊕ *www.galleriaborghese.it* ⛾ *€5* ⊘ *Closed Tues.*

Fodor's Choice **Pantheon.** One of the wonders of the ancient world, this onetime pagan
★ temple, a marvel of architectural harmony and proportion, is the best-preserved ancient building in Rome—the result of its consecration as a church in AD 608. It was entirely rebuilt (and likely designed) by the emperor Hadrian around AD 120 on the site of an earlier pantheon erected in 27 BC. The most striking thing is not the Pantheon's size, immense though it is (until 1960 the dome was the largest ever built), nor even the phenomenal technical difficulties posed by so vast a construction; rather, it's the remarkable unity of the building: the diameter described by the dome is exactly equal to its height. It's why some call it the world's only architecturally perfect building. Today the Pantheon serves as one of the city's important burial places, with its most famous tomb that of Raphael. ⊠ *Piazza della Rotonda, Piazza Navona* ☎ *06/68300230* ⊕ *www.pantheonroma.com* ⛾ *Free; audio guide €5* Ⓜ *Closest bus hub: Argentina (Bus Nos. 40, 85, 53, 46, 64, 87, and 571; Tram No. 8).*

Piazza Navona. Here, everything that makes Rome unique is compressed into one beautiful Baroque piazza. Always camera-ready, Piazza Navona has Bernini sculptures, three gorgeous fountains, a magnificently Baroque church (Sant'Agnese in Agone), and the excitement of so many people strolling, admiring the fountains, and enjoying the view. Although undoubtedly more touristy today, the square still has the carefree air of the days when it was the scene of medieval jousts and 17th-century carnivals. At center stage is the Fontana dei Quattro Fiumi, created for Innocent X by Bernini in 1651. Bernini's powerful figures of the four rivers represent the four corners of the world: the Nile; the Ganges; the Danube; and the Plata, with its hand raised. If you want a caffè with one of the most beautiful (if pricey) views in Rome, grab a seat; just be aware that the restaurants are geared toward tourists, so while lovely, you can find cheaper and more authentic meals elsewhere. ⊠ *Piazza Navona.*

Fodor's Choice **San Luigi dei Francesi.** A pilgrimage spot for art lovers, San Luigi's Con-
★ tarelli Chapel is adorned with three stunningly dramatic works by Caravaggio (1571–1610), the Baroque master of the heightened approach to light and dark. At the altar end of the left nave, they were commissioned for San Luigi, the official church of Rome's French colony (San Luigi is St. Louis, patron saint of France). The inevitable coin machine will light up his *Calling of St. Matthew, Saint Matthew and the Angel,* and *Martyrdom of Saint Matthew* (seen from left to right), and Caravaggio's mastery of light takes it from there. When painted, they caused

considerable consternation to the clergy of San Luigi, who thought the artist's dramatically realistic approach was scandalously disrespectful. A first version of the altarpiece was rejected; the priests were not particularly happy with the other two, either. Time has fully vindicated Caravaggio's patron, Cardinal Francesco del Monte, who secured the commission for these works and stoutly defended them. ⊠ *Piazza di San Luigi dei Francesi, Piazza Navona* ☎ *06/688271* ⊕ *www.saintlouis-rome.net* Ⓜ *Bus Nos. 40 and 87.*

FodorśChoice **Santa Maria sopra Minerva.** The name of the church reveals that it was
★ built *sopra* (over) the ruins of a temple of Minerva, the ancient goddess of wisdom. Erected in 1280 by Dominicans along severe Italian Gothic lines, it has undergone a number of more or less happy restorations to the interior. Certainly, as the city's major Gothic church, it provides a refreshing contrast to Baroque flamboyance. Have a €1 coin handy to illuminate the **Cappella Carafa** in the right transept, where Filippino Lippi's (1457–1504) glowing frescoes are well worth the small investment, opening up the deepest azure expanse of sky where musical angels hover around the Virgin. Under the main altar is the tomb of St. Catherine of Siena, one of Italy's patron saints. Left of the altar you'll find Michelangelo's *Risen Christ* and the tomb of the gentle artist Fra Angelico. Bernini's unusual and little-known monument to the Blessed Maria Raggi is on the fifth pier from the door on the left as you leave the church. In front of the church, the little obelisk-bearing elephant carved by Bernini is perhaps the city's most charming sculpture. An inscription on the base of **Bernini's Elephant Obelisk,** which was recently cleaned and restored, references the church's ancient patroness, reading something to the effect that it takes a strong mind to sustain solid wisdom. ⊠ *Piazza della Minerva, Piazza Navona* ☎ *06/6793926* ⊕ *www.santamariasopraminerva.it.*

FodorśChoice **Sant'Ignazio.** Rome's second Jesuit church, this 17th-century landmark
★ harbors some of the most city's magnificent trompe-l'oeil. To get the full effect of the marvelous illusionistic ceiling by priest-artist Andrea Pozzo, stand on the small disk set into the floor of the nave. The heavenly vision above you, seemingly extending upward almost indefinitely, represents the *Allegory of the Missionary Work of the Jesuits* and is part of Pozzo's cycle of works in this church exalting the early history of the Jesuit Order, whose founder was the reformer Ignatius of Loyola. The saint soars heavenward, supported by a cast of thousands; not far behind is Saint Francis Xavier, apostle of the Indies, leading a crowd of Eastern converts; a bare-breasted, spear-wielding America in American Indian headdress rides a jaguar; Europe with crown and scepter sits serene on a heftily rumped horse; while a splendid Africa with gold tiara perches on a lucky crocodile. The artist repeated this illusionist technique, so popular in the late 17th century, in the false dome, which is actually a flat canvas—a trompe-l'oeil trick used when the budget drained dry. The overall effect of the frescoes is dazzling (be sure to have coins handy for the machine that switches on the lights) and was fully intended to rival that produced by Baciccia in the nearby mother church of Il Gesù. Scattered around the nave are several awe-inspiring altars; their soaring columns, gold-on-gold decoration,

and gilded statues make these the last word in splendor. The church is often host to concerts of sacred music performed by choirs from all over the world. Look for posters at the church doors or see ⊕ *www.chiesasantignazio.it* for more information. ⊠ *Piazza Sant'Ignazio, Piazza Navona* ☎ *06/6794406* ⊕ *www.chiesasantignazio.it.*

Fodor'sChoice ★ **Via Giulia.** Still a Renaissance-era diorama and one of Rome's most exclusive addresses, Via Giulia was the first street in Rome since ancient times to be laid out in a straight line. Named for Pope Julius II (of Sistine Chapel fame), who commissioned it in the early 1500s as part of a scheme to open up a grandiose approach to St. Peter's Basilica (using funds from a prostitution tax), it became flanked with elegant churches and palaces. Although the pope's plans to change the face of the city were only partially completed, Via Giulia became an important thoroughfare in Renaissance Rome. Today, after more than four centuries, it remains the "salon of Rome," address of choice for Roman aristocrats, although controversy has arisen about a recent change—the decision to add a large parking lot along one side of the street—that meant steamrolling through ancient and medieval ruins underneath. A stroll will reveal elegant palaces and churches (one, **San Eligio,** on the little side street Via di Sant'Eligio, was designed by Raphael himself). The area around Via Giulia is wonderful to wander through and get the feel of daily life as carried on in a centuries-old setting. Among the buildings that merit your attention are **Palazzo Sacchetti** (Via Giulia 66), with an imposing stone portal (inside are some of Rome's grandest state rooms, still, after 300 years, the private quarters of the Marchesi Sacchetti), and the forbidding brick building that housed the **Carceri Nuove** (New Prison; Via Giulia 52), Rome's prison for more than two centuries and now the offices of Direzione Nazionale Antimafia. Near the bridge that arches over the southern end of Via Giulia is the church of **Santa Maria dell'Orazione e Morte** (Holy Mary of Prayer and Death), with stone skulls on its door. These are a symbol of a confraternity that was charged with burying the bodies of the unidentified dead found in the city streets. Home since 1927 to the Hungarian Academy, the **Palazzo Falconieri** (Via Giulia 1 ☎ 06/6889671) was designed by Borromini—note the architect's rooftop belvedere adorned with statues of the family "falcons," best viewed from around the block along the Tiber embankment. (The Borromini-designed salons and loggia are sporadically open as part of a guided tour; call the Academy for information.) Remnant of a master plan by Michelangelo, the arch over the street was meant to link massive Palazzo Farnese, on the east side of Via Giulia, with the building across the street and a bridge to the Villa Farnesina, directly across the river. Finally, on the right and rather green with age, dribbles that star of many a postcard, the Fontana del Mascherone. ⊠ *Via Giulia, between Piazza dell'Oro and Piazza San Vincenzo Palloti, Campo de' Fiori.*

WORTH NOTING

Sant'Andrea della Valle. Topped by the highest dome in Rome after St. Peter's (designed by Maderno), this huge and imposing 17th-century church is remarkably balanced in design. Fortunately, its facade, which had turned a sooty gray from pollution, has been cleaned to a near-sparkling white. Use one of the handy mirrors to examine the early-17th-century frescoes by Domenichino in the choir vault and those by Lanfranco in the dome. One of the earliest ceilings done in full Baroque style, its upward vortex was influenced by Correggio's dome in Parma, of which Lanfranco was also a citizen. (Bring a few coins to light the paintings, which can be very dim.) The three massive paintings of Saint Andrew's martyrdom are by Maria Preti (1650–51). Richly marbled and decorated chapels flank the nave, and in such a space, Puccini set the first act of *Tosca*. ⊠ *Piazza Vidoni 6, Corso Vittorio Emanuele II, Campo de' Fiori* ☎ *06/6861339.*

Sant'Ivo alla Sapienza. The main facade of this eccentric Baroque church, probably Borromini's best, is on the stately courtyard of an austere building that once housed Rome's university. Sant'Ivo has what must surely be one of the most delightful "domes" in all of Rome—a dizzying spiral said to have been inspired by a bee's stinger. The apian symbol is a reminder that Borromini built the church on commission from the Barberini pope Urban VIII (a swarm of bees figure on the Barberini family crest). The interior, open only for three hours on Sunday, is worth a look, especially if you share Borromini's taste for complex mathematical architectural idiosyncrasies. "I didn't take up architecture solely to be a copyist," he once said. Sant'Ivo is certainly the proof. ⊠ *Corso del Rinascimento 40, Piazza Navona* ☎ *06/6864987* ⊕ *www.060608. it* ⊙ *Closed July and Aug., and Mon.–Sat.* Ⓜ *Bus Nos. 130, 116, 186, 492, 30, 70, 81, and 87.*

THE JEWISH GHETTO

Although today most of Rome's Jews live outside the Ghetto, the area remains the spiritual and cultural home of Jewish Rome, and that heritage permeates its small commercial area of Judaica shops, kosher bakeries, and restaurants. The Jewish Ghetto was established by papal decree in the 16th century. It was by definition a closed community, where Roman Jews lived under lock and key until Italian unification in 1870. In 1943–44, the already small Jewish population there was decimated by deportations. Today there are a few Judaica shops and kosher groceries, bakeries, and restaurants (especially on Via di Portico d'Ottavia), but the neighborhood mansions are now being renovated and much coveted by rich and stylish expats.

GETTING HERE AND AROUND
From the Vatican or the Spanish Steps, it's a 30-minute walk to the Jewish Ghetto, or take the No. 40 Express or the No. 64 bus from Termini station to Largo Torre Argentina.

TOP ATTRACTIONS

Fodor'sChoice
★ **Fontana delle Tartarughe.** Designed by Giacomo della Porta in 1581 and sculpted by Taddeo Landini, this 16th-century fountain, set in venerable Piazza Mattei, is one of Rome's most charming. The focus of the fountain is four bronze boys, each grasping a dolphin spouting water into a marble shell. Bronze turtles held in the boys' hands drink from the upper basin. The turtles are thought to have been added in the 17th century by Bernini. ⊠ *Piazza Mattei, Jewish Ghetto.*

FodorśChoice **Portico d'Ottavia.** Looming over the Jewish Ghetto, this huge portico
★ enclosure, with a few surviving columns, is one of the area's most
picturesque set pieces, with the time-stained church of Sant'Angelo in
Pescheria (seemingly under perpetual restoration) built right into its
ruins. Named by Augustus in honor of his sister Octavia, it was originally 390 feet wide and 433 feet long, encompassed two temples, a
meeting hall, and a library, and served as a kind of grandiose entrance
foyer for the adjacent Teatro di Marcello. The ruins of the portico
became Rome's *pescheria* (fish market) during the Middle Ages. A
stone plaque on a pillar (a copy; the original is in the Musei Capitolini) states in Latin that the head of any fish surpassing the length
of the plaque was to be cut off "up to the first fin" and given to the
city fathers, or else the vendor was to pay a fine of 10 gold florins.
The heads were used to make fish soup and were considered a great
delicacy. ⊠ *Via Tribuna di Campitelli 6, Jewish Ghetto.*

WORTH NOTING

Sinagoga. This synagogue has been the city's largest Jewish temple, and
a Roman landmark with its aluminium dome, since its 1904 construction. The building also houses the Jewish Museum, with its precious
ritual objects and other exhibits, which document the uninterrupted
presence of a Jewish community in the city for nearly 22 centuries.
Until the 16th century, Jews were esteemed citizens of Rome. Among
them were bankers and physicians to the popes, who had themselves
given permission for the construction of synagogues. But in 1555,
during the Counter-Reformation, Pope Paul IV decreed the building of the walls of the Ghetto, confining the Jews to this small area
and imposing a series of restrictions, some of which continued to be
enforced until 1870. For security reasons, guided visits are mandatory, and tours in English start every hour at about 10 minutes past
the hour; entrance to the synagogue is through the museum located
in Via Catalana (*Largo 16 Ottobre 1943*). ⊠ *Lungotevere Cenci 15,
Jewish Ghetto* ☎ *06/68400661* ⊕ *www.museoebraico.roma.it* ☑ *€11*
☉ *Closed Sat.* Ⓜ *Bus Nos. 46, 64, and 87; Tram No. 8.*

PIAZZA DI SPAGNA

In spirit (and in fact) this section of the city is its most grandiose.
The overblown Vittoriano monument, the labyrinthine treasure-chest
palaces of Rome's surviving aristocracy, even the diamond-draped
denizens of Via Condotti's shops—all embody the exuberant ego of
a city at the center of its own universe. Here's where you'll see ladies
in furs gobbling pastries at café tables, and walk through a thousand
snapshots as you climb the famous Spanish Steps, admired by generations from Byron to Versace. Cultural treasures abound around
here: gilded 17th-century churches, glittering palaces, and the greatest
example of portraiture in Rome, Velázquez's incomparable *Innocent
X* at the Galleria Doria Pamphilj. Have your camera ready—along
with a coin or two—for that most beloved of Rome's landmarks, the
Trevi Fountain.

GETTING HERE AND AROUND

The Piazza di Spagna is a short walk from Piazza del Popolo, the Pantheon, and the Trevi Fountain. One of Rome's handiest subway stations, Spagna, is tucked just left of the steps. Bus Nos. 117 (from the Colosseum) and 119 (from Piazza del Popolo) hum through the area; the latter tootles up Via del Babuino, famed for its shopping.

TOP ATTRACTIONS

Fodor'sChoice
★
Ara Pacis Augustae (*Altar of Augustan Peace*). This vibrant monument of the Imperial age is housed in one of Rome's newest architectural landmarks: a gleaming, rectangular glass-and-travertine structure designed by American architect Richard Meier. Overlooking the Tiber on one side and the ruins of the marble-clad **Mausoleo di Augusto** (Mausoleum of Augustus) on the other, the result is a serene, luminous oasis right in the center of Rome. The altar itself dates back to 13 BC; it was commissioned to celebrate the Pax Romana, the era of peace ushered in by Augustus's military victories. Like all ancient Roman monuments of this kind, you have to imagine its spectacular and moving relief sculptures painted in vibrant colors, now long gone. The reliefs on the short sides portray myths associated with Rome's founding and glory; the long sides display a procession of the imperial family. It's fun to try to play "who's who"—although half of his body is missing, Augustus is identifiable as the first full figure at the procession's head on the south-side frieze—but academics still argue over exact identifications of other figures. The small museum has a model and useful information about the Ara Pacis's original location and the surrounding Augustan monuments. ⊠ *Lungotevere in Augusta, Piazza di Spagna* ☎ *06/0608* ⊕ *www.arapacis.it* 🎫 *€13* Ⓜ *Flaminio.*

Monumento a Vittorio Emanuele II, or Altare della Patria (*Victor Emmanuel II Monument, or Altar of the Nation*). The huge white mass of the "Vittoriano" is an inescapable landmark—Romans say you can avoid its image only if you're actually standing on it. Some have likened it to a huge wedding cake; others, to an immense typewriter. To create this elaborate marble monster and the vast piazza on which it stands, architects blithely destroyed many ancient and medieval buildings and altered the slope of the Campidoglio (Capitoline Hill), which abuts it. Built to honor the unification of Italy and the nation's first king, Victor Emmanuel II, it also shelters the eternal flame at the tomb of Italy's Unknown Soldier killed during World War I. The flame is guarded day and night by sentinels, while inside the building there is the (rather dry) Institute of the History of the Risorgimento. Take the elevator up to the top to see some of Rome's most panoramic views. ⊠ *Entrances on Piazza Venezia, Piazza del Campidoglio, and Via di San Pietro in Carcere, Piazza di Spagna* ☎ *06/0608* ⊕ *www.060608.it* 🎫 *Free, elevator €7* Ⓜ *Colosseo.*

Fodor'sChoice
★
Palazzo Colonna. Rome's grandest family built themselves Rome's grandest private palazzo, a fusion of 17th- and 18th-century buildings on a spot they have occupied for a millennium. It's so immense that it faces Piazza dei Santi Apostoli on one side and the Quirinale (Quirinal Hill) on the other (a little bridge over Via della Pilotta links the palace with the gardens on the hill). While still home to some Colonna patricians, the palace also holds the family picture gallery, which is open to the public on

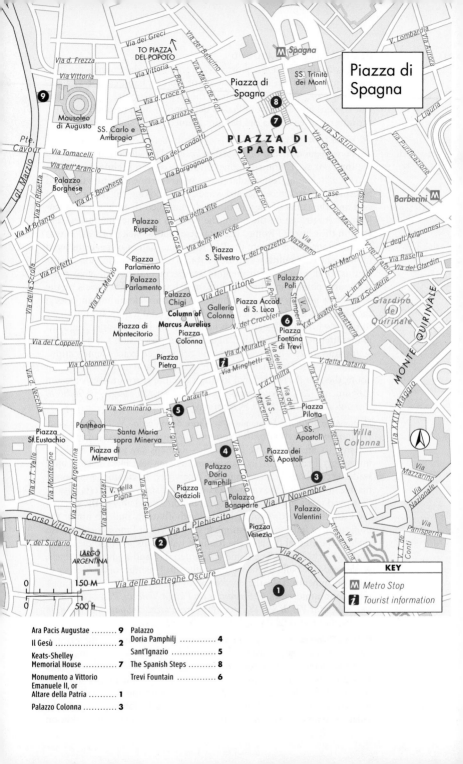

Piazza di Spagna

KEY

- **M** Metro Stop
- **i** Tourist information

2

Saturday mornings. The gallery is itself a setting of aristocratic grandeur; you might recognize the **Sala Grande** as the site where Audrey Hepburn meets the press in *Roman Holiday.* At one end looms the ancient red marble column (*colonna* in Italian), which is the family's emblem; above the vast room is the spectacular ceiling fresco of the Battle of Lepanto painted by Giovanni Coli and Filippo Gherardi in 1675—the center scene almost puts the computer-generated special effects of Hollywood to shame. Adding redundant luster to the opulently stuccoed and frescoed salons are works by Poussin, Tintoretto, and Veronese, and a number of portraits of illustrious members of the family such as Vittoria Colonna, Michelangelo's muse and longtime friend, and Marcantonio Colonna, who led the papal forces in the great naval victory at Lepanto in 1577. Lost in the array of madonnas, saints, goddesses, popes, and cardinals is Annibale Carracci's lonely *Beaneater,* spoon at the ready and front teeth missing. (As W. H. Auden put it, "Grub first, art later.") At noon, there's a guided tour in English, included in your entrance fee. The gallery also boasts a caffè with a pleasant terrace when weather permits. ⊠ *Via della Pilotta 17, Piazza di Spagna* ☎ *06/6784350* ⊕ *www.galleriacolonna.it* 🎟 *€12* ☉ *Closed Sun.–Fri.* Ⓜ *Barberini.*

Fodor's Choice
★
Palazzo Doria Pamphilj. Along with the Palazzo Colonna and the Galleria Borghese, this spectacular 15th-century family palace provides the best glimpse of aristocratic Rome. The main attractions are the legendary old master paintings, including treasures by Velázquez and Caravaggio, the splendor of the main galleries, and a unique suite of private family apartments. It passed through several hands before becoming the property of the famous seafaring Doria family of Genoa, who had married into the Roman Pamphilj (also spelled Pamphili) clan. The picture gallery contains 550 paintings, including three by Caravaggio—a young St. John the Baptist, Mary Magdalene, and the breathtaking *Rest on the Flight to Egypt.* Off the eye-popping Galleria degli Specchi (Gallery of Mirrors)—a smaller version of the one at Versailles—are the famous Velázquez *Pope Innocent X,* considered by some historians as the greatest portrait ever painted, and the Bernini bust of the same. ⊠ *Via del Corso 305, Piazza di Spagna* ☎ *06/6797323* ⊕ *www.doriapamphilj.it* 🎟 *€12* Ⓜ *Barberini.*

FAMILY
Fodor's Choice
★
The Spanish Steps. That icon of postcard Rome, the Spanish Steps (often called simply *la scalinata,* or "the staircase," by Italians) and the Piazza di Spagna from which they ascend both get their names from the Spanish Embassy to the Vatican on the piazza—even though the staircase was built with French funds in 1723. In honor of a diplomatic visit by the king of Spain, the hillside was transformed by architect Francesco de Sanctis to link the church of Trinità dei Monti at the top with the Via dei Condotti below. In an allusion to the church, the staircase is divided by three landings (beautifully banked with azaleas from mid-April to mid-May). For centuries, the scalinata has welcomed tourists, dukes, and writers in search of inspiration—among them Stendhal, Honoré de Balzac, William Makepeace Thackeray, and Byron. Bookending the bottom of the steps are the 18th-century Keats-Shelley House and Babington's Tea Rooms, both beautifully redolent of the Grand Tour era. ⊠ *Piazza di Spagna* Ⓜ *Spagna.*

Trevi Fountain. An aquatic marvel in a city filled with them, the unique drama of the Fontana di Trevi is largely due to the site: its vast basin is squeezed into the tight meeting of three little streets (the *tre vie,* which may give the fountain its name) with cascades emerging as if from the wall of Palazzo Poli. The dazzling Baroque pyrotechnics—the sculpted seashells, the roaring sea beasts, the divalike mermaids—have been slyly incorporated in a stately triumphal arch. To ensure a return trip to the Eternal City, the famous legend has it that you should throw a coin into the fountain; the right way involves tossing it with your right hand over your left shoulder, with your back to the fountain. One coin means you'll return to Rome; two, you'll return and fall in love; three, you'll return, find love, and marry. ⊠ *Piazza di Trevi, Piazza di Spagna* Ⓜ *Barberini.*

WORTH NOTING

Keats-Shelley Memorial House. Sent to Rome in a last-ditch attempt to treat his consumptive condition, English Romantic poet John Keats lived—and died—in this house at the foot of the Spanish Steps. At that point, this was the heart of the colorful bohemian quarter of Rome that was especially favored by the English. Keats had become celebrated through such poems as "Ode to a Nightingale" and "Endymion," but his trip to Rome was fruitless. He took his last breath here on February 23, 1821, at only 25, forevermore the epitome of the doomed poet. In this "Casina di Keats," you can visit his rooms, though all his furnishings were burned after his death, as a sanitary measure by the local authorities. You'll also find a rather quaint collection of memorabilia of English literary figures of the period—Lord Byron, Percy Bysshe Shelley, Joseph Severn, and Leigh Hunt, as well as Keats—and an exhaustive library of works on the Romantics. ⊠ *Piazza di Spagna 26, Piazza di Spagna* ☎ *06/6784235* ⊕ *www.keats-shelley-house.org* 🎟 *€5* ⊗ *Closed Sun.* Ⓜ *Spagna.*

REPUBBLICA AND THE QUIRINALE

This sector of Rome stretches down from the 19th-century district built up around the Piazza della Repubblica—originally laid out to serve as a monumental foyer between the Termini train station and the rest of the city—and over the rest of the Quirinale. The highest of ancient Rome's famed seven hills, it's crowned by the massive Palazzo Quirinale, home to the popes until 1870 and now Italy's presidential palace. Along the way, you can see ancient Roman sculptures, early Christian churches, and highlights from the 16th and 17th centuries, when Rome was conquered by the Baroque—and by Bernini.

Although Bernini's work feels omnipresent in much of the city center, the Renaissance-man range of his work is particularly notable here. The artist as architect considered the church of Sant'Andrea al Quirinale one of his best; Bernini the urban designer and water worker is responsible for the muscle-bound sea god who blows his conch so provocatively in the fountain at the center of whirling Piazza Barberini. And Bernini the master gives religious passion a joltingly corporeal treatment in what is perhaps his greatest work, the *Ecstasy of St. Teresa,* in the church of Santa Maria della Vittoria.

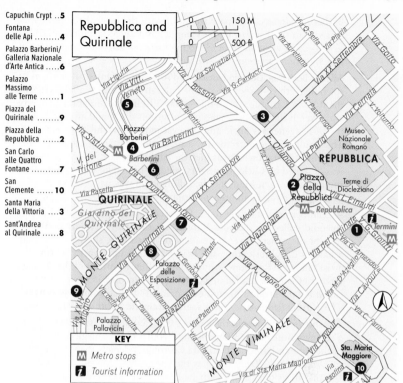

KEY

Ⓜ️ *Metro stops*

🛈 *Tourist information*

GETTING HERE AND AROUND

Located between Termini station and the Spanish Steps, this area is about a 15-minute walk from either. Bus No. 40 will get you from Termini to the Quirinale in two stops; from the Vatican take Bus No. 64. The very busy and convenient Repubblica Metro stop is on the piazza of the same name.

TOP ATTRACTIONS

Capuchin Crypt. Not for the easily spooked, the crypt under the church of Santa Maria della Concezione holds the bones of some 4,000 dead Capuchin monks. Arranged in odd decorative designs around the shriveled and decayed skeletons of their kinsmen, a macabre reminder of the impermanence of earthly life, the crypt is strangely touching and beautiful. As one sign proclaims: "What you are, we once were. What we are, you someday will be." After a recent renovation, the crypt was reopened to the public with a new museum devoted to teaching visitors about the Capuchin order; the crypt is now located at the end of the museum circuit. Upstairs in the church, the first chapel on the right contains Guido Reni's mid-17th-century *St. Michael Trampling the Devil*. The painting caused great scandal after an astute contemporary observer remarked that the face of the devil bore a surprising resemblance to the Pamphilj Pope Innocent X, archenemy of Reni's

Barberini patrons. Compare the devil with the bust of the pope that you saw in the Palazzo Doria Pamphilj and judge for yourself. ⊠ *Via Veneto 27, Quirinale* ☎ *06/88803695* ⊕ *www.cappucciniviaveneto.it* 🖅 *€8, includes museum* Ⓜ *Barberini.*

Fodor's Choice **Palazzo Barberini/Galleria Nazionale d'Arte Antica.** One of Rome's most ★ splendid 17th-century palaces, the Palazzo Barberini is a landmark of the Roman Baroque style. Pope Urban VIII had acquired the property and given it to a nephew, who was determined to build an edifice worthy of his generous uncle and the ever-more-powerful Barberini clan. The result was, architecturally, a precedent-shattering affair: a "villa suburbana" set on what was then the edge of the city. The grand facade was designed by Carlo Maderno (aided by his nephew, Francesco Borromini), but when Maderno died, Borromini was passed over in favor of his great rival, Gianlorenzo Bernini.

Ascend Bernini's staircase to the Galleria Nazionale d'Arte Antica. The splendid collection includes Raphael's *La Fornarina*, a luminous portrait of the artist's lover (a resident of Trastevere, she was reputedly a baker's daughter): study the bracelet on her upper arm bearing the artist's name. Also noteworthy are Guido Reni's portrait of the doomed *Beatrice Cenci* (beheaded in Rome for patricide in 1599)—Hawthorne called it "the saddest picture ever painted" in his Rome-based novel, *The Marble Faun*—and Caravaggio's dramatic *Judith and Holofernes.*

The showstopper here is the palace's Gran Salone, a vast ballroom with a ceiling painted in 1630 by the third (and too-often-neglected) master of the Roman Baroque, Pietro da Cortona. It depicts the *Glorification of Urban VIII's Reign* and has the spectacular conceit of glorifying Urban VIII as the agent of Divine Providence, escorted by a "bomber squadron" (to quote art historian Sir Michael Levey) of huge Barberini bees, the heraldic symbol of the family.

Part of the family of museums that make up the Galleria Nazionale d'Arte (others include the Palazzo Corsini, Galleria Borghese, Palazzo Spada, Palazzo Venezia), the Palazzo Barberini has gone into marketing in a big way—visit the shop for some distinctive gifts for Aunt Ethel back home, including tote bags bearing the beloved visage of Raphael's La Fornarina, bookmarks with Caravaggio's Judith slicing off Holofernes's head, and coffee mugs bearing the famous Barberini heraldic bees. ⊠ *Via Barberini 18, Quirinale* ☎ *06/32810* ⊕ *www.galleriaborghese.it* 🖅 *€7; €9, includes Palazzo Corsini* ☉ *Closed Mon.* Ⓜ *Barberini; Bus Nos. 52, 56, 60, 95, 116, 175, and 492.*

Fodor's Choice **Palazzo Massimo alle Terme.** Come here to get a real feel for ancient ★ Roman art—the collection rivals even the Vatican's. The Museo Nazionale Romano, with a collection ranging from striking classical Roman paintings to marble bric-a-brac, has four locations: Palazzo Altemps, Crypta Balbi, the Museo delle Terme di Diocleziano, and this, the Palazzo Massimo alle Terme. This vast structure holds the great ancient treasures of the archaeological collection and also the coin collection. Highlights include the Dying Niobid, the famous bronze Boxer, and the Discobolus Lancellotti. Pride of place goes, however, to the great ancient frescoes on view on the top floor, stunningly set up to "re-create" the look of the homes they once decorated. These include stuccoes and wall paintings found in the area of the Villa della Farnesina (in Trastevere) and the legendary frescoes from Empress Livia's villa at Prima Porta, delightful depictions of a garden in bloom and an orchard alive with birds. Their colors are remarkably well preserved. These delicate decorations covered the walls of cool, sunken rooms in Livia's summer house outside the city. ⊠ *Largo Villa Peretti 1, Repubblica* ☎ *06/39967700* ⊕ *www.coopculture.it* 🎫 *€7, includes Crypta Balbi, Museo delle Terme di Diocleziano, Palazzo Altemps (valid for 3 days)* ⊘ *Closed Mon.* Ⓜ *Repubblica.*

Piazza del Quirinale. This strategic location atop the Quirinale has long been of great importance. It served as home of the Sabines in the 7th century BC—at that time, deadly enemies of the Romans, who lived on the Campidoglio and Palatino (all of 1 km [½ mile] away). Today, it's the foreground for the presidential residence, Palazzo del Quirinale, and home to the **Palazzo della Consulta,** where Italy's Constitutional Court sits. The open side of the piazza has an impressive vista over the rooftops and domes of central Rome and St. Peter's. The **Fontana di Montecavallo,** or Fontana dei Dioscuri, comprises a huge Roman statuary group and an obelisk from the tomb of the emperor Augustus. The group of the Dioscuri trying to tame two massive marble steeds was found in the Baths of Constantine, which occupied part of the summit of the Quirinale. Unlike just about every other ancient statue in Rome, this group survived the Dark Ages intact and accordingly became one of the city's great sights, especially during the Middle Ages. Next to the figures, the ancient obelisk from the Mausoleo di Augusto (Tomb of Augustus) was put here by Pope Pius VI at the end of the 18th century. ⊠ *Quirinale* Ⓜ *Barberini.*

Fodor's Choice ★ **San Carlo alle Quattro Fontane.** Sometimes known as San Carlino because of its tiny size, this is one of Borromini's masterpieces. In a space no larger than the base of one of the piers of St. Peter's Basilica, he created a church that is an intricate exercise in geometric perfection, with a coffered dome that seems to float above the curves of the walls. Borromini's work is often bizarre, definitely intellectual, and intensely concerned with pure form. In San Carlo, he invented an original treatment of space that creates an effect of rippling movement, especially evident in the double-S curves of the facade. Characteristically, the interior decoration is subdued, in white stucco with no more than a few touches of gilding, so as not to distract from the form. Don't miss the cloister: a tiny, understated Baroque jewel, with a graceful portico and loggia above, echoing the lines of the church. ⊠ *Via del Quirinale 23, Quirinale* ☎ *06/4883109* ⊕ *www.sancarlino.eu* Ⓜ *Barberini.*

Fodor's Choice ★ **San Clemente.** One of the most impressive archaeological sites in Rome, San Clemente is a historical triple-decker. A 12th-century church was built on top of a 4th-century church, which had been built over a 2nd-century pagan temple to the god Mithras and 1st-century Roman apartments. The layers were uncovered in 1857, when a curious prior, Friar Joseph Mullooly, started excavations beneath the present basilica. Today, you can descend to explore all three.

The **upper church** (at street level) is a gem in its own right. In the apse, a glittering 12th-century mosaic shows Jesus on a cross that turns into a living tree. Green acanthus leaves swirl and teem with small scenes of everyday life. Early Christian symbols, including doves, vines, and fish, decorate the 4th-century marble choir screens. In the left nave, the Castiglioni chapel holds frescoes painted around 1400 by the Florentine artist Masolino da Panicale (1383–1440), a key figure in the introduction of realism and one-point perspective into Renaissance painting. Note the large Crucifixion and scenes from the lives of Saints Catherine, Ambrose, and Christopher, plus the Annunciation (over the entrance).

To the right of the sacristy (and bookshop), descend the stairs to the **4th-century church,** used until 1084, when it was damaged beyond repair during a siege of the area by the Norman prince Robert Guiscard. Still intact are some vibrant 11th-century frescoes depicting stories from the life of St. Clement. Don't miss the last fresco on the left, in what used to be the central nave. It includes a particularly colorful quote—including "Go on, you sons of harlots, pull!"—that's not only unusual for a religious painting, but one of the earliest examples of written vernacular Italian.

Descend an additional set of stairs to the **mithraeum,** a shrine dedicated to the god Mithras. His cult spread from Persia and gained a foothold in Rome during the 2nd and 3rd centuries AD. Mithras was believed to have been born in a cave and was thus worshipped in cavernous, underground chambers, where initiates into the all-male cult would share a meal while reclining on stone couches, some visible here along with the altar block. Most such pagan shrines in Rome were destroyed by Christians, who often built churches over their remains, as happened here. ⊠ *Via San Giovanni in Laterano 108, Celio* ☎ *06/7740021* ⊕ *www. basilicasanclemente.com* ☒ *Archaeological area €10* Ⓜ *Colosseo.*

Fodor's Choice
★

Santa Maria della Vittoria. Like the church of Santa Susanna across Piazza San Bernardo, this church was designed by Carlo Maderno, but this one is best known for Bernini's sumptuous Baroque decoration of the **Cappella Cornaro** (Cornaro Chapel, the last on the left as you face the altar), which houses his interpretation of divine love, the *Ecstasy of St. Teresa.* Your eye is drawn effortlessly from the frescoes on the ceiling down to the marble figures of the angel and the swooning saint to the earthly figures of the Cornaro family (some living, some dead at the time), who observe the scene from the opera boxes on either side, to the two inlays of marble skeletons in the pavement, representing the hope and despair of souls in purgatory.

As evinced in other works of the period, the theatricality of the chapel is the result of Bernini's masterly fusion of sculpture, light, architecture, painting, and relief; it's a multimedia extravaganza, and one of the key examples of the Roman High Baroque. Bernini's audacious conceit was to model the chapel as a theater. The members of the Cornaro family meditate on the communal vision of the great moment of divine love before them: the swooning saint's robes appear to be on fire, quivering with life, and the white marble group seems suspended in the heavens as golden rays illuminate the scene. An angel assists at the mystical moment of Teresa's vision as the saint abandons herself to the joys of heavenly love. Bernini represented this mystical experience in what, to modern eyes, may seem very earthly terms. Or, as the visiting French dignitary President de Brosses put it in the 18th century, "If this is divine love, I know all about it." No matter what your reaction, you'll have to admit it's great theater. ⊠ *Via XX Settembre 17, Largo Santa Susanna, Repubblica* ☎ *06/42740571* ⊕ *www.chiesasantamariavittoriaroma.it* Ⓜ *Repubblica.*

Fodor'sChoice
★

Sant'Andrea al Quirinale. Designed by Bernini, this small church is one of the triumphs of the Roman Baroque period. His son wrote that Bernini considered it his best work and that he used to come here occasionally, just to sit and contemplate. Bernini's simple oval plan, a classic form in Baroque architecture, is given drama and movement by the church's decoration, which carries the story of St. Andrew's martyrdom and ascension into heaven, starting with the painting over the high altar, up past the figure of the saint above, to the angels at the base of the lantern and the dove of the Holy Spirit that awaits on high. ⊠ *Via del Quirinale 29, Quirinale* ☎ *06/4740807* ⊕ *www.santandrea.gesuiti.it* ⊗ *Closed Mon.* Ⓜ *Barberini.*

WORTH NOTING

Fontana delle Api (*Fountain of the Bees*). Decorated with the famous heraldic bees of the Barberini family, the upper shell and the inscription are from a fountain that Bernini designed for Pope Urban VIII; the rest was lost when the fountain was moved to make way for a new street. The inscription was the cause of a considerable scandal when the fountain was first built in 1644. It said that the fountain had been erected in the 22nd year of the pontiff's reign, although in fact the 21st anniversary of Urban's election to the papacy was still some weeks away. The last numeral was hurriedly erased, but to no avail—Urban died eight days before the beginning of his 22nd year as pope. The superstitious Romans, who had immediately recognized the inscription as a foolhardy tempting of fate, were vindicated. ⊠ *Via Veneto at Piazza Barberini, Quirinale* Ⓜ *Barberini.*

Piazza della Repubblica. Often the first view that spells "Rome" to weary travelers walking from Termini station, this round piazza was laid out in the late 1800s and follows the line of the caldarium of the vast ancient Terme di Diocleziano. At its center, the exuberant **Fontana delle Naiadi** (Fountain of the Naiads) teems with voluptuous bronze ladies happily wrestling with marine monsters. The nudes weren't there when the pope unveiled the fountain in 1870—sparing him any embarrassment—but when the figures were added in 1901, they caused a scandal. It's said that the sculptor, Mario Rutelli, modeled them on the ample figures of two musical-comedy stars of the day. The colonnades now house the luxe Hotel Exedra, and a branch of foodie superstore Eataly recently opened in a former McDonald's, gradually helping Piazza della Repubblica to return to its original status as a smart section of town. ⊠ *Repubblica* Ⓜ *Repubblica.*

VILLA BORGHESE AND PIAZZA DEL POPOLO

Touring Rome's artistic masterpieces while staying clear of its hustle and bustle can be, quite literally, a walk in the park. Some of the city's finest sights are tucked away in or next to green lawns and pedestrian piazzas, offering a breath of fresh air for weary sightseers, especially in the Villa Borghese park. One of Rome's largest, this park can alleviate gallery gout by offering an oasis in which to cool off under the ilex, oak, and umbrella pine trees. If you feel like a picnic, have an *alimentari* (food shop) make you some panini before you go; food carts within the park are overpriced.

GETTING HERE AND AROUND

The Metro stop for Piazza del Popolo is Flaminio on Line A. The Villa Giulia, the Galleria Nazionale d'Arte Moderna e Contemporanea, and the Bioparco in Villa Borghese are accessible from Via Flaminia, 1 km (½ mile) from Piazza del Popolo. Tram No. 19 and Bus No. 3 stop at each. Bus No. 119 connects Piazza del Popolo to Piazza Venezia. From the Colosseum, take No. 117 to Piazza del Popolo. Bus No. 116, starting near the Galleria Borghese, is the only bus that goes through the park.

TOP ATTRACTIONS

Fodor'sChoice
★
Galleria Borghese. The villa built for Cardinal Scipione Borghese in 1612 houses one of the finest collections of Baroque sculpture anywhere in the world. One of the most famous works in the collection is Canova's neoclassical sculpture of Pauline Borghese as *Venus Victrix*. The next three rooms hold three key early Baroque sculptures: Bernini's *David, Apollo and Daphne,* and *Rape of Proserpina.* The Caravaggio Room houses works by this hotheaded genius; upstairs, the Pinacoteca (Picture Gallery) boasts paintings by Raphael (including his moving *Deposition*), Pinturicchio, Perugino, Bellini, and Rubens. Probably the gallery's most famous painting is Titian's allegorical *Sacred and Profane Love,* a mysterious and yet-unsolved image with two female figures, one nude, one clothed. ■TIP→ Admission to the Galleria is by reservation only. Visitors are admitted in two-hour shifts 9–5. Prime-time slots can sell out days in advance, so in high season reserve directly through the Borghese's website. ⊠ *Piazza Scipione Borghese 5, off Via Pinciana, Villa Borghese* 🕾 *06/32810 for reservations, 06/8413979 for info* ⊕ *www. galleriaborghese.it* 🔁 *€15, includes €2 reservation fee; audio guide €5* ⊙ *Closed Mon.* Ⓜ *Bus No. 910 from Piazza della Repubblica; Tram No. 19 or Bus No. 3 from Policlinico.*

MAXXI—Museo Nazionale delle Arti del XXI Secolo (*National Museum of 21st-Century Arts*). It took 10 years and cost some €150 million, but for art lovers, Italy's first national museum devoted to contemporary art and architecture was worth it. The building alone impresses, as it should: the design, by the late Anglo-Iraqi star-architect Zaha Hadid, triumphed over 272 other contest entries. The building plays with lots of natural light, curving and angular lines, and big open spaces, all meant to question the division between "within" and "without" (think glass ceilings and steel staircases that twist through the air). The MAXXI hosts temporary exhibitions of art, architecture, film, and more. The permanent collection, exhibited on a rotating basis, boasts more than

Villa Borghese and
Piazza del Popolo

350 works from artists including Andy Warhol, Francesco Clemente, and Gerhard Richter. ✉ *Via Guido Reni 4, Flaminio* ☎ *06/32810* ⊕ *www.fondazionemaxxi.it* 🎟 *€10* ⊗ *Closed Mon.* Ⓜ *Flaminio, then Tram No. 2 to Apollodoro; Bus Nos. 53, 217, 280, and 910.*

Fodor'sChoice ★ **Santa Maria del Popolo.** Standing inconspicuously in a corner of the vast Piazza del Popolo, this church often goes unnoticed, but the treasures inside make it a must for art lovers, as they include an entire chapel designed by Raphael and one adorned with two striking Caravaggio masterpieces. Bramante enlarged the apse of the church, which was rebuilt in the 15th century on the site of a much older place of worship. Inside, in the first chapel on the right, you'll see some frescoes by Pinturicchio from the mid-15th century; the adjacent **Cybo Chapel** is a 17th-century exercise in decorative marble. Raphael's famous **Chigi Chapel,** the second on the left, was built around 1513 and commissioned by the banker Agostino Chigi (who also had the artist decorate his home across the Tiber, the Villa Farnesina). Raphael provided the cartoons for the vault mosaic—showing God the Father in benediction—and the designs for the statues of Jonah and Elijah. More than a century later, Bernini added the oval medallions on the tombs and the statues of Daniel and Habakkuk, when, in the mid-17th century another Chigi, Pope Alexander VII, commissioned him to restore and decorate the building. The organ case by Bernini in the right transept bears the Della Rovere family oak tree, part of the Chigi family's coat of arms. Behind the main altar the **choir,** with vault frescoes by Pinturicchio, contains the handsome tombs of Ascanio Sforza and Girolamo della Rovere—both designed by Andrea Sansovino—and 16th-century stained glass, a rarity in central Italy. ■TIP→ **To visit the choir ask at the information booth; tours are free.** The best is for last: the **Cerasi Chapel,** to the left of the high altar, holds two Caravaggios: the *Crucifixion of St. Peter* and *Conversion of St. Paul.* Exuding drama and realism, both are key early Baroque works that show how "modern" 17th-century art can appear. Compare their style with the much more restrained and classically "pure" *Assumption of the Virgin* by Caravaggio's contemporary and rival, Annibale Carracci, which hangs over the altar of the chapel. ⊠ *Piazza del Popolo 12, near Porta Pinciana, Piazza del Popolo* ☎ *06/3610836* ⊕ *www.santamariadelpopolo.it* Ⓜ *Flaminio.*

THE VATICAN

Climbing the steps to St. Peter's Basilica feels monumental, like a journey that has reached its climactic end. Suddenly, all is cool and dark … and you are dwarfed by the gargantuan nave and its magnificence. Above is a ceiling so high it must lead to heaven itself. Great, shining marble figures of saints frozen mid-whirl loom from niches and corners. And at the end, a throne for an unseen king whose greatness, it is implied, must mirror the greatness of his palace. For this basilica is a palace, the dazzling center of power for a king and a place of supplication for his subjects. Whether his kingdom is earthly or otherwise may lie in the eye of the beholder.

For good Catholics and sinners alike, the Vatican is an exercise in spirituality, requiring patience but delivering joy. Some come here for a transcendent glimpse of a heavenly Michelangelo fresco; others come in search of a direct connection with the divine. But what all visitors share, for a few hours, is an awe-inspiring landscape that offers a famous sight for every taste: rooms decorated by Raphael, antique sculptures like the Apollo Belvedere, famous paintings by Giotto and Bellini, and, perhaps most of all, the Sistine Chapel—for the lover of beauty, few places are as historically important as this epitome of faith and grandeur.

GETTING HERE AND AROUND

Metro stops Cipro or Ottaviano will get you within about a 10-minute walk of the entrance to the Musei Vaticani. Or, from Termini station, Bus No. 40 Express or the famously crowded No. 64 will take you to Piazza San Pietro. Both routes swing past Largo Argentina, where you can also get Bus No. 571 or 46.

A leisurely meander from the centro storico, across the exquisite Ponte Sant'Angelo, will take about a half hour.

TOP ATTRACTIONS

Fodor's Choice **Basilica di San Pietro.** The world's largest church, built over the tomb of ★ St. Peter, is the most imposing and breathtaking architectural achievement of the Renaissance (although much of the lavish interior dates to the Baroque). No fewer than five of Italy's greatest artists—Bramante,

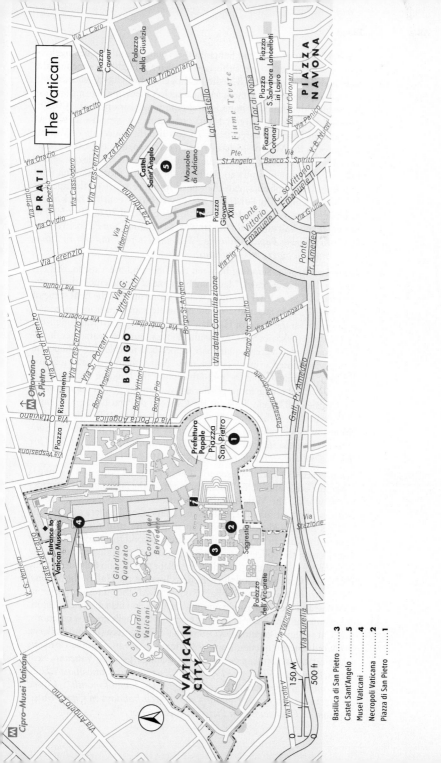

The Vatican

PRATI

BORGO

PIAZZA NAVONA

Castel Sant'Angelo

Mausoleo di Adriano

Fiume Tevere

VATICAN CITY

Prefettura Papale

Piazza San Pietro

Giardino Quadrato

Cortile del Belvedere

Giardini Vaticani

Entrance to Vatican Museums

Palazzo dell'Arciprete

Raphael, Peruzzi, Antonio Sangallo the Younger, and Michelangelo—died while striving to erect this new St. Peter's. Highlights include the **Loggia delle Benedizioni** (Benediction Loggia), the balcony where newly elected popes are proclaimed; **Michelangelo's Pietà;** and Bernini's great bronze **Baldacchino,** a huge, spiral-columned canopy—at 100,000 pounds, perhaps the largest bronze object in the world—as well as many other Bernini masterpieces. There's also the collection of Vatican treasures in the **Museo Storico-Artistico e Tesoro,** and the **Grotte Vaticane** crypt. For views of both the dome above and the piazza below, take the elevator or stairs to the roof; those with more stamina (and without claustrophobia) can then head up more stairs to the apex of the dome. ■TIP→ The Basilica is free to visit but a security check at the entrance can create very long lines. Arrive before 8:30 or after 5:30 to minimize the wait and avoid the crowds. ⊠ *Piazza di San Pietro, Vatican* ⊗ *Closed during Papal Audience (Wed. until 1 pm) and during other ceremonies in piazza* Ⓜ *Ottaviano.*

FAMILY   **Castel Sant'Angelo.** Standing between the Tiber and the Vatican, this circular and medieval "castle" has long been one of Rome's most distinctive landmarks. Opera lovers know it well as the setting for the final scene of Puccini's *Tosca*. In fact, the structure began life many centuries before as a mausoleum for the emperor Hadrian. Started in AD 135, it was completed by the emperor's successor, Antoninus Pius, about five years later. It initially consisted of a great square base topped by a marble-clad cylinder on which was planted a ring of cypress trees. Above them towered a gigantic statue of Hadrian. From the mid-6th century the building became a fortress, a place of refuge for popes during wars and sieges. In the rooms off the Cortile dell'Angelo, look for the Cappella di Papa Leone X (Chapel of Pope Leo X), with a facade by Michelangelo. The Sala Paolina (Pauline Room) was decorated in the 16th century with lavish frescoes. ⊠ *Lungotevere Castello 50, Prati* ☎ *06/6819111 for central line, 06/6896003 for tickets* ⊕ *castelsantangelo.beniculturali.it* 🎟 *€10* Ⓜ *Lepanto.*

Fodor'sChoice   **Musei Vaticani** (*Vatican Museums*). Other than the pope and his papal
★   court, the occupants of the Vatican are some of the most famous artworks in the world. The **Vatican Palace,** residence of the popes since 1377, consists of an estimated 1,400 rooms, chapels, and galleries. The pope and his household occupy only a small part; most of the rest is given over to the Vatican Library and Museums. Beyond the glories of the Sistine Chapel, the collection is extraordinarily rich; highlights include the great antique sculptures (including the celebrated Apollo Belvedere in the **Octagonal Courtyard** and the Belvedere Torso in the **Hall of the Muses**); the **Stanzi de Raffaello** (Raphael Rooms), with their famous gorgeous frescoes; and the old master paintings, such as Leonardo da Vinci's beautiful (though unfinished) St. Jerome, some of Raphael's greatest creations, and Caravaggio's gigantic *Deposition* in the **Pinacoteca** (Picture Gallery). To avoid lengthy queues, book your ticket in advance online (⊕ *www.biglietteriamusei.vatican.va*) for a €4 surcharge. ⊠ *Viale Vaticano, near intersection with Via Leone IV, Vatican* ⊕ *www.museivaticani.va* 🎟 *€20 with online reservations, €16 without; free last Sun. of month* ⊗ *Closed Sun. (except last Sun. of month) and church holidays* Ⓜ *Cipro–Musei Vaticani or Ottaviano–San Pietro. Bus No. 64 or 40.*

Necropoli Vaticana (*Vatican Necropolis*). With advance notice you can take a 1¼-hour guided tour in English of the Vatican Necropolis, under the Basilica di San Pietro, which gives a rare glimpse of Early Christian Roman burial customs and a closer look at the tomb of St. Peter. Apply by fax or email at least two months in advance, specifying the number of people in the group (all must be age 15 or older), preferred language, preferred time, available dates, and your contact information in Rome. ✉ *Piazza di San Pietro, Vatican* ☎ *06/69885318* ⊕ *www. vatican.va* ☜*€13* ⊙ *Closed Sun.* Ⓜ *Ottaviano–San Pietro.*

Fodor'sChoice **Piazza di San Pietro.** Mostly enclosed within high walls that recall the
★ papacy's stormy history, the Vatican opens the spectacular arms of Bernini's colonnade to embrace the world only at St. Peter's Square, scene of the pope's public appearances. One of Bernini's most spectacular masterpieces, the elliptical Piazza di San Pietro was completed in 1667 after only 11 years' work and holds about 100,000 people. Surrounded by a pair of quadruple colonnades, it is gloriously studded with 140 statues of saints and martyrs. At the piazza center, the 85-foot-high Egyptian obelisk was brought to Rome by Caligula in AD 37 and moved here in 1586 by Pope Sixtus V. The famous Vatican post offices (known for fast handling of outgoing mail) can be found on both sides of St. Peter's Square and inside the Vatican Museums complex. ■TIP→ The main Information Office is just left of the basilica as you face it. ✉ *West end of Via della Conciliazione, Vatican* ☎ *06/69881662* Ⓜ *Cipro–Musei Vaticani or Ottaviano–San Pietro.*

TRASTEVERE

Across the Tiber from the Jewish Ghetto is Trastevere (literally "across the Tiber"), long cherished as Rome's Greenwich Village and now subject to rampant gentrification. In spite of this, Trastevere remains about the most tightly knit community in the city, the Trasteverini proudly proclaiming their descent from the ancient Romans. Ancient bridges— the Ponte Fabricio and the Ponte Cestio—link the Ghetto to the Isola Tiberina (Tiber Island), a diminutive sandbar and one of Rome's most picturesque sights.

GETTING HERE AND AROUND

It's easy to get to Trastevere from Piazza Venezia: just take Tram No. 8 to the first stop on the other side of the river. You'll probably want to head right to the Piazza di Santa Maria in Trastevere, the heart of this lively area. Heading to the opposite side of Viale di Trastevere, though, is a treat many tourists miss. The cobblestone streets around Piazza in Piscinula and Via della Luce—locals peering down from balconies and the smell of fresh-baked bread floating from bakeries—are much more reminiscent of how Trastevere used to be than the touristic area to the north. Either way, remember that many of Trastevere's lovely small churches close, like others in Rome, in the afternoons. In the evenings, the neighborhood heats up with locals and visitors alike, drinking, eating, and going for *passeggiate* (strolls)—a not-to-be-missed atmosphere, especially for those with energy to burn.

Continued on page 78

HEAVEN'S ABOVE:
THE SISTINE CEILING

Forming lines that are probably longer than those
waiting to pass through the Pearly Gates, hordes of
visitors arrive at the Sistine Chapel daily to view what
may be the world's most sublime example of artistry:

Michelangelo: *The Creation of Adam*, Sistine Chapel, The Vatican, circa 1511.

Michelangelo's Sistine Ceiling. To paint this 12,000-square-foot barrel vault, it took four years, 343 frescoed figures, and a titanic battle of wits between the artist and Pope Julius II. While in its typical fashion, Hollywood focused on the element of agony, not ecstasy, involved in the saga of creation, a recently completed restoration of the ceiling has revolutionized our appreciation of the masterpiece of masterpieces.

By Martin Bennett

View of the Cappella Sistina

MICHELANGELO'S
MISSION IMPOSSIBLE

Designed to match the proportions of Solomon's Temple described in the Old Testament, the Sistine Chapel is named after Pope Sixtus VI, who commissioned it as a place of worship for himself and as the venue where new popes could be elected. Before Michelangelo, the barrel-vaulted ceiling was an expanse of azure fretted with golden stars. Then, in 1504, an ugly crack appeared. Bramante, the architect, managed do some patchwork using iron rods, but when signs of a fissure remained, the new Pope Julius II summoned Michelangelo to cover it with a fresco 135 feet long and 44 feet wide.

Taking in the entire span of the ceiling, the theme connecting the various participants in this painted universe could be said to be mankind's anguished waiting. The majestic panel depicting the Creation of Adam leads, through the stages of the Fall and the expulsion from Eden, to the tragedy of Noah found naked and mocked by his own sons; throughout all runs the underlying need for man's redemption. Witnessing all from the side and end walls, a chorus of ancient Prophets and Sibyls peer anxiously forward, awaiting the Redeemer who will come to save both the Jews and the Gentiles.

APOCALYPSE NOW

The sweetness and pathos of his Pietà, carved by Michelangelo only ten years earlier, have been left behind. The new work foretells an apocalypse, its congregation of doomed sinners facing the wrath of heaven through hanging, beheading, crucifixion, flood, and plague. Michelangelo, by nature a misanthrope, was already filled with visions of doom thanks to the fiery orations of Savonarola, whose thunderous preachments he had heard before leaving his hometown of Florence. Vasari, the 16th-century art historian, coined the word "terribilità" to describe Michelangelo's tension-ridden style, a rare case of a single word being worth a thousand pictures.

Michelangelo wound up using a *Reader's Digest* condensed version of the stories from Genesis, with the dramatis personae overseen by a punitive and terrifying God. In real life, poor Michelangelo answered to a flesh-and-blood taskmaster who was almost as vengeful: Pope Julius II. Less vicar of Christ than latter-day Caesar, he was intent on uniting Italy under the power of the Vatican, and was eager to do so by any means, including riding into pitched battle. Yet this "warrior pope" considered his most formidable adversary to be Michelangelo. Applying a form of blackmail, Julius threatened to wage war on Michelangelo's Florence, to which the artist had fled after Julius canceled a commission for a grand papal tomb unless Michelangelo agreed to return to Rome and take up the task of painting the Sistine Chapel ceiling.

MICHELANGELO, SCULPTOR

A sculptor first and foremost, however, Michelangelo considered painting an inferior genre—"for rascals and sissies" as he put it. Second, there was the sheer scope of the task, leading Michelangelo to suspect he'd been set up by a rival, Bramante, chief architect of the new St. Peter's Basilica. As Michelangelo was also a master architect, he regarded this fresco commission as a Renaissance mission-impossible. Pope Julius's powerful will prevailed—and six years later the work of the Sistine Ceiling was complete. Irving Stone's famous novel *The Agony and the Ecstasy*—and the granitic 1965 film that followed—chart this epic battle between artist and pope.

THINGS ARE LOOKING UP

To enhance your viewing of the ceiling, bring along opera-glasses, binoculars, or just a mirror (to prevent your neck from becoming bent like Michelangelo's). Note that no photos are permitted. Insiders know the only time to get the chapel to yourself is during the papal blessings and public audiences held in St. Peter's Square. Failing that, get there during lunch hour. Admission and entry to the Sistine Chapel is only through the Musei Vaticani (Vatican Museums).

SCHEMATIC OF THE SISTINE CEILING

Libyan Sibyl — Daniel — Cumean Sibyl — Isaiah — Delphic Sibyl

Jonah | NOAH STORIES [1] [2] [3] | ADAM & EVE STORIES [4] [5] [6] | THE CREATION [7] [8] [9] | Zacheriah

ENTRANCE

Jeremiah — Persian Sibyl — Ezekiel — Eritrean Sibyl — Joel

☐ Prophets ☐ Sibyls ➤ Ignudi

PAINTING THE BIBLE

The ceiling's biblical symbols were ideated by three Vatican theologians, Cardinal Alidosi, Egidio da Viterbo, and Giovanni Rafanelli, along with Mi-

chelangelo. As for the ceiling's painted "framework," this *quadratura* alludes to Roman triumphal arches because Pope Julius II was fond of mounting "triumphal entries" into his conquered cities (in imitation of Christ's

procession into Jerusalem on Palm Sunday).

THE CENTER PANELS

Prophet turned art-critic or, perhaps doubling as ourselves, the ideal viewer, Jonah the prophet (painted at the altar end) gazes up at the

Creation, or Michelangelo's version of it.

1 The first of three scenes taken from the Book of Genesis: God separates Light from Darkness.

2 God creates the sun and a craterless pre-Galilean moon

while the panel's other half offers an unprecedented rear view of the Almighty creating the vegetable world.

3 In the panel showing God separating the Waters from the Heavens, the Creator

tumbles towards us as in a self-made whirlwind.

4 Pausing for breath, next admire probably Western Art's most famous image—God giving life to Adam.

5 The Creation of Eve from Adam's rib leads to the sixth panel.

6 In a sort of diptych divided by the trunk of the Tree of Knowledge of Good and Evil, Michelangelo retells the Temptation and the Fall.

7 Illustrating Man's fallen nature, the last three panels narrate, in un-chronological order, the Flood. In the first Noah offers a pre-Flood sacrifice of thanks.

8 Damaged by an explosion in 1794, next comes Michelangelo's version of Flood itself.

9 Finally, above the monumental Jonah, you can just make out the small, wretched figure of Noah, lying drunk— in pose, the shrunken anti-type of the majestic Adam five panels down the wall.

THE CREATION OF ADAM

Michelangelo's Adam was partly inspired by the Creation scenes Michelangelo had studied in the sculpted doors of Jacopo della Quercia in Bologna and Lorenzo Ghiberti's Doors of Paradise in Florence. Yet in Michelangelo's version Adam's hand hangs limp, waiting God's touch to impart the spark of life. Facing his Creation, the Creator—looking a bit like the pagan god Jupiter—is for the first time ever depicted as horizontal, mirroring the Biblical "in his own likeness." Decades after its completion, a crack began to appear, amputating Adam's fingertips. Believe it or not, the most famous fingers in Western art are the handiwork, at least in part, of one Domenico Carnevale.

TOP ATTRACTIONS

Isola Tiberina. It's easy to overlook this tiny island in the Tiber. Don't. In terms of history and sheer loveliness, the charming Isola Tiberina— shaped like a boat about to set sail—gets high marks.

Cross onto the island via Ponte Fabricio, constructed in 62 BC, Rome's oldest remaining bridge; on the north side of the island crumbles the romantic ruin of the Ponte Rotto (Broken Bridge), which dates back to 179 BC. Descend the steps to the lovely river embankment to see the island's claim to fame: a Roman relief of the intertwined-snakes symbol of Aesculapius, the great god of healing. In 291 BC, a temple to Aesculapius was erected on the island. A ship had been sent to Epidaurus in Greece, heart of the cult of Aesculapius, to obtain a statue of the god. As the ship sailed back up the Tiber, a great serpent was seen escaping from it and swimming to the island—a sign that a temple to Aesculapius should be built here. In Imperial times, Romans sheathed the entire island with marble to make it look like Aesculapius's ship, replete with a towering obelisk as a mast. Amazingly, a fragment of the ancient sculpted ship's prow still exists. You can marvel at it on the downstream end of the embankment.

Today, medicine still reigns here. The island is home to the hospital of Fatebenefratelli (literally, "Do good, brothers"). Nearby is San Bartolomeo, built at the end of the 10th century by the Holy Roman Emperor Otto III and restored in the 18th century. Sometimes called the world's most beautiful movie theater, the open-air Cinema d'Isola di Tiberina operates from mid-June to early September as part of Rome's big summer festival, Estate Romana (⊕ *www.estateromana.comune.roma.it*). The 450-seat Arena unfolds its silver screen against the backdrop of the ancient Ponte Fabricio, while the 50-seat CineLab is set against Ponte Garibaldi facing Trastevere. Screenings usually start at 9:30 pm; admission is €6 for the Arena, €5 CineLab. Call ☎ *06/58333113* or go to ⊕ *isoladelcinema.com* for more information. Line up at the kiosk of La Grattachecca del 1915 (near the Ponte Cestio) for the most yumptious frozen ices in Rome. ⊠ *Isola Tiberina can be accessed by Ponte Fabricio or Ponte Cestio, Trastevere.*

Fodor'sChoice   **Santa Cecilia in Trastevere.** This basilica commemorates the aristocratic ★   St. Cecilia, patron saint of musicians. One of ancient Rome's most celebrated Early Christian martyrs, she was most likely put to a supernaturally long death by the Emperor Diocletian just before the year AD 300. After an abortive attempt to suffocate her in the baths of her own house (a favorite means of quietly disposing of aristocrats in Roman days), she was brought before the executioner. But not even three blows of the executioner's sword could dispatch the young girl. She lingered for several days, converting others to the Christian cause, before finally dying. In 1595, her body was exhumed—it was said to look as fresh as if she still breathed—and the heart-wrenching sculpture by eyewitness Stefano Maderno that lies below the main altar was, the sculptor insisted, exactly how she looked. Time your visit to enter the cloistered convent to see what remains of Pietro Cavallini's *Last Judgment,* dating to 1293. It's the only major fresco in existence known to have been painted by Cavallini, a contemporary of Giotto. To visit the frescoes, ring the bell of the convent to the left of the

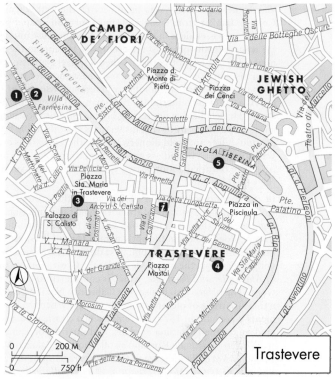

church entrance. ⊠ *Piazza di Santa Cecilia in Trastevere 22, Trastevere* ☎ *06/5899289* ✉ *Frescoes €2.50, underground €2.50.*

FodorśChoice
★
Santa Maria in Trastevere. Originally built during the 4th century and rebuilt in the 12th century, this is one of Rome's oldest and grandest churches. It is also the earliest foundation of any Roman church to be dedicated to the Virgin Mary. With a nave framed by a processional of two rows of gigantic columns (22 in total) taken from the ancient Baths of Caracalla, and an apse studded with gilded mosaics, the interior conjures the splendor of ancient Rome better than any other in the city. Overhead is Domenichino's gilded ceiling (1617). The 18th-century portico draws attention to the facade's 800-year-old mosaics, which represent the parable of the Wise and Foolish Virgins. They enhance the whole piazza, especially at night, when the church front and bell tower are illuminated. The church's most important mosaics, Pietro Cavallini's six panels of the *Life of the Virgin,* cover the semicircular apse. Note the building labeled "Taberna Meritoria" just under the figure of the Virgin in the Nativity scene, with a stream of oil flowing from it; it recalls the legend that a fountain of oil appeared on this spot, prophesying the birth of Christ. Off the piazza's northern side is a street called Via delle Fonte dell'Olio in honor of this miracle. ⊠ *Piazza Santa Maria in Trastevere, Trastevere* ☎ 06/5814802.

Fodor's Choice **Villa Farnesina.** Money was no object to the extravagant Agostino
★ Chigi, a banker from Siena who financed many papal projects. His
munificence is evident in this elegant villa, built for him about 1511.
He was especially proud of the decorative frescoes in the airy loggias,
now glassed in to protect them. When Raphael could steal a little time
from his work on the Vatican Stanze, he came over to execute some
of the frescoes himself, notably a luminous *Triumph of Galatea*. In
his villa, Agostino entertained the popes and princes of 16th-century
Rome. He delighted in impressing his guests at alfresco suppers held in
riverside pavilions by having his servants clear the table by casting the
precious silver and gold dinnerware into the Tiber. (His extravagance
was not quite so boundless as he wished to make it appear, however:
nets were unfurled a foot or two beneath the water's surface to catch
the valuable ware.)

In the magnificent **Loggia of Psyche** on the ground floor, Giulio
Romano and others worked from Raphael's designs. Raphael's lovely
Galatea is in the adjacent room. On the floor above you can see the
trompe-l'oeil effects in the aptly named **Hall of Perspectives** by Peruzzi. Agostino Chigi's bedroom, next door, was frescoed by Il Sodoma
with scenes from the life of Alexander the Great, notably the *Wedding
of Alexander and Roxanne*, which is considered to be the artist's best
work. The palace also houses the **Gabinetto Nazionale delle Stampe,**
a treasure trove of old prints and drawings. When the Tiber embank-
ments were built in 1879, the remains of a classical villa were discovered under the Farnesina gardens, and their decorations are now in
the Museo Nazionale Romano's collections in Palazzo Massimo alle
Terme. ⊠ *Via della Lungara 230, Trastevere* ☎ *06/68027268 for info,
06/68027397 for tour reservations* ⊕ *www.villafarnesina.it* 🎫 *€6.*

WORTH NOTING
Palazzo Corsini. A brooding example of Baroque style, the palace (once
home to Queen Christina of Sweden) is across the road from the Villa
Farnesina and houses part of the 16th- and 17th-century sections of
the collection of the Galleria Nazionale d'Arte Antica. Among the
star paintings in this manageably sized collection are Rubens's *St.
Sebastian* and Caravaggio's *St. John the Baptist.* Stop in if only to
climb the 17th-century stone staircase, itself a drama of architectural
shadows and sculptural voids. Behind, but separate from, the palazzo
is the University of Rome's **Orto Botanico**, home to 3,500 species of
plants, with various greenhouses around a stairway/fountain with 11
jets. ⊠ *Via della Lungara 10, Trastevere* ☎ *06/68802323 for Galleria
Corsini, 06/32810 for Galleria Corsini tickets, 06/49912436 for Orto
Botanico* ⊕ *galleriacorsini.beniculturali.it* 🎫 *€5* ☉ *Closed Tues.*

VIA APPIA ANTICA

Far south of the Celio lies catacomb country—the haunts of the fabled
underground graves of Rome's earliest Christians, arrayed to either
side of the Queen of Roads, the Via Appia Antica (Appian Way).
Strewn with classical ruins and dotted with grazing sheep, the road
stirs images of chariots and legionnaires returning from imperial

conquests. It was completed in 312 BC by Appius Claudius, who laid it out to connect Rome with settlements in the south, in the direction of Naples. Though time and vandals have taken their toll on the ancient relics along the road, the catacombs remain to cast their spirit-warm spell. Although Jews and pagans also used the catacombs, the Christians expanded the idea of underground burials to a massive scale. Persecution of Christians under pagan emperors made martyrs of many, whose bones, once interred underground, became objects of veneration. Today, the dark, gloomy catacombs contrast strongly with the Appia Antica's fresh air, verdant meadows, and evocative classical ruins.

GETTING HERE AND AROUND

The initial stretch of the Via Appia Antica is not pedestrian-friendly—there is fast, heavy traffic and no sidewalk all the way from Porta San Sebastiano to the Catacombe di San Callisto. To reach the catacombs, take Bus No. 218 from San Giovanni in Laterano. Alternatively, take Metro Line A to Colli Albani and then Bus No. 660 to the Tomba di Cecilia Metella. A more expensive option is the big, green Archeobus from Piazza Venezia (Friday–Sunday, early June–early November only); with an open-top deck, these buses allow you to hop on and off as you please (€20 for 24 hours). Another attractive alternative is to rent a bike—for example, at the Appia Antica Caffè near the Cecilia Metella bus stop.

TOP ATTRACTIONS

Fodor'sChoice ★ **Catacombe di San Sebastiano** (*Catacombs of St. Sebastian*). The 4th-century church was named after the saint who was buried in the catacomb, which burrows underground on four different levels. This was the only early Christian cemetery to remain accessible during the Middle Ages, and it was from here that the term *catacomb* is derived—it's in a spot where the road dips into a hollow, known to the Romans as *catacumba* (Greek for "near the hollow"). The Romans used the name to refer to the cemetery that had existed here since the 2nd century BC, and it came to be applied to all the underground cemeteries discovered in Rome in later centuries. As well as Christian burial areas, some very well preserved pagan mausolea were found here in the early 20th century making this one of the more varied catacomb complexes in the area. ⊠ *Via Appia Antica 136, Via Appia Antica* ☎ *06/7850350* ⊕ *www.catacombe.org* 🖾 *€8* ☉ *Closed Sun.* Ⓜ *Bus No. 118, 218, or 660.*

Tomba di Cecilia Metella. For centuries, sightseers have flocked to this famous landmark, one of the most complete surviving tombs of ancient Rome. One of the many round mausoleums that once lined the Appian Way, this tomb is a smaller version of the Mausoleum of Augustus, but impressive nonetheless. It was the burial place of a Roman noblewoman: the wife of the son of Crassus, who was one of Julius Caesar's rivals and known as the richest man in the Roman Empire (infamously entering the English language as "crass"). The original decoration includes a frieze of bulls' skulls near the top. The travertine stone walls were made higher and the medieval-style crenellations were added when the tomb was transformed into a fortress by

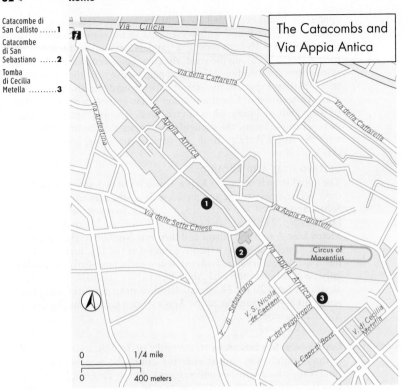

The Catacombs and
Via Appia Antica

the Caetani family in the 14th century. An adjacent chamber houses a small museum of the area's geological phases. Entrance to this museum also includes the Terme di Caracalla (Baths of Caracalla) and the Villa dei Quintili, but you can also get a super view without going in. ⊠ *Via Appia Antica 162, Via Appia Antica* ☎ *06/39967700* ⊕ *www.archeoroma.beniculturali.it* ⊠ *€6, includes Terme di Caracalla and Villa dei Quintili (valid for 7 days)* ⊙ *Closed Mon.*

WORTH NOTING

Catacombe di San Callisto (*Catacombs of St. Calixtus*). Burial place of several 3rd-century popes, this is Rome's oldest and best-preserved underground cemetery. One of the (English-speaking) friars who act as custodians of the catacomb will guide you through its crypts and galleries, some adorned with early Christian frescoes. Watch out for wrong turns: this catacomb is five stories deep! ■ TIP➔ **The large parking garage makes a visit easy—both for you and for large groups— and it can get busy.** ⊠ *Via Appia Antica 110/126, Via Appia Antica* ☎ *06/5310151* ⊕ *www.catacombe.roma.it* ⊠ *€8* ⊙ *Closed Wed., and mid-Jan.–Feb.* Ⓜ *Bus Nos. 118, 218.*

MONTI, CELIO, ESQUILINO, AND SAN LORENZO

Monti is the oldest *rione* in Rome. Gladiators, prostitutes, and even Caesar made their homes in this area that stretches from Santa Maria Maggiore down to the Forum. Today, Monti is one of the best-loved neighborhoods in Rome, known for its appealing mix of medieval streets, old-school trattorias, and hip boutiques. Bordering it is **Celio**— named after the hill across from the Palatine and from the Colosseum— which has residential cobblestone streets, ancient churches, and some good authentic restaurants and wine bars. **Esquilino,** covering Rome's most sprawling hill—the Esquiline—lies at the edge of the tourist maps, near the Termini station. Today, it's where many multinational inhabitants live and work. It's not the cobblestone-street atmosphere that most think of when they think of Rome.

AVENTINO AND TESTACCIO

The **Aventino** district is somewhat rarefied, where some houses still have their own bell towers and private gardens are called "parks," without exaggeration. Like the emperors of old on the Palatine, the fortunate residents here look out over the Circus Maximus and the river, winding its way far below. **Testaccio** is perhaps the world's only district built on broken pots: the hill of the same name was born from discarded pottery used to store oil, wine, and other goods loaded from the nearby Ripa, when Rome had a port and the Tiber was once a mighty river to an empire. It's quiet during the day, but on Saturday buzzes with the loud music from rows of discos and clubs.

WHERE TO EAT

In Rome, the Eternal(ly culinarily conservative) City, simple yet traditional cuisine reigns supreme. Most chefs prefer to follow the mantra of freshness over fuss, and simplicity of flavor and preparation over complex cooking techniques.

Rome has been known since antiquity for its grand feasts and banquets, and dining out has alway been a favorite Roman pastime. Until recently, the city's *buongustai* (gourmands) would have been the first to tell you that Rome is distinguished more by its enthusiasm for eating out than for a multitude of world-class restaurants—but this is changing. There is an ever-growing promotion of slow-food practices, a focus on sustainably and locally sourced produce. The economic crisis has forced the food industry in Rome to adopt innovative ways to maintain a clientele who are increasingly looking to dine out but want to spend less. The result has been the rise of "street food" restaurants, selling everything from inexpensive and novel takes on classic *supplì* (Roman fried-rice balls) to sandwich shops that use a variety of organic ingredients.

Generally speaking, Romans like Roman food, and that's what you'll find in many of the city's trattorias and wine bars. For the most part, today's chefs cling to the traditional and excel at what has taken hundreds, sometimes thousands, of years to perfect. This is why the basic trattoria menu is more or less the same wherever you go. And it's why even the top Roman chefs feature their versions of simple trattoria classics like carbonara, and why those who attempt to offer it in a "deconstructed" or slightly varied way will often come under criticism. To a great extent, Rome is still a town where the Italian equivalent of "What are you in the mood for?" still gets the answer, "Pizza or pasta."

WHAT IT COSTS				
	$	$$	$$$	$$$$
At dinner	under €14	€14–€24	€25–€34	Over €34

Restaurant prices are the average cost of a main course at dinner or, if dinner is not served, at lunch.

Use the coordinate (✛ B2) at the end of each listing to locate a site on the Where to Eat in Rome map.

PIAZZA NAVONA AND THE CAMPO DE' FIORI

PIAZZA NAVONA

$$
ROMAN
✕ **Armando al Pantheon.** In the shadow of the Pantheon, this trattoria, open since 1961, delights the tourists who tend to come for lunch. There's an air of authenticity here, and you'll see Roman antiques-shop owners who've been regulars here for decades. This is the place to try Roman artichokes or *vignarola* (a fava bean, asparagus, pea, and guanciale stew) in the spring, or the wild boar bruschetta in winter. Pastas are wonderful and filling, and secondi deliver all the Roman staples: oxtail, baby lamb chops, tripe, meatballs, and other hearty fare. Ⓢ *Average main: €15* ✉ *Salita dei Crescenzi 31, Piazza Navona* ☎ *06/68803034* ⊕ *www.armandoalpantheon.it* ☾ *Closed Sun., and Dec.–Jan. 6. No dinner Sat.* ✛ *E4.*

$
ITALIAN
FAMILY
✕ **Bar del Fico.** Everyone in Rome knows Bar del Fico, located right behind Piazza Navona, so if you're looking to hang out with the locals, this is the place to come. Just about every evening of the year, it's packed with people sipping cocktails in the square. Inside, diners sit on mismatched chairs, at eclectic tables, and order local specialties like their excellent rendition of *cacio e pepe* (cheese and pepper). For dessert, order the profiteroles. An Italian-style brunch is served on Sunday, in the style of lunch at nonna's (grandma's), complete with pasta *al forno* (baked) and crumbed schnitzel—though you can also order pancakes and American-style coffee. Ⓢ *Average main: €12* ✉ *Piazza de Fico 26, Piazza Navona* ☎ *06/68891373* ⊕ *www.bardelfico. com* ✛ *D4.*

$
CAFÉ
✕ **Caffè Sant'Eustachio.** Traditionally frequented by Rome's literati, this café is considered by many to make Rome's best coffee. Servers are hidden behind a huge espresso machine, where they vigorously mix the sugar and coffee to protect their "secret method" for the perfectly prepared cup. (If you want your caffè without sugar here, ask for it *amaro*.) Note that as in most cafés in Rome, it costs more if you want

to sit and sip your coffee—but there is nice outdoor seating when the weather is pleasant, so it's often worth it. $ *Average main: €2* ☒ *Piazza Sant'Eustachio 82, Piazza Navona* ☎ *06/68802048* ⊕ *www.santeusta-chioilcaffe.it* ✛ *E4.*

$$
WINE BAR
Fodor's Choice
★

✕ **Cul de Sac.** This popular wine bar near Piazza Navona is among the city's oldest and offers a book-length selection of wines from Italy, France, the Americas, and elsewhere. The food is eclectic, ranging from a huge assortment of Italian meats and cheeses (try the delicious *lonza*, cured pork loin, or *speck*, a northern Italian smoked prosciutto) and various Mediterranean dishes, including delicious baba ghanoush, a tasty Greek salad, and a spectacular wild boar pâté. Outdoor tables get crowded fast, so arrive early, or come late—they usually serve food until just past midnight, though they're closed in the late afternoon (about 4–5:30). $ *Average main: €14* ☒ *Piazza Pasquino 73, Piazza Navona* ☎ *06/68801094* ⊕ *www.enotecaculdesacroma.it* ✛ *D4.*

$
MEDITERRANEAN
Fodor's Choice
★

✕ **Etablì.** On a narrow *vicolo* (alley) off lovely cobblestone Piazza del Fico, this multifunctional restaurant and lounge space is decorated according to what could be called a modern Italian farmhouse-chic aesthetic, with vaulted wood-beam ceilings, wrought-iron touches, plush leather sofas, and chandeliers. The food is Mediterranean, with touches of Asia in the raw-fish appetizers. Pastas are more traditionally Italian, and secondi range from land to sea. It gets busy *dopo cena* (after dinner), when it becomes a popular spot for sipping and posing. If you want a more low-key experience, come for breakfast or lunch, served daily. $ *Average main: €12* ☒ *Vicolo delle Vacche 9/a, Piazza Navona* ☎ *06/97616694* ⊕ *www.etabli.it* ✛ *D3.*

$$$$
MODERN ITALIAN
Fodor's Choice
★

✕ **Il Convivio.** In a tiny, nondescript alley north of Piazza Navona, the three Troiani brothers—Angelo in the kitchen, and brothers Giuseppe and Massimo presiding over the dining room and wine cellar—have quietly been redefining the experience of Italian *alta cucina* (haute cuisine) for many years. Antipasti include "speck" of amberjack fish, herbs, pears, pomegranate, nuts, and raspberry oil, while pastas include spelt spaghetti with shrimp, mint, cocoa beans, and chili peppers. The renowned secondi might include options like Ischian-style rabbit or "cannoli" of sole, artichokes, and saffron. Service is attentive without being overbearing, and the wine list is exceptional. $ *Average main: €40* ☒ *Vicolo dei Soldati 31, Piazza Navona* ☎ *06/6869432* ⊕ *www.ilconviviotroiani.it* ☾ *Closed Sun., and 1 wk in Aug. No lunch* ✛ *D3.*

$$
ITALIAN

✕ **La Ciambella.** The sprawling space is styled after American restaurants, with a lively bar in front, but the structure itself is all Roman, with brick archways, high ceilings, and a skylight in one of the dining rooms that allows guests to gaze at the fantastic Roman sky. The emphasis here is on high-quality ingredients and classic Italian culinary traditions, evident in the incomparable Pugliese burrata, thin-crust pizzas, flavorful pastas (both classic and seasonal specialties), and grilled meats on offer. $ *Average main: €17* ☒ *Via dell'Arco della Ciambella 20, Piazza Navona* ☎ *06/6832930* ⊕ *www.laciambellaroma.com* ☾ *Closed Sun. No lunch in Aug.* ✛ *E4.*

CAMPO DE' FIORI

$$ ITALIAN

🍴 **Ditirambo.** Don't let the country-kitchen ambience fool you: at this little spot off Campo de' Fiori, the constantly changing selection of offbeat takes on Italian classics makes this a step beyond the ordinary. Antipasti can be delicious and unexpected, like Gorgonzola-and-pear soufflé drizzled with aged balsamic vinegar, or a mille-feuille of mozzarella, sundried tomatoes, and fresh mint. But people really love this place for rustic dishes like roast lamb, suckling pig, and hearty pasta with guinea fowl and porcini mushrooms. Vegetarians love the cheesy potato gratin with truffle shavings. Desserts, though homemade, can be skipped in favor of a *digestivo.* [$] *Average main: €16* ✉ *Piazza della Cancelleria 74, Campo de' Fiori* ☎ *06/6871626* 🌐 *www.ristoranteditirambo.it* 🕓 *Closed Aug. No lunch Mon.* ✣ *D4.*

$$ ROMAN FAMILY Fodor's Choice ★

🍴 **Emma.** Opened by Rome's renowned family of bakers, the Roscliolis, this large, sleek, modern pizzeria is smack in the middle of the city, with the freshest produce right outside the door. Start your meal with the artichoke salad if it's in season and an order of golden-fried supplì, then choose among the excellent pastas and thin-crust pizzas. The pancetta and chicory pizza is simple but outstanding—you really can't go wrong here. The wine list features many local Lazio options. If you have room, the warm apple cake with vanilla bean gelato, is deliciously decadent. You can walk it off tomorrow. [$] *Average main: €15* ✉ *Via Monte della Farina 28–29, Campo de' Fiori* ☎ *06/64760475* 🌐 *www.emmapizzeria.com* ✣ *D5.*

$ ITALIAN

🍴 **Filetti di Baccalà.** The window reads "Filetti di Baccalà," but the official name of this small restaurant that specializes in one thing—deliciously battered and deep-fried fillets of salt cod—is Dar Filettaro a Santa Barbara. There are a few basic starters on the menu, like *bruschette al pomodoro* (garlic-rubbed toast topped with fresh tomatoes and olive oil), and sautéed zucchini, and, in the winter, the cod is served alongside *puntarelle* (chicory stems tossed with a delicious anchovy-garlic-lemon vinaigrette). The location, down the street from Campo de' Fiori in a little piazza in front of the beautiful Santa Barbara church, practically begs you to eat at one of the outdoor tables. Be prepared for the service to be as Roman as the food: that is, brusque. [$] *Average main: €12* ✉ *Largo dei Librari 88, Campo de' Fiori* ☎ *06/6864018* 💳 *No credit cards* 🕓 *Closed Sun., and Aug. No lunch* ✣ *D5.*

$$$$ SEAFOOD Fodor's Choice ★

🍴 **Il Sanlorenzo.** This gorgeous space with its chandeliers and soaring original brickwork ceilings, houses one of the best seafood restaurants in the Eternal City. The eight-course tasting menu is extremely tempting—it might include the likes of cuttlefish-ink tagliatelle with mint, artichokes, and roe, or shrimp from the island of Ponza with rosemary, bitter herbs, and porcini mushrooms—and, for Rome, a relative bargain at €85. There are also plenty of à la carte items: a *crudo* (raw fish) appetizer, for instance, might include a perfectly seasoned fish tartare trio, sweet scampi, and a wispy carpaccio of red shrimp. The restaurant's version of spaghetti with sea urchin is exquisite and delicate; follow up with a main course of freshly caught seasonal fish prepared to order. [$] *Average main: €36* ✉ *Via dei Chiavari 4/5, Campo de' Fiori* ☎ *06/6865097* 🌐 *www.ilsanlorenzo.it* 🕓 *Closed 2 wks in Aug. No lunch Sat.–Mon.* ✣ *D4.*

$$ WINE BAR 🍴 **L'Angolo Divino.** There's something about this cozy wine bar that feels as if it's in a small university town instead of a bustling metropolis. Serene blue-green walls lined with wooden shelves of wines from around the Italian peninsula add to the warm atmosphere. There are always a few fresh pastas to choose from, and you can order smoked fish, cured meats, cheeses, and salads to make a nice lunch or light dinner. The kitchen stays open until the wee hours on weekends. [$] *Average main: €15* ✉ *Via dei Balestrari 12, Campo de' Fiori* ☎ *06/6864413* 🌐 *www.angolodivino.it* ⏲ *Closed 2 wks in Aug.* ✥ *D5.*

$$ BURGER 🍴 **Open Baladin.** The craft beer movement has taken hold in Italy and this gorgeous, sprawling space down the road from Campo de' Fiori is headed up by the Baladin beer company. Staff members take their jobs—and brews—seriously, and they're helpful with recommendations from the more than 40 options on tap and the more than 100 bottles to choose from. The food is mostly burgers and sandwiches, in many, many incarnations, and the hand-cut potato chips come in interesting flavors like cacio e pepe or paprika. [$] *Average main: €14* ✉ *Via Degli Specchi 5–6, Campo de' Fiori* ☎ *06/6838989* 🌐 *www.baladin.it* ✥ *E5.*

$$ ROMAN 🍴 **Osteria La Quercia.** Looking for a pleasant escape from the chaos of the Campo de' Fiori? The menu at this casual trattoria is simple and traditional, but the setting in the pretty piazza with tables under the gorgeous, looming oak tree is undoubtedly the real highlight. [$] *Average main: €15* ✉ *Piazza della Quercia 23, Campo de' Fiori* ☎ *06/68300932* 🌐 *www.osterialaquercia.com* ✥ *D5.*

$$ SOUTHERN ITALIAN 🍴 **Pesci Fritti.** This cute jewel box of a restaurant on the amphitheater-shape street behind Campo de' Fiori serves the namesake fried fish and much more. Step inside, and the whitewashed walls with touches of pale sea blue will make you feel like you've escaped to the Mediterranean. Much of the cuisine echoes this theme, with heavy incorporation of seaside favorites like octopus, *spigola* (sea bass), and *bottarga* (salted, cured fish roe). The pasta with clams is a highlight, as is the fish prepared many different ways. The few missteps happen when the cooks try to get too creative, so stick to the southern classics and enjoy this virtual seaside escape. [$] *Average main: €18* ✉ *Via della Grottapinta 8, Campo de' Fiori* ☎ *06/68806170* ⏲ *Closed Mon., and Aug. No lunch* ✥ *D4.*

$$$ ITALIAN 🍴 **Pierluigi.** This popular seafood restaurant is a fun spot on balmy summer evenings with tables out on the pretty piazza de'Ricci. As at many Italian fish ristoranti, any antipasto featuring crudi is always a smart choice: delicious tartare, carpaccio, shrimp, clams, and oysters are all in abundance. So are pastas and risotto with seafood, and secondi like roasted turbot with potatoes, cherry tomatoes, and black olives. Make sure to end your meal with a refreshing *sgroppino* (lemon sorbet, vodka, and prosecco). If you're ordering fresh fish, double-check the cost after it's been weighed so you don't get overcharged. [$] *Average main: €28* ✉ *Piazza de Ricci 144, Campo de' Fiori* ☎ *06/6861302* 🌐 *www.pierluigi.it* ⏲ *Closed Mon.* ✥ *D4.*

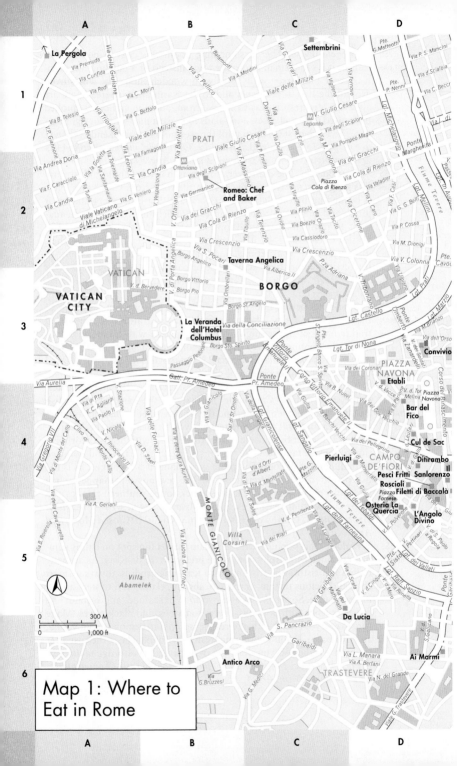

Map 1: Where to
Eat in Rome

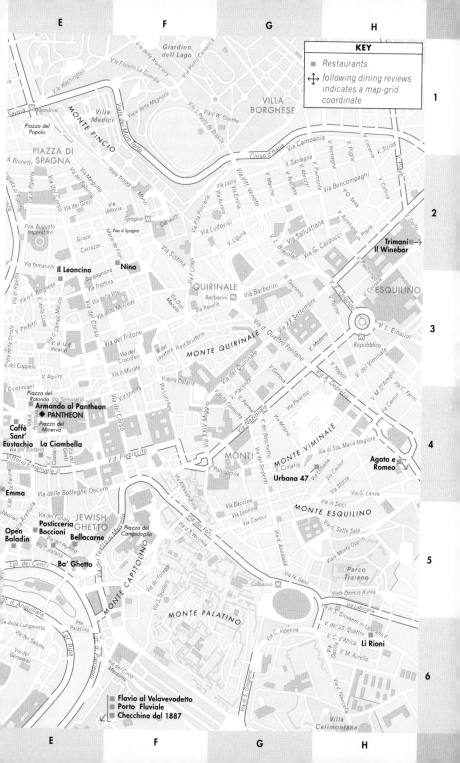

$$ WINE BAR Fodor's Choice ★ 🍴 **Roscioli.** The shop in front of this wine bar will beckon you in with top-quality comestibles like hand-sliced cured ham from Italy and Spain, more than 300 cheeses, and a dizzying array of wines—but venture further inside to where you can sit and order artisanal cheeses and smoked meats, as well as an extensive selection of unusual dishes and interesting takes on classics. Try the burrata with Norwegian herring caviar, pasta with sardines, or Sicilian linguine with red prawns and cumin. The menu ranges from meat, seafood (including a nice selection of crudi), to vegetarian-friendly items. You can also reserve a table in the cozy wine cellar downstairs for an even more intimate experience. After your meal, head around the corner to their bakery for rightfully famous breads and sweets. [$] *Average main: €22* ✉ *Via dei Giubbonari 21/22, Campo de' Fiori* ☎ *06/6875287* 🌐 *www.salumeriaroscioli.com/restaurant* 🕘 *Closed Sun., and 1 wk in Aug.* ✣ *D4.*

THE JEWISH GHETTO

$$ ISRAELI Fodor's Choice ★ 🍴 **Ba' Ghetto.** This hot spot on the main promenade in the Jewish Ghetto has been going strong for years, with pleasant indoor and outdoor seating. The kitchen is kosher (many places featuring Roman Jewish fare are not) and serves meat dishes (so no dairy); the menu features an assortment of Roman Jewish delights, as well as Mediterranean and Middle Eastern Jewish fare. Enjoy starters like phyllo "cigars" stuffed with ground meat and spices, or the mixed appetizer platter with hummus. Forego pasta for couscous (the spicy fish is delicious) or baccalà with raisins and pine nuts. Down the street is **Ba'Ghetto Milky** (*Via del Portico d'Ottavia 2/a*), the kosher dairy version of the original. [$] *Average main: €22* ✉ *Via del Portico d'Ottavia 57, Jewish Ghetto* ☎ *06/68892868* 🌐 *www.kosherinrome.com* 🕘 *No dinner Fri.; no lunch Sat.* ✣ *E5.*

$$ ROMAN 🍴 **Bellacarne.** *Bellacarne* means "beautiful meat," and that's the focus of the menu here, though the double entendre is that it's also what a Jewish Italian grandmother might say while pinching her grandchild's cheek. The kosher kitchen makes its own pastrami—a pretty good version of what one might find in Jewish delis in NYC, but the difference is that here the meat is served on its own, thinly sliced, at room temperature, and on a platter with mustard—much like how cured meats are served in Italy. It's culturally on-point, though it might leave you longing for two slices of rye bread to make a sandwich—and the setting is definitely more fine-dining than deli. The fried artichokes are excellent, as is the shawarma with hummus, and the chopped Israeli salad. [$] *Average main: €17* ✉ *Via Portico d'Ottavia 51, Jewish Ghetto* ☎ *06/6833104* 🌐 *www.bellacarne.it* 🕘 *No dinner Fri.; no lunch Sat.* ✣ *E5.*

$ CAFÉ 🍴 **Pasticceria Boccioni.** *Forno* means "oven" in Italian, but it's also the word for a bakery that specializes in bread and simple baked goods, like biscotti and pine-nut tarts. A *pasticceria,* on the other hand, specializes in more complicated Italian sweets, like fruit tarts, *montebianco* (a chestnut-cream creation resembling an alpine mountain), and *millefoglie* (puff pastry layered with pastry cream). Straddling the line between a forno and a pasticceria, Boccioni—commonly known as

Forno del Ghetto (or "the Burnt Bakery," for the dark brown crust most everything here seems to have)—is famed for its Roman Jewish specialties. Try the delicious ricotta cheesecake, filled with cherries or chocolate, baked in an almond crust. Come early on Friday, as they sell out before closing for the Sabbath. [$] *Average main: €4* ✉ *Via del Portico d'Ottavia 1, Jewish Ghetto* ☎ *06/6878637* ⏲ *Closed Sat.* ✥ *E5.*

PIAZZA DI SPAGNA

$ PIZZA Fodor's Choice ★

🍴 **Il Leoncino.** The no-reservations policy and long lines of locals out the door attest to the popularity of this fluorescent-lighted pizzeria in the otherwise big-ticket neighborhood around Piazza di Spagna, but if you arrive early (between 7 and 8), you probably won't have to wait. The atmosphere is noisy and cheerful, and the service is dished out by a Fellinian cast of characters that falls just on the right side of chaotic. The Tridente area might not have much in the way of budget dinner options, but a pizza at Il Leoncino is a good start. [$] *Average main: €12* ✉ *Via del Leoncino 28, Piazza di Spagna* ☎ *06/6876306* ⏲ *Closed Wed., and Aug.* [M] *Spagna* ✥ *E3.*

$$$ ITALIAN Fodor's Choice ★

🍴 **Nino.** A favorite among international journalists and the rich and famous for decades, Nino is Rome's best-loved dressed-up trattoria. The interior is country rustic *alla toscana,* and the menu accordingly sticks to the classics, featuring Roman and Tuscan staples. Start with a selection of antipasti or the warm crostini spread with pâté. Move on to pappardelle *al lepre* (in a rich hare sauce) or hearty Tuscan ribollita, and go for the gold with a piece of juicy grilled beef. If you're not Italian or a regular or a celebrity, the chance of brusque service multiplies—insist on good service and you'll win the waiters' respect. [$] *Average main: €28* ✉ *Via Borgognona 11, Piazza di Spagna* ☎ *06/6786752* 🌐 *www.ristorantenino.it* ⏲ *Closed Sun., and Aug.* [M] *Spagna* ✥ *F2.*

REPUBBLICA

$$ WINE BAR

🍴 **Trimani Il Winebar.** Operating nonstop 11 am–midnight, this wine bar serves hot food at lunch and dinner. The interior is minimalist in style, but the second floor provides a subdued, candlelit space to sip wine. There's always a choice of soup and pasta, as well as second courses and *torte salate* (savory tarts). Around the corner is a wine shop, one of the oldest in Rome, by the same name. They also offer wine tastings and classes (in Italian). [$] *Average main: €15* ✉ *Via Cernaia 37/b, Repubblica* ☎ *06/4469630* 🌐 *www.trimani.com* ⏲ *Closed Sun., and Aug.* [M] *Castro Pretorio* ✥ *H2.*

AROUND THE VATICAN

$$$ ROMAN Fodor's Choice ★

🍴 **La Veranda dell'Hotel Columbus.** Deciding where to sit at La Veranda isn't easy, because both the shady courtyard (torchlit at night), and the frescoed dining room are among Rome's most spectacular settings. While La Veranda is known for classic Roman cuisine, some dishes are served with refreshing twists on the familiar. The seasonal menu may include an eggplant caponata with *burrata* (fresh cheese made from mozzarella and cream) and bottarga from Sardinia; Piedmontese oxtail soup; a risotto with Barolo wine and blue cheese; or quail carpaccio with mustard seeds. $ *Average main: €25* ✉ *Hotel Columbus, Borgo Santo Spirito 73, Borgo* ☎ *06/6872973* ⊕ *www.laveranda.net* ⊗ *Closed Mon. No lunch* ✛ *B3*.

$$
MODERN ITALIAN

✕ **Romeo: Chef and Baker.** The sprawling space here—it used to be an Alfa Romeo workshop; hence, the name—is an übermodern, multifaceted affair. In front is a casual bakery and deli counter, serving pizzas; gourmet sandwiches like pita stuffed with chicken, walnuts, celery, and pomegranate; and freshly baked breads, cakes, muffins, and tarts. In back, a more upscale menu is available, with pasta dishes like the classic carbonara, and secondi like lamb, or calamari stuffed with ricotta, sea urchin, ginger, and orange. This is the second restaurant from Michelin-starred chef Cristina Bowerman; the other is Glass Hostaria, in Trastevere. $ *Average main: €20* ✉ *Via Silla 26A, Prati* ☎ *06/32110120* ⊕ *www.romeo.roma.it* Ⓜ *Ottaviano* ✛ *B2*.

$$
MODERN ITALIAN
Fodor's Choice
★

✕ **Settembrini.** The modern, intimate dining room here hints at what to expect from the kitchen and staff: elegant and restrained cooking, friendly yet unobtrusive service, and an interesting and well-curated wine list. The menu puts creative twists on classic Italian ingredients—think risotto with sea urchins, basil, and licorice, or cod with burrata, watermelon, and cardamom. This is a gem in a reasonably quiet neighborhood. $ *Average main: €20* ✉ *Via Luigi Settembrini 21, Prati* ☎ *06/3232617* ⊕ *www.viasettembrini.com* ⊗ *Closed Sun., and 2 wks in Aug. No lunch Sat.* Ⓜ *Lepanto* ✛ *C1*.

$$
MODERN ITALIAN

✕ **Taverna Angelica.** The Borgo area near St. Peter's Basilica hasn't been known for culinary excellence, but this is starting to change, and Taverna Angelica was one of the first refined restaurants in this part of town. The dining room is small, which allows the chef to create a menu that's inventive without being pretentious: perhaps pasta with pistachio pesto and shrimp, or turbot with crushed almonds and white wine sauce. Spaghetti with crunchy pancetta and leeks is wonderful, as is the warm seafood soup. Fresh sliced tuna in a pistachio crust with orange sauce is light and delicious. Desserts here go beyond the staples of tiramisù and panna cotta. $ *Average main: €22* ✉ *Piazza A. Capponi 6, Borgo* ☎ *06/6874514* ⊕ *www.tavernaangelica.it* ⊗ *Closed 2 wks in Aug. No lunch Mon.–Sat.* Ⓜ *Ottaviano* ✛ *B3*.

TRASTEVERE

$
PIZZA
FAMILY

✕ **Ai Marmi** (*Panattoni*). The official name of this popular pizzeria is Panattoni, but everyone calls it "Ai Marmi" or "L'Obitorio" (the morgue) for its marble-slab tables. Contrary to what that might imply, this place is actually about as lively as it gets—indeed, it's packed pretty much every night, with diners munching on crisp pizzas that come out of the wood-burning ovens at top speed. The fried starters, like a nice baccalà, are light and tasty. The restaurant stays open well past midnight, convenient for a late meal after the theater or a movie nearby. $ *Average main: €12* ✉ *Viale Trastevere 53–57, Trastevere* ☎ *06/5800919* ⊗ *Closed Wed., and 3 wks in Aug. No lunch* ✛ *D6*.

2

$$$ ✕**Antico Arco.** Founded by three friends with a passion for wine and
MODERN ITALIAN   fine food, Antico Arco attracts foodies from Rome and beyond with
Fodor'sChoice   its refined culinary inventiveness. The location on top of the Janiculum
★   Hill makes for a charming setting, and inside, the dining rooms are
plush, modern spaces, with whitewashed brick walls, dark floors, and
black velvet chairs. The seasonal menu offers delights such as amberjack
tartare with lime, ginger, and a salad of chicory stems; classic pasta alla
carbonara enriched with black truffle; and duck with artichokes and
foie gras. The molten chocolate cake has made a name for itself among
chocoholics the city over. **$** *Average main: €28* ⊠ *Piazzale Aurelio 7,
Trastevere* ☎ *06/5815274* ⊕ *www.anticoarco.it* ✛ *B6.*

$$ ✕**Da Lucia.** There's no shortage of old-school trattorias in Trastevere, but
ROMAN   Da Lucia has a strong following among them. Both locals and expats
enjoy the brusque but "authentic" service and the hearty Roman fare,
like classic *bombolotti* all'amatriciana (short, fat tubular pasta) and
spaghetti cacio e pepe; and meat dishes like beef *involtini* (meat rolls)
with peas and Roman-style tripe. Snag a table outside in warm weather
for the true Roman experience of cobblestone-terrace dining. **$** *Aver-
age main: €14* ⊠ *Vicolo del Mattonato 2b, Trastevere* ☎ *06/5803601*
☾ *Closed Mon., and Aug.* ✛ *C5.*

MONTI, CELIO, AND ESQUILINO

MONTI

$$ ✕**Urbana 47.** This restaurant serving breakfast through dinner embod-
MODERN ITALIAN   ies the *kilometro zero* concept, highlighting hyper-local food from the
Fodor'sChoice   surrounding Lazio region. The local boho crowd comes in the morning
★   for a Continental or "American" breakfast (with free Wi-Fi); lunch
means tasty "fast slow-food" options like grain salads and healthy
panini. From 6 pm onward, there are tapas and drinks, then leisurely
dinners like homemade pasta with broccoli, anchovies, and orange
zest, or a local free-range chicken stuffed with potatoes and chic-
ory. **$** *Average main: €15* ⊠ *Via Urbana 47, Monti* ☎ *06/47884006*
⊕ *www.urbana47.it* Ⓜ *Cavour* ✛ *G4.*

ESQUILINO

$$ ✕**Agata e Romeo.** For the perfect combination of fine dining, creative
MODERN ITALIAN   cuisine, and rustic Roman tradition, this restaurant run by husband-
Fodor'sChoice   and-wife team of Agata Parisella (in the kitchen) and Romeo Carac-
★   cio (in the front of the house) is a must. The intimate dining room
and personal service make you feel as if you're dining in a friend's
house; and the food is outstanding. Chef Agata was one of the first
in the capital to put a gourmet spin on Roman ingredients and classic
preparations, so even though the menu might look familiar, the quality of the food is several steps above. The cacio e pepe is particularly
renowned. **$** *Average main: €20* ⊠ *Via Carlo Alberto 45, Esquilino*
☎ *06/4466115* ⊕ *www.agataeromeo.it* ☾ *Closed Sun., and 2 wks in
Aug. No lunch Sat. and Mon.* Ⓜ *Vittorio Emanuele* ✛ *H4.*

$ ✕**Li Rioni.** This busy pizzeria conveniently close to the Colosseum has
PIZZA   been serving real-deal Roman-style pizza—super thin and cooked
FAMILY   to a crisp—since the mid-1980s. The magic might be due to the
fact that they let their pizza dough rise 24–48 hours before baking

to guarantee an extra-light pizza, said to be more easily digested than others. The Napoli and Margherita reign supreme here, as well as anything with buffalo mozzarella and pork sausage. Do as the Romans do, and start your meal with fritti; the olive ascolane are particularly good. $ *Average main: €12* ⊠ *Via dei Santi Quattro 24, Esquilino* ☎ *06/70450605* ⊕ *www.lirioni.it* ☉ *Closed 2 wks in Aug. No lunch* Ⓜ *Colosseo* ✛ *H6.*

TESTACCIO

$$ ✕ **Checchino dal 1887.** Literally carved out of a hill of ancient shards of
ROMAN   amphorae, Checchino is an example of a classic, upscale, family-run Roman restaurant, with one of the best wine cellars in the region. Although the slaughterhouses of Testaccio are long gone, their echo carries on in the restaurant's classic dishes—mostly offal and other cuts like *trippa* (tripe), *pajata* (intestines), and *coratella* (sweetbreads and beef heart) are all still on the menu for Roman purists. For the less adventurous, other house specialties include braised milk-fed lamb with seasonal vegetables. $ *Average main: €23* ⊠ *Via di Monte Testaccio 30, Testaccio* ☎ *06/5746318* ⊕ *www.checchino-dal-1887. com* ☉ *Closed Mon., Aug., and 1 wk at Christmas. No dinner Sun.* Ⓜ *Piramide* ✛ *F6.*

$$ ✕ **Flavio al Velavevodetto.** It's everything you're looking for in a true
ROMAN   Roman eating experience: authentic, in a historic setting, and filled
Fodor'sChoice   with Italians eating good food at good prices. In this very *romani di*
★   *Roma* working-class neighborhood, surrounded by discos and bars sharing Monte Testaccio, you can enjoy a meal of classic Roman pasta dishes (carbonara, amatriciana, etc.) and delicious fettucine with baby calamari and cherry tomatoes with some very good antipasti (try the mixed vegetable plate); and great meat mains like *polpette di bollito* (broiled meatballs) and flame-grilled lamb. The menu is simple and seasonal, and served either in the cozy, cavelike indoor dining rooms or outside under the umbrellas. For dessert order the tiramisù with a Nutella chocolate center. $ *Average main: €16* ⊠ *Via di Monte Tes-taccio 97, Testaccio* ☎ *06/5744194* ⊕ *www.ristorantevelavevodetto. it* Ⓜ *Piramide* ✛ *F6.*

$$ ✕ **Porto Fluviale.** This massive structure is on a stretch of street that's
ITALIAN   gone from gritty clubland to popular night spot, thanks largely to Porto Fluviale, which has come to mean all things to all people: bar, café, pizzeria, lunch buffet, and lively evening restaurant. The food, too, is all-encompassing, featuring cuisine from all over Italy. As one might expect from such a cavernous, busy place, the service is not perfect, but it's a fun place to be and the food is tasty, from pizza made in wood-burning ovens to pasta and grilled meats and inter-esting salads. Cocktails at the bar, if you can get a spot, are a fun option—accompany your drink with *cicchetti* (the Venetian word for tapas-style snacks). $ *Average main: €14* ⊠ *Via del Porto Fluviale 22, Testaccio* ☎ *06/5743199* ⊕ *www.portofluviale.com* Ⓜ *Piramide* ✛ *F6.*

MONTE MARIO

$$$$ MODERN ITALIAN Fodor's Choice ★ 🍴 **La Pergola.** Dinner here is a truly spectacular and romantic event, with incomparable views across the city matched by the spectacular three–Michelin star dining experience. The difficulty comes in choosing from among Chef Heinz Beck's alta cucina specialties. Expect such temptations as John Dory fillet with white truffles, pumpkin puree, and mushrooms, or deep-fried zucchini flowers with caviar in a shellfish-and-saffron consommé. Everything from the bread to the wine to the service is top-notch, and the dessert course is always an extravagant, multicourse event. [$] *Average main: €65* ✉ *Waldorf Astoria Rome Cavalieri, Via Alberto Cadlolo 101, Monte Mario* ☎ *06/35092152* 🌐 *www.romecavalieri.com/lapergola.php* ⏲ *Closed Sun. and Mon., 3 wks in Aug., and most of Jan. No lunch* 👔 *Jacket and tie* ✥ *A1.*

WHERE TO STAY

It's the click of your heels on inlaid marble, the whisper of 600-thread-count Frette sheets, the murmured *buongiorno* of a coat-tailed porter bowing low as you pass. It's a rustic attic room with a wood-beam ceiling, a white umbrella on a roof terrace, a 400-year-old palazzo. Maybe it's birdsong pouring into your room as you swing open French windows to a sun-kissed view of the Colosseum, a timeworn piazza, or a flower-filled marketplace.

When it comes to accommodations, Rome offers a wide selection of high-end hotels, bed-and-breakfasts, designer boutique hotels—options that run the gamut from whimsical to luxurious. Whether you want a simple place to rest your head or a complete cache of exclusive amenities, you have plenty to choose from. *Hotel reviews have been shortened. For full information, visit Fodors.com.*

WHAT IT COSTS

	$	$$	$$$	$$$$
For two people	under €125	€125–€200	€201–€300	over €300

Prices are for a standard double room in high season.

Use the coordinate (✥ B2) at the end of each listing to locate a site on the Where to Stay in Rome map.

PIAZZA NAVONA AND THE CAMPO DE' FIORI

PIAZZA NAVONA

$$$ HOTEL Fodor's Choice ★ 🏨 **Albergo Santa Chiara.** If you're looking for a good location and top-notch service at great rates—not to mention comfortable beds and a quiet stay—look no further than this historic hotel, run by the same family for some 200 years. **Pros:** great location; free Wi-Fi; lovely terrace/sitting area in front, overlooking the piazza. **Cons:** some rooms are on the small side and need updating; breakfast

selection isn't always the best; Wi-Fi can be slow. $ *Rooms from:* €270 ✉ *Via Santa Chiara 21, Piazza Navona* ☎ *06/6872979* ⊕ *www. albergosantachiara.com* ⤵ *99 rooms, 3 apartments* ⦿ *Breakfast* Ⓜ *Spagna* ✛ *E4.*

$$ | 🏨 **Hotel Genio.** Just outside one of Rome's most beautiful piazzas—
HOTEL | Piazza Navona—this pleasant hotel has a lovely rooftop terrace perfect for enjoying a cappuccino or a glass of wine while taking in the view. **Pros:** friendly staff; breakfast buffet is abundant; free Wi-Fi; spacious, elegant bathrooms. **Cons:** rooms facing the street can be noisy; spotty Internet; beds can be too firm for some. $ *Rooms from: €160* ✉ *Via Giuseppe Zanardelli 28, Piazza Navona* ☎ *06/6833781* ⊕ *www.hotel-genioroma.it* ⤵ *60 rooms* ⦿ *Breakfast* Ⓜ *Spagna* ✛ *D3.*

$$$ | 🏨 **Relais Palazzo Taverna.** This little hidden gem on a side street behind
HOTEL | the lovely Via dei Coronari is a good compromise for those looking for boutique-style accommodations on a budget. **Pros:** centrally located; boutique-style accommodations at moderate prices; free Wi-Fi; friendly, responsive staff; spacious rooms. **Cons:** staff on duty until 11 pm (can be contacted after-hours in an emergency); some rooms are starting to show wear and tear. $ *Rooms from: €210* ✉ *Via dei Gabrielli 92, Piazza Navona* ☎ *06/20398064* ⊕ *www.relaispalazzotaverna.com* ⤵ *11 rooms* ⦿ *Breakfast* Ⓜ *Spagna* ✛ *D3.*

CAMPO DE' FIORI

$$ | 🏨 **Albergo del Sole al Biscione.** This affordable and comfortable hotel,
HOTEL | centrally located in the heart of Campo de' Fiori and built atop the ruins of the ancient Theatre of Pompey, has warm, cozy decor and a rooftop terrace with a stunning view of Sant'Andrea delle Valle. **Pros:** parking garage in the hotel; reasonable rates for the location; nice rooftop terrace. **Cons:** some rooms are small and lack a/c; no elevator at the entrance of hotel; area can be a bit noisy. $ *Rooms from: €130* ✉ *Via del Biscione 76, Campo de' Fiori* ☎ *06/68806873* ⊕ *www.sole-albiscione.it* ⤵ *59 rooms* ⦿ *No meals* Ⓜ *Barberini* ✛ *D4.*

$$$ | 🏨 **Casa di Santa Brigida.** The friendly sisters of Santa Brigida oversee
B&B/INN | simple, straightforward, and centrally located accommodations in
Fodor'sChoice | one of Rome's loveliest convents, with a rooftop terrace overlooking
★ | Palazzo Farnese. **Pros:** no curfew in this historic convent; insider papal tickets; location in the Piazza Farnese; large library and sunroof; free Wi-Fi. **Cons:** weak a/c; no TVs in the rooms (though there is a common TV room); not equipped for guests with disabilities. $ *Rooms from: €210* ✉ *Piazza Farnese 96, entrance around the corner at Via Monserrato 54, Campo de' Fiori* ☎ *06/68892596* ⊕ *www.brigidine. org* ⤵ *20 rooms* ⦿ *Breakfast; All meals* ✛ *D4.*

$$$$ | 🏨 **D.O.M. Hotel.** In an old convent on Via Giulia, one of Rome's
HOTEL | romantic ivy-covered streets, the D.O.M. (Deo Optimo Maximo) is an ultrachic luxury hotel that resembles an aristocratic *casa nobile*. **Pros:** complimentary Aqua di Parma toiletries; heated towel racks; hip decor. **Cons:** pricey breakfast; delicious but expensive cocktails; rooms are small for a five-star standard. $ *Rooms from: €380* ✉ *Via Giulia, 131, Campo de' Fiori* ☎ *06/683–2144* ⊕ *www.domhotelroma. com* ⤵ *18 rooms* ⦿ *Breakfast* ✛ *C4.*

$$$
HOTEL
Fodor'sChoice
★
 ⌃ **Hotel Ponte Sisto.** Situated in a restored Renaissance palazzo with one of the prettiest patio-courtyards in Rome, this hotel is a relaxing retreat close to Trastevere and Campo de' Fiori. **Pros:** friendly staff; rooms with views (and some with balconies and terraces); luxury bathrooms; beautiful courtyard garden. **Cons:** streetside rooms can be a bit noisy; some upgraded rooms are small and not worth the price difference; carpets starting to show signs of wear; aside from breakfast, restaurant caters only to groups and must be booked in advance. $\boxed{\$}$ *Rooms from: €260* ✉ *Via dei Pettinari 64, Campo de' Fiori* ☎ *06/6863100* ⊕ *www.hotelpontesisto.it* 🛏 *107 rooms* ⎟◉⎟ *Breakfast* ✛ *D5.*

JEWISH GHETTO

$$
HOTEL
 ⌃ **Arenula.** If you're looking for no-frills bargain accommodations in the center of Rome, this budget hotel is a good option with an almost unbeatable location. **Pros:** a real bargain; conveniently located, near Campo de' Fiori and Trastevere; spotless. **Cons:** totally no-frills accommodations; no elevator; breakfast is nothing to write home about. $\boxed{\$}$ *Rooms from: €145* ✉ *Via Santa Maria dei Calderari 47, off Via Arenula, Jewish Ghetto* ☎ *06/6879454* ⊕ *www.hotelarenula.com* 🛏 *50 rooms* ⎟◉⎟ *Breakfast* ✛ *E5.*

PIAZZA DI SPAGNA AND PIAZZA DEL POPOLO

$$$$
HOTEL
 ⌃ **Babuino 181.** Named for the street it's on, which is also known for high-end boutiques and antiques shops, this stylish hotel, spread through two historic buildings, has spacious rooms and personalized service. **Pros:** spacious suites; luxury Frette linens; iPhone docks and other handy in-room amenities. **Cons:** rooms can be a bit noisy; breakfast is nothing special. $\boxed{\$}$ *Rooms from: €350* ✉ *Via Babuino 181, Piazza di Spagna* ☎ *06/32295295* ⊕ *www.romeluxurysuites.com/babuino* 🛏 *24 rooms* ⎟◉⎟ *No meals* Ⓜ *Flaminio, Spagna* ✛ *E2.*

$
B&B/INN
 ⌃ **Daphne Trevi.** This urban B&B is run by people who love Rome and want to make sure you do, too—the staff will happily act as your personal travel planners, helping you map out destinations, plan day trips, choose restaurants, and organize transportation. **Pros:** kosher, gluten-free, and vegetarian breakfast options; friendly, helpful staff; beds have Simmons mattresses and fluffy comforters; free Wi-Fi. **Cons:** no TVs; two rooms share a bathroom. $\boxed{\$}$ *Rooms from: €115* ✉ *Via degli Avignonesi 20, Piazza di Spagna* ☎ *06/89345781* ⊕ *www.daphne-rome.com* 🛏 *10 rooms* ⎟◉⎟ *Breakfast* Ⓜ *Barberini* ✛ *G3.*

$$$$
HOTEL
Fodor'sChoice
★
 ⌃ **The Hassler.** When it comes to million-dollar views, the best place to stay in the whole city is the Hassler. **Pros:** exclusive toiletries from hotel Amorvero SPA; prime location and panoramic views; stunning rooms. **Cons:** VIP rates (10% V.A.T. not included); breakfast not included (continental option is €29 plus 10% V.A.T. per person). $\boxed{\$}$ *Rooms from: €600* ✉ *Piazza Trinità dei Monti 6, Piazza di Spagna* ☎ *06/699340, 800/223–6800 from U.S.* ⊕ *www.hotelhasslerroma.com* 🛏 *96 rooms* ⎟◉⎟ *No meals* Ⓜ *Spagna* ✛ *F2.*

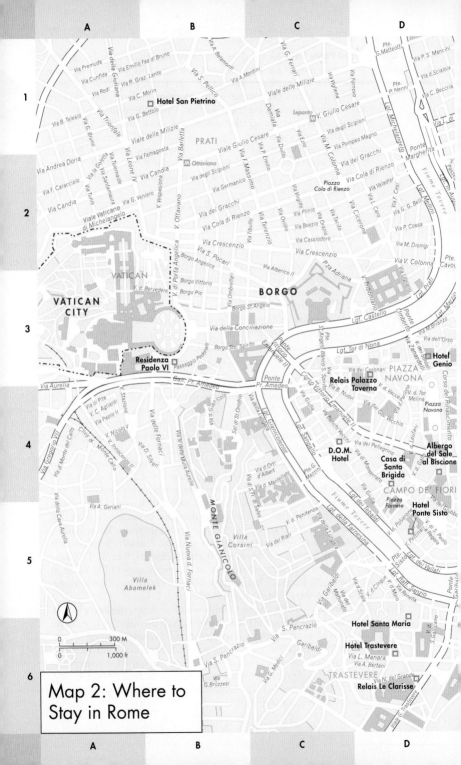

Map 2: Where to Stay in Rome

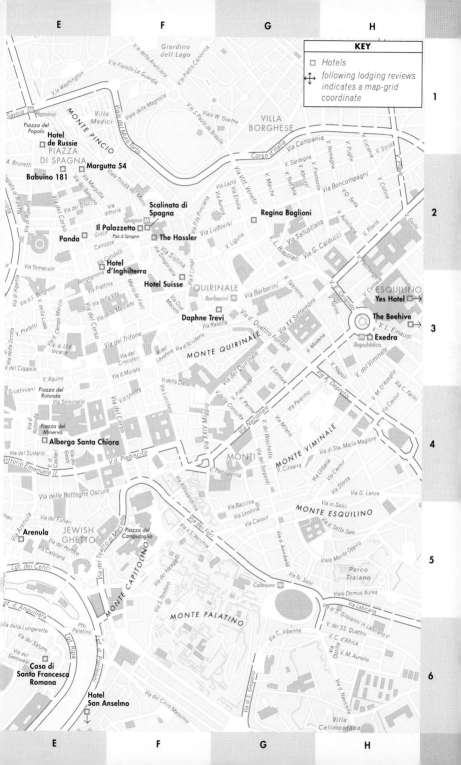

$$$$ **Hotel d'Inghilterra.** Situated in a 17th-century guesthouse and founded
HOTEL   in 1845, Hotel D'Inghilterra has a long, storied history. **Pros:** distinct character and opulence; turndown service (with chocolates); genuinely friendly and attentive staff; excellent in-house restaurant. **Cons:** elevator is small and slow; the location, despite soundproofing, is still noisy; bathrooms are surprisingly petite; some rooms badly in need of renovations and maintenance. $ *Rooms from: €400* ⊠ *Via Bocca di Leone 14, Piazza di Spagna* ☎ *06/699811* ⊕ *www.hoteldinghilterrarome.com* ⟿ *88 rooms* ⊚ *Breakfast* Ⓜ *Spagna* ✚ *E3.*

$$$$ **Hotel de Russie.** A ritzy retreat for government bigwigs and Hollywood
HOTEL   high rollers, the Hotel de Russie is just steps from the famed
FAMILY   Piazza del Popolo and occupies a 19th-century hotel that once hosted
Fodor'sChoice   royalty, Picasso, and Cocteau. **Pros:** big potential for celebrity sightings;
★   extensive gardens (including a butterfly reserve); first-rate luxury spa; Wi-Fi included. **Cons:** some rooms need updating; breakfast not included. $ *Rooms from: €700* ⊠ *Via del Babuino 9, Piazza del Popolo* ☎ *06/328881* ⊕ *www.roccofortehotels.com* ⟿ *122 rooms* ⊚ *No meals* Ⓜ *Flaminio* ✚ *E1.*

$$ **Hotel Suisse.** Located on a picturesque street around the corner from
HOTEL   the Spanish Steps, this warm and inviting hotel has been run by the same family for three generations. **Pros:** a good value; rooms are obviously cared for; great location. **Cons:** breakfast selection isn't that ample and is served in your room; bathrooms are on the small side. $ *Rooms from: €175* ⊠ *Via Gregoriana 54, Piazza di Spagna* ☎ *06/6783649* ⊕ *www.hotelsuisserome.com* ⟿ *12 rooms* ⊚ *Breakfast* Ⓜ *Barberini, Spagna* ✚ *F3.*

$$$$ **Il Palazzetto.** This 15th-century house, once a retreat for one of
B&B/INN   Rome's richest noble families, is one of the most intimate and luxurious
Fodor'sChoice   hotels in Rome, with gorgeous terraces where you can watch
★   the never-ending theater of the Scalinatella. **Pros:** location and view; free Wi-Fi; guests have full access to the Hassler's services; continental breakfast included (served at the Hassler). **Cons:** restaurant often rented out for crowded special events; bedrooms do not access communal terraces; with just four bedrooms, often books up far in advance, particularly in high season; only three rooms have a view of Piazza di Spagna. $ *Rooms from: €350* ⊠ *Vicolo del Bottino 8, Piazza di Spagna* ☎ *06/699341000* ⊕ *www.ilpalazzettoroma.com* ⟿ *4 rooms* ⊚ *No meals* Ⓜ *Spagna* ✚ *F2.*

$$$$ **Margutta 54.** Tucked away on a quiet, leafy street known for its art
B&B/INN   galleries, this four-suite property is like your very own hip, New York–
Fodor'sChoice   style loft in the center of old-world Rome, with top-drawer amenities,
★   contemporary design, and an ivy-draped courtyard. **Pros:** studio-loft feel in center of town; complete privacy; deluxe furnishings. **Cons:** breakfast not included (€20 per person), served at sister hotel Babuino 181; no staff available on-site after 8 pm. $ *Rooms from: €380* ⊠ *Via Margutta 54, Piazza di Spagna* ☎ *06/69921907* ⊕ *www.romeluxurysuites.com/margutta* ⟿ *4 suites* ⊚ *No meals* Ⓜ *Spagna* ✚ *E2.*

$$ **Panda.** Located near the Spanish Steps, this little gem of a hotel has
HOTEL   excellent service that gives you more bang for your buck. **Pros:** 10% discount if you pay in cash; free Wi-Fi; on a quiet street, but still close

2

to the Spanish Steps; very high ceilings. **Cons:** dim lighting; no elevator directly to floor; breakfast not included. $ *Rooms from: €130* ✉ *Via della Croce 35, Piazza di Spagna* ☎ *06/6780179* ⊕ *www.hotelpanda.it* ⇱ *28 rooms (20 with bath)* ❍| *No meals* Ⓜ *Spagna* ✥ *E2.*

$$$$ ⛵ **Regina Baglioni.** The former playground of kings and poets, the Regina
HOTEL   Baglioni, which enjoys a prime spot on the Via Veneto, is a favorite among today's international jetsetters. **Pros:** nice decor; luxury on-site spa; excellent on-site restaurant and bar. **Cons:** some rooms are noisy; service is hit-or-miss; spotty Internet. $ *Rooms from: €380* ✉ *Via Veneto 72, Piazza di Spagna* ☎ *06/421111* ⊕ *www.reginabaglioni.com* ⇱ *143 rooms* ❍| *Breakfast* Ⓜ *Barberini* ✥ *G2.*

$$ ⛵ **Scalinata di Spagna.** Perched atop the Spanish Steps, this charming
B&B/INN   boutique hotel makes guests fall in love over and over again—so popu-
FodorśChoice   lar, in fact, it's often booked far in advance. **Pros:** friendly and helpful
★   concierge; fresh fruit in guest rooms; free Wi-Fi throughout. **Cons:** it's a hike up the hill to the hotel; small rooms; no porter and no elevator. $ *Rooms from: €190* ✉ *Piazza Trinità dei Monti 17, Piazza di Spagna* ☎ *06/45686150* ⊕ *www.hotelscalinata.com* ⇱ *16 rooms* ❍| *Breakfast* Ⓜ *Spagna* ✥ *F2.*

REPUBBLICA

$$ ⛵ **The Beehive.** Living the American dream *dolce vita*–style is exactly
B&B/INN   what one Los Angeles couple started to do in 1999, when they opened
FodorśChoice   the Beehive, a hip, alternative budget hotel near Termini station. **Pros:**
★   massage and other therapies offered on-site; convenient to Termini station; very good prices, even in high season. **Cons:** some rooms do not have private baths; standard rooms lack TV and a/c; breakfast not included. $ *Rooms from: €180* ✉ *Via Marghera 8, Repubblica* ☎ *06/44704553* ⊕ *www.the-beehive.com* ⇱ *8 rooms, 1 dormitory* ❍| *No meals* Ⓜ *Termini* ✥ *H3.*

$$$$ ⛵ **Exedra.** Located in one of the most spectacular piazzas in the city, this
HOTEL   is the "it girl" of Rome's hotel scene, where high-rollers come to party
FodorśChoice   by the rooftop pool—you'll experience exquisite service and pampering
★   from the minute you waltz through the door. **Pros:** top-notch concierge and staff; great spa and pool overlooking one of the most beautiful piaz-zas in Rome; terrace with cocktail service; free Wi-Fi; close to Termini station. **Cons:** food and beverages are expensive; beyond the immediate vicinity of many sights. $ *Rooms from: €400* ✉ *Piazza della Repubblica 47, Repubblica* ☎ *06/489381* ⊕ *www.exedra-roma.boscolohotels.com* ⇱ *238 rooms* ❍| *Breakfast* Ⓜ *Repubblica, Termini* ✥ *H3.*

$$ ⛵ **Yes Hotel.** This chic hotel may fool you into thinking the digs are
HOTEL   expensive, but the contemporary coolness of Yes Hotel, located around
FodorśChoice   the corner from Termini station, actually comes at a bargain. **Pros:**
★   around the corner from Termini station; discount if you pay in cash; a great value without the budget feel. **Cons:** small rooms; fee for in-room Wi-Fi. $ *Rooms from: €140* ✉ *Via Magenta 15, Repubblica* ☎ *06/44363836* ⊕ *www.yeshotelrome.com* ⇱ *40 rooms* ❍| *Breakfast* Ⓜ *Termini, Castro Pretorio* ✥ *H3.*

AROUND THE VATICAN

$ HOTEL Fodor's Choice ★ **Hotel San Pietrino.** This cute, simple hotel on the third floor of a 19th-century palazzo offers rock-bottom rates at a five-minute walk from the Vatican. **Pros:** heavenly rates near the Vatican; free Wi-Fi; close to Rome's famous farmers' market, Mercato Trionfale. **Cons:** a couple of Metro stops from the centro storico; no breakfast (coffee/tea machine for guest use); no bar. *Rooms from: €110 Via Giovanni Bettolo 43, Prati 06/3700132 www.sanpietrino.it 12 rooms No meals Ottaviano B1.*

$$$$ HOTEL Fodor's Choice ★ **Residenza Paolo VI.** Set in a former monastery—still an extraterritorial part of the Vatican—magnificently abutting Bernini's colonnade of St. Peter's Square, the Paolo VI (pronounced "Sesto," a reference to Pope Paul VI) is unbeatably close to St. Peter's, with guest rooms that are luxurious, comfortable, and amazingly quiet. **Pros:** unparalleled views of St. Peter's from the rooftop terrace; quiet rooms; huge breakfast spread. **Cons:** small rooms are really small; bathrooms are small; atmosphere at night is a little too quiet. *Rooms from: €350 Via Paolo VI 29, Borgo 06/684870 www.residenzapaolovi.com 35 rooms Breakfast Ottaviano B3.*

TRASTEVERE

$$ HOTEL Fodor's Choice ★ **Casa di Santa Francesca Romana.** In the heart of Trastevere but tucked away from the hustle and bustle of the medieval quarter, this cheap, clean, comfortable hotel in a former monastery is centered on a lovely green courtyard. **Pros:** rates can't be beat; excellent restaurants nearby; away from rowdy side of Trastevere. **Cons:** thin walls; interior is a bit bland; spotty Wi-Fi. *Rooms from: €130 Via dei Vasceillari 61, Trastevere 06/5812125 www.sfromana.it 37 rooms Breakfast Piramide, Circo Massimo E6.*

$$$ HOTEL Fodor's Choice ★ **Hotel Santa Maria.** A Trastevere treasure with a pedigree going back four centuries, this ivy-covered, mansard-roof, rosy-brick-red, erstwhile Renaissance-era convent—just steps away from the glorious Santa Maria in Trastevere church and a few blocks from the Tiber—has sweet and simple guest rooms: a mix of brick walls, "cotto" tile floors, modern oak furniture, and matching bedspreads and curtains. **Pros:** a quaint and pretty oasis in a central location; relaxing courtyard; fully stocked wine bar; free bicycles to use during your stay; kettle for tea and coffee in room. **Cons:** tricky to find; some of the showers drain slowly; finding a cab is not always easy in Trastevere. *Rooms from: €230 Vicolo del Piede 2, Trastevere 06/5894626 www.hotelsantamariatrastevere.it 20 rooms Breakfast D6.*

$ HOTEL **Hotel Trastevere.** This tiny hotel captures the villagelike charm of the Trastevere district and offers basic, clean, comfortable rooms in a great location. **Pros:** good rates for location; convenient to tram and bus; free Wi-Fi; friendly staff. **Cons:** no frills; rooms are a little worn on the edges; few amenities. *Rooms from: €103 Via Luciano Manara 24/a–25, Trastevere 06/5814713 www.hoteltrastevere.net 18 rooms Breakfast Trastevere, Mastai D6.*

$$ B&B/INN Fodor's Choice ★ **Relais Le Clarisse.** Set within the former cloister grounds of the Santa Chiara order, with beautiful gardens, Le Clarisse makes you feel like a personal guest at a friend's villa, thanks to the comfortable size of the guest rooms and personalized service. **Pros:** spacious rooms with comfy beds; high-tech showers/tubs with good water pressure; complimentary Wi-Fi. **Cons:** this part of Trastevere can be noisy at night; rooms fill up quickly; reception unavailable after 10:30 pm. [$] *Rooms from: €180* ✉ *Via Cardinale Merry del Val 20, Trastevere* ☎ *06/58334437* 🌐 *www.leclarissetrastevere.com* *16 rooms, 1 apartment* 🍴 *Breakfast* ✣ *D6.*

AVENTINO

$$ HOTEL **Hotel San Anselmo.** This refurbished 19th-century villa is a romantic retreat from the city, set in a *molto* charming garden atop the Aventine Hill. **Pros:** free Wi-Fi; historic building with artful interior; great showers with jets; a garden where you can enjoy breakfast. **Cons:** a bit of a hike to sights; limited public transportation. [$] *Rooms from: €160* ✉ *Piazza San Anselmo 2, Aventino* ☎ *06/570057* 🌐 *www.aventinohotels.com* *35 rooms* 🍴 *Breakfast* [M] *Circo Massimo* ✣ *E6.*

NIGHTLIFE AND PERFORMING ARTS

NIGHTLIFE

"*E mo' che fammo?*" ("And now what do we do?" in local dialect) ... For a great night out in Rome, all you need to do is to wander, because ready entertainment is sure to find you on every corner. It's important to follow Rome's rule of thumb: if you see an enoteca, stop in. Although most enoteche are tiny and offer a limited antipasti menu, they cover more ground in their wine lists and often have a charming gang of regulars. For the linguistically timid, there are also several stereotypical English and Irish pubs peppered around the city, complete with a steady stream of Guinness, darts, and rugby on their satellite televisions. Those oversize flat-screen TVs also show American football, baseball, and basketball—ideal for those who don't want to miss a playoff game.

Most visitors head out in the centro storico to find some fun; Piazza Navona, Pantheon, Campo de' Fiori, and even Trastevere may be filled with tourists, but more recently, several niche and boutique bars have opened. (In contrast, the Spanish Steps area is a ghost town by 9 pm.) If you want to get out of the comfort zone, head to the Testaccio and San Lorenzo areas. When it comes to clubs, discos, and DJs in Rome, Testaccio is considered a mecca—Via Galvani is Rome's Sunset Strip, where hybrid restaurant-clubs, largely identical in music and crowd, jockey for top ranking. And wherever you go, remember: Romans love an after-party, so plenty of nightlife doesn't start until midnight.

PIAZZA NAVONA AND CAMPO DE' FIORI

Fodor'sChoice
★

Etablì. If you set up a wine bar in your living room, it'd feel a lot like Etablì. This is the perfect spot for meeting friends before a night out on the town. ⊠ *Vicolo delle Vacche 9, Piazza Navona* ☎ *06/97616694* ⊕ *www.etabli.it.*

La Cabala. Atop the medieval Hostaria dell'Orso, La Cabala is an after-dinner club and late-night dance party whose VIP room hosts wannabe models. Depending on the evening, the vibe can be chic, hipster, or clubby. Rome's version of a supper club, La Cabala is part of the Hostaria dell'Orso trio of restaurant, disco, and piano bar. Dress code is "stylish." ⊠ *Hostaria dell'Orso, Via dei Soldati 23, Piazza Navona* ☎ *06/68301192* ⊕ *www.hdo.it.*

L'Angolo Divino. Nestled on a quiet side street around the corner from the ever vivacious Campo de' Fiori, this wood-paneled enoteca is a hidden treasure of wines. Its extensive selection lists more than 1,000 labels to go along quite nicely with its quaint menu of delicious homemade pastas and local antipasti. And because it's open every night until 1:30 am, it's the ideal place for a late-night tipple. ⊠ *Via dei Balestrari 12, Campo de' Fiori* ☎ *06/6864413* ⊕ *www.angolodivino.it.*

Fodor'sChoice
★

Roof Garden Bar at Grand Hotel della Minerve. During warm months, this lofty perch offers perhaps the most inspiring view in Rome—directly over the Pantheon's dome. The Roof Garden has an equally impressive cocktail menu. Take advantage of summer sunsets and park yourself in a front-row seat as the dome glows. ⊠ *Grand Hotel della Minerve, Piazza della Minerve 69, Piazza Navona* ☎ *06/695201* ⊕ *www.grand-hoteldelaminerve.com.*

Vinoteca Novecento. A lovely, tiny enoteca with a very old-fashioned vibe, Vinoteca Novecento has a seemingly unlimited selection of wines, proseccos, vini santi, and grappe, along with salami-and-cheese tasting menus. Inside is standing-room only; in good weather, sit outside on one of the oak barriques. ⊠ *Piazza delle Coppelle 47, Piazza Navona* ☎ *06/6833078.*

PIAZZA DI SPAGNA

Fodor'sChoice
★

Antica Birreria Peroni. For beer lovers, the Art Nouveau–style halls of Antica Birreria Peroni will enchant you with their turn-of-the-century atmosphere, not to mention the always-flowing taps. Expect filling canteen-style meals and big steins, with several taps featuring Peroni favorites. It's also the best place for hot dogs in Rome, however tasteless their presentation. ⊠ *Via di San Marcello 19, Piazza di Spagna* ☎ *06/6795310* ⊕ *www.anticabirreriaperoni.net.*

Fodor'sChoice
★

Enoteca Regionale Palatium. Just down the street from the Piazza di Spagna hub is this modern gem run by Lazio's Regional Food Authority as a chic showcase for the best of Lazio's pantry and wine cellar. You can sample fine wines, olive oils, cheeses, and meats, and also a full seasonal menu of Lazio cuisine, including classics from top-notch ingredients (think gnocchi with ragù of mutton) and dishes with a twist (like lentil and calamari soup, or durum wheat rigatoni with zucchini sauce). Located where famed aesthete and poet Gabriele d'Annunzio once lived, this is not your garden-variety corner wine bar. ■TIP→ Stop by during aperitivo, from 6:30 pm onward (reservations recommended), to enjoy this burst of local flavor. ⊠ *Via Frattina 94, Piazza di Spagna* ☏ *06/69202132* ⊕ *www.enotecaregionalepalatium.it.*

Wine Bar at the Palazzetto. The prize for perfect aperitivo spot goes to the Palazzetto, with excellent drinks and appetizers, as well as a breathtaking view of Rome's domes and rooftops—all from its fifth-floor rooftop overlooking Piazza di Spagna. Keep an eye on the sky, as any chance for a rainy day will close the terrace (as do special events). ⊠ *Vicolo del Bottino 8, Piazza di Spagna* ☏ *06/69934711* ⊕ *www.ilpalazzettoroma. com* Ⓜ *Spagna.*

REPUBBLICA

Fodor'sChoice **Champagnerie Tazio.** A chic Champagne bar named after the original Ital-
★ ian *paparazzo* Tazio Secchiaroli, this spot brings a very *dolce vita* vibe with its red, black, and white lacquered interior with crystal chandeliers. The favorite pastime at Tazio is sipping Champagne while watching people parade through the colonnade of the lobby. In summer, the hotel's rooftop Posh bar is the place to be, with its infinity pool and terrace view overlooking downtown. ⊠ *Hotel Exedra, Piazza della Repubblica 47, Repubblica* ☏ *06/489381* ⊕ *exedra-roma.boscolohotels.com/ restaurant-and-bar/champagnerie-tazio* Ⓜ *Repubblica.*

PIAZZA DEL POPOLO

Stravinskij Bar at the Hotel de Russie. The Stravinskij Bar, in the Hotel de Russie's gorgeous garden, is the best place to catch a glimpse of la dolce vita. Celebrities, blue bloods, and VIPs hang out in the private courtyard garden where mixed drinks and cocktails are well above par. ⊠ *Hotel de Russie, Via del Babuino 9, Piazza del Popolo* ☏ *06/328881* ⊕ *www. roccofortehotels.com/hotels-and-resorts/hotel-de-russie/restaurant-and-bar/stravinskij-bar* Ⓜ *Flaminio.*

TRASTEVERE

Fodor'sChoice **Freni e Frizioni.** This hipster hangout has a cute artist vibe, and is great
★ for an afternoon coffee, tea, or aperitivo, or for late-night socializing. In warmer weather, the crowd overflows the large terrazzo overlooking the Tiber and the side streets of Trastevere. ⊠ *Via del Politeama 4, Trastevere* ☏ *06/45497499* ⊕ *www.freniefrizioni.com.*

MONTI

Fodor'sChoice **Ai Tre Scalini.** An ivy-covered wine bar in the center of Monti, Rome's
★ trendiest 'hood, Ai Tre Scalini has a warm and cozy menu of delicious antipasti and light entrées to go along with its enticing wine list. After about 8 pm, if you haven't booked, be prepared to wait—this is one extremely popular spot with locals. ⊠ *Via Panisperna 251, Monti* ☏ *06/48907495* ⊕ *www.aitrescalini.org* Ⓜ *Cavour.*

TESTACCIO

Ketum Bar. One of Rome's few "organic" happy hours, the price of a drink will buy you a spread of healthy and organic vegetarian appetizers. It also serves up a great weekend brunch. Aperitivo starts at 6:30 pm. ⊠ *Via Galvani 24, Testaccio* ☏ *06/57305338* ⊕ *www.ketumbar.it.*

PERFORMING ARTS

One of the pleasures of Rome is seeing a performance in one of the city's stunning venues, ancient or modern. This is the city where you might experience classical opera performed in a 3rd-century-AD theater, or enjoy an experimental dance show in a postindustrial detergent, or see a contemporary performance at the Renzo Piano–designed Auditorium Parco della Musica.

In summertime, most of the performing arts events move outdoors—any public space is fair game. Keep an eye on the Estate Romana website (⊕ *www.estateromana.comune.roma.it*) to find out what's happening in Rome on any night of the week. There is enough entertainment in Rome to take your breath away, in any season and in any location.

TICKETS

Orbis. An in-person, cash-only ticket vendor, Orbis stocks a wide array of tickets for music, cultural, and performance events. ⊠ *Piazza dell'Esquilino 37, Repubblica* ☎ *06/4827403* ⊕ *www.boxofficelazio.it.*

VivaTicket. One of Italy's largest ticket vendors (both online and at ticket offices), VivaTicket covers major musical performances and cultural events in Rome and throughout Italy. ⊕ *www.vivaticket.it.*

DANCE

Teatro Olimpico. Part of Rome's theater circuit, the 1930s-era Teatro Olimpico is one of the main venues for cabaret, contemporary dance companies, visiting international ballet companies, touring Broadway shows, and TEDxRoma. ⊠ *Piazza Gentile da Fabriano 17, Flaminio* ☎ *06/3265991* ⊕ *www.teatroolimpico.it.*

MAJOR VENUES

Fodor's Choice ★ **Auditorium Parco della Musica.** Rome became a world-class arts contender when world-renowned architect Renzo Piano conceived and constructed the Parco della Musica, fondly known as "the Auditorium." The futuristic music complex is made up of three enormous, pod-shape concert halls, which have heard the live melodies of Luciano Pavarotti, Philip Glass, Tracy Chapman, Peter Gabriel, Burt Bacharach, Woody Allen, and many more. Likened to anything from beetles to computer "mice," the musical pods are consistently jammed with people: the Sala Santa Cecilia is a massive hall for grand orchestra and choral concerts; the Sala Sinopoli is more intimately scaled for smaller troupes; and the Sala Petrassi was designed for alternative events. All three are arrayed around the Cavea, a vast Greco-Roman-style theater.

The auditorium is more than just music. The music park also hosts seasonal festivals—including the Rome Film Fest, a Christmas Village, and a springtime science, math, and philosophy festival. The grounds also have restaurants, a charming café, a bookstore, an outdoor amphitheater, an archaeological site, and an outstanding children's playground. If you're here in summer, there will be outdoor concerts and festivals.

Located in the Flaminio neighborhood, the Auditorium is just 10 minutes from the city center, reachable by local tram transport. To book guided tours, email *visiteguidate@musicaperroma.it.* ⊠ *Viale Pietro de Coubertin 30, Flaminio* ☎ *06/80241281* ⊕ *www.auditorium.com.*

OPERA

Fodor'sChoice **Teatro dell'Opera.** Long considered a far younger sibling of La Scala in
★   Milan and La Fenice in Venice, the company commands an audience
during its mid-November–May season. In the hot summer months,
the company moves to the Terme di Caracalla for its outdoor opera
series. As can be expected, the oft-preferred performance is *Aida*,
for its spectacle, which once included real elephants. The company
has lately taken a new direction, using projections atop the ancient
ruins to create cutting-edge sets. ⊠ *Piazza Beniamino Gigli 8, Repubblica* ☎ *06/481601, 06/48160255 for tickets* ⊕ *www.operaroma.it*
Ⓜ *Repubblica.*

THEATER

Fodor'sChoice **Teatro Argentina.** A gorgeous 18th-century theater, the Teatro Argentina
★   evokes glamour and sophistication with its velvet upholstery, large
crystal chandeliers and beautifully dressed theatergoers, who come
to see international productions of stage and dance performances.
⊠ *Largo di Torre Argentina 52, Campo de' Fiori* ☎ *06/684000311*
⊕ *www.teatrodiroma.net.*

SHOPPING

In Rome, shopping is an art form. Perhaps it's the fashionably bespec-
tacled commuter wearing Giorgio Armani as he deftly zips through
traffic on his Vespa, or all those Anita Ekberg, Audrey Hepburn, and
Julia Roberts films that make us long to be Roman for a day. But with
limited time and no Hollywood studio backing you, the trick is to find
what you're looking for and still not miss out on the city's museums
and monuments—and, of course, leave yourself plenty of euros to enjoy
the rest of your trip.

SHOPPING DISTRICTS

The city's most famous shopping district, **Piazza di Spagna,** is conveniently compact, fanning out at the foot of the Spanish Steps in a galaxy
of boutiques selling gorgeous wares with glamorous labels. Here you
can prance back and forth from Gucci to Prada to Valentino to Versace
with less effort than it takes to pull out your credit card. If your budget
is designed for lower altitudes, you also can find great clothes and accessories at less extravagant prices. But here, buying is not necessarily the
point—window displays can be works of art in themselves, and dream-
ing may be satisfaction enough. Via dei Condotti is the neighborhood's
central axis, but there are shops on every street in the area bordered
by Piazza di Spagna on the east, Via del Corso on the west, between
Piazza San Silvestro and Via della Croce, and extending along Via del
Babuino to Piazza del Popolo. Via Margutta, a few blocks north of the
Spanish Steps, is a haven for contemporary art galleries.

Running from Piazza Venezia to Piazza del Popolo, the **Via del Corso**
has more than a mile of shops. Unfortunately, these days most of it is
taken up by the same chain stores you find worldwide (including Gap,
H&M, and even an Athlete's Foot), rendering it little more interesting

than a trip to one's local shopping mall. Running west from Piazza Navona, Via del Governo Vecchio has numerous women's boutiques and secondhand-clothing stores.

The Termini train station has become a good one-stop place for many shopping needs, although again, most stores are the same you see worldwide. Its 60-plus shops are open until 10 pm and include a Nike store, the Body Shop, Sephora, Mango (women's clothes), a UPIM department store, a grocery store, and a three-story bookstore with selections in English. For local designers and independent boutiques, don't miss the trendy shopping districts of **Monti** near the Forum and **Trastevere** across the Tiber from the centro storico.

PIAZZA NAVONA

CLOTHING

Arsenale. Roman designer Patrizia Pieroni's sleek, unique, high-end fashion items stand out no matter the season. Her store, Arsenale, features everything from cleverly cut, stylish overcoats and seductive bustiers to sexy, flowing dresses perfect for the summer. ⊠ *Via del Pellegrino 172, Piazza Navona* ☎ *06/68802424* ⊕ *www.patriziapieroni.it.*

Le Tartarughe. A familiar face on the catwalk of Rome's fashion shows, designer Susanna Liso, a Rome native, adds suggestive elements of playful experimentation to her haute couture and ready-to-wear lines, which are much loved by Rome's aristocracy and intelligentsia. With intense, enveloping designs, she mixes raw silks or cashmere and fine merino wool together to form captivating garments that mix seduction and linear form. ⊠ *Via Piè di Marmo 17, Piazza Navona* ☎ *06/6792240* ⊕ *www.letartarughe.eu.*

Mado. A leader in nostalgia styling, often appearing on the pages of *Vogue Italia* and *Vanity Fair,* Mado has been vintage cool in Rome since 1969. The shop is funky, glamorous, and often over-the-top wacky. Whether you are looking for a robin's egg–blue empire-waist dress or a 1950s gown evocative of a Lindy Hop, Mado understands the challenges of incorporating vintage pieces into a modern wardrobe. ⊠ *Via del Governo Vecchio 89/a, Piazza Navona* ☎ *06/6798660.*

Vestiti Usati Cinzia. Vintage clothes hunters, costume designers, and stylists alike love browsing through the racks at Vestiti Usati Cinzia. The shop is fun and very inviting and stocked with wall-to-wall funky 1960s and '70s apparel and loads of goofy sunglasses. There's definitely no shortage of flower power bell bottoms and hippie shirts, embroidered tops, trippy and psychedelic boots, and other awesome accessories that will take you back to the days of peace and love. ⊠ *Via del Governo Vecchio 45, Piazza Navona* ☎ *06/6832945.*

FOOD AND WINE

Enoteca al Parlamento Achilli. The proximity of this traditional enoteca to Montecitorio, the Italian Parliament building, makes it a favorite with journalists and politicos, who often stop in for a glass of wine after work. But it's the tantalizing smell of truffles from the snack counter, where a sommelier waits to organize your tasting, that will probably lure you into Enoteca al Parlamento Achilli. There's also a lovely little restaurant where you can book a table and munch on a lovely array of cheese, salumi, and other cured meats. Don't forget to check out their wine shop to take home a bottle of your favorite wine. ⊠ *Via dei Prefetti 15, Piazza Navona* ☎ *06/6873446* ⊕ *www.enotecaalparlamento.it.*

Moriondo e Gariglio. Not exactly Willy Wonka (but in the same vein), Moriondo e Gariglio is a chocolate lover's paradise, churning out some of the finest chocolate delicacies in town. The shop dates back to 1850 and adheres strictly to family recipes passed on from generation to generation. In 2009, the shop partnered with Bulgari and placed 300 pieces of jewelry in their Easter eggs to benefit cancer research. While you may not find diamonds in your bonbons, marrons glacés, or dark-chocolate truffles, you'll still delight in choosing from more than 80 delicacies. ⊠ *Via Piè di Marmo 21, Piazza Navona* ☎ *06/6990856.*

JEWELRY

MMM—Massimo Maria Melis. Drawing heavily on ancient Roman and Etruscan designs, Massimo Maria Melis jewelry will carry you back in time. Working with 21-carat gold, he often incorporates antique coins in many of his exquisite bracelets and necklaces. Some of his pieces are done with an ancient technique, much-loved by the Etruscans, in which tiny gold droplets are soldered together to create intricately patterned designs. ⊠ *Via dell'Orso 57, Piazza Navona* ☎ *06/6869188* ⊕ *www. massimomariamelis.com.*

Quattrocolo. This historic shop dating to 1938 showcases exquisite antique micro-mosaic jewelry painstakingly crafted in the style perfected by the masters at the Vatican mosaic studio. You'll also find 18th- and 19th-century cameos and beautiful engraved stones. Their small works were beloved by cosmopolitan clientele of the Grand Tour age and offer modern-day shoppers a taste of yesteryear's grandeur. ⊠ *Via della Scrofa 48, Piazza Navona* ☎ *06/68801367* ⊕ *www.quattrocolo.com.*

SHOES AND ACCESSORIES

Spazio IF. In a tiny piazza alongside Rome's historic Via dei Coronari, designers Irene and Carla Ferrara have created a tantalizing hybrid between fashion paradise and art gallery. Working with unconventional designers and artists who emphasize Sicilian design, the shop has more to say about the style of Sicily and the creativity of the island's inhabitants than flat caps, puppets, and rich pastries. Perennial favorites include handbags cut by hand in a shop in Palermo, swimsuits, designer textiles, jewelry, and sportswear. ⊠ *Via dei Coronari 44a, Piazza Navona* ☎ *06/64760639* ⊕ *www.spazioif.it.*

TOYS

FAMILY **Al Sogno.** If you're looking for quality toys that encourage imaginative play and learning, look no further than Al Sogno. With an emphasis on the artistic as well as the multisensory, the shop has a selection of toys that are both discerning and individual, making them perfect for children of all ages. Carrying an exquisite collection of fanciful puppets, collectible dolls, masks, stuffed animals, and illustrated books, this Navona jewel, around since 1945, is crammed top-to-bottom with beautiful, well-crafted playthings. If you believe that children's toys don't have to be high-tech, you will adore reliving some of your best childhood memories here. ⊠ *Piazza Navona 53, corner of Via Agonale, Piazza Navona* ☎ *06/6864198* ⊕ *www.alsogno.net.*

FAMILY

Fodor'sChoice

★

Bartolucci. For more than 60 years and three generations, the Bartolucci family has been making whimsical, handmade curiosities out of pine, including cuckoo clocks, bookends, bedside lamps, and wall hangings. You can even buy a child-size vintage car entirely made of wood (wheels, too!). Don't miss the life-size Pinocchio pedaling furiously on a wooden bike ⊠ *Via dei Pastini 98, Piazza Navona* ☎ *06/69190894* ⊕ *www.bartolucci.com.*

CAMPO DE' FIORI

SHOES, HANDBAGS, AND LEATHER GOODS

Ibiz–Artigianato in Cuoio. In business since 1970, this father-and-daughter team creates colorful, stylish leather handbags, belts, and sandals near Piazza Campo de' Fiori. Choose from the premade collection or order something made to measure; their workshop is right next door to the boutique. ⊠ *Via dei Chiavari 39, Campo de' Fiori* ☎ *06/68307297.*

PIAZZA DI SPAGNA

ACCESSORIES

Furla. Furla sells high-end quality handbags and purses at affordable prices. There are multiple locations throughout the Eternal City (including one at Fiumicino Airport), but its flagship store can be found in the heart of Piazza di Spagna. Be prepared to fight your way through crowds of passionate handbag lovers, all anxious to possess one of the delectable bags, wallets, or watch straps in ice-cream colors. ⊠ *Piazza di Spagna 22, Piazza di Spagna* ☎ *06/69200363* ⊕ *www.furla.com* Ⓜ *Spagna.*

CLOTHING

Dolce & Gabbana. Dolce and Gabbana met in 1980 when both were assistants at a Milan fashion atelier, and they opened their first store in 1982. With a modern aesthetic that screams sex appeal, the brand has always thrived on excess. The Rome store can be more than a little overwhelming, with its glossy decor and blaring music, but at least there's plenty of eye candy—masculine and feminine alike. There is a second location on Via dei Condotti. ⊠ *Piazza di Spagna 94–95, Piazza di Spagna* ☎ *06/6991592* ⊕ *www.dolcegabbana.it* Ⓜ *Spagna.*

Elena Mirò. Elena Mirò is a high-end brand that specializes in sophisticated, beautifully sexy clothes for curvy, European-styled women size 46 (U.S. size 12, U.K. size 14) and up. There are several locations in Rome, including one in Prati and one in the San Giovanni neighborhood. ⊠ *Via Frattina 11–12, Piazza di Spagna* ☎ *06/6784367* ⊕ *www. elenamiro.it* Ⓜ *Spagna.*

Fodor'sChoice

★

Fendi. Fendi has been a fixture of the Roman fashion landscape since "Mamma" Fendi first opened shop with her husband in 1925. With an eye for crazy genius, she hired Karl Lagerfeld, who began working with the group at the start of his career. His furs and runway antics have made him one of the most influential designers of the 20th century and brought

2

international acclaim to Fendi along the way. Recent Lagerfeld triumphs include new collections marrying innovative textures and fabrics (cashmere, felt, and duchesse satin) with exotic skins like crocodile. Keeping up with technology, they even have an iPad case that will surely win a fashionista's seal of approval. The atelier, now owned by the Louis Vuitton group, continues to symbolize Italian glamour at its finest, though the difference in ownership is noticeable. It's also gotten new life in the Italian press for its "Fendi for Fountains" campaign, which recently included funding the restoration of Rome's Trevi Fountain. ⊠ *Largo Carlo Goldoni 419–421, Piazza di Spagna* ☏ *06/3344501* ⊕ *www.fendi.com* Ⓜ *Spagna.*

Giorgio Armani. One of the most influential designers of Italian haute couture, Giorgio Armani creates fluid silhouettes and dazzling evening gowns with décolletage so deep they'd make a grown man blush; his signature cuts are made with the clever-handedness and flawless technique achievable only by working with tracing paper and Italy's finest fabrics over the course of a lifetime. His menswear collection uses traditional textiles like wide-ribbed corduroy and stretch jersey in nontraditional ways while staying true to a clean, masculine aesthetic. It's true that exotic runway ideas and glamorous celebrities give Armani strong selling points, but his staying power is casual Italian elegance with just the right touch of whimsy and sexiness. ⊠ *Via dei Condotti 77–79, Piazza di Spagna* ☏ *06/6991460* ⊕ *www.giorgioarmani.com* Ⓜ *Spagna.*

Fodor'sChoice ★ **Gucci.** As the glamorous fashion label approaches its centennial, the success of the double-G trademark is unquestionable. The fashion house is still seeking to maintain the label's trendiness while bringing in a breath of fresh air. Tom Ford may have made Gucci the sexiest label in the world, but it's today's reinterpreted horsebit styles and Jackie Kennedy scarves that keep the design house on top. And while Gucci remains a fashion must for virtually every A-list celebrity, their designs have moved from heart-stopping sexy rock star to something classically subdued and retrospectively feminine. There's another store on Via Borgognona. ⊠ *Via dei Condotti 8, Piazza di Spagna* ☏ *06/6790405* ⊕ *www.gucci.com* Ⓜ *Spagna.*

Fodor'sChoice ★ **Laura Biagiotti.** For 40 years Laura Biagiotti has been a worldwide ambassador of Italian fashion. Considered the Queen of Cashmere, her soft-as-velvet pullovers have been worn by Sophia Loren, and her snow-white cardigans were said to be a favorite of the late pope John Paul II. Princess Diana even sported one of Biagiotti's cashmere maternity dresses. Be sure to indulge in sampling her line of his-and-her perfumes. ⊠ *Via Mario de' Fiori 26, Piazza di Spagna* ☏ *06/6791205* ⊕ *www.laurabiagiotti.it* Ⓜ *Spagna.*

Fodor'sChoice ★ **Patrizia Pepe.** One of Florence's best-kept secrets for up-and-coming fashions, Patrizia Pepe first emerged on the scene in 1993 with designs both minimalist and bold, combining classic styles with low-slung jeans and jackets with oversize lapels that are bound to draw attention. Her line of shoes are hot-hot-hot for those who can walk on stilts. It's still not huge on the fashion scene as a stand-alone brand, but take a look at this shop before the line becomes the next fast-tracked craze. ⊠ *Via Frattina 44, Piazza di Spagna* ☏ *06/6781851* ⊕ *www.patriziapepe.com* Ⓜ *Spagna.*

Fodor'sChoice   **Prada.** Besides the devil, plenty of serious shoppers wear Prada season
★   after season, especially those willing to sell their souls for one of their
ubiquitous handbags. If you are looking for that blend of old-world
luxury with a touch of fashion-forward finesse, you'll hit pay dirt here.
Recent handbag designs have a bit of a 1960s Jackie Kennedy feel, and
whether you like them will hinge largely on whether you find Prada's
signature retro-modernism enchanting. You'll find the Rome store more
service-oriented than the New York City branches—a roomy elevator delivers you to a series of thickly carpeted rooms where a flock
of discreet assistants will help you pick out dresses, shoes, lingerie,
and fashion accessories. The men's store is located at Via dei Condotti
88/90, women's down the street at 92/95. ⊠ *Via dei Condotti 88/90 and
92/95, Piazza di Spagna* ☏ *06/6790897* ⊕ *www.prada.com* Ⓜ *Spagna.*

Save the Queen! A hot Florentine design house with exotic and creative
pieces for women with artistic and eccentric frills, cutouts, and textures,
Save the Queen! has one of the most beautiful shops in the city, with
window displays that are works of art unto themselves. The store is
chock-full of baroque-inspired dresses, shirts, and skirts that are ultra-
feminine and not the least bit discreet. Pieces radiate charming excess,
presenting a portrait of youthful chic. ⊠ *Via del Babuino 49, Piazza di
Spagna* ☏ *06/36003039* ⊕ *www.savethequeen.com* Ⓜ *Spagna.*

Schostal. A Piazza di Spagna fixture since 1870, the shop was once the
go-to place for women looking to stock up on corsets, bonnets, stock-
ings and petticoats. Today, it's the place to stop for fine-quality shirts,
underwear, and handkerchiefs made of wool and pure cashmere at
affordable prices. There's a second location at Piazza Euclide. ⊠ *Via
Fontanella Borghese 29, Piazza di Spagna* ☏ *06/6791240* ⊕ *www.schos-
talroma.com* Ⓜ *Spagna.*

Fodor'sChoice   **Valentino.** Since taking the Valentino reins nearly 10 years ago, cre-
★   ative directors Maria Grazia Chiuri and Pierpaolo Piccioli have faced
numerous challenges, the most basic of which is keeping Valentino
true to Valentino after the designer's retirement in 2008. Both served
as accessories designers under Valentino for more than a decade and
understand exactly how to make the next generation of Hollywood
stars swoon. Valentino has taken over most of Piazza di Spagna, where
multiple boutiques showcase designs with a romantic edginess; think
kitten heels or a show-stopping prêt-à-porter evening gown worthy of
the Oscars. ⊠ *Via dei Condotti 15, Piazza di Spagna* ☏ *06/6739420*
⊕ *www.valentino.com* Ⓜ *Spagna.*

Versace. Versace's new Rome flagship, which opened in a palazzo at
the Piazza di Spagna in fall 2013, is a gem of architecture and design,
with Byzantine-inspired mosaic floors and futuristic interiors, not to
mention, of course, fashion: here shoppers will find apparel, jewelry,
watches, fragrances, cosmetics, and home furnishings in designs every
bit as flamboyant as Donatella and Allegra (Gianni's niece), drawing
heavily on the sexy rocker gothic underground vibe. There's also a
smaller boutique on the Via Veneto with prêt-à-porter and jewelry.
⊠ *Piazza di Spagna 12, Piazza di Spagna* ☏ *06/6691773* ⊕ *www.ver-
sace.com* Ⓜ *Spagna.*

2

DEPARTMENT STORES

La Rinascente. Located inside the chic Galleria Alberto Sordi, La Rinascente is Italy's best-known department store. It's also the store where Italian fashion genius Giorgio Armani got his start as a window dresser. Here, one can find oodles of cosmetics on the ground floor, as well as a phalanx of ready-to-wear designer sportswear and blockbuster handbags and accessories. The Piazza Fiume location has more floor space and a wider range of goods, including a homeware department. ⊠ *Galleria Alberto Sordi, Piazza Colonna, Piazza di Spagna* ☎ *06/6784209* ⊕ *www.rinascente.it* Ⓜ *Spagna.*

JEWELRY

Bulgari. Every capital city has its famous jeweler, and Bulgari is to Rome what Tiffany is to New York and Cartier to Paris. The jewelry giant has developed a reputation for meticulous craftsmanship melding noble metals with precious gems. In the middle of the 19th century, the great-grandfather of the current Bulgari brothers began working as a silver jeweler in his native Greece and is said to have moved to Rome with less than 1,000 lire in his pocket. Today the megabrand emphasizes colorful and playful jewelry as the principal cornerstone of its aesthetic. Popular collections include Parentesi, Bulgari-Bulgari, and B.zero1. The Rome flagship store was refurbished in honor of the 130th anniversary, in 2015, and the restoration was hailed by critics for its savvy update that also stayed true to its 1930s modernist style. ⊠ *Via dei Condotti 10, Piazza di Spagna* ☎ *06/696261* ⊕ *www.bulgari.com* Ⓜ *Spagna.*

MEN'S CLOTHING

Fodor'sChoice
★
Brioni. Founded in 1945 and hailed for its impeccable craftsmanship and flawless execution, the Brioni label is known for attracting and keeping the best men's tailors in Italy, where the exacting standards require that custom-made suits are designed from scratch and measured to the millimeter. For this personalized line, the menswear icon has 5,000 spectacular fabrics to select from. As thoughtful as expensive, one bespoke suit made from wool will take a minimum of 32 hours to create. Their prêt-à-porter line is also praised for peerless cutting and stitching. Past and present clients include Clark Gable, Barack Obama and, of course, James Bond. ⊠ *Via del Babuino 38/40, Piazza di Spagna* ☎ *06/484517* ⊕ *www.brioni.com* Ⓜ *Spagna.*

SHOES

A. Testoni. Amedeo Testoni, the brand's founder and original designer, was born in 1905 in Bologna, the heart of Italy's shoemaking territory. In 1929, he opened his first shop and began producing shoes as artistic as the Cubist and Art Deco artwork of the period. His shoes have adorned the feet of Fred Astaire, proving that lightweight shoes can be comfortable and luxurious and still turn heads. Today the Testoni brand includes an extraordinary women's collection and a sports line that is relaxed without losing its artistic heritage. The soft, calfskin sneakers are a dream, as are the matching messenger bags. ⊠ *Via del Babuino 152, Piazza di Spagna* ☎ *06/6788944* ⊕ *www. testoni.com* Ⓜ *Spagna.*

Fodor's Choice **Braccialini.** Founded in 1954 by Florentine stylist Carla Braccialini and
★ her husband, Braccialini—currently managed by their sons—makes
bags that are authentic works of art in delightful shapes, such as little
gold taxis or Santa Fe stagecoaches. The delightfully quirky beach bags
have picture-postcard scenes of Italian resorts made of brightly colored
appliquéd leather: be sure to check out their eccentric Temi (Theme)
creature bags; the opossum-shape handbag made out of crocodile skin
makes a richly whimsical fashion statement. There's a second location at
the Galleria Alberto Sordi. ⊠ *Via Mario De' Fiori 73, Piazza di Spagna*
☏ *06/6785750* ⊕ *www.braccialini.it* Ⓜ *Spagna.*

Fausto Santini. Shoe lovers with a passion for minimalist design flock
to Fausto Santini to get their hands on his preppy-hipster/nerdy-chic
shoes. Santini has been in business since 1970 and caters to a sophisticated, avant-garde clientele looking for elegant, classic shoes with a
kick. An outlet at Via Cavour 106 sells last season's shoes at a deep
discount. ⊠ *Via Frattina 120, Piazza di Spagna* ☏ *06/6784114* ⊕ *www.*
faustosantini.it Ⓜ *Spagna.*

Gherardini. In business since 1885, Gherardini has taken over a decon-
secrated church and slickly transformed it into a showplace for their
label. Gherardini's leather totes, sling bags, and soft luggage have
become classics, and the quality of each piece is worth the investment.
⊠ *Via Belsiana 48, Piazza di Spagna* ☏ *06/6795501* ⊕ *www.gherardini.*
it Ⓜ *Spagna.*

Fodor's Choice **Saddlers Union.** Reborn on the mythical artisan's street, Via Margutta,
★ across the street from Federico Fellini's old house, Saddlers Union
first launched in 1957 and quickly gained a cult following among
those who valued Italian artistry and a traditional aesthetic. Jacque-
line Kennedy set the trend of classical elegance by sporting Saddlers
Union's rich saddle-leather bucket bag. If you're searching for a sinfully fabulous handbag in a graceful, classic shape or that "I have
arrived" attorney's briefcase, you will find something guaranteed to
inspire envy. Items are made on-site with true artistry and under the
watchful eye of Angelo Zaza, one of Saddlers Union's original master
artisans. Prices are a bit steep, but the quality is definitely worth it.
⊠ *Via Margutta 11, Piazza di Spagna* ☏ *06/32120237* ⊕ *www.sad-*
dlersunion.com Ⓜ *Flaminio, Spagna.*

Fodor's Choice **Tod's.** With just 30 years under its belt, Tod's has grown from a small
★ family brand into a global powerhouse so wealthy that its owner, Diego
Della Valle, donated €20 million to the Colosseum restoration project.
The shoe baron's trademark is his simple, classic, understated designs.
Sure to please are his light and flexible slip-on Gommini driving shoes
with rubber-bottomed soles for extra driving-pedal grip—now you just
need a Ferrari. There are also locations on Via dei Condotti and Via
Borgogona. ⊠ *Via Fontanella di Borghese 56a–57, Piazza di Spagna*
☏ *06/68210066* ⊕ *www.tods.com* Ⓜ *Spagna.*

THE VATICAN

RELIGIOUS SOUVENIRS

Savelli Arte e Tradizione. Here you'll find a fully stocked selection of holier-than-thou gifts and sacred trinkets for you to take home. This family business has been around for more than 100 years and specializes in everything from rosaries, crosses, religious artwork, statues, and Pope Francis memorabilia. The family name, Savelli, dates back to an old Roman family that boasts four popes in its bloodline: Benedict II, Gregory II, Honorius III, and Honorius IV. The store has three other locations: Galleria Savelli in St. Peter's Square; Savelli Gift in Via della Concilliazione; and Art Studio Cafè in Via dei Gracchi. ⊠ *Via Paolo VI 27, Borgo* ☎ *06/68307017* ⊕ *www.savellireligious. com* Ⓜ *Ottaviano.*

MONTI AND SAN LORENZO

CLOTHING

Hydra 2. Italian teens and college students looking to make a bold statement are frequent shoppers at Hydra 2. The store stocks up on everything from Betty Boop dresses and indie underground wear to heavy-metal T-shirts that would make your nonna's hair stand up. ⊠ *Via Urbana 139, Monti* ☎ *06/48907773* Ⓜ *Cavour.*

L'Anatra all'Arancia. Repetto ballerinas, chunky handbags, and funky dresses make L'Anatra all'Arancia one of the best local secrets of boho San Lorenzo. The shop showcases innovative designer clothes from Marina Spadafora, Antik Batik, See by Chloé, and Donatella Baroni (the store's owner). Leaning toward the alternative with an eclectic selection of handpicked Italian and French labels, Donatella also carries luxurious perfumes and beautiful jewelry. ⊠ *Via Tiburtina 105, San Lorenzo* ☎ *06/4456293* Ⓜ *Termini, Castro Pretorio.*

Fodor'sChoice **Le Gallinelle.** This tiny boutique may live in a former butcher's shop,
★ but it houses some of the most sophisticated retro-inspired fashion garments around Rome. Its owner, Wilma Silvestri, cleverly combines ethnic and contemporary fabrics, evolving them into stylish clothing with a modern edge made for everyday wear. There is a second shop at Via del Boschetto 22. ⊠ *Via Panisperna 61, Monti* ☎ *06/4881017* ⊕ *www.legallinelle.it* Ⓜ *Cavour.*

TRASTEVERE

BOOKSTORES

Almost Corner Bookshop. Busting at the seams, with not an ounce of space left on its shelves, this tiny little bookshop is a favorite meeting point for English speakers in Trastevere. Irish owner Dermot O'Connell goes out of his way to find what you're looking for, and if he doesn't have it in stock he'll make a special order for you. The shop carries everything from popular best sellers to translated Italian classics. ⊠ *Via del Moro 45, Trastevere* ☎ *06/5836942.*

FLEA MARKETS

Porta Portese. One of the biggest flea markets in Italy—even in Europe, perhaps—Porta Portese welcomes visitors in droves every Sunday 7 am–2 pm. One can literally find anything and everything under the kitchen sink. Treasure seekers and bargain hunters love scrounging around tents for new and used clothing, antique furniture, used books, accessories, and other odds 'n' ends—all at rock-bottom prices. Bring your haggling skills, and cash (preferably small bills—it'll work in your favor when driving a bargain); stallholders don't accept credit cards, and the nearest ATM is a hike. Keep your valuables close; pickpockets lurk nearby. Tram No. 8 is the best way to reach the market. ⊠ *Via Portuense and adjacent streets between Porta Portese and Via Ettore Rolli, Trastevere.*

SHOES

Fodor'sChoice
★

Joseph DeBach. The best-kept shoe secret in Rome and open only in the evenings (or by appointment), Joseph DeBach has eccentric creations that are more art than footwear. Entirely handmade from wood, metal, and leather in his small and chaotic studio, his abacus wedge is worthy of a museum. Styles are outrageous "wow" and sometimes finished with hand-painted strings, odd bits of comic books, newspapers, or other unexpected baubles. ⊠ *Piazza de' Renzi 21, Trastevere* ☎ *3460255265* ⊕ *www.josephdebach.it.*

VENICE

WELCOME TO VENICE

TOP REASONS TO GO

★ **Cruising the Grand Canal:** The beauty of its palaces, enhanced by light playing on the water, make a trip down Venice's "main street" unforgettable.

★ **Basilica di San Marco:** Don't miss the gorgeous mosaics inside—they're worth standing in line for.

★ **Santa Maria Gloriosa dei Frari:** Its austere, cavernous interior houses Titian's Assunta—one of the world's most beautiful altarpieces—plus several other spectacular art treasures.

★ **Gallerie dell'Accademia:** Legendary masterpieces of Venetian painting will overwhelm you in this fabled museum.

★ **Sipping wine and snacking at a bacaro:** For a sample of tasty local snacks and excellent Veneto wines in a uniquely Venetian setting, head for one of the city's many wine bars.

1 San Marco. The neighborhood at the center of Venice is filled with fashion boutiques, art galleries, and grand hotels. Piazza San Marco is one of the world's most beautiful and historically significant urban spaces.

2 Dorsoduro. This graceful residential area is home to the Santa Maria della Salute, the Gallerie dell'Accademia, the Peggy Guggenheim Collection, the François Pinault Collection at the Punta della Dogana, and the Campo Santa Margherita, a lively hangout for students from Venice's three universities. The sunny Zattere promenade is one of the best spots to stroll with a gelato or linger at an outdoor café.

3 San Polo and Santa Croce. These bustling sestieri are both residential and commercial, with all sorts of shops and artisan studios, several major churches and museums, and the Rialto fish and produce markets.

4 Cannaregio. Brimming with residential Venetian life, this sestiere provides some of the sunniest open-air canalside walks in town. The Fondamenta della Misericordia is a strand of restaurants and cafés

interspersed among Gothic, Renaissance, and Baroque residences, and the Jewish Ghetto has a fascinating history and tradition.

THE JEWISH GHETTO

Stazione Ferrovia Santa Luca

Santa Maria Gloriosa dei Frari

Campo Santa Margherita

Canal Della

LA GIUDECCA

5 Castello. Along with Cannaregio, this area is home to most of the residents. With its gardens, park, and narrow, winding walkways, it's the sestiere least influenced by Venice's tourist culture.

6 San Giorgio Maggiore and the Giudecca. San Giorgio, across from Piazza San Marco, is graced with Palladio's magnificent church, San Giorgio Maggiore. His elegant Church of the Santissimo Redentore is the major landmark on the Giudecca, where the main attractions are the wonderful views of Venice.

7 Islands of the Lagoon. Torcello, Burano, and Murano are the islands of Venice's northern lagoon; each has its own allure. The Lido is the barrier island that closes the Venetian lagoon off from the Adriatic—it's Venice's beach.

GETTING ORIENTED

Venice proper is divided into six *sestieri,* or districts (the word *sestiere* means, appropriately, "sixth"): Cannaregio, Santa Croce, San Polo, Dorsoduro, San Marco, and Castello. More sedate outer islands float around them: San Giorgio and the Giudecca just to the south; beyond them to the east, the Lido, the barrier island; and to the north, Murano, Burano, and Torcello.

CANNAREGIO

SANTA CROCE

SAN POLO

SAN MARCO

CASTELLO

DORSODURO

SAN GIORGIO MAGGIORE

Giudecca

Fondamenta della Misericordia
Ca' d'Oro
Grand Canal
Basilica di San Marco
François Pinault Collection
Piazza San Marco
Palazzo Ducale
Gallerie dell' Accademia
Peggy Guggenheim Collection
Santa Maria della Salute
Zatterre
San Giorgio Maggiore
Church of the Santissimo Redentore

0 1/4 mi
0 1/4 km

EATING AND DRINKING WELL IN VENICE

The catchword in Venetian restaurants is "fish." How do you learn about the catch of the day? A visit to the Rialto's *pescheria* (fish market) is more instructive than any book, and when you're dining at a well-regarded restaurant, ask for a recommendation.

Traditionally, fish is served with a bit of salt, maybe some chopped parsley, and a drizzle of olive oil—no lemon; lemon masks the flavor. Ask for an entire sea-caught fish; it's much more expensive than its farmed cousin, but certainly worth it. Antipasto may be *prosciutto di San Daniele* (cured ham of the Veneto region) or *sarde in saor* (fresh panfried sardines marinated with onions, raisins, and pine nuts). Risotto, cooked with shellfish or veggies, is a great first course. Pasta? Enjoy it with seafood sauce: this is *not* the place to order spaghetti with tomato sauce. Other pillars of regional cooking include *pasta e fagioli* (thick bean soup with pasta), polenta, often with *fegato alla veneziana* (liver with onion), and that dessert invented in the Veneto: *tiramisù.*

GOING BACARO

You can sample regional wines and scrumptious *cicheti* (small snacks) in *bacari* (wine bars), a great Venetian tradition. *Crostini* (toast with toppings) and *polpette* (meat, fish, or vegetable croquettes) are popular cicheti, as are small sandwiches, seafood salads, *baccalà mantecato* (creamy, whipped salt cod), and toothpick-speared items such as roasted peppers, marinated artichokes, and mozzarella balls.

3

SEAFOOD

Granseola (crab), *moeche* (tiny, locally caught soft-shell crabs), sweet *canoce* (mantis shrimp), *capelunghe* (razor clams), calamari, and *seppie* or *seppioline* (cuttlefish) are all prominently featured, as well as *rombo* (turbot), *branzino* (sea bass), *San Pietro* (John Dory), *sogliola* (sole), *orate* (gilthead bream), and *triglia* (mullet). Trademark dishes include sarde in saor, *la frittura mista* (tempura-like fried fish and vegetables), and baccalà mantecato.

RISOTTO, PASTA, POLENTA

Although legend has it that Venetian traveler Marco Polo brought pasta back from China, it isn't a traditional staple of Venetian cuisine. As a first course, Venetians favor the creamy rice dish risotto *all'onda* ("undulating," as opposed to firm), prepared with vegetables or shellfish. When pasta is served, it's generally accompanied by seafood sauces, too: *pasticcio di pesce* is lasagna-type pasta baked with fish, and *bigoli* is a strictly local whole wheat pasta shaped like thick spaghetti, usually served *in salsa* (an anchovy-onion sauce with a dash of cinnamon), or with *nero di seppia* (cuttlefish-ink sauce). Pasta e fagioli is a classic first course. *Polenta* (cornmeal gruel) is another staple that's served creamy or fried in wedges, generally as an accompaniment to stews or *seppie in nero* (cuttlefish in black ink).

VEGETABLES

The larger islands of the lagoon are legendary for fine vegetables, such as the Sant'Erasmo *castraure,* sinfully expensive but heavenly tiny white artichokes that appear for a few days in spring. Other regions produce baby artichokes, but only Sant'Erasmo has true castraure. Spring treats are fat white asparagus from neighboring Bassano or Verona, and artichoke bottoms (*fondi*), usually sautéed with olive oil, parsley, and garlic. From December to March the prized *radicchio di Treviso,* a local red endive, is grilled and served frequently with a bit of melted *taleggio* cheese from Lombardy. Fall brings small wild mushrooms called *chiodini,* and *zucca di Mantova,* a yellow squash with a gray-green rind used in soups, puddings, and to stuff ravioli.

SWEETS

Tiramisù lovers will have ample opportunity to sample this creamy delight made from ladyfingers soaked in espresso and rum or brandy and covered with mascarpone cream and cinnamon—a dessert invented in the Veneto. Gelati, *sgropini* (prosecco, vodka, and lemon sorbet), and *semifreddi* (soft, homemade ice cream) are other sweets frequently seen on Venetian menu, as are almond cakes and dry cookies served with dessert wine. Try *focaccia veneziana,* a sweet raised cake made in the late fall and winter.

Updated
by Bruce
Leimsidor

Venice is often called La Serenissima, or "the most serene," a reference to the majesty, wisdom, and power of this city that was for centuries a leader in trade between Europe and Asia, and a major center of European culture. Built on water by people who saw the sea as a defense and ally, and who constantly invested in its splendor with magnificent architectural projects, Venice is a city unlike any other.

No matter how often you've seen it in photos and films, the real thing is more dreamlike than you could ever imagine. Its most notable landmarks, the Basilica di San Marco and the Palazzo Ducale, are exotic mixes of Byzantine, Romanesque, Gothic, and Renaissance styles, reflecting Venice's ties with the rest of Italy and with Constantinople in the east. Shimmering sunlight and silvery mist soften every perspective here; it's easy to understand how the city became renowned in the Renaissance for its artists' use of color. It's full of secrets, inexpressibly romantic, and frequently given over to pure, sensuous enjoyment.

You'll see Venetians going about their daily affairs in *vaporetti* (water buses), in the *campi* (squares), and along the *calli* (narrow streets). They are proud of their city and its history, and are still quite helpful to tourists, as long as the tourist shows proper respect for the city and its way of life.

VENICE PLANNER

MAKING THE MOST OF YOUR TIME

The hordes of tourists visiting Venice are legendary, especially in spring and fall, but during other seasons too—there's really no "off-season" in Venice. Unfortunately, tales of impassable, tourist-packed streets and endless queues to get into the Basilica di San Marco are not exaggerated. A little bit of planning, however, will help you avoid the worst of the crowds.

The majority of tourists do little more than take the vaporetto down the Grand Canal to Piazza San Marco, see the piazza and the basilica, and walk up to the Rialto and back to the station. You'll want to visit these areas, too, but do so in the early morning, before most tourists have finished their breakfast cappuccinos. Because many of the tourists are other Italians who come for a weekend outing, you can further decrease your competition for Venice's pleasures by choosing weekdays to visit the city.

Away from San Marco and the Rialto, the streets and quays of Venice's beautiful medieval and Renaissance residential districts receive only a moderate amount of traffic. Besides the Grand Canal and the Piazza San Marco, and perhaps Torcello, the other historically and artistically important sites are seldom overcrowded. Even on weekends you probably won't have to queue up to get into the Gallerie dell'Accademia.

Venice proper is quite compact, and you should be able to walk across it in a couple of hours, counting even a few minutes for getting lost. The water buses will save wear and tear on tired feet, but won't always save you much time.

PASSES AND DISCOUNTS

Avoid lines and save money by booking services and venue entry online with **Venezia Unica City Pass** (⊕ *www.veneziaunica.it*). The seven-day pass costs €39.90 (with discounts for those under 30) and gives you free entry to the Palazzo Ducale, 10 of Venice's Civic Museums, the Quirini-Stampalia museum, and the Jewish Museum. Note that the Gallerie dell'Accademia, the Guggenheim, the Ca' d'Oro, the Scuola di San Rocco and the Scuola di San Giorgio, and the Pinault collection at the Punta della Dogana are not Civic Museums, and therefore not included. It also gives you access to 15 of the most important churches in Venice. A reduced version of this pass gives you access to the Palazzo Ducale, three museums in Piazza San Marco, three churches of your choice, and the Quirini-Stampalia museum for €25.90. You can also include public transportation in the pass for an additional cost.

Fifteen of Venice's most significant churches covered by the Venezia Unica City Pass are part of the **Chorus Foundation** umbrella group (☎ *041/2750462* ⊕ *www.chorusvenezia.org*), which coordinates their administration, hours, and admission fees. Churches in this group are open to visitors all day except Sunday morning. Single church entry costs €3; you have a year to visit all 15 with the €12 **Chorus Pass**, which you can get at any participating church or online.

The **MUVE Pass** (€45) from **Musei Civici** (☎ *041/2715911* ⊕ *www.museicivicivenezia.it*) includes multiple entry to 12 Venice city museums for one year. Since the Venezia Unica City Pass is limited to one week, visitors who plan an extended stay, or who plan more than one visit to Venice in a year, may prefer to take the MUVE Pass plus the Chorus Pass, which would provide most of the same privileges as the Venezia Unica pass, but is valid for multiple entries for a year, instead of only for one week.

GETTING HERE AND AROUND
AIR TRAVEL
Aeroporto Marco Polo. Venice's Aeroporto Marco Polo is on the mainland, 10 km (6 miles) north of the city. It's served by domestic and international flights, including connections from 21 European cities, plus direct flights from New York's JFK and other U.S. cities. It is reachable from Venice either by bus or by special vaporetto (Alilaguna). ☎ *041/2609260* ⊕ *www.veniceairport.it.*

LAND TRANSFERS **ATVO.** Buses run by ATVO make a quick (20-minute) and cheap (€8) trip from the airport to Piazzale Roma, from where you can get a vaporetto to the stop nearest your hotel. Tickets are sold from machines and at the airport ground transportation booth (daily 9–7:30), and on the bus when tickets are otherwise unavailable. The public ACTV Bus No. 5 also runs to the Piazzale Roma in about the same time; tickets (€8) are available at the airport ground transportation booth. ☎ *0421/383672* ⊕ *www.atvo.it.*

WATER TRANSFERS From Marco Polo terminal, it's a mostly covered seven-minute walk to the dock where boats depart for Venice's historic center. The ride is in a closed boat so you won't get much of a view; plus, it's more expensive and generally slower than the bus to Piazzale Roma (unless your hotel is near a boat station).

Alilaguna. This company has regular, scheduled ferry service from pre-dawn until nearly midnight. During most of the day there are two departures from the airport to Venice every hour, at 15 and 45 minutes after. Early-morning and evening departures are less frequent, but there is at least one per hour. The charge is €15, including bags, and it takes about 1½ hours to reach the landing near Piazza San Marco; some ferries also stop at Fondamente Nove, Murano, Lido, the Cannaregio Canal, and the Rialto. Slight reductions are possible if you book a round trip online. ☎ *041/2401701* ⊕ *www.alilaguna.it.*

CAR TRAVEL
Venice is at the end of SR11, just off the east–west A4 autostrada. There are no cars in Venice; if possible, return your rental when you arrive.

A warning: don't be waylaid by illegal touts, often wearing fake uniforms, who try to flag you down and offer to arrange parking and hotels. Use one of the established garages and consider reserving a space in advance. The **Autorimessa Comunale** (☎ *041/2727211* ⊕ *www. asmvenezia.it*) costs €26–€29 for 24 hours (slight discounts if you book online). The **Garage San Marco** (☎ *041/5232213* ⊕ *www.garag-esanmarco.it*) costs €26 for up to 14 hours and €30 for 24 hours, slight discounts for prepaid online reservations. On its own island, **Tronchetto** (☎ *041/5207555*) charges €21 for 5–24 hours. Watch for signs coming over the bridge—you turn right just before Piazzale Roma. Many hotels and the casino have guest discounts with San Marco or Tronchetto garages. A cheaper alternative is to park in Mestre, on the mainland, and take a train (10 minutes, €1) or bus into Venice. The garage across from the station and the Bus No. 2 stop costs €8–€10 for 24 hours.

PUBLIC TRANSPORTATION

WATER BUSES **ACTV.** The ACTV operates the land and water bus service in Venice. A single tourist ticket valid for 60 minutes costs €7.50, but there are also one-, two-, and three-day tickets plus a one-week ticket available, which represent considerable savings if you plan to move frequently around the city by public transportation. Water buses run 24 hours in Venice, because there are parts of the city that are accessible only by water. Service is quite frequent during the day. Routes and schedules are available on the ACTV website, or at individual vaporetto stations. Tickets are available at main vaporetto stops, at tobacconists, and at some newspaper kiosks. The tickets are valid on both the vaporetti in Venice and on the bus lines to Mestre and on the Lido. Controls are frequent and fines for traveling without a valid ticket are steep. If you plan an extended stay in Venice, or plan to make several trips, and have a local address (not a hotel or B&B), you can apply for a Carta Venezia (€50) valid for several years, which will give you substantially reduced rates on public transportation. ☎ *041/2424* ⊕ *www.actv.it.*

WATER TAXIS A *motoscafo* isn't cheap: you'll spend about €60 for a short trip in town, €80 to the Lido, and €90 or more per hour to visit the outer islands. It is strongly suggested to book through the Consorzio Motoscafi Venezia (☎ *041/5222303* ⊕ *www.motoscafivenezia.it*) to avoid having to argue with the driver over prices. A water taxi can carry up to 10 passengers, with an additional charge of €10 per person for more than five people, so if you're traveling in a group, it may not be that much more expensive than a vaporetto.

TRAIN TRAVEL

Venice has rail connections with many major cities in Italy and Europe. Note that Venice's train station is **Venezia Santa Lucia,** not to be confused with Venezia Mestre, which is the mainland stop prior to arriving in the historic center. Some trains don't continue beyond the Mestre station; in such cases you can catch the next Venice-bound train. Get a €1 ticket from the newsstand on the platform and validate it (in the yellow time-stamp machine) to avoid a fine.

TOURS

If you want some expert guidance around Venice, you may opt for private, semiprivate, or large group tours. Any may include a boat tour as a portion of a longer walking tour. For private tours, make sure to choose an authorized guide.

LARGE-GROUP TOURS

Venice Tourism Office. Visit any Venice tourism office to book walking tours of the San Marco area (no Sunday tour in winter). There's also an afternoon walking tour that ends with a gondola ride, and a daily serenaded gondola ride. Check the main branch of the city's tourist office or their website for additional scheduled offerings, meeting places, prices, and times. ✉ *San Marco 2637* ☎ *041/5298711* ⊕ *www.turismovenezia.it.*

PRIVATE TOURS

A Guide in Venice. This popular company offers a wide variety of innovative, entertaining, and informative themed tours for groups of up to eight people. Individual tours are also available and generally last two to three hours. The guide fee is €75 per hour, and does not include admissions or transportation fees. Small group tours are also available at €62.50 per person. ☎3477876846 *for Sabrina Scaglianti* ⊕ *www.aguideinvenice.com.*

Walks Inside Venice. For a host of particularly creative group and private tours, from historic to artistic to gastronomic, opt for one run by Walks Inside Venice. Tours are for groups up to six people and guides include people with advanced university degrees and published authors. ⊕ *www.walksinsidevenice.com.*

VISITOR INFORMATION

The multilingual staff of the **Venice tourism office** (☎ *041/5298711* ⊕ *www. turismovenezia.it*) can provide directions and up-to-the-minute information. Their free, quarterly *Show and Events Calendar* lists current happenings and venue hours. Tourist office branches are at Marco Polo Airport; the Venezia Santa Lucia train station; Garage Comunale, on Piazzale Roma; at Piazza San Marco near Museo Correr at the southwest corner; the Venice Pavilion (including a Venice-centered bookstore), on the *riva* (canal-front street) between the San Marco vaporetto stop and the Royal Gardens; and at the main vaporetto stop on the Lido. The train-station branch is open daily 8–6:30; other branches generally open at 9:30.

EXPLORING VENICE

Venice proper is divided into six sestieri: Cannaregio, Castello, Dorso-duro, San Marco, San Polo, and Santa Croce. More sedate outer islands float around them—San Giorgio Maggiore and the Giudecca just to the south, beyond them the Lido, the barrier island; to the north, Murano, Burano, and Torcello.

SAN MARCO

Extending from the Piazza San Marco to the Rialto bridge, San Marco comprises the historical and commercial heart of Venice. Aside from the Piazza itself—San Marco is the only square in Venice given full stature as a "piazza" and accordingly is often known simply as "the Piazza"—this sestiere is graced with some of Venice's finest churches and best-endowed museums. San Marco is also the shopping district of Venice, and its mazes of streets are lined with Venetian glass, fine clothing, and elegantly wrought jewelry. Most of the famous Venetian glass producers from Murano have boutiques in San Marco, as do most Italian designers.

TIMING

You can easily spend several days seeing the historical and artistic monuments in and around the Piazza San Marco alone, but at a bare minimum, plan on at least an hour for the basilica, with its wonderful mosaics. Add on another half hour if you want to see its Pala d'Oro, Galleria, and Museo di San Marco. You'll want at least an hour to appreciate the Palazzo Ducale. Leave another hour for the Museo Correr, through which you also enter the archaeological museum and the Libreria Sansoviniana. If you choose to take in the piazza itself from a café table with an orchestra, keep in mind there will be an additional charge for the music.

Continued on page 134

CRUISING THE GRAND CANAL

THE BEST INTRODUCTION TO VENICE
IS A TRIP DOWN MAIN STREET

Venice's Grand Canal is one of the world's great thoroughfares. It winds its way from Piazzale Roma to Piazza San Marco, passing 200 palazzi built from the 13th to the 18th centuries by Venice's richest and most powerful families. There's a theatrical quality to a boat ride on the canal: it's as if each pink- or gold-tinted façade is trying to steal your attention from its rival across the way.

In medieval and Renaissance cities, wars and sieges required defense to be an element of design; but in rich, impregnable Venice, you could safely show off what you had. But more than being simply an item of conspicuous consumption, a Venetian's palazzo was an embodiment of his person—not only his wealth, but also his erudition and taste.

The easiest and cheapest way to see the Grand Canal is to take the Line 1 vaporetto (water bus) from Piazalle Roma to San Marco. The ride takes about 35 minutes. Invest in a day ticket and you can spend the better part of a day hopping on and off at the vaporetto's many stops, visiting the sights along the banks. Keep your eyes open for the highlights listed here; some have fuller descriptions later in this chapter.

FROM PIAZZALE ROMA TO RIALTO

Palazzo Labia
Tiepolo's masterpiece, the cycle of Antony and Cleopatra, graces the grand ballroom in this palazzo. The Labia family, infamous for their ostentation, commissioned the frescos to celebrate a marriage and had Tiepolo use the face of the family matriarch, Maria Labia, for that of Cleopatra. Luckily, Maria Labia was known not only for her money, but also for her intelligence and her beauty.

Santa Maria di Nazareth

Ponte di Scalzi

R. DI BIASIO

Stazione Ferrovia Santa Lucia

FERROVIA

SANTA CROCE

Ponte di Calatrava

After you pass the Ferrovia, the baroque church immediately to your left is the baroque **Santa Maria di Nazareth**, called the Chiesa degli Scalzi (Church of the Barefoot).

After passing beneath the Ponte di Scalzi, ahead to the left, where the Canale di Cannaregio meets the Grand Canal, you'll spy **Palazzo Labia**, an elaborate 18th-century palace built for

the social-climbing Labia family. Known for their ostentation even in this city where modesty was seldom a virtue, the Labias chose a location that required three façades instead of the usual one.

A bit farther down, across the canal, is the 13th-century **Fondaco dei Turchi**, an elegant residence that served as a combination commercial center and ghetto for the Turkish com-

munity. Try not to see the side towers and the crenellations; they were added during a 19th-century restoration.

Beyond it is the obelisk-topped **Ca' Belloni-Battagia**, designed for the Belloni family by star architect Longhena. Look for the family crest he added prominently on the façade.

On the opposite bank is architect Mauro Codussi's magnificent **Palazzo Vendramin-Calergi**, designed just before 1500. Codussi ingeniously married the fortress-like Renaissance style of the Florentine Alberti's Palazzo Rucellai to the lacy delicacy of the Venetian Gothic, creating the prototype of

Palazzo Vendramin-Calergi
Venice's first Renaissance palazzo. Immediately recognized as a masterpiece, it was so highly regarded that later, when its subsequent owners, the Calergi, were convicted of murder and their palace was to be torn down as punishment, the main building was spared.

Ca' d'Oro
Inspired by stories of Nero's Domus Aurea (Golden House) in Rome, the first owner had parts of the façade gilded with 20,000 sheets of gold leaf. The gold has long worn away, but the Ca' D'Oro is still Venice's most beautiful Gothic palazzo.

Ca' da Mosto
Venice's oldest surviving palazzo gives you an idea of Marco Polo's Venice. More than any other Byzantine palazzo in town, it maintains its original 13th-century appearance.

GHETTO

S. MARCUOLA

Ca' Belloni-Battagia

S. STAE

Ca' Pesaro

Fondaco dei Turchi

Depositi del Megio

San Stae Church

SAN POLO

Ca' Corner della Regina

CA' D'ORO

Rialto Mercato

Pescheria
Stop by in the morning to see the incredible variety of fish for sale. Produce stalls fill the adjacent fondamenta. Butchers and cheesemongers occupy the surrounding shops.

Fondaco dei Tedeschi

Ca' dei Camerlenghi

RIALTO

SAN MARCO

the Venetian Renaissance palazzo. The palazzo is now Venice's casino.

The whimsically baroque church of **San Stae** on the right bank is distinguished by a host of marble saints on its façade.

Farther along the bank is one of Longhena's Baroque masterpieces, **Ca' Pesaro**. It is now the Museum of Modern Art.

Next up on the left is **Ca' d'Oro** (1421-1438), the canal's most spendid example of Venetian Gothic domestic design. Across from this palazzo is the loggia of the neo-Gothic **pescheria**, Venice's fish market.

Slightly farther down, on the bank opposite from the vegetable market, is the early 13th-century **Ca' da Mosto**, the oldest building on the Grand Canal. The upper two floors are later additions, but the ground floor and piano nobile give you a good idea of a rich merchant's house during the time of Marco Polo.

As you approach the Rialto Bridge, to the left, just before

the bridge, is the **Fondaco dei Tedeschi**. German merchants kept warehouses, offices, and residences here; its façade was originally frescoed by Titian and Giorgione.

FROM RIALTO TO THE PONTE DELL' ACCADEMIA

SAN POLO

Ponte di Rialto

▲ **RIALTO**

Ca' Foscari
The canal's most imposing Gothic masterpiece, Ca' Foscari was built to blot out the memory of a traitor to the Republic.

Palazzo Barzizza

Ca' Loredan

▲ *S. SILVESTRO*

Ca' Farsetti

Palazzo Pisani Moretta

Ca' Grimani

▲ *S. ANGELO*

Ca' Garzoni

TOMA ▲

Ca' Balbi

Palazzo Grassi

Ca' Rezzonico

REZZONICO ▲

SAN MARCO

ACCADEMIA ▲

Gallerie dell'Accademia

DORSODURO

The shop-lined **Ponte di Rialto** was built in stone after former wooden bridges had burned or collapsed. As you pass under the bridge, on your left stands star architect Sansovino's Palazzo Dolfin Manin. The white stone–clad Renaissance palace was built at huge expense and over the objections of its conservative neighbors.

A bit farther down stand **Ca' Loredan** and **Ca' Farsetti**, 13th-century Byzantine palaces that today make up Venice's city hall.

Along the same side is the **Ca' Grimani**, by the Veronese architect Sanmichele. Legend has it that the palazzo's oversized windows were demanded by the young Grimani's fiancée, who insisted that he build her a palazzo on the Canale Grande with windows larger than the portal of her own house.

At the Sant'Angelo landing, the vaporetto passes close to Codussi's **Ca' Corner-Spinelli**. Back on the right bank, in a lovely salmon color, is the graceful **Palazzo Pisani Moretta**, built in the mid-15th century and typical of the Venetian Gothic palazzo of the generation after the Ca' D'Oro.

A bit farther down the right bank, crowned by obelisks, is **Ca' Balbi**. Niccolò Balbi built this elegant palazzo in order to upstage his former landlord, who had insulted him in public.

Farther down the right bank, where the Canale makes a sharp turn, is the imposing **Ca' Foscari**. Doge Francesco Foscari tore down an earlier palazzo on this spot and built this splendid palazzo to erase memory of the traitorous former owner. It is now the seat of the University of Venice.

Continuing down the right bank you'll find Longhena's **Ca' Rezzonico**, a magnificent baroque palace. Opposite stands the Grand Canal's youngest palace, Giorgio Massari's **Palazzo Grassi**, commissioned in 1749. It houses part of the François Pinot contemporary art collection.

Near the canal's fourth bridge, is the former church and monastery complex that houses the world-renowned **Gallerie dell'Accademia**, the world's largest and most distinguished collection of Venetian art.

ARCHITECTURAL STYLES ALONG THE GRAND CANAL

BYZANTINE: 13th century
Distinguishing characteristics: high, rounded arches, relief panels, multicolored marble.

Examples: Fondaco dei Turchi, Ca' Loredan, Ca' Farsetti, Ca' da Mosto

GOTHIC: 14th and 15th centuries
Distinguishing characteristics: pointed arches, high ceilings, and many windows.

Examples: Ca' d'Oro, Ca' Foscari, Palazzo Pisani Moretta, Ca' Barbaro (and, off the canal, Palazzo Ducale)

RENAISSANCE: 16th century
Distinguishing characteristics: classically influenced emphasis on harmony and motifs taken from classical antiquity.

Examples: Palazzo Vendramin-Calergi, Ca' Grimani, Ca' Corner-Spinelli, Ca' dei Camerlenghi, Ca' Balbi, Palazzo Corner della Ca' Granda, Palazzo Dolfin Manin, and, off the canal, Libreria, Sansoviniana on Piazza San Marco

BAROQUE: 17th century
Distinguishing characteristics: Renaissance order wedded with a more dynamic style, achieved through curving lines and complex decoration.

Examples: churches of Santa Maria di Nazareth, San Stae, and Santa Maris della Salute; Ca' Belloni Battaglia, Ca' Pesaro, Ca' Rezzonico

FROM THE PONTE DELL'ACCADEMIA TO SAN ZACCARIA

Ca' Barbaro
John Singer Sargent, Henry James, and Cole Porter are among the guests who have stayed at Ca' Barbaro. It was a center for elegant British and American society during the turn of the 20th century.

Santa Maria Della Salute
Baldessare Longhena was only 26 when he designed this church, which was to become one of Venice's major landmarks. Its rotunda form and dynamic Baroque decoration predate iconic Baroque churches in other Italian cities.

SAN MARCO

Ponte dell' Accademia

Ca' Pisani-Gritti

Palazzo Corner della Ca' Granda

△ ACCADEMIA

Casetta Rossa

△ *S. M. DEL GIGLIO*

DORSODURO

Ca' Barbarigo

△ *SALUTE*

Palazzo Salviati

Palazzo Venier dei Leoni
Eccentric art dealer Peggy Guggenheim's personal collection of modern art is here. At the Grand Canal entrance to the palazzo stands Marino Marini's sexually explicit equestrian sculpture, the Angel of the Citadel. Numerous entertaining stories have been spun around the statue and Ms. Guggenheim's overtly libertine ways.

S. Maria della Salute

Ca' Dario
Graceful and elegant Ca' Dario is reputed to carry a curse. Almost all its owners since the 15th century have met violent deaths or committed suicide. It was, nevertheless, a center for elegant French society at the turn of the 20th century.

Down from the Accademia bridge, on the left bank next door to the fake Gothic Ca' Franchetti, is the beautiful **Ca' Barbaro**, designed by Giovanni Bon, who was also at work about that time on the Ca' D'Oro.

Farther along on the left bank Sansovino's first work in Venice, the **Palazzo Corner della Ca' Granda**, begun in 1533, still shows the influence of his Roman Renaissance contemporaries, Bramante and Giulio Romano. It faces the uncompleted **Palazzo Venier dei Leoni**, which holds the Peggy Guggenheim Collection, a good cross-section of the visual arts from 1940 to 1960.

Ca' Dario a bit farther down, was originally a Gothic palazzo, but in 1487 it was given an early Renaissance multicolored marble façade.

At this point on the canal the cupola of **Santa Maria della Salute** dominates the scene. The commission for the design of the church to celebrate the Virgin's rescuing Venice from the disastrous plague of 1630, was given to the 26-year-old

Longhena. The young architect stressed the new and inventive aspects of his design, likening the rotunda shape to a crown for the Virgin.

Across from the Salute, enjoying the magnificent view across the canal, are a string of luxury hotels whose historic

Basilica di S. Marco

Palazzo Ducale

PIAZZA SAN MARCO

S. ZACCARIA

VALLARESSO

Palazzo Dandolo a San Moise

Punta della Dogana

The Grand Canal is 2½ miles long, has an average depth of 9 feet, and is 76 yards wide at its broadest point and 40 yards at its narrowest.

façades have either been radically modified or are modern neo-Gothic fantasies. The main interest here is the rather unimposing Hotel Monaco e Gran Canal, the former Palazzo Dandolo a San Moise, which contains Europe's first casino, the famous ridotto, founded in 1638. It was a stomping ground of Casanova, and was closed by the Republic in 1774 because too much money was being lost to foreigners.

At the **Punta della Dogana** on the tip of Dorsoduro, Japanese architect Tadao Ando,

using Zen-inspired concepts of space, has transformed a 17th–century customs house into a museum for contemporary art. It is a fitting coda to the theme of Venice as living center for international artistic creativity, as set by Calatrava's bridge at the beginning of the Grand Canal.

At the Vallaresso vaporetto stop you've left the Grand Canal, but stay on board for a view of the **Palazzo Ducale**, with **Basilica di San Marco** behind it, then disembark at San Zaccaria.

SAN GIORGI MAGGIORE

TOP ATTRACTIONS

Fodor's Choice
★

Basilica di San Marco. The basilica is not only Venice's religious center, but also an expression of the political, intellectual, and economic aspiration and accomplishments of a city that for centuries was at the forefront of European culture. It was the doge's personal chapel, endowed with all the riches the Republic's admirals and merchants could carry off from the Orient (as the Byzantine Empire was known). When the present church was begun in the 11th century, rare colored marbles and gold leaf mosaics were used in its decoration. The 12th and 13th centuries were a period of intense military expansion, and by the early 13th century, the facades began to bear testimony to Venice's conquests, including gilt-bronze ancient Roman horses taken from Constantinople in 1204. The glory of the basilica is its 12th- and 13th-century medieval mosaic work. ■TIP→ Make a reservation, at no extra cost, on the website. Guards will deny admission to people in shorts, sleeveless dresses, and tank tops. ⊠ *Piazza San Marco, San Marco 328, San Marco* ☎ *041/2413817 for tour info (weekdays 10–noon)* ⊕ *www.basilicasanmarco.it* ⊠ *Basilica free, Treasury €3, sanctuary and Pala d'Oro €2, museum €5* Ⓜ *Vallaresso/San Zaccaria.*

Fodor's Choice
★

Museo Correr. This museum of Venetian art and history contains an important sculpture collection by Antonio Canova and important paintings by Giovanni Bellini, Vittore Carpaccio (Carpaccio's famous painting of the Venetian courtesans is here), and other major local painters. It's the main repository of Venetian drawings and prints, which, unfortunately, can be seen only by special arrangement, or during special exhibitions. It also houses curiosities such as the absurdly high-soled shoes worn by 16th-century Venetian ladies (who walked with the aid of a servant). The city's proud naval history is evoked in several rooms through highly descriptive paintings and numerous maritime objects, including ships' cannons and some surprisingly large iron mast-top navigation lights. The museum also has a significant collection of antique gems. The Correr exhibition rooms lead directly into the **Museo Archeologico,** which houses the Grimani collection—an important 16th- and 17th-century collection of Greek and Roman art, still impressive even after the transfer of many objects to Paris and Vienna during the Napoleonic and Austrian occupations—and the Stanza del Sansovino, the only part of the **Biblioteca Nazionale Marciana** open to visitors. ⊠ *Piazza San Marco, Ala Napoleonica, opposite basilica, Piazza San Marco* ☎ *041/2405211* ⊕ *www.museiciviciveneziani. it* ⊠ *Museums of San Marco Pass €19, includes Museo Archeologico, Biblioteca Nazionale Marciana, and Palazzo Ducale. Free with MUVE pass* Ⓜ *Vaporetto: Vallaresso, San Zaccaria.*

Fodor's Choice
★

Palazzo Ducale (*Doge's Palace*). Rising majestically above the Piazzetta San Marco, this Gothic fantasia of pink-and-white marble—the doges' residence from the 10th century and the central administrative center of the Venetian Republic—is a majestic expression of Venetian prosperity and power. Upon entering, you'll find yourself in an immense courtyard with some of the first evidence of Venice's Renaissance architecture, including Antonio Rizzo's 15th-century *Scala dei Giganti* (Stairway of the Giants). The palace's sumptuous chambers have walls and ceilings covered with works by Venice's greatest artists. In the Anticollegio

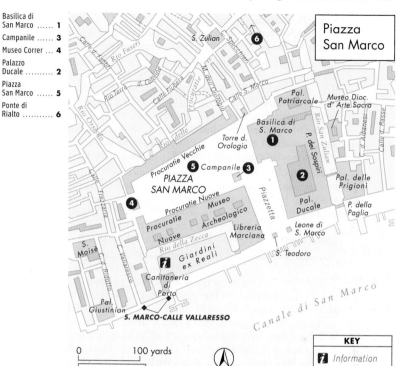

Piazza
San Marco

KEY

🛈 *Information*

◆ *Vaporetto Stop*

you'll find the *Rape of Europa* by Veronese and Tintoretto's *Bacchus and Ariadne Crowned by Venus*. The ceiling of the Sala del Senato (Senate Chamber), featuring *The Triumph of Venice* by Tintoretto, is magnificent, but it's dwarfed by his masterpiece *Paradise* in the Sala del Maggiore Consiglio (Great Council Hall), the world's largest oil painting. The popular Secret Itineraries tour lets you visit the doge's private apartments and hidden passageways. ✉ *Piazzetta San Marco, Piazza San Marco* ☎ *041/2715911, 041/5209070 for Secret Itineraries tour* ⊕ *www.museiciviciveneziani.it* ✉ *Museums of San Marco Pass €19, includes Museo Correr, Museo Archeologico, and Biblioteca Nazionale Marciana; free with MUVE pass. Secret Itineraries tour €20* Ⓜ *Vaporetto: San Zaccaria, Vallaresso.*

Fodor'sChoice
★ **Piazza San Marco.** One of the world's most beautiful squares, Piazza San Marco (St. Mark's Square) is spiritual and artistic heart of Venice, a vast open space bordered by an orderly procession of arcades marching toward the fairy-tale cupolas and marble lacework of the Basilica di San Marco. From midmorning on, it is generally packed with tourists. (If Venetians have business in the piazza, they try to conduct it in the early morning, before the crowds swell.) At night the piazza can be magical, especially in winter, when mists swirl around the lampposts and the campanile.

Facing the basilica, on your left, the long, arcaded building is the **Procuratie Vecchie,** renovated to its present form in 1514 as offices and residences for the powerful procurators (magistrates).

On your right is the **Procuratie Nuove,** built half a century later in a more imposing, classical style. It was originally planned by Venice's great Renaissance architect Jacopo Sansovino (1486–1570), to carry on the look of his Libreria Sansoviniana (Sansovinian Library), but he died before construction on the Nuove had begun. Vincenzo Scamozzi (circa 1552–1616), a pupil of Andrea Palladio (1508–80), completed the design and construction. Still later, the Procuratie Nuove was modified by architect Baldassare Longhena (1598–1682), one of Venice's Baroque masters.

When Napoléon (1769–1821) entered Venice with his troops in 1797, he expressed his admiration for the piazza and promptly gave orders to alter it. His architects demolished a church with a Sansovino facade in order to build the Ala Napoleonica (Napoleonic Wing), or Fabbrica Nuova (New Building), which linked the two 16th-century *procuratie* (procurators' offices) and effectively enclosed the piazza.

Piazzetta San Marco is the "little square" leading from Piazza San Marco to the waters of Bacino San Marco (St. Mark's Basin); its *molo* (landing) once served as the grand entrance to the Republic. Two imposing columns tower above the waterfront. One is topped by the winged lion, a traditional emblem of St. Mark that became the symbol of Venice itself; the other supports St. Theodore, the city's first patron, along with his dragon. (A third column fell off its barge and ended up in the bacino before it could be placed alongside the others.) Although the columns are a glorious vision today, the Republic traditionally executed convicts between them. Even today, some superstitious Venetians avoid walking between the two. ⊠ *San Marco* 🚇 Ⓜ *Vaporetto Calle Valaresso or San Zaccaria.*

Fodor's Choice
★   **Ponte di Rialto** (*Rialto Bridge*). The competition to design a stone bridge across the Grand Canal attracted the best architects of the late 16th century, including Michelangelo, Palladio, and Sansovino, but the job went to the less famous (but appropriately named) Antonio da Ponte (1512–95). His pragmatic design, completed in 1591, featured shop space and was high enough for galleys to pass beneath. Putting practicality and economy over aesthetic considerations—and unlike the classical plans proposed by his more famous contemporaries—Da Ponte's bridge essentially followed the design of its wooden predecessor; it kept decoration and cost to a minimum at a time when the Republic's coffers were low, due to continual wars against the Turks and the competition brought about by the Spanish and Portuguese opening of oceanic trade routes. Along the railing you'll enjoy one of the city's most famous views: the Grand Canal vibrant with boat traffic. ⊠ *San Marco* Ⓜ *Vaporetto: Rialto.*

WORTH NOTING

Campanile. Construction of Venice's famous brick bell tower (325 feet tall, plus the angel) began in the 9th century; it took on its present form in 1514. During the 15th century, the tower was used as a place of punishment: immoral clerics were suspended in wooden cages from the

VENICE THROUGH THE AGES

BEGINNINGS

Venice was founded in the 5th century when the Veneti, inhabitants of the mainland region roughly corresponding to today's lower Veneto, fled their homes to escape invading Germanic and other barbarian tribes. The unlikely city, built on islands in the lagoon and later atop wooden posts driven into the marshes, would evolve into a maritime republic lasting over a thousand years. After liberating the Adriatic from marauding pirates, its early fortunes grew as a result of its active role in the Crusades, beginning in 1095 and culminating in the Venetian-led sacking of Constantinople in 1204. The defeat of rival Genoa in the Battle of Chioggia (1380) established Venice as the dominant sea power in Europe.

EARLY GOVERNMENT

As early as the 7th century, Venice was governed by a ruler, the *doge*, elected by the nobility to a lifetime term; however, since the common people had little political input or power, the city wasn't a democracy by modern definition. Beginning in the 12th century, the doge's power was increasingly subsumed by a growing number of councils, commissions, and magistrates. In 1268 a complicated procedure for the doge's election was established to prevent nepotism, but by that point power rested foremost with the Great Council, which at times numbered as many as 2,000 members.

A LONG DECLINE

Venice reached the height of its wealth and territorial expansion in the early 15th century, during which time its domain included all of the Veneto region and part of Lombardy, but the seeds of its decline were soon to be sown, with the fall of Constantinople to the Turks in 1453 and the opening up of Atlantic trade routes, starting, of course, with Columbus in 1492.

By the beginning of the 16th century, the pope, threatened by Venice's mainland expansion, organized the League of Cambrai, defeated Venice in 1505, and effectively put a stop to the Republic's mainland territorial designs. The Ottoman Empire blocked Venice's Mediterranean trade routes, and newly emerging sea powers such as Britain, Spain, Portugal, and the Netherlands ended Venice's monopoly.

When Napoléon arrived in 1797, he first offered Venice an alliance and then, having been betrayed by the Venetians' violation of a pledge of neutrality, took the city without a fight. Venice was ceded again to the Austrians at the Council of Vienna in 1815, and they ruled (save for a brief Venetian revolt in 1848) until the formation of the Italian Republic in 1866. During their occupation, the Austrians helped themselves to many of the city's artistic treasures—very few of them have been returned. Ironically, Venice's greatest contributions to Western culture, and those that leave a lasting impression upon the visitor, took place during periods of political humiliation and economic decline. While some of the Romanesque and Gothic palaces along the Grand Canal were built during a period of undisputed power, its most marvelous palaces and churches were built after Venice's sun had begun to set.

tower, some forced to subsist on bread and water for as long as a year; others were left to starve. In 1902, the tower unexpectedly collapsed, taking with it Jacopo Sansovino's marble loggia (1537–49) at its base. The largest original bell, called the *marangona*, survived. The crushed loggia was promptly reconstructed, and the new tower, rebuilt to the old plan, reopened in 1912. Today, on a clear day the stunning view includes the Lido, the lagoon, and the mainland as far as the Alps, but, strangely enough, none of the myriad canals that snake through the city. Currently, the Campanile is undergoing foundation restoration due to deterioration caused by flooding (*acqua alta*); however, this hasn't affected the visiting hours. ⊠ *Piazza San Marco* ☎ *041/5224064* 🖃 *€8* Ⓜ *Vaporetto: Vallaresso, San Zaccaria.*

Palazzo Grassi. Built between 1748 and 1772 by Giorgio Massari for a Bolognese family, this palace is one of the last of the great noble residences on the Grand Canal. Once owned by auto magnate Giovanni Agnelli, it was bought by French businessman François Pinaut in 2005 to showcase his highly important collection of modern and contemporary art (which has now grown so large that Pinaut rented the Punta della Dogana, at the entryway to the Grand Canal, for his newest acquisitions). Pinaut brought in Japanese architect Tadao Ando to remodel the Grassi's interior. Check online for a schedule of temporary art exhibitions. ⊠ *Campo San Samuele, San Marco* ☎ *041/5231680* ⊕ *www.palazzograssi.it* 🖃 *€15, €20 with Punta della Dogana* ☉ *Closed Tues.* Ⓜ *Vaporetto: San Samuele.*

DORSODURO

The sestiere Dorsoduro (named for its "hard back" solid clay foundation) is across the Grand Canal to the south of San Marco. It is a place of meandering canals, the city's finest art museums, monumental churches, and *scuole* (Renaissance civic institutions) filled with works by Titian, Veronese, and Tiepolo, and a promenade called the Zattere, where on sunny days you'll swear half the city is out for a passeggiata, or stroll. The eastern tip of the peninsula, the Punta della Dogana, is capped by the dome of Santa Maria della Salute and was once the city's customs point; the old customs house is now a museum of contemporary art.

Dorsoduro is home to the Gallerie dell'Accademia, with an unparalleled collection of Venetian painting, and the gloriously restored Ca' Rezzonico, which houses the Museo del Settecento Veneziano. Another of its landmark sites, the Peggy Guggenheim Collection, has a fine selection of 20th-century art.

TIMING

You can easily spend a full day in the neighborhood. Devote at least a half hour to admiring the Titians in the imposing and monumental Santa Maria della Salute, and another half hour for the wonderful Veroneses in the peaceful, serene church of San Sebastiano. The Gallerie dell'Accademia demands a few hours, but if time is short an audio guide can help you cover the highlights in about an hour. Ca' Rezzonico deserves at least an hour, as does the Peggy Guggenheim collection.

TOP ATTRACTIONS

Fodor'sChoice
★

Ca' Rezzonico. Designed by Baldassare Longhena in the 17th century, this gigantic palace was completed nearly 100 years later by Giorgio Massari and became the last home of English poet Robert Browning (1812–89). Stand on the bridge by the Grand Canal entrance to spot the plaque with Browning's poetic excerpt, "Open my heart and you will see graved inside of it, Italy ..." on the palace's left side. The eye-popping Grand Ballroom has hosted some of the grandest parties in the city's history, from its 18th-century heyday to the 1969 Bal Fantastica (a Save Venice charity event that attracted notables from Elizabeth Taylor to Aristotle Onassis) to balls re-created for Heath Ledger's 2005 film *Casanova*. Today the upper floors of the Ca' Rezzonico are home to the especially delightful Museo del Settecento (Museum of Venice in the 1700s), decorated with period furniture and tapestries in gilded salons, as well as Tiepolo ceiling frescoes and oil paintings. ⊠ *Fondamenta Rezzonico, Dorsoduro 3136, Dorsoduro* ☏ *041/2410100* ⊕ *www. museiciviciveneziani.it* 🎫 *€10 (free with MUVE pass)* ⊗ *Closed Tues.* Ⓜ *Vaporetto: Ca' Rezzonico.*

Fodor'sChoice
★

Gallerie dell'Accademia. The greatest collection of Venetian paintings in the world hangs in these galleries founded by Napoléon in 1807 on the site of a religious complex he had suppressed. They were carefully and subtly restructured between 1945 and 1959 by the renowned architect Carlo Scarpa. Highlights include works by Jacopo Bellini, the father of the Venetian Renaissance, as well as the richly colored paintings of his more accomplished son Giovanni; *Tempest* by Giorgione, a revolutionary work that has intrigued viewers and critics for centuries; *Feast in the House of Levi*, which got Veronese summoned to the Inquisition; and several of Tintoretto's finest works. Don't miss the views of 15th- and 16th-century Venice by Carpaccio and Gentile Bellini, Giovanni's brother—you'll see how little the city has changed. Booking tickets in advance isn't essential but costs only an additional €1.50. ⊠ *Dorsoduro 1050, Campo della Carità just off Accademia Bridge, Dorsoduro* ☏ *041/5222247, 041/5200345 for reservations* ⊕ *www. gallerieaccademia.org* 🎫 *€12, subject to increases for special exhibitions* Ⓜ *Vaporetto: Accademia.*

FAMILY

Peggy Guggenheim Collection. Housed in the incomplete but nevertheless charming Palazzo Venier dei Leoni, this choice selection of 20th-century painting and sculpture represents the taste and extraordinary style of the late heiress Peggy Guggenheim. Through wealth, social connections, and a sharp eye for artistic trends, Guggenheim (1898–1979) became an important art dealer and collector from the 1930s through the 1950s, and her personal collection here includes works by Picasso, Kandinsky, Pollock, Motherwell, and Ernst (her onetime husband). The museum serves beverages, snacks, and light meals in its refreshingly shady and artistically sophisticated garden. On Sundays at 3 pm (except in August) the museum offers a free tour and art workshop for children (ages 4–10); it's conducted in Italian, but anglophone interns are generally on hand to help those who don't *parla italiano*. ⊠ *Fondamenta Venier dei Leoni, Dorsoduro 701, Dorsoduro* ☏ *041/2405411* ⊕ *www. guggenheim-venice.it* 🎫 *€15* ⊗ *Closed Tues.* Ⓜ *Vaporetto: Accademia.*

Fodor's Choice
★

Punta della Dogana. Funded by the billionaire who owns a major share in Christie's Auction House, the François Pinault Foundation had Japanese architect Tadao Ando redesign this fabled customs house—sitting at the *punta,* or very head, of the Grand Canal—and now home to a changing roster of works from Pinault's collection of contemporary art. The streaming light, polished surfaces, and clean lines of Ando's design contrast beautifully with the brick, massive columns, and sturdy beams of the original Dogana. Even if you aren't into contemporary art, a visit is worthwhile just to see Ando's amazing architectural transformation. Be sure to walk down to the punta for a magnificent view of the Venetian basin. Check online for a schedule of temporary exhibitions. ⊠ *Punta della Dogana, Dorsoduro* ☎ *041/5231680* ⊕ *www.palazzograssi.it* ⌑ *€15, €20 with Palazzo Grassi* ⊘ *Closed Tues.* Ⓜ *Vaporetto: Salute.*

Fodor's Choice
★

San Sebastiano. Paolo Veronese (1528–88), although still in his twenties, was already the official painter of the Republic when he began the oil panels and frescoes at San Sebastiano, his parish church, in 1555. For decades he continued to embellish the church with very beautiful illusionistic scenes. The cycles of panels in San Sebastiano are considered to be his supreme accomplishment. Veronese is buried beneath his bust near the organ. The church itself, remodeled by Antonio Scarpagnino and finished in 1548, offers a rare opportunity to see a monument in Venice where both the architecture and the pictorial decoration all date from the same period. Be sure to check out the portal of the ex-convent, now part of the University of Venice, to the left of the church; it was designed in 1976–78 by Carlo Scarpa, one of the most important Italian architects of the 20th century. ⊠ *Campo San Sebastiano, Dorsoduro* ☎ *041/2750462* ⊕ *www.chorusvenezia.org* ⌑ *€3 (free with Chorus Pass)* Ⓜ *Vaporetto: San Basilio.*

Fodor's Choice
★

Santa Maria della Salute. The most iconic landmark of the Grand Canal, La Salute (as this church is commonly called) is best viewed from the Riva degli Schiavoni at sunset or from the Accademia Bridge by moonlight. Baldassare Longhena (later Venice's most important Baroque architect) won a competition in 1631 to design a shrine honoring the Virgin Mary for saving Venice from a plague that over two years (1629–30) killed 47,000 residents, or one-third of the city's population. Outside, this ornate, white Istrian stone octagon is topped by a colossal cupola with snail-like ornamental buttresses. Inside, a white-and-gray color scheme is echoed in the polychrome marble floor and six chapels. An icon of Madonna della Salute (Madonna of Health) sits above the main altar; above is a sculpture showing Venice on her knees before the Madonna as she drives the plague from the city. Do not leave without visiting the Sacrestia Maggiore, which contains a dozen works by Titian. ⊠ *Punta della Dogana, Dorsoduro* ☎ *041/2411018* ⌑ *Church free, sacristy €2* Ⓜ *Vaporetto: Salute.*

QUICK BITES

Il Caffè. For more than a portable munch, bask in the sunshine at the popular Il Caffè, commonly called Bar Rosso for its bright red exterior. It dishes up the best *tramezzini* (snack sandwiches) in the campo, is open until midnight, and serves drinks and other light refreshments every day except Sunday. ⊠ *Campo Santa Margherita, Dorsoduro 2963, Dorsoduro* ☎ *041/5287998.*

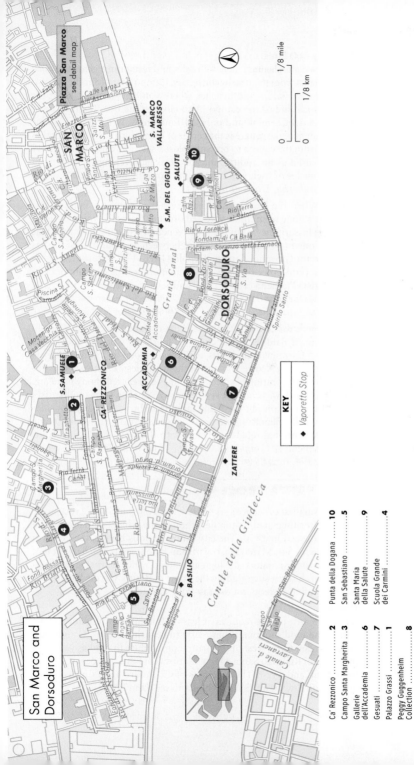

San Marco and Dorsoduro

Ca' Rezzonico **2**

Campo Santa Margherita ... **3**

Gallerie
dell'Accademia **6**

Gesuati **7**

Palazzo Grassi **1**

Peggy Guggenheim
Collection **8**

Punta della Dogana **10**

San Sebastiano **5**

Santa Maria
della Salute **9**

Scuola Grande
dei Carmini **4**

WORTH NOTING

Campo Santa Margherita. Lined with cafés and restaurants generally filled with students from the nearby university, Campo Santa Margherita also has produce vendors and benches where you can sit and take in the bustling local life of the campo. Also close to the Ca' Rezzonico and the Scuola dei Carmini, and only a 10-minute walk from the Gallerie dell'Accademia, the square is the center of Dorsoduro social life. It takes its name from the church to one side, closed since the early 19th century and now used as an auditorium. On weekend evenings it sometimes attracts hordes of high school students from the mainland. ⊠ *Campo Santa Margherita, Dorsoduro.*

Gesuati. When the Dominicans took over the church of Santa Maria della Visitazione from the suppressed order of Gesuati laymen in 1668, Giorgio Massari, the last of the great Venetian Baroque architects, was commissioned to build this structure between 1726 and 1735. It has an important Giovanni Battista Tiepolo (1696–1770) illusionistic ceiling and several other of his works, plus those of his contemporaries, Giambattista Piazzetta (1683–1754) and Sebastiano Ricci (1659–1734). ⊠ *Zattere, Dorsoduro* ☎ *041/2750462* ⊕ *www.chorusvenezia.org* ⊠ €3 *(free with Chorus Pass)* ☉ *Closed Sun.* Ⓜ *Vaporetto: Zattere.*

Scuola Grande dei Carmini. When the order of Santa Maria del Carmelo commissioned Baldassare Longhena to finish the work on the Scuola Grande dei Carmini in the 1670s, their brotherhood of 75,000 members was the largest in Venice and one of the wealthiest. Little expense was spared in the decorating of stuccoed ceilings and carved ebony paneling, and the artwork was choice, even before 1739, when Giovanni Battista Tiepolo began painting the **Sala Capitolare.** In what many consider his best work, Tiepolo's nine great canvases vividly transform some rather conventional religious themes into dynamic displays of color and movement. ⊠ *Campo dei Carmini, Dorsoduro 2617, Dorsoduro* ☎ *041/5289420* ⊠ €5 Ⓜ *Vaporetto: Ca' Rezzonico.*

SAN POLO AND SANTA CROCE

The two smallest of Venice's six sestieri, San Polo and Santa Croce, were named after their main churches, though the Chiesa di Santa Croce was demolished in 1810. The city's most famous bridge, the Ponte di Rialto, unites San Marco (east) with San Polo (west). The Rialto takes its name from Rivoaltus, the high ground on which it was built. Shops abound in the area surrounding the Ponte di Rialto. On the San Marco side you'll find fashion, on the San Polo side, food.

TIMING

To do the area justice requires at least half a day. If you want to take part in the food shopping, come early to beat the crowds. Campo San Giacomo dell'Orio, west of the main thoroughfare that takes you from the Ponte di Rialto to Santa Maria Gloriosa dei Frari, is a peaceful place for a drink and a rest. The museums of Ca' Pesaro are a time commitment—you'll want at least two hours to see them both.

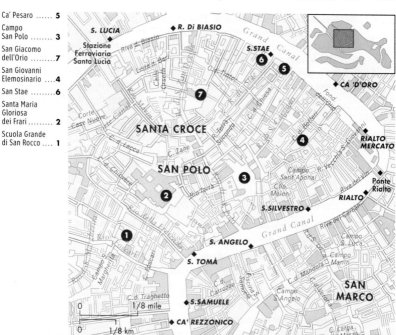

San Polo and
Santa Croce

KEY

◆ *Vaporetto Stop*

TOP ATTRACTIONS

Fodor's Choice
★

Santa Maria Gloriosa dei Frari. Completed in 1442, this immense Gothic church of russet-color brick—known locally as I Frari—is famous worldwide for its array of spectacular Venetian paintings. In the sacristy, see Giovanni Bellini's 1488 triptych *Madonna and Child with Saints*, painted for precisely this spot. The Corner Chapel is graced by Bartolomeo Vivarini's altarpiece *St. Mark Enthroned* and *Saints John the Baptist, Jerome, Peter, and Nicholas*. In the first south chapel of the chorus, there is a fine sculpture of St. John the Baptist by Donatello, dated 1438, with a psychological intensity rare for early Renaissance sculpture. You can see the rapid development of Venetian Renaissance painting by contrasting Bellini with the heroic energy of Titian's *Assumption*, over the main altar, painted only 30 years later. Titian's beautiful *Madonna di Ca' Pesaro* is in the left aisle; Titian disregarded the conventions of his time by moving the Virgin out of center and making the saints active participants. ⊠ *Campo dei Frari, San Polo* ☎ *041/2728618, 041/2750462 for Chorus Foundation* ⊕ *www.chorusvenezia.org* ⊠ *€3 (free with Chorus Pass)* Ⓜ *Vaporetto: San Tomà.*

Fodor'sChoice
★
Scuola Grande di San Rocco. This elegant example of Venetian Renaissance architecture, built between 1517 and 1560, was built for the essentially secular charitable confraternity bearing the saint's name. The Venetian "scuole" were organizations that sometimes had loose religious affiliations, through which the artisan class could exercise some influence upon civic life. Although San Rocco is bold and dramatic outside, its contents are even more stunning—a series of more than 60 paintings by Tintoretto. In 1564 Tintoretto edged out competition for a commission to decorate a ceiling by submitting not a sketch, but a finished work, which he moreover offered free of charge. *Moses Striking Water from the Rock, The Brazen Serpent,* and *The Fall of Manna* represent three afflictions—thirst, disease, and hunger—that San Rocco and later his brotherhood sought to relieve. ⊠ *Campo San Rocco, San Polo 3052, San Polo* ☎ *041/5234864* ⊕ *www.scuolagrandesanrocco.it* 🎟 *€10, includes audio guide* Ⓜ *Vaporetto: San Tomà.*

QUICK BITES

Caffè dei Frari. Just over the bridge in front of the Frari church is this old-fashioned place where you'll find an assortment of sandwiches and snacks, but it is the atmosphere, and not the food, that is the main attraction. Established in 1870, it's one of the last Venetian tearooms with its original decor. It's frequented more by residents and students than by tourists. Prices are a bit higher than in cafés in nearby Campo Santa Margherita, but the decor and the friendly "retro" atmosphere seem to make the added cost worthwhile. ⊠ *Fondamenta dei Frari, San Polo 2564, San Polo* ☎ *No phone* ☉ *No dinner.*

Pasticceria Tonolo. Venice's premier confectionary has been in operation since 1886. During Carnevale it's still one of the best places in town for *fritelle,* or fried doughnuts (traditional raisin, or cream-filled), and before Christmas and Easter, Venetians order their *focaccia,* the traditional raised cake eaten especially at holidays, from here well in advance. ⊠ *Calle Crosera, Dorsoduro 3764, Dorsoduro* ☎ *041/5237209* ☉ *Closed Mon. and Sun. afternoon.*

WORTH NOTING

Ca' Pesaro. Baldassare Longhena's grand Baroque palace, begun in 1676, is the beautifully restored home of two impressive collections. The **Galleria Internazionale d'Arte Moderna** has works by 19th- and 20th-century artists such as Klimt, Kandinsky, Matisse, and Miró. It also has a collection of representative works from Venice's Biennale art show that amounts to a panorama of 20th-century art. The pride of the **Museo Orientale** is its collection of Japanese art, and especially armor and weapons, of the Edo period (1603–1868). It also has a small but striking collection of Chinese and Indonesian porcelains and musical instruments. ⊠ *San Stae, Santa Croce 2076, Santa Croce* ☎ *041/721127 for Galleria, 041/5241173 for Museo Orientale* ⊕ *www.museicivecivene-neziani.it* 🎟 *€10, includes both museums (free with MUVE pass)* ☉ *Closed Mon.* Ⓜ *Vaporetto: San Stae.*

Campo San Polo. Only Piazza San Marco is larger than this square, and the echo of children's voices bouncing off the surrounding palaces makes the space seem even bigger. Campo San Polo once hosted bull races, fairs, military parades, and packed markets, and now comes especially alive on summer nights, when it's home to the city's outdoor cinema. The **Chiesa di San Polo** has been restored so many times that little remains of the original 9th-century church, and sadly, 19th-century alterations were so costly that the friars sold off many great paintings to pay bills. Although Giambattista Tiepolo is represented here, his work is outdone by 16 paintings by his son Giandomenico (1727–1804), including the *Stations of the Cross* in the oratory to the left of the entrance. The younger Tiepolo also created a series of expressive and theatrical renderings of the saints. Look for altarpieces by Tintoretto and Veronese that managed to escape auction. San Polo's bell tower (begun 1362) remained unchanged through the centuries—don't miss the two lions playing with a disembodied human head and a serpent that guard it. Tradition has it that the head refers to that of Martin Falier, the doge executed for treason in 1355. ⊠ *Campo San Polo, San Polo* ☎ *041/2750462 for Chorus Foundation* ⊕ *www.chorusvenezia.org* ✉ *€3 (free with Chorus Pass)* ⊗ *Closed Sun.* Ⓜ *Vaporetto: San Silvestro, San Tomà.*

San Giacomo dell'Orio. This lovely square was named after a laurel tree (*orio*), and today trees lend it shade and character. Add benches and a fountain (with a drinking bowl for dogs), and the pleasant, oddly shaped campo becomes a welcoming place for friendly conversation and neighborhood kids at play. Legend has it the **Chiesa di San Giacomo dell'Orio** was founded in the 9th century on an island still populated by wolves. The current church dates from 1225; its short, unmatched Byzantine columns survived renovation during the Renaissance, and the church never lost the feel of an ancient temple sheltering beneath its 14th-century ship's-keel roof. In the sanctuary, large marble crosses are surrounded by a group of small medieval Madonnas. The altarpiece is *Madonna with Child and Saints* (1546) by Lorenzo Lotto (1480–1556), and the sacristies contain 12 works by Palma il Giovane (circa 1544–1628). ⊠ *Campo San Giacomo dell'Orio, Santa Croce* ☎ *041/2750462 for Chorus Foundation* ⊕ *www.chorusvenezia.org* ✉ *Church €3 (free with Chorus Pass)* ⊗ *Church closed Sun.* Ⓜ *Vaporetto: San Stae.*

San Giovanni Elemosinario. Storefronts make up the facade, and the altars were built by market guilds—poulterers, messengers, and fodder merchants—at this church intimately bound to the Rialto Market. The original church was completely destroyed by a fire in 1514 and rebuilt in 1531 by Antonio Abbondi, who had also worked on the Scuola di San Rocco. During a recent restoration, workers stumbled upon a frescoed cupola by Pordenone (1484–1539) that had been painted over centuries earlier. Don't miss Titian's *St. John the Almsgiver* and Pordenone's *Sts. Catherine, Sebastian, and Roch.* ⊠ *Rialto Ruga Vecchia San Giovanni, Santa Croce* ☎ *041/2750462 for Chorus Foundation* ⊕ *www.chorusvenezia.org* ✉ *€3 (free with Chorus Pass)* ⊗ *Closed Sun.* Ⓜ *Vaporetto: San Silvestro, Rialto.*

San Stae. The church of San Stae—the Venetian name for San Eustacchio (Eustace)—was reconstructed in 1687 by Giovanni Grassi and given a new facade in 1707 by Domenico Rossi. Renowned Venetian painters and sculptors of the early 18th century decorated this church around 1717 with the legacy left by Doge Alvise Mocenigo II, who's buried in the center aisle. San Stae affords a good opportunity to see the early works of Gianbattista Tiepolo, Sebastiano Ricci, and Piazzetta, as well as those of the previous generation of Venetian painters, with whom they had studied. ⊠ *Campo San Stae, Santa Croce* ☎ *041/2750462 for Chorus Foundation* ⊕ *www.chorusvenezia.org* ⊠ *€3 (free with Chorus Pass)* ⊘ *Closed Sun.* Ⓜ *Vaporetto: San Stae.*

CANNAREGIO

Seen from above, this part of town seems like a wide field plowed by several long, straight canals that are linked by intersecting straight streets—not typical of Venice, where the shape of the islands usually defines the shape of the canals. Cannaregio's main thoroughfare, the Strada Nova (literally, "New Street," as it was converted from a canal in 1871), is the longest street in Venice; it runs parallel to the Grand Canal. Today the Strada Nova serves as a pedestrian walkway from the train station almost to the Rialto. Cannaregio, first settled in the XIV century, is one of the more "modern" of Venice's neighborhoods, with walkways, or *fondamente,* along its major canals north of the Strada Nova, making it ideal for canalside strolls where you can view some spectacular Gothic and Baroque facades.

TOP ATTRACTIONS

Fodor'sChoice
★

Ca' d'Oro. One of the postcard sights of Venice, this exquisite Venetian Gothic palace was once literally a "Golden House," when its marble traceries and ornaments were embellished with gold. It was created by Giovanni and Bartolomeo Bon between 1428 and 1430 for the patrician Marino Contarini, who had read about the Roman emperor Nero's golden house in Rome, and wished to imitate it as a present to his wife. Her family owned the land and the Byzantine *fondaco* (palace-trading house) previously standing on it; you can still see the round Byzantine arches on the entry porch incorporated into the Gothic building. The last proprietor, Baron Giorgio Franchetti, left Ca' d'Oro to the city, after having had it carefully restored and furnished with antiquities, sculptures, and paintings that today make up the Galleria Franchetti. It also contains the type of fresco that once adorned the exteriors of Venetian buildings (commissioned by those who could not afford a marble facade). ⊠ *Calle Ca' d'Oro, Cannaregio 3933, Cannaregio* ☎ *041/5238790* ⊕ *www.cadoro.org* ⊠ *€8.50 (free 1st Sun. of month)* Ⓜ *Vaporetto: Ca' d'Oro.*

Fodor'sChoice
★

Jewish Ghetto. The neighborhood that gave the world the word *ghetto* is today a quiet place surrounding a large campo. The area has Europe's highest density of Renaissance-era synagogues, and visiting them is interesting not only culturally but also aesthetically. In 1516 relentless local opposition forced the Senate to confine Jews to an island in Cannaregio, named for its *geto* (foundry). The term "ghetto" also

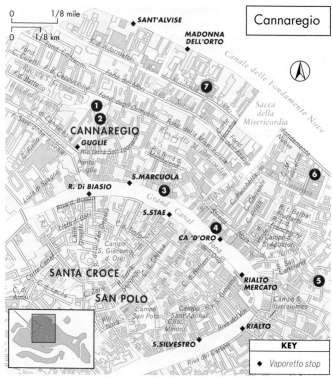

may come from the Hebrew "ghet," meaning separation or divorce. Gates at the entrance were locked at night, and boats patrolled the surrounding canals. In the 16th century the community grew with refugees from the Inquisition. Although the gates were pulled down after Napoleon's 1797 arrival, the ghetto was reinstated during the Austrian occupation. Full freedom wasn't realized until 1866 with the founding of the Italian state. Many Jews fled Italy as a result of Mussolini's 1938 racial laws. During World War II, the remaining 247 were deported by the Nazis; only eight returned. ⊠ *Campo del Ghetto Nuovo, Cannaregio* ⊡ *Synagogue tour €8.50, arranged through Jewish Museum in Campo del Ghetto Nuovo; museum €4; combination ticket €10* ⊗ *No tours Sat.*

Fodor'sChoice **Madonna dell'Orto.** Though built toward the middle of the 14th century, this church takes its character from its beautiful late-Gothic
★ facade, added between 1460 and 1464; it's one of the most beautiful Gothic churches in Venice. Tintoretto lived nearby, and this, his parish church, contains some of his most powerful work. Lining the chancel are two huge (45 feet by 20 feet) canvases, *Adoration of the Golden Calf* and *Last Judgment.* In glowing contrast to this awesome spectacle is Tintoretto's *Presentation of the Virgin at the Temple* and the simple chapel where he and his children, Marietta and Domenico,

are buried. Paintings by Domenico, Cima da Conegliano, Palma il Giovane, Palma il Vecchio, and Titian also hang in the church. A chapel displays a photographic reproduction of a precious *Madonna with Child* by Giovanni Bellini. The original was stolen one night in 1993. Don't miss the beautifully austere, late-Gothic cloister (1460), which you enter through the small door to the right of the church; it is frequently used for exhibitions but may be open at other times as well. ⊠ *Campo della Madonna dell'Orto, Cannaregio* ☎ *041/719933* ⬚ *€3* Ⓜ *Vaporetto: Orto.*

Museo Ebraico. The small but well-arranged museum highlights centuries of Venetian Jewish culture with splendid silver Hanukkah lamps and Torahs, and handwritten, beautifully decorated wedding contracts in Hebrew. Hourly tours in Italian and English (on the half hour) of the ghetto and its five synagogues leave from the museum. ⊠ *Campo del Ghetto Nuovo, Cannaregio 2902/B, Cannaregio* ☎ *041/715359* ⊕ *www.museoebraico.it* ⬚ *€4, €10 with guided tour* ⊗ *Closed Sat.* Ⓜ *Vaporetto: San Marcuola, Guglie.*

Santa Maria dei Miracoli. Tiny yet harmoniously proportioned, this Renaissance gem, built between 1481 and 1489, is sheathed in marble and decorated inside with exquisite marble reliefs. Architect Pietro Lombardo (circa 1435–1515) miraculously compressed the building into its confined space, then created the illusion of greater size by varying the color of the exterior, adding extra pilasters on the building's canal side and offsetting the arcade windows to make the arches appear deeper. The church was built to house *I Miracoli,* an image of the Virgin Mary by Niccolò di Pietro (1394–1440) that is said to have performed miracles—look for it on the high altar. ⊠ *Campo Santa Maria Nova, Cannaregio* ☎ *041/2750462 for Chorus Foundation* ⊕ *www.chorusvenezia.org* ⬚ *€3 (free with Chorus Pass)* Ⓜ *Vaporetto: Rialto.*

WORTH NOTING

Gesuiti. The interior walls of this early-18th-century church (1715–30) resemble brocade drapery, and only touching them will convince skeptics that rather than embroidered cloth, the green-and-white walls are inlaid marble. This trompe-l'oeil decor is typical of the late Baroque's fascination with optical illusion. Toward the end of his life, Titian tended to paint scenes of suffering and sorrow in a nocturnal ambience. A dramatic example of this is on display above the first altar to the left: Titian's daring *Martyrdom of St. Lawrence* (1578), taken from an earlier church that stood on this site. To the left of the church is the Oratory of the Crociferi, which features some of Palma Giovane's best work, painted between 1583 and 1591. ⊠ *Campo dei Gesuiti, Cannaregio* ☎ *041/5286579* ⊗ *Oratory closed Nov.–Mar. and Sun.–Thurs.* Ⓜ *Vaporetto: Fondamente Nove.*

Palazzo Vendramin-Calergi. Hallowed as the place of Richard Wagner's death and today's Venice's most glamorous casino, this magnficent edifice found its fame centuries before: Venetian star architect Mauro Codussi (1440–1504) essentially invented Venetian Renaissance architecture with this design. Built for the Loredan family around 1500,

Codussi's palace married the fortresslike design of the Florentine Alberti's Palazzo Ruccelai with the lightness and delicacy of Venetian Gothic. Note how Codussi beautifully exploits the flickering light of Venetian waterways to play across the building's facade and to pour in through the generous windows.

Venice has always prized the beauty of this palace. In 1652 its owners were convicted of a rather gruesome murder, and the punishment would have involved, as was customary, the demolition of their palace. The murderers were banned from the Republic, but the palace, in view of its beauty and historical importance, was spared. Only the newly added wing was torn down. ⊠ *Cannaregio 2040, Cannaregio* ☎ *041/5297111* ⊕ *www.casinovenezia.it* 🎫 *Casinò €10* Ⓜ *Vaporetto: San Marcuola.*

CASTELLO

Castello, Venice's largest sestiere, includes all of the land from east of Piazza San Marco to the city's easternmost tip. Its name probably comes from a fortress that once stood on one of the eastern islands. Not every well-off Venetian family could find a spot or afford to build a palazzo on the Grand Canal. Many who couldn't instead settled in western Castello, taking advantage of its proximity to the Rialto and San Marco, and built the noble palazzos that today distinguish this area from the fishermen's enclave in the more easterly streets of the sestiere. During the days of the Republic, eastern Castello was the primary neighborhood for workers in the shipbuilding Arsenale, which is located in its midst.

TOP ATTRACTIONS

Arsenale. Visible from the street, the impressive Renaissance gateway, the **Porta Magna** (1460), designed by Antonio Gambello, was the first classical structure to be built in Venice. It is guarded by four lions— war booty of Francesco Morosini, who took the Peloponnese from the Turks in 1687. The 10-foot-tall lion on the left stood sentinel more than 2,000 years ago near Athens, and experts say its mysterious inscription is runic "graffiti" left by Viking mercenaries hired to suppress 11th-century revolts in Piraeus. If you look at the winged lion above the doorway, you'll notice that the Gospel at his paws is open, but lacks the customary *Pax* inscription; praying for peace perhaps seemed inappropriate above a factory that manufactured weapons. The interior is not regularly open to the public, since it belongs to the Italian Navy, but it opens for the Biennale di Arte and for Venice's festival of traditional boats, **Mare Maggio** (⊕ *www.maremaggio.it*), held every May. If you're here during those times, don't miss the chance for a look inside; you can enter from the back via a northern-side walkway leading from the Ospedale vaporetto stop.

The Arsenale is said to have been founded in 1104 on twin islands. The immense facility that evolved—it was the largest industrial complex in Europe built prior to the Industrial Revolution—was given the old Venetian dialect name *arzanà*, borrowed from the Arabic *darsina'a*, meaning "workshop." At the height of its activity, in the early 16th century, it employed as many as 16,000 *arsenalotti,* workers who were among the most respected shipbuilders in the world. The Arsenale developed a type of pre-Industrial Revolution assembly line, which allowed it to build ships with astounding speed and efficiency. (This innovation existed even in Dante's time, and he immortalized these toiling workers armed with boiling tar in his *Inferno,* canto 21.) The Arsenale's efficiency was confirmed time and again—whether building 100 ships in 60 days to battle the Turks in Cyprus (1597) or completing one perfectly armed warship, start to finish, while King Henry III of France attended a banquet. ⊠ *Campo dell'Arsenale, Castello* Ⓜ *Vaporetto: Arsenale.*

Fodor'sChoice
★
San Francesco della Vigna. Although this church contains some interesting and beautiful paintings and sculptures, it's the architecture that makes it worth the hike through a lively, middle-class, residential neighborhood. The Franciscan church was enlarged and rebuilt by Jacopo Sansovino in 1534, giving it the first Renaissance interior in Venice; its proportions are said to reflect the mystic significance of the numbers three and seven dictated by Renaissance neo-Platonic numerology. The soaring but harmonious facade was added in 1562 by Palladio. The church represents a unique combination of the work of the two great stars of Veneto 16th-century architecture. As you enter, a late Giovanni Bellini *Madonna with Saints* is down some steps to the left, inside the Cappella Santa. In the Giustinian chapel to the left is Veronese's first work in Venice, an altarpiece depicting the Virgin and child with saints. In another, larger chapel, on the left, are bas-reliefs by Pietro and his son Tullio Lombardo. Be sure to ask to see the attached cloisters, which are usually open to visitors and quite lovely. ⊠ *Campo di San Francesco della Vigna, Castello* ☎ *041/5206102* ⬚ *Free* ⊘ *Closed weekends* Ⓜ *Vaporetto: Celestia.*

Fodor'sChoice
★
Santi Giovanni e Paolo. This gorgeous Italian Gothic church of the Dominican order, consecrated in 1430, looms over one of the most picturesque squares in Venice: the Campo Giovanni e Paolo, centered around the magnificent 15th-century equestrian statue of Bartolomeo Colleoni by the Florentine Andrea Verrocchio. Bartolomeo Bon's portal, combining Gothic and classical elements, was added between 1458 and 1462, using columns salvaged from Torcello. The 15th-century Murano stained-glass window near the side entrance is breathtaking for its beautiful colors and figures. The second official church of the Republic after San Marco, San Zanipolo is the Venetian equivalent of London's Westminster Abbey, with a great number of important people, including 25 doges, buried here. Artistic highlights include an early polyptych by Giovanni Bellini, Alvise Vivarini's *Christ Carrying the Cross,* and Lorenzo Lotto's *Charity of St. Antonino.* Don't miss the Cappella del Rosario (Rosary Chapel), built in the 16th century, or the Pietro Mocenigo tomb to the right of the main entrance. ⊠ *Campo dei Santi Giovanni e Paolo, Castello* ☎ *041/5235913* ⬚ *€2.50* Ⓜ *Vaporetto: Fondamente Nove, Rialto.*

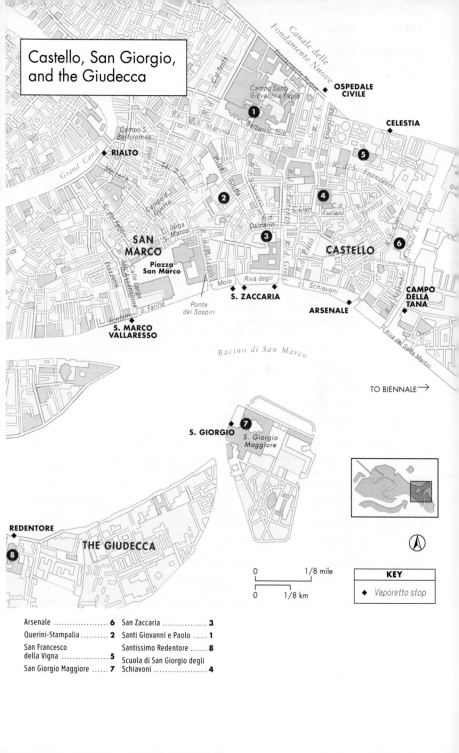

Castello, San Giorgio, and the Giudecca

Canale delle Fondamente Nuove

OSPEDALE CIVILE

Campo Santi Giovanni e Paolo

1

CELESTIA

Campo S. Bartolomeo

RIALTO

Merceria

Grand Canal

Campo d. Guerra

Rio M.ai Marina

Barbari d. Tole

5

2

Rio di S. Lorenzo

Osmarin

4

C. d. Furlani

6

CASTELLO

SAN MARCO

Salizad Larga Marco

3

C. Lion

Campo d. Greci

Rio del Greci

Calle d. Caselleria

Piazza San Marco

Calle Larga dell'Ascensione

Frezzeria

Molo

Riva degli

Schiavoni

CAMPO DELLA TANA

Ponte dei Sospiri

S. ZACCARIA

ARSENALE

Riva Ca' di Dio

Fontam. d. Farine

S. MARCO VALLARESSO

Fontam.

Riva dei Sette Martiri

Bacino di San Marco

TO BIENNALE →

S. GIORGIO

7

S. Giorgio Maggiore

REDENTORE

8

THE GIUDECCA

0   1/8 mile

0   1/8 km

KEY

◆ *Vaporetto stop*

Didovich Pastry Shop. To satisfy your sweet tooth, head for Campo Santa Marina and the family-owned and -operated shop. It's a local favorite, especially for Carnevale-time fritelle (fried doughnuts). There is limited seating inside, but in the warmer months you can sit outside. ⊠ *Campo Santa Marina, Castello 5909, Castello* ☎ *041/5230017* ⊘ *Closed Sun.*

Fodor'sChoice
★
San Zaccaria. Practically more a museum than a church, San Zaccaria bears a striking Renaissance facade, with central and upper portions representing some of Mauro Codussi's best work. The lower portion of the facade and the interior were designed by Antonio Gambello. The original structure of the church was 14th-century Gothic, with its facade completed in 1515, some years after Codussi's death in 1504, and it retains the proportions of the rest of the essentially Gothic structure. Inside is one of the great treasures of Venice, Giovanni Bellini's celebrated altarpiece, *La Sacra Conversazione*, easily recognizable in the left nave. Completed in 1505, when the artist was 75, it shows Bellini's ability to incorporate the aesthetics of the High Renaissance into his work. It bears a closer resemblance to the contemporary works of Leonardo (it dates from approximately the same time as the *Mona Lisa*) than it does to much of Bellini's early work. The **Cappella di San Tarasio** displays frescoes by Tuscan Renaissance artists Andrea del Castagno (1423–57) and Francesco da Faenza (circa 1400–51). Castagno's frescoes (1442) are considered the earliest examples of Renaissance painting in Venice. The three outstanding Gothic polyptychs attributed to Antonio Vivarini earned it the nickname "Golden Chapel." ⊠ *Campo San Zaccaria, 4693 Castello, Castello* ☎ *041/5221257* ⊡ *Church free, chapels and crypt €1* Ⓜ *Vaporetto: San Zaccaria.*

Fodor'sChoice
★
Scuola di San Giorgio degli Schiavoni. Founded in 1451 by the Dalmatian community, this small scuola, or confraternity, was, and still is, a social and cultural center for migrants from what is now Croatia. It contains one of Italy's most beautiful rooms, harmoniously decorated between 1502 and 1507 by Vittore Carpaccio. While Carpaccio generally painted legendary and religious figures against backgrounds of contemporary Venetian architecture, here is perhaps one of the first instances of "Orientalism" in Western painting. Note the turbans and exotic dress of those being baptized and converted, and even the imagined, arid Middle Eastern or North African landscape in the background of several of the paintings. In this scuola for immigrants, Carpaccio focuses on "foreign" saints especially venerated in Dalmatia: Sts. George, Tryphone, and Jerome. He combined keen empirical observation with fantasy, a sense of warm color, and late medieval realism. (Look for the priests fleeing St. Jerome's lion, or the body parts in the dragon's lair.) ■TIP➔ **Opening hours are quite flexible. Since this is a "must-see" site, check in advance so you won't be disappointed.** ⊠ *Calle dei Furlani, Castello 3259/A, Castello* ☎ *041/5228828* ⊡ *€5* Ⓜ *Vaporetto: Arsenale, San Zaccaria.*

WORTH NOTING

Querini-Stampalia. A connoisseur's delight, this art collection at this late-16th-century palace includes Giovanni Bellini's *Presentation in the Temple* and Sebastiano Ricci's triptych *Dawn, Afternoon, and Evening.* Portraits of newlyweds Francesco Querini and Paola Priuli were left unfinished on the death of Giacomo Palma il Vecchio (1480–1528); note the groom's hand and the bride's dress. Original 18th-century furniture and stuccowork are a fitting background for Pietro Longhi's portraits. Nearly 70 works by Gabriele Bella (1730–99) capture scenes of Venetian street life; downstairs is a café. The entrance hall and the small, charming rear garden were designed by famous Venetian architect Carlo Scarpa during the 1950s. ⊠ *Campo Santa Maria Formosa, Castello 5252, Castello* ☎ *041/2711411* ⊕ *www.querinistampalia.org* ▧ *€10* ⊘ *Closed Mon.* Ⓜ *Vaporetto: San Zaccaria.*

3

SAN GIORGIO MAGGIORE AND THE GIUDECCA

Beckoning travelers across St. Mark's Basin is the island of San Giorgio Maggiore, separated by a small channel from the Giudecca. A tall brick campanile on that distant bank nicely complements the Campanile of San Marco. Beneath it looms the stately dome of one of Venice's greatest churches, San Giorgio Maggiore, the creation of Andrea Palladio. To the west, on the Giudecca, is Palladio's other masterpiece, the Church of the Santissimo Redentore.

You can reach San Giorgio Maggiore via Vaporetto Line 2 from San Zaccaria. The next three stops on the line take you to the Giudecca. The island's past may be shrouded in mystery, but despite recent gentrification by artists and well-to-do bohemians, it's still down-to-earth and one of the city's few remaining primarily working-class neighborhoods. Interestingly, you find that most Venetians don't even consider the Giudecchini Venetians at all.

TIMING

A half day should be plenty of time to visit the area. Allow about a half hour to see each of the churches and an hour or two to look around the Giudecca.

TOP ATTRACTIONS

Fodor's Choice ★ **San Giorgio Maggiore.** There's been a church on this island since the 8th century, with a Benedictine monastery added in the 10th century. Today's refreshingly airy and simply decorated church of brick and white marble was begun in 1566 by Palladio and displays his architectural hallmarks of mathematical harmony and classical influence. *The Last Supper* and the *Gathering of Manna*, two of Tintoretto's later works, line the chancel. To the right of the entrance hangs *The Adoration of the Shepherds* by Jacopo Bassano (1517–92); his affection for his home in the foothills, Bassano del Grappa, is evident in the bucolic subjects and terra-firma colors he chooses. The monks are happy to show Carpaccio's *St. George and the Dragon*, hanging in a private room, if they have time. The campanile dates from 1791, the previous structures having collapsed twice.

Adjacent to the church is the complex now housing the **Cini Foundation**, containing a very beautiful cloister designed by Palladio in 1560, his refectory, and a library designed by Longhena. Guided tours are given on weekends 10–5, April through September; reservations are not required. ⊠ *Isola di San Giorgio Maggiore, San Giorgio Maggiore* ☎ *041/5227827* ▧ *Church free, campanile €6* Ⓜ *Vaporetto: San Giorgio.*

Santissimo Redentore. After a plague in 1576 claimed some 50,000 people—nearly one-third of the city's population (including Titian)—Andrea Palladio was asked to design a commemorative church. Giudecca's Capuchin friars offered land and their services, provided the building was in keeping with the simplicity of their hermitage. Consecrated in 1592, after Palladio's death, the Redentore (considered Palladio's supreme achievement in ecclesiastical design) is dominated by a dome and a pair of slim, almost minaretlike bell towers. Its deceptively simple, stately facade leads to a bright, airy interior. There aren't any paintings or sculptures of note, but the harmony and elegance of the interior makes a visit worthwhile.

For hundreds of years, on the third weekend in July the doge would make a pilgrimage here to give thanks to the Redeemer for ending the 16th-century plague. The event has become the Festa del Redentore, a favorite Venetian festival featuring boats, fireworks, and outdoor feasting. It's the one time of year you can walk to Giudecca—across a temporary pontoon bridge connecting Redentore with the Zattere. ⊠ *Fondamenta San Giacomo, Giudecca* ☎ *041/5231415, 041/2750462 for Chorus Foundation* ☞ *€3 (free with Chorus Pass)* Ⓜ *Vaporetto: Redentore.*

ISLANDS OF THE LAGOON

The perfect vacation from your Venetian vacation is an escape to Murano, Burano, and sleepy Torcello, the islands of the northern lagoon. Torcello is legendary for its beauty and offers ancient mosaics, greenery, breathing space, and picnic opportunities (remember to pack a lunch). Burano is an island of fishing traditions and houses painted in a riot of colors—blue, yellow, pink, ocher, and dark red. Visitors still love to shop here for "Venetian" lace, even though the vast majority of it is machine-made in Asia; visit the island's Museo del Merletto (Lace Museum) to discover the undeniable difference between the two.

Murano is renowned for its glass, plenty of which you can find in Venice itself. It's also notorious for high-pressure sales on factory tours, even those organized by top hotels. Vaporetto connections to Murano aren't difficult, and for the price of a boat ticket (included in any vaporetto pass) you'll buy your freedom and more time to explore. The Murano "guides" herding new arrivals follow a rotation so that factories take turns giving tours, but you can avoid the hustle by just walking away. ■ TIP→ Don't take a "free" taxi to Murano; it only means that should you choose to buy (and you'll be strongly encouraged), your taxi fare and commission will be included in the price you pay.

The Lido is Venice's barrier island, forming the southern border of the Venetian Lagoon and protecting Venice from the waters of the Adriatic. It forms the beach of Venice, and is home to a series of bathing establishments both public and private—some luxurious and elegant, some quite simple and catering to Venetian families and their children. Buses run the length of the island.

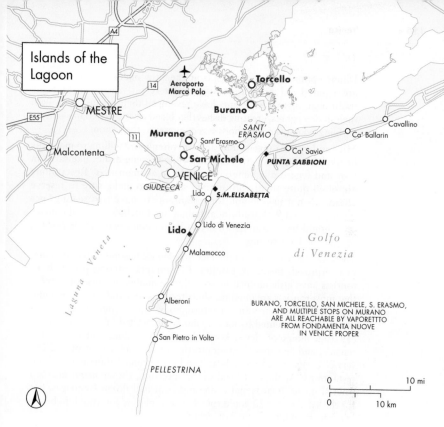

Islands of the Lagoon

MESTRE

Malcontenta

Murano

VENICE

GIUDECCA

Lido

Lido

Malamocco

Alberoni

San Pietro in Volta

PELLESTRINA

Aeroporto Marco Polo

Torcello

Burano

SANT' ERASMO

Sant'Erasmo

San Michele

S.M.ELISABETTA

Lido di Venezia

Ca' Savio

PUNTA SABBIONI

Ca' Ballarin

Cavallino

Golfo di Venezia

Laguna Veneta

BURANO, TORCELLO, SAN MICHELE, S. ERASMO, AND MULTIPLE STOPS ON MURANO ARE ALL REACHABLE BY VAPORETTO FROM FONDAMENTA NUOVE IN VENICE PROPER

0   10 mi

0   10 km

■TIP➔ San Michele, a vaporetto stop on the way to Murano, is the cemetery island of Venice, the resting place of many international artists who have chosen to spend eternity in this beautiful city. It also hosts Venice's first church to exhibit features of Renaissance architecture.

TIMING

Hitting all the sights on all the islands takes a busy, full day. If you limit yourself to Murano and San Michele, you can easily explore for an ample half day; the same goes for Burano and Torcello. In summer the express Vaporetto Line 7 will take you to Murano from San Zaccaria (the Jolanda landing) in 25 minutes; Line 3 will take you from Piazzale Roma to Murano via the Canale di Cannaregio in 21 minutes; otherwise, local Line 4.1 makes a 45-minute trip from San Zaccaria every 20 minutes, circling the east end of Venice, stopping at Fondamente Nove and San Michele island cemetery on the way. To see glassblowing, get off at Colonna; the Museo stop will put you near the Museo del Vetro.

Line 12 goes from Fondamente Nove direct to Murano and Burano every 30 minutes (Torcello is a five-minute ferry ride—Line 9—from there); the full trip takes 45 minutes each way. To get to Burano and Torcello from Murano, pick up Line 12 at the Faro stop (Murano's lighthouse).

WHERE TO EAT

Dining options in Venice range from the ultra–high end, where jackets are required and shorts are a no-go, to the very casual. Once staunchly traditional, many restaurants have revamped their menus along with their dining rooms, creating dishes that blend classic Venetian elements with ingredients and methods less common to the region.

Mid- and upper-range restaurants are often more willing to make the break, offering innovative options while keeping dishes like sarde in saor and fegato alla veneziana available as mainstays. Restaurants are often quite small with limited seating, so make sure to reserve ahead. It's not uncommon for restaurants to have two seatings per night, at 7 and 9. A traditional Italian meal includes several courses and should be a leisurely affair; so if you don't want to be rushed, opt for the later sitting.

There's no getting around the fact that Venice has more than its share of overpriced, mediocre eateries. Restaurants catering primarily to tourists have little motivation to maintain quality, because they know that most tourists are onetime, short-term visitors and will, even under the best circumstances, never return. So, you are better off selecting a restaurant frequented by locals, who are interested in the food, not in canalside dining or views. Avoid places with cajoling waiters standing outside, and beware of restaurants that don't display their prices. The service desks at many hotels are paid off to funnel tourists to certain restaurants. At the other end of the spectrum, showy *menu turistico* (tourist menu) boards make offerings clear in a dozen languages, but for the same €15–€20 you'd spend at such places, you could do better at a bacaro making a meal of cicheti.

Use the coordinate (⊹ B2) at the end of each listing to locate a site on the Where to Eat and Stay in Venice map.

WHAT IT COSTS				
	$	$$	$$$	$$$$
At dinner	under €15	€15–€24	€25–€35	over €35

Prices in the dining reviews are the average cost of a main course at dinner, or, if dinner is not served, at lunch.

SAN MARCO

$
CAFÉ

✕ **Bar all'Angolo.** This corner of Campo Santo Stefano is one of the most pleasing locations to sit and watch the Venetian world go by. The constant motion of the café staff assures you'll receive your coffee, spritz, panino, or *tramezzino* (sandwich on untoasted white bread, usually with a mayonnaise-based filling) in short order; consume it at your leisure either at one of the outdoor tables, at the bar, or take refuge at the tables in the back. They'll whip you up a fresh salad, and they offer a delectable tiramisù for dessert—homemade, just like the sandwiches. The pasta dishes, however, are not homemade. As in most bars, it is better to stick to cold dishes. Closing time is 9 pm, making the Angolo a good alternative to a more elaborate evening meal. $ *Average main:* €10 ⊠ *Campo Santo Stefano (just in front of Santo Stefano church), San Marco 3464, San Marco* ☎ *041/5220710* ⊘ *Closed Sun., and Jan.* Ⓜ *Vaporetto: Sant'Angelo* ⊹ *C4.*

$$$
CAFÉ
Fodor's Choice
★

✕ **Caffè Florian.** Because of the prices and the tourist mobs, Venetians tend to avoid the cafés in the Piazza San Marco. But when they want to indulge and regain control of their city, they go to Florian. Founded in 1720, it's not only Italy's first café, but with its glittering neo-baroque decor and attractive 19th-century wall panels (depicting Venetian heroes), it's undisputedly the most beautiful. Florian is steeped in local history: favored by Venetians during the long Austrian occupation, it was the only café to serve women during the 18th century (hence Casanova's patronage), and it was the café of choice for artistic notables such as Wagner, Goethe, Goldoni, Lord Byron, Marcel Proust, and Charles Dickens. It was also the birthplace of the international art exhibition, which later blossomed into the Venice Biennale. The coffee, drinks, and snacks are quite good (think chocolate, hot or otherwise), but you really come here for the atmosphere and to be part of Venetian history. There's a surcharge for music, so savvy Venetians and travelers in a hurry opt for lower prices at the comfortable bar in the back. $ *Average main:* €27 ⊠ *Piazza San Marco, San Marco, 56, San Marco* ☎ *041/5205641* ⊕ *www.caffeflorian.com* ⊹ *E4.*

$
VENETIAN

✕ **Enoteca al Volto.** A short walk from the Rialto Bridge, this bar has been around since 1936; the satisfying cicheti and primi have a lot to do with its staying power. Grab one of the tables out front, or take refuge in two small, dark rooms with a ceiling plastered with wine labels that provide a classic backdrop for simple fare, including a delicious risotto that is served daily at noon. The place prides itself on its solid wine list of both Italian and foreign vintages. If you stick to a panino or some cicchetti at the bar, you'll eat well for relatively little. If you take a table and opt for one of the day's exceptional primi, the price category goes up a notch; however, this is still a good bargain for San Marco. There are, of course, traditional secondi, such as a very good seppie in nero. Al Volto is open every day of the year but Christmas (and closes a bit early on Christmas Eve). $ *Average main:* €12 ⊠ *Calle Cavalli, San Marco 4081, San Marco* ☎ *041/5228945* ▭ *No credit cards* Ⓜ *Vaporetto: Rialto* ⊹ *E3.*

$$$$
VENETIAN
Fodor's Choice
★

✕ **Harry's Bar.** For those who can afford it, and despite its recently having become the watering place of Russian oligarchs and their female stiletto-heeled retinues, lunch or dinner at Harry's Bar is as much a part of a visit to Venice as a walk across the Piazza San Marco or a vaporetto ride down the Grand Canal. Harry's is not just a fine restaurant; it's a cultural institution. When founder Giuseppe Cipriani opened the doors in 1931, the place became a favorite of almost every famous name to visit Venice (including Charlie Chaplin, Orson Welles, and Ernest Hemingway) and still attracts much of Venetian high society as regulars. Today, many still remember Harry's as one of the few restaurants in town that continued to serve Jewish patrons during the period of the fascist racial laws. Inside, the suave, subdued beige-on-white decor is unchanged from the 1930s, and the classic Venetian fare is carefully and excellently prepared. Try the delicate baked sea bass with artichokes, and don't miss the signature crepes flambées or famous Cipriani chocolate cake for dessert. Because a meal at Harry's is as much about being seen, book one of the cramped tables on the ground floor—the upper floor of the restaurant is the Venetian equivalent of Siberia (take heart if seated there: views from the second-floor windows look like framed paintings). Be sure to order a Bellini cocktail—a refreshing mix of white peach puree and sparking prosecco—this is its birthplace, after all. On the other hand, true to its retro atmosphere, Harry's makes one of the best martinis in town. Ⓢ *Average main: €38* ⊠ *Calle Vallaresso, San Marco 1323, San Marco* ☎ *041/5285777* ⊕ *www.harrysbarvenezia. com* 🎩 *Jacket required* Ⓜ *Vaporetto: San Marco (Calle Vallaresso)* ✛ *E5.*

$$$$ ✕ **Ristorante Quadri.** Located above the famed café of the same name sits
VENETIAN one of the most widely discussed restaurants in Italy: Quadri, a name steeped in history (as a café, it was the first to introduce Turkish coffee to an already overcaffeinated city in the 1700s) and overstated Venetian ambience. The Alajmo family (of the celebrated Le Calandre restaurant near Padua) have taken over the restaurant and put their accomplished sous-chef from Padua in charge of the kitchen. The menu has developed increasing complexity, which runs contrary to the inherent simplicity and directness of classic Italian cuisine. With tasting menus (€185–€235, exclusive of wine), you can savor such creative delights as pumpkin lasagnetta noodles with lobster, squid, ginger, and almonds, but you can also be more conservative and enjoy burrata ravioli with a seafood-tomato sauce spiked with oregano. Note also that any tasting menu must be ordered by the entire table. Downstairs, the simpler **abc-Quadri** (located next to the café)—with impeccably restored neo-rococo wall paintings—serves more traditional Venetian fare and some of the best martinis in town. As for Quadri itself—the prices, cuisine, and decor are all *alta,* so beware: some food critics find the fare not worth the ticket. Be sure, also, to book one of the few tables with a Piazza San Marco view; otherwise, the ambience offered is lavish, but not really extraordinary. Ⓢ *Average main: €65* ⊠ *Piazza San Marco 121, San Marco* ☎ *041/5222105* ⊕ *www.caffequadri.it* ☉ *Closed Mon.* ✛ *E4.*

DORSODURO

$ ✕ **Caffè Bar Ai Artisti.** Sitting on a campo made famous in films with
CAFÉ Katharine Hepburn and Indiana Jones, Caffè Ai Artisti gives locals, students, and travelers alike good reason to pause and refuel. The location is central, pleasant, and sunny—perfect for people-watching and taking a break before the next destination—and the hours are long: you can come here for a morning cappuccino, or drop by late for an after-dinner spritz. The panini are composed on-site from fresh, seasonal ingredients, their names scribbled in front of each on the glass case. There's a varied selection of wines by the glass, as well as herbal teas, and even caffè with ginseng. Ⓢ *Average main: €8* ⊠ *Campo San Barnaba, Dorsoduro 2771, Dorsoduro* ☎ *041/5238994* ▭ *No credit cards* Ⓜ *Vaporetto: Ca' Rezzonico* ✛ *C5.*

$ **✕Cantinone già Schiavi.** A mainstay for anyone living or working in
WINE BAR the area, this beautiful, family-run, 19th-century bacaro across from
Fodor'sChoice the *squero* (gondola repair shop) of San Trovaso has original furnish-
★ ings and one of the best wine cellars in town—the walls are covered
floor to ceiling by bottles for purchase. The cicheti here are some of
the most inventive—and freshest—in Venice (feel free to compliment
the Signora, who makes them up to twice a day). Try the crostini-style
layers of bread, smoked swordfish, and slivers of raw zucchini, or pun-
gent slices of *parmigiano,* fig, pistachio, and toast. They also have a
creamy version of baccalà mantecato spiced with herbs, and there are
nearly a dozen open bottles of wine for experimenting at the bar. You'll
have no trouble spotting the Cantinone as you approach; it's the one
with throngs of chatty patrons enjoying themselves. $ *Average main:*
€8 ⊠ *Fondamenta Nani, Dorsoduro 992, Dorsoduro* ☎ *041/5230034*
▭ *No credit cards* ⊗ *Closed Sun., and 2 wks in Aug.* M *Vaporetto:*
Zattere, Accademia ✛ *C5.*

$ **✕Imagina Caffè.** This friendly café and art gallery, located between
ITALIAN Campo Santa Margherita and Campo San Barnaba, is a great place to
stop for a spritz, or even for a light lunch or dinner. The highlights are
the freshly made salads, but their panini and tramezzini are also among
the best in the area. The staff prepare a freshly made pasta and a soup
every day—this is one of the very few cafés where the pasta is recommended. The well-stocked bar has a good assortment of wines, and
the talented bartenders can even whip up a decent American martini.
There's also seating outside, where you can watch the locals making
their way between the two major campi. $ *Average main: €10* ⊠ *Rio*
Terà Canal, Dorsoduro 3126, Dorsoduro ☎ *041/2410625* ⊕ *www.*
imaginacafe.it/english.html M *Vaporetto Ca' Rezonnico* ✛ *B4.*

$ **✕Impronta Cafe.** This sleek café is a favorite lunchtime haunt for pro-
VENETIAN fessors from the nearby university and local businesspeople. Unlike
Fodor'sChoice in more traditional places, it's quite acceptable to order only pasta
★ or a secondo, without an antipasto or dessert. Although the restaurant is also open for dinner—and you can dine well and economi-
cally in the evening—the real bargain is lunch, where you can easily
have a beautifully prepared primo or secondo, plus a glass of wine,
for around €12–€18. There's also a good selection of sandwiches and
salads. The attentive staff speak English, although you may be the only
non-Venetian in the place. Unlike most local eateries, this spot is open
from breakfast through late dinner (with tea and chocolate served late
afternoon). $ *Average main: €12* ⊠ *Crosera - San Pantalon, Dorsoduro*
3815–3817, Dorsoduro ☎ *041/2750386* ⊕ *www.improntacafevenice.*
com ⊗ *Closed Sun., and 2 wks in Aug.* ✛ *B3.*

$$ **✕La Bitta.** The decor is more discreet, the dining hours longer, and the
NORTHERN service friendlier and more efficient here than in many small restau-
ITALIAN rants in Venice—and the nonfish menu (inspired by the cuisine of the
Fodor'sChoice Venetian terra firma) is a temptation at every course. Market avail-
★ ability keeps the menu changing almost every day, although typically
you can start with a savory barley soup or gnocchi with winter squash
and aged ricotta cheese. Then choose a secondo such as lamb chops
with thyme, *anatra in pevarada* (duck in a pepper sauce), or guinea

hen in cream. The homemade desserts are all luscious, and it's been said that La Bitta serves the best panna cotta in town. Trust owner Deborah Civiero's selection from her excellent wine and grappa lists. $ *Average main: €20* ⊠ *Calle Lunga San Barnaba, Dorsoduro 2753/A, Dorsoduro* ☎ *041/5230531* ▭ *No credit cards* ⊗ *Closed Sun. No lunch* Ⓜ *Vaporetto: Ca' Rezzonico* ✛ *B5.*

$ ✕ **Osteria al Squero.** It wasn't long after this lovely little locale appeared
WINE BAR   across from the Squero San Trovaso that it became a neighborhood—and citywide—favorite. The Venetian owner of this wine bar (not, as its name implies, a restaurant) has created a personal vision of what a good one should offer: a variety of sumptuous cicheti, panini, and cheeses to be accompanied by just the right regional wines (ask for his recommendation). You can linger along the fondamenta outdoors, and there are places to perch and even sit inside, in front of a sunny picture window that brings the outside view in. $ *Average main: €12* ⊠ *Fondamenta Nani, Dorsoduro 943/944, Dorsoduro* ☎ *335/6007513* ⊕ *osteriaalsquero.wordpress.com* ⊗ *Closed Mon.* Ⓜ *Vaporetto: Accademia, Zattere* ✛ *C5.*

$$ ✕ **Osteria alla Bifora.** A beautiful and atmospheric bacaro, Alla Bifora has
VENETIAN   such ample and satisfying food and wine selections that most Venetians
Fodor'sChoice   consider it a full-fledged restaurant. Most of the offerings consist of
★   overflowing trays of cold, sliced meats and cheeses, various preparations of baccalà, or Venetian classics such as polpette, sarde in saor, or marinated anchovies; there's a good selection of regional wines by the glass as well. La Bifora also serves up a couple of excellent hot dishes; the seppie in nero is among the best in the city. Owner and barman Franco Bernardi and his sister Mirella are warm and friendly—after a few visits, you'll be greeted like a member of the family. $ *Average main: €18* ⊠ *Campo Santa Margherita, Dorsoduro 2930, Dorsoduro* ☎ *041/5236119* ▭ *No credit cards* ✛ *B4.*

SAN POLO

$$$ ✕ **Al Paradiso.** In a small dining room made warm and cozy by its pleas-
MODERN ITALIAN   ing and unpretentious decor, proprietor Giordano makes all diners feel
Fodor'sChoice   like honored guests. Pappardelle "al Paradiso" takes pasta with sea-
★   food sauce to new heights, while risotto with shrimp, Champagne, and grapefruit puts a delectable twist on a traditional dish. The inspired and original array of entrées includes meat and fish selections such as a salmon with honey and balsamic vinegar in a stunning presentation. Unlike many elegant restaurants, Al Paradiso serves generous portions, and many of the delicious antipasti and primi are quite satisfying; you may want to follow the traditional Italian way of ordering and wait until you've finished your antipasto or your primo before you order your secondo. $ *Average main: €26* ⊠ *Calle del Paradiso, San Polo 767, San Polo* ☎ *041/5234910* ⊗ *Closed 3 wks in Jan. and Feb.* Ⓜ *Vaporetto: San Silvestro* ✛ *D3.*

$$$ ✕ **Alla Madonna.** "The Madonna" used to be world famous as "the"
VENETIAN   classic Venetian trattoria but in the past decades has settled down into middle age. Owned and run by the Rado family since 1954, this Venetian institution looks like one, with its wood beams, stained-glass

windows, and panoply of paintings on white walls. It is frequented more by regular Italian visitors to Venice and people from the provinces than by Venetians themselves. Folks still head here to savor the classic Venetian repertoire as most dishes are properly prepared, albeit for stiff prices and without much variation or imagination. $ *Average main: €30 ⊠ Calle della Madonna, San Polo 594, San Polo ☎ 041/5223824 ⊕ www.ristoranteallamadonna.com ⊗ Closed Wed., Jan., and 2 wks in Aug.* Ⓜ *Vaporetto: San Silvestro* ✛ *D3.*

$ ✕**All'Arco.** Just because it's noon and you only have time between
CAFÉ sights for a sandwich doesn't mean that it can't be a satisfying, even awe-inspiring one. There's no menu at All'Arco, but a scan of what's behind the glass counter is all you need. Order what entices you, or have Roberto or Matteo (father and son) suggest a cicheto or panino. Options here are broad enough to satisfy both conservative and adventurous eaters. Wine choices are well suited to the food. Arrive early or at the tail end of lunchtime to snag one of the few tables in the calle. $ *Average main: €8 ⊠ Calle Arco, San Polo 436, San Polo ☎ 041/5220619 ⊗ Closed weekends. No dinner* Ⓜ *Vaporetto: San Silvestro* ✛ *D3.*

$$$ ✕**Antiche Carampane.** Judging from its rather modest and unremarkable
VENETIAN appearance, you wouldn't guess that Piera Bortoluzzi Librai's trattoria is among the finest fish restaurants in the city both because of the quality of the ingredients and because of the chef's creative magic. You can choose from a selection of classic dishes with a modern and creative touch. The perfectly grilled fish is always freshly caught, and in spring, try the local, fried soft-shell crabs. $ *Average main: €26 ⊠ Rio Terà della Carampane, San Polo 1911, San Polo ☎ 041/5240165 ⊕ www. antichecarampane.com ⊗ Closed Sun. and Mon., 10 days in Jan., and 3 wks in July and Aug.* Ⓜ *Vaporetto: San Silvestro* ✛ *D3.*

$ ✕**Cantina Do Mori.** This is the original bacaro—in business continually
WINE BAR since 1462. Cramped but warm and cozy under hanging antique copper pots, it has been catering to the workers of the Rialto Market for generations. In addition to young local whites and reds, the well-stocked cellar offers more refined labels, many available by the glass. Between sips you can choose to munch the myriad cicheti on offer, or a few well-stuffed, tiny tramezzini, appropriately called *francobolli* (postage stamps). Don't leave without tasting the delicious baccalà mantecato, with or without garlic and parsley. If you choose to create a light lunch, snag one of the stools at the bar that lines the wall across from the banco. $ *Average main: €8 ⊠ Calle dei Do Mori, San Polo 429, San Polo ☎ 041/5225401* ▭ *No credit cards ⊗ Closed Sun., 3 wks in Aug., and 1 wk in Jan.* Ⓜ *Vaporetto: Rialto Mercato* ✛ *D3.*

$$$ ✕**Osteria Da Fiore.** The understated atmosphere, simple decor, and quiet
VENETIAN elegance featured alongside Da Fiore's modern take on traditional Vene-
Fodor'sChoice tian cuisine certainly merit its international reputation. With such beauti-
★ fully prepared cuisine, you would expect the kitchen to be manned by a chef with a household name; however, the kitchen is headed by owner Maurizio Martin's wife, Mara, who learned to cook from her grandmother. The other surprise is that, while this restaurant is in a higher price category, it is hardly among the priciest in Venice. The menu is constantly changing, but generally fritto misto or Da Fiore's tender, aromatic version

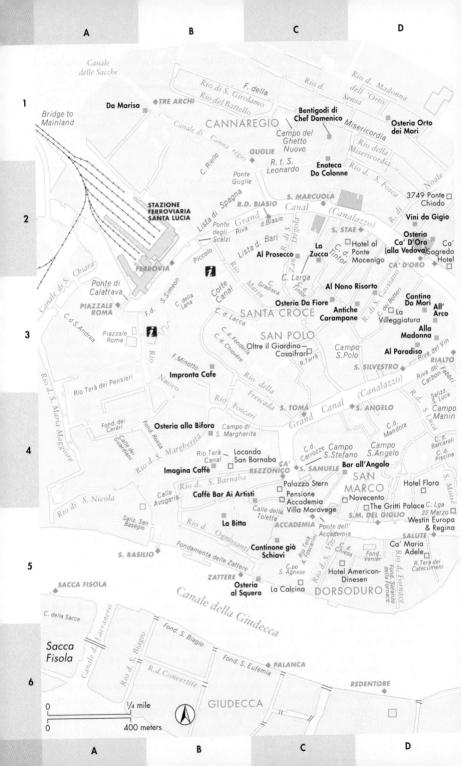

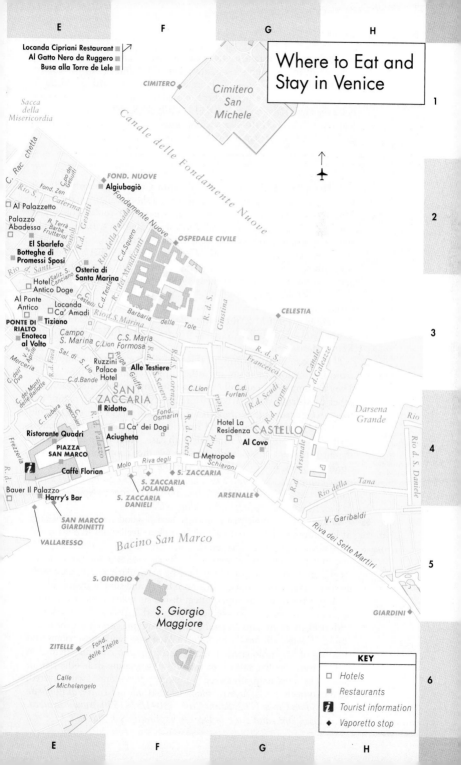

of seppie in nero is almost always available. Reservations, made a few days in advance in high season, are essential for dinner, but you can try just dropping in for lunch. Da Fiore is consistently awarded a Michelin star, although—unlike many other honored restaurants—it does not publicize the fact. $ *Average main: €34* ⊠ *Calle del Scaleter, San Polo 2002, San Polo* ☎ *041/721308* ⊕ *www.dafiore.net* ☾ *Closed Sun. and Mon., and 3 wks in Jan.* Ⓜ *Vaporetto San Tomà* ⊹ *C3.*

SANTA CROCE

$ ✕ **Al Nono Risorto.** Although in the Santa Croce neighborhood, this friendly and popular trattoria is really only a short walk from the Rialto Market. You may not be the only tourist here, but you'll probably be outnumbered by the locals (and if just a couple or a trio, the friendly staff may ask you to share a table). There's no English menu, but a server can usually help you out. The pizza—not a Venetian specialty, generally speaking—is pretty good here, but the star attractions are the generous appetizers and excellent shellfish pastas. The house wine is quite drinkable, and in good weather, you can enjoy your meal in the pergola-covered courtyard (do reserve if you want to snag a table there). $ *Average main: €11* ⊠ *Ramo de l'Arsenal, Santa Croce 2337, Santa Croce* ☎ *041/5241169* ▬ *No credit cards* ☾ *Closed Wed.* Ⓜ *Vaporetto: Rialto Mercato* ⊹ *D3.*

VENETIAN
FAMILY

$$ ✕ **Al Prosecco.** Locals drop into this friendly bacaro to explore wines from this region, or from any other in the country for that matter. They accompany a carefully chosen selection of meats, cheeses, and other food from small, artisanal producers, used in tasty panini like the *porchetta romane verdure* (roast pork with greens), or elegant cold platters. Proprietors Davide and Stefano preside over a young, friendly staff who reel off the day's specials with ease. There are a few tables in the intimate back room, and when the weather cooperates you can sit outdoors on the lively campo, watching the Venetian world go by. $ *Average main: €20* ⊠ *Campo San Giacomo dell'Orio, Santa Croce 1503, Santa Croce* ☎ *041/5240222* ⊕ *www.alprosecco.com* ▬ *No credit cards* ☾ *Closed Sun.* Ⓜ *Vaporetto: San Stae* ⊹ *C2.*

WINE BAR

$$ ✕ **La Zucca.** The simple place settings, lattice-wood walls, and mélange of languages make La Zucca (the pumpkin) feel much like a typical, somewhat sophisticated vegetarian restaurant that you could find in any European city. What makes La Zucca special is the use of fresh, local ingredients (many of which, like the particularly sweet *zucca* itself, aren't normally found outside northern Italy), and simply great cooking. Although the menu has superb meat dishes such as the *piccata di pollo ai caperi e limone con riso* (sliced chicken with capers and lemon served with rice), more attention is paid to dishes from the garden: try the radicchio *di Treviso con funghi e scaglie di Montasio* (with mushrooms and shavings of Montasio cheese), the *finocchi piccanti con olive* (fennel in a spicy tomato–olive sauce), or the house's signature dish—the *flan di zucca,* a luscious, naturally sweet, pumpkin pudding topped with slivered, aged ricotta cheese. $ *Average main: €18* ⊠ *Calle del Tintor, at Ponte de Megio, Santa Croce 1762, Santa Croce* ☎ *041/5241570* ⊕ *www.lazucca. it* ☾ *Closed Sun., and 1 wk in Dec.* Ⓜ *Vaporetto: San Stae* ⊹ *C2.*

NORTHERN
ITALIAN

CANNAREGIO

$$$ ITALIAN 🍴 **Algiubagiò.** A waterfront table is more affordable at lunchtime here on Venice's northern Fondamente Nove, where instead of a grand palazzo, the wide-open lagoon is the backdrop—on a clear day, the majestic Dolomites put on quite a show. Algiubagiò has a dual personality: big salads at lunch (a better bet than the pizza); at dinner, creative primi like ravioli stuffed with *pecorino di fossa* (a hard sheep's-milk cheese) followed by elegant secondi such as Angus fillets with vodka and Gorgonzola. The young, friendly staff also serve ice cream, drinks, and sandwiches all day. A lunch table is an airy respite; while quite romantic, dinnertime sees a considerable rise in prices. [$] *Average main: €30* ✉ *Fondamente Nove, Cannaregio 5039, Cannaregio* ☎ *041/5236084* 🌐 *www.algiubagio.net* 🕓 *Closed Sun.* [M] *Vaporetto: Fondamente Nove* ⊕ *E2.*

$$ VENETIAN 🍴 **Bentigodi di Chef Domenico.** Many claim that owner Domenico Iacuzio is one of Venice's best chefs, even though he hails from Italy's deep south. The chef marries delicious Venetian culinary traditions with southern accents; try sarde in saor, which perfectly balances sweet and savory, and the diced raw tuna *cipolata,* enlivened by sautéed onions and oranges. His seafood risottos are always made to order, and his preparations of freshly caught—never farmed—fish are magical. For the Venetian traditionalist, Domenico prepares a first-class *fritto misto* (deep-fried seafood). If you've missed his southern accent up to now, you'll find it at dessert with homemade southern specialties such as cannoli or *cassata* (candied Sicilian cake). Portions are ample, the atmosphere is informal, and the service is helpful. [$] *Average main: €22* ✉ *Calesele, Cannargio 1423, Cannaregio* ☎ *041/8223714* 🌐 *www.bentigodi.com* 🕓 *Closed Tues.* [M] *Vaporetto San Marcuola* ⊕ *C1.*

$$ VENETIAN 🍴 **Botteghe di Promessi Sposi.** Join locals at the *banco* (counter) premeal for an *ombra* (small glass of wine) and cicheti like polpette croquettes or violet eggplant rounds, or reserve a sit-down meal in the dining room or the intimate courtyard. A varied, seasonal menu includes local standards like calf's liver or grilled *canestrelli* (tiny Venetian scallops), along with creative, regional fusion variations incorporating classic Venetian fare, like homemade ravioli stuffed with *radicchio di Treviso* (red chicory leaves) or *orecchiette* ("small ear"–shape pasta) with a scrumptious sauce of minced duck. The service is friendly and helpful, but it's very popular among locals, so be sure to make a reservation (later is better for a more relaxed environment). [$] *Average main: €18* ✉ *Calle de l'Oca, just off Campo Santi Apostoli, Cannaregio 4367, Cannaregio* ☎ *041/2412747* 🕓 *No lunch Mon. and Wed.* [M] *Vaporetto: Ca' d'Oro* ⊕ *E2.*

$$ VENETIAN Fodor's Choice ★ 🍴 **Da Marisa.** This is the most famous workingman's restaurant in Venice. If you can get a table for lunch, you'll eat, without any choice, what Marisa prepares for her workmen clientele—generally enormous portions of excellently prepared pasta, followed by a hearty roast meat course, frequently game, more infrequently fish, for an unbelievably inexpensive fixed price. Dinner is a bit more expensive, and you may have a bit of a choice, but not much; for the authentic "Marisa" experience, go for lunch. In good weather, you'll have a better chance getting

a table, because tables are set up along the fondamenta. Generally, reservations aren't taken, and locals and steady customers are given preference for seating. Don't be put off by the occasional gruff service; it's part of the scene. $ *Average main: €15* ✉ *Cannaregio 625b, Fondamenta di San Giobbe, Cannaregio* ☎ *041/720211* ▭ *No credit cards* ⊗ *No dinner Sun.–Tues.* ✛ *B1.*

$ ✕ **El Sbarlefo.** This odd name is Venetian for "smirk," although you'd
WINE BAR   be hard-pressed to find one of those around this cheery, familiar wine bar with a wine selection as ample as the cicheti on offer. Sbarlefo has expanded to a new location in Dorsoduro, in the calle just behind the church of San Pantalon. Making the most of their limited space, owners Alessandro and Andrea have installed counters and stools inside, tables outside, and external banco access for ordering a second round. And order you will, selecting from a spread of delectable cicheti from classic polpette of meat and tuna to tomino cheese rounds to speck and robiolo rolls, and more. They've paid equal attention to their wine selection—ask for a recommendation and you're likely to make a new discovery. $ *Average main: €8* ✉ *Salizzada del Pistor, off Campo Santi Apostoli, Cannaregio 4556/C, Cannaregio* ☎ *041/5233084* ▭ *No credit cards* Ⓜ *Vaporetto: Ca d'Oro* ✛ *E2.*

$ ✕ **Enoteca Do Colonne.** Venetians from this working-class neighborhood
WINE BAR   frequent this friendly bacaro, not just for a glass of very drinkable wine, but also because of its excellent selection of traditional Venetian cicheti for lunch. There's not only a large selection of sandwiches and panini, but also luscious tidbits like grilled vegetables, breaded and fried sardines and shrimp, and a superb version of baccalà mantecato. For the more adventurous, there are Venetian working-class specialties such as *musetto* (a sausage made from pigs' snouts served warm with polenta) and *nervetti* (veal tendons with lemon and parsley). These dishes are worth trying at least once when in Venice, and Do Colonne offers the best musetto in town. $ *Average main: €8* ✉ *Rio Terà Cristo, Cannaregio 1814, Cannaregio* ☎ *041/5240453* ⊕ *www.docolonne.it* ▭ *No credit cards* ⊗ *Closed Sun.* Ⓜ *Vaporetto: San Marcuola* ✛ *C2.*

$ ✕ **Osteria Ca' D'Oro (alla Vedova).** "The best polpette in town," you'll
VENETIAN   hear fans of the venerable Vedova say, and that explains why it's an obligatory stop on any *giro d'ombra* (bacaro tour). The polpette are always hot and crunchy—and also gluten-free, as they're made with polenta. Ca' d'Oro is a full-fledged trattoria as well, but make sure to reserve ahead: it's no secret to those seeking traditional Venetian fare at a reasonable cost, locals and travelers alike. Vedova is one of the few places that still serves house wine in tiny, traditional *palline* glasses; never fear, if you order a bottle you'll get a fancier glass. $ *Average main: €12* ✉ *Calle del Pistor, off Strada Nova, Cannaregio 3912, Cannaregio* ☎ *041/5285324* ▭ *No credit cards* ⊗ *Closed Thurs., and Aug. No lunch Sun.* Ⓜ *Vaporetto: Ca d'Oro* ✛ *D2.*

$$ ✕ **Osteria Orto dei Mori.** This small and popular Cannaregio neighbor-
ITALIAN   hood restaurant specializes in creative versions of classic Italian (but not necessarily Venetian) dishes. Try the *fagotti* (bundles of beef marinated in Chianti with goat cheese) or a seafood version with prawns, zucchini,

and ricotta. Their signature dish is parchment-baked monkfish. Co-owner Micael has artfully created a regional wine list. The osteria is located canalside, just under the nose of the campo's famous corner statue. $ *Average main: €16* ⊠ *Campo dei Mori, Fondamenta dei Mori, Cannaregio 3386, Cannaregio* ☎ *041/5235544* ⊘ *Closed Tues.* Ⓜ *Vaporetto: Orto, Ca d'Oro, or San Marcuola* ⊹ *D1.*

$ ╳**Tiziano.** A fine variety of excellent tramezzini lines the display cases
ITALIAN at this *tavola calda* (roughly the Italian equivalent of a cafeteria) on the main thoroughfare from the Rialto to Santi Apostoli; inexpensive salad plates and daily pasta specials are also served. This is a great place for a light meal or snack before a performance at the nearby Teatro Malebran. Whether you choose to sit or stand, it's a handy—and popular—spot for a quick meal or a snack at very modest prices. Service is efficient, if occasionally grumpy. $ *Average main: €8* ⊠ *Salizzada San Giovanni Crisostomo, Cannaregio 5747, Cannaregio* ☎ *041/5235544* ⊟ *No credit cards* Ⓜ *Vaporetto: Rialto* ⊹ *E3.*

$$$ ╳**Vini da Gigio.** Paolo and Laura, a brother–sister team, run this refined
VENETIAN trattoria as if they've invited you to dinner in their home, while keeping
Fodor'sChoice the service professional. Deservedly popular with Venetians and visitors
★ alike, it's one of the best values in the city. Indulge in pastas such as rigatoni with duck sauce and arugula-stuffed ravioli. The seafood risotto, made to order, has the patrons raving. Fish is well represented—try the sesame-encrusted tuna—but the meat dishes steal the show. The steak with red-pepper sauce and the *tagliata di agnello* (sautéed lamb fillet with a light, crusty coating) are both superb, and you'll never enjoy a better *fegato alla veneziana* (Venetian-style liver with onions). This is a place for wine connoisseurs, as the cellar is one of the best in the city. Come at lunch or for the second sitting in the evening for more relaxed service. $ *Average main: €25* ⊠ *Fondamenta San Felice, Cannaregio 3628/A, Cannaregio* ☎ *041/5285140* ⊕ *www.vinidagigio.com* ⊘ *Closed Mon. and Tues., and 2 wks in Aug.* Ⓜ *Vaporetto: Ca' d'Oro* ⊹ *D2.*

CASTELLO

$ ╳**Aciugheta.** Almost an institution, the "Tiny Anchovy" (as the name
WINE BAR translates) doubles as a pizzeria–trattoria, but the real reason for coming is the tasty cicheti offered at the bar, like the eponymous anchovy minipizzas, the *arancioni* rice balls, and the polpette. The selection of wines by the glass changes daily, but there is always a good selection of local wines on hand, as well as some Tuscan and Piedmontese choices thrown in for good measure. Don't miss the *tonno con polenta* (tuna with polenta) if it's offered. $ *Average main: €12* ⊠ *Campo SS. Filippo e Giacomo, Castello 4357, Castello* ☎ *041/5224292* Ⓜ *Vaporetto: San Zaccaria* ⊹ *F4.*

$$$ ╳**Al Covo.** For years, Diane and Cesare Binelli's Al Covo has set the
VENETIAN standard of excellence for traditional, refined Venetian cuisine. The Binellis are dedicated to providing their guests with the freshest, highest-quality fish from the Adriatic, and vegetables, when at all possible, from the islands of the Venetian lagoon and the fields of the adjacent Veneto region. Although their cuisine could be correctly termed "classic Venetian," it always offers surprises like the juicy crispness of

their legendary fritto misto—reliant upon a secret, nonconventional ingredient in the batter—or the heady aroma of their fresh anchovies marinated in wild fennel, an herb somewhat foreign to Veneto. The main exception to Al Covo's distinct local flavor is Diane's wonderful Texas-inspired desserts, especially her dynamite chocolate cake. [$] *Average main: €30* ✉ *Campiello Pescaria, Castello 3968, Castello* ☎ *041/5223812* 🌐 *www.ristorantealcovo.com* ⏲ *Closed Wed. and Thurs.* [M] *Vaporetto: Arsenale* ✥ *G4.*

$$$ VENETIAN Fodor's Choice ★

🍴 **Alle Testiere.** The name is a reference to the old headboards that adorn the walls of this tiny, informal restaurant, but the food (not the decor) is undoubtedly the focus. Local foodies consider this one of the most refined eateries in the city thanks to chef Bruno Cavagni's gently creative take on classic Venetian fish dishes. The chef's artistry seldom draws attention to itself, but simply reveals new dimensions to familiar fare, creating dishes that stand out for their lightness and balance. A classic black risotto of cuttlefish, for example, is surrounded by a brilliant coulis of mild yellow peppers; tiny potato gnocchi are paired with tender newborn squid. The menu changes regularly to capitalize on the freshest produce of the moment, and the wine selection is top-notch. To enjoy a more leisurely meal, be sure to book the second dinner sitting. [$] *Average main: €30* ✉ *Calle del Mondo Novo, Castello 5801, Castello* ☎ *041/5227220* 🌐 *www.osterialletestiere.it* ⏲ *Closed Sun. and Mon., 3 wks in Jan. and Feb., and 4 wks in July and Aug.* ✥ *F3.*

$$$ MODERN ITALIAN Fodor's Choice ★

🍴 **Il Ridotto.** Longtime restaurateur Gianni Bonaccorsi (proprietor of the popular Aciugheta nearby) has established an eatery where he can pamper a limited number of lucky patrons with his imaginative cuisine and impeccable taste in wine. *Ridotto* means a small, private place, which this very much is, evoking an atmosphere of secrecy and intimacy. The innovative menu employing traditional elements is revised daily, with the offerings tending toward lighter, but wonderfully tasty versions of classic dishes. The tasting menus—one meat, one fish—where Gianni "surprises" you with a selection of his own creations, never fail to satisfy. Ask for a wine recommendation from the excellent cantina. [$] *Average main: €28* ✉ *Campo SS Filippo e Giacomo, Castello 4509, Castello* ☎ *041/5208280* 🌐 *www.ilridotto.com* ⏲ *Closed Wed. No lunch Thurs.* [M] *Vaporetto: San Zaccaria* ✥ *F4.*

$$$ VENETIAN Fodor's Choice ★

🍴 **Osteria di Santa Marina.** The candlelit tables on this romantic campo are inviting enough, but it's this intimate restaurant's imaginative kitchen creations that are likely to win you over. Star dishes include *tortino di baccalà mantecato* (cod torte) with baby arugula and fried polenta; *passatina di piselli* (fresh pea puree with scallops and tiny calamari); scampi in saor, a turn on a Venetian classic with leeks and ginger; and fresh ravioli stuffed with mussels and turbot in a creamed celery sauce. You can also opt for one of the rewarding tasting menus (fish or meat, €55–€85). The wine list is ample and well thought out. Service is gracious and cordial—just don't be in a terrible rush, or expect the server to be your new best friend. [$] *Average main: €26* ✉ *Campo Santa Marina, Castello 5911, Castello* ☎ *041/5285239* 🌐 *www.osteriadisantamarina.com* ⏲ *Closed Sun. No lunch Mon.* [M] *Vaporetto: Rialto* ✥ *E2.*

ISLANDS OF THE LAGOON

$$$
SEAFOOD
✕ **Al Gatto Nero da Ruggero.** Around since 1965, Al Gatto Nero da Ruggero offers the best fish on Burano. "Each day our fisherman return with the best the lagoon has to offer," says the owner, who upon understanding he could not pursue his dream of being a musician, instead decided to make the kitchen sing. The fish is top quality and couldn't get any fresher; all pastas and desserts are made in-house; the fritto misto is outstanding for its lightness and variety of fish. *Risotto de Gò* (*ghiozzo*) is a Burano *cucina povera* standard that had almost disappeared from local menus until Anthony Bourdain introduced it to travelers. No matter what you order though, you'll savor the pride the owner and his family have in their lagoon, their island, and the quality of their cucina (maybe even more so when enjoying it on the picturesque fondamenta). $ *Average main: €26* ✉ *Fondamenta della Giudecca 88, Burano* ☎ *041/730120* ⊕ *www.gattonero.com* ⊙ *Closed Mon., and 3 wks in Nov. No dinner Sun.* Ⓜ *Vaporetto: Burano* ✠ *F1.*

$$
VENETIAN
✕ **Busa alla Torre da Lele.** If you're shopping for glass on Murano and want to sample some first-rate home cooking for lunch, you can't do better than stopping in this unpretentious trattoria in the island's central square. The friendly waiters will bring you ample portions of pasta with freshly made seafood-based sauces. There is also a substantial variety of carefully grilled or baked fish. There are some decent meat dishes, too, but this is, essentially, a fish restaurant. $ *Average main: €20* ✉ *Campo Santo Stefano 3, Murano* ☎ *041/739662* ⊙ *Closed Mon. No dinner* Ⓜ *Vaporetto Murano Colonna* ✠ *F1.*

$$$
VENETIAN
✕ **Locanda Cipriani Restaurant.** A nearly legendary restaurant established by a nephew of Giuseppe Cipriani (the founder of Harry's Bar), this inn profits from its idyllic location on the island of Torcello. Hemingway, who loved the silence of the lagoon, came here often to eat, drink, and brood under the green veranda. The food is not exceptional, especially considering the high-end prices, but dining here is more about getting lost in Venetian magic. The menu features pastas, *vitello tonnato* (chilled poached veal in a tuna and caper sauce), baked *orata* (gilthead bream) with potatoes, and lots of other seafood. $ *Average main: €34* ✉ *Piazza Santa Fosca 29, Locanda Cipriani, Torcello* ☎ *041/730150* ⊙ *Closed Tues., and early Jan.–early Feb.* Ⓜ *Vaporetto: Torcello* ✠ *F1.*

WHERE TO STAY

Venetian magic lingers when you retire for the night, whether you're staying in a grand hotel or budget *locanda* (inn). Some of the finest Venetian hotel rooms are lighted with Murano chandeliers and swathed in famed fabrics of Rubelli and Bevilacqua, with gilded mirrors and furnishing styles from Baroque to Biedermeier and Art Deco.

Even if well renovated, most hotels occupy very old buildings. Preservation laws prohibit elevators in some, so if climbing stairs is an issue, check before you book. In the lower price categories, hotels may not have lounge areas, and rooms may be cramped, and the same is true of standard rooms in more expensive hotels. Space is at a premium in Venice, and even exclusive hotels have carved out small, dowdy,

Cinderella-type rooms in the "standard" category. It's not at all unusual for each room to be different even on the same floor: windows overlooking charming canals and bleak alleyways are both common. En suite bathrooms have become the norm; they're usually well equipped but sizes range from compact to more than ample; tubs are considered a luxury but are not unheard-of, even in less expensive lodging. Air-conditioning is rarely a necessity until mid-June. A few of the budget hotels make do with fans.

WHAT NEIGHBORHOOD SHOULD I STAY IN?

"Only a stone's throw from St. Mark's square" is the standard hotel claim. Whether that's the case, it's not necessarily an advantage. In Venice, you can't go terribly wrong in terms of "good" areas in which to stay, and once you get your bearings, you'll find you're never far from anything.

You may, however, want to consider how close your hotel is to a vaporetto stop, and how many bridges there are to cross between your hotel and the vaporetto station. If you have lots of heavy baggage, carrying them over the bridges to and from your hotel can be quite a chore.

The area in and around San Marco will always be the most crowded and touristy and almost always more expensive: even two- and three-star hotels cost more here than they do in other parts of town. If you want to stay in less-trafficked surroundings, consider still convenient but more tranquil locations in Dorsoduro, Santa Croce, and Cannaregio (though hotels near the train station in Cannaregio can have their own crowd issues), or even Castello in the area beyond the Pietà church. A stay on the Lido in shoulder season offers serenity and beaches for the kids, but it also includes about a half-hour boat ride to the centro storico, and in summer it's crowded with beachgoers.

Substantial savings can be had by staying in a hotel in Mestre or Marghera, or near the airport, but you must count on at least an hour each way until you get into the centro storico. Touring in Venice can be physically taxing, involving a lot of walking on stone pavement, climbing stairs and foot bridges, and a paucity of places to sit down unless you've ordered a drink or a snack at a café. You may want to return to your hotel for a brief rest, or for a shower on a hot, humid summer day. Booking a hotel in the historic center will make a brief rest possible; a hotel on the mainland simply won't.

Venice is saturated with lodging options, but it is also one of the most popular destinations on earth—so book your lodging as far in advance as possible.

FINDING YOUR HOTEL

It is essential to have detailed arrival directions along with the address, including the sestiere and preferably a nearby landmark; conveniently, most hotels include maps on their websites. Even if you choose a pricey water taxi, you may still have a walk, depending on where the boat leaves you. Nothing is obvious on Venice's streets (even if you have GPS); turn-by-turn directions can help you avoid wandering back and forth along side streets and across bridges, luggage in tow. *Use the coordinate (⊕ B2) at the end of each listing to locate a site on the Where to Eat and Stay in Venice map.*

PRICES

Hotel rates are about 20% higher than in Rome and Milan but can be reduced by as much as half off-season, from November to March (excluding Christmas, New Year's, and Carnevale), and likely in August as well. *Hotel reviews have been shortened. For full information, visit Fodors.com.*

WHAT IT COSTS				
	$	$$	$$$	$$$$
For two people	under €125	€125–€200	€201–€300	over €300

Prices in the reviews are the lowest cost of a standard double room in high season.

SAN MARCO

$$$$ HOTEL **Bauer Il Palazzo.** This palazzo with an ornate, 1930s neo-Gothic facade facing the Grand Canal has lavishly decorated guest rooms (large by Venetian standards) featuring high ceilings, tufted walls of Bevilacqua and Rubelli fabrics, Murano glass, marble bathrooms, damask drapes, and imitation antique furniture. **Pros:** pampering service; high-end luxury. **Cons:** Wi-Fi is additional fee; furnishings are, as is the facade, an imitation. [$] *Rooms from: €1050 ✉ Campo San Moisè, San Marco 1413/D, San Marco ☎ 041/5207022 🌐 www.ilpalazzovenezia.com 🛏 72 rooms 🍴 No meals [M] Vaporetto: Vallaresso ✥ E5.*

$$$$ HOTEL Fodor's Choice ★ **The Gritti Palace.** This hotel represents aristocratic Venetian living at its best, complete with handblown chandeliers, sumptuous textiles, and sweeping canal views. **Pros:** historic setting; Grand Canal location; classic Venetian experience. **Cons:** major splurge; some extra fees (not for Wi-Fi). [$] *Rooms from: €874 ✉ Campo Santa Maria del Giglio, San Marco 2467, San Marco ☎ 041/794611 🌐 www.thegrittipalace.com 🛏 82 rooms 🍴 No meals [M] Vaporetto Santa Maria del Giglio ✥ D5.*

$$ HOTEL Fodor's Choice ★ **Hotel Flora.** The elegant and refined facade announces truly special place; the hospitable staff, the tastefully decorated rooms, and magical garden do not disappoint. **Pros:** central location; lovely garden; excellent breakfast. **Cons:** some rooms can be on the small side. [$] *Rooms from: €200 ✉ Calle Bergamaschi, just off Calle Larga XXII Marzo, San Marco 2283/A, San Marco ☎ 041/5228217 🌐 www.hotelflora.it 🛏 40 rooms 🍴 Breakfast [M] Vaporetto: San Marco (Vallaresso) ✥ D4.*

$$$ HOTEL **Novecento.** A stylish yet intimate retreat tucked away on a quiet calle midway between Piazza San Marco and the Accademia Bridge offers exquisite rooms tastefully decorated with original furnishings and tapestries from the Mediterranean and Far East. **Pros:** intimate, romantic atmosphere; free Wi-Fi. **Cons:** some rooms are small, and some can be noisy. [$] *Rooms from: €240 ✉ Calle del Dose, off Campo San Maurizio, San Marco 2683/84, San Marco ☎ 041/2413765 🌐 www.novecento.biz 🛏 9 rooms 🍴 Breakfast [M] Vaporetto: Santa Maria del Giglio ✥ C4.*

$$$$ HOTEL **Fodor's Choice** ★ 🏨 **Westin Europa & Regina.** Spread across five historic palazzi (is there anything else in Venice?) in the lee of San Marco, this amalgamation of the former Hotel Britannia and Hotel Regina is easily one of Venice's still-undiscovered gems. **Pros:** ideal location, with the über-boutiques of Via XXII Marzo and the Piazza San Marco a stone's throw away. **Cons:** slightly dated public areas and restaurants. [$] *Rooms from: €550* ✉ *Corte Barozzi, San Marco 2159, San Marco* ☎ *041/2400001* 🌐 *www.westineuropareginavenice.com* 🛏 *185 rooms* 🍴 *No meals* ✥ *D5.*

DORSODURO

$$$$ HOTEL 🏨 **Ca' Maria Adele.** One of the city's most intimate and elegant getaways immerses guests in a mix of classic style (terrazzo floors, dramatic Murano chandeliers, antique-style furnishings) and touches of the contemporary, found in the African-wood reception area and breakfast room. **Pros:** quiet and romantic; imaginative contemporary decor; tranquil yet convenient spot near Santa Maria della Salute. **Cons:** small rooms, even for Venice; few good restaurants nearby. [$] *Rooms from: €330* ✉ *Campo Santa Maria della Salute, Dorsoduro 111, Dorsoduro* ☎ *041/5203078* 🌐 *www.camariaadele.it* 🛏 *12 rooms, 4 suites* 🍴 *Breakfast* [M] *Vaporetto: Salute* ✥ *D5.*

$$$$ HOTEL 🏨 **Hotel American–Dinesen.** The exceptional service here will help you feel at home in spacious guest rooms furnished in Venetian brocade fabrics with lacquered Venetian-style furniture; some front rooms have terraces with canal views. **Pros:** high degree of personal service; on a bright, quiet, exceptionally picturesque canal; free Wi-Fi. **Cons:** no elevator; rooms with a canal view are more expensive; some rooms could stand refurbishing. [$] *Rooms from: €330* ✉ *San Vio, Dorsoduro 628, Dorsoduro* ☎ *041/5204733* 🌐 *www.hotelamerican.com* 🛏 *30 rooms* 🍴 *Breakfast* [M] *Vaporetto: Accademia, Salute, and Zattere* ✥ *C5.*

$$$ HOTEL **Fodor's Choice** ★ 🏨 **La Calcina.** Time-burnished and elegant rooms with parquet floors, original 19th-century furniture, and firm beds enjoy an enviable position along the sunny Zattere, with front rooms offering vistas across the wide Giudecca Canal; a few have private terraces. **Pros:** panoramic views from some rooms; elegant, historic atmosphere; cheaper in low season. **Cons:** not for travelers who prefer ultramodern surroundings; no elevator; rooms with views are more expensive. [$] *Rooms from: €240* ✉ *Zattere, Dorsoduro 780, Dorsoduro* ☎ *041/5206466* 🌐 *www.lacalcina.com* 🛏 *27 rooms* 🍴 *Breakfast* [M] *Vaporetto: Zattere* ✥ *C5.*

$$ HOTEL 🏨 **Locanda San Barnaba.** This family-run, value-for-money establishment is housed in a 16th-century palazzo and, if you're lucky, you'll bag one of the superior rooms or the double that have original 18th-century wall paintings; one junior suite has two small balconies and is exceptionally luminous. **Pros:** traditional furnishings make spacious rooms attractive and welcoming; free Wi-Fi; close to many restaurants and cafés. **Cons:** no elevator. [$] *Rooms from: €175* ✉ *Calle del Traghetto, Dorsoduro 2785–2786, Dorsoduro* ☎ *041/2411233* 🌐 *www.locanda-sanbarnaba.com* 🛏 *13 rooms* 🍴 *Breakfast* [M] *Vaporetto: Ca' Rezzonico* ✥ *B4.*

$$$$ HOTEL **Palazzo Stern.** This opulently refurbished neo-Gothic palazzo features marble-columned arches, terrazzo floors, frescoed ceilings, mosaics, and a majestic carved staircase, and some rooms have tufted walls and parquet flooring, but the gracious terrace that overlooks the Grand Canal is almost reason alone to stay here. **Pros:** excellent hotel service; lovely views from many rooms; modern renovation retains historic ambience; steps from vaporetto stop, but set back from the canal, so there is little noise. **Cons:** terrace bar and service are substandard; quality of the rooms varies and inferior rooms are not offered at reduced prices. [$] *Rooms from: €320* ✉ *Calle del Traghetto, Dorsoduro 2792, Dorsoduro* ☎ *041/2770869* 🌐 *www.palazzostern.com* 🛏 *24 rooms* 🍴 *Breakfast* [M] *Vaporetto: Ca' Rezzonico* ✥ *C4.*

$$$ HOTEL Fodor's Choice ★ **Pensione Accademia Villa Maravege.** Behind iron gates in one of the most densely packed parts of the city you'll find yourself in front of a large and elegant garden and Gothic-style villa where accommodations are charmingly decorated with a connoisseur's eye. **Pros:** a unique villa in the heart of Venice; one of the city's most enchanting hotels. **Cons:** standard rooms are smaller than is usual in Venice, and seem to be more sparsely decorated than the more expensive options. [$] *Rooms from: €250* ✉ *Fondamenta Bollani, Dorsoduro 1058, Dorsoduro* ☎ *041/5210188* 🌐 *www.pensioneaccademia.it* 🛏 *29 rooms* 🍴 *Breakfast* [M] *Vaporetto: Accademia* ✥ *C5.*

SAN POLO

$$ HOTEL **La Villeggiatura.** If eclectic Venetian charm is what you seek, this luminous residence offers six individually decorated rooms, each with its own original, theatrically themed wall painting by a local artist. **Pros:** relaxed atmosphere; meticulously maintained; well located near markets, artistic monuments, and restaurants. **Cons:** no elevator and lots of stairs; modest breakfast; no view to speak of, despite the climb. [$] *Rooms from: €195* ✉ *Calle dei Botteri, San Polo 1569, San Polo* ☎ *041/5244673* 🌐 *www.lavilleggiatura.it* 🛏 *6 rooms* 🍴 *Breakfast* [M] *Vaporetto: Rialto Mercato* ✥ *D3.*

$$$ HOTEL **Oltre il Giardino–Casaifrari.** It's easy to overlook—and it can be a challenge to find—this secluded palazzo, sheltered as it is behind a brick wall just over the bridge from the Frari church, but the search is well worth it: airy, individually decorated guest rooms face a large garden, an oasis of peace (especially in high season). **Pros:** a peaceful, gracious, and convenient setting; walled garden. **Cons:** a beautiful, but not particularly Venetian, ambience. [$] *Rooms from: €250* ✉ *Fondamenta Contarini, San Polo 2542, San Polo* ☎ *041/2750015* 🌐 *www.oltreilgiardino-venezia.com* 🛏 *6 rooms* 🍴 *Breakfast* [M] *Vaporetto: San Tomà* ✥ *C3.*

SANTA CROCE

$$ HOTEL Fodor's Choice ★ **Hotel al Ponte Mocenigo.** A columned courtyard welcomes you to this elegant, charming palazzo, former home of the Santa Croce branch of the Mocenigo family (which has a few doges in its past), and the canopied beds, striped damask fabrics, lustrous terrazzo flooring, and gilt-accented furnishings keep the sense of Venice's past strong in the

guest rooms. **Pros:** enchanting courtyard; friendly and helpful staff; fantastic value. **Cons:** beds are on the hard side; standard rooms are small; rooms in the annex can be noisy. $ *Rooms from: €145* ✉ *Fondamento de Rimpeto a Ca' Mocenigo, Santa Croce 2063, Santa Croce* ☎ *041/5244797* ⊕ *www.alpontemocenigo.com* ⬦ *11 rooms* ⦿ *Breakfast* Ⓜ *Vaporetto: San Stae* ✛ *C2.*

CANNAREGIO

$
B&B/INN
FAMILY

🖾 **Al Palazzetto.** Understated yet gracious Venetian decor, original open-beam ceilings and terrazzo flooring, spotless marble baths, and friendly, attentive service are hallmarks of this intimate, family-owned guesthouse. **Pros:** standout service; owner on-site; very good value for money. **Cons:** old-fashioned decor; not many amenities. $ *Rooms from: €100* ✉ *Calle delle Vele, Cannaregio 4057, Cannaregio* ☎ *041/2750897* ⊕ *www.guesthouse.it* ⬦ *7 rooms* ⦿ *Breakfast* Ⓜ *Vaporetto: Ca' d'Oro* ✛ *E2.*

$$$$
HOTEL
Fodor's Choice
★

🖾 **Al Ponte Antico.** This 16th-century palace inn has lined its Gothic windows with tiny white lights, creating an inviting glow that's emblematic of the hospitality and sumptuous surroundings that await you inside: rich brocade-tufted walls, period-style furniture, and hand-decorated beamed ceilings. **Pros:** upper-level terrace overlooks Grand Canal; family run; superior service. **Cons:** in one of the busiest areas of the city, although not particularly noisy; check-in is late (4 pm). $ *Rooms from: €315* ✉ *Calle dell'Aseo, Cannaregio 5768, Cannaregio* ☎ *041/2411944* ⊕ *www.alponteantico.com* ⬦ *13 rooms* ⦿ *Breakfast* Ⓜ *Vaporetto: Rialto* ✛ *E3.*

$$$$
HOTEL
Fodor's Choice
★

🖾 **Ca' Sagredo Hotel.** A study in Venetian opulence, this expansive palace has been the Sagredo family residence since the mid-1600s and has the decor to prove it: the massive staircase has Longhi wall panels soaring above it, and the large common areas are adorned with original art by Tiepolo, Longhi, and Ricci, among others. **Pros:** excellent location; authentic yet comfortable renovation of Venice's patrician past; about as close as you can get to an authentic 18th-century Venetian experience. **Cons:** more opulent than intimate; views of the canal aren't as great as other hotels. $ *Rooms from: €450* ✉ *Campo Santa Sofia, Cannaregio 4198/99, Cannaregio* ☎ *041/2413111* ⊕ *www.casagredohotel.com* ⬦ *42 rooms, 2 junior suites, 3 suites* ⦿ *Breakfast* Ⓜ *Vaporetto: Ca' d'Oro* ✛ *D3.*

$$
HOTEL

🖾 **Hotel Antico Doge.** Once the home of Doge Marino Falier, the 14th-century doge who was executed for treason, this palazzo has been attentively modernized in elegant 18th-century Venetian style: all rooms are adorned with brocades, damask-tufted walls, gilt mirrors, and parquet floors, and even the breakfast room comes fitted out with a stuccoed ceiling and Murano chandelier. **Pros:** romantic, atmospheric decor; convenient to the Rialto and beyond. **Cons:** no outdoor garden or terrace; no elevator. $ *Rooms from: €170* ✉ *Campo Santi Apostoli, Cannaregio 5643, Cannaregio* ☎ *041/2411570* ⊕ *www.anticodoge.com* ⬦ *20 rooms* ⦿ *Breakfast* Ⓜ *Vaporetto: Ca' d'Oro or Rialto* ✛ *E3.*

$$
HOTEL

🖾 **Locanda Ca' Amadi.** A historic palazzo is a welcome retreat on a tranquil *corte,* and individually decorated rooms have tufted walls and views of a lively canal or a quiet courtyard. **Pros:** classic Venetian style;

personal service; handy for sightseeing. **Cons:** standard rooms are small; not ideal for guests with mobility issues; canal-view rooms can be noisy at night. $ *Rooms from: €140* ✉ *Corte Amadi, Cannaregio 5815, Cannaregio* ☎ *041/5285210* ⊕ *www.caamadi.it* 🛏 *6 rooms* ⏏ *Breakfast* Ⓜ *Vaporetto: Rialto* ✛ *E3.*

$$$ 🛏 **Palazzo Abadessa.** At this late-16th-century palazzo, you can experience gracious hospitality, a luxurious atmosphere, and unusually spacious guest rooms well-appointed with antique-style furniture (although the hotel's website claims that they are original antiques), frescoed or stuccoed ceilings, and silk fabrics. **Pros:** enormous walled garden, a rare and delightful treat in crowded Venice; superb guest service. **Cons:** some bathrooms are small. $ *Rooms from: €220* ✉ *Calle Priuli off Strada Nova, Cannaregio 4011, Cannaregio* ☎ *041/2413784* ⊕ *www.abadessa.com* 🛏 *15 rooms* ⏏ *Breakfast* Ⓜ *Vaporetto: Ca' d'Oro* ✛ *E2.*

HOTEL

$$ 🛏 **3749 Ponte Chiodo.** Attractively appointed guest rooms handy to the Ca' d'Oro vaporetto stop look past geranium-filled windows to the bridge leading to its entrance (one of the only bridges without hand railings remaining) and canals below or the spacious enclosed garden. **Pros:** highly attentive service; warm, relaxed atmosphere; good value. **Cons:** no elevator; some bathrooms are smallish. $ *Rooms from: €180* ✉ *Calle Racchetta, Cannaregio 3749, Cannaregio* ☎ *041/2413935* ⊕ *www.pontechiodo.it* 🛏 *6 rooms* ⏏ *Breakfast* Ⓜ *Vaporetto: Ca' d'Oro* ✛ *D2.*

B&B/INN

CASTELLO

$$ 🛏 **Ca' dei Dogi.** A quiet courtyard secluded from the San Marco melee offers an island of calm in six individually decorated guest rooms (some with private terraces) that feature contemporary furnishings and accessories. **Pros:** some rooms have terraces with views of the Doge's Palace; peaceful amid a busy part of the town. **Cons:** rooms are on the small side; furnishings are spartan and look a bit cheap. $ *Rooms from: €150* ✉ *Corte Santa Scolastica, Castello 4242, Castello* ☎ *041/2413751* ⊕ *www.cadeidogi.it* ☉ *Closed Dec.* 🛏 *6 rooms* ⏏ *Breakfast* Ⓜ *Vaporetto: San Zaccaria* ✛ *F4.*

HOTEL

$$ 🛏 **Hotel La Residenza.** Most rooms at this renovated Gothic-Byzantine palazzo are spacious and elegant, with imitation period furnishings and 18th-century paintings as well as modern amenities. **Pros:** free Wi-Fi; quiet, residential area. **Cons:** not the warmest staff; disappointing breakfast; a/c in rooms not controlled by guest. $ *Rooms from: €140* ✉ *Campo Bandiera e Moro (or Bragora), Castello 3608, Castello* ☎ *041/5285315* ⊕ *www.venicelaresidenza.com* 🛏 *15 rooms* ⏏ *Breakfast* Ⓜ *Vaporetto: Arsenale* ✛ *G4.*

HOTEL

$$$ 🛏 **Metropole.** Atmosphere prevails in this labyrinth of intimate, opulent spaces featuring classic Venetian decor combined with exotic Eastern influences: the owner—a lifelong collector of unusual objects—fills common areas and the sumptuously appointed guest rooms with an assortment of antiques and curiosities. **Pros:** hotel harkens back to a gracious Venice of times past; fine bar (and great martinis); good but expensive restaurant. **Cons:** one of the most densely touristed locations in the city;

HOTEL
Fodor's Choice
★

rooms with views are considerably more expensive. $ *Rooms from: €300* ✉ *Riva degli Schiavoni, Castello 4149, Castello* ☎ *041/5205044* ⊕ *www.hotelmetropole.com* ↪ *89 rooms* ⦿ *Breakfast* Ⓜ *Vaporetto: San Zaccaria* ⊹ *F4.*

$$$$ 🏨 **Ruzzini Palace Hotel.** Public rooms are Renaissance- and Baroque-style,
HOTEL with soaring spaces, Venetian terrazzo flooring, frescoed and exposed-beam ceilings, and Murano chandeliers, while guest rooms are essays in historic style but come integrated with contemporary furnishings and appointments. **Pros:** excellent service; a luminous, aristocratic ambience; located on a lively Venetian campo not frequented by tourists. **Cons:** the 5- to 10-minute walk from San Zaccaria or Rialto includes two bridges and can be cumbersome for those with mobility issues or significant amounts of luggage; relatively far from a vaporetto stop; no restaurant. $ *Rooms from: €350* ✉ *Campo Santa Maria Formosa, Castello 5866, Castello* ☎ *041/2410447* ⊕ *www.ruzzinipalace.com* ↪ *28 rooms* ⦿ *Breakfast* Ⓜ *Vaporetto: San Zaccaria or Rialto* ⊹ *E3.*

NIGHTLIFE AND PERFORMING ARTS

NIGHTLIFE

Venice's offerings for nightlife are, even by rather sedate standards, fairly tame. Most bars must close by midnight, especially those that offer outdoor seating. Piazza San Marco is a popular meeting place in nice weather, when the cafés stay open relatively late and all seem to compete to offer the best live music. The younger crowd, Venetians and visitors alike, tend to gravitate toward the area around Rialto Bridge, with Campi San Bartolomeo and San Luca on one side and Campo Rialto Nuovo on the other. Especially popular with university students and young people from the mainland are the bars around Campo Santa Margherita. Pick up a booklet of *2Night* or visit ⊕ *venezia.2night.it* for nightlife listings and reviews.

SAN MARCO AND DORSODURO

Al Chioschetto. While this popular place consists only of a kiosk set up to serve some outdoor tables, it is located on the Zattere, and thus provides panoramic views. It's a handy meet-up for locals and a stop-off for tourists in nice weather for a spritz, a panino, or a sunny read as the Venetian world eases by. But go for the view and the sunshine; the food and drink, while acceptable, are not exceptional. ✉ *Near Ponte Lungo, Dorsoduro 1406/A, Dorsoduro* ☎ *338/1174077* Ⓜ *Vaporetto: Zattere.*

Corte dell'Orso. It is easy to see why this place is popular with the locals, offering fairly priced cocktails, a reasonable assortment of cicheti, and a good selection of Italian wine, but the warm ambience, friendly staff, and occasional live jazz are the main draws. The kitchen stays open until late. ✉ *Tucked away in alley across from Church of San Giovanni Grisostomo, San Marco 5495, San Marco* ☎ *041/5224673* Ⓜ *Vaporetto: Rialto.*

Fodor's Choice
★

Il Caffè. Commonly called "Bar Rosso" for its bright-red exterior, Il Caffè has far more tables outside than inside. A favorite with students and faculty from the nearby university, it's a good place to enjoy a spritz—the preferred Venetian aperitif of white wine, Campari or Aperol, soda water, an olive, and a slice of orange. It has excellent tramezzini (among the best in town) and panini, and a hip, helpful staff. It's been recently frequented by high-school students from the mainland on weekend nights, so it can be more enjoyable around lunchtime, or in the early evening. ⊠ *Campo Santa Margherita, Dorsoduro 2963, Dorsoduro* ☎ *041/5287998* ⊘ *Closed Sun.*

Orange. Modern, hip, and complemented by an internal garden, this welcoming bar anchors the south end of Campo Santa Margherita, the liveliest campo in Venice. You can have *piadine* sandwiches, salads, and drinks while watching soccer games on a massive screen inside, or sit at the tables in the campo. Despite being close to the university, Orange is frequented primarily by young working people from the mainland and tourists. ⊠ *Campo Santa Margherita, Dorsoduro 3054/A, Dorsoduro* ☎ *041/5234740.*

SAN POLO

Naranzaria. At the friendliest of the several bar-restaurants that line the Erbaria, near the Rialto Market, enjoy a cocktail outside along the Canal Grande or at a cozy table inside of the renovated 16th-century warehouse. Although the food is acceptable, the ambience is really the main attraction. After the kitchen closes at 10:30, light snacks are served until midnight, and live music (usually jazz, Latin, or rock) occasionally plays on Sunday evening. ⊠ *L'Erbaria, along Canal Grande, San Polo 130, San Polo* ☎ *041/7241035* Ⓜ *Vaporetto: Rialto Mercato.*

CASTELLO

Zanzibar. This kiosk bar is very popular on warm summer evenings with upper-class Venetians and tourists. It offers food, but that is mostly limited to conventional Venetian sandwiches and commercial ice cream. The most interesting thing about the place is its location with a view of the church of Santa Maria Formosa, which makes it a pleasant place for a drink and a good place for people-watching. ⊠ *Campo Santa Maria Formosa, Castello 5840, Castello* ☎ *041/962640* Ⓜ *Vaporetto: San Zaccaria.*

PERFORMING ARTS

Visit ⊕ *www.aguestinvenice.com* for a preview of musical, artistic, and sporting events. *Venezia News* (*VENews*), available at newsstands, has similar information but also includes in-depth articles about noteworthy events. The tourist office publishes a handy, free quarterly *Calendar* in Italian and English, listing daily events and current museum and venue hours. *Venezia da Vivere* is a seasonal guide listing nightspots and live music. For a Venice website that allows you to scan the cultural horizon before you arrive, try ⊕ *www.turismovenezia.it*. And don't ignore the posters you see plastered on the walls as you walk—they're often the most up-to-date information you can find.

CARNEVALE

Although Carnevale has traditionally been associated with the time leading up to the Roman Catholic period of Lent, it originally started out as a principally secular annual period of partying and feasting to celebrate Venice's victory over the patriarch of Ulrich Aquileia in 1162. To commemorate the annual tribute Ulrich was forced to pay, a bull and 12 pigs were slaughtered each year on the day before Lent in Piazza San Marco. The use of masks for Carnevale was first mentioned in 1268, and its direct association with Lent was not made until the end of the 13th century. Since then, for centuries the city marked the days preceding *quaresima* (Lent) with abundant feasting and wild celebrations. The word *carnevale* is derived from the words *carne* (meat) and *levare* (to remove), as eating meat was restricted during Lent.

Venice earned its international reputation as the "city of Carnevale" in the 18th century, when partying would begin several months before Lent and the city seemed to be one continuous masquerade. During this time, income from tourists became a major source of funds in La Serenissima's coffers. With the Republic's fall in 1797, Carnevale was prohibited by the French and the Austrians. From Italian reunification in 1866 until the fall of fascism in the 1940s, the event was alternately resumed and banned, depending on the government's stance.

It was revived for good in the 1970s, when residents began taking to the calli and campi in their own impromptu celebrations. It didn't take long for the tourist industry to embrace the revival as a means to stimulate business during low season. The efforts were successful. Each year over the 10- to 12-day Carnevale period (ending on the Tuesday before Ash Wednesday), more than a half-million people attend concerts, theater and street performances, masquerade balls, historical processions, fashion shows, and contests. Since 2008 Carnevale has been organized by **Venezia Marketing & Eventi** (⊕ *www.carnevale.venezia.it*). *A Guest in Venice* is also a complete guide to public and private Carnevale festivities. Stop by the **tourist office** (☎ *041/5298711* ⊕ *www.turismovenezia.it*) or Venice Pavilion for information, but be aware they can be mobbed. If you're not planning on joining in the revelry, you'd be wise to choose another time to visit Venice. Crowds throng the streets (which become one-way, with police directing foot traffic), bridges are designated "no-stopping" zones to avoid gridlock, and prices skyrocket.

FESTIVALS

The **Biennale** (⊕ *www.labiennale.org*) cultural institution organizes events year-round, including the **Venice Film Festival,** which begins the last week of August. **La Biennale di Venezia,** an international exhibition of contemporary art, is held in odd-numbered years, usually from mid-June to early November, at the Giardini della Biennale, and in the impressive Arsenale.

Festa del Redentore. On the third Sunday in July, crowds cross the Canale della Giudecca by means of a pontoon bridge, built every year to commemorate the doge's annual visit to Palladio's Chiesa del Redentore, to offer thanks for the end of a 16th-century plague. The evening before, Venetians, accompanied each year with an increasing number of tourists, set up tables and chairs along the canals. As evening falls, practically the whole city takes to the streets and tables, and thousands more take to the water. Boats decorated with colored lanterns (and well provisioned with traditional Redentore meals) jockey for position to watch the grand event. Half an hour before midnight, Venice kicks off a fireworks display over the Bacino, with the fireworks reflecting in its waters. Anywhere along the Riva degli Schiavoni you'll find good viewing; or try Zattere, as close to Punta Dogana as you can get, or on the Zitelle end of the Giudecca. After the fireworks you can join the young folks in staying out all night and greeting sunrise on the Lido beach, or rest up and make the procession to Mass on Sunday morning. If you're on a boat, allow for a couple of hours to dislodge yourself from the nautical traffic jam when the festivities break up.

SHOPPING

Globalization has made most goods available in Venice and items like Venetian glass widely available in major cities throughout the world. While the selection of Italian and Venetian made goods may be a bit better in Venice than at home, the prices may actually be lower in the United States, especially considering that U.S. retailers discount sale goods quite radically. Venetian antiques, especially antique Venetian glass, is almost invariably cheaper in other places, because Venetians are ready to pay high prices for their own heritage. So, before your trip, check the prices at home on what you may wish to buy abroad before you leave.

Alluring shops abound in Venice. You'll find countless vendors of trademark Venetian wares such as glass and lace. The authenticity of some goods can be suspect, but they're often pleasing to the eye regardless of their place of origin. There are also some interesting craft and art studios, where you can find high-quality, one-of-a-kind articles, but Venice is a design center only for glass, lace, and high-end textiles. You will probably find a better choice of leather, clothing, and furnishings in other Italian cities.

Regular store hours are usually 9 to 12:30 and 3:30 or 4 to 7:30; some stores close Saturday afternoon or Monday morning. Food shops are open 8 to 1 and 5 to 7:30, and may close Wednesday afternoon and all day Sunday. Supermarkets are generally open every day, including Sunday, and have longer opening hours than independent stores. Many tourist-oriented shops are open all day, every day. Some shops close for both a summer and a winter vacation.

The **San Marco** area is full of shops and couture boutiques such as Armani, Missoni, Valentino, Fendi, and Versace. Le Mercerie, the Frezzeria, Calle dei Fabbri, and Calle Larga XXII Marzo, all leading from Piazza San Marco, are some of Venice's busiest shopping streets. Other good shopping areas surround Calle del Teatro and Campi San Salvador, Manin, San Fantin, and San Bartolomeo. You can find somewhat less expensive, more varied and imaginative shops between the Rialto Bridge and San Polo and in Santa Croce, and art galleries in Dorsoduro from the Salute to the Accademia.

Venetian Art Glass

The glass of Murano is Venice's number-one product, and you'll be confronted by mind-boggling displays of traditional and contemporary glassware—much of it kitsch and not made in Venice. Traditional Venetian glass is hot, blown glass, not lead crystal; it comes in myriad forms that range from the classic ornate goblets and chandeliers, to beads, vases, sculpture, and more. Beware of paying "Venetian" prices for glass made elsewhere. A piece claiming to be made in Murano may guarantee its origin, but not its value or quality; the prestigious Venetian glassmakers—like Venini, Seguso, Salviati, and others—sign their pieces, but never use the "made in Murano" label. To make a smart purchase, take your time and be selective. You can learn a great deal without sales pressure at the Museo del Vetro on Murano; unfortunately, you'll likely find the least-attractive glass where public demonstrations are offered. Although prices in Venice and on Murano are comparable, shops in Venice with wares from various glassworks may charge slightly less. ■TIP➔ A "free" taxi to Murano always comes with sales pressure. Take the vaporetto that's included in your transit pass, and, if you prefer, a private guide who specializes in the subject but has no affinity to any specific furnace.

SAN MARCO AND DORSODURO

GIFTS

Giuliana Longo. A hat shop that's been around since 1901 offers an assortment of Venetian and gondolier straw hats, Panama hats from Ecuador, caps and berets, and some select scarves of silk and fine wool; there's even a special corner dedicated to accessories for antique cars. ⊠ *Calle del Lovo, San Marco 4813, San Marco* ☎ *041/5226454* ⊕ *www. giulianalongo.com* ☉ *Closed Sun.* Ⓜ *Vaporetto: San Marco.*

GLASS

Marina and Susanna Sent. The beautiful and elegant glass jewelry of Marina and Susanna Sent has been featured in *Vogue.* Look also for vases and other exceptional design pieces. Other locations are near San Moise in San Marco, on Murano on the Fondamenta Serenella, and in San Polo in the Sottoportico dei Oresi. ⊠ *Campo San Vio, Dorsoduro 669, Dorsoduro* ☎ *041/5208136 for Dorsoduro, 041/5204014 for San Marco, 041/5274665 for Murano* ⊕ *www.marinaesusannasent. com* ☉ *Closed weekends* Ⓜ *Vaporetto: Accademia/Zattere, Giglio, Murano Serenella.*

Pauly & C. Established in 1866, Pauly & Company features a truly impressive selection of authentic Murano art glass (both traditional and contemporary styles) by accomplished masters. The showroom in Piazza San Marco at No. 73 houses the more traditional collection while at No. 77 you can find works by artists and designers. ⊠ *Piazza San Marco, San Marco 73 and 77, San Marco* ☎ *041/5235484, 041/2770279.*

Venini. When connoisseurs of Venetian glass think of the firms who have restored Venice to its place as the epicenter of artistic glass production, Venini is, without any major discussion, the firm that immediately comes to mind. Since the beginning of the 20th century, Venini has found craftsmen and designers that have made their trademark synonymous with the highest quality both in traditional and in creative glass design. A piece of Venini glass, even one of modest price and proportions, will be considered not only a charming decorative object, but also a work of art that will maintain its value for years to come. While Venini's more exciting and innovative pieces may cost thousands of dollars, the Venini showrooms in the Piazza San Marco and on Murano also have small, more conventional designs for prices as low as € 100. ⊠ *314 Piazzetta Leoncini, San Marco* ☎ *041/5224045* ⊕ *www.venini.com.*

LEATHER

Il Grifone. Very few artisan leather shops remain in Venice, and Il Grifone is the standout with respect to quality, tradition, and a guarantee for an exquisite product. For more than 30 years, Antonio Peressin has been making bags, purses, belts, and smaller leather items that have a wide following because of his precision and attention to detail. His prices remain reasonable and accessible. ⊠ *Fondamenta del Gaffaro, Dorsoduro 3516, Dorsoduro* ☎ *041/5229452* ⊕ *www.ilgrifonevenezia.it* ☾ *Closed Sun. and Mon.* Ⓜ *Vaporetto: Piazzale Roma.*

SHOPPING CENTERS

Fondaco dei Tedeschi. This 15th-century Renaissance commercial center served as Venice's main post office for many years, but has now been remodeled and returned to its historical roots as a luxury department store. Here you can find a large assortment of high-end jewelry, clothing, and other luxury items. ⊠ *Calle Fondaco dei Tedeschi, near San Marco end of Rialto Bridge, San Marco* ☎ *041/3142000* Ⓜ *Rialto.*

TEXTILES

Fodor'sChoice
★

Bevilacqua. This renowned studio has kept the weaving tradition alive in Venice since 1875, using 18th-century hand looms for its most precious creations. Its repertoire of 3,500 different patterns and designs yields a ready-to-sell selection of hundreds of brocades, Gobelins, damasks, velvets, taffetas, and satins. You'll also find tapestry, cushions, and braiding. Fabrics made by this prestigious firm have been used to decorate the Vatican, the Royal Palace of Stockholm, and the White House. This listing is for the main retail outlet of the Bevilacqua establishment; there's another behind the San Marco Basilica. If you're interested in seeing the actual 18th-century looms in action making the most precious fabrics, request an appointment at the Luigi Bevilacqua production center in Santa Croce. ⊠ *Campo di Santa Maria del Giglio, San Marco 2520, San Marco* ☎ *041/2410662 for main retail outlet, 041/5287581 for retail outlet behind Basilica, 041/721566 for Santa Croce production center* ⊕ *www.bevilacquatessuti.com* ☾ *Closed Sun.* Ⓜ *Vaporetto: Giglio.*

Jesurum. A great deal of so-called Burano-Venetian lace is now machine made in China—and there really is a difference. Unless you have some experience, you're best off going to a trusted place. Jesurum has been the major producer of handmade Venetian lace since 1870. Its lace is, of course, all modern production, but if you want an antique piece, the people at Jesurum can point you in the right direction. ✉ *Calle Larga XII Marzo, San Marco 2401, San Marco* ☎ *041/5238969* ⊕ *www.jesurum.it.*

4

NORTHERN ITALY

With the Veneto, Milan, Cinque Terre,
and Emilia-Romagna

Visit Fodors.com for advice, updates, and bookings

WELCOME TO NORTHERN ITALY

TOP REASONS TO GO

★ **Giotto's frescoes in the Cappella degli Scrovegni:** In this Padua chapel, Giotto's expressive and innovative frescoes fore-shadowed the Renaissance.

★ **Leonoardo's Last Supper:** Behold one of the world's most famous works of art for yourself house within Santa Maria delle Grazie in Milan.

★ **Hiking in the Cinque Terre:** Hike the famous Cinque Terre trails past gravity-defying vineyards, colorful, rock-perched villages, and the deep blue Mediterranean Sea.

★ **The signature food of Emilia-Romagna:** This region's food—prosciutto crudo, Parmigiano-Reggiano, balsamic vinegar, and above all, pasta—makes the trip to Italy worthwhile.

★ **Breathtaking mosaics:** The intricate tiles in Ravenna's Mausoleo di Galla Placidia, in brilliantly well-preserved colors, depict vivid portraits and pastoral scenes.

1 The Veneto. A city of both high-rises and history, **Padua** is most noted for Giotto's frescoes in the Cappella degli Scrovegni, where Dante's contemporary painted with a human focus that foreshadowed the Renaissance. **Vicenza**, an elegant art city, is on the green plain reaching inland from Venice's lagoon, bears the signature of the great 16th-century architect Andrea Palladio, including several palazzi and other important buildings. Shakespeare placed Romeo, Juliet, and a couple of gentlemen in Verona, one of the best-preserved and most beautiful cities in Italy. Try to catch *Aida* at the gigantic Roman arena.

2 Milan. The country's center of finance and commerce is constantly looking to the future. Home of the Italian stock exchange, it's also one of the world's fashion capitals

GETTING ORIENTED

Northern Italy holds some of the country's most memorable towns, cities, and regions. The Veneto region, just west of Venice, holds the beautiful, artistically rich cities of Padua, Vincenza, and Verona. Farther west, Milan is a major transportation hub and may be your point of entry into the country. South of Milan, you'll find the gorgeous beaches of the Italian Riviera, with the colorful villages of the Cinque Terre being a highlight. Between Florence and Venice, the region of Emilia-Romagna holds prosperous, highly cultured cities, where the locals have mastered the art of living—and especially eating—well.

and has cultural and artistic treasures that rival those of Florence and Rome.

3 Cinque Terre. Five isolated seaside villages seem removed from the modern world—despite the many hikers who populate the trails between them.

4 Emilia-Romagna. **Bologna**, Emilia's principal cultural and intellectual center, is famed for its arcaded sidewalks, grandiose medieval towers, and

sublime restaurants. North of Bologna, the prosperous, tidy city of **Ferrara** has a rich medieval past and its own distinctive cuisine. The main attractions of the well-preserved Romagna city of **Ravenna** are its memorable mosaics— glittering treasures left from Byzantine rule.

EATING AND DRINKING WELL IN THE VENETO AND FRIULI–VENEZIA GIULIA

With the decisive seasonal changes of the Venetian Arc, it's little wonder that many restaurants shun printed menus. Elements from field and forest define much of the region's cuisine, including white asparagus, herbs, chestnuts, radicchio, and wild mushrooms.

Restaurants of the Venetian Arc tend to cling to tradition, not only in the food they serve, but also when they serve it. From 2:30 in the afternoon until about 7:30 in the evening most places are closed (though you can pick up a snack at a bar during these hours), and on Sunday afternoon restaurants are packed with Italian families and friends indulging in the weekly ritual of lunching out.

Meals are still sacred for most Italians, so don't be surprised if you get disapproving looks when you gobble down a sandwich or a slice of pizza while seated on the church steps or a park bench. In many places it's actually illegal to do so. If you want to fit in with the locals, snack while standing at the bar or seated in a café, and they may not even notice that you're a tourist.

THE BEST IN BEANS

Pasta e fagioli, a thick bean soup with pasta, served slightly warm or at room temperature, is made all over Italy. Folks in the Veneto, though, take special pride in their version, made from particularly fine beans grown around the village of Lamon, near Belluno.

Even when they're bought in the Veneto, the beans from Lamon cost more than double the next-most-expensive variety, but their rich and delicate taste is considered well worth the added expense. You never knew that bean soup could taste so good.

FISH

The catch of the day is always a good bet, whether it's sweet and succulent Adriatic shellfish, sea bream, bass, or John Dory, or freshwater fish from Lake Garda, near Verona. A staple in the Veneto is *baccalà*, dried salt cod, introduced to Italy during the Renaissance by northern European traders. Dried cod is soaked in water or milk and then prepared in a different way in each city. In Vicenza, baccalà *alla vicentina* is cooked with onions, milk, and cheese, and is generally served with polenta.

MEAT

Because grazing land is scarce in the Veneto, beef is a rarity, but pork and veal are standards, and goose, duck, and guinea fowl are common poultry options. In Friuli–Venezia Giulia, menus show the influences of Austria–Hungary: you may find deer and hare on the menu, as well as Eastern European–style goulash. Throughout the Veneto an unusual treat is *nervetti*—cubes of gelatin from a calf's knee prepared with onions, parsley, olive oil, and lemon.

PASTA, RISOTTO, POLENTA

For *primi* (first courses), the Veneto dines on *bigoli* (thick whole-wheat pasta), generally served with an anchovy-onion sauce delicately flavored with cinnamon, or risotto, creamy rice generally flavored with vegetables or

shellfish. *Polenta* (cornmeal gruel) is everywhere, whether it's a stiff porridge topped with Gorgonzola, or a stew, or a patty grilled alongside meat or fish. Spaghetti and other types of pasta are widely available, but they are considered practically foreign. The same holds true for pizza. You can find fairly good pizza in the Veneto, but it has little in common with the local cuisine.

RADICCHIO DI TREVISO

In fall and winter be sure to try the radicchio di Treviso, *pictured above,* a red endive grown near that town but popular all over the region. Cultivation is very labor-intensive, so it can be expensive. It's best in a stew with chicken or veal, in a risotto, or just grilled or baked with a drizzle of olive oil and perhaps a little taleggio cheese from neighboring Lombardy.

WINE

The Veneto produces more D.O.C. (Denominazione di Origine Controllata) wines than any other region in Italy. Amarone, the region's crowning achievement, is a robust, full-bodied red. The best of the whites are Soave, prosecco, and *pinot bianco* (pinot blanc). In Friuli–Venezia Giulia the local wines include *tocai friulano,* a dry, lively white made from the sauvignon vert grape, and *piccolit,* perhaps Italy's most highly prized dessert wine.

EATING AND DRINKING WELL IN EMILIA-ROMAGNA

Italians rarely agree about anything, but many concede that some of the country's finest foods originated in Emilia-Romagna. Tortellini, fettuccine, Parmesan cheese, prosciutto crudo, and balsamic vinegar are just a few of the Italian delicacies born here.

One of the beauties of Emilia-Romagna is that its exceptional food can be had without breaking the bank. Many trattorias serve up classic dishes, mastered over the centuries, at reasonable prices. Cutting-edge restaurants and wine bars are often more expensive; their inventive menus are full of *fantasia*—reinterpretations of the classics. For the budget-conscious, Bologna, a university town, has great places for cheap eats.

Between meals, you can sustain yourself with the region's famous sandwich, the *piadina*. It's made with pitalike thin bread, usually filled with prosciutto or mortadella, cheese, and vegetables; then put under the grill and served hot, with the cheese oozing at the sides. These addictive sandwiches can be savored at sit-down places or ordered to go.

THE REAL RAGÙ

Emilia-Romagna's signature dish is *tagliatelle al ragù* (flat noodles with meat sauce), known as "spaghetti Bolognese" most everywhere else. This *primo* (first course) is on every menu, and no two versions are the same. The sauce starts in a sauté pan with finely diced carrots, onions, and celery. Purists add nothing but minced beef, but some use *guanciale* (pork cheek), sausage, veal, or chicken. Regular ministrations of broth are added, and sometimes wine, milk, or cream. After a couple of hours of cooking, the ragù is ready to be joined with pasta and Parmigiano-Reggiano and brought to the table.

PORK PRODUCTS

It's not just mortadella and cured pork products like prosciutto crudo and *culatello* that Emilia-Romagnans go crazy for—they're wild about the whole hog.

You'll frequently find cotechino and zampone, both *secondi* (second courses), on menus. *Cotechino* is a savory, thick, fresh sausage served with lentils on New Year's Eve (the combination is said to augur well for the new year) and with mashed potatoes year-round. *Zampone*, a stuffed pig's foot, is redolent of garlic and deliciously fatty.

BOLLITO MISTO

The name means "mixed boil," and they do it exceptionally well in this part of Italy. According to Emilia-Romagnans, it was invented here, although other Italians—especially those from Milan and the Piedmont—might argue this point. Chicken, beef, tongue, and zampone are tossed into a stockpot and boiled; they're then removed from the broth and served with a fragrant *salsa verde* (green sauce), made green by parsley and spiced with anchovies, garlic, and capers. This simple yet rich dish is usually served with mashed potatoes on the side, and savvy diners will mix some of the piquant salsa verde into the potatoes as well.

STUFFED PASTA

Among the many Emilian variations on stuffed pasta, *tortellini* are the smallest. *Tortelli* and *cappellacci* are larger pasta "pillows," about the size of a brussels sprout, but with the same basic form as tortellini. They're often filled with pumpkin or spinach and cheese.

Tortelloni are, in theory, even bigger, although their sizes vary. Stuffed pastas are generally served simply, with melted butter, sage, and Parmigiano-Reggiano cheese or, in the case of tortellini, *in brodo* (in beef, chicken, or capon broth or a combination of any of them), which brings out the subtle richness of the filling.

WINES

Emilia-Romagna's wines accompany the region's fine food rather than vying with it for accolades. The best-known is *lambrusco*, a sparkling red produced on the Po Plain that has some admirers and many detractors. It's praised for its tartness and condemned for the same; it does, however, pair brilliantly with the local fare. The region's best wines include Sangiovese di Romagna (somewhat similar to Chianti), from the Romagnan hills, and barbera from the Colli Piacetini and Apennine foothills. Castelluccio, Bonzara, Zerbina, Leone Conti, and Tre Monti are among the region's top producers.

Updated
by Bruce
Leimsidor, Liz
Humphreys,
Megan
McCaffrey-
Guerrera,
and Patricia
Rucidlo

The prosperous north has Italy's most diverse landscape. Venice is a rare jewel of a city, while Milan and Turin are centers of commerce and style. Along the country's northern border, the mountain peaks of the Dolomites and Valle d'Aosta attract skiers in winter and hikers in summer, while the Lake District and the coastline of the Italian Riviera are classic summertime playgrounds. Food here is exceptional, from the French-influenced cuisine of Piedmont to Italian classics prepared with unrivaled skill in Emilia-Romagna.

NORTHERN ITALY PLANNER

WHEN TO GO

The ideal times to visit are late spring and early summer (May and June) and in early fall (September and October). Summers tend to be hot and humid—though if you're an opera buff, it's worth tolerating the heat in order to see a performance at the Arena di Verona (where the season runs from July through September).

Winter is a good time to avoid travel to these regions; although the dense fog can be beautiful, it makes for bad driving conditions, and wet, bone-chilling cold isn't unusual November through March. That being said, you'll get some of the best rates and some of the smallest crowds if you do decide to visit during this time.

MAKING THE MOST OF YOUR TIME

Lined up in a row west of Venice are Padua, Vicenza, and Verona—three prosperous small cities that are each worth at least a day on a northern Italy itinerary. Verona has the most charm and the widest selection of hotels and restaurants, so it's probably the best choice for a base in the area, even though it also draws the most tourists. The hills north of Venice make for good drives, with appealing villages set amid a visitor-friendly wine country.

Italy's commercial hub isn't usually at the top of the list for visiting tourists, but Milan is the nation's most modern city, with its own sophisticated appeal: its fashionable shops rival those of New York and Paris, its soccer teams are Italy's answer to the Yankees and the Mets, its opera performances set the standard for the world, and its art treasures are well worth the visit.

The Italian Riviera and Cinque Terre is extremely seasonal. From April to October, the area's bustling with shops, cafés, clubs, and restaurants that stay open late. In high season (Easter and June–August), it can be very crowded and lively. Yet, the rest of the year, the majority of resorts close down, and you'll be hard-pressed to find accommodations or restaurants open.

Plan on spending at least two days in Bologna, the region's cultural and historical capital. Also plan on visiting Ferrara, a misty, mysterious medieval city. If you have time, go to Ravenna for its memorable Byzantine mosaics and Modena for its harmonious architecture and famous balsamic vinegar.

GETTING HERE AND AROUND

Aeroporto Malpensa, 50 km (31 miles) northwest of Milan, is the major northern Italian hub for intercontinental flights and also sees substantial European and domestic traffic. Venice's **Aeroporto Marco Polo** also serves international destinations. There are regional airports in Turin, Genoa, Bologna, Verona, Trieste, Treviso, Bolzano, and Parma, and Milan has a secondary airport, Linate. You can reach all of these on connecting flights from within Italy and from other European cities. You can also get around northern Italy by train using the Italian national rail system, **Ferrovie dello Stato** (☎ *199303060 toll-free within Italy* ⊕ *www.trenitalia.com*). Shuttle buses run three times an hour (less often after 10 pm) between Malpensa and Milan's main train station, Stazione Centrale; the trip takes about 75 minutes, depending on traffic. The Malpensa Express Train, which leaves twice an hour, takes 40 minutes and delivers you to Cadorna metro station in central Milan.

The cities in these regions are connected by well-maintained highways and an efficient railway system. A car provides added freedom, but city driving and parking can be a challenge.

RESTAURANTS

You'll find lots of traditional northern Italian restaurants in this region, and can pretty much count on menus divided into pasta, fish, and meat options. As in the rest of Italy, it's common for dishes to feature seasonal and local ingredients. Although the Veneto is not considered one of Italy's major cuisine areas, the region offers many opportunities for exciting gastronomic adventures. The fish offerings are among the most varied and freshest in Italy, and possibly Europe, and the vegetables from the islands in the Venetian lagoon are considered a national treasure. Take a break from pasta and try the area's wonderful, creamy risottos and hearty polenta. Meal prices in Milan tend to be higher than in the rest of the region (and quite high for European cities in general), though this is also where you'll see examples of the latest food trends and more adventurous choices on the menus. While fine dining can be found in Cinque Terre, you are more likely to enjoy a casual atmosphere, often with an amazing sea view. Expect both the decor and dishes to be simple but flavorful.

In Emilia-Romagna, dining options range from mom-and-pop-style informal trattorias to three-star Michelin restaurants. Food here is not for the faint of heart (or those on diets): it is rich, creamy, and cheesy. Local wines pair remarkably well with this sumptuous fare. You may want to rethink Lambrusco, as it marries well with just about everything on the menu.

HOTELS

Rates tend to be higher in Padua and Verona; in Verona especially, seasonal rates vary widely and soar during trade fairs and the opera season. There are fewer good lodging choices in Vicenza, perhaps because more overnighters are drawn to the better restaurant scenes in Verona and Padua. *Agriturismo* (farm stay) information is available at tourist offices and sometimes on their websites. High-season in Milan depends on what fairs and exhibitions are being staged. Prices in almost all hotels can go up dramatically during the Furniture Fair in early April. Fashion, travel, and tech fairs also draw big crowds throughout the year, raising prices. In contrast to other cities in Italy, however, you can often find discounts on weekends. In Cinque Terre, lodging tends to be pricey in high season, particularly June to August; reservations for this region should also be made far in advance as places book up very quickly. Emilia-Romagna has a reputation for demonstrating a level of efficiency uncommon in most of Italy. Even the smallest hotels are usually well run, with high standards of quality and service. Bologna is very much a businessperson's city, and many hotels here cater to the business traveler, but there are smaller, more intimate hotels as well. It's smart to book in advance—the region hosts many fairs and conventions that can fill up hotels even during low season. *Hotel reviews have been shortened. For full information, visit Fodors.com.*

WHAT IT COSTS				
	$	$$	$$$	$$$$
Restaurants	under €15	€15–€24	€25–€35	over €35
Hotels	under €125	€125–€200	€201–€300	over €300

Prices in the dining reviews are the average cost of a main course at dinner, or, if dinner is not served, at lunch. Prices in the reviews are the lowest cost of a standard double room in high season.

THE VENETO

The arc around Venice—stretching from Verona to Trieste, encompassing the Veneto and Friuli–Venezia Giulia regions—is undisputedly one of most culturally rich areas in Italy, an intellectual and spiritual feast of architecture, painting, and sculpture. Since the 16th century, the art, architecture, and way of life here have all reflected Venetian splendor. Whether coastal or inland, the emblem of Venice, St. Mark's winged lion, is emblazoned on palazzi and poised on pedestals.

It wasn't always this way. Back in the Middle Ages, Padua and Verona were independent cities that developed substantial cultural traditions of their own, leaving behind many artistic treasures. And even while it was under Venice's political domination, 16th-century Vicenza contributed more to the cultural heritage of La Serenissima than it took from her, in large part because of its master architect, Andrea Palladio.

The area is primarily flat, green farmland. As you move inland, though, you encounter low hills, which swell and rise in a succession of plateaus and high meadows, culminating in the snowcapped Dolomite Alps. Much of the pleasure of exploring here comes from discovering the variations on the Venetian theme that give a unique character to each of the towns. Some, such as Verona, Treviso, and Udine, have a solid medieval look. Padua, with its narrow arcaded streets, is romantic; Vicenza, ennobled by the architecture of Palladio, is more elegant. Udine, in Friuli–Venezia Giulia, is a genteel, intricately sculpted city that's home to the first important frescoes by Gianbattista Tiepolo. In Trieste, once the main port of the Austro-Hungarian Empire, you can find survivors of those days in its Viennese-inspired coffeehouses and *buffets*—hole-in-the-wall eateries serving sausages and other pork dishes.

Unlike the western regions of northern Italy, the Veneto and Friuli–Venezia Giulia were slow to move from an agricultural to an industrial economy, and even now depend upon small and medium-size businesses, many of which are still family-run. The area, therefore, attracted far fewer migrants from elsewhere in Italy, and it was able to maintain its local cultures to a substantial degree. Local dialects may have all but died out in places like Milan and Turin, but they still thrive in the Veneto and Friuli–Venezia Giulia, and even when the residents speak standard Italian, it is frequently laced with local words and usage.

PADUA

A romantic warren of arcaded streets, Padua is a major cultural center in northern Italy. It has first-rate artistic monuments and, along with Bologna, is one of the few cities in the country where you can catch a glimpse of student life.

Its university, founded in 1222 and Italy's second oldest, attracted such cultural icons as Dante (1265–1321), Petrarch (1304–74), and Galileo (1564–1642), thus earning the city the sobriquet "La Dotta" (the Learned). Padua's Basilica di Sant'Antonio, begun around 1238, attracts droves of pilgrims, especially on his feast day, June 13. Three great artists—Giotto (1266–1337), Donatello (circa 1386–1466), and Mantegna (1431–1506)—left significant works in Padua. Giotto's Capella degli Scrovegni here is one of the best-known and most meticulously preserved works of art in the country. Today, a bicycle-happy student body—some 50,000 strong—flavors every aspect of local culture. Don't be surprised if you spot a *laurea* (graduation) ceremony marked by laurel leaves, mocking lullabies, and X-rated caricatures.

GETTING HERE AND AROUND

Many people visit Padua from Venice: the train trip between the cities is short, and regular bus service originates from Venice's Piazzale Roma. By car from Milan or Venice, Padua is on the Autostrada Torino–Trieste (A4/E70). Take the San Carlo exit and follow Via Guido Reni to Via Tiziano Aspetti into town. From the south, take the Autostrada Bologna–Padova (A13) to its Padua terminus at Via Ballaglia. Regular bus service connects Venice's Marco Polo airport with downtown Padua.

Padua is a walker's city—parking is difficult, and cars are prohibited in much of the city center. If you arrive by car, leave your vehicle in one of the parking lots on the outskirts, or at your hotel. Unlimited bus service is included with the Padova Card (€16 or €21, valid for 48 or 72 hours), which allows entry to all the city's principal sights (€1 extra for a Capella degli Scrovegni reservation). It's available at tourist information offices and at some museums.

VISITOR INFORMATION

Padova Card. ☒ *Padua* ⊕ *www.padovacard.it.*

Padua Tourism Office. ☒ *Padova Railway Station* ☎ *049/2010080* ⊕ *www.turismopadova.it.*

EXPLORING

TOP ATTRACTIONS

Fodor's Choice ★ **Basilica di Sant'Antonio** (*Basilica del Santo*). Thousands of faithful make the pilgrimage here each year to pray at the tomb of St. Anthony, while others come to admire works by the 15th-century Florentine master Donatello. His equestrian statue (1453) of the *condottiere* (mercenary general) Erasmo da Narni, known as Gattamelata, in front of the church is one of the great masterpieces of Italian Renaissance sculpture. It was inspired by the ancient statue of Marcus Aurelius in Rome's Campidoglio. Donatello also sculpted the beautiful series of bronze reliefs in the imposing interior illustrating the miracles of St. Anthony, as well as the bronze statues of the Madonna and saints, on the high altar.

The huge church, which combines elements of Byzantine, Romanesque, and Gothic styles, was probably begun around 1238, seven years after the death of the Portuguese-born saint. It was completed in 1310, with structural modifications added from the end of the 14th century into the mid-15th century. Because of the site's popularity with pilgrims, masses are held in the basilica almost constantly, which makes it difficult to see these works. More accessible is the restored **Cappella del Santo** (housing the tomb of the saint), which dates from the 16th century. Its walls are covered with impressive reliefs by various important Renaissance sculptors, including Jacopo Sansovino (1486–1570), the architect of the library in Venice's Piazza San Marco, and Tullio Lombardo (1455–1532), the greatest in a family of sculptors who decorated many churches in the area, among them Venice's Santa Maria dei Miracoli. The **Museo Antoniano** (€2.50; closed Monday), part of the basilica complex, contains a Mantegna fresco and works by Tiepolo, Carpaccio, and Piazzetta. ☒ *Piazza del Santo* ☎ *049/8225652* ⊕ *www.basilicadelsanto.it.*

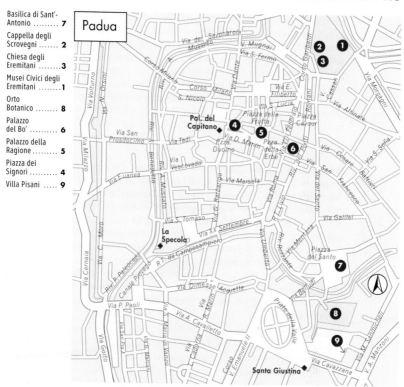

Fodor's Choice **Cappella degli Scrovegni** (*The Arena Chapel*). The spatial depth, emo-
★   tional intensity, and naturalism of the frescoes illustrating the lives of
Mary and Jesus in this world-famous chapel—note the use of blue
sky instead of the conventional, depth-destroying gold background of
medieval painting—broke new ground in Western art. Enrico Scrovegno
commissioned these frescoes to atone for the sins of his deceased father,
Reginaldo, the usurer condemned to the Seventh Circle of the Inferno
in Dante's *Divine Comedy*. Giotto and his assistants worked on the
frescoes from 1303 to 1305, arranging them in tiers to be read from
left to right. Opposite the altar is a *Last Judgment*, most likely designed
and painted by Giotto's assistants, where Enrico offers his chapel to the
Virgin, celebrating her role in human salvation—particularly appropriate, given the penitential purpose of the chapel.

■TIP→ Mandatory reservations, nonrefundable and for a specific
time, can be made in advance at the ticket office, online, or by phone.
Payments online or by phone by credit card must be made one day in
advance. Reservations are necessary even if you have a Padova Card.
In order to preserve the artwork, doors are opened only every 15
minutes. A maximum of 25 visitors at a time must spend 15 minutes
in an acclimatization room before making a 15-minute (20-minute in
winter, late June, and July) chapel visit. Punctuality is essential; tickets

should be picked up at least one hour before your reservation time. If you don't have a reservation, it's sometimes possible to buy your chapel admission on the spot—but you might have to wait a while until there's a group with an opening. You can see fresco details as part of a virtual tour at the Musei Civici degli Eremitani. A good place to get some background before visiting the chapel is the multimedia room, where there are films and interactive computer presentations. Between Christmas and Epiphany (January 6), the chapel sometimes has special late hours. ⊠ *Piazza Eremitani 8* ☎ *049/2010020 for reservations* ⊕ *www.cappelladegliscrovegni.it* ⌑ *€13, includes Musei Civici (€1 with PadovaCard).*

Palazzo della Ragione. Also known as Il Salone, the spectacular arcaded reception hall in Padua's original law courts is as notable for its grandeur—it's 85 feet high—as for its colorful setting, surrounded by shops, cafés, and open-air fruit and vegetable markets. Niccolò Miretto and Stefano di Ferrara, working from 1425 to 1440, painted the frescoes, following the plan of frescoes by Giotto destroyed by a fire in 1420. The stunning space hosts art shows, and an enormous wooden horse, crafted for a public tournament in 1466, commands pride of place. It is patterned after the famous equestrian statue by Donatello in front of the Basilica di San Antonio, and may, in fact, have been designed by Donatello himself in the last year of his life. ⊠ *Piazza della Ragione* ☎ *049/8205006* ⌑ *Salone €4 (free with PadovaCard).*

Piazza dei Signori. Some fine examples of 15th- and 16th-century buildings line this square. On the west side, the **Palazzo del Capitanio** (facade constructed 1598–1605) has an impressive **Torre dell'Orologio**, with an astronomical clock dating from 1344 and a portal made by Falconetto in 1532 in the form of a Roman triumphal arch. The 12th-century **Battistero del Duomo** (Cathedral Baptistry), with frescoes by Giusto de Menabuoi (1374–78), is a few steps away. ⊠ *Piazza dei Signori* ☎ *049/656914* ⌑ *Battistero €3 (free with PadovaCard).*

FAMILY **Villa Pisani.** Extensive grounds with rare trees, ornamental fountains, and garden follies surround this extraordinary palace in Stra, 13 km (8 miles) southeast of Padua. Built in 1721 for the Venetian doge Alvise Pisani, it recalls Versailles more than a Veneto villa. This was one of the last and grandest of many stately residences constructed along the Brenta River from the 16th to 18th century by wealthy Venetians for their *villeggiatura*—vacation and escape from the midsummer humidity. Gianbattista Tiepolo's (1696–1770) spectacular fresco on the ballroom ceiling, *The Apotheosis of the Pisani Family* (1761), alone is worth the visit. For a relaxing afternoon, explore the gorgeous park and maze. To get here from Venice, take Bus No. 53 from Piazzale Roma. The villa is a five-minute walk from the bus stop in Stra. ■ **TIP→ Mussolini invited Hitler here for their first meeting, but they stayed only one night because of the mosquitoes, which remain. If visiting on a late afternoon in summer, carry bug repellent.** ⊠ *Via Doge Pisani 7, Stra* ☎ *049/502074* ⊕ *www.villapisani.beniculturali.it* ⌑ *€10, €7.50 park only* ☉ *Closed Mon.*

THE VENETIAN ARC, PAST AND PRESENT

Long before Venetians made their presence felt on the mainland in the 15th century, Ezzelino III da Romano (1194–1259) laid claim to Verona, Padua, and the surrounding lands and towns. He was the first of a series of brutal and aggressive rulers who dominated the cities of the region until the rise of Venetian rule.

After Ezzelino was ousted, powerful families such as Padua's Carrara and Verona's della Scala (Scaligeri) vied throughout the 14th century to dominate these territories. With the rise of Venetian rule came a time of relative peace, when noble families from the lagoon and the mainland commissioned Palladio and other accomplished architects to design their palazzi and villas. This rich classical legacy, superimposed upon medieval castles and fortifications, is central to the identities of present-day Padua, Vicenza, and Verona.

The region remained under Venetian control until the Napoleonic invasion and the fall of the Venetian Republic in 1797. The Council of Vienna ceded it, along with Lombardy, to Austria in 1815. The region revolted against Austrian rule and joined the Italian Republic in 1866.

Friuli–Venezia Giulia's complicated history is reflected in its architecture, language, and cuisine. It's been marched through, fought over, hymned by patriots, and romanticized by writers that include James Joyce, Rainer Maria Rilke, Ernest Hemingway, Pier Paolo Pasolini, Italo Svevo, and Jan Morris. The region has seen Fascists and Communists, Romans, Habsburgs, and Huns. It survived by forging sheltering alliances—Udine beneath the wings of San Marco (1420), Trieste choosing Duke Leopold of Austria (1382) over Venetian domination.

Some of World War I's fiercest fighting took place in Friuli–Venezia Giulia, where memorials and cemeteries commemorate the hundreds of thousands who died before the arrival of Italian troops in 1918 finally liberated Trieste from Austrian rule. Trieste, along with the whole of Venezia Giulia, was annexed to Italy in 1920. During World War II, Germany occupied the area and placed Trieste in an administrative zone along with parts of Slovenia. The only Nazi extermination camp on Italian soil, the Risiera di San Sabba, was in a suburb of Trieste. After the war, during a period of Cold War dispute, Trieste was governed by an allied military administration; it was officially re-annexed to Italy in 1954, when Italy ceded the Istrian peninsula to the south to Yugoslavia. These arrangements were not finally ratified by Italy and Yugoslavia until 1975.

WORTH NOTING

Chiesa degli Eremitani. This 13th-century church houses substantial fragments of Andrea Mantegna's frescoes (1448–50), which were damaged by Allied bombing in World War II. Despite their fragmentary condition, Mantegna's still beautiful and historically important depictions of the martyrdom of St. James and St. Christopher show the young artist's mastery of extremely complex problems of perspective. ⊠ *Piazza degli Eremitani* ☎ *049/8756410.*

Musei Civici degli Eremitani (*Civic Museum*). This former monastery now houses works of Venetian masters, as well as fine collections of archaeological finds and ancient coins. Notable are the Giotto Crucifix, which once hung in the Scrovegni Chapel, and the *Portrait of a Young Senator,* by Giovanni Bellini (1430–1516). ✉ *Piazza Eremitani 8* ☎ *049/82045450* 🎟 *€10, €13 with Scrovegni Chapel (free with Padova Card)* 🕒 *Closed Mon.*

Orto Botanico (*Botanical Garden*). The Venetian Republic ordered the creation of Padua's botanical garden in 1545 to supply the university with medicinal plants, and it retains its original layout. You can stroll the arboretum—still part of the university—and wander through hothouses and beds of plants that were introduced to Italy in this late-Renaissance garden. A St. Peter's palm, planted in 1585, inspired Goethe to write his 1790 essay, "The Metamorphosis of Plants." ✉ *Via Orto Botanico 15* ☎ *049/8272119* 🌐 *www.ortobotanico.unipd.it* 🎟 *€10 (€5 with PadovaCard).*

Palazzo del Bo'. The University of Padua, founded in 1222, centers around this predominantly16th-century palazzo with an 18th-century facade. It's named after the Osteria del Bo' (*bo'* means "ox"), an inn that once stood on the site. It's worth a visit to see the perfectly proportioned anatomy theater (1594), the beautiful "Old Courtyard," and a hall with a lectern used by Galileo. You can enter only as part of a guided tour; most guides speak English, but it is worth checking ahead by phone. ✉ *Via VIII Febbraio* ☎ *049/8275111 for university switchboard* 🌐 *www.unipd.it* 🎟 *€7* 🕒 *Closed holidays and when the university is on vacation.*

WHERE TO EAT

$$ ITALIAN
🍴 **Enoteca dei Tadi.** In this cozy and atmospheric cross between a wine bar and a restaurant you can put together an inexpensive dinner from the various classic dishes from all over Italy on offer. Portions are small, but so are the prices—just follow the local custom and order a selection. Dishes are made with first-rate ingredients and are coupled with a fine selection of wines. Start with fresh *burrata* (mozzarella's creamier cousin) with tomatoes, or choose from a selection of prosciutto *crudo* or salamis. Don't pass up the house specialty: lasagna—there are several kinds are on the menu. Main courses are limited, but they include a savory Veneto stew with polenta. [$] *Average main: €18* ✉ *Via dei Tadi 16* ☎ *049/8364099, 388/4083434 mobile* 🌐 *www.enotecadeitadi.it* 🕒 *Closed Mon., and 2 wks late June–July. No lunch.*

$$ WINE BAR
🍴 **L'Anfora.** This mix between a traditional *bacaro* (wine bar) and an *osteria* (tavernlike restaurant) is a local institution. Stand at the bar shoulder-to-shoulder with a cross section of Padovano society, from construction workers to professors, and let the friendly and knowledgeable proprietors help you choose a wine. The reasonably priced menu offers simple *casalinga* (home-cooked dishes), plus salads and a selection of cheeses. Portions are ample, and no one will look askance if you don't order the full meal. The place is packed with loyal regulars at lunchtime, so come early or expect a wait, and don't expect to have an intimate conversation. [$] *Average main: €20* ✉ *Via Soncin 13* ☎ *049/656629* 🕒 *Closed Sun. (except in Dec.), 1 wk in Jan., and 1 wk in Aug.*

$$$$ MODERN ITALIAN 🍴 **Le Calandre.** If you're willing to shell out around €600 for a dinner for two and are gastronomically adventurous but not very hungry, then consider this quietly elegant restaurant that critics often rave about. Traditional Veneto recipes are given a highly sophisticated and creative treatment—traditional squid in its ink comes as a "cappuccino," in a glass with a crust of potato foam—while dishes such as sole with a grapefruit and curry sauce leave the Veneto far behind. Owner-chef Massimiliano Alajmo's creative impulses, together with seasonal changes, augment the signature dishes, but Alajmo considers food to be an art form rather than nourishment, so be prepared for minuscule portions. There's a very reduced tasting menu (only three dishes) at €145, exclusive of wine, but it must be ordered by the entire table. Reserve well in advance. [$] *Average main: €235* ✉ *Via Liguria 1, Sarmeola* ✥ *7 km (4 miles) west of Padua* ☎ *049/630303* 🌐 *www.calandre.com* ⏲ *Closed Sun. and Mon., and Jan. 1–15.*

$$ VENETIAN 🍴 **Osteria Dal Capo.** A friendly trattoria in the heart of what used to be Padua's Jewish ghetto serves almost exclusively traditional Veneto dishes, and it does so with refinement and care. The liver and onions is extraordinarily tender. Even the accompanying polenta is grilled to perfection—slightly crisp on the outside and moist on the inside. The desserts are nothing to scoff at, either. This tiny place fills up quickly, so reservations are a must. [$] *Average main: €20* ✉ *Via degli Oblizzi 2* ☎ *049/663105* ⏲ *Closed Sun. No lunch Mon.*

WHERE TO STAY

$ HOTEL 🏨 **Al Fagiano.** The delightfully funky surroundings in this boutique hotel include sponge-painted walls, brush-painted chandeliers, and some views of the spires and cupolas of the Basilica di Sant'Antonio. **Pros:** large rooms; relaxed atmosphere; convenient location; free Wi-Fi. **Cons:** no room service or help with baggage; some find the eccentric decoration a bit much. [$] *Rooms from: €80* ✉ *Via Locatelli 45* ☎ *049/8750073* 🌐 *www.alfagiano.com* 🛏 *40 rooms* 🍽 *No meals.*

$$ HOTEL 🏨 **Albergo Verdi.** One of the best-situated hotels in the city provides tastefully renovated rooms that tend toward the minimalist without being severe; they also have the rare virtue of being absolutely quiet. **Pros:** excellent location close to the Piazza dei Signori; attentive staff; pleasant and warm atmosphere; discounts available depending on time of year. **Cons:** rooms are not that large; few views; charge for Wi-Fi; hefty parking fee. [$] *Rooms from: €150* ✉ *Via Dondi dell'Orlogio 7* ☎ *049/8364163* 🌐 *www.albergoverdipadova.it* 🛏 *14 rooms* 🍽 *Breakfast.*

$ HOTEL 🏨 **Methis.** Four floors of sleekly designed guest rooms reflect the elements: gentle earth tones, fiery red, watery cool blue, and airy white in the top-floor suites. **Pros:** attractive rooms; helpful and attentive staff; pleasant extras such as umbrellas; better breakfast than usual for Italy. **Cons:** a 15-minute walk from major sights and restaurants; uninviting public spaces. [$] *Rooms from: €120* ✉ *Riviera Paleocapa 70* ☎ *049/8725555* 🌐 *www.methishotel.com* 🛏 *59 rooms* 🍽 *Breakfast.*

NIGHTLIFE

Caffè Pedrocchi. No visit to Padua is complete without taking time to sit in this massive café, as the French novelist Stendhal did shortly after it was established, in 1831. Nearly 200 years later, it remains central to the city's social life. The café was built in the Egyptian Revival style, which became popular after Napoléon's expeditions in Egypt. The accomplished restaurant serves only lunch regularly, and dinner on special occasions, and is proud of its innovative menu. ⊠ *Piazzetta Pedrocchi* ☎ *049/8781231* ⊕ *www.caffepedrocchi.it.*

VICENZA

A visit to Vicenza is a must for any student or fan of architecture. This elegant, prosperous city bears the distinctive signature of the architect Andrea Palladio (1508–80), whose name has been given to the "Palladian" style of architecture.

Palladio emphasized the principles of order and harmony using the classical style of architecture established by Renaissance architects such as Brunelleschi, Alberti, and Sansovino. He used these principles and classical motifs not only for public buildings but also for private dwellings. His elegant villas and palaces were influential in propagating classical architecture in Europe, especially Britain, and later in America—most notably at Thomas Jefferson's Monticello.

In the mid-16th century Palladio was commissioned to rebuild much of Vicenza, which had been greatly damaged during wars waged against Venice by the League of Cambrai (1505), an alliance of the papacy, France, the Holy Roman Empire, and several neighboring city-states. He made his name with the renovation of Palazzo della Ragione, begun in 1549 in the heart of Vicenza, and then embarked on a series of noble buildings, all of which adhere to the same principles of classicism and harmony.

GETTING HERE AND AROUND

Vicenza is midway between Padua and Verona, and several trains leave from both cities every hour. By car, take the Autostrada Brescia–Padova/Torino–Trieste (A4/E70) to SP247 North directly into Vicenza.

VISITOR INFORMATION

Vicenza Tourism Office. ⊠ *Piazza Giacomo Matteotti 12* ☎ *0444/320854* ⊕ *www.vicenzae.org.*

EXPLORING

TOP ATTRACTIONS

Palazzo Barbaran da Porto (Palladio Museum). Palladio executed this beautiful city palace for the Vicentine noble Montano Barbarano between 1570 and 1575. The noble patron, however, did not make things easy for Palladio; the plan had to incorporate at least two preexisting medieval houses, with irregularly shaped rooms, into his classical, harmonious plan, and to support the great hall of the *piano nobile* above the fragile walls of the original medieval structure. The wonder of it is that this palazzo is one of Palladio's most harmonious constructions; the viewer has little indication that this is actually a transformation of a medieval structure. The palazzo also contains a museum dedicated to Palladio and is the seat of a center for Palladian studies. ⊠ *Contra' Porti 11* ☎ *0444/323014* 💳 *€6; €15, includes Palazzo Chiericati and Teatro Olimpico, plus other museums in Musei Civici group* ⊗ *Closed Mon.*

Fodor'sChoice ★ **Teatro Olimpico.** Palladio's last, and perhaps most spectacular work, was begun in 1580 and completed in 1585, after his death, by Vincenzo Scamozzi (1552–1616). Based closely on the model of ancient Roman theaters, it represents an important development in theater and stage design and is noteworthy for its acoustics and the cunning use of perspective in Scamozzi's permanent backdrop. The anterooms are frescoed with images of important figures in Venetian history. One of the few Renaissance theaters still standing, it is used for concerts, operas, and other performances. ⊠ *Ticket office, Piazza Matteotti 12* ☎ *0444/222800* ⊕ *www.teatrolimpico.it* 💳 *€11; €15, includes Palazzo Chiericati and Palazzo Barbaran da Porto, plus other museums in Musei Civici group* ⊗ *Closed Mon.*

Fodor'sChoice ★ **Villa della Rotonda** (*Villa Almerico Capra*). This beautiful Palladian villa, commissioned in 1556 as a suburban residence for Paolo Almerico, is the purest expression of Palladio's architectural theory and aesthetic. More a villa-temple than a residence, it contradicts the rational utilitarianism of Renaissance architecture and demonstrates the priority Palladio gave to the architectural symbolism of celestial harmony over practical considerations. A visit to view the interior can be difficult to schedule—the villa remains privately owned—but this is a worthwhile stop, if only to see how Palladio's harmonious arrangement of smallish, interconnected rooms around a central domed space paid little attention to the practicalities of living. The interior decoration, mainly later Baroque stuccowork, contains some allegorical frescoes in the cupola by Palladio's contemporary, Alessando Maganza. Even without a peek inside, experiencing the exterior and the grounds is a must for any visit to Vicenza. The villa is a 20-minute walk from town or a short ride on Bus No. 8 from Vicenza's Piazza Roma. ⊠ *Via della Rotonda* ☎ *0444/321793* ⊕ *www.villalarotonda.it* 💳 *€10 villa and grounds, €5 grounds only.*

Fodor'sChoice ★ **Villa Valmarana ai Nani.** Inside this 17th- to 18th-century country house, named for the statues of dwarfs adorning the garden, is a series of frescoes executed in 1757 by Gianbattista Tiepolo depicting scenes from classical mythology, *The Iliad*, Tasso's *Gerusalemme Liberata*, and Ariosto's *Orlando Furioso*. They include his *Sacrifice of Iphigenia*, a major masterpiece of 18th-century painting. The neighboring *foresteria* (guesthouse) is also part of the museum; it contains frescoes showing 18th-century life at its most charming, and scenes of chinoiserie popular in the 18th century, by Tiepolo's son Giandomenico (1727–1804). The garden dwarfs are probably taken from designs by Giandomenico. You can reach the villa on foot by following the same path that leads to Palladio's Villa della Rotonda. ⊠ *Via dei Nani 2/8* ☎ *0444/321803* ⊕ *www.villavalmarana.com/en* 💳 *€10* ⊗ *Closed Mon.*

WORTH NOTING

Palazzo Chiericati. This imposing Palladian palazzo (1550) would be worthy of a visit even if it didn't house Vicenza's **Museo Civico.** Because of the ample space surrounding the building, Palladio combined elements of an urban palazzo with those he used in his country villas. The museum's important Venetian holdings include significant paintings by Cima, Tiepolo, Piazzetta, and Tintoretto, but its main attraction is an extensive collection of rarely found works by painters from the Vicenza area, among them Jacopo Bassano (1515–92) and the eccentric and innovative Francesco Maffei (1605–60), whose work foreshadowed important currents of Venetian painting of subsequent generations. ⊠ *Piazza Matteotti* ☎ *0444/325071* ✆ *€7; €15, includes Palazzo Barbaran da Porto and Teatro Olimpico, plus other museums in Musei Civici group* ✆ *Closed Mon.*

Piazza dei Signori. At the heart of Vicenza, this square contains the **Palazzo della Ragione** (1549), the project with which Palladio made his name by successfully modernizing a medieval building, grafting a graceful two-story exterior loggia onto the existing Gothic structure. Commonly known as Palladio's basilica, the palazzo served as a courthouse and public meeting hall (the original Roman meaning of the term *basilica*) and is now open only when it houses exhibits. The main point of interest, though, the loggia, is visible from the piazza. Take a look also at the **Loggia del Capitaniato,** opposite, which Palladio designed but never completed. ✉ *Vicenza.*

Santa Corona. An exceptionally fine *Baptism of Christ* (1502), a work of Giovanni Bellini's maturity, hangs over the altar on the left, just in front of the transept. The church also houses the elegantly simple Valmarana chapel, designed by Palladio. ✉ *Contrà S. Corona* ☎ *0444/222811* 🎟 *€3 (free with Musei Civici pass)* 🕒 *Closed Mon.*

WHERE TO EAT

$$ VENETIAN 🍴 **Antico Ristorante agli Schioppi.** When they want to eat well, Vicentini generally head to the countryside, so it is telling that this is one of the few restaurants in the city frequented by local families and the business community. Done in Veneto country style, with enormous murals, agli Schioppi serves simple, well-prepared regional cuisine with some modern touches. The risotto, delicately flavored with wild mushrooms and zucchini flowers, is creamy and beautifully textured—or try the Vicenza specialty, baccalà. The "Menu Palladiana" presents 16th-century dishes featuring spices common during that period, such as cinnamon and cloves, and omitting New World items like tomatoes and potatoes. [$] *Average main: €18* ✉ *Contrà Piazza del Castello 26* ☎ *0444/543701* 🕒 *Closed Mon. No dinner Sun.*

$ PIZZA 🍴 **Da Vittorio.** You'll find little in the way of atmosphere or style at this tiny, casual place, but Vicentini flock here for what may be the best pizza north of Naples. There's an incredible array of toppings, from the traditional to the exotic (mango), but the pizzas taste so authentic you may feel transported to the Bay of Naples. The service is friendly and efficient, and it's open late. ■ **TIP→ This is a good stop for lunch if you're walking to Palladio's Rotonda or the Villa Valmarana.** [$] *Average main: €12* ✉ *Borgo Berga 52* ☎ *0444/525059* 💳 *No credit cards* 🕒 *Closed Tues., and 2 wks in July.*

$$ NORTHERN ITALIAN 🍴 **Ponte delle Bele.** Many of Vicenza's wealthier residents spend at least part of the summer in the Alps to escape the heat, and the dishes of this popular and friendly trattoria reflect the Alpine influences on local cuisine. The house specialty, *stinco di maiale al forno* (roast pork shank), is wonderfully fragrant, with herbs and aromatic vegetables. Game dishes include venison with blueberries, and guinea fowl roasted with white grapes. The restaurant's also justly proud of its baccalà *alla vicentina* (in an onion, herb, and Parmesan sauce, served with polenta). Though a little kitschy, the interior doesn't detract from the good, hearty food. [$] *Average main: €22* ✉ *Contrà Ponte delle Bele 5* ☎ *0444/320647* 🌐 *www.pontedellebele.it* 🕒 *No dinner Sun. Closed 2 wks in Aug.*

$ ITALIAN 🍴 **Righetti.** For a city of its size, Vicenza has few outstanding restaurants. That's why many people gravitate to this popular cafeteria, which serves well-prepared classic dishes without putting a dent in your wallet. There's frequently a hearty soup such as *orzo e fagioli* (barley and bean) on the menu. The classic baccalà alla vicentina is a great reason to stop by on Tuesday or Friday. Righetti tends to be a bit crowded at lunch, so be patient. [$] *Average main: €12* ✉ *Piazza Duomo 3* ☎ *0444/543135* 💳 *No credit cards* 🕒 *Closed weekends, and 1 wk in Jan. and Aug.*

4

Palladio's Architecture

Wealthy 16th-century patrons commissioned Andrea Palladio to design villas that would reflect their sense of cultivation and status. Using a classical vocabulary of columns, arches, and domes, he gave them a series of masterpieces in the towns and hills of the Veneto that exemplify the neo-Platonic ideals of harmony and proportion. Palladio's creations are the perfect expression of how a learned 16th-century man saw himself and his world, and as you stroll through them today, their serene beauty is as powerful as ever. Listen closely and you might even hear that celestial harmony, the music of the spheres, that so moved Palladio and his patrons.

TOWN AND COUNTRY

Although the *villa*, or country residence, was still a relatively new phenomenon in the 16th century, it quickly became all the rage once the great lords of Venice turned their eyes from the sea toward the fertile plains of the Veneto. They were forced to do this once their trade routes had faltered when Ottoman Turks conquered Constantinople in 1456 and Columbus opened a path for Spain to the riches of America in 1492. In no time, canals were built, farms were laid out, and the fashion for *villeggiatura*—the attraction of idyllic country retreats for the nobility—became a favored lifestyle. As a means of escaping an overheated Rome, villas had been the original brainchild of the ancient emperors and it was no accident that the Venetian lords wished to emulate this palatial style of country residence. Palladio's method of evaluating the standards, and standbys, of ancient Roman life through the eye of the

Italian Renaissance, combined with his innate sense of proportion and symmetry, became the lasting foundation of his art. In turn, Palladio threw out the jambalaya of styles prevalent in Venetian architecture—Byzantine, Gothic, and Renaissance—for the pure, noble lines found in the buildings of the Caesars.

ANDREA PALLADIO (1508–80)

"Face dark, eyes fiery. Dress rich. His appearance that of a genius." So was Palladio described by his wealthy mentor, Count Trissino. Trissino encouraged the young student to trade in his birth name, Andrea di Pietro della Gondola, for the elegant Palladio. He did, and it proved a wise move indeed. Born in Padua in 1508, Andrea moved to nearby Vicenza in 1524 and was quickly taken up by the city's power elite. He experienced a profound revelation on his first trip, in 1541, to Rome, where he sensed the harmony of the ancient ruins and saw the elements of classicism that were working their way into contemporary architecture. This experience led to his spectacular conversion of the Vicenza's Palazzo della Ragione into a Roman basilica, recalling the great meeting halls of antiquity. In years to come, after relocating to Venice, he created some memorable churches, such as S. Giorgio Maggiore (1564). Despite these varied projects, Palladio's unassailable position as one of the world's greatest architects is tied to the countryside villas, which he spread across the Veneto plains like a firmament of stars. Nothing else in the Veneto illuminates more clearly the idyllic beauty of the region than these elegant residences, their stonework now nicely mellowed and suntanned after five centuries.

4

VICENZIA

To see Palladio's pageant of palaces, head for Vicenza. His Palazzo della Ragione marks the city's heart, the Piazza dei Signori. This building rocketed young Palladio from an unknown to an architectural star. Across the way is his redbrick Loggia dei Capitaniato. One block past the Loggia is Vicenza's main street, appropriately named Corso Andrea Palladio. Just off this street is the Contrà Porti, where you'll find the Palazzo Barbaran da Porto (1570) at No. 11, with its fabulously rich facade erupting with Ionic and Corinthian pillars. Today, this is the Centro Internazionale di Studi di Architettura Andrea Palladio (⊕ *www. cisapalladio. org*), a study center which mounts impressive temporary exhibitions. A few steps away, on the Contrà San Gaetano Thiene, is the Palazzo Thiene (1542–58), designed by Giulio Romano and completed by Palladio. Doubling back to Contrà Porti 21, you find the Palazzo Iseppo da Porto (1544), the first palazzo where you can see the neoclassical effects of young Palladio's trip to Rome. Following the Contrà Reale, you come to Corso Fogazzaro 16 and the Palazzo Valmarana Braga (1565). Its gigantic pilasters were a first for domestic architecture. Returning to the Corso Palladio, head left to the opposite end of the Corso, about five blocks, to the Piazza Mattoti and Palazzo Chiericati (1550). This was practically a suburban area in the 16th century, and for the palazzo Palladio combined elements of urban and rural design. The pedestal raising the building and the steps leading to the entrance—unknown in urban palaces—were to protect from floods and to keep cows from

wandering in the front door. Across the Corso Palladio is Palladio's last and one of his most spectacular works, the Teatro Olimpico (1580). By careful study of ancient ruins and architectural texts, he reconstructed a Roman theater with archaeological precision. Palladio died before it was completed, but he left clear plans for the project. Although it's on the outskirts of town, the Villa Almerico Capra, better known as La Rotonda (1566), is an indispensable part of any visit to Vicenza. It's the iconic Palladian building, the purest expression of his aesthetic.

PALLADIO COUNTRY

At the Villa Barbaro (1554) near the town of Maser in the province of Treviso, 48 km (30 miles) northeast of Vicenza, you can see the results of a onetime collaboration between two of the greatest artists of their age. Palladio was the architect, and Paolo Veronese decorated the interior with an amazing cycle of trompe-l'oeil frescoes—walls dissolve into landscapes, and illusions of courtiers and servants enter rooms and smile down from balustrades. Legend has it a feud developed between Palladio and Veronese, with Palladio feeling the illusionistic frescoes detracted from his architecture; but there is practically nothing to support the idea of such a rift. It's also noteworthy that Palladio for the first time connected the two lateral granaries to the main villa. This was a working farm, and Palladio thus created an architectural unity by connecting with graceful arcades the working parts of the estate to the living quarters, bringing together the Renaissance dichotomy of the active and the contemplative life.

WHERE TO STAY

During annual gold fairs in January, May, and September, it may be quite difficult to find lodging. If you're coming then, be sure to reserve well in advance and expect to pay higher rates.

$$ HOTEL **Campo Marzio.** Rooms at this comfortable, full-service hotel, a five-minute walk from the train station and right in front of the city walls, are ample and furnished in various styles, from modern to traditional and romantic. **Pros:** central; more amenities than its competitors; set back from the street, so it's quiet and bright; free Wi-Fi in rooms. **Cons:** public spaces are uninspiring; expensive during fairs. [$] *Rooms from: €125* ✉ *Viale Roma 21* ☎ *0444/5457000* 🌐 *www.hotelcampomarzio.com* 🛏 *36 rooms* 🍴 *Breakfast.*

$ HOTEL Fodor's Choice ★ **Due Mori.** Rooms at one of the oldest (1883) hotels in the city, just off the Piazza dei Signori, are filled with turn-of-the-20th-century antiques, and regulars favor the place because the high ceilings in the main building make it feel light and airy. **Pros:** comfortable, tastefully furnished rooms; friendly staff; central location; rate same year-round; free Wi-Fi. **Cons:** no a/c (although ceiling fans minimize the need for it); no help with baggage; no TVs. [$] *Rooms from: €90* ✉ *Contrà Do Rode 24* ☎ *0444/321886* 🌐 *www.hotelduemori.com* ⏲ *Closed 1st 2 wks in Aug., 2 wks in late Dec.* 🛏 *53 rooms* 🍴 *No meals.*

VERONA

On the banks of the fast-flowing River Adige, enchanting Verona, 60 km (37 miles) west of Vicenza, has timeless monuments, a picturesque town center, fascinating museums, and a romantic reputation as the setting of Shakespeare's *Romeo and Juliet.* Verona grew to power and prosperity within the Roman Empire as a result of its key commercial and military position in northern Italy. With its Roman arena, theater, and city gates, it has the most significant monuments of Roman antiquity north of Rome. After the fall of the empire, the city continued to flourish under the guidance of barbarian kings such as Theodoric, Alboin, Pepin, and Berenger I. It reached its cultural and artistic peak in the 13th and 14th centuries under the della Scala (Scaligeri) dynasty. (Look for the *scala,* or ladder, emblem all over town.) In 1404 Verona traded its independence for security and placed itself under the control of Venice. (The other recurring architectural motif is the lion of St. Mark, a symbol of Venetian rule.)

With its lively Venetian air and proximity to Lake Garda, Verona attracts many tourists, especially Germans and Austrians. Tourism peaks during summer's renowned season of open-air opera in the arena and during spring's Vinitaly, one of the world's most important wine and spirits expos.

If you're going to visit more than one or two sights, it's worth purchasing a VeronaCard, available at museums, churches, and tobacconists for €15 (for 24 hours) or €20 (72 hours). It buys a single admission to most of the city's significant museums and churches, plus you can ride for free on city buses. If you're mostly interested in churches, a €6 Chiese Vive Card is sold at Verona's major houses of worship and gains you entry to the Duomo, San Fermo Maggiore, San Zeno Maggiore, and Sant'Anastasia (all also covered also by the VeronaCard). Verona's churches enforce a dress code: no sleeveless shirts, shorts, or short skirts.

GETTING HERE AND AROUND

Verona is midway between Venice and Milan. Its small Aeroporto Valerio Catullo accommodates domestic and European flights, though many travelers fly into Venice or Milan and drive or take the train to Verona. Several trains per hour depart from any point on the Milan–Venice line. By car, from the east or west, take the Autostrada Trieste–Torino (A4/E70) to the SS12 and follow it north into town. From the north or south, take the Autostrada del Brennero (A22/E45) to the SR11 East (initially, called the Strada Bresciana) directly into town.

VISITOR INFORMATION

VeronaCard. ⊠ *Verona* ⊕ *www.turismoverona.eu.*

Verona Tourism Office (IAT Verona). ⊠ *Via degli Alpini 9, Piazza Bra* ⊕ *www.tourism.verona.it.*

EXPLORING

TOP ATTRACTIONS

Fodor's Choice ★ **Arco dei Gavi.** This stunning structure is simpler and less imposing, but also more graceful, than the triumphal arches in Rome. Built in the 1st century AD by the architect Lucius Vitruvius Cerdo to celebrate the accomplishments of the patrician Gavia family, it was highly esteemed by several Renaissance architects, including Palladio. ⊠ *Corso Cavour.*

FAMILY **Arena di Verona.** Only Rome's Colosseum and Capua's arena would dwarf this amphitheater, built for gymnastic competitions, choreographed sacrificial rites, and games involving hunts, fights, battles, and wild animals. Although four arches are all that remain of the arena's outer arcade, the main structure is complete and dates from AD 30. In summer, you can join up to 16,000 people packing the stands for spectacular opera productions. Even those not crazy about opera can sit in the stands and enjoy Italians enjoying themselves—including, at times, singing along with their favorite hits. ■TIP➔ The opera's the main thing here: when there is no opera performance, you can still enter the interior, but the arena is less impressive inside than the Colosseum or other Roman amphitheaters. ⊠ *Piazza Bra 5* ☎ *045/596517* ⊕ *www.arena.it* 🖃 *€10 (free with VeronaCard).*

Fodor's Choice ★ **Castelvecchio.** This crenellated, russet brick building with massive walls, towers, turrets, and a vast courtyard was built for Cangrande II della Scala in 1354 and presides over a street lined with attractive old buildings and palaces of the nobility. Only by going inside the **Museo di Castelvecchio** can you really appreciate this massive castle complex with its vaulted halls. You also get a look at a significant collection of Venetian and Veneto art, medieval weapons, and jewelry. The interior of the castle was restored and redesigned as a museum between 1958 and 1975 by Carlo Scarpa, one of Italy's most accomplished architects. Behind the castle is the Ponte Scaligero (1355), which spans the River Adige. ⊠ *Corso Castelvecchio 2* ☎ *045/8062611* 🖃 *€6 (free with VeronaCard).*

Duomo. The present church was begun in the 12th century in the Romanesque style; its later additions are mostly Gothic. On pilasters guarding the main entrance are 12th-century carvings thought to represent Oliver and Roland, two of Charlemagne's knights and heroes of several medieval epic poems. Inside, Titian's *Assumption* (1532) graces the first chapel on the left. ⊠ *Via Duomo* ☎ *045/595627* ⊕ *www.chieseverona. it* ⌧ *€2.50 (free with Chiese Vive or VeronaCard).*

Piazza delle Erbe. Frescoed buildings surround this medieval square, where a busy Roman forum once stood. During the week it's still bustling, as vendors sell produce and trinkets, much as they have been doing for generations. Relax at one of the cafés and take in the lively scene. ⊠ *Verona.*

Fodor's Choice   **Porta dei Borsari.** As its elegant decoration suggests, this is the main ★   entrance to ancient Verona, and, in its present state, dates from the 1st century AD. It's at the beginning of Corso Porta Borsari, just a few steps from Piazza della Erbe. ⊠ *Corso Porta Borsari.*

Porta dei Leoni. The oldest of Verona's elegant and graceful Roman portals, the Porta dei Leoni (on Via Leoni, just a few steps from Piazza delle Erbe), dates from the 1st century BC, but its original earth-and-brick structure was sheathed in local marble during early Imperial times. Like the city's other Roman structures, the gate gives us an idea of the high aesthetic standards of the time. ⊠ *Via Leoni.*

Fodor's Choice   **San Zeno Maggiore.** One of Italy's finest Romanesque churches is filled ★   with treasures. A rose window by the 13th-century sculptor Brioloto represents a wheel of fortune, with six of the spokes formed by statues depicting the rising and falling fortunes of mankind. The 12th-century porch is the work of Maestro Niccolò; it's flanked by marble reliefs by Niccolò and Maestro Guglielmo depicting scenes from the Old and New Testaments and from the legend of Theodoric. The bronze doors date from the 11th and 12th centuries; some were probably imported from Saxony and some are from Veronese workshops. They combine allegorical representations with scenes from the lives of saints. Inside, look for the 12th-century statue of San Zeno to the left of the main altar. In modern times it has been dubbed the "Laughing San Zeno" because of a misinterpretation of its conventional Romanesque grin. A justly famous *Madonna and Saints* triptych by Andrea Mantegna (1431–1506) hangs over the main altar, and a peaceful cloister (1120–38) lies to the left of the nave. The detached bell tower was begun in 1045, before the construction of much of the present church, and finished in 1173. ⊠ *Piazza San Zeno* ☎ *045/592813* ⊕ *www.chieseverona.it* ⌧ *€2.50 (free with Chiese Vive or VeronaCard).*

Sant'Anastasia. Verona's largest church, begun in 1290 but only consecrated in 1471, is a fine example of Gothic brickwork and has a grand doorway with elaborately carved biblical scenes. The main reason for visiting this church, however, is *St. George and the Princess* (dated 1434, but perhaps earlier) by Pisanello (1377–1455). It's above the Pellegrini Chapel off the main altar. As you come in, look also for the *gobbi* (hunchbacks) supporting the holy-water basins. ⊠ *Vicolo Sotto Riva 4* ☎ *045/8004925* ⌧ *€2.50 (free with Chiese Vive or VeronaCard).*

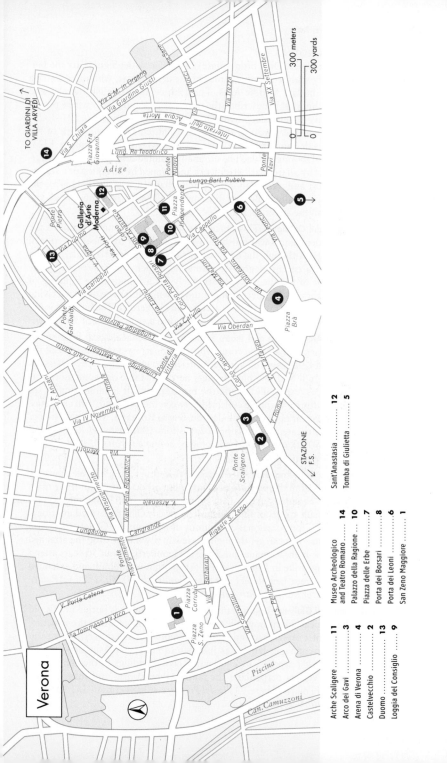

Verona

Arche Scaligere **11**
Arco dei Gavi **3**
Arena di Verona **4**
Castelvecchio **2**
Duomo **13**
Loggia del Consiglio **9**

Museo Archeologico
and Teatro Romano **10**
Palazzo della Ragione ... **10**
Piazza delle Erbe **7**
Porta dei Borsari **8**
Porta dei Leoni **6**
San Zeno Maggiore **1**

Sant'Anastasia **12**
Tomba di Giulietta **5**

WORTH NOTING

Arche Scaligere. On a little square off the Piazza dei Signori are the fantastically sculpted Gothic tombs of the della Scalas, who ruled Verona during the late Middle Ages. The 19th-century English traveler and critic John Ruskin described the tombs as graceful places where people who have fallen asleep live. The tomb of Cangrande I (1291–1329) hangs over the portal of the adjacent church and is the work of the Maestro di Sant'Anastasia. The tomb of Mastino II, begun in 1345, has an elaborate baldachin, originally painted and gilded, and is surrounded by an iron grillwork fence and topped by an equestrian statue. The latest and most elaborate tomb is that of Cansignorio (1375), the work principally of Bonino di Campione. The major tombs are all visible from the street. ✉ *Via Arche Scaligere.*

Loggia del Consiglio. This graceful structure on the north flank of the Piazza dei Signori was finished in 1492 and built to house city council meetings. Although the city was already under Venetian rule, Verona still had a certain degree of autonomy, which was expressed by the splendor of the loggia. Very strangely for a Renaissance building of this quality, its architect remains unknown, but it's the finest surviving example of late-15th-century architecture in Verona. The building is not open to the public, but the exterior is worth a visit. ✉ *Piazza dei Signori.*

Museo Archeologico and Teatro Romano. The archaeological holdings of this museum in a 15th-century former monastery consist largely of the donated collections of Veronese citizens proud of their city's classical past. You'll find few blockbusters here, but there are some noteworthy pieces (especially among the bronzes), and it is interesting to see what cultured Veronese collected between the 17th and 19th centuries. The museum complex includes the Teatro Romano, Verona's 1st-century-AD theater, which is open to visitors. ✉ *Rigaste del Redentore 2* ☎ *045/8000360* ⊕ *museoarcheologico.comune.verona.it* ✍ *€4.50 (free with VeronaCard).*

Palazzo della Ragione. An elegant 15th-century pink marble staircase leads up from the *mercato vecchio* (old market) courtyard to the magistrates' chambers in this 12th-century palace, built at the intersection of the main streets of the ancient Roman city. The renovated interior is now used for occasional exhibitions of art from the Galleria dell'Arte Moderna. You can get the highest view in town from atop the attached 270-foot-high, Romanesque Torre dei Lamberti. About 50 years after a lightning strike in 1403 knocked its top off, it was rebuilt and extended to its current height. ✉ *Piazza dei Signori* ☎ *045/8032726* ✍ *Palace free, tower €6 (free with VeronaCard).*

OFF THE BEATEN PATH

Tomba di Giulietta. If you want to believe that Juliet is buried in this old chapel near the river, you'll have to put aside the fact that the structure is a former orphanage and Franciscan monastery. In the crypt there's an open sarcophagus labeled as Juliet's tomb that was fashioned in 1937 for tourist purposes; by conducting civil weddings in the chapel, the city of Verona perpetuates the fantasy that Romeo and Juliet existed and were married here. ✉ *Via del Pontiere 35* ☎ *045/8000361* ✍ *€4.50 (free with VeronaCard).*

WHERE TO EAT

$$ NORTHERN ITALIAN Fodor's Choice ★ 🍴 **Antica Osteria al Duomo.** This side-street eatery, lined with old wood paneling and decked out with musical instruments, serves Veronese food to a Veronese crowd; they come for the local wine and to savor excellent versions of local dishes such as *bigoli con sugo di asino* (thick whole-wheat spaghetti with sauce made from donkey meat) and *pastissada con polenta* (horsemeat stew with polenta). Don't be deterred by the unconventional meats—they're tender and delicious, and this is probably the best place in town to sample them. This first-rate home cooking is reasonably priced and served by helpful, efficient staff. It's popular, so arrive early. Reservations are not always taken. [$] *Average main: €18* ✉ *Via Duomo 7/A* ☎ *045/8004505* 🕑 *Closed Sun. (except in Dec. and during wine fair).*

4

$$$$ MODERN ITALIAN Fodor's Choice ★ 🍴 **Il Desco.** *Cucina dell'anima*—food of the soul—is how chef Elia Rizzo describes his cuisine. True to Italian culinary traditions, he preserves natural flavors through quick cooking and selective ingredients, but tradition gives way to invention, even daring, in the combination of ingredients in dishes such as dumplings with cod tripe and black olives. Some find Rizzo's creative combinations, such as adding truffles to a fish fillet, difficult to fathom. For an extravagant gastronomic adventure, try the multicourse tasting menu (€150 per person, not including wine), or the limited pre-opera tasting menu at €100. Il Desco's interior is elegant, if overdone, with tapestries, paintings, and an impressive 16th-century lacunar ceiling. The service, though efficient, is not exactly friendly. [$] *Average main: €45* ✉ *Via Dietro San Sebastiano 7* ☎ *045/595358* 🌐 *www.ristoranteildesco.it* 🕑 *Closed Sun. and Mon. (but open for dinner Mon. in July, Aug., and Dec.), and 2 wks in June.*

$$$ MODERN ITALIAN 🍴 **Ostaria La Fontanina.** Veronese come to this restaurant on a quiet street in one of the oldest sections of town to enjoy a sumptuous meal under vine-covered balconies. The Tapparini family takes great pride in the kitchen's modern variations on traditional dishes. Risotto *al Amarone* is made with Verona's treasured red wine, and there's an excellent baccalà, a staple of Veneto cuisine. The service does not always merit the 10% charge automatically added to the bill. [$] *Average main: €25* ✉ *Portichiette fontanelle S. Stefano 3* ☎ *045/913305* 🌐 *www.ristorantelafontanina.com* 🕑 *Closed Sun., 1 wk in Jan., and 2 wks in Aug. No lunch Mon.*

$$$ NORTHERN ITALIAN 🍴 **Ristorante 12 Apostoli.** In a city where many high-end restaurants tend toward nouvelle cuisine, this is an exceptional place to enjoy classic dishes made with elegant variations on traditional recipes. Near Piazza delle Erbe, it stands on the foundations of a Roman temple. Specialties include gnocchi *di zucca e ricotta* (with squash and ricotta cheese) and *vitello alla Lessinia* (veal with mushrooms, cheese, and truffles) and a signature pasta e fagioli. [$] *Average main: €30* ✉ *Vicolo Corticella San Marco 3* ☎ *045/596999* 🌐 *www.12apostoli.com* 🕑 *Closed Mon., 2 wks in Jan., and 2 wks in June. No dinner Sun.*

WHERE TO STAY

$$ HOTEL 🏨 **Armando.** In a residential area a few minutes' walk from the Arena, this contemporary Best Western hotel offers respite from the busy city as well as easier parking. **Pros:** large rooms for Italy; central location; helpful staff; good breakfast; free Wi-Fi. **Cons:** no parking valet;

simple room decor. $ *Rooms from: €125* ⊠ *Via Dietro Pallone 1* ☎ *045/8000206* ⊕ *www.hotelarmando.it* ⊙ *Closed 2 wks late Dec.– early Jan.* ⤵ *19 rooms* ⑩ *Breakfast.*

$$$$ ⊞ **Gabbia d'Oro.** Occupying a historic building off Piazza delle Erbe
HOTEL in the ancient heart of Verona, this hotel is a romantic fantasia of ornamentation, rich fabrics, and period-style furniture. **Pros:** central location; great breakfast; romantic atmosphere. **Cons:** some very small rooms, especially considering the price; small bathrooms; some guests may find the decor overly ornate, even stuffy. $ *Rooms from: €350* ⊠ *Corso Porta Borsari 4/a* ☎ *045/8003060* ⊕ *www.hotelgabbiadoro.it* ⤵ *8 rooms, 19 suites* ⑩ *Breakfast.*

$$ ⊞ **Hotel Accademia.** The exterior columns and arches of this hotel in
HOTEL old Verona hint at what guests discover inside: elegance, gracious service, and comfortable, traditional furnishings. **Pros:** central location; old-world charm; up-to-date. **Cons:** expensive parking; prices increase greatly during summer opera season and trade fairs. $ *Rooms from: €180* ⊠ *Via Scala 12* ☎ *045/596222* ⊕ *www.accademiavr.it* ⤵ *93 rooms* ⑩ *Breakfast.*

$$$ ⊞ **Palazzo Victoria.** Business types and tourists experience tasteful luxury
HOTEL at the Victoria, whose rooms blend traditional and contemporary style. **Pros:** quiet and tasteful rooms; central location near the Piazza delle Erbe; good business center. **Cons:** no views; expensive parking (and rates); staff not particularly helpful. $ *Rooms from: €300* ⊠ *Via Adua 8* ☎ *045/5905664* ⊕ *www.palazzovictoria.com* ⤵ *71 rooms* ⑩ *No meals.*

$ ⊞ **Torcolo.** In addition to a central location close to the arena and Piazza
HOTEL Bra, you can count on this budget choice for a warm welcome, helpful service, and pleasant rooms with late-19th-century furniture. **Pros:** nice rooms; staff give reliable advice. **Cons:** some street noise; showers but no tubs; pricey parking. $ *Rooms from: €95* ⊠ *Vicolo Listone 3* ☎ *045/8007512* ⊕ *www.hoteltorcolo.it* ⊙ *Closed 2 wks in Jan. and Feb.* ⤵ *19 rooms* ⑩ *No meals.*

PERFORMING ARTS

Fodor's Choice **Arena di Verona.** Milan's La Scala and Parma's Teatro Regio offer per-
★ formances more likely to attract serious opera fans, but neither offers a greater spectacle than the Arena di Verona. Many Italian opera lovers claim their enthusiasm began when they were taken as children to a production at the arena. During the venue's summer season (July to September) as many as 16,000 attendees sit on the original stone terraces or in modern cushioned stalls. Most of the operas presented are the big, splashy ones, like *Aida* or *Turandot,* which demand huge choruses, lots of color and movement, and, if possible, camels, horses, or elephants. Order tickets by phone or through the Arena website: if you book a spot on the cheaper terraces, be sure to take or rent a cushion—four hours on a 2,000-year-old stone bench can be an ordeal. ⊠ *Box office, Via Dietro Anfiteatro 6/b* ☎ *045/8005151* ⊕ *www.arena.it* ⊠ *From €20 (for unnumbered, open seating).*

MILAN

Milan is Italy's business hub and crucible of chic. Between the Po's rich farms and the industrious mountain valleys, it's long been the country's capital of commerce, finance, fashion, and media. Rome may be bigger and have the political power, but Milan and the affluent north are what really make the country go. It's also Italy's transport hub, with the biggest international airport, the most rail connections, and the best subway system. Leonardo da Vinci's *Last Supper* and other great works of art are here, as well as a spectacular Gothic Duomo, the finest of its kind. Milan even reigns supreme where it really counts (in the minds of many Italians), routinely trouncing the rest of the nation with its two premier soccer teams.

And yet, Milan hasn't won the battle for hearts and minds when it comes to tourism. Most visitors prefer Tuscany's hills and Venice's canals to Milan's hectic efficiency and wealthy indifference, and it's no surprise that in a country of medieval hilltop villages and skilled artisans a city of grand boulevards and global corporations leaves visitors asking the real Italy to please stand up. They're right, of course: Milan is more European than Italian, a new buckle on an old boot, and although its old city can stand cobblestone for cobblestone against the best of them, seekers of Roman ruins and fairy-tale towns may pass. But Milan's secrets reveal themselves slowly to those who look. A side street conceals a garden complete with flamingos (Giardini Invernizzi, on Via dei Cappuccini, just off Corso Venezia; closed to the public, but you can still catch a glimpse), and a renowned 20th-century art collection hides modestly behind an unspectacular facade a block from Corso Buenos Aires (the Casa-Museo Boschi di Stefano). Visitors lured by the world-class shopping will appreciate Milan's European sophistication while discovering unexpected facets of a country they may have only thought they knew.

Virtually every invader in European history—Gaul, Roman, Goth, Lombard, and Frank—as well as a long series of rulers from France, Spain, and Austria, took a turn at ruling the city. After being completely sacked by the Goths in AD 539 and by the Holy Roman Empire under Frederick Barbarossa in 1157, Milan became one of the first independent city-states of the Renaissance. Its heyday of self-rule proved comparatively brief. From 1277 until 1500 it was ruled first by the Visconti and then the Sforza dynasties. These families were known, justly or not, for a peculiarly aristocratic mixture of refinement, classical learning, and cruelty; much of the surviving grandeur of Gothic and Renaissance art and architecture is their doing. Be on the lookout in your wanderings for the Visconti family emblem—a viper, its jaws straining wide, devouring a child.

GETTING HERE AND AROUND

The city center is compact and walkable; trolleys and trams make it even more accessible, and the efficient Metropolitana (subway) and buses provide access to locations farther afield. Driving in Milan is difficult and parking a real pain, so a car is a liability. In addition, drivers within the second ring of streets (the *bastioni*) must pay a daily congestion charge on weekdays between 7:30 am and 7:30 pm (till 6 pm on Thursday). You can pay the charge at news vendors, tobacconists, Banca Intesa Sanpaolo ATMs, or online at ⊕ *areac.atm-mi.it*; parking meters and parking garages in the area also include it in the cost.

BICYCLE TRAVEL

BikeMI. This innovative sharing system has hundreds of designated spots for picking up or dropping off both traditional and electric bicycles around the city. Weekly and daily rates for tourists are available. Buy your subscription by phone or online; the site has a map showing stations and availability. Keep in mind, though, that traffic makes biking in the city risky for inexperienced cyclists, and be careful not to get your tires caught on the tram tracks. ☎ *02/48607607* ⊕ *www.bikemi.com.*

PUBLIC TRANSPORTATION

A standard public transit ticket costs €1.50 and is valid for a 90-minute trip on a subway, bus, or tram. An all-inclusive subway, bus, and tram pass costs €4.50 for 24 hours or €8.25 for 48 hours. Individual tickets and passes can be purchased from news vendors, tobacconists, at ticket machines at all subway stops, at ticket offices at the Duomo and other subway stops, and on your phone via the ATM Milano app. Another option is a *carnet* (€13.80), good for 10 tram or subway rides, or a *B14 4-journey integrated ticket* (€6), good for four rides. Once you have your ticket or pass, either stamp it or insert it into the slots in station turnstiles or on poles inside trolleys and buses. (The electronic tickets won't function if they become bent or demagnetized. If you have a problem, contact a station manager, who can usually issue a new ticket.) Trains run from 6 am to 12:30 am.

ATM (*Azienda Trasporti Milanesi*). Milan's transit authority has information offices at the Duomo, Stazione Cadorna, Stazione Centrale, Garibaldi, Loreto, and Romolo stops. ☎ *02/48607607* ⊕ *www.atm-mi.it/en.*

Radiobus. From 10 pm to 2 am, Radiobus will pick you up at Milan transit stations and drop you off at your destination in the neighborhood; you can use your public transit pass, or purchase a ticket online for €1.50. Advance booking is recommended, starting at 1 pm for same-day travel. ☎ *02/48034803* ⊕ *www.atm-mi.it/en.*

TAXI TRAVEL

Taxi fares in Milan are higher than in American cities; a short ride can run about €15 during rush hour or during fashion week. You can get a taxi at a stand with an orange "Taxi" sign, or by calling one of the taxi companies. Most also have apps you can download to order taxis from your phone; some let you text or use WhatsApp to hail a cab.

Dispatchers may speak some English; they'll ask for the phone number you're calling from, and they'll tell you the number of your taxi and how long it'll take to arrive. If you're in a restaurant or bar, ask the staff to call a cab for you.

Taxi Contacts **Autoradiotaxi.** ☎ *02/8585* ⊕ *www.028585.it.* **Radio Taxi Freccia.** ☎ *02/4000* ⊕ *www.024000.it.* **Taxiblu.** ☎ *02/4040* ⊕ *www.taxiblu.it.* **Yellow Taxi.** ☎ *02/6969* ⊕ *www.026969.it.*

TOURS

City Sightseeing Milano. Open-top double-decker buses provide hop-on, hop-off tours on three routes departing from Piazza Castello. An all-inclusive day pass costs €22. ☎ 02/867131 ⊕ *www.milano.city-sightseeing.it.*

VISITOR INFORMATION

Milan Tourism Office. The tourism office in Galleria Vittorio Emanuele II is the perfect place to begin your visit. There are excellent maps, booklets with museum descriptions, itineraries on a variety of themes, and a selection of brochures about smaller museums and cultural initiatives. ✉ *Galleria Vittorio Emanuele II, Piazza del Duomo, corner of Piazza della Scala, Duomo* ☎ 02/884555555 ⊕ *www.turismo.milano.it.*

EXPLORING

DUOMO

Milan's main streets radiate out from the massive Duomo, a late-Gothic cathedral begun in 1386. Heading north is the handsome Galleria Vittorio Emanuele, an enclosed shopping arcade that opens at one end to the world-famous opera house known as La Scala. Heading northeast from La Scala is Via Manzoni, which leads to the Quadrilatero della Moda, or fashion district.

Heading northeast from the Duomo is the pedestrians-only street Corso Vittorio Emanuele. Northwest of the Duomo is Via Dante, at the top of which is the imposing outline of the Castello Sforzesco.

TOP ATTRACTIONS

Fodor'sChoice ★ **Duomo.** There is no denying that for sheer size and complexity, the Duomo is unrivaled in Italy. It is the second-largest church in the country—the largest being St. Peter's in Rome—and the fifth largest in the world. This intricate Gothic structure has been fascinating and exasperating visitors and conquerors alike since it was begun by Galeazzo Visconti III (1351–1402), first duke of Milan, in 1386. Consecrated in the 15th or 16th century, it was not completed until just before the coronation of Napoléon as king of Italy in 1809. Although the capacity is estimated to be 40,000, it is usually empty, a sanctuary from the frenetic pace of life outside and the perfect place for solitary contemplation.

The building is adorned with 135 marble spires and 2,245 marble statues. The oldest part is the apse. Its three colossal bays of curving and counter-curved tracery, especially the bay adorning the exterior of the stained-glass windows, should not be missed. At the end of the southern transept down the right aisle lies the **tomb of Gian Giacomo Medici.** The tomb owes some of its design to Michelangelo but was executed by Leone Leoni (1509–90) and is generally considered to be his masterpiece; it dates from the 1560s. Directly ahead is the Duomo's most famous sculpture, the gruesome but anatomically instructive figure of San Bartolomeo (St. Bartholomew), who was flayed alive. As you enter the apse to admire those splendid windows, glance at the sacristy doors to the right and left of the altar. The lunette on the right dates from 1393 and was decorated by Hans von Fernach. The one on the left also dates from the 14th century and is ascribed jointly to Giacomo da Campione and Giovanni dei Grassi.

The roof is worth a look: walk out the left (north) transept to the stairs and elevator. As you stand among the forest of marble pinnacles, remember that virtually every inch of this gargantuan edifice, including the roof itself, is decorated with precious white marble dragged from quarries near Lake Maggiore by Duke Visconti's team along road laid fresh for the purpose and through the newly dredged canals. Exhibits at the **Museo del Duomo** shed light on the cathedral's history and include some of the treasures removed from the exterior for preservation purposes, while the early Christian **Bapistry of St. John** can be seen in the **archaeological area** underneath the cathedral. ⊠ *Piazza del Duomo, Duomo* ☎ *02/72022656* ⊕ *www.duomomilano.it* ✐ *Cathedral and museum €2 (€6 with archaeological area), stairs to roof €9, elevator €13* Ⓜ *Duomo.*

Fodor'sChoice ★ **Galleria Vittorio Emanuele II.** This spectacular, late-19th-century, Belle Époque tunnel is essentially one of the planet's earliest and most select shopping malls, with upscale tenants that include Gucci, Prada, Versace, and Louis Vuitton. This is the city's heart, midway between the Duomo and La Scala. It teems with life, inviting people-watching from the tables that spill from the bars and restaurants, where you can enjoy an overpriced coffee. Books, clothing, food, hats, and jewelry are all for sale. Known as Milan's "parlor," the Galleria is often viewed as a barometer of the city's well-being. The historic, if somewhat overpriced and inconsistent, Savini restaurant hosts the beautiful and powerful of the city, just across from McDonald's. Even in poor weather the great glass dome above the octagonal center is a splendid sight. The paintings at the base of the dome represent Europe, Asia, Africa, and America. Those at the entrance arch are devoted to science, industry, art, and agriculture. And the floor mosaics are a vastly underrated source of pleasure, even if they are not to be taken too seriously. Be sure to follow tradition and spin your heels once or twice on the more "delicate" parts of the bull beneath your feet in the northern apse; the Milanese believe it brings good luck. ⊠ *Piazza del Duomo, Duomo* Ⓜ *Duomo.*

QUICK BITES

Camparino in Galleria. One thing has remained constant in the Galleria: the Camparino, formerly known as Caffè Zucca. Its inlaid counter, mosaics, and wrought-iron fixtures have been welcoming tired shoppers since 1867. Enjoy a Campari aperitif as well as the entire range of Italian coffees, served either in the Galleria or in an elegant upstairs room where lunch is also available. ⊠ *Galleria Vittorio Emanuele, Duomo* ☎ *02/86464435* ⊕ *www.camparino.it* ⊗ *Closed Mon.*

Fodor'sChoice ★ **Palazzo Reale.** This elaborately decorated former royal palace close to the Duomo with painted ceilings and grand staircases is almost worth a visit in itself, but it also functions as one of Milan's major art exhibition spaces, with a focus on modern artists. Recent exhibits have highlighted works by Chagall, Escher, Warhol, Pollock, and Kandinsky. Check the website before you visit to see what's on; purchase tickets online in advance to save time in the queues, which are often long and chaotic. ⊠ *Piazza Duomo 12, Duomo* ☎ *02/8929711* ⊕ *www.artpalazzoreale. it* ✐ *€12 for exhibitions* Ⓜ *Duomo.*

Pinacoteca Ambrosiana. Cardinal Federico Borromeo, one of Milan's native saints, founded this picture gallery in 1618 with the addition of his personal art collection to a bequest of books to Italy's first public library. The core works of the collection include such treasures as Cara-vaggio's *Basket of Fruit,* Raphael's monumental preparatory drawing (known as a "cartoon") for *The School of Athens,* which hangs in the Vatican, and Leonardo da Vinci's *Portrait of a Musician.* The highlight for many is Leonardo's *Codex Atlanticus,* which features thousands of his sketches and drawings. In addition to works by Lombard artists are paintings by Botticelli, Luini, Titian, and Jan Brueghel. A wealth of charmingly idiosyncratic items on display include 18th-century scientific instruments and gloves worn by Napoléon at Waterloo. Access to the library, the Biblioteca Ambrosiana, is limited to researchers who apply for entrance tickets. ⊠ *Piazza Pio XI 2, Duomo* ☎ *02/806921* ⊕ *www. leonardo-ambrosiana.it* 🎫 *€15* ⊙ *Closed Mon.* Ⓜ *Duomo.*

WORTH NOTING

Battistero Paleocristiano/Baptistry of San Giovanni alle Fonti. More spe-cifically known as the Baptistry of San Giovanni alle Fonti, this 4th-century baptistry is one of two that lie beneath the Duomo. Although opinion remains divided, it is widely believed to be where Ambrose, Milan's first bishop and patron saint, baptized Augustine. Tickets also include a visit to the Duomo and its museum. ⊠ *Piazza del Duomo, enter through Duomo, Duomo* ☎ *02/72022656* ⊕ *www.duomomilano. it* 🎫 *€6* Ⓜ *Duomo.*

CASTELLO

Castello Sforzesco. Wandering the grounds of this tranquil castle and park near the center of Milan is a great respite from the often-hectic city, and the interesting museums inside are an added bonus. The castle's crypts and battlements, including a tunnel that emerges well into the Parco Sempione behind, can be visited with privately reserved guides from **Ad Artem** (☎ *02/6596937* ⊕ *www.adartem.it*) or **Opera d'Arte** (☎ *02/45487400* ⊕ *www.operadartemilano.it*).

For the serious student of Renaissance military engineering, the Castello must be something of a travesty, so often has it been remodeled or rebuilt since it was begun in 1450 by the *condottiere* (hired mercenary) who founded the city's second dynastic family, Francesco Sforza, fourth duke of Milan. Although today "mercenary" has a pejorative ring, dur-ing the Renaissance all Italy's great soldier-heroes were professionals hired by the cities and principalities they served. Of them—and there were thousands—Francesco Sforza (1401–66) is considered one of the greatest, most honest, and most organized. It is said he could remember the names not only of all his men but of their horses as well. His rule signaled the enlightened age of the Renaissance but preceded the next foreign rule by a scant 50 years.

Since the turn of the 20th century, the Castello has been the deposi-tory of several city-owned collections of Egyptian and other antiquities, musical instruments, arms and armor, decorative arts and textiles, prints and photographs (on consultation), paintings, and sculpture. Highlights include the **Sala delle Asse,** a frescoed room still sometimes attributed to

Leonardo da Vinci (1452–1519), which is currently undergoing restoration, though it's still open to the public. Michelangelo's unfinished *Rondanini Pietà*, believed to be his last work—an astounding achievement for a man nearly 90, and a moving coda to his life—is housed in the **Museo Pieta Rondanini**. The *pinacoteca* (picture gallery) features 230 paintings from medieval times to the 18th century, including works by Antonello da Messina, Canaletto, Andrea Mantegna, and Bernardo Bellotto. The **Museo dei Mobili** (furniture museum), which illustrates the development of Italian furniture from the Middle Ages to current design, includes a delightful collection of Renaissance treasure chests of exotic woods with tiny drawers and miniature architectural details. A single ticket purchased in the office in an inner courtyard admits visitors to these separate installations, which are dispersed around the castle's two immense courtyards. ✉ *Piazza Castello, Castello* ☎ *02/88463700* ⊕ *www.milanocastello.it* 🖱 *Castle free, museums €5 (free Tues. 2–5:30, Wed.–Fri. and weekends 4:30–5:30)* ◷ *Museums closed Mon.* Ⓜ *Cadorna, Lanza, or Cairoli; Tram No. 1, 2, 4, 12, 14, or 19; Bus No. 18, 37, 50, 58, 61, or 94.*

SEMPIONE

Parco Sempione. Originally the gardens and parade grounds of the Castello Sforzesco, this open space was reorganized during the Napoleonic era, when the arena on its northeast side was constructed, and then turned into a park during the building boom at the end of the 19th century. It is still the lungs of the city's fashionable western neighborhoods, and the **Aquarium** still attracts Milan's schoolchildren (Viale Gadio 2 ☎ *02/88445392* ⊕ *www.acquariocivicomilano.eu*; €5). The park became a bit of a design showcase in 1933 with the construction of the Triennale. ✉ *Sempione* ◷ *Aquarium closed Mon.* Ⓜ *Cairoli, Lanza, or Cadorna; Tram No. 1, 2, 4, 12, 14, 19, or 27; Bus No. 43, 57, 61, 70, or 94.*

Torre Branca. It is worth visiting Parco Sempione just to see the Torre Branca. Designed by the architect Gio Ponti (1891–1979), who was behind so many of the projects that made Milan the design capital that it is, this steel tower rises 330 feet over the Triennale. Take the elevator to get a nice view of the city, then have a drink at the glitzy Just Cavalli Restaurant and Club at its base. ✉ *Parco Sempione, Sempione* ☎ *02/3314120* ⊕ *www.turismo.milano.it* 🖱 *€5* ◷ *Closed Mon. year-round and Tues., Thurs., and Fri. in mid-Sept.–mid-May* Ⓜ *Cadorna; Tram No. 1; Bus No. 61.*

BRERA

Fodor'sChoice ★ **Pinacoteca di Brera** (*Brera Gallery*). The collection here is star-studded even by Italian standards. The museum has nearly 40 rooms, arranged in chronological order—so pace yourself. One highlight is the somber, moving *Cristo Morto* (Dead Christ) by Mantegna, which dominates Room VI with its sparse palette of umber and its foreshortened perspective. Mantegna's shocking, almost surgical precision tells of an all-too-human agony. It's one of Renaissance painting's most quietly wondrous achievements, finding an unsuspected middle ground between the excesses of conventional gore and beauty in representing the Passion's saddest moment.

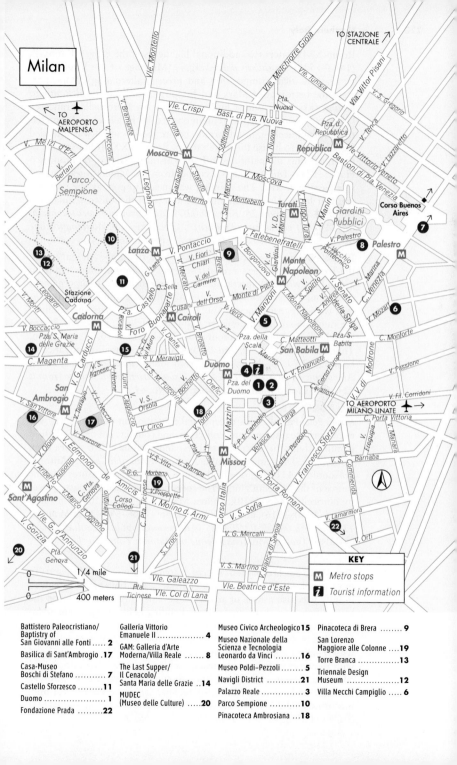

Milan

TO STAZIONE
CENTRALE

TO
AEROPORTO
MALPENSA

Parco
Sempione

Moscova Ⓜ

Pta.
Nuova

Pza. d.
Repubblica

Republica Ⓜ

Corso Buenos
Aires

Giardini
Pubblici

Palestro Ⓜ

Lanza Ⓜ

Monte
Napoleone

Stazione
Cadorna

Cadorna Ⓜ

Cairoli Ⓜ

Pza. della
Scala

San Babila Ⓜ

San
Ambrogio

Duomo

Pza. del
Duomo

TO AEROPORTO
MILANO LINATE

Sant'Agostino Ⓜ

Missori Ⓜ

San Lorenzo

Corso
Collodi

Pta.
Genova

Navigli

Fondazione Prada

Pta.
Ticinese

Vle. Galeazzo   Vle. Beatrice d'Este

KEY	
Ⓜ	Metro stops
🛈	Tourist information

Room XXIV offers two additional highlights of the gallery. Raphael's (1483–1520) *Sposalizio della Vergine* (Marriage of the Virgin) with its mathematical composition and precise, alternating colors, portrays the betrothal of Mary and Joseph. *La Vergine con il Bambino e Santi* (Madonna with Child and Saints), by Piero della Francesca (1420–92), is an altarpiece commissioned by Federico da Montefeltro (shown kneeling, in full armor, before the Virgin); it was intended for a church to house the duke's tomb. Room XXXVII houses one of the most romantic paintings in Italian history: *Il Bacio*, by Francesco Hayez (1791–1882), depicts a couple from the Middle Ages engaged in a passionate kiss. The painting was meant to portray the patriotic spirit of Italy's Unification and freedom from the Austro-Hungarian empire. ⊠ *Via Brera 28, Brera* 🕾 *02/722631* ⊕ *www.pinacotecabrera. org* 🖃 *€10 (free 1st Sun. of month)* ⊘ *Closed Mon.* Ⓜ *Montenapoleone or Lanza; Tram No. 1, 4, 12, 14, or 27; Bus No. 61.*

Triennale Design Museum. In addition to honoring Italy's design talent, the Triennale also offers a regular series of exhibitions on design from around the world. A spectacular bridge entrance leads to a permanent collection, an exhibition space, and a stylish café and rooftop restaurant with expansive views. The Triennale also manages the fascinating museum-studio of designer Achille Castiglioni, in nearby Piazza Castello (hour-long guided tours Tuesday–Friday at 10, 11, and noon, Thursday at 6:30, 7:30, and 8:30; €10. Call or email in advance to book: 🕾 *02/805–3606* or ⊕ *www.fondazioneachillecastiglioni.it*). ⊠ *Via Alemagna 6, Brera* 🕾 *02/724341* ⊕ *www.triennaledesignmuseum.it* 🖃 *€10* ⊘ *Closed Mon.* Ⓜ *Cadorna; Bus No. 61.*

QUADRILATERO

Museo Poldi-Pezzoli. This exceptional museum, opened in 1881, was once a private residence and collection, and contains not only pedigreed paintings but also porcelain, textiles, and a cabinet with scenes from Dante's life. The gem is undoubtedly the *Portrait of a Lady* by Antonio Pollaiuolo (1431–98), one of the city's most prized treasures and the source of the museum's logo. The collection also includes masterpieces by Botticelli (1445–1510), Andrea Mantegna (1431–1506), Giovanni Bellini (1430–1516), and Fra Filippo Lippi (1406–69). ⊠ *Via Manzoni 12, Quadrilatero* 🕾 *02/794889* ⊕ *www.museopoldipezzoli.it* 🖃 *€10* ⊘ *Closed Tues.* Ⓜ *Montenapoleone or Duomo; Tram No. 1.*

BUENOS AIRES

Casa-Museo Boschi di Stefano (*Boschi di Stefano House and Museum*). To most people, Italian art means Renaissance art, but the 20th century in Italy was also a time of artistic achievement. An apartment on the second floor of a stunning Art Deco building designed by Milan architect Portaluppi houses this collection, which was donated to the city of Milan in 2003 and is a tribute to the enlightened private collectors who replaced popes and nobles as Italian patrons. The walls are lined with the works of postwar greats, such as Fontana, De Chirico, and Morandi. Along with the art, the museum holds distinctive postwar furniture and stunning Murano glass chandeliers. ⊠ *Via Jan 15, Buenos Aires* 🕾 *02/20240568* ⊕ *www.fondazioneboschidistefano.it* 🖃 *Free* ⊘ *Closed Mon.* Ⓜ *Lima; Tram No. 33; Bus No. 60.*

PALESTRO

GAM: Galleria d'Arte Moderna/Villa Reale. One of the city's most beautiful buildings is an outstanding example of Neoclassical architecture, built between 1790 and 1796 as a residence for a member of the Belgioioso family. It later became known as the Villa Reale when it was donated to Napoléon, who lived here briefly with Empress Josephine. Its origins as a residence are reflected in the elegance of its proportions and its private garden behind. The museum provides a unique glimpse of the splendors hiding behind Milan's discreet and often stern facades.

The collection comes from private donations from prominent Milanese art collectors and their families. It focuses mainly on 18th- and 19th-century Italian works, with a smattering of 20th-century pieces from Italian artists as well as international works from Van Gogh and Picasso, among others. ⊠ *Via Palestro 16, Palestro* ☎ *02/88445947* ⊕ *www.gam-milano.com* ⊠ *€5 (free Wed.–Sun. after 4:30 and Tues. after 2)* ۞ *Closed Mon.* Ⓜ *Palestro or Turati; Tram No. 1 or 2; Bus No. 94 or 61.*

Villa Necchi Campiglio. In 1932, architect Piero Portaluppi designed this sprawling estate in an art deco style, with inspiration coming from the decadent cruise ships of the 1920s. Once owned by the Necchi Campiglio industrial family, the tasteful and elegant home—which sits on Via Mozart, one of Milan's most exclusive streets—is a reminder of the refined, modern culture of the nouveau riche who accrued financial power in Milan during that era. Tickets can be purchased at the ticket counter on the estate grounds; there's a small additional charge for a photography permit. There is also a well-regarded café on the grounds that is open for lunch. ■TIP➔ Tours of the estate run about every 30 minutes and include English-speaking guides if needed. ⊠ *Via Mozart 14, Palestro* ☎ *02/76340121* ⊕ *www.visitfai.it/villanecchi* ⊠ *€10* ۞ *Closed Mon. and Tues.* Ⓜ *Palestro, San Babila, or Montenapoleone; Bus No. 54, 61, or 94.*

SANT'AMBROGIO

If the part of the city to the north of the Duomo is dominated by its shops, Sant'Ambrogio and other parts to the south are known for their works of art. The most famous is *Il Cenacolo*—known in English as *The Last Supper*. If you have time for nothing else, make sure you see this masterpiece. You will need reservations to see this fresco, which is housed in the refectory of Santa Maria delle Grazie. Make these at least three weeks before you depart for Italy, so you can plan the rest of your time in Milan.

TOP ATTRACTIONS

Basilica di Sant'Ambrogio (*Basilica of St. Ambrose*). Milan's bishop, St. Ambrose (one of the original Doctors of the Catholic Church), consecrated this church in AD 387. St. Ambroeus, as he is known in Milanese dialect, is the city's patron saint, and his remains—dressed in elegant religious robes, a miter, and gloves—can be viewed inside a glass case in the crypt below the altar. Until the construction of the more imposing Duomo, this was Milan's most important church. Much restored and reworked over the centuries (the gold-and-gem-encrusted altar dates from the 9th century), Sant'Ambrogio still preserves its Romanesque characteristics (5th-century mosaics may be seen for €2). The church is often closed for weddings on Saturday. ⊠ *Piazza Sant'Ambrogio 15, Sant'Ambrogio* ☎ *02/86450895* ⊕ *www.basilicas-antambrogio.it* Ⓜ *Sant'Ambrogio; Bus No. 50, 58, or 94.*

Fodor'sChoice
★

The Last Supper/Il Cenacolo/Santa Maria delle Grazie. Leonardo da Vinci's *The Last Supper,* housed in this church and former Dominican monastery, has had an almost unbelievable history of bad luck and neglect—its near destruction in an American bombing raid in August 1943 was only the latest chapter in a series of misadventures, including, if one 19th-century source is to be believed, being whitewashed over by monks. Well-meant but disastrous attempts at restoration have done little to rectify the problem of the work's placement: it was executed on a wall unusually vulnerable to climatic dampness. Yet Leonardo chose to work slowly and patiently in oil pigments—which demand dry plaster—instead of proceeding hastily on wet plaster according to the conventional fresco technique. After years of restorers patiently shifting from one square centimeter to another, Leonardo's masterpiece is now free of centuries of retouching, grime, and dust. Astonishing clarity and luminosity have been regained.

Despite Leonardo's carefully preserved preparatory sketches, in which the apostles are clearly labeled by name, there still remains some small debate about a few identities in the final arrangement. But there can be no mistaking Judas, small and dark, his hand calmly reaching forward to the bread, isolated from the terrible confusion that has taken the hearts of the others. One critic, Frederick Hartt, offers an elegantly terse explanation for why the composition works: it combines "dramatic confusion" with "mathematical order." Certainly, the amazingly skillful and unobtrusive repetition of threes—in the windows, in the grouping of the figures, and in their placement—adds a mystical aspect to what at first seems simply the perfect observation of spontaneous human gesture.

Reservations are required to view the work. Viewings are in 15-minute, timed-entry slots, and visitors must arrive 15 minutes before their assigned time in order not to lose their place. Reservations can be made by phone or online; it is worthwhile to call, as a number of tickets are set aside for phone reservations. Call at least three weeks ahead if you want a Saturday slot, two weeks for a weekday slot. The telephone reservation office is open Monday–Saturday 8–6:30. Operators do speak English, though not fluently, and to reach one you must wait for the Italian introduction to finish and then press "2." However, you can sometimes get tickets from one day to the next. Some city bus tours include a visit in their regular circuit, which may be a good option.

The painting was executed in what was the order's refectory, which is now referred to as the **Cenacolo Vinciano.** Take a moment to visit Santa Maria delle Grazie itself. It's a handsome, completely restored church, with a fine dome, which Bramante added along with a cloister about the time that Leonardo was commissioned to paint *The Last*

Supper. ⊠ *Piazza Santa Maria delle Grazie 2, off Corso Magenta, Sant'Ambrogio* ☎ *02/92800360 for reservations, 02/4676111 for church* ⊕ *www.cenacolovinciano.net, www.grazieop.it* ✉ *Last Supper €10 plus €2 reservation fee (free 1st Sun. of month)* ⊙ *Closed Mon.* Ⓜ *Cadorna or Conciliazione; Tram No. 18.*

WORTH NOTING

Museo Civico Archeologico (*Municipal Archaeological Museum*). Appropriately situated in the heart of Roman Milan, this museum housed in a former monastery displays everyday utensils, jewelry, silver plate, and several fine examples of mosaic pavement from Mediolanum, the ancient Roman name for Milan. The museum opens into a garden that is flanked by the square tower of the Roman circus and the polygonal Ansperto tower, adorned with frescoes dating to the end of the 13th and 14th centuries, portraying St. Francis and other saints receiving the stigmata. ⊠ *Corso Magenta 15, Sant'Ambrogio* ☎ *02/88445208* ⊕ *www.comune.milano.it/museoarcheologico* ✉ *€5* ⊙ *Closed Mon.* Ⓜ *Cadorna or Cairoli; Tram No. 16 or 27; Bus No. 50, 58, or 94.*

FAMILY **Museo Nazionale della Scienza e Tecnologia Leonardo da Vinci** (*National Museum of Science and Technology*). This converted cloister is best known for the collection of models based on Leonardo da Vinci's sketches. One of the most visited rooms features interactive, moving models of the famous *vita aerea* (aerial screw) and *ala battente* (beating wing), thought to be forerunners of the modern helicopter and airplane, respectively. The museum also houses a varied collection of industrial artifacts including trains and several reconstructed workshops including a watchmaker's, a lute maker's, and an antique pharmacy. Reserve tickets for the celebrated Italian-built submarine and helicopter simulator in advance online or by phone to avoid disappointment. Displays also illustrate papermaking and metal founding, which were fundamental to Milan's—and the world's—economic growth. There's a bookshop and a bar. ■TIP➔ Avoid this museum on weekends. It's a popular spot for families, and there are long lines on those days. ⊠ *Via San Vittore 21, Sant'Ambrogio* ☎ *02/48555558* ⊕ *www.museoscienza.org* ✉ *€10* ⊙ *Closed Mon.* Ⓜ *Sant'Ambrogio; Bus No. 50, 58, or 94.*

NAVIGLI

Navigli District. In medieval times, a network of *navigli*, or canals, crisscrossed the city. Almost all have been covered over, but two—Naviglio Grande and Naviglio Pavese—are still navigable. The area's chock-full of boutiques, art galleries, cafés, bars, and restaurants, and at night the Navigli serves up a scene about as close as you will get to southern-style Italian street life in Milan. On weekend nights, it is difficult to walk among the youthful crowds thronging the narrow streets along the canals. Check out the antiques fair on the last Sunday of the month from 9 am to 6 pm. ■TIP➔ During the summer months, be sure to put on some mosquito repellent. ⊠ *South of Corso Porta Ticinese, Navigli* Ⓜ *Porta Genova; Tram No. 2, 3, 9, 14, 15, 29, or 30.*

TICINESE

MUDEC (Museo delle Culture). Home to a permanent collection of ethnographic displays as well as temporary exhibitions of big-name artists such as Basquiat and Miró, MUDEC is in the vibrant and developing Zona Tortona area of the city. British architect David Chipperfield designed the soaring space in a former factory. The permanent collection includes art, objects, and documents from Africa, Asia, and the Americas. Book in advance for the most popular temporary exhibits. There's also a highly rated restaurant, Enrico Bartolini Mudec, as well as a more casual bistro. ⊠ *Via Tortona 56, Ticinese* ☎ *02/54917* ⊕ *www.mudec.it* ⌨ *€5 for permanent collection, €12 for exhibitions* ⊗ *Closed Mon. until 2:30 pm* Ⓜ *Sant'Agostino or Porta Genova; Tram No. 2 or 14; Bus No. 68 or 90/91.*

San Lorenzo Maggiore alle Colonne. Sixteen ancient Roman columns line the front of this sanctuary; 4th-century paleo-Christian mosaics survive in the Cappella di Sant'Aquilino (Chapel of St. Aquilinus). ⊠ *Corso di Porta Ticinese 39, Ticinese* ☎ *02/89404129* ⊕ *www.sanlorenzomaggiore.com* ⌨ *Mosaics €2* Ⓜ *Missori.*

LARGO ISARCO

Fodor's Choice
★

Fondazione Prada. Housed in former distillery buildings from the 1910s and revamped alongside new structures of metal and glass, this collection of modern art in about 120,000 square feet of exhibition space is not for the faint of heart. Permanent pieces, such as Louise Bourgeois's *Haunted House,* are avant-garde and challenging, while temporary exhibitions highlight cutting-edge Italian and international artists. Although navigating the expansive grounds can be confusing, the knowledgeable staff will help guide loft visitors. Don't miss the Wes Anderson–designed café, Luce Bar, for a drink or snack before you leave. The Fondazione is a hike from the city center; expect a 10-minute walk from the metro station to the galleries. ⊠ *Largo Isarco 2* ☎ *02/56662611* ⊕ *www.fondazioneprada.org* ⌨ *€10* ⊗ *Closed Tues.* Ⓜ *Lodi TIBB; Tram No. 24; Bus No. 65.*

WHERE TO EAT

DUOMO

$$$
ITALIAN

✕ **Don Carlos.** One of the few restaurants open after La Scala lets out, Don Carlos, in the Grand Hotel et de Milan, is nothing like its indecisive operatic namesake (whose betrothed was stolen by his father). Flavors are bold, presentation is precise and full of flair, and the service is attentive. The walls are blanketed with sketches of the theater, and the low-key opera recordings are every bit as well chosen as the wine list, setting the perfect stage for discreet business negotiation or, better yet, refined romance. Ⓢ *Average main: €34* ⊠ *Grand Hotel et de Milan, Via Manzoni 29, Duomo* ☎ *02/72314640* ⊕ *www.ristorantedoncarlos.it* ⊗ *No lunch* Ⓜ *Montenapoleone; Tram No. 1 or 2.*

$$$
ITALIAN

✕ **Giacomo Arengario.** Join businesspeople, ladies who lunch, and in-the-know tourists at this elegant restaurant with a glorious view of the Duomo atop the Museo del Novecento. To complement the vistas, renowned Milanese restaurateur Giacomo Bulleri offers up a mix of well-prepared seafood, pasta, and meat courses for lunch and dinner. The servers are happy to recommend pairings from the extensive wine list. Just make sure you request seating by the windows when you book, to gaze at some of the best views in town; otherwise, you may be relegated to the viewless back room. $ *Average main: €30* ⊠ *Via Marconi 1, Duomo* ☎ *02/72093814* ⊕ *giacomoarengario.com* Ⓜ *Duomo.*

$ ✕ **La Vecchia Latteria.** With only two small dining rooms, this family-
VEGETARIAN   owned lunch spot dishes out an impressive amount of vegetarian cuisine. Nestled on a small street just steps away from the Duomo, it offers an array of freshly prepared, in-season dishes. The menu changes daily; try the mixed plate (*misto forno*), which offers a taste of several different small dishes. Between the months of February and July, on Tuesday and Thursday nights, as well as occasional times throughout the year, the restaurant hosts an aperitivo called "Eppi Auar" (Happy Hour) from 7 to 10 pm with live music and an all-you-can-eat buffet for €9. $ *Average main: €9* ⊠ *6 Via dell'Unione, Duomo* ☎ *02/874401* ⊘ *Closed Sun. No dinner Mon., Wed., Fri., or Sat.* Ⓜ *Duomo or Missori.*

$ ✕ **Piz.** Fun, lively, and full of locals, this casual and inexpensive pizzeria
PIZZA   on a side street near the Duomo has just three kinds of thin-crust pizza
FAMILY   on the menu—luckily, all are excellent. Choose from margherita, bianca (white, with no tomato), and marinara (with no mozzarella); although you'll inevitably need to wait, you'll get a free glass of prosecco and a slice of pizza with cheese while you do. When you finish, a complimentary shot of limoncello or melon liqueur, given to all customers, is a pleasant way to end the meal. $ *Average main: €9* ⊠ *Via Torino 34, Duomo* ☎ *02/86453482* Ⓜ *Duomo; Tram No. 2, 3, or 14.*

$ ✕ **Rinascente Food & Restaurants.** The seventh floor of this famous Ital-
ECLECTIC   ian department store is a gourmet food market surrounded by several small restaurants that can be a good option for lunch, an aperitivo overlooking the Duomo, or dinner after a long day of shopping. There are several places to eat, including the popular mozzarella bar Obica, My Sushi, De Santis for "slow food" sandwiches, and the sophisticated Maio restaurant. A terrace overlooking the Duomo is shared by three locations. It's best to get here early—it's popular, and there are often lines at mealtimes. $ *Average main: €10* ⊠ *Piazza Duomo, Duomo* ☎ *02/8852471* ⊕ *www.rinascente.it* Ⓜ *Duomo.*

BRERA

$$$ ✕ **Fioraio Bianchi Caffe.** A French-style bistro in the heart of Milan, Fio-
MODERN ITALIAN   raio Bianchi Caffe was opened more than 40 years ago by Raimondo Bianchi, a great lover of flowers. In fact, eating at this restaurant is like dining in the middle of a boutique Parisian flower shop. Despite the French atmosphere, the many pasta and meat dishes have Italian flair and ensure a classy, inventive meal. It's also a popular place for a morning coffee and pastry. $ *Average main: €28* ⊠ *Via Montebello 7, Brera* ☎ *02/29014390* ⊕ *www.fioraiobianchicaffe.it* ⊘ *Closed Sun., and 3 wks in Aug.* Ⓜ *Turati.*

QUADRILATERO

$$$$ MODERN ITALIAN Fodor's Choice ★

🍴 **Seta.** Modern Italian dishes with interesting ingredients are on offer in this sophisticated restaurant located within Milan's Mandarin Oriental Hotel. In a masculine setting with brown and green decor, sample such signature dishes as *cavolfiore* (cauliflower with almond-milk sauce, yuzu juice, and seafood) and *riso* (risotto with vegetables, Maccagno cheese, and raspberry powder). The best way to get a sense of the intricate dishes is through the five-course tasting menu; for a less expensive option, opt for the two- or three-course "business lunch." With more than 500 labels on the extensive wine list and a focus on Italian producers, you're guaranteed to find something wonderful to accompany your meal. [$] *Average main: €45* ✉ *Via Andegari 9, Quadrilatero* ☎ *02/87318897* 🌐 *www.mandarinoriental.com/milan/fine-dining/seta* ⏲ *Closed Sun., and 1st wk of Jan. No lunch Sat.* [M] *Montenapoleone; Tram No. 1.*

CINQUE GIORNATE

$$$ ITALIAN

🍴 **Da Giacomo.** The fashion and publishing crowd, as well as international bankers and businesspeople, favor this Tuscan-Ligurian restaurant. The emphasis is on fish; even the warm slice of pizza served while you study the menu has seafood on it. The specialty, *gnocchetti alla Giacomo,* has a savory seafood-and-tomato sauce. With its tile floor and bank of fresh seafood, the place has a refined neighborhood-bistro style. [$] *Average main: €28* ✉ *Via P. Sottocorno 6, entrance in Via Cellini, Cinque Giornate* ☎ *02/76023313* 🌐 *www.giacomoristorante.com* [M] *Tram No. 9, 12, 23, or 27; Bus No. 60 or 73.*

GARIBALDI

$$$ CONTEMPORARY Fodor's Choice ★

🍴 **Ceresio 7 Pools & Restaurant.** Book well in advance for one of Milan's most fashionable eateries, where the tables are lacquered red and modern artwork crowds the walls—exactly what you'd expect from the twin brothers Dean and Dan Caten behind the fashion label Dsquared2. The food cred matches the scene, with sophisticated dishes using luxe ingredients like lobster, king crab, and truffles. Pastas are fresh and creative, and elegant meat and seafood mains include nontraditional accompaniments. When the weather's warm, people-watch while enjoying drinks and aperitivo on the expansive terrace alongside two swimming pools and a fabulous skyline view. [$] *Average main: €35* ✉ *Via Ceresio 7, Garibaldi* ☎ *02/31039221* 🌐 *www.ceresio7.com* [M] *Garibaldi; Tram No. 2, 4, 12, or 14; Bus No. 37 or 190.*

$ PIZZA

🍴 **Pizzeria Fabbrica.** This lively pizzeria has two wood-burning ovens going full-steam every day of the week. Skip the appetizers and go straight to the pizzas, which vary from traditional (*quattro stagioni*) to vegetable based (with zucchini, spinach, rucola, and more) to in-house specialties like the *tartufona* (with truffle oil). The menu also offers antipasti, pastas like *pici* with fresh pecorino and pepper, and secondi. Save room for a worthy dessert—though after pizza, you might want to share. The Fabbrica is large enough to handle groups; seek out a seat in the garden when the weather's nice. [$] *Average main: €9* ✉ *Viale Pasubio 2, Garibaldi* ☎ *02/6552771* 🌐 *www.lafabbricapizzeria.it* [M] *Garibaldi.*

LORETO

$$ ✕ **Da Abele.** If you love risotto, then make a beeline for this neighbor-
ITALIAN hood trattoria. The superb risotto dishes change with the season, and
every day there are three on the menu: one meat, one fish, and one veg-
etarian. It is tempting to try them all. The setting is relaxed, the service
informal, the prices strikingly reasonable. Outside the touristy center
of town but quite convenient by subway, this trattoria is invariably
packed with locals. $ *Average main: €15* ⊠ *Via Temperanza 5, Loreto*
☎ *02/2613855* ⊕ *www.trattoriadaabele.it* ⊘ *Closed Mon., Aug., and
Dec. 24–Jan. 3. No lunch* Ⓜ *Pasteur.*

PORTA ROMANA

$ ✕ **U Barba.** Simple, fresh, authentic Ligurian specialties (in Ligurian
NORTHERN dialect the name means "the uncle") will take you back to lazy summer
ITALIAN days on the Italian Riviera—even during Milan's wet winter weather.
Such classic coastal specialties as *trofie al pesto* (an egg-free pasta served
with pesto) and *cozze ripieni* (stuffed mussels), coupled with a basket
of warm focaccia, reign supreme in this favorite of Milan's fashion
crowd overlooking a lively bocce court. $ *Average main: €13* ⊠ *Via
Pier Candido Decembrio 33, Porta Romana* ☎ *02/45487032* ⊕ *www.
ubarba.it* ⊘ *Closed Mon. No lunch Tues.–Fri.* Ⓜ *Lodi TIBB; Tram No.
16; Bus No. 90.*

PORTA VENEZIA

$$$ ✕ **Joia.** At this haute-cuisine vegetarian haven near Piazza della Repub-
VEGETARIAN blica, delicious dishes—all without eggs and many without flour—are
artistically prepared by chef Pietro Leemann. Vegetarians, who often get
short shrift in Italy, will marvel at the variety of culinary offerings and
artistry here. The ever-changing dishes here are presented in unusual
formats: tiny glasses of creamed vegetables or ravioli in the shape of a
human hand. For the best sampling of the creative foods on offer, try
one of the interesting tasting menus: the five-course Discovery menu,
the eight-course Emphasis on Nature, the 11-course Zenith, or, for a
better deal, the less pricey tasting menu at lunch. $ *Average main: €35*
⊠ *Via Panfilo Castaldi 18, Porta Venezia* ☎ *02/29522124* ⊕ *www.joia.
it* ⊘ *Closed Sun., 3 wks in Aug., and Dec. 24–Jan. 7* Ⓜ *Repubblica or
Porta Venezia; Tram No. 1, 5, 9, or 33.*

$ ✕ **Pizza OK.** The thin-crust pizza wins raves from locals at this family-
PIZZA run pizzeria with four locations, the oldest near Corso Buenos Aires
in the Porta Venezia area. The pizza is extra thin and large, and pos-
sibilities for toppings seem endless. A good choice for families, this
dining experience will be easy on your pocketbook. Other locations
are on Via San Siro 9 in Corso Vercelli, Piazza Sempione 8, and Via
Chiesa Rossa 109. $ *Average main: €8* ⊠ *Via Lambro 15, Porta Vene-
zia* ☎ *02/29401272* ⊘ *Closed Aug. 7–20 and Dec. 24–Dec. 26* Ⓜ *Porta
Venezia; Tram No. 5, 23, or 33.*

WHERE TO STAY

DUOMO

$$$$ HOTEL **Grand Hotel et de Milan.** Only blocks from La Scala you'll find everything you hope for in a traditionally elegant European hotel, with ancient tapestries and persimmon velvet enlivening the 19th-century look without sacrificing dignity and luxury. **Pros:** traditional and elegant; great location off Milan's main shopping streets; staff goes above and beyond to meet guests' needs. **Cons:** gilt decor may not suit those who like more modern design; no spa; some small rooms. [$] *Rooms from: €415* ✉ *Via Manzoni 29, Duomo* ☎ *02/723141* 🌐 *www.grandhoteletdemilan.it* 🛏 *95 rooms* 🍴 *No meals* [M] *Montenapoleone.*

$$ HOTEL **Hotel Gran Duca di York.** These spare but classically elegant and efficient rooms are arranged around a courtyard—four have private terraces—and are very good value for pricey Milan. **Pros:** central; friendly staff. **Cons:** rooms are simple, with many on the small side; dated decor. [$] *Rooms from: €157* ✉ *Via Moneta 1/a, Duomo* ☎ *02/874863* 🌐 *www.ducadiyork.com* ⏲ *Closed Aug.* 🛏 *33 rooms* 🍴 *Breakfast* [M] *Cordusio or Duomo; Tram No. 2, 12, 14, 16, or 27.*

$$$ HOTEL **Hotel Spadari al Duomo.** The fact that this chic city center inn is owned by an architect's family shows in the details, including custom-designed furniture and paintings by young Milanese artists on rotating display in the stylish guest rooms. **Pros:** good breakfast; central location; attentive staff. **Cons:** some rooms on the small side; street noise can be a problem. [$] *Rooms from: €280* ✉ *Via Spadari 11, Duomo* ☎ *02/72002371* 🌐 *www.spadarihotel.com* 🛏 *40 rooms* 🍴 *Breakfast* [M] *Duomo; Tram No. 2, 3, 12, 14, 16, 24, or 27.*

$$ HOTEL **Hotel Star.** The price is extremely reasonable, the staff are helpful, and the rooms are well equipped and comfortable, some with touches like Jacuzzi tubs and balconies. **Pros:** central; reasonably priced; breakfast is included. **Cons:** Wi-Fi can be iffy; street noise in some rooms. [$] *Rooms from: €155* ✉ *Via dei Bossi 5, Duomo* ☎ *02/801501* 🌐 *www.hotelstar.it* 🛏 *30 rooms* 🍴 *Breakfast.*

$$$$ HOTEL Fodor's Choice ★ **Park Hyatt Milan.** Extensive use of warm travertine stone and modern art creates a sophisticated yet inviting and tranquil backdrop in these spacious and opulent guest rooms. **Pros:** central; contemporary; refined. **Cons:** not particularly intimate; very expensive; some rooms showing a little wear. [$] *Rooms from: €580* ✉ *Via Tommaso Grossi 1, Duomo* ☎ *02/88211234* 🌐 *milan.park.hyatt.com* 🛏 *106 rooms* [M] *Duomo; Tram No. 1.*

$$$ HOTEL Fodor's Choice ★ **Room Mate Giulia.** For a hip and affordable design-focused place to stay with a friendly feel and prime location right next to the Galleria and around the corner from the Duomo, Milan visitors can't do much better than the city's first outpost from Spanish hotel chain Room Mate. **Pros:** amazing central location; fresh, appealing design; affordable rates for Milan. **Cons:** breakfast room a bit cramped; gym on the small side; busy location means some noise in rooms. [$] *Rooms from: €279* ✉ *Via Silvio Pellico 4, Duomo* ☎ *02/80888900* 🌐 *www.room-matehotels.com/en/giulia* 🛏 *85 rooms* 🍴 *No meals* [M] *Duomo; Tram No. 1.*

QUADRILATERO

$$$$ | **Armani Hotel Milano.** Located in Milan's fashion district, this minimal-
HOTEL | ist boutique hotel looks like it has been plucked from the pages of a
Fodor's Choice | sleek shelter magazine. **Pros:** complimentary minibar (minus alcohol);
★ | lovely spa area and 24-hour gym; great location near major shopping
streets. **Cons:** exclusive vibe not for everyone; some noise issues from
neighboring rooms; a few signs of wear and tear. $ *Rooms from: €480*
⊠ *Via Manzoni 31, Quadrilatero* ☎ *02/88838888* ⊕ *milan.armaniho-*
tels.com ⤳ *95 rooms* ⦿*No meals* Ⓜ *Montenapoleone.*

$$$$ | **Four Seasons.** Built in the 15th century as a convent and surrounding
HOTEL | a colonnaded cloister, this sophisticated retreat in the heart of Milan's
upscale shopping district certainly exudes a feeling that is anything
but urban. **Pros:** quiet, elegant setting that feels removed from noisy
central Milan; friendly and helpful staff; large rooms. **Cons:** rooms feel
a little bland and old-fashioned; breakfast isn't included in the rate;
extremely expensive. $ *Rooms from: €725* ⊠ *Via Gesù 6–8, Quadri-*
latero ☎ *02/77088* ⊕ *www.fourseasons.com/milan* ⤳ *118 rooms* ⦿*No*
meals Ⓜ *Montenapoleone; Tram No. 1.*

$$$$ | **Mandarin Oriental, Milan.** A sense of refined luxury pervades the guest
HOTEL | rooms and public spaces of the first Mandarin Oriental in Italy, located
FAMILY | just off the main Via Montenapoleone shopping street. **Pros:** wonder-
Fodor's Choice | ful and attentive service; tranquil spa and 24-hour fitness center; top
★ | restaurant on-site. **Cons:** very expensive. $ *Rooms from: €700* ⊠ *Via*
Andegari 9, Quadrilatero ☎ *02/87318888* ⊕ *www.mandarinoriental.*
com/milan ⤳ *104 rooms* ⦿*No meals* Ⓜ *Montenapoleone; Tram No. 1.*

SANT'AMBROGIO

$$ | **Antica Locanda Leonardo.** Half the rooms in this 19th-century building
HOTEL | face a courtyard and the others a back garden; many have balconies,
and one ground-floor room has a private garden with table and chairs.
Pros: very quiet and homey; breakfast is ample. **Cons:** more like a
bed-and-breakfast than a hotel; old-fashioned decor. $ *Rooms from:*
€125 ⊠ *Corso Magenta 78, Sant'Ambrogio* ☎ *02/48014197* ⊕*www.*
anticalocandaleonardo.com ⊗ *Closed 1st wk in Jan. and 3 wks in*
Aug. ⤳ *16 rooms* ⦿*Breakfast* Ⓜ *Conciliazione, Sant'Ambrogio, or*
Cadorna; Tram No. 1, 16, 19, or 27.

REPUBBLICA

$$$ | **Hotel Principe di Savoia Milano.** Milan's grande dame has all the trap-
HOTEL | pings of an exquisite traditional luxury hotel: lavish mirrors, drapes,
and carpets, limousine services, and the city's largest guest rooms, outfitted with eclectic fin-de-siècle furnishings. **Pros:** substantial spa–health
club; close to Central Station. **Cons:** located in a not-very-central or
attractive neighborhood; breakfast and other meals overly expensive. $ *Rooms from: €255* ⊠ *Piazza della Repubblica 17, Repubblica*
☎ *02/62301* ⊕ *www.hotelprincipedisavoia.com* ⤳ *301 rooms* ⦿*No*
meals Ⓜ *Repubblica; Tram No. 1, 9, or 33.*

$$$ | **ME Milan Il Duca.** The first Italian hotel from the Spanish ME by Melia
HOTEL | brand has a lively party atmosphere, with rousing music playing in
the lobby, a design-conscious vibe, and a happening rooftop bar with
panoramic city views. **Pros:** great rooftop bar; spacious rooms; young,

vibrant atmosphere. **Cons:** no spa; may feel overdesigned to some; can be noisy. [$] *Rooms from: €275* ✉ *Piazza della Repubblica 13, Repubblica* ☎ *02/84220107* 🌐 *www.melia.com/en/hotels/italy/milan/home.htm* 🛏 *132 rooms* 🍴 *No meals* [M] *Repubblica; Tram No. 1, 5, 9, 10, or 33.*

TICINESE

$$$ HOTEL Fodor's Choice ★ 🏨 **The Yard.** Knickknacks and memorabilia from sports including golf, horseback riding, and boxing inspire the room decor in this electic and extremely hip hotel at the foot of the lively Corso di Porta Ticinese by the Navigli canals—but even if you're not a sports fan, you'll appreciate this friendly boutique hotel's contemporary flair. **Pros:** extremely attractive and comfortable; interesting location near many restaurants and bars; ultrafriendly staff. **Cons:** lacking some of the amenities of large hotels; about a half-hour hike from the Duomo and central Milan attractions. [$] *Rooms from: €274* ✉ *Piazza XXIV Maggio 8, Porta Ticinese* ☎ *02/89415901* 🌐 *www.theyardmilano.com* 🛏 *14 rooms* 🍴 *Breakfast* [M] *Tram 3 or 9.*

NIGHTLIFE AND PERFORMING ARTS

NIGHTLIFE

The aperitivo, or prelunch or predinner drink, is available everywhere in Italy, but in Milan it is a big part of life and a must-try. Milan bar owners have enriched the usual nibbles of olives, nuts, and chips with full finger (and often fork) buffets serving cubes of pizza and cheese, fried vegetables, rice salad, sushi, and even pasta, and they've baptized it "Appy Hour," with the first "h" dropped and the second one pronounced. For the price of a drink (around €8), you can make a meal of hors d'oeuvres—but don't be greedy.

DUOMO

Bar STRAF. This architecturally stimulating but dimly lit place has such artistic features as recycled fiberglass panels and vintage 1970s furnishings. The music is an eclectic mix of chilling tunes during the daytime, with more upbeat and vibrant tracks pepping it up at night. Located on a quiet side street near the Duomo, STRAF draws a young and lively, if tourist-heavy, crowd. ✉ *Via San Raffaele 3, Duomo* ☎ *02/805081* 🌐 *www.straf.it* [M] *Duomo.*

Café Trussardi. Open throughout the day, this is a great place for coffee and bumping into Milan's elite, who are entertained by video art on an enormous plasma screen. ✉ *Piazza della Scala 5, Duomo* ☎ *02/80688295* 🌐 *www.trussardiallascala.com* [M] *Tram No. 1.*

Fodor's Choice ★ **Peck Italian Bar.** This foodie paradise near the Duomo with an enormous deli featuring Italian specialty foods also has a bar and restaurant that serves up traditional—and excellent—pastas, pizza slices, olives, toasted nuts, and a good selection of wines by the glass in a refined setting. ✉ *Via Cesare Cantù 3, Duomo* ☎ *02/8693017* 🌐 *www.peck.it* 🕒 *Closed Sun.* [M] *Duomo; Tram No. 2, 12, 14, 16, or 27.*

BRERA

Bulgari Hotel Bar. Having drinks or a light lunch at the Bulgari Hotel Bar lets you step off the asphalt and into one of the city's most impressive, private urban gardens—even indoors you seem to be outside, separated from the elements by a spectacular wall of glass. This is a great place to run into international hotel guests and jet-setting Milanese, and the bar staff mixes up a wide range of traditional and novel drinks—including the Bulgari Cocktail with gin, aperol, and orange, pineapple, and lime juices. ⊠ *Via Privata Fratelli Gabba 7/b, Brera* ☎ *02/8058051* ⊕ *www. bulgarihotels.com* Ⓜ *Montenapoleone; Tram No. 1.*

'N Ombra de Vin. This highly rated enoteca serves wine by the glass and, in addition to the plates of sausage and cheese nibbles, has light food and not-so-light desserts. It's a great place for people-watching on Via San Marco, while indoors offers a more dimly lit, romantic setting. Check out the impressive vaulted basement, where bottled wine and spirits are sold. ⊠ *Via S. Marco 2, Brera* ☎ *02/6599650* ⊕ *www.nombradevin.it* Ⓜ *Lanza, Turati, or Montenapoleone; Tram No. 1, 2, 4, 12, or 14.*

QUADRILATERO

Armani/Bamboo Bar. The Bamboo Bar at the Armani Hotel Milano has kept Milan abuzz since its opening. A modern architectural marvel, it's got high ceilings, louvered windows, and expansive views of the city's rooftops. It's great for a relaxing after-work tea with friends or a predinner aperitivo. ⊠ *Via Manzoni 31, Quadrilatero* ☎ *02/88838888* ⊕ *milan.armanihotels.com* Ⓜ *Montenapoleone; Tram No. 1.*

REPUBBLICA

Radio Rooftop Bar. Milan's most beautiful people congregate for aperol spritz and a selection of international tapas on this terrace with panoramic views of the city. Located at the top of the ME Milan Il Duca, there are heat lamps to keep visitors here even in cooler weather. There's also lunch Monday through Saturday and brunch on Sunday. ⊠ *Piazza della Repubblica 13, Repubblica* ☎ *02/84220109* ⊕ *www.radiorooftop. com/Milan* Ⓜ *Repubblica; Tram No. 1, 5, 9, 10, or 33.*

GARIBALDI

Blue Note. The first European branch of the famous New York nightclub features regular performances by some of the most famous names in jazz, as well as blues and rock concerts. Dinner is available, and there's a popular jazz brunch on Sunday. It's closed Monday. ⊠ *Via Borsieri 37, Garibaldi* ☎ *02/69016888* ⊕ *www.bluenotemilano.com* Ⓜ *Isola; Tram No. 7, 31, or 33.*

Dry Cocktails & Pizza. A hot spot for both classic and creative cocktails, this trendy industrial space packed with hip locals has a pizza joint in the back if you get hungry. ⊠ *Via Solferino 33, Garibaldi* ☎ *02/63793414* ⊕ *www.drymilano.it* Ⓜ *Moscova, Turati, or Repubblica; Tram No. 1, 9, or 33; Bus No. 37.*

NAVIGLI

Brellin Café. This popular spot in the arty Navigli district has live music. It serves late-night snacks as well as traditional Milanese dishes for lunch and dinner. ⊠ *Vicolo dei Lavandai at Alzaia Naviglio Grande,*

Navigli ☎*02/58101351, 02/89402700* ⊕*www.brellin.it* Ⓜ*Porta Genova; Tram No. 2 or 9.*

PORTA VIGENTINA

Magazzini Generali. What was once an abandoned warehouse is now a fun, futuristic venue for dancing. It also is a popular spot for fashion shows, and its concert schedule attracts well-known international acts. It's usually standing room only for concerts. ✉ *Via Pietrasanta 16, Porta Vigentina* ☎ *02/5393948* ⊕ *www.magazzinigenerali.it* Ⓜ *Tram No. 24; Bus No. 79, 90, or 91.*

CORSO COMO

Tocqueville 13. Regular nightclub fare from Thursday through Sunday is embellished with occasional live music, featuring young and emerging talent. ✉ *Via Alexis de Tocqueville 13, Corso Como* ☎ *3939527044* ⊕ *www.tocqueville13.club* ⊘ *Closed Mon.–Wed.* Ⓜ *Porta Garibaldi.*

BEYOND CITY CENTER

Plastic. Its venerable age notwithstanding (it opened in 1980), this is still one of Milan's most avant-garde and fun clubs, complete with drag-queen shows. The action starts late, even by Italian standards— don't bother going before midnight. They don't take reservations, and there aren't any tables. Entrance on Sunday is free. ✉ *Via Gargano 15* ☎ *02/733996* ⊘ *Closed Mon.–Thurs.* Ⓜ *Tram No. 27; Bus No. 60, 62, 66, 73, or K511.*

PERFORMING ARTS

For events likely to be of interest to non–Italian speakers, see *Hello Milano* (⊕ *www.hellomilano.it*), a monthly magazine available online and in print at the tourist office in Piazza Duomo; *Easy Milano* (⊕ *www. easymilano.it*); or the *American* (⊕ *www.theamericanmag.com*), which has a thorough cultural calendar.

MUSIC

Auditorium di Milano. This modern hall, known for its excellent acoustics, is home to the **Orchestra Verdi** and **Choir of Milano,** founded by the Milan-born conductor Richard Chailly. The season, which runs from September to June, includes many top international performers and rotating guest conductors. ✉ *Largo Gustav Mahler Corso, San Gottardo 39, at Via Torricelli, Conchetta, Castello* ☎ *02/83389401* ⊕ *www. laverdi.org* Ⓜ *Tram No. 3 or 15; Bus No. 59 or 91.*

Conservatorio. The two halls belonging to the Conservatorio host some of the leading names in classical music. Series are organized by several organizations, including the venerable chamber music society the **Società del Quartetto** (☎ *02/76005500* ⊕ *www.quartettomilano.it*). ✉ *Via del Conservatorio 12, Duomo* ☎ *02/762110* ⊕ *www.consmilano.it* Ⓜ *San Babila; Tram No. 9, 12, 23, or 27; Bus No. 60 or 73.*

Teatro Dal Verme. Frequent classical music concerts are staged here from October to May. ✉ *Via San Giovanni sul Muro 2, Castello* ☎ *02/87905* ⊕ *www.dalverme.org* Ⓜ *Cairoli; Tram No. 1 or 4.*

OPERA

Fodor's Choice ★ **Teatro alla Scala.** You need know nothing of opera to sense that La Scala is closer to a cathedral than an auditorium. Hearing opera sung in the magical setting of La Scala is an unparalleled experience. Here, Verdi established his reputation and Maria Callas sang her way into opera lore. It looms as a symbol—both for the performer who dreams of singing here and for the opera buff. Audiences are notoriously demanding and are apt to jeer performers who do not measure up.

If you are lucky enough to be here during the opera season, do whatever is necessary to attend. Tickets go on sale two months before the first performance and are usually sold out the same day. The season runs from December 7, the feast day of Milan patron St. Ambrose, through June. For tickets, visit the **Biglietteria Centrale** (Galleria del Sagrato, Piazza Del Duomo ; *daily noon–6*), which is in the Duomo subway station. Tickets are also available online or via La Scala's automated booking system (☎ *02/860775*). To pick up tickets for performances—from two hours prior to 15 minutes after the start of a performance—go to the box office at the theater, which is around the corner at Via Filodrammatici 2. Although you might not get seats for the more popular operas with big-name stars, it is worth trying; ballets are easier. There are also 140 tickets available on a first-come, first-served basis starting 2½ hours before the start of each performance at the theater box office. The theater is closed from the end of July through August and on national and local holidays.

At the **Museo Teatrale alla Scala** you can admire an extensive collection of librettos, paintings of the famous names of Italian opera, posters, costumes, antique instruments, and design sketches for the theater. It is also possible to take a look at the theater itself. Special exhibitions reflect current productions. ✉ *Piazza della Scala, Largo Ghiringhelli 1, Duomo* ☎ *02/72003744 for theater, 02/88797473 for museum* ⊕ *www. teatroallascala.org* 🎫 *Museum €7* Ⓜ *Duomo or Cordusio; Tram No. 1.*

SHOPPING

Milan is the birthplace of many of the world's most celebrated brands and high-ticket retail establishments: Prada, Versace, and Armani all call Milan home. The city has produced some of the industry's biggest talents, and reigns as one of the most important fashion capitals in the world. "Fashion tourists" come from cities like Shanghai, Moscow, and Tokyo to shop here.

Weekly open markets selling fruits and vegetables—and a great deal more—are still a regular sight in Milan. Many also sell clothing and shoes.

DUOMO

Borsalino. The kingpin of milliners, Borsalino has managed to stay trendy since it opened in 1857. ✉ *Galleria Vittorio Emanuele II 92, Duomo* ☎ *02/89015436* ⊕ *www.borsalino.com* Ⓜ *Duomo; Tram No. 1.*

Gucci. This Florence-born brand attracts lots of fashion-forward tourists in hot pursuit of its monogrammed bags, shoes, and accessories. ✉ *Galleria Vittorio Emanuele II, Duomo* ☎ *02/8597991* ⊕ *www.gucci. com* Ⓜ *Duomo; Tram No. 1.*

La Rinascente. The flagship location of this always-bustling and very central department store—adjacent to both the Duomo and the Galleria Vittorio Emanuele—carries a wide range of Italian and international brands, both high-end and casual, for men, women, and children. There's also a fine selection of beauty and home products. ⊠ *Piazza Duomo, Duomo* ☎ *02/88521* ⊕ *www.rinascente.it* Ⓜ *Duomo; Tram No. 1, 2, 12, 14, 16, or 27.*

Trussardi. This family-run label offers sleek, fashion-forward accessories, leather goods, and clothes at its flagship store. ⊠ *Piazza della Scala 5, Duomo* ☎ *02/80688242* ⊕ *www.trussardi.com* Ⓜ *Duomo; Tram No. 1.*

Versace. Run by flamboyant Donatella Versace and known for its rock-and-roll styling, Versace's first store opened on Via della Spiga in 1978 and its latest flagship is inside the Galleria Vittorio Emanuele II. ⊠ *Galleria Vittorio Emanuele II 33/35, Duomo* ☎ *02/89011479* ⊕ *www.versace.com* Ⓜ *Duomo; Tram No. 1.*

BRERA

With its narrow streets and outdoor cafés, Brera is one of Milan's most charming neighborhoods. Wander through it to find smaller shops with some appealing offerings from lesser-known names that cater to the well-schooled taste of this upscale area. The densest concentration is along Via Brera, Via Solferino, and Corso Garibaldi.

Mercato di Via S. Marco. The Monday- and Thursday-morning markets here cater to the wealthy residents of the central Brera neighborhood. In addition to food stands where you can get cheese, roast chicken, and dried beans and fruits, there are several clothing and shoe stalls that are important stops for some of Milan's most elegant women. Check out the knitwear at Valentino, about midway down on the street side. ⊠ *Brera* Ⓜ *Lanza; Tram No. 2, 4, 12, or 14.*

QUADRILATERO

The heart of Milan's shopping reputation is the Quadrilatero della Moda district north of the Duomo. Here the world's leading designers compete for shoppers' attention, showing off their ultrastylish clothes in stores that are works of high style themselves. It's difficult to find any bargains, but regardless of whether you're making a purchase, the area is a great place for window-shopping and people-watching.

Armani Megastore. Armani Casa (furniture), Armani Junior, Emporio Armani, Amani Fiori (flowers), Armani Dolci (chocolate), Armani Jeans, and Armani Libri (books) are all under this monumental store's roof. ⊠ *Via Manzoni 31, Quadrilatero* ☎ *02/72318600* ⊕ *www.armani.com* Ⓜ *Montenapoleone; Tram No. 1.*

Fodor'sChoice ★ **DMagazine Outlet.** This store boasts some of the best prices in the area for luxury items such as Prada, Gucci, Lanvin, and Cavalli. DMagazine has two other locations, at Via Forcella 13 and Via Bigli 4. ⊠ *Via Manzoni 44, Quadrilatero* ☎ *02/36514365* ⊕ *www.dmagazine.it* Ⓜ *Montenapoleone; Tram No. 1.*

Fodor'sChoice ★ **Dolce & Gabbana.** This fabulous duo has created an empire based on sultry designs for men and women. The gorgeous flagship store, in a 19th-century palazzo, features two floors of women's wear and accessories, and one floor of menswear. ⊠ *Montenapoleone 4, Quadrilatero* ☎ *02/77123711* ⊕ *www.dolcegabbana.it* Ⓜ *Montenapoleone; Tram No. 1.*

Giorgio Armani. Find Armani's women's, men's, and ready-to-wear collections inside a historic palazzo. ⊠ *Via Montenapoleone 2, Quadrilatero* ☎ *02/76003234* ⊕ *www.armani.com* Ⓜ *San Babilo.*

Missoni. Famous for their kaleidoscope-patterned knits, this family-run brand sells whimsical designs for men and women. ⊠ *Via Montenapoleone 8, Quadrilatero* ☎ *02/76003555* ⊕ *www.missoni.com* Ⓜ *Montenapoleone or San Babila; Tram No. 1.*

Miu Miu. Prada's more upbeat, youthful brand has a wide offering of boldly printed women's fashions and accessories. ⊠ *Via Sant'Andrea 21, Quadrilatero* ☎ *02/76001799* ⊕ *www.miumiu.com* Ⓜ *Montenapoleone, San Babila, or Palestro; Tram No. 1.*

Moschino. Known for its bold prints, colors, and appliqués, Moschino is a brand for daring fashionistas. ⊠ *Via Sant'Andrea 25, Quadrilatero* ☎ *02/76022639* ⊕ *www.moschino.com* Ⓜ *Montenapoleone, San Babila, or Palestro; Tram No. 1.*

Prada. Founded in Milan, Prada has several locations throughout the city. Its Via della Spiga location carries upscale accessories and bags coveted by women worldwide, while its stores on Via Montenapoleone showcase its women's (Via Montenapoleone 8) and men's fashions (Via Montenapoleone 6). ⊠ *Via della Spiga 18, Quadrilatero* ☎ *02/780465* ⊕ *www.prada.com* Ⓜ *Montenapoleone, San Babila, or Palestro; Tram No. 1.*

Roberto Cavalli. Famous for his wild-animal prints, Roberto Cavalli creates sexy designs for men and women. ⊠ *Via Montenapoleone 6, Quadrilatero* ☎ *02/7630771* ⊕ *www.robertocavalli.com* Ⓜ *San Babila.*

Salvatore Ferragamo Donna. This Florence-based brand is a leader in leather goods and accessories, and carries designs for women in this store. ⊠ *Via Montenapoleone 3, Quadrilatero* ☎ *02/76000054* ⊕ *www.ferragamo.com* Ⓜ *San Babila.*

Tod's. This leather-goods leader sells luxury handbags as well as a variety of shoes for men and women. It also sells a complete line of men's and women's clothing. ⊠ *Via della Spiga 22, Quadrilatero* ☎ *02/76002423* ⊕ *www.tods.com* Ⓜ *Montenapoleone, San Babila, or Palestro; Tram No. 1.*

Valentino. Even after the departure of its founding father, Valentino Garavani, this Roman-based fashion brand still flourishes. ⊠ *Via Montenapoleone 20, Quadrilatero* ☎ *02/76006182* ⊕ *www.valentino.com* Ⓜ *Montenapoleone; Tram No. 1.*

CENTRO DIREZIONALE

Antonioli. Antonioli raises the bar for Milan's top trendsetters. Uniting the most cutting-edge looks of each season, it is perhaps the most fashion-forward concept store in the city. Aside from Italian brands like Valentino, it also stocks a competitive international array of designers like Ann Demeulemeester, Rick Owens, Givenchy, Gareth Pugh, Haider Ackermann, Maison Martin Margiela, and Christopher Kane. ⊠ *Via Pasquale Paoli 1, Centro Direzionale* ☎ *02/36561860* ⊕ *www.antonioli.eu* Ⓜ *Porta Genova; Tram No. 2; Bus No. 47 or 74.*

VIA TORINO

For inexpensive and trendy clothes—for the under-25 set—stroll **Via Torino,** which begins in Piazza Duomo. Stay away on Saturday afternoon if you don't like crowds.

CORSO COMO

Fodor'sChoice **10 Corso Como.** A shrine to Milan's creative fashion sense, 10 Corso
★ Como was founded by the former fashion editor and publisher Carla Sozzani. The clothing and design establishment also includes a restaurant-café, gallery, and small hotel. ✉ *Corso Como 10, Corso Como* ☎ *02/29002674* ⊕ *www.10corsocomo.com* Ⓜ *Porta Garibaldi.*

CINQUE TERRE

The photogenic and preposterously beautiful Cinque Terre is the heart of the Italian Riviera. In their rugged simplicity, the five old fishing towns of Monterosso, Vernazza, Corniglia, Manarola, and Riomaggiore seem to mock the caked-on artifice of glitzy neighboring resorts. With a clear blue sea in the foreground, spectacularly multicolor buildings emerge almost seamlessly from cliffs, and rocky mountains rise precipitously to gravity-defying vineyards and dusty olive groves. The five small villages (Cinque Terre literally means "Five Lands") cling to the cliffs along a gorgeous stretch of the Ligurian coast. The geography here prevents expansion or extensive technological advancement, which allows these small towns to retain most of their enchanting old-world charm.

The terrain is so steep that for centuries, footpaths were the only way to get from place to place. These footpaths provide beautiful views of the rocky coast tumbling into the sea, as well as access to secluded beaches and grottoes. Since its designation in 1997 as a UNESCO World Heritage Site, Cinque Terre has become one of Italy's most popular destinations. Despite summer crowds and some lingering damage from the 2011 flash floods, the villages remain alluringly characteristic and the views from the trails in between are as breathtaking as ever.

RIOMAGGIORE

17 km (11 miles) southwest of La Spezia, 101 km (60 miles) southeast of Genoa.

At the eastern end of the Cinque Terre, Riomaggiore is built into a river gorge (thus the name, which means "major river") and is easily accessible from La Spezia by train or car. The landscape is terraced and steep—be prepared for many stairs!—and leads down to a small harbor, protected by large slabs of alabaster and marble that serve as tanning beds for sunbathers. The harbor is also the site of several outdoor cafés with fine views. According to legend, the settlement of Riomaggiore dates as far back as the 8th century, when Greek religious refugees came here to escape persecution by the Byzantine emperor.

CLOSE UP

Accessing the Trails of the Cinque Terre

WHEN TO GO

The ideal times to visit the Cinque Terre are September and May, when the weather is mild and the summer tourist season isn't in full swing (between June and August it can be unbearably hot and crowded).

GETTING HERE AND AROUND

There is now a local train between La Spezia and Levanto that stops at each of the Cinque Terre villages, and runs approximately every 30 minutes throughout the day. Tickets for each leg of the journey (€2.30) are available at the five train stations. In Corniglia, the only one of the Cinque Terre that isn't at sea level, a shuttle service (€1) is provided for those who don't wish to climb (or descend) 300-plus steps that link the train station with the clifftop town.

Along the Cinque Terre coast two ferry lines operate. From June to September, Golfo Paradiso runs from Genoa and Camogli to Monterosso al Mare and Vernazza. The smaller but more frequent Golfo dei Poeti stops at each village from Lerici (east of Riomaggiore) to Monterosso, with the exception of Corniglia, four times a day. A one-day ticket costs €32.

ADMISSION

Entrance tickets for using the trails are available at ticket booths located at the start of each section of Trail No. 2, and at information offices in the Levanto, Monterosso, Vernazza, Corniglia, Manarola, Riomaggiore, and La Spezia train stations.

A one-day pass costs €7.50, which includes a trail map and an information leaflet; a two-day pass is €14.50. The Cinque Terre Card combines park entrance fees with unlimited daily use of the regional train between La Spezia, the five villages, and Levanto just north of Monterosso, and costs €19.50 for a one-day pass and €31.50 for a two-day pass.

FOR MORE INFORMATION

⊕ www.cinqueterre.com; ⊕ www.lecinqueterre.org; ⊕ www.parconazionale-5terre.it; ⊕ www.rebuildmonterosso.com; ⊕ savevernazza.com; ⊕ www.littleparadiso.com (blog); ⊕ lifeinliguria.blogspot.it (blog).

The village is divided into two parts. If you arrive by train, you will have to pass through a tunnel that flanks the train tracks in order to reach the historic side of town. To avoid the crowds and get a great view of the Cinque Terre coast, walk straight uphill as soon as you exit the station. This winding road takes you over the hill to the 14th-century **church of St. John the Baptist,** toward the medieval town center and the Genovese-style tower houses that dot the village. Follow Via Roma (the Old Town's main street) downhill, pass under the train tracks, and you'll arrive in the charming fishermen's port of the village. Lined with traditional fishing boats and small trattorias, this is a lovely spot for a romantic lunch or dinner. Unfortunately, Riomaggiore doesn't have as much old-world charm as its sister villages; its easy accessibility has brought traffic and more modern construction here than elsewhere in the Cinque Terre.

GETTING HERE AND AROUND

The enormous parking problems presented by these cliff-dwelling villages have been mitigated somewhat by a large, covered parking structure at La Spezia Centrale station, which costs €1.50 per hour. It's clean and secure (you cannot enter without a ticket code to open the door), and it's open 24/7. This is a good backup solution for those with cars, although others may choose to take a day trip from Pisa or Lucca and rely on bus and train services. Arrive early as it can fill up by midmorning, especially in the high season.

WHERE TO EAT

$$$ LIGURIAN 🍴 **Dau Cila.** There's wonderful seaside dining on Riomaggiore harbor, with a vast menu of local Ligurian dishes and an extensive wine list. **■ TIP→ On bad-weather days, take advantage of the lovely dining room with vaulted ceilings, built into the rock.** [$] *Average main: €25* ✉ *Via San Giacomo 65* ☎ *0187/760032* 🕓 *Closed Nov.–Mar.*

MANAROLA

16 km (10 miles) southwest of La Spezia, 117 km (73 miles) southeast of Genoa.

Fodor's Choice ★ The enchanting pastel houses of Manarola spill down a steep hill overlooking a spectacular turquoise swimming cove and a bustling harbor. The whole town is built on black rock. Above the town, ancient terraces still protect abundant vineyards and olive trees. This village is the center of wine and olive-oil production in the region, and its streets are lined with shops selling local products.

Surrounded by steep terraced vineyards, Manarola's one road tumbles from the **Chiesa di San Lorenzo** (14th century) high above the village, down to the rocky port below. Since the Cinque Terre wine cooperative is located in **Groppo,** a hamlet overlooking the village (and reachable by foot or by the green Park bus; ask at Park offices for schedules), the vineyards are accessible. If you'd like to snap a shot of the most famous view of the town, you can walk from the port area to the cemetery above. Along the way you'll pass the town's play yard, uncrowded bathrooms, and a tap with clean drinking water.

WHERE TO STAY

$$ HOTEL Fodor's Choice ★ 🏨 **La Torretta.** The Cinque Terre's only "boutique" hotel is in a 17th-century tower that sits high on the hill above the rainbow-hue village of Manarola with truly lovely views of the terraced vineyards, colorful village homes, and the Mediterranean sea; inside, decor is chic, sleek, and antiques bedecked. **Pros:** well maintained; a cut above most lodging in the Cinque Terre. **Cons:** if the luggage shuttle is not running during its limited hours, it is a steep walk up to the hotel. [$] *Rooms from: €200* ✉ *Vico Volto 20, Cinque Terre* ☎ *0187/920327* 🌐 *www.torrettas.com* 🕓 *Closed Nov.–mid-Mar.* 🛏 *4 rooms, 7 suites* 🍽 *Breakfast.*

Continued on page 243

HIKING THE CINQUE TERRE

FIVE REMOTE VILLAGES MAKE ONE MUST-SEE DESTINATION

"Charming" and "breathtaking" are adjectives that get a workout when you're traveling in Italy, but it's rare that both apply to a single location. The Cinque Terre is such a place, and this combination of characteristics goes a long way toward explaining its tremendous appeal.

The area is made up of five tiny villages (Cinque Terre literally means "Five Lands") clinging to the cliffs along a gorgeous stretch of the Ligurian coast. The terrain is so steep that for centuries footpaths were the only way to get from place to place. It just so happens that these paths provide beautiful views of the rocky coast tumbling into the sea, as well as access to secluded beaches and grottoes.

Backpackers "discovered" the Cinque Terre in the 1970s, and its popularity has been growing ever since. Despite summer crowds, much of the original appeal is intact. Each town has maintained its own distinct charm, and views from the trails in between are as breathtaking as ever.

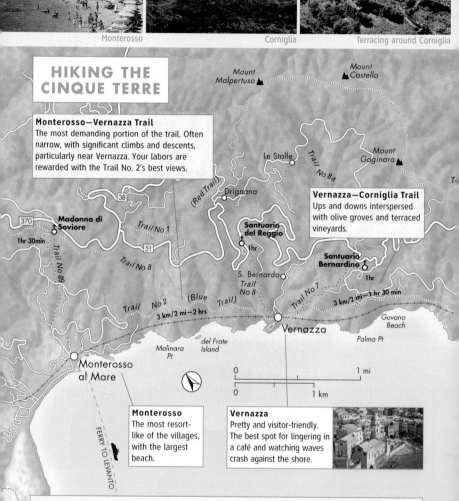

Monterosso

Corniglia

Terracing around Corniglia

HIKING THE CINQUE TERRE

Mount Malpertuso ▲

Mount Castello ▲

Monterosso—Vernazza Trail
The most demanding portion of the trail. Often narrow, with significant climbs and descents, particularly near Vernazza. Your labors are rewarded with the Trail No. 2's best views.

Le Stalle

Mount Gaginara ▲

(Red Trail)

Drignana

Trail No 8a

38

Vernazza—Corniglia Trail
Ups and downs interspersed with olive groves and terraced vineyards.

370

Madonna di Soviore

Trail No 1

Santuario del Reggio

51

1hr

1hr 30min

Trail No 89

Trail No 8

S. Bernardo

Santuario Bernardino

1hr

Trail No 8

Trail No 7

3 km/2 mi—1 hr 30 min

Trail No 2 *(Blue Trail)*

3 km/2 mi—2 hrs

Vernazza

Guvano Beach

Molinara Pt

del Frate Island

Palma Pt

Monterosso al Mare

0 ———— 1 mi

0 ———— 1 km

FERRY TO LEVANTO

Monterosso
The most resort-like of the villages, with the largest beach.

Vernazza
Pretty and visitor-friendly. The best spot for lingering in a café and watching waves crash against the shore.

THE CLASSIC HIKE

Hiking is the most popular way to experience the Cinque Terre, and Trail No. 2, the Sentiero Azzurro (Blue Trail), is the most traveled path. To cover the entire trail is a full day: it's approximately 13 km (8 miles) in length, takes you to all five villages, and requires about five hours, not including stops, to complete. The best approach is to start at the eastern-

most town of Riomaggiore and warm up your legs on the easiest segment of the trail. As you work your way west, the hike gets progressively more demanding. Between Corniglia and Manarola take the ferry (which provides its own beautiful views) or the inland train running between the towns instead.

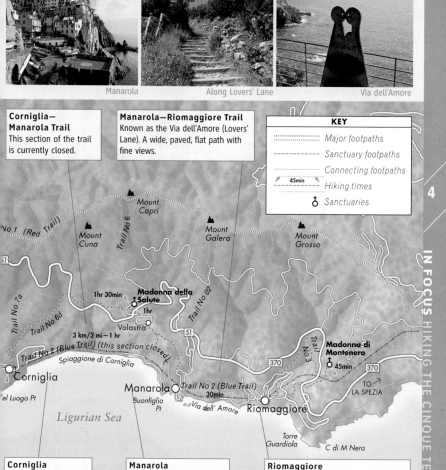

Manarola

Along Lovers' Lane

Via dell'Amore

Corniglia–Manarola Trail
This section of the trail is currently closed.

Manarola–Riomaggiore Trail
Known as the Via dell'Amore (Lovers' Lane). A wide, paved, flat path with fine views.

KEY

··············	*Major footpaths*
– – – – –	*Sanctuary footpaths*
- - - - - -	*Connecting footpaths*
▱ 45min	*Hiking times*
♀	*Sanctuaries*

Mount Capri

No 1 (Red Trail)

Mount Cuna

Trail No 6

Mount Galera

Mount Grosso

Trail No 7a

Trail No 6d

1hr 30min

Madonna della Salute

1hr

Volastra

Trail No 02

3 km/2 mi – 1 hr

Trail No 2 (Blue Trail) (this section closed)

Spiaggione di Corniglia

51

Madonna di Montenero
♀ 45min

Trail No 3

370

370

TO → LA SPEZIA

Corniglia

el Luogo Pt

Manarola

Buonfiglio Pt

Trail No 2 (Blue Trail)

30min

Via dell' Amore

Riomaggiore

Ligurian Sea

Torre Guardiola

C di M Nero

Corniglia
Perched on a cliff 500 ft. above the sea, reached by a switchback path (or by shuttle bus).

Manarola
The most photogenic of the villages, best seen from the cemetery a few minutes up the path toward Corniglia.

Riomaggiore
Cliff-clinging buildings are almost as striking as those in Manarola. Stairs to the left of the train station entrance cross over the tracks and lead to the trailhead.

BEYOND TRAIL NO.2

Trail No. 2 is just one of a network of trails crisscrossing the hills. If you're a dedicated hiker, spend a few nights and try some of the other routes. Trail No. 1, the Sentiero Rosso (Red Trail), climbs from Portovenere (east of Riomaggiore) and returns to the sea at Levanto (west of Monterosso al Mare). To hike its length takes from 9 to 12 hours; the ridge-top trail provides spectacular views from high above the villages, each of which can be reached via a steep path. Other shorter trails go from the villages up into the hills, some leading to religious sanctuaries. Trail No. 9, for example, starts from the old section of Monterosso and ends at the Madonna di Soviore Sanctuary.

Hiking the Cinque Terre

Although often described as relaxing and easy, the Cinque Terre also have several hiking options if you wish to exert yourself a little. Many people do not realize just how demanding parts of these trails can be—it's best to come prepared. We recommend bringing a Cinque Terre Card and cash (smaller shops, eateries, and the park entrances do not accept credit cards).

When all trails are completely open, a hike through the entire region takes about four to five hours; add time for exploring each village and taking a lunch break. It's an all-day, if not two-day trek. We recommend an early start, especially in summer when midday temperatures can rise to 90°F. Note that only Sentiero Azzuro (Trail No. 2) requires the Cinque Terre Card. The other 20-plus trails in the area are free. All trails are well marked with a red-and-white hiking-trail sign. The trails from village to village get progressively steeper as you move from south (Riomaggiore) to the north (Monterosso). If you're a day-tripper arriving by car, use the new underground lot at La Spezia Centrale train station (€2.30 per hour in summer) and take the train to Riomaggiore (6–8 minutes) to begin your hiking adventure.

OUR FAVORITES

Other trails to consider include: **Monterosso to Santuario Madonna di Soviore**, a fairly strenuous but rewarding 1½ hours up to a lovely 8th-century sanctuary. There is also a restaurant and a priceless view.

Riomaggiore to Montenero and Portovenere is one hour up to the sanctuary and another three hours on to Portovenere, passing through some gorgeous, less-traveled terrain. **Manarola to Volastra to Corniglia** runs high above the main trail and through vineyards and lesser-known villages. **Monterosso to Levanto** is a good 2½-hour hike, passing over Punta Mesco with glorious views of the Cinque Terre to the south, Corsica to the west, and the Alps to the north.

Each town has something that passes for a beach (usually with lots of pebbles or slabs of terraced rock), but there is only one option for both sand and decent swimming—in Monterosso, just across from the train station. It's equipped with chairs, umbrellas, and snack bars.

PRECAUTIONS

If you're hitting the trails, carry water with you, wear sturdy shoes (hiking boots are best), and have a hat and sunscreen handy. Note that the lesser-used trails aren't as well maintained as Trail No. 2. If you're undertaking the full Trail No. 1 hike, bring something to snack on as well as your water bottle. Note that currently the Via dell'Amore and the portion of Trail No. 2 between Manarola and Corniglia were closed indefinitely due to landslides. ■TIP➜ Check weather reports; especially in late fall and winter, thunderstorms can make shelterless trails slippery and dangerous. Rain in October and November can cause landslides and close the trails.

CORNIGLIA

27 km (17 miles) northwest of La Spezia, 100 km (60 miles) southeast of Genoa.

Fodor's Choice ★

The buildings, narrow lanes, and stairways of Corniglia are strung together amid vineyards high on the cliffs. On a clear day, views of the entire coastal strip are excellent, from Elba in the south to the Italian Alps in the north. The high perch and lack of harbor make this farming community the most remote and therefore least crowded of the Cinque Terre. In fact, the 365 steps that lead from the train station to the town center dissuade many tourists from making the hike to the village. You can also take the green Park bus, but they run infrequently and are usually packed with tired hikers.

Corniglia is built along one road edged with small shops, bars, gelaterias, and restaurants. Midway along Via Fieschi is the **Largo Taragio,** the main square and heart of the village. Shaded by leafy trees and umbrellas, this is a lovely spot for a midhike gelato break. Here you'll find the 14th-century **Chiesa di San Pietro.** Its rose window of marble imported from Carrara is impressive, particularly considering the work required to get it here!

VERNAZZA

27 km (17 miles) west of La Spezia, 96 km (59 miles) southeast of Genoa.

Fodor's Choice ★

With its narrow streets and small squares, Vernazza is arguably the most charming of the five Cinque Terre towns, and usually the most crowded. Historically, it was the most important of them, since it was the only one fortunate enough to have a natural port and, therefore, became wealthier than its neighbors—as evinced by the elaborate arcades, loggias, and marble work lining Via Roma and Piazza Marconi.

The village's pink, slate-roof houses and colorful squares contrast with the remains of the medieval fort and castle, including two towers, in the Old Town. The Romans first inhabited this rocky spit of land in the 1st century.

Today, Vernazza has a fairly lively social scene. **Piazza Marconi** looks out across Vernazza's small sandy beach to the sea, towards Monterosso. The numerous restaurants and bars crowd their tables and umbrellas on the outskirts of the piazza, creating a patchwork of sights and sounds that form one of the most unique and beautiful places in the world.

EXPLORING

If mass is not going on (there will be a cord blocking the entrance if it is), take a peek into the **church of St. Margaret of Antioch.** Little changed since its enlargement in the 1600s, this 14th-century edifice has simple interiors but truly breathtaking views toward the sea: a stark contrast to the other, elaborate churches of the Cinque Terre.

On the other side of the piazza, stairs lead to a lookout **fortress and cylindrical watchtower,** built in the 11th century as protection against pirate attacks. For a small fee you can climb to the top of the tower for a spectacular view of the coastline.

4

WHERE TO EAT AND STAY

$$
LIGURIAN

✕ **Gambero Rosso.** Relax on Vernazza's main square at this fine trattoria looking out at a church. Enjoy such delectable dishes as shrimp salad, vegetable torte, and squid-ink risotto. The creamy pesto, served atop spaghetti, is some of the best in the Cinque Terre. End your meal with Cinque Terre's own *sciacchetrà*, a dessert wine served with semisweet biscotti. Don't drink it out of the glass—dip the biscotti in the wine instead. $ *Average main: €22* ✉ *Piazza Marconi 7* ☎ *0187/812265* ⊕ *www.ristorantegamberorosso.net* ⊘ *Closed Mon., and Nov.–Mar.*

$$$
LIGURIAN
Fodor'sChoice
★

✕ **Ristorante Belforte.** High above the sea in one of Vernazza's remaining stone towers is this unique spot serving delicious Cinque Terre cuisine such as branzino *sotto sale* (sea bass cooked under salt), stuffed mussels, and *insalata di polpo* (octopus salad). The setting is magnificent, so try for an outdoor table. Reservations are a must. $ *Average main: €25* ✉ *Via Guidoni 42* ☎ *0187/812222* ⊕ *www.ristorantebelforte.it* ⊘ *Closed Tues., and Nov.–Easter.*

$$
B&B/INN

▦ **La Malà.** A cut above other lodging options in the Cinque Terre, these small guest rooms are equipped with flat-screen TVs, a/c, marble showers, comfortable bedding, and have views of the sea or the port, which can also be enjoyed at their most bewitching from the shared terrace literally suspended over the Mediterranean. **Pros:** clean, fresh-feeling rooms; oh, the views. **Cons:** there are some stairs involved; for the price, one should not have to go to a bar for a small continental breakfast. $ *Rooms from: €160* ✉ *Giovanni Battista 29* ☎ *334/2875718* ⊕ *www.lamala.it* ⊘ *Closed Jan. 8–Mar. 1* ⊷ *4 rooms* ⦿ *No meals.*

MONTEROSSO AL MARE

32 km (20 miles) northwest of La Spezia, 89 km (55 miles) southeast of Genoa.

Fodor'sChoice
★

It's the combined draw of beautiful beaches, rugged cliffs, crystal clear turquoise waters, and plentiful small hotels and restaurants that make Monterosso al Mare into the largest of the Cinque Terre villages (population 1,800) and also the busiest in midsummer.

Monterosso has the most festivals of the five villages, starting with the Lemon Feast on the Saturday preceding Ascension Sunday, followed by the Flower Festival of Corpus Christi, celebrated yearly on the second Sunday after Pentecost. During the afternoon, the streets and alleyways of the historic center are decorated with thousands of colorful flower petals set in beautiful designs that the evening procession passes over. Finally, the Salted Anchovy and Olive Oil Festival takes place each year during the second weekend of September.

EXPLORING

From the train station, heading west, you pass through a tunnel and exit into the *centro storico* (historic center) of the village. Nestled into the wide valley that leads to the sea, Monterosso is built above numerous streams, which have been covered to make up the major streets of the village. Via Buranco, the oldest street in Monterosso, leads out to the most characteristic piazza of the village, Piazza Matteotti (locals pass through here daily to shop at the supermarket and butcher). This piazza also contains the oldest and most typical wineshop in the village, Enoteca da Eliseo—stop here between 6 pm and midnight to share tables with fellow tourists and locals over a bottle of Cinque Terre wine. There's also the **Chiesa di San Francesco,** built in the 12th century, which is an excellent example of the Ligurian Gothic style. Its distinctive black stripes and marble rose window make it one of the most photographed sites in the Cinque Terre.

Fegina, the newer side of the village (and site of the train station), has relatively modern homes ranging from Liberty style (Art Nouveau) to the early 1970s. At the far eastern end of town, you'll run into a private sailing club sheltered by a vast rock carved with an impressive statue of Neptune. From here, you can reach the challenging trail to Levanto (a great 2½ hour hike). This trail has the added bonus of a five-minute detour to the **ruins of a 14th-century monastery.** The expansive view from this vantage point allowed the monks who were housed here to easily scan the waters for enemy ships that might invade the villages and alert residents to coming danger. Have your camera ready for this Cinerama-like vista.

Although it has the most nightlife on the Cinque Terre (thanks to its numerous wine bars and pubs), Monterosso is also the most family-friendly. With its expanse of free and equipped beaches, extensive pedestrian areas, large children's play park, and summer activities, Monterosso is a top spot for kids.

The **local outdoor market** is held on Thursday and attracts crowds of tourists and villagers from along the coast to shop for everything from pots, pans, and underwear to fruits, vegetables, and fish. Often a few stands sell local art and crafts, as well as olive oil and wine.

WHERE TO EAT

$$ ✕ **Enoteca Internazionale.** Located on the main street, this wine bar offers
WINE BAR a large variety of vintages, both local and from farther afield, plus delicious light fare; its umbrella-covered patio is a welcoming spot to recuperate after a day of hiking. Susanna, the owner, is a certified sommelier who's always forthcoming with helpful suggestions on pairing local wines with their tasty bruschettas. $ *Average main: €15* ✉ *Via Roma 62* ☎ *0187/817278* ⊕ *www.enotecainternazionale. com* ⊗ *Closed Tues., and Jan.–Mar.*

$$$ ✕ **Miky.** This is arguably the best restaurant in Monterosso, special-
SEAFOOD izing in tasty, fresh seafood dishes including grilled calamari and monkfish ravioli. The *catalana* (poached lobster and shrimp with finely sliced raw fennel and carrot) is a winner. It has a beautiful little garden in the back, perfect for lunch on a sunny day. If the restaurant is full (and reservations are advised), try their *cantina* just a few doors down, for more casual seaside dining with a view. $ *Average main: €28* ✉ *Via Fegina 104* ☎ *0187/817608* ⊕ *www.ristorantemiky. it* ⊗ *Closed mid-Nov.–mid-Mar.*

WHERE TO STAY

$$ 🛏 **Bellambra B&B.** Modern rooms with charm and comfort in the heart
B&B/INN of the old town make this a terrific base for exploring the Cinque Terre. **Pros:** relatively new; spacious rooms and bathrooms; location; helpful

service. **Cons:** can be a bit noisy; no elevator with steep, narrow stairs. $ *Rooms from: €170* ⊠ *Via Roma 64* ☎ *39/3920121912* ⊕ *www.bellambra5terre.com* ➟ *4 rooms, 1 apartment* ⏐○⏐ *Breakfast.*

$$
B&B/INN
⚅ **Il Giardino Incantato.** With wood-beam ceilings and stone walls, the stylishly restored and updated rooms in this 16th-century house in the historic center of Monterosso ooze comfort and old-world charm. **Pros:** spacious rooms; gorgeous garden; excellent hosts. **Cons:** no views. $ *Rooms from: €180* ⊠ *Via Mazzini 18* ☎ *0185/818315* ⊕ *www.ilgiardinoincantato.net* ☉ *Closed Nov.–early Apr.* ➟ *3 rooms, 1 junior suite* ⏐○⏐ *Breakfast.*

$$$$
HOTEL
⚅ **Porto Roca.** Far from the madding crowds, Cinque Terre's only high-end hotel is perched on the famous terraced cliffs right over the main beach and magnificent sea with large balconies to savor all the panoramic views. **Pros:** unobstructed sea views; tranquil location; pool. **Cons:** some of the rooms could use a revamp; back-facing rooms can be a bit dark; expensive for level of comfort offered. $ *Rooms from: €340* ⊠ *Via Corone 1* ☎ *0187/817502, 0187/817692* ⊕ *www.portoroca.it* ☉ *Closed Nov.–Mar.* ➟ *39 rooms, 3 junior suites, 3 apartments* ⏐○⏐ *No meals.*

EMILIA-ROMAGNA

Gourmets the world over claim that Emilia-Romagna's greatest contribution to humankind has been gastronomic. Birthplace of fettuccine, tortellini, lasagna, prosciutto, and Parmigiano-Reggiano cheese, the region has a spectacular culinary tradition. But there are many reasons to come here aside from the desire to be well fed: Parma's Correggio paintings, Giuseppe Verdi's villa at Sant'Agata, the medieval splendor of Bologna's palaces, Ferrara's medieval alley, the rolling hills of the Romagna countryside, and, perhaps foremost, the Byzantine beauty of mosaic-rich Ravenna—glittering as brightly today as it did 1,500 years ago.

As you travel through Emilia, the western half of the region, you'll encounter the sprawling plants of Italy's industrial food giants, like Barilla and Fini, standing side by side with the fading villas and farmhouses that have long punctuated the flat, fertile land of the Po Plain. Bologna, the principal city of Emilia, is a busy cultural and, increasingly, business center, less visited but in many ways just as engaging as the country's more famous tourist destinations—particularly given its acknowledged position as the leading city of Italian cuisine. The rest of the region follows suit: eating is an essential part of any Emilian experience.

The area's history is laden with culinary legends, such as how the original tortellino was modeled on the shape of Venus's navel and the original *tagliolini* (long, thin egg pasta) was served at the wedding banquet of Annibale Bentivoglio and Lucrezia d'Este—a marriage uniting two of the noblest families in the region. You'll need to stay focused just to make sure you try all the basics: Parma's famed prosciutto and Parmigiano-Reggiano cheese, Modena's balsamic vinegar, the ragù whose poor imitations are known worldwide as "Bolognese"—and, of course, the best pasta in the world.

The historic border between Emilia to the west and Romagna to the east lies near the fortified town of Dozza. Emilia is flat; but just east of the Romagnan border the landscape gets hillier and more sparsely settled, in places covered with evergreen forests and steaming natural springs. Finally, it flattens again into the low-lying marshland of the Po Delta, which meets the Adriatic Sea. Each fall, in both Romagna and Emilia, the trademark fog rolls in off the Adriatic to hang over the flatlands in winter, coloring the region with a spooky, gray glow.

BOLOGNA

Bologna, a city rich with cultural jewels, has long been one of the best-kept secrets in northern Italy. Tourists in the know can bask in the shadow of its leaning medieval towers and devour the city's wonderful food.

The charm of the centro storico, with its red-arcaded passageways and sidewalks, can be attributed to wise city counselors who, at the beginning of the 13th century, decreed that roads couldn't be built without *portici* (porticoes). Were these counselors to return to town eight centuries later, they'd marvel at how little has changed.

Bologna, with a population of about 373,000, has a university-town vibe—and it feels young and lively in a way that many other Italian cities don't. It also feels full of Italians in a way that many other towns, thronged with tourists, don't. Bolognesi come out at aperitivo time, and you might be struck by the fact that it's not just youngsters who are out doing the passeggiata, or having a glass of wine with affettati misti.

From as early as the Middle Ages the town was known as "Bologna the Fat" for the agricultural prosperity that resulted in a well-fed population. In the 21st century Bolognese food remains, arguably, the best in Italy. With its sublime cuisine, lively spirit, and largely undiscovered art, Bologna is a memorable destination.

GETTING HERE AND AROUND

Frequent train service from Florence to Bologna makes getting here easy. The Italo and Frecciarossa and Frecciaargento (high-speed trains) run several times an hour and take just under 40 minutes.

Otherwise, you're left with the *regionali* (regional) trains, which putter along and get you to Bologna in just over two hours. The historic center is an interesting and relatively effortless walk from the station—though it takes about 20 minutes.

If you're driving from Florence, take the A1, exiting onto the A14, and then get on the RA1 to Uscita 7–Bologna Centrale. The trip takes about an hour. From Milan, take the A1, exiting to the A14 as you near the city; from there, take the A13 and exit at Bologna; then follow the RA1 to Uscita 7–Bologna Centrale. The trip takes just under three hours.

VISITOR INFORMATION

Bologna Tourism Offices. ✉ *Aeroporto di Bologna* ☎ *051/6472201* ⊕ *www.bolognawelcome.it.*

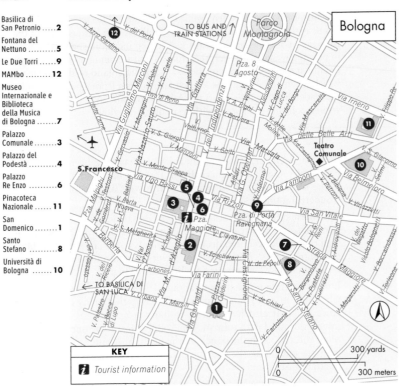

EXPLORING

Piazza Maggiore and the adjacent Piazza del Nettuno are the historic centers of the city. Arranged around these two squares are the imposing Basilica di San Petronio, the massive Palazzo Comunale, the Palazzo del Podestà, the Palazzo Re Enzo, and the Fontana del Nettuno—one of the most visually harmonious groupings of public buildings in the country. From here, sights that aren't on one of the piazzas are but a short walk away, along delightful narrow cobblestone streets or under the ubiquitous arcades that double as municipal umbrellas. Take at least a full day to explore Bologna; it's compact and lends itself to easy exploration, but there's plenty to see.

TOP ATTRACTIONS

Basilica di San Petronio. Construction on this vast cathedral began in 1390; and the work, as you can see, still isn't finished more than 600 years later. The wings of the transept are missing and the facade is only partially decorated, lacking most of the marble that was intended to adorn it. The main doorway was carved in 1425 by the great Sienese master Jacopo della Quercia. Above the center of the door is a Madonna and Child flanked by saints Ambrose and Petronius, the city's patrons. Michelangelo, Giulio Romano, and Andrea Palladio (among others), submitted designs for the facade, which were all eventually rejected.

The interior of the basilica is huge. The Bolognesi had planned an even bigger church—you can see the columns erected to support the larger version outside the east end—but had to tone down construction when the university seat was established next door in 1561. The **Museo di San Petronio** contains models showing how it was originally supposed to look. The most important art in the church is in the fourth chapel on the left: these frescoes by Giovanni di Modena date to 1410–15. ⊠ *Piazza Maggiore* ☏ *051/22544* ⊒ *Free.*

Fontana del Nettuno. Sculptor Giambologna's elaborate 1563–66 Baroque fountain and monument to Neptune occupying Piazza Nettuno has been aptly nicknamed "Il Gigante" (The Giant). Its exuberantly sensual mermaids and undraped god of the sea drew fire when it was constructed, but not enough, apparently, to dissuade the populace from using the fountain as a public washing stall for centuries. Restoration efforts are planned for most of 2017. ⊠ *Piazza Nettuno, next to Palazzo Re Enzo, Piazza Maggiore.*

Le Due Torri. Two landmark towers, mentioned by Dante in *The Inferno,* stand side by side in the compact Piazza di Porta Ravegnana. Once every family of importance had a tower as a symbol of prestige and power—and as a potential fortress. Now only 60 remain out of more than 200 that once presided over the city. **Torre Garisenda** (late 11th century), which tilts 10 feet off perpendicular, was shortened to 165 feet in the 1300s and is now closed to visitors. **Torre degli Asinelli** (circa 1109) is 320 feet tall and leans 7½ feet. If you're up to a serious physical challenge—and not claustrophobic—you may want to climb its 500 narrow, wooden steps to get the view over Bologna. ⊠ *Piazza di Porta Ravegnana, East of Piazza Maggiore* ⊒ €3.

FAMILY

Fodor'sChoice

★

Santo Stefano. This splendid and unusual basilica contains between four and seven connected churches (authorities differ). A 4th-century temple dedicated to Isis originally occupied this site, but much of what you see was erected between the 10th and 12th centuries. The oldest existing building is **Santi Vitale e Agricola,** parts of which date from the 5th century. The exquisite beehive-shape San Sepolcro contains a Nativity scene much loved by Bologna's children, who come at Christmastime to pay their respects to the Christ child. Just outside the church, which probably dates from the 5th century (with later alterations), is the **Cortile di Pilato** (Pilate's Courtyard), named for the basin in the center. Despite the fact that the basin was probably crafted around the 8th century, legend has it that Pontius Pilate washed his hands in it after condemning Christ. Also in the building are a museum displaying various medieval religious works and its shop, which sells honey, shampoos, and jams made by the monks. ⊠ *Via Santo Stefano 24, Piazza Santo Stefano, University area* ☏ *051/223256* ☽ *Closed daily noon–3:30.*

Università di Bologna. Take a stroll through the streets of the university area: a jumble of buildings, some dating as far back as the 15th century and most to the 17th and 18th. The neighborhood, as befits a college town, is full of bookshops, coffee bars, and inexpensive restaurants. Though not particularly distinguished, they're characteristic of student life in the city. Try eating at the *mensa universitaria* (cafeteria) if you want to strike up a conversation with local students (most speak English). Political slogans and sentiments are scrawled on walls all around the university and tend to be ferociously leftist, sometimes juvenile, and often entertaining. Among the university museums, the most interesting is the **Museo di Palazzo Poggi,** which displays scientific instruments plus paleontological, botanical, and university-related artifacts. ✉ *Via Zamboni 33, University area* ☎ *051/2099610* ⊕ *www.museopalazzopoggi.unibo.it* ▨ *€3.*

WORTH NOTING

MAMbo. The name of this museum stands for Museo d'Arte Moderna di Bologna, or Bologna's Museum of Modern Art. It houses a permanent collection of modern art (defined as post–World War II until five minutes ago) and stages a revolving series of temporary exhibitions by cutting-edge artists. All of this is set within a remarkable space: you might have a hard time telling that the sleek minimalist structure was built in 1915 as the Forno del Pane, a large bakery that made bread for city residents. A bookshop and a restaurant complete the complex, the latter offering Sunday brunch and delicious aperitivi. ✉ *Via Don Minzoni 14* ☎ *051/6496611* ⊕ *www.mambo-bologna.org* ▨ *€6* ☾ *Closed Mon.*

Museo Internazionale e Biblioteca della Musica di Bologna. The music museum in the spectacular Palazzo Aldini Sanguinetti, with its 17th- and 18th-century frescoes, offers among its exhibits a 1606 harpsichord and a collection of beautiful music manuscripts dating from the 1500s. ✉ *Strada Maggiore 34, University area* ☎ *051/2757720* ⊕ *www.museo-musicabologna.it* ▨ *Free* ☾ *Closed Sun. and Mon., and 2 wks in Aug.*

Palazzo Comunale. A mélange of building styles and constant modifications characterize this huge palace dating from the 13th to 15th century. When Bologna was an independent city-state, this was the seat of government—a function it still serves today. Over the door is a statue of Bologna-born Pope Gregory XIII (reigned 1572–85), most famous for reorganizing the calendar. There are good views from the upper stories of the palace. The first-floor **Sala Rossa** (Red Room) is open on advance request and during some exhibitions, and the **Sala del Consiglio Comunale** (City Council Hall) is open to the public for a few hours in the late morning. The old stock exchange, part of the Palazzo Comunale, which you enter from Piazza Nettuno, has been turned into a library. Dubbed the **Sala Borsa** (⊕ *www.bibliotecasalaborsa.it*), it has an impressive interior courtyard. Within the palazzo are two museums. The **Collezioni Comunali d'Arte** exhibits paintings from the Middle Ages as well as some Renaissance works by Luca Signorelli (circa 1445–1523) and Tintoretto (1518–94). Underground caves and the foundations of the old cathedral can be visited by appointment made through the tourist office. ✉ *Piazza Maggiore 6, Piazza Maggiore* ☎ *051/2194400 Palazzo/Sala Borsa,* ▨ *€5, except during special art exhibitions* ☾ *Closed Sun. and Mon.*

Palazzo del Podestà. This classic Renaissance palace facing the Basilica di San Petronio was erected in 1484, and attached to it is the soaring **Torre dell'Arengo.** The bells in the tower have rung whenever the city has celebrated, mourned, or called its citizens to arms. ✉ *Piazza Nettuno, Piazza Maggiore.*

Palazzo Re Enzo. Built in 1244, this palace became home to King Enzo of Sardinia, who was imprisoned here in 1249 after he was captured during the fierce battle of Fossalta. He died here 23 years later. The palace has other macabre associations as well: common criminals received last rites in the tiny courtyard chapel before being executed in Piazza Maggiore. The courtyard is worth peeking into, but the palace merely houses government offices. ✉ *Piazza Re Enzo, Piazza Maggiore* ☎ *051/6375111.*

Pinacoteca Nazionale. Bologna's principal art gallery contains many works by the immortals of Italian painting. Its prize possession is the *Ecstasy of St. Cecilia* by Raphael (1483–1520). There's also a beautiful polyptych by Giotto (1267–1337), as well as *Madonna and Child with Saints Margaret, Jerome, and Petronio* by Parmigianino (1503–40): note the rapt eye contact between St. Margaret and the Christ child. ✉ *Via delle Belle Arti 56, University area* ☎ *051/4209411* 🌐 *www.pinacotecabologna.beniculturali.it* 🎟 *€6* ⏲ *Closed Mon.*

4

San Domenico. The tomb of St. Dominic, who died here in 1221, is called the **Arca di San Domenico,** and is found in this church in the sixth chapel on the right. Many artists participated in its decoration, notably Niccolò di Bari, who was so proud of his 15th-century contribution that he changed his name to Niccolò dell'Arca to recall this famous work. The young Michelangelo (1475–1564) carved the angel on the right. In the right transept of the church is a tablet marking the last resting place of hapless King Enzo, the Sardinian ruler imprisoned in the Palazzo Re Enzo. The attached museum contains religious relics. ✉ *Piazza San Domenico 13, off Via Garibaldi, South of Piazza Maggiore* ☎ *051/6400411* 🌐 *www.conventosandomenico.org.*

WHERE TO EAT

$$ EMILIAN Fodor's Choice ★

🍴 **Da Cesari.** Just off Piazza Maggiore, this one-room restaurant has white tablecloths, dark-wood paneling, and wine-bottle-lined walls. Host Paolino Cesari has been presiding over his eatery since 1955, and he and his staff go out of their way to make you feel at home. The food's terrific—if you love pork products, try anything on the menu with *mora romagnola.* Paolino has direct contact with the people who raise this breed that nearly became extinct (he calls it "my pig"). The highly flavorful meat makes divine salame, among other things. All the usual Bolognesi classics are here, as well as—in fall and winter—an inspired *scaloppa all Petroniano* (veal cutlet with prosciutto and fontina) that comes smothered in white truffles. [$] *Average main: €15* ✉ *Via de' Carbonesi 8, South of Piazza Maggiore* ☎ *051/237710* 🌐 *www.da-cesari.it* ⏲ *Closed Sun., and Aug. and 1 wk in Jan.*

$ EMILIAN Fodor's Choice ★

🍴 **Da Gianni a la Vecia Bulagna.** Locals simply call it "Da Gianni," and they fill these two unadorned rooms at lunch and dinner. Though the interior is plain and unremarkable, it doesn't much matter—this place is all about food. The usual starters such as a tasty tortellini in brodo are on hand, as are daily specials such as gnocchi made with pumpkin, then sauced with melted cheese. Bollito misto is a fine option here, and the cotechino *con purè di patate* (a deliciously oily sausage with mashed potatoes) is elevated to sublimity by the accompanying salsa verde. [$] *Average main: €12* ✉ *Via Clavature 18, Piazza Maggiore* ☎ *051/229434* ⏲ *Closed Mon. No dinner Sun.*

$ ✕ **Tamburini.** Two small rooms inside plus kegs and bar stools outside
WINE BAR   make up this lively, packed little spot. At lunchtime, office workers swarm to the "bistrot self service" for remarkably tasty primi and secondi. After lunch, Tamburini becomes a wine bar with a vast array of selections by the glass and the bottle. The overwhelming plate of affettati misti is crammed with top-quality local ham products and succulent cheeses (including, sometimes, a goat Brie). An adjacent salumeria offers many wonderful things to take away. $ *Average main: €10* ⊠ *Via Drapperie 1, Piazza Maggiore* ☎ *051/234726* ⊕ *www.tamburini. com* ☾ *No dinner.*

$ ✕ **Trattoria del Rosso.** Although its interior—glaring yellow walls and the
EMILIAN   oddly placed ceramic plate—is nothing to write home about, this trattoria pulls in the locals. A mostly young crowd chows down on basic regional fare at rock-bottom prices. Nimble staff bearing multiple plates sashay neatly between the closely spaced tables delivering such standards as *crescentine con salumi e squacquerone* (deep-fried flour puffs with cured meats and soft cheese) and tortellini in brodo. It is the kind of place where there's always a line of hungry people outside waiting to get in, but where the waiters don't glare at you if you only order a plate of pasta—another reason, perhaps, why it's a favorite of university students. $ *Average main: €9* ⊠ *Via Augusto Righi 30, University area* ☎ *051/236730* ⊕ *www.trattoriadelrosso.com* ☾ *Closed Thurs.*

WHERE TO STAY

$ ⛺ **Albergo Centrale.** A stone's throw from Piazza Maggiore, this place
HOTEL   that started out as a pensione in 1875 has been brought firmly into the 21st century and offers the winning combination of comfort, affordability, and some family-size rooms. **Pros:** very good value; excellent location. **Cons:** might be too plain for some tastes; street-facing rooms can get some noise; some rooms have a shared bath. $ *Rooms from: €90* ⊠ *Via della Zecca 2, Piazza Maggiore* ☎ *051/225114* ⊕ *www.albergocentralebologna.it* ⤴ *31 rooms* ⦿ *Breakfast.*

$$ ⛺ **Art Hotel Novecento.** This swank place, inspired by the 1930s Vien-
HOTEL   nese Secession movement, is in a little piazza just minutes from Piazza
Fodor'sChoice   Maggiore. **Pros:** spacious single rooms ideal for solo travelers; friendly,
★   capable concierge service; sumptuous buffet breakfast. **Cons:** some standard doubles are small; might be too trendy for some. $ *Rooms from: €140* ⊠ *Piazza Galileo 4/3, Piazza Maggiore* ☎ *051/7457311* ⊕ *www. bolognarthotels.it/novecento* ⤴ *25 rooms* ⦿ *Breakfast.*

$ ⛺ **Art Hotel Orologio.** The location of this stylish and welcoming family-
HOTEL   run hotel can't be beat: it's right around the corner from Piazza Mag-
Fodor'sChoice   giore on a quiet piazza. **Pros:** central location; family-friendly rooms;
★   welcomes all animals. **Cons:** some steps to elevator; pet-friendly environment may not appeal to allergy sufferers. $ *Rooms from: €120* ⊠ *Via IV Novembre 10, Piazza Maggiore* ☎ *051/7457411* ⊕ *www. bolognarthotels.it/orologio* ⤴ *32 rooms, 1 apartment* ⦿ *Breakfast.*

EMILIA-ROMAGNA THROUGH THE AGES

Ancient History. Emilia-Romagna owes its beginnings to a road. In 187 BC the Romans built the Via Aemilia—a long road running northwest from the Adriatic port of Rimini to the central garrison town of Piacenza—and it was along this central spine that the primary towns of the region developed.

Despite the unifying factor of what came to be known as the Via Emilia, this section of Italy has had a fragmented history. Its eastern part, roughly the area from Faenza to the coast (known as Romagna), looked first to the Byzantine east and then to Rome for art, political power, and, some say, national character. The western part, from Bologna to Piacenza (Emilia), looked more to the north with its practice of self-government and dissent.

Bologna was founded by the Etruscans and eventually came under the influence of the Roman Empire. The Romans established a garrison here, renaming the old Etruscan settlement Bononia. It was after the fall of Rome that the region began its fragmentation. Romagna, centered in Ravenna, was ruled from Constantinople. Ravenna eventually became the capital of the empire in the west in the 5th century, passing to papal control in the 8th century. Even today, the city is still filled with reminders of two centuries of Byzantine rule.

Family Ties. The other cities of the region, from the Middle Ages on, became the fiefdoms of important noble families—the Este in Ferrara and Modena, the Pallavicini in Piacenza, and the Bentivoglio in Bologna. Today all these cities bear the marks of their noble patrons. When in the 16th century the papacy managed to exert its power over the entire area, some of these cities were divided among the papal families—hence the stamp of the Farnese family on Parma and Piacenza.

A Leftward Tilt. Bologna and Emilia-Romagna have established a robust tradition of rebellion and dissent. The Italian socialist movement was born in the region, as was Benito Mussolini. In keeping with the political climate of his home state, he was a firebrand socialist during the early part of his career. Despite having Mussolini as a native son, Emilia-Romagna didn't take to Fascism: it was here that the anti-Fascist resistance was born, and during World War II the region suffered terribly at the hands of the Fascists and the Nazis.

NIGHTLIFE AND PERFORMING ARTS
NIGHTLIFE

As a university town, Bologna has long been known for its busy nightlife. As early as 1300 it was said to have 150 taverns. Most of the city's current 200-plus pubs and bars are frequented by Italian students, young adults, and international students, with the university district forming the hub. In addition to the university area, the pedestrian zone on Via del Pratello, lined with plenty of bars, has a hopping nightlife scene; as does Via delle Moline, which promises cutting-edge cafés and bars. A more upscale, low-key evening experience can be had at one of Bologna's many wine bars, where the food is often substantial enough to constitute dinner.

BARS **Bar Calice.** A year-round indoor-outdoor operation (with heat lamps), this bar is extremely popular with thirtysomethings, sometimes pushing baby carriages. Its large menu includes raw oysters. ☒ *Via Clavature 13/a, at Via Marchesana, Piazza Maggiore* ☎ *051/6569296* ⊕ *www. barilcalice.it.*

Fodor'sChoice ★ **Nu Bar Lounge.** This high-energy place draws a cocktail-loving crowd that enjoys fun drinks such as "I'm Too Sexy for This Place," a combination of vodka, triple sec, apple juice, and lemon. ☒ *Via de' Musei 6, off Buca San Petronio, Piazza Maggiore* ☎ *051/222532* ⊕ *www.nu-lounge.com.*

Osteria del Sole. Although "osteria" in an establishment's name suggests that food will be served, such is not the case here. This place is all about drinking wine; the entrance door has warnings such as "He who doesn't drink will please stay outside" and "Dogs who don't drink are forbidden to come in." It's been around since 1465, and locals pack in, bearing food from outside to accompany the wine. ☒ *Vicolo Ranocchi 1/d, Piazza Maggiore* ☎ *347/9680171* ⊕ *www.osteriadelsole.it.*

CAFÉS **Zanarini.** Chic Bolognesi congregate at this bar that serves coffee in Fodor'sChoice the morning and swank aperitivi in the evening. Tasty sandwiches and ★ pastries are also available. ☒ *Piazza Galvani 1* ☎ *051/2750041.*

MUSIC VENUES **Cantina Bentivoglio.** With live music staged every evening, Cantina Bentivoglio is one of Bologna's most appealing nightspots. You can enjoy light and more substantial meals here as well. ☒ *Via Mascarella 4/b, University area* ☎ *051/265416* ⊕ *www.cantinabentivoglio.it.*

Osteria Buca delle Campane. In a 13th-century building, this underground tavern has good, inexpensive food and the after-dinner scene is popular with locals, including students, who come to listen to live music. The kitchen stays open until long past midnight. Reservations are strongly advised. ☒ *Via Benedetto XIV 4/a, University area* ☎ *051/220918* ⊕ *www.bucadellecampane.it.*

PERFORMING ARTS

MUSIC AND **Teatro Comunale.** This 18th-century theater presents concerts by Ital-
OPERA ian and international orchestras throughout the year, but the highly acclaimed opera performances from November through May are the main attraction. Reserve seats for those performances well in advance. ☒ *Largo Respighi 1, University area* ☎ *051/529958* ⊕ *www.tcbo.it.*

SHOPPING

CLOTHING

Castel Guelfo Outlet City. If you don't feel like paying Galleria Cavour prices, this mall is about 20 minutes outside Bologna. It includes about 50 discounted stores, some from top designers such as Ferré. ☒ *Via del Commercio 20/a, Loc. Poggio Piccolo, Castel Guelfo* ⊕ *Take A14 toward Imola, Castel San Pietro Terme exit; 980 feet after tollbooth, turn right onto Via San Carlo* ☎ *0542/670765* ⊕ *www.thestyleoutlets. it* ⊗ *Closed Mon. morning.*

Galleria Cavour. One of the most upscale malls in Italy, the Galleria houses many of the fashion giants, including Gucci, Versace, and jeweler-watchmaker Bulgari. ☒ *Via Luigi Carlo Farini, South of Piazza Maggiore* ⊕ *www.galleriacavour.it.*

WINE AND FOOD

Bologna is a good place to buy wine. Several shops have a bewilderingly large selection—to go straight to the top, ask the managers which wines have won the prestigious Tre Bicchieri (Three Glasses) award from Gambero Rosso's wine bible, *Vini d'Italia.*

Eataly. At this lively shop—the original location in the now ubiquitous Italian cuisine empire—with an attached bookstore you can grab a bite to eat or have a glass of wine while stocking up on high-quality olive oil, vinegar, cured meats, and artisanal pasta. On the top floor, you can have a full-fledged trattoria meal, but what you can't have is anything decaffeinated: it's considered "chemical." ⊠ *Via degli Orafici 19, Piazza Maggiore* ☎ *051/0952820* ⊕ *www.eataly.it.*

Enoteca Italiana. Consistently recognized as one of the best wine stores in the country, Enoteca Italiana lives up to its reputation with shelves lined with excellent selections from all over Italy at reasonable prices. The delicious sandwiches, served with wines by the glass, make a great light lunch. ⊠ *Via Marsala 2/b, North of Piazza Maggiore* ☎ *051/235989* ⊕ *www.enotecaitaliana.it.*

La Baita. Fresh tagliolini, tortellini, and other Bolognese pasta delicacies are sold here, along with sublime food to take away. The cheese counter is laden with superlative local specimens. ⊠ *Via Pescherie Vecchia 3/a, Piazza Maggiore* ☎ *051/223940.*

Majani. Classy Majani has been producing chocolate since 1796. Its staying power may be attributed to high-quality confections that are as pretty to look at as they are to eat. ⊠ *Via de'Carbonesi 5, Piazza Maggiore* ☎ *051/234302* ⊕ *www.majani.com.*

Mercato delle Erbe. This food market that's more than a century old bustles year-round. ⊠ *Via Ugo Bassi 25, Piazza Maggiore* ☎ *051/230186* ⊕ *www.mercatodelleerbe.it* ⊗ *Closed Sun.*

Fodor's Choice ★ **Mercato di Mezzo.** Formerly a fruit and vegetable market, the Mercato has morphed into a food hall. Various stalls offer the best that Bologna has to offer, and the Bolognesi are gobbling it up. Order from whatever place strikes your fancy, and sit anywhere there's room. ⊠ *Via Peschiere Vecchie, Piazza Maggiore.*

Paolo Atti & Figli. This place has been producing some of Bologna's finest pastas, cakes, and other delicacies for more than 130 years. ⊠ *Via Caprarie 7, Piazza Maggiore* ☎ *051/220425* ⊕ *www.paoloatti.com.*

Fodor's Choice ★ **Roccati.** Sculptural works of chocolate, as well as basic bonbons and simpler sweets, have been crafted here since 1909. ⊠ *Via Clavature 17/a, Piazza Maggiore* ☎ *051/261964* ⊕ *www.roccaticioccolato.com.*

Scaramagli. Friendly owners run this midsize, down-to-earth wine store. ⊠ *Strada Maggiore 31/d, University area* ☎ *051/227132* ⊕ *www.scaramagli.it.*

FERRARA

47 km (29 miles) northeast of Bologna, 74 km (46 miles) northwest of Ravenna.

When the legendary Ferrarese filmmaker Michelangelo Antonioni called his beloved hometown "a city that you can see only partly, while the rest disappears to be imagined," perhaps he was referring to the low-lying mist that rolls in off the Adriatic each winter and shrouds Ferrara's winding knot of medieval alleyways, turreted palaces, and ancient wine bars—once inhabited by the likes of Copernicus—in a ghostly fog. But perhaps Antonioni was also suggesting that Ferrara's striking beauty often conceals a dark and tortured past.

Today you're likely to be charmed by Ferrara's prosperous air and meticulous cleanliness, its excellent restaurants and chic bars (for coffee and any other liquid refreshment), and its lively wine-bar scene. You'll find aficionados gathering outside any of the wine bars near the Duomo even on the foggiest of weeknights. Although Ferrara is a UNESCO World Heritage Site, the city draws amazingly few tourists—which only adds to its appeal.

■TIP➔ If you plan to explore the city fully, consider buying a Card Musei (Museum Card, also known as "My Ferrara Tourist Card"). Two days cost €10, three days €12, and six days €18. Purchase the card at the Palazzo dei Diamanti or any of Ferrara's museums; it grants admission to every museum, palace, and castle in town. The first Monday of the month is free at many museums.

GETTING HERE AND AROUND

Train service is frequent from Bologna (usually three trains per hour) and takes either a half hour or 45 minutes, depending on which train type you take. It's 37 minutes from Florence to Bologna, and then about a half hour from Bologna to Ferrara. The walk from the station is easy, takes about 20 minutes, and is not particularly interesting. You can take either Bus No. 1 or No. 9 from the station to the center; buy your ticket at the newsagent inside the station and remember to stamp your ticket upon boarding the bus. If you're driving from Bologna, take the RA1 out of town, then the A13 in the direction of Padova, exiting at Ferrara Nord. Follow the SP19 directly into the center of town. The trip should take about 45 minutes.

VISITOR INFORMATION

Ferrara Tourism Office. ✉ *Castello Estense, Piazza Castello* ☎ *0532/299303* ⊕ *www.ferrarainfo.com.*

EXPLORING

TOP ATTRACTIONS

Fodor'sChoice ★ **Castello Estense.** The former seat of Este power, this massive castle dominates the center of town. The building was a suitable symbol for the ruling family: cold and menacing on the outside, lavishly decorated within. The public rooms are grand, but deep in the bowels of the castle are chilling dungeons where enemies of the state were held in wretched conditions—a function these quarters served as recently as 1943, when anti-Fascist prisoners were detained there. In particular, the **Prisons of Don Giulio, Ugo,** and **Parisina** have some fascinating features, like 15th-century graffiti protesting the imprisonment of lovers Ugo and Parisina, who were beheaded in 1425 because Ugo's father, Niccolò III, didn't like the fact that his son was cavorting with Niccolò's wife.

The castle was established as a fortress in 1385, but work on its luxurious ducal quarters continued into the 16th century. Representative of Este grandeur are the **Sala dei Giochi,** extravagantly painted with athletic scenes, and the **Sala dell'Aurora,** decorated to show the times of the day. The terraces of the castle, and the hanging garden—once reserved for the private use of the duchesses—have fine views of the town and the surrounding countryside. You can cross the castle's moat, traverse its drawbridge, and wander through many of its arcaded passages at any time. ⊠ *Piazza Castello* ☎ *0532/299233* ⊕ *www.castelloestense.it* 🎫 *€8 (€12 during special exhibitions)* ☾ *Closed Mon.*

Duomo. The magnificent Gothic cathedral, a few steps from the Castello Estense, has a three-tier facade of slender arches and beautiful sculptures over the central door. Work began in 1135 and took more than 100 years to complete. The interior was completely remodeled in the 17th century. At this writing, the facade was scaffolded and undergoing a major restoration. ⊠ *Piazza delle Cattedrale* ☎ *0532/207449.*

Palazzo dei Diamanti (*Palace of Diamonds*). Named for the 12,600 small, pink-and-white marble pyramids (or "diamonds") that stud its facade, this building was designed to be viewed in perspective—both faces at once—from diagonally across the street. Work began in the 1490s and finished around 1504. Today the palazzo contains the **Pinacoteca Nazionale,** an extensive art gallery that also hosts temporary exhibits. ⊠ *Corso Ercole I d'Este 19–21* ☎ *0532/244949* ⊕ *www.palazzodiamanti.it* 🎫 *€10.*

Fodor'sChoice ★ **Palazzo Schifanoia.** The oldest, most characteristic area of Ferrara is south of the Duomo, stretching between the Corso Giovecca and the city's ramparts. Here various members of the Este family built pleasure palaces, the best known of which is the Palazzo Schifanoia (*schifanoia* means "carefree" or, literally, "fleeing boredom"). Begun in the late 14th century, the palace was remodeled between 1464 and 1469. Now part of the Museo Schifanoia, the lavish interior is well worth visiting—particularly the **Salone dei Mesi,** which contains an extravagant series of frescoes showing the months of the year and their mythological attributes. Since a 2013 earthquake, only the Salone and the adjacent Ala degli Stucchi have remained open to the public. ⊠ *Via Scandiana 23* ☎ *0532/64178* ⊕ *www.artecultura.fe.it* 🎫 *€3* ☾ *Closed Mon.*

Via delle Volte. One of the best-preserved medieval streets in Europe, the Via delle Volte clearly evokes Ferrara's past. The series of ancient *volte* (arches) along the narrow cobblestone alley once joined the merchants' houses on the south side of the street to their warehouses on the north side. The street ran parallel to the banks of the Po River, which was home to Ferrara's busy port. ⊠ *Ferrara.*

WORTH NOTING

Casa Romei. This ranks among Ferrara's loveliest Renaissance palaces. Built by the wealthy banker Giovanni Romei (1402–83), it's a vast structure with a graceful courtyard. Mid-15th-century frescoes decorate rooms on the ground floor; the piano nobile contains detached frescoes from local churches as well as lesser-known Renaissance sculptures. The Sala delle Sibelle has a very large 15th-century fireplace and beautiful wood-coffered ceilings. ✉ *Via Savonarola 30* ☎ *0532/234130 for tickets, 0532/234100 for info* 🌐 *www.soprintendenzaravenna.beniculturali.it* 🎫 *€3 (free 1st Sun. of month).*

Museo della Cattedrale. Some of the original decorations of the town's main church, the former church, and cloister of San Romano, reside in the Museo della Cattedrale, which is across the piazza from the Duomo. Inside you'll find 22 codices commissioned between 1477 and 1535; early-13th-century sculpture by the Maestro dei Mesi; a mammoth oil on canvas by Cosmé Tura from 1469; and an exquisite Jacopo della Quercia, the *Madonna della Melograno*. Although this last work dates from 1403 to 1408, the playful expression on the Christ child seems very 21st century. ✉ *Via San Romano 1* ☎ *0532/761299* 🌐 *www.artecultura.fe.it* 🎫 *€6* 🕒 *Closed Mon.*

WHERE TO EAT

$ EMILIAN 🍴 **Enoteca Enotria.** This little two-room enoteca opened in 1986 in the old Jewish section of town and since then has been pouring significant French and other wines. The first room has just a counter where the wine is poured, a couple of stools, and a table; two more tables in the other room, lined with wine bottles, complete the space. Locals come for the wine but also the simple but good food—plates of affettati misti and cheeses to pair with the wines. Enotria opens at 8:30 in the morning, closes at 2, and reopens in the late afternoon, making it a wonderful quick stop before the usual lunch and dinner opening hours (12:30 pm and 7 pm). [$] *Average main: €11* ✉ *Via Saraceno 39/A–41* ☎ *0532/209166* 🌐 *www.enotecaenotria.it* 🕒 *Closed Mon.*

$$$ MODERN ITALIAN 🍴 **Il Don Giovanni.** Just down the street from Castello Estense, this warm and inviting restaurant consists of a handful of tables inside a 17th-century palace. Chef Pier Luigi Di Diego pays strict attention to what's seasonal. Here tortellini are stuffed with guinea fowl and sauced with *zabaione* (custard), Parmesan, and prosciutto *croccante* (fried prosciutto). Equally inventive is the delicate *tegame di pernice rossa ai frutti di bosco* (partridge in a fruit sauce), which delights the palate. Next door, the same proprietors run the less expensive but more crowded **La Borsa.** The trendy wine bar has excellent cured meats, cheeses, lovely primi and secondi, and a fantastic by-the-glass wine list. **TIP→ The wine bar is open for lunch and dinner, the restaurant for dinner only.** [$] *Average main: €29* ✉ *Corso Ercole I d'Este 1* ☎ *0532/243363* 🌐 *www.ildongiovanni.com* 🕒 *Closed Mon. No lunch.*

$$ EMILIAN 🍴 **L'Oca Giuliva.** Food, service, and ambience harmonize blissfully at this casual but elegant restaurant inside a 12th-century building. Patrons enter through a tiny wine bar, some pausing for glass of wine before proceeding into the restaurant. The chef shows a deft hand with area specialties and shines with the fish dishes: his *scampo saltato su una crema di fave e cime di rape* (a sweet crustacean, quickly sautéed, with

a fava-bean puree with cooked bitter greens) shifts the palate into gear. Dishes such as the *gnocchi al cacao con ragù di cervo* (cocoa potato gnocchi with a venison sauce) show his more fanciful side. If the chestnut ice cream happens to be on the menu, don't miss it. A terrific cheese plate complements the amazing wines poured here. $\$$ *Average main: €18* ✉ *Via Boccanale di Santo Stefano 38* ☎ *0532/207628* ⊕ *www.ristorantelocagiuliva.it* ⊗ *Closed Mon. No lunch Tues.*

$

WINE BAR

Fodor's Choice

★

✕ **Osteria al Brindisi.** Ferrara is a city of wine bars, beginning with this one—allegedly Europe's oldest—which opened in 1435. Copernicus drank here while a student in the late 1400s, and the place still has a somewhat undergraduate aura. Most of the staff and clientele are twentysomethings. Perfectly dusty wine bottles line the walls, and there are wooden booths in another small room for those who want to eat while they drink. A young staff pours well-selected wines by the glass, and offers three different sauces (butter and sage, tomato, or ragù) with the *cappellacci di zucca* (pasta stuffed with butternut squash). Those in search of lighter fare might enjoy any of the salads or the grilled vegetable plate with melted pecorino. $\$$ *Average main: €8* ✉ *Via degli Adelardi 11* ☎ *0532/209142* ⊕ *www.albrindisi.net.*

$$

EMILIAN

Fodor's Choice

★

✕ **Quel Fantastico Giovedì.** Locals and other cognoscenti frequent this sleek eatery just minutes away from Piazza del Duomo. Two small rooms—one white, the other with red accents—have linen tablecloths and jazz playing softly in the background. Chef Gabriele Romagnoli uses prime local ingredients to create gustatory taste sensations on a menu that changes daily. His *sformatino di patate* (potato flan) resembles a French gratin, but he sauces it with *salamina e Parmigiano* (that deliciously unctuous pork product made into a smooth sauce with the help of Parmesan cheese), thus rendering it deliciously Ferraresi. Fish figures prominently among his dishes. The restaurant's tasting menu is well priced, its wine list is divine, and the service, led by hands-on, gregarious proprietor Mara Farinelli, is always top-notch. $\$$ *Average main: €16* ✉ *Via Castelnuovo 9* ☎ *0532/760570* ⊕ *www.quelfantasticogiovedi.it* ⊗ *Closed Wed. No lunch Tues.*

$$

EMILIAN

✕ **Ristorante Centrale.** Pasta constantly being produced from scratch is the big draw here. Order a plate of cappellaci di zucca *alla ferrarese* (pumpkin-stuffed pasta with a hearty meat ragù), and depending on where you sit you might actually witness your pasta being rolled out, stuffed, and sauced. Centrale is an unassuming place, with white walls, white linens, and an ebullient owner-host. Servings tend to be huge, though mercifully the *salamina in sugo*—a delicious local specialty of salame atop creamy mashed potatoes—comes in smaller portions. $\$$ *Average main: €15* ✉ *Via Boccaleone 8* ☎ *0532/470940* ⊗ *Closed Sun.*

WHERE TO STAY

$

HOTEL

🏨 **Hotel Annunziata.** Brightly colored fittings enliven the white-walled, hardwood-floor guest rooms—think minimalism with a splash—at this hotel on a quiet little piazza near the forbiddingly majestic Castello Estense. **Pros:** perfect location (you can't get much more central); stellar staff; terrific buffet breakfast. **Cons:** it books up quickly. $\$$ *Rooms from: €114* ✉ *Piazza, Repubblica 5* ☎ *0532/201111* ⊕ *www.annunziata.it* ⇥ *27 rooms* ⦿ *Breakfast.*

$ B&B/INN Fodor's Choice ★ **Locanda Borgonuovo.** In the early 18th century this lodging began life as a convent (later suppressed by Napoléon) but now it's a delightful city-center bed-and-breakfast, popular with performers at the city's Teatro Comunale. **Pros:** phenomenal breakfast featuring local foods and terrific cakes made in-house; bicycles can be borrowed for free. **Cons:** steep stairs to reception area and rooms; must reserve far in advance as this place books quickly. [$] *Rooms from: €100* ✉ *Via Cairoli 29* ☎ *0532/211100* 🌐 *www.borgonuovo.com* *4 rooms, 2 apartments* 🍴 *Breakfast.*

RAVENNA

76 km (47 miles) east of Bologna, 93 km (58 miles) southeast of Ferrara.

A small, quiet, well-heeled city, Ravenna has brick palaces, cobblestone streets, magnificent monuments, and spectacular Byzantine mosaics. The high point in its civic history occurred in the 5th century, when Pope Honorious moved his court here from Rome. Gothic kings Odoacer and Theodoric ruled the city until it was conquered by the Byzantines in AD 540. Ravenna later fell under the sway of Venice, and then, inevitably, the Papal States.

Because Ravenna spent much of its past looking east, its greatest art treasures show that Byzantine influence. Churches and tombs with the most unassuming exteriors contain within them walls covered with sumptuous mosaics. These beautifully preserved Byzantine mosaics put great emphasis on nature, which you can see in the delicate rendering of sky, earth, and animals. Outside Ravenna, the town of Classe hides even more mosaic gems.

GETTING HERE AND AROUND

By car from Bologna, take the SP253 to the RA1, and then follow signs for the A14/E45 in the direction of Ancona. From here, follow signs for Ravenna, taking the A14dir Ancona–Milano–Ravenna exit. Follow signs for the SS16/E55 to the center of Ravenna. From Ferrara the drive is more convoluted, but also more interesting. Take the SS16 to the RA8 in the direction of Porto Garibaldi taking the Roma/Ravenna exit. Follow the SS309/E55 to the SS309dir/E55, taking the SS253 Bologna/Ancona exit. Follow the SS16/E55 into the center of Ravenna.

VISITOR INFORMATION

Ravenna Tourism Office. ✉ *Via Salara 8* ☎ *0544/35404* 🌐 *www.turismo.ra.it.*

EXPLORING

A combination ticket (available at ticket offices of all included sights) admits you to four of Ravenna's important monuments: the Mausoleo di Galla Placidia, the Basilica di San Vitale, the Battistero Neoniano, and Sant'Apollinare Nuovo. Start out early in the morning to avoid lines (reservations are necessary for the Mausoleo and Basilica in May and June). A half day should suffice to walk the town; allow a half hour for the Mausoleo and the Basilica.

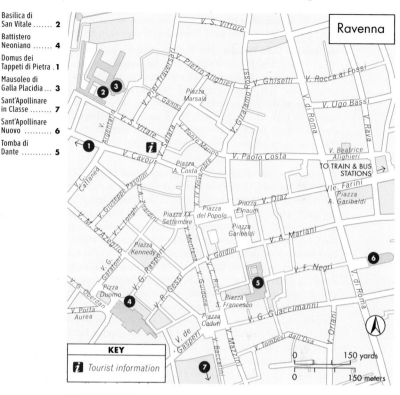

Ravenna

KEY

🛈 *Tourist information*

0 ⟶ 150 yards
0 ⟶ 150 meters

TOP ATTRACTIONS

Fodor'sChoice ★ **Basilica di San Vitale.** The octagonal church of San Vitale was built in AD 547, after the Byzantines conquered the city, and its interior shows a strong Byzantine influence. The area behind the altar contains the most famous works, depicting Emperor Justinian and his retinue on one wall, and his wife, Empress Theodora, with her retinue, on the opposite one. Notice how the mosaics seamlessly wrap around the columns and curved arches on the upper sides of the altar area. ■TIP→ Reservations are recommended March–mid-June. ✉ *Via San Vitale, off Via Salara* ☏ *0544/541688 for reservations* ⊕ *www.raven-namosaici.it* ✉ *Combination ticket €9.50 mid-June–Feb., €11.50 Mar.–mid-June (includes all diocesan monuments).*

Fodor'sChoice ★ **Battistero Neoniano.** Next door to Ravenna's 18th-century cathedral, the baptistery has one of the town's most important mosaics. It dates from the beginning of the 5th century AD, with work continuing through the century. In keeping with the building's role, the great mosaic in the dome shows the baptism of Christ, and beneath are the Apostles. The lowest register of mosaics contains Christian symbols, the Throne of God, and the Cross. Note the naked figure kneeling next to Christ—he is the personification of the River Jordan. ✉ *Via Battistero* ☏ *0544/541688 for reservations, 800/303999 for info (toll-free)*

⊕ *www.ravennamosaici.it* ✉ *Combination ticket €9.50 mid-June–Feb., €11.50 Mar.–mid-June (includes all diocesan monuments).*

FodorśChoice **Mausoleo di Galla Placidia.** The little tomb and the great church stand
★ side by side, but the tomb predates the Basilica di San Vitale by at
least 100 years. These two adjacent sights are decorated with the
best-known, most elaborate mosaics in Ravenna. Galla Placidia was
the sister of the Roman emperor Honorius, who moved the imperial
capital to Ravenna in AD 402. She is said to have been beautiful and
strong-willed, and to have taken an active part in the governing of
the crumbling empire. This mausoleum, constructed in the mid-5th
century, is her memorial.

Viewed from the outside, it's a small, unassuming redbrick building: the
exterior's seeming poverty of charm only serves to enhance by contrast
the richness of the interior mosaics, in deep midnight blue and glittering gold. The tiny central dome is decorated with symbols of Christ,
the evangelists, and striking gold stars. Over the door is a depiction of
the Good Shepherd. Eight of the Apostles are represented in groups of
two on the four inner walls of the dome; the other four appear singly
on the walls of the two transepts. Notice the small doves at their feet,
drinking from the water of faith. Also in the tiny transepts are some
delightful pairs of deer (representing souls), drinking from the fountain
of resurrection. There are three sarcophagi in the tomb, none of which
are believed to contain the remains of Galla Placidia. She died in Rome
in AD 450, and there's no record of her body's having been transported
back to the place where she wished to lie. ■TIP→ **Reservations are
required for the Mausoleo from March through mid-June.** ✉ *Via San
Vitale, off Via Salara* ☎ *0544/541688 for reservations* ⊕ *www.raven-
namosaici.it* ✉ *Combination ticket €9.50 mid-June–Feb., €11.50 Mar.–
mid-June (includes all diocesan monuments).*

FodorśChoice **Sant'Apollinare Nuovo.** The mosaics displayed in this church date from
★ the early 6th century, making them slightly older than those in San
Vitale. Since the left side of the church was reserved for women, it's only
fitting that the mosaics on that wall depict 22 virgins offering crowns to
the Virgin Mary. On the right wall are 26 men carrying the crowns of
martyrdom. They approach Christ, surrounded by angels. ✉ *Via Roma,
at Via Guaccimanni* ☎ *0544/219518, 0544/541688 for reservations*
⊕ *www.ravennamosaici.it* ✉ *Combination ticket €9.50 mid-June–Feb.,
€11.50 Mar.–mid-June (includes all diocesan monuments).*

WORTH NOTING

Domus dei Tappeti di Pietra (*Ancient Home of the Stone Carpets*). This
archaeological site was uncovered in 1993 during digging for an underground parking garage near the 18th-century church of Santa Eufemia.
Ten feet below ground level lie the remains of a Byzantine palace dating from the 5th and 6th century AD. Its beautiful and well-preserved
network of floor mosaics displays elaborately designed patterns, creating the effect of luxurious carpets. ✉ *Via Barbiani, enter through
Sant'Eufemia* ☎ *0544/32512* ⊕ *www.domusdeitappetidipietra.it* ✉ *€4*
⊘ *Closed Mon. Nov.–Feb.*

Sant'Apollinare in Classe. This church about 5 km (3 miles) southeast of Ravenna is landlocked now, but when it was built it stood in the center of the busy shipping port known to the ancient Romans as Classis. The arch above and the area around the high altar are rich with mosaics. Those on the arch, older than the ones behind it, are considered superior. They show Christ in Judgment and the 12 lambs of Christianity leaving the cities of Jerusalem and Bethlehem. In the apse is the figure of Sant'Apollinare himself, a bishop of Ravenna, and above him is a magnificent Transfiguration against blazing green grass, animals in odd perspective, and flowers. ✉ *Via Romea Sud 224, off SS71, Classe* ☎ *0544/473569* 🎟 *€5.*

Tomba di Dante. The tomb of Dante is in a small Neoclassical building next door to the large church of St. Francis. Exiled from his native Florence, the author of *The Divine Comedy* died here in 1321. The Florentines have been trying to reclaim their famous son for hundreds of years, but the Ravennans refuse to give him up, arguing that since Florence did not welcome Dante in life it does not deserve him in death. Perhaps as penance, every September the Florentine government sends olive oil that's used to fuel the light hanging in the chapel's center. ✉ *Via Dante Alighieri 4 and 9* 🎟 *Free.*

4

WHERE TO EAT

$$ EMILIAN ✕ **Bella Venezia.** Pale yellow walls, crisp white tablecloths, and warm light provide the backdrop for some seriously good regional food. The menu offers local specialties, but also gives a major nod to Venice—Ravenna's conqueror of long ago. The flavorful and delicate *cappelletti romagnoli* (stuffed "little hats" in broth) is a lovely pasta starter. Follow up with *cotoletta alla Bisanzio* (a fried veal cutlet topped with cherry tomatoes and arugula), a house specialty. Desserts are made daily on the premises; save room for the killer tiramisù. [$] *Average main: €15* ✉ *Via IV Novembre 16* ☎ *0544/212746* 🌐 *www.bellavenezia.it* 🕒 *Closed Sun., and 3 wks in Dec. and Jan.*

$ EMILIAN ✕ **Ca' de' Ven.** Some may quibble with the notion that the exiled Dante ever set foot in the two structures that house this restaurant, but Lord Byron irrefutably did. The buildings, joined by a glass-ceilinge courtyard, securely date from the 15th century. The setting itself is reason enough to come; that the food is so good makes a visit here all the more satisfying. At lunchtime Ca' de' Ven teems with locals tucking in to piadine, stuffed or topped with various ingredients, and the grilled dishes—including *tagliata di pollo* (sliced chicken breast tossed with arugula and set atop exquisitely roasted potatoes)—are among the highlights. One dish to consider: *insalatina di radicchio con bruciatini,* a local specialty with raw radicchio, a bacon dressing, and heaps of bacon bits. [$] *Average main: €13* ✉ *Via Corrado Ricci 24* ☎ *0544/30163* 🌐 *www.cadeven.it.*

$ EMILIAN ✕ **I Battibecchi.** Simple, honest food doesn't get any tastier than what's served at this tiny venue (there are about 20 seats) with an even tinier kitchen. Nicoletta Molducci, chef and owner, takes pride in turning out terrific regional dishes. The short menu provides the usual local specialties, such as cappelletti in broth or al ragù, supplemented by an ever-changing list of daily specials. The *polpettini al lesso* (little meatballs) in a lively tomato sauce with peas and pancetta is one of many winning dishes that might be on offer. Attentive service and a fine wine list make a meal here a true pleasure. [$] *Average main: €14* ✉ *Via della Tesoreria Vecchia 16* ☎ *0544/219536* 🌐 *www.osteriadeibattibecchi.it.*

$$ EMILIAN Fodor's Choice ★ 🍴 **Osteria del Tempo Perso.** A couple of jazz-, rock-, and food-loving friends joined forces to open this smart little restaurant in the center. The interior's warm, terra-cotta-sponged walls give off an orange glow, and wine bottles line the walls, interspersed with photographs of musical greats. The classics are cooked well here, like the cappelletti prepared three different ways—sauced with butter, with a meat ragù, or in broth. But the kitchen also produces contemporary fare. The *gamberi croccanti con riso venere e vellutata di zucca*—shrimp so lightly fried you'd hardly know it, served with wild rice and pumpkin puree—is an absolute winner. The carefully culled wine list includes many local wines, and the service is stellar. [$] *Average main: €18* ✉ *Via Gamba 12* ☎ *0544/215393* 🌐 *www.osteriadeltempoperso.it* ⏲ *No lunch weekdays, and in July and Aug.*

WHERE TO STAY

$$ HOTEL 🏨 **Albergo Cappello.** In operation since the late 19th century and restored a century later, this charming place reflects a Venetian influence, with many Murano chandeliers hanging in the high-ceiling, wood-coffered public rooms. **Pros:** good location; accommodating staff; good restaurant. **Cons:** only seven rooms. [$] *Rooms from: €139* ✉ *Via IV Novembre 41* ☎ *0544/219876* 🌐 *www.albergocappello.it* 🛏 *7 rooms* 🍽 *No meals.*

$ B&B/INN 🏨 **Sant'Andrea.** For a lovely little B&B on a residential street a stone's throw from the Basilica of San Vitale, look no further—it even has a delightful garden. **Pros:** children under 12 stay free; discounts for stays of three nights or more; cheery and helpful staff. **Cons:** can get a little noisy; staff goes home in the early evening. [$] *Rooms from: €90* ✉ *Via Carlo Cattaneo 33* ☎ *0544/215564* 🌐 *www.santandreahotel.com* 🛏 *12 rooms* 🍽 *Breakfast.*

NIGHTLIFE AND PERFORMING ARTS

Mosaics by Night. On Friday nights from June to August, the Byzantine mosaic masterpieces at the Basilica of San Vitale and the Mauseleo di Galla Placida are illuminated. The event is also held on certain Tuesdays. To check, call the tourist office, which offers guided tours. ✉ *Ravenna* 🌐 *www.ravennamosaici.it.*

Ravenna Festival. Orchestras from all over the world perform in city churches and theaters during this music festival that takes place in June and July. ✉ *Ravenna* 🌐 *www.ravennafestival.org.*

FLORENCE

WELCOME TO FLORENCE

TOP REASONS TO GO

★ **Galleria degli Uffizi:**
Italian Renaissance art doesn't get much better than this vast collection bequeathed to the city by the last Medici, Anna Maria Luisa.

★ **Brunelleschi's Dome:**
His work of engineering genius is the city's undisputed centerpiece.

★ **Michelangelo's *David*:**
One look and you'll know why this is one of the world's most famous sculptures.

★ **The view from Piazzale Michelangelo:** From this perch the city is laid out before you. The colors at sunset heighten the experience.

★ **Piazza Santa Croce:**
After you've had your fill of Renaissance masterpieces, hang out here and watch the world go by.

1 Around the Duomo.
You're in the heart of Florence here. Among the numerous highlights are the city's greatest museum (the Uffizi) and arguably its most impressive square (Piazza della Signoria).

2 San Lorenzo. The blocks from the basilica of San Lorenzo to the Galleria dell'Accademia bear the imprints of the Medici and of Michelangelo, culminating in the latter's masterful *David*. Just to the north, the former convent of San Marco is an oasis of artistic treasures decorated with ethereal frescoes.

3 Santa Maria Novella.
This part of town includes the train station, 16th-century palaces, and the city's most swank shopping street, Via Tornabuoni.

4 Santa Croce. The district centers on its namesake basilica, which is filled with the tombs of Renaissance (and other) luminaries. The area is also known for its leather shops.

5 The Oltrarno. Across the Arno you encounter the massive Palazzo Pitti and the narrow streets of the Santo Spirito neighborhood, filled with artisans' workshops and antiques stores. A climb to Piazzale Michelangelo gives you a spectacular view of the city.

GETTING ORIENTED

The historic center of Florence is flat and compact—you could walk from one end to the other in half an hour. In the middle of everything is the Duomo, with its huge dome towering over the city's terra-cotta rooftops. Radiating from the Duomo are Renaissance-era neighborhoods identified by their central churches and piazzas. Although the majority of sights are north of the Arno River, the area to the south, known as the Oltrarno, has its charms as well.

5

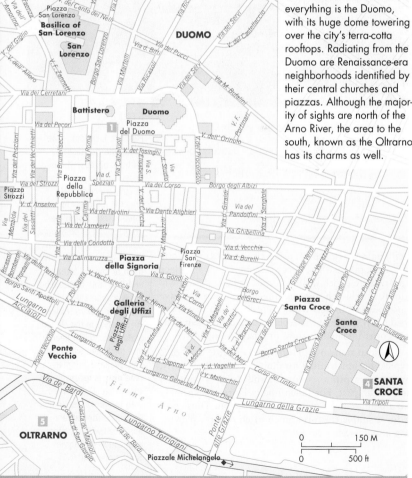

Galleria dell'Accademia

Via Panicale · Via Taddea · Via Sant' Orsola · Via Guelfa · Via G. B. Zannoni · Via Chiara · Via Rosina · Via degli Alfani · Via Ariento · Via dell'Aranto · Via Sant'Antonino · V. Faenza · Via dell'Amorino · Piazza San Lorenzo · V. del Canto dei Nelli · Borgo la Noce · Via della Stufa · Via de' Ginori · Via Cavour · Via Ricasoli · Via de' Servi

Basilica of San Lorenzo

San Lorenzo

Via del Giglio · V. dell'Alloro · V. S. Zanobi · Borgo San Lorenzo · Via de' Pucci · Via de' Martelli · Via Ricasoli · Via de' Servi · V. del Castellaccio

DUOMO

Via de' Birti · Via M. Bufalini

Via dei Cerretani

Battistero · **Duomo**

Via del Pecori · Piazza del Duomo · V. F. Portinari

Piazza della Repubblica · V. del Studio · V. dell'Orinolo

Piazza Strozzi · V. d. Anselmi · Via Monalda · Via del Sassetti · V. dei Sassetti · Via dei Pescioni · Via de' Vecchietti · Via de' Brunelleschi · Via Roma · Via Calzaioli · V. dei Tosinghi · V. d. Speziali · Via dei Tavolini · Via del Corso · Borgo degli Albizi

Via d. Pellicceria · Via della Condotta · Via dei Cerchi · Via Dante Alighieri · Via del Pandolfini · Via d. Isola · Via d. Giraldi · V. d. Magazzini

Via Calimaruzza · Via della Calza · Via dei Lamberti · Via Ghibellina

Piazza della Signoria

Via Calimaruzza · Via delle Terme · Pol. Santa · V. Vacchereccia · V. Lambertesca · V. d. Gondi · Via d. Vecchia · Via d. Buretti

Borgo Santi Apostoli · Lungarno Acciaioli · Piazza San Firenze

Galleria degli Uffizi

Via d. Nimna · Via d. Cimatori · Via d. Corno · Borgo dei Greci

Piazza degli Uffizi · V. d. Castellani · Via de' Neri · Via de' Magazzini · Via de' Rustici · Via de' Bracche · Via de' Neri

Piazza Santa Croce

Santa Croce

Borgo Santa Croce · V. Antonio Magliabechi · V. Giuseppe Verdi · V.-G.-d.-Ferrazzina · Via de' Pepi · Via de' Macci · Viale Pinzochere · Via Sant' Cristoforo · Via San Giuseppe · Borgo Allegri

Ponte Vecchio

Lungarno Archibusieri · Via d. Saponai · Via Vinegia · V. d. Mosca · V.-V. Matenchini · V. d. Vagellai · Corso dei Tintori

Via de' Bardi · Coasta de' Magnoli · Coasta di San Giorgio · Lungarno Generale Armando Diaz · Lungarno della Grazie · Via Tripoli

4 SANTA CROCE

Fiume Arno

Lungarno Torrigiani · Via de' Bardi · Ponte alle Grazie

5 OLTRARNO

Piazzale Michelangelo

0	150 M
0	500 ft

EATING AND DRINKING WELL IN FLORENCE

In Florence simply prepared meats, grilled or roasted, are the culinary stars, usually paired with seasonal vegetables like artichokes or porcini. Bistecca's big here, but there's plenty more that tastes great on the grill, too.

Traditionalists go for their gustatory pleasures in trattorie and osterie, places where decor is unimportant and place mats are mere paper. Culinary innovation comes slowly in this town, though some cutting-edge restaurants have been appearing, usually with young chefs who've worked outside Italy. Some of these places lack charm, but their menus offer updated versions of Tuscan standards.

By American standards, Florentines eat late: 1:30 or 2 is typical for lunch and 9 for dinner is considered early. Consuming a primo, secondo, and dolce is largely a thing of the past. For lunch, many Florentines simply grab a panino and a glass of wine at a bar. Those opting for a simple trattoria lunch often order a plate of pasta and dessert.

STALE AND STELLAR

Florence lacks signature pasta and rice dishes, perhaps because it has raised frugality with bread to culinary craft. Stale bread is the basis for three classic Florentine primi: *pappa al pomodoro*, *ribollita*, and *panzanella*. Pappa is made with either fresh or canned tomatoes and that stale bread. Ribollita is a vegetable soup with *cavolo nero* (called Tuscan kale in the United States), cannellini beans, and thickened with bread. Panzanella, a summertime dish, is reconstituted Tuscan bread combined with tomatoes, cucumber, and basil. They all are enhanced with a generous application of fragrant Tuscan olive oil.

A CLASSIC ANTIPASTO: *CROSTINI DI FEGATINI*

This beloved dish consists of a chicken-liver spread, served warm or at room temperature, on toasted, garlic-rubbed bread. It can be served smooth, like a pâté, or in a chunkier, more rustic version. It's made by sautéing chicken livers with finely diced carrot and onion, enlivened with the addition of wine, broth, or Marsala reductions, and mashed anchovies and capers.

A CLASSIC SECONDO: *BISTECCA FIORENTINA*

The town's culinary pride and joy is a thick slab of beef, resembling a T-bone steak, from large white oxen called Chianina. The meat's slapped on the grill and served rare, sometimes with a pinch of salt.

It's always seared on both sides, and just barely cooked inside (experts say 5 minutes per side, and then 15 minutes with the bone sitting perpendicularly on the grill). To ask for it more well-done is to incur disdain; if you can't eat it this way, do please order something else.

A CLASSIC CONTORNO: *CANNELLINI BEANS*

Simply boiled, they provide the perfect accompaniment to bistecca. The small white beans are best when they go straight from the garden into the pot. They should be anointed with a generous dose of Tuscan olive oil; the

combination is oddly felicitous, and it goes a long way toward explaining why Tuscans are referred to as *mangiafagioli* (bean eaters) by other Italians.

A CLASSIC DOLCE: *BISCOTTI DI PRATO*

These are sometimes the only dessert on offer (if you find yourself in such a restaurant, you'll know you're in a really, truly Tuscan eatery) and are more or less an afterthought to the glories that have preceded them. *Biscotti* means twice-cooked (or, in this case, twice baked). They are hard almond cookies that soften considerably when dipped languidly into *vin santo* ("holy wine"), a sweet dessert wine, or into a simple *caffè*.

A CLASSIC WINE: *CHIANTI CLASSICO*

This blend from the region just south of Florence relies mainly on the local, hardy *sangiovese* grape; it's aged for at least one year before hitting the market. (*Riserve*—reserves—are aged at least an additional six months.)

Chianti is usually the libation of choice for Florentines, and it pairs magnificently with grilled foods and seasonal vegetables. Traditionalists opt for the younger, fruitier (and usually less expensive) versions often served in straw flasks. You can sample Chianti Classico all over town, and buy it in local supermarkets.

Updated
by Patricia
Rucidlo

Why visit Florence, the city that shook up the Western world in the Middle Ages and gifted it with what would later be called the Renaissance? There are many reasons: its biggest draw is its unsurpassable art, from the sensuousness of Botticelli's nudes to the muscularity, masculinity, and virtual perfection of Michelangelo's *David*. Also to see firsthand Brunelleschi's engineering and architectural genius, from the powerful cupola crowning the cathedral to his fledging Ospedale degli Innocenti (arguably the first Renaissance building in Italy).

Visitors have been captivated by this city along the Arno for centuries, and it has always been high on the list of places to visit on the Grand Tour. For centuries it has captured the imaginations of travelers in search of rooms with views and phenomenal art. Florence's is a subtle beauty—its staid palaces built in local stone are not showy, even though they are very large. A walk along the Arno offers views that don't quit and haven't much changed in 700 years. Navigating Piazza della Signoria and other major squares, always packed with tourists, requires patience. There's a reason why everyone wants to be here. Florence's *centro storico* (historic center) is little changed since Lorenzo de' Medici roamed its streets; outside the center, where most of the city's residents live, is less picturesque, but full of Florentines (they tend not to hang out in the historic center if they can help it).

When the sun sets over the Arno and, as Mark Twain described it, "overwhelms Florence with tides of color that make all the sharp lines dim and faint and turn the solid city to a city of dreams," it's hard not to fall under the city's spell.

FLORENCE PLANNER

MAKING THE MOST OF YOUR TIME

With some planning, you can see Florence's most famous sights in a couple of days. Start off at the city's most awe-inspiring architectural wonder, the **Duomo**, climbing to the top of the dome if you have the stamina (and are not claustrophobic: it gets a little tight going up and coming back down). On the same piazza, check out Ghiberti's bronze doors at the **Battistero**. (They're actually high-quality copies; the Museo dell'Opera del Duomo has the originals.) Set aside the afternoon for the **Galleria degli Uffizi**, making sure to reserve tickets in advance.

On Day 2, visit Michelangelo's *David* in the **Galleria dell'Accademia**—reserve tickets here, too. Linger in **Piazza della Signoria**, Florence's central square, where a copy of *David* stands in the spot the original occupied for centuries, then head east a couple of blocks to **Santa Croce**, the city's most artistically rich church. Double back and walk across Florence's landmark bridge, the **Ponte Vecchio**.

Do all that, and you'll have seen some great art, but you've just scratched the surface. If you have more time, put the **Bargello**, the **Museo di San Marco**, and the **Cappelle Medicee** at the top of your list. When you're ready for an art break, stroll through the **Boboli Gardens** or explore Florence's lively shopping scene, from the food stalls of the **Mercato Centrale** to the chic boutiques of the **Via Tornabuoni**.

HOURS

Florence's sights keep tricky hours. Some are closed Wednesday, some Monday, some every other Monday. Quite a few shut their doors each day (or on most days) by 2 in the afternoon. Things get even more confusing on weekends. Make it a general rule to check the hours closely for any place you're planning to visit; if it's someplace you have your heart set on seeing, it's worthwhile to call to confirm.

Here's a selection of major sights that might not be open when you'd expect *(consult the sight listings within this chapter for the full details)*. And be aware that, as always, hours can and do change. Also note that on the first Sunday of the month, all state museums are free. That means that the Accademia and the Uffizi, among others, do not accept reservations. Unless you are a glutton for punishment (i.e., large crowds), these museums are best avoided on that day.

The **Accademia** and the **Uffizi** are both closed Monday.

The **Battistero** is open Monday through Saturday 11–7 and Sunday 8:15–1:30.

The **Bargello** closes at 1:50 pm, and is closed entirely on alternating Sundays and Mondays. However, it's often open much later during high season and when there's a special exhibition on.

The **Cappelle Medicee** are closed alternating Sundays and Mondays (those Sundays and Mondays when the Bargello is open).

The **Duomo** closes at 4 , as opposed to 5 other weekdays, 4:45 Saturday, and Sunday it's open only 1:30–4:45. The dome of the Duomo is closed Sunday.

Museo di San Marco closes at 1:50 weekdays but stays open until 7 weekends—except for alternating Sundays and Mondays, when it's closed entirely.

Palazzo Medici-Riccardi is closed Wednesday.

RESERVATIONS

At most times of day you'll see a line of people snaking around the Uffizi. They're waiting to buy tickets, and you don't want to be one of them. Instead, call ahead for a reservation (☎ 055/294883; reservationists speak English). You'll be given a reservation number and a time of admission—the sooner you call, the more time slots you'll have to choose from. Go to the museum's reservation door 10 minutes before the appointed hour, give the clerk your number, pick up your ticket, and go inside. (Know that often in high season, there's at least a half-hour wait to pick up the tickets.) You'll pay €4 for this privilege, but it's money well spent. You can also book tickets online through the website ⊕ *www.polomuseale. firenze.it*; the booking process takes some patience, but it works.

Use the same reservation service to book tickets for the Galleria dell'Accademia, where lines rival those of the Uffizi. (Reservations can also be made for the Palazzo Pitti, the Bargello, and several other sights, but they usually aren't needed—although, lately, in summer, lines can be long at Palazzo Pitti.) An alternative strategy is to check with your hotel—many will handle reservations.

GETTING HERE AND AROUND

AIR TRAVEL

Aeroporto A. Vespucci. Florence's small Aeroporto A. Vespucci, commonly called **Peretola**, is just outside of town, and receives flights from Milan, Rome, London, and Paris. ⊠ *10 km (6 miles) northwest of Florence* ☎ *055/30615* ⊕ *www.aeroporto.firenze.it.*

To get into the city center from the airport by car, take the autostrada A11. A SITA bus will take you directly from the airport to the center of town. Buy the tickets within the train station.

Aeroporto Galileo Galilei. Pisa's Aeroporto Galileo Galilei is the closest landing point with significant international service, including a few direct flights from New York each week on Delta. Sadly, the flight is seasonal and shuts down when it's cold outside. It's a straight shot down the SS67 to Florence. A train service, which used to connect Pisa's airport station with Santa Maria Novella, has as of press time been temporarily suspended. It's easy to take the shuttle bus to the train station at Pisa Centrale, and then go on to Florence Santa Maria Novella. ⊠ *12 km (7 miles) south of Pisa and 80 km (50 miles) west of Florence* ☎ *050/849300* ⊕ *www.pisa-airport.com.*

BUS TRAVEL

Florence's flat, compact city center is made for walking, but when your feet get weary you can use the efficient bus system, which includes small electric buses making the rounds in the center. Buses also climb to Piazzale Michelangelo and San Miniato south of the Arno.

Maps and timetables for local bus service are available for a small fee at the ATAF (Azienda Trasporti Area Fiorentina) booth next to the train station, or for free at visitor information offices. Tickets must be bought in advance from tobacco shops, newsstands, automatic ticket machines near main stops, or ATAF booths. The ticket must be canceled in the small validation machine immediately upon boarding.

You have several ticket options, all valid for one or more rides on all lines. A €1.20 ticket is good for one hour from the time it is first canceled. A multiple ticket—four tickets, each valid for 70 minutes—costs €4.50. A 24-hour tourist ticket costs €5. Two-, three-, and seven-day passes are also available.

Long-distance buses provide inexpensive service between Florence and other cities in Italy and Europe. **SITA** (✉ *Via Santa Caterina da Siena 17/r* ☎ *055/47821* ⊕ *www.sitabus.it*) is the major line.

CAR TRAVEL

Florence is connected to the north and south of Italy by the Autostrada del Sole (A1). It takes about 1½ hours of driving on scenic roads to get to Bologna (although heavy truck traffic over the Apennines often makes for slower going), about three hours to Rome, and 3–3½ hours to Milan. The Tyrrhenian Coast is an hour west on the A11.

An automobile in Florence is a major liability. If your itinerary includes parts of Italy where you'll want a car (such as Tuscany), pick the vehicle up on your way out of town.

TAXI TRAVEL

Taxis usually wait at stands throughout the city (in front of the train station and in Piazza della Repubblica, for example), or you can call for one (☎ *055/4390 or 055/4242*). The meter starts at €3.30 from any taxi stand; if you call Radio Dispatch (that means that a taxi comes to pick you up wherever it is you are), it starts at €5.40. Extra charges apply at night, on Sunday, for radio dispatch, and for luggage. Women out on the town after midnight seeking taxis are entitled to a 10% discount on the fare; you must, however, request it.

TRAIN TRAVEL

Florence is on the principal Italian train route between most European capitals and Rome, and within Italy it is served frequently from Milan, Venice, and Rome by Intercity (IC) and nonstop Eurostar trains. Avoid trains that stop only at the Campo di Marte or Rifredi station, which are not convenient to the city center.

Stazione Centrale di Santa Maria Novella. Florence's main train station is in the center of town. ✉ *Florence* ☎ *892021* ⊕ *www.trenitalia.com*.

VISITOR INFORMATION

The Florence tourist office, known as the APT (☎ *055/290832* ⊕ *www. firenzeturismo.it*), has branches next to the Palazzo Medici-Riccardi, across the street from Stazione di Santa Maria Novella (the main train station), and at the Bigallo, in Piazza del Duomo. The offices are generally open from 9 in the morning until 7 in the evening. The multilingual staff will give you directions and the latest on happenings in the city. It's particularly worth a stop if you're interested in finding out about performing-arts events. The APT website provides information in both Italian and English.

EXPLORING

AROUND THE DUOMO

The heart of Florence, stretching from the Piazza del Duomo south to the Arno, is as dense with artistic treasures as any place in the world. Its churches, medieval towers, Renaissance palaces, and world-class museums and galleries contain some of the most outstanding achievements of Western art.

Much of the *centro storico* (historic center) is closed to automobile traffic, but you still must dodge mopeds, cyclists, and masses of fellow tourists as you walk the narrow streets, especially in the area bounded by the Duomo, Piazza della Signoria, Galleria degli Uffizi, and the Ponte Vecchio. Via dei Calzaiuoli, between Piazza del Duomo and Piazza della Signoria, is the city's favorite *passeggiata*.

TOP ATTRACTIONS

Bargello. This building started out as the headquarters for the Capitano del Popolo (captain of the people) during the Middle Ages, and was later used as a prison. The exterior served as a "most wanted" billboard: effigies of notorious criminals and Medici enemies were painted on its walls. Today it houses the Museo Nazionale, home to what is probably the finest collection of Renaissance sculpture in Italy. The concentration of masterworks by Michelangelo, Donatello, and Benvenuto Cellini is remarkable; the works are distributed among an eclectic collection of arms, ceramics, and miniature bronzes, among other things. For Renaissance art lovers, the Bargello is to sculpture what the Uffizi is to painting. In 1401 Filippo Brunelleschi and Lorenzo Ghiberti competed to earn the most prestigious commission of the day: the decoration of the north doors of the Baptistery in Piazza del Duomo. Though the judges chose Ghiberti, view both artists' bronze bas-relief panels to see if you agree. ✉ *Via del Proconsolo 4, Bargello* ☎ *055/294883* ⊕ *www.polomuseale.firenze.it* 🎟 *€4.*

Battistero (*Baptistery*). The octagonal Baptistery is one of the supreme monuments of the Italian Romanesque style and one of Florence's oldest structures. Modern excavations suggest that its foundations date from the 1st century AD. The round Romanesque arches on the exterior date from the 11th century, and the interior dome mosaics from the beginning of the mid-13th century are justly renowned, but they could never outshine the building's famed bronze Renaissance doors decorated with panels crafted by Lorenzo Ghiberti. These doors—or at least copies of them—on which Ghiberti worked most of his adult life are on the north and east sides of the Baptistery (the original doors are now on display in the Museo dell'Opera del Duomo), and the Gothic panels on the south door were designed by Andrea Pisano in 1330. Michelangelo declared them so beautiful that they could serve as the Gates of Paradise. ✉ *Piazza del Duomo* ☎ *055/2302885* ⊕ *www.operaduomo.firenze.it* 🎟 *€10.*

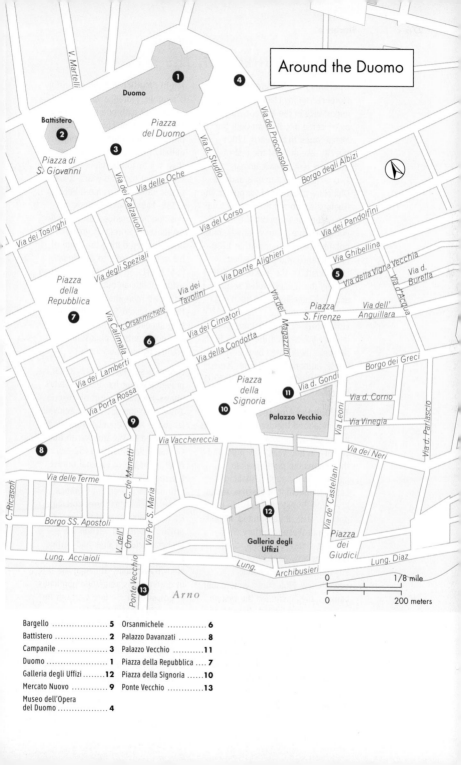

Around the Duomo

Duomo

Battistero

Piazza del Duomo

Piazza di S. Giovanni

V. Martelli

Via del Proconsolo

Borgo degli Albizi

Via dei Tosinghi

Via delle Oche

Via d. Studio

Via del Corso

Via dei Pandolfini

Via dei Calzaiuoli

Via degli Speziali

Via Dante Alighieri

Via Ghibellina

Via della Vigna Vecchia

Via d. Buretta

Piazza della Repubblica

Via dei Tavolini

V. Orsanmichele

Via dei Cimatori

Via dei Magazzini

Piazza S. Firenze

Via dell' Anguillara

Via dell'Acqua

Via Calimala

Via della Condotta

Borgo dei Greci

Via dei Lamberti

Piazza della Signoria

Via d. Gondi

Via d. Corno

Via Porta Rossa

Palazzo Vecchio

Via Leoni

Via Vinegia

Via d. Parlascio

Via Vacchereccia

Via dei Neri

C. de Manetti

Via delle Terme

C. Ricasoli

Via Por S. Maria

Via de' Castellani

Piazza dei Giudici

Borgo SS. Apostoli

V. dell' Oro

Galleria degli Uffizi

Lung. Acciaioli

Lung. Diaz

Ponte Vecchio

Lung. Archibusieri

Arno

0   1/8 mile

0   200 meters

Bargello .... **5**   Orsanmichele **6**
Battistero .... **2**   Palazzo Davanzati **8**
Campanile .... **3**   Palazzo Vecchio **11**
Duomo .... **1**   Piazza della Repubblica **7**
Galleria degli Uffizi .... **12**   Piazza della Signoria **10**
Mercato Nuovo .... **9**   Ponte Vecchio **13**
Museo dell'Opera
del Duomo **4**

FLORENCE THROUGH THE AGES

Guelph vs. Ghibelline. Although Florence can lay claim to a modest importance in the ancient world, it didn't come into its own until the Middle Ages. In the early 1200s the city, like most of the rest of Italy, was rent by civic unrest. Two factions, the Guelphs and the Ghibellines, competed for power. The Guelphs supported the papacy, and the Ghibellines supported the Holy Roman Empire. Bloody battles—most notably one at Montaperti in 1260—tore Florence and other Italian cities apart. By the end of the 13th century the Guelphs ruled securely, and the Ghibellines had been vanquished. This didn't end civic strife, however: the Guelphs split into the Whites and the Blacks for reasons still debated by historians. Dante, author of *The Divine Comedy*, was banished from Florence in 1301 because he was a White.

The Guilded Age. Local merchants had organized themselves into guilds by sometime beginning in the 12th century. In that year, they proclaimed themselves the *primo popolo* (literally, "first people"), making a landmark attempt at elective, republican rule. Though the episode lasted only 10 years, it constituted a breakthrough in Western history. Such a daring stance by the merchant class was a by-product of Florence's emergence as an economic powerhouse. Florentines were papal bankers; they instituted the system of international letters of credit; and the gold florin became the international standard of currency. With this economic strength came a building boom. Sculptors such as Donatello and Ghiberti decorated them; painters such as Giotto and Botticelli frescoed their walls.

Mighty Medici. Though ostensibly a republic, Florence was blessed (or cursed) with one very powerful family, the Medici, who came to prominence in the 1430s and were initially the de facto rulers and then the absolute rulers of Florence for several hundred years. It was under patriarch Cosimo il Vecchio (1389–1464) that the Medici's position in Florence was securely established. Florence's golden age occurred during the reign of his grandson Lorenzo de' Medici (1449–92). Lorenzo was not only an astute politician but also a highly educated man and a great patron of the arts. Called "Il Magnifico" (the Magnificent), he gathered around him poets, artists, philosophers, architects, and musicians.

Lorenzo's son Piero (1471–1503) proved inept at handling the city's affairs. He was run out of town in 1494, and Florence briefly enjoyed its status as a republic while dominated by the Dominican friar Girolamo Savonarola (1452–98). After a decade of internal unrest, the republic fell and the Medici returned to power, but Florence never regained its former prestige. By the 1530s most of the major artistic talent had left the city—Michelangelo, for one, had settled in Rome. The now-ineffectual Medici, eventually attaining the title of grand dukes, remained nominally in power until the line died out in 1737, after which time Florence passed from the Austrians to the French and back again until the unification of Italy (1865–70), when it briefly became the capital under King Vittorio Emanuele II.

Fodor's Choice ★ **Duomo.** *(See the highlighted listing in this chapter.)* ✉ *Piazza del Duomo* ☎ *055/2302885* ⊕ *www.operaduomo.firenze.it* ✒ *Church free; combination ticket €15, includes Baptistery, Crypt, Museo, Campanile, cupola.*

Fodor's Choice ★ **Galleria degli Uffizi.** The Medici installed their art collections at Europe's first modern museum, open to the public (at first only by request) since 1591. Among the highlights are Paolo Uccello's *Battle of San Romano*; the *Madonna and Child with Two Angels,* by Fra Filippo Lippi; the *Birth of Venus* and *Primavera* by Sandro Botticelli; the portraits of the Renaissance duke Federico da Montefeltro and his wife Battista Sforza, by Piero della Francesca; the *Madonna of the Goldfinch* by Raphael; Michelangelo's *Doni Tondo*; the *Venus of Urbino* by Titian; and the splendid *Bacchus* by Caravaggio. Don't forget to see the Caravaggios and the Raphaels, which you'll pass through during the exiting process. Late in the afternoon is the least crowded time to visit. ■ TIP➔ **For a €4 fee, advance tickets can be reserved by phone, online, or at the Uffizi reservation booth on the Piazza Pitti at least one day in advance of your visit. That's a very good idea.** ✉ *Piazzale degli Uffizi 6, Piazza della Signoria* ☎ *055/23885* ⊕ *www.uffizi.firenze.it; www.polomuseale.firenze.it for reservations* ✒ *€12.50 during special exhibitions; reservation fee €4.*

Piazza della Signoria. This is by far the most striking square in Florence. It was here, in 1497, that the famous "bonfire of the vanities" took place, when the fanatical friar Savonarola induced his followers to hurl their worldly goods into the flames. The statues in the square and in the 14th-century Loggia dei Lanzi on the south side vary in quality. Cellini's famous bronze *Perseus* holding the severed head of Medusa is certainly the most important; other works include *The Rape of the Sabine* and *Hercules and the Centaur,* both late-16th-century works by Giambologna. In the square, the Neptune Fountain was created by Bartolomeo Ammannati between 1550 and 1575, who considered it a failure. Giambologna's equestrian statue, to the left of the fountain, portrays Grand Duke Cosimo I. Occupying the steps of the Palazzo Vecchio are copies of famous sculptures now housed in museums around the city, including Michelangelo's *David,* as well as Baccio Bandinelli's *Hercules.* ✉ *Florence.*

Ponte Vecchio (*Old Bridge*). This charmingly simple bridge was built in 1345 to replace an earlier bridge swept away by flood. Its shops first housed butchers, then grocers, blacksmiths, and other merchants. But in 1593 the Medici grand duke Ferdinand I, whose private corridor linking the Medici palace (Palazzo Pitti) with the Medici offices (the Uffizi) crossed the bridge atop the shops, decided that all this plebeian commerce under his feet was unseemly. So he threw out the butchers and blacksmiths and installed 41 goldsmiths and eight jewelers. The bridge has been devoted solely to these two trades ever since. The **Corridoio Vasariano** (*Piazzale degli Uffizi 6, Piazza della Signoria, 055/23885, 055/294–883*), the private Medici elevated passageway, was built by Vasari in 1565; it was most likely designed so that the Medici family wouldn't have to walk amid the commoners. It can sometimes be visited by prior special arrangement. Call for the most up-to-date details. ✉ *Florence.*

Continued on page 283

THE DUOMO
FLORENCE'S BIGGEST MASTERPIECE

For all its monumental art and architecture, Florence has one undisputed centerpiece: the Cathedral of Santa Maria del Fiore, better known as the Duomo. Its cupola dominates the skyline, presiding over the city's rooftops like a red hen over her brood. Little wonder that when Florentines feel homesick, they say they have *"nostalgia del cupolone."*

The Duomo's construction began in 1296, following the design of Arnolfo da Cambio, Florence's greatest architect of the time. By modern standards, construction was slow and haphazard—it continued through the 14th and into the 15th century, with some dozen architects having a hand in the project.

In 1366 Neri di Fioravante created a model for the hugely ambitious cupola: it was to be the largest dome in the world, surpassing Rome's Pantheon. But when the time finally came to build the dome in 1418, no one was sure how—or even if—it could be done. Florence was faced with a 143-ft hole in the roof of its cathedral, and one of the greatest challenges in the history of architecture.

Fortunately, local genius Filippo Brunelleschi was just the man for the job. Brunelleschi won the 1418 competition to design the dome, and for the

next 18 years he oversaw its construction. The enormity of his achievement can hardly be overstated. Working on such a large scale (the dome weighs 37,000 tons and uses 4 million bricks) required him to invent hoists and cranes that were engineering marvels. A "dome within a dome" design and a novel herringbone bricklaying pattern were just two of the innovations used to establish structural integrity. Perhaps most remarkably, he executed the construction without a supporting wooden framework, which had previously been thought indispensable.

Brunelleschi designed the lantern atop the dome, but he died soon after its first stone was laid in 1446; it wouldn't be completed until 1461. Another 400 years passed before the Duomo received its façade, a 19th-century neo-Gothic creation.

DUOMO TIMELINE

1296 Work begins, following design by Arnolfo di Cambio.

1302 Arnolfo dies; work continues, with sporadic interruptions.

1331 Management of construction taken over by the Wool Merchants guild.

1334 Giotto appointed project overseer, designs campanile.

1337 Giotto dies; Andrea Pisano takes leadership role.

1348 The Black Plague; all work ceases.

1366 Vaulting on nave completed; Neri di Fioravante makes model for dome.

1417 Drum for dome completed.

1418 Competition is held to design the dome.

1420 Brunelleschi begins work on the dome.

1436 Dome completed.

1446 Construction of lantern begins; Brunelleschi dies.

1461 Antonio Manetti, a student of Brunelleschi, completes lantern.

1469 Gilt copper ball and cross added by Verrocchio.

1587 Original façade is torn down by Medici court.

1871 Emilio de Fabris wins competition to design new façade.

1887 Façade completed.

WHAT TO LOOK FOR INSIDE THE DUOMO

The interior of the Duomo is a fine example of Florentine Gothic with a beautiful marble floor, but the space feels strangely barren—a result of its great size and the fact that some of the best art has been moved to the nearby **Museo dell'Opera del Duomo**.

Notable among the works that remain are two towering equestrian frescoes of famous mercenaries: *Niccolò da Tolentino* (1456), by Andrea del Castagno, and *Sir John Hawkwood* (1436), by Paolo Uccello. There's also fine terra-cotta work by Luca della Robbia. Ghiberti,

Brunelleschi's great rival, is responsible for much of the stained glass, as well as a reliquary urn with gorgeous reliefs. A vast fresco of the Last Judgment, painted by Vasari and Zuccari, covers the dome's interior. Brunelleschi had wanted mosaics to go there; it's a pity he didn't get his wish.

In the crypt beneath the cathedral, you can explore excavations of a Roman wall and mosaic fragments from the late sixth century; entry is near the first pier on the right. On the way down you pass Brunelleschi's modest tomb.

1. Entrance; stained glass by Ghiberti
2. Fresco of Niccolò da Tolentino by Andrea del Castagno
3. Fresco of John Hawkwood by Paolo Uccello
4. *Dante and the Divine Comedy* by Domenico di Michelino
5. Lunette: *Ascension* by Luca della Robbia
6. Above altar: two angels by Luca della Robbia. Below the altar: reliquary of St. Zenobius by Ghiberti.
7. Lunette: *Resurrection* by Luca della Robbia
8. Entrance to dome
9. Bust of Brunelleschi by Buggiano
10. Stairs to crypt
11. Campanile

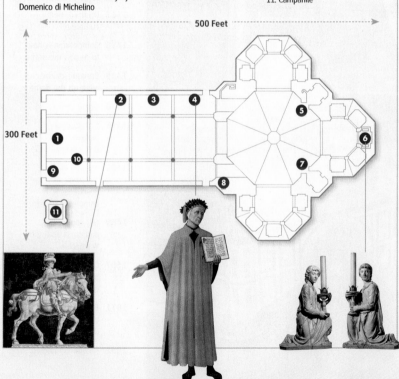

MAKING THE CLIMB

Climbing the 463 steps to the top of the dome is not for the faint of heart—or for the claustrophobic—but those who do it will be awarded a smashing view of Florence ❶. Keep in mind that the way up is also the way down, which means that while you're huffing and puffing in the ascent, people very close to you in a narrow staircase are making their way down ❷.

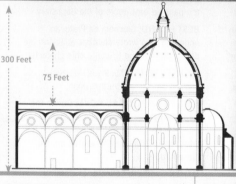

300 Feet

75 Feet

DUOMO BASICS

- Even first thing in the morning during high season (May through September), a line is likely to have formed to climb the dome. Expect an hour wait.

- For an alternative to the dome, consider climbing the less trafficked campanile, which gives you a view from on high of the dome itself.

- Dress code essentials: covered shoulders, no short shorts, and hats off upon entering.

THE CRYPT

The crypt is worth a visit: computer modeling allows visitors to see its ancient Roman fabric and subsequent rebuilding. A transparent plastic model shows exactly what the earlier church looked like.

BRUNELLESCHI vs. GHIBERTI
The Rivalry of Two Renaissance Geniuses

In Renaissance Florence, painters, sculptors, and architects competed for major commissions, with the winner earning the right to undertake a project that might occupy him (and keep him paid) for a decade or more. Stakes were high, and the resulting rivalries fierce—none more so than that between Filippo Brunelleschi and Lorenzo Ghiberti.

The two first clashed in 1401, for the commission to create the bronze doors of the Baptistery. When Ghiberti won, Brunelleschi took it hard, fleeing to Rome, where he would remain for 15 years. Their rematch came in 1418, over the design of the Duomo's cupola, with Brunelleschi triumphant. For the remainder of their lives, the two would miss no opportunity to belittle each other's work.

FILIPPO BRUNELLESCHI (1377–1446)

MASTERPIECE: The dome of Santa Maria del Fiore.

BEST FRIENDS: Donatello, whom he stayed with in Rome after losing the Baptistery doors competition; the Medici family, who rescued him from bankruptcy.

SIGNATURE TRAITS: Paranoid, secretive, bad tempered, practical joker, inept businessman.

SAVVIEST POLITICAL MOVE: Feigned sickness and left for Rome after his dome plans were publicly criticized by Ghiberti, who was second-in-command. The project proved too much for Ghiberti to manage on his own, and Brunelleschi returned triumphant.

MOST EMBARRASSING MOMENT: In 1434 he was imprisoned for two weeks for failure to pay a small guild fee. The humiliation might have been orchestrated by Ghiberti.

OTHER CAREER: Shipbuilder. He built a huge vessel, *Il Badalone*, to transport marble for the dome up the Arno. It sank on its first voyage.

INSPIRED: The dome of St. Peter's in Rome.

LORENZO GHIBERTI (1378–1455)

MASTERPIECE: *The Gates of Paradise*, the ten-paneled east doors of the Baptistery.

BEST FRIEND: Giovanni da Prato, an underling who wrote diatribes attacking the dome's design and Brunelleschi's character.

SIGNATURE TRAITS: Instigator, egoist, know-it-all, shrewd businessman.

SAVVIEST POLITICAL MOVE: During the Baptistery doors competition, he had an open studio and welcomed opinions on his work, while Brunelleschi labored behind closed doors.

OTHER CAREER: Collector of classical artifacts, historian.

INSPIRED: *The Gates of Hell* by Auguste Rodin.

The Gates of Paradise detail

WORTH NOTING

Campanile. The Gothic bell tower designed by Giotto (circa 1266–1337) is a soaring structure of multicolor marble originally decorated with sculptures by Donatello and reliefs by Giotto, Andrea Pisano, and others (which are now in the Museo dell'Opera del Duomo). A climb of 414 steps rewards you with a close-up of Brunelleschi's cupola on the Duomo next door and a sweeping view of the city. ⊠ *Piazza del Duomo* ☎ *055/2302885* ⊕ *www.operaduomo.firenze.it* 🎫 *€15.*

FAMILY **Mercato Nuovo** (*New Market*). The open-air loggia, built in 1551, teems with souvenir stands, but the real attraction is a copy of Pietro Tacca's bronze *Porcellino* (which translates as "little pig" despite the fact the animal is, in fact, a wild boar). The *Porcellino* is Florence's equivalent of the Trevi Fountain: put a coin in his mouth, and if it falls through the grate below (according to one interpretation), it means you'll return to Florence someday. What you're seeing is a copy of a copy: Tacca's original version, in the Museo Bardini, is actually a copy of an ancient Greek work. ⊠ *Corner of Via Por Santa Maria and Via Porta Rossa, Piazza della Repubblica.*

Museo dell'Opera del Duomo (*Cathedral Museum*). A seven-year restoration of this museum and its glorious reopening in October 2015 have given Florence one of its most modern, up-to-date museums. Exhibition space has doubled in size, and the old facade of the cathedral, torn down in the 1580s, has been recreated with a 1:1 relationship to the real thing. Both sets of Ghiberti's doors adorn the same room. Michelangelo's *Pietà* finally has the space it deserves, as does Donatello's *Mary Magdalene.* ⊠ *Piazza del Duomo 9, Duomo* ☎ *055/2302885* ⊕ *www.operaduomo.firenze.it* 🎫 *€15.*

Orsanmichele. This multipurpose structure began as an 8th-century oratory and then in 1290 was turned into an open-air loggia for selling grain. Destroyed by fire in 1304, it was rebuilt as a loggia-market. Between 1367 and 1380 the arcades were closed and two stories were added above; finally, at century's end it was turned into a church. Inside is a beautifully detailed 14th-century Gothic tabernacle by Andrea Orcagna (1308–68). The exterior niches contain sculptures (all copies) dating from the early 1400s to the early 1600s by Donatello and Verrocchio (1435–88), among others, which were paid for by the guilds. Although it is a copy, Verrocchio's *Doubting Thomas* (circa 1470) is particularly deserving of attention. Here you see Christ, like the building's other figures, entirely framed within the niche, and St. Thomas standing on its bottom ledge, with his right foot outside the niche frame. This one detail, the positioning of a single foot, brings the whole composition to life. It's possible to see the original sculptures at the **Museo di Orsanmichele,** which is open Monday only. ⊠ *Via dei Calzaiuoli, Piazza della Repubblica* ☎ *055/284944* ⊕ *www.polomuseale.firenze.it* 🎫 *Free.*

Palazzo Davanzati. The prestigious Davanzati family owned this 14th-century palace in one of Florence's swankiest medieval neighborhoods. The place is a delight, as you can wander through the surprisingly light-filled courtyard, and climb the steep stairs to the piano nobile (there's also an elevator), where the family did most of its living. The beautiful *Sala dei Pappagalli* (Parrot Room) is adorned with trompe-l'oeil tapestries and gaily painted birds. ⊠ *Piazza Davanzati 13, Piazza della Repubblica* ☎ *055/2388610* ⊕ *www.polomuseale. firenze.it* 🎫 *€6.*

FAMILY **Palazzo Vecchio** (*Old Palace*). Florence's forbidding, fortresslike city hall was begun in 1299, presumably designed by Arnolfo di Cambio, and its massive bulk and towering campanile dominate Piazza della Signoria. It was built as a meeting place for the guildsmen governing the city at the time; today it is still City Hall. The main attraction is on the second floor, the opulently vast **Sala dei Cinquecento** (Room of the Five Hundred), named for the 500-member Great Council that met here. Giorgio Vasari and others decorated the room, around 1563–65, with gargantuan frescoes celebrating Florentine history. In comparison, the little **Studiolo,** just off the Sala dei Cinquecento's entrance, was a private room meant for the duke and those whom he invited in. ⊠ *Piazza della Signoria* ☎ *055/2768465* ⊕ *museicivicifiorentini.comune.fi.it* 🎫 *Museo €10, Torre €10, Museo and Torre €14.*

Piazza della Repubblica. The square marks the site of the ancient forum that was the core of the original Roman settlement. While the street plan around the piazza still reflects the carefully plotted Roman military encampment, the Mercato Vecchio (Old Market), which had been here since the Middle Ages, was demolished and the current piazza was constructed between 1885 and 1895 as a Neoclassical showpiece. The piazza is lined with outdoor cafés, affording an excellent opportunity for people-watching. ⊠ *Florence.*

SAN LORENZO

A sculptor, painter, architect, and poet, Florentine native son Michelangelo was a consummate genius, and some of his finest creations remain in his hometown. The Biblioteca Medicea Laurenziana is perhaps his most fanciful work of architecture. A key to understanding Michelangelo's genius can be found in the magnificent Cappelle Medicee, where both his sculptural and architectural prowess can be clearly seen. Planned frescoes were never completed, sadly, for they would have shown in one space the artistic triple threat that he certainly was. The towering yet graceful *David,* perhaps his most famous work, resides in the Galleria dell'Accademia.

After visiting San Lorenzo, resist the temptation to explore the market that surrounds the church: the market is open until 7 pm, while the churches and museums you may want to visit are not. Come back to the market later, after other sites have closed. Note that the Museo di San Marco closes at 1:50 on weekdays.

TOP ATTRACTIONS

Cappelle Medicee (*Medici Chapels*). This magnificent complex includes the Cappella dei Principi, the Medici chapel and mausoleum begun in 1605 that kept marble workers busy for several hundred years, and the Sagrestia Nuova (New Sacristy), designed by Michelangelo and so called to distinguish it from Brunelleschi's Sagrestia Vecchia

Florence's Trial by Fire

One of the most striking figures of Renaissance Florence was Girolamo Savonarola, a Dominican friar who, for a moment, captured the spiritual conscience of the city. In 1491 he became prior of the convent of San Marco, where he adopted a life of austerity and delivered sermons condemning Florence's excesses and the immorality of his fellow clergy. Following the death of Lorenzo de' Medici in 1492, Savonarola was instrumental in the re-formation of the republic of Florence, ruled by a representative council with Christ enthroned as monarch. In one of his most memorable acts he urged Florentines to toss worldly possessions—from sumptuous dresses to Botticelli paintings—onto a "bonfire of the vanities" in Piazza della Signoria. Savonarola's antagonism toward church hierarchy led to his undoing: he was excommunicated in 1497, and the following year was hanged and burned on charges of heresy. Today, at the Museo di San Marco, you can visit Savonarola's cell.

(Old Sacristy). Michelangelo received the commission for the New Sacristy in 1520 from Cardinal Giulio de' Medici, who later became Pope Clement VII. The cardinal wanted a new burial chapel for his cousins Giuliano, Duke of Nemours, and Lorenzo, Duke of Urbino, and he also wanted to honor his father, also named Giuliano, and his uncle, Lorenzo il Magnifico. The result was a tour de force of architecture and sculpture. Architecturally, Michelangelo was as original here as ever, but it is the powerfully sculpted tombs that dominate the room. The figures on the tomb on the right represent Day and Night; those on the tomb to the left represent Dawn and Dusk. ⊠ *Piazza di Madonna degli Aldobrandini, San Lorenzo* ☎ *055/294883 for reservations* ⊕ *www.polomuseale.firenze.it* ⊠ *€6 (€8 during special exhibits).*

FAMILY **Galleria dell'Accademia** (*Accademia Gallery*). The collection of Florentine paintings, dating from the 13th to the 18th centuries, is largely unremarkable, but the sculptures by Michelangelo are worth the price of admission. The unfinished *Slaves*, fighting their way out of their marble prisons, were meant for the tomb of Michelangelo's overly demanding patron Pope Julius II. But the focal point is the original *David*, commissioned in 1501 by the Opera del Duomo (Cathedral Works Committee), which gave the 26-year-old sculptor a leftover block of marble that had been ruined 40 years earlier by two other sculptors. Michelangelo didn't give the statue perfect proportions—the head is slightly too large for the body, the arms too large for the torso, and the hands dramatically large for the arms. But he did it to express and embody an entire biblical story. ■TIP→ Today David is beset not by Goliath but by tourists; save yourself a long wait in line by reserving tickets in advance. ⊠ *Via Ricasoli 60, San Marco* ☎ *055/294883 for reservations, 055/2388609 for gallery* ⊕ *www.gallerieaccademia.org* ⊠ *€8, special exhibitions €12.50; reservation fee €4.*

Fodor's Choice **Mercato Centrale.** Some of the food at this huge, two-story market hall is
★ remarkably exotic. The ground floor contains meat and cheese stalls, as
well as some very good bars that have panini. In June 2014, a second-
floor food hall opened, eerily reminiscent of food halls everywhere.
The quality of the food served, however, more than makes up for this.
⊠ *Piazza del Mercato Centrale, San Lorenzo* ⊕ *www.mercatocentrale.it.*

Museo di San Marco. A Dominican convent adjacent to the church of
San Marco now houses this museum, which contains many stunning
works by Fra Angelico (circa 1400–55), the Dominican friar famous
for his piety as well as for his painting. When the friars' cells were
restructured between 1439 and 1444, he decorated many of them with
frescoes meant to spur religious contemplation. His unostentatious and
direct paintings exalt the simple beauties of the contemplative life. Fra
Angelico's works are everywhere, from the friars' cells to the superb
panel paintings on view in the museum. Don't miss the famous *Annunciation,* on the upper floor, and the works in the gallery off the cloister
as you enter. Here you can see his beautiful *Last Judgment*; as usual,
the tortures of the damned are far more inventive and interesting than
the pleasures of the redeemed. ⊠ *Piazza San Marco 1* ☎ *055/2388608*
⊕ *www.polomuseale.firenze.it/en/musei/index.php?m=sanmarco* 💳 €4.

San Lorenzo. Filippo Brunelleschi designed this basilica, as well as that
of Santo Spirito in the Oltrarno, in the 15th century. He never lived to
see either finished. The two interiors are similar in design and effect. San
Lorenzo, however, has a grid of dark, inlaid marble lines on the floor,
which considerably heightens the dramatic effect. The grid makes the
rigorous geometry of the interior immediately visible, and is an illumi-
nating lesson on the laws of perspective. If you stand in the middle of
the nave at the church entrance, on the line that stretches to the high
altar, every element in the church—the grid, the nave columns, the side
aisles, the coffered nave ceiling—seems to march inexorably toward
a hypothetical vanishing point beyond the high altar, exactly as in a
single-point-perspective painting. Brunelleschi's **Sagrestia Vecchia** (Old
Sacristy) has stucco decorations by Donatello; it's at the end of the left
transept. ⊠ *Piazza San Lorenzo* 💳 €4.50.

WORTH NOTING

Biblioteca Medicea Laurenziana (*Laurentian Library*). Michelangelo the
architect was every bit as original as Michelangelo the sculptor. Unlike
Brunelleschi (the architect of the Spedale degli Innocenti), however, he
wasn't obsessed with proportion and perfect geometry. He was interested in experimentation and invention and in the expression of a personal vision that was at times highly idiosyncratic.

It was never more idiosyncratic than in the Laurentian Library, begun
in 1524 and finished in 1568 by Bartolomeo Ammannati. Its famous
vestibolo, a strangely shaped anteroom, has had scholars scratching
their heads for centuries. In a space more than two stories high, why
did Michelangelo limit his use of columns and pilasters to the upper
two-thirds of the wall? Why didn't he rest them on strong pedestals
instead of on huge, decorative curlicue scrolls, which rob them of all
visual support? Why did he recess them into the wall, which makes

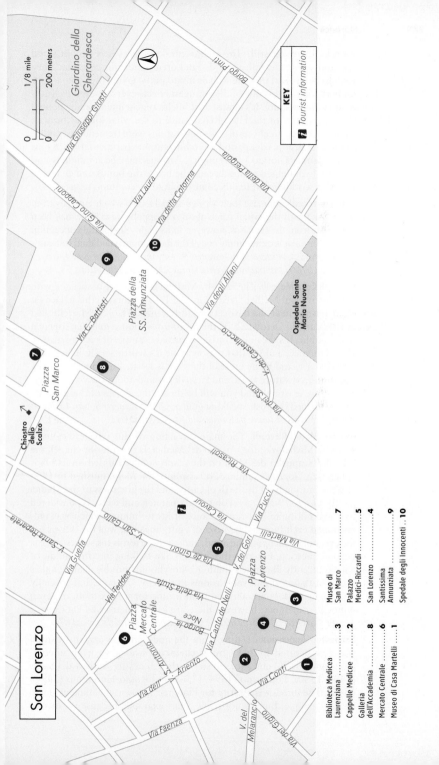

San Lorenzo

Giardino della Gherardesca

0 — 1/8 mile
0 — 200 meters

Chiostro dello Scalzo

Piazza San Marco

Piazza della SS. Annunziata

Piazza Mercato Centrale

Piazza S. Lorenzo

Ospedale Santa Maria Nuova

Via Giuseppi Giusti
Via Gino Capponi
Via Laura
Via della Colonna
Via della Pergola
Borgo Pinti
Via C. Battisti
Via degli Alfani
Via del Castellaccio
Via dei Servi
Via Ricasoli
Via Cavour
Via Pucci
Via Martelli
V. dei Gori
V. S. Gallo
Via de Ginori
Via della Stufa
Via Canto de Nelli
Borgo la Noce
Via dell' S. Antonio
Via Tadda
Via Guelfa
V. Santa Reparata
Via Faenza
V. del Melarancio
V. del Giglio
Via Conti
Via dell' Ariento

KEY

𝐢 Tourist information

Biblioteca Medicea
Laurenziana **3**
Cappelle Medicee **2**
Galleria
dell'Accademia **8**
Mercato Centrale **6**
Museo di Casa Martelli **1**

Museo di
San Marco **7**
Palazzo
Medici-Riccardi **5**
San Lorenzo **4**
Santissima
Annunziata **9**
Spedale degli Innocenti .. **10**

them look weaker still? The architectural elements here do not stand firm and strong and tall, as inside San Lorenzo, next door; instead, they seem to be pressed into the wall as if into putty, giving the room a soft, rubbery look that is one of the strangest effects ever achieved by 16th-century architecture. It's almost as if Michelangelo intentionally flouted the conventions of the High Renaissance to see what kind of bizarre, mannered effect might result. His innovations were tremendously influential, and produced a period of architectural experimentation. As his contemporary Giorgio Vasari put it, "Artisans have been infinitely and perpetually indebted to him because he broke the bonds and chains of a way of working that had become habitual by common usage."

The anteroom's staircase (best viewed straight on), which emerges from the library with the visual force of an unstoppable lava flow, has been exempted from the criticism, however. In its highly sculptural conception and execution, it is quite simply one of the most original and fluid staircases in the world. ⊠ *Piazza San Lorenzo 9, entrance to left of San Lorenzo* ☎ *055/210760* ⊕ *www.bml.firenze.sbn.it* ⌨ *Special exhibitions €3.*

Museo di Casa Martelli. The wealthy Martelli family, long associated with the all-powerful Medici, lived, from the 16th century, in this palace on a quiet street near the basilica of San Lorenzo. The last Martelli died in 1986, and in October 2009 the *casa-museo* (house-museum) opened to the public. It's the only nonreconstructed example of such a house in all of Florence, and for that reason alone it's worth a visit. The family collected art, and while most of the stuff is B-list, a couple of gems by Beccafumi, Salvatore Rosa, and Piero di Cosimo adorn the walls. Reservations are essential, and you will be shown the glories of this place by well-informed, English-speaking guides. ⊠ *Via Zanetti 8, San Lorenzo* ☎ *055/290383* ⊕ *www.polomuseale.firenze.it* ⌨ *€3.*

Palazzo Medici-Riccardi. The main attraction of this palace, begun in 1444 by Michelozzo for Cosimo de' Medici, is the interior chapel, the so-called **Cappella dei Magi** on the piano nobile. Painted on its walls is Benozzo Gozzoli's famous *Procession of the Magi,* finished in 1460 and celebrating both the birth of Christ and the greatness of the Medici family. Gozzoli wasn't a revolutionary painter, and today is considered by some not quite first-rate because of his technique, which was old-fashioned even for his day. Gozzoli's gift, however, was for entrancing the eye, not challenging the mind, and on those terms his success here is beyond question. Entering the chapel is like walking into the middle of a magnificently illustrated children's storybook, and this beauty makes it one of the most enjoyable rooms in the city. Do note that officially only eight visitors are allowed in at a time for a maximum of seven minutes; sometimes, however, there are lenient guards. ⊠ *Via Cavour 1, San Lorenzo* ☎ *055/2760340* ⊕ *www.palazzo-medici.it* ⌨ *€7.*

Santissima Annunziata. Dating from the mid-13th century, this church was restructured in 1447 by Michelozzo, who gave it an uncommon (and lovely) entrance cloister with frescoes by Andrea del Sarto (1486–1530), Pontormo (1494–1556), and Rosso Fiorentino (1494–1540). The interior is a rarity for Florence: an overwhelming example of the Baroque. But it's not really a fair example, because it's merely

CLOSE UP

Meet the Medici

The Medici were the dominant family of Renaissance Florence, wielding political power and financing some of the world's greatest art. You'll see their names at every turn around the city. These are some of the clan's more notable members:

Cosimo il Vecchio (1389–1464), incredibly wealthy banker to the popes, was the first in the family line to act as de facto ruler of Florence. He was a great patron of the arts and architecture; he was the moving force behind the family palace and the Dominican complex of San Marco.

Lorenzo il Magnifico (1449–92), grandson of Cosimo il Vecchio, presided over a Florence largely at peace with her neighbors. A collector of cameos, a writer of sonnets, and lover of ancient texts, he was the preeminent Renaissance man.

Leo X (1475–1521), also known as Giovanni de' Medici, became the first Medici pope, helping extend the family power base to include Rome and the Papal States. His reign was characterized by a host of problems, the biggest one being a former friar named Martin Luther.

Catherine de' Medici (1519–89) was married by her great uncle Pope Clement VII to Henry of Valois, who later became Henry II of France. Wife of one king and mother of three, she was the first Medici to marry into European royalty. Lorenzo il Magnifico, her great-grandfather, would have been thrilled.

Cosimo I (1537–74), the first grand duke of Tuscany, should not be confused with his ancestor Cosimo il Vecchio.

17th-century Baroque decoration applied willy-nilly to an earlier structure—exactly the sort of violent remodeling exercise that has given the Baroque a bad name. The **Cappella dell'Annunziata,** immediately inside the entrance to the left, illustrates the point. The lower half, with its stately Corinthian columns and carved frieze bearing the Medici arms, was commissioned by Piero de' Medici in 1447; the upper half, with its erupting curves and impish sculpted cherubs, was added 200 years later. Fifteenth-century-fresco enthusiasts should also note the very fine *Holy Trinity with St. Jerome* in the second chapel on the left. Done by Andrea del Castagno (circa 1421–57), it shows a wiry and emaciated St. Jerome with Paula and Eustochium, two of his closest followers. ✉ *Piazza di Santissima Annunziata* ☎ *055/266186.*

Spedale degli Innocenti. The orphanage built by Brunelleschi in 1419 to serve as an orphanage takes the historical prize as the very first Renaissance building. Brunelleschi designed its portico with his usual rigor, constructing it from the two shapes he considered mathematically (and therefore philosophically and aesthetically) perfect: the square and the circle. Below the level of the arches, the portico encloses a row of perfect cubes; above the level of the arches, the portico encloses a row of intersecting hemispheres. The entire geometric scheme is articulated with Corinthian columns, capitals, and arches borrowed directly from antiquity. At the time he designed the portico, Brunelleschi was also designing

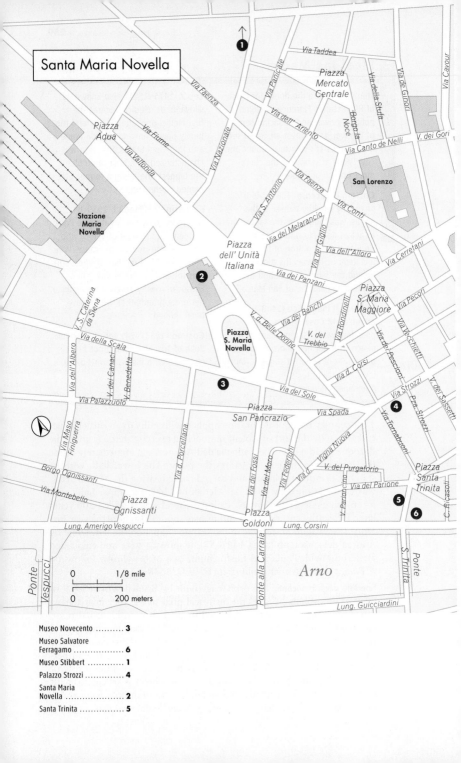

Santa Maria Novella

Via Taddea

Piazza Mercato Centrale

Via Faenza

Via Panicale

Via della Stufa

Via de' Ginori

Via Cavour

Via dell' Ariento

Borgo la Noce

Piazza Adua

Via Fiume

Via Nazionale

Via Vallonda

San Lorenzo

V. dei Gori

Via Canto de' Nelli

Via Conti

Stazione Maria Novella

Via S. Antonio

Via Faenza

Via del Melarancio

Via del Giglio

Via dell'Alloro

Via Cerretani

Piazza dell' Unità Italiana

Via dei Panzani

Piazza S. Maria Maggiore

Via Pecori

Via S. Caterina da Siena

Via della Scala

V. d. Belle Donne

Via dei Banchi

V. del Trebbio

Via Rondinelli

Via de' Pescioni

Via de' Vecchietti

Piazza S. Maria Novella

Via d. Corsi

Via dell'Albero

Via del Canaco

V. Benedetta

Via Palazzuoto

Via d. Porcellana

Via del Sole

Via Spada

Via Strozzi

Pza. Strozzi

V. de' Sassetti

Piazza San Pancrazio

Via Maso Finiguerra

Vigna Nuova

V. del Purgatorio

Piazza Santa Trinita

Via Federighi

V. d.

Via Tornabuoni

C. Ricasoli

Borgo Ognissanti

Via del Fossi

Via del Moro

Via del Parione

Via Montebello

Piazza Ognissanti

V. Parioncino

Piazza Goldoni

Lung. Amerigo Vespucci

Lung. Corsini

Ponte alla Carraia

S. Trinita

Ponte Vespucci

Ponte S. Trinita

Arno

0   1/8 mile

0   200 meters

Lung. Guicciardini

the interior of San Lorenzo, using the same basic ideas. But because the portico was finished before San Lorenzo, the Spedale degli Innocenti can claim the honor of ushering in Renaissance architecture. The 10 ceramic medallions depicting swaddled infants that decorate the portico are by Andrea della Robbia (1435–1525/28), done in about 1487.

Within the Spedale degli Innocenti is a small museum, or **Pinacoteca** (€7; *Thurs.–Tues. 9–7*). Most of the objects are minor works by major artists, but well worth a look is Domenico Ghirlandaio's (1449–94) *Adorazione dei Magi (Adoration of the Magi)*, executed in 1488. His use of color, and his eye for flora and fauna, shows that art from north of the Alps made a great impression on him. ⊠ *Piazza di Santissima Annunziata 12* ☎ *055/20371* ⊕ *www.istitutodegliinnocenti.it* ☜ *€7.*

SANTA MARIA NOVELLA

Piazza Santa Maria Novella is a gorgeous, pedestrian-only square, with grass (laced with roses) and plenty of places to sit and rest your feet. The streets in and around the piazza have their share of architectural treasures, including some of Florence's most tasteful palaces. Between Santa Maria Novella and the Arno is Via Tornabuoni, Florence's swankiest shopping street.

TOP ATTRACTIONS

Santa Maria Novella. The facade of this church looks distinctly clumsy by later Renaissance standards, and with good reason: it is an architectural hybrid. The lower half was completed mostly in the 14th century; its pointed-arch niches and decorative marble patterns reflect the Gothic style of the day. About 100 years later (around 1456), architect Leon Battista Alberti was called in to complete the job, adding architectural motifs in an entirely different style. Don't miss the church's store of remarkable art treasures. Highlights include the 14th-century stained-glass rose window depicting the *Coronation of the Virgin*; the Cappella Filippo Strozzi, containing late-15th-century frescoes and stained glass by Filippino Lippi; the cappella maggiore, displaying frescoes by Ghirlandaio; and the Cappella Gondi, containing Filippo Brunelleschi's famous wood crucifix, carved around 1410. Of special interest for its great historical importance and beauty is Masaccio's *Trinity*; painted around 1426–27, it unequivocally announced the arrival of the Renaissance. ⊠ *Piazza Santa Maria Novella 19* ☎ *055/210113, 055/282187 for museo* ⊕ *www.chiesasantamarianovella.it* ☜ *€5.*

Santa Trinita. Started in the 11th century by Vallombrosian monks and originally Romanesque in style, the church underwent a Gothic remodeling during the 14th century. (Remains of the Romanesque construction are visible on the interior front wall.) The major works are the fresco cycle and altarpiece in the Cappella Sassetti, the second to the high altar's right, painted by Ghirlandaio between 1480 and 1485. His work here possesses such graceful decorative appeal as well as a proud depiction of his native city (most of the cityscapes show 15th-century Florence in all her glory). The wall frescoes illustrate scenes from the life of St. Francis, and the altarpiece, depicting the *Adoration of the Shepherds,* veritably glows. ⊠ *Piazza Santa Trinita, Santa Maria Novella* ☎ *055/216912.*

WORTH NOTING

Museo Novecento. It began life as a 13th-century Franciscan hostel offering shelter to tired pilgrims. It later became a convalescent home, and in the late 18th century it was a school for poor girls. Now the former Ospedale di San Paolo houses a museum devoted to Italian art of the 20th century. Admittedly, most of these artists are not exactly household names, but the museum is so beautifully well done that it's worth a visit. The second floor contains works by artists from the second half of the century; start on the third floor, and go directly to the collection of Alberto della Ragione, a naval engineer determined to be on the cutting edge of art collecting. ⊠ *Piazza, Santa Maria Novella 10, Santa Maria Novella* ☎ *055/286 132* ⊕ *www.museonovecento.it.*

Museo Salvatore Ferragamo. If there's such a thing as a temple for footwear, this is it. The shoes in this dramatically displayed collection were designed by Salvatore Ferragamo (1898–1960) beginning in the early 20th century. Born in southern Italy, the late master jump-started his career in Hollywood by creating shoes for the likes of Mary Pickford and Rudolph Valentino. He then returned to Florence and set up shop in the 13th-century Palazzo Spini Ferroni. The collection includes about 16,000 shoes, and those on exhibition are frequently rotated. Special exhibitions are also mounted here and are well worth visiting—past shows have been devoted to Audrey Hepburn, Greta Garbo, and Marilyn Monroe. ⊠ *Via dei Tornabuoni 2, Santa Maria Novella* ☎ *055/3561* ⊕ *www.museoferragamo.it* 🖾 €6.

Museo Stibbert. Federico Stibbert (1838–1906), born in Florence to an Italian mother and an English father, liked to collect things. Over a lifetime of doing so, he amassed some 50,000 objects. This museum, which was also his home, displays many of them. He had a fascination with medieval armor and also collected costumes, particularly Uzbek costumes, which are exhibited in a room called the Moresque Hall. These are mingled with an extensive collection of swords, guns, and other devices whose sole function was to kill people. The paintings, most of which date from the 15th century, are largely second-rate. The house itself is an interesting amalgam of neo-Gothic, Renaissance, and English eccentric. To get here, take Bus No. 4 (across the street from the station at Santa Maria Novella) and get off at the stop marked "Fabbroni 4," then follow signs to the museum. ⊠ *Via Federico Stibbert 26* ☎ *055/475520* ⊕ *www.museostibbert.it* 🖾 €8.

Palazzo Strozzi. The Strozzi family built this imposing palazzo in an attempt to outshine the nearby Palazzo Medici. Based on a model by Giuliano da Sangallo (circa 1452–1516) dating from around 1489 and executed between 1489 and 1504 under il Cronaca (1457–1508) and Benedetto da Maiaino (1442–97), it was inspired by Michelozzo's earlier Palazzo Medici-Riccardi. The palazzo's exterior is simple, severe, and massive: it's a testament to the wealth of a patrician, 15th-century Florentine family. The interior courtyard, entered from the rear of the palazzo, is another matter altogether. It is here that the classical vocabulary—columns, capitals, pilasters, arches, and cornices—is given uninhibited and powerful expression. The palazzo frequently hosts blockbuster art shows. ⊠ *Via Tornabuoni, Piazza della Repubblica* ☎ *055/264 5155* ⊕ *www.palazzostrozzi.org* 🖾 *Free.*

SANTA CROCE

The Santa Croce quarter, on the southeast fringe of the historic center, was built up in the Middle Ages outside the second set of medieval city walls. The centerpiece of the neighborhood was (and is) the basilica of Santa Croce, which could hold great numbers of worshippers; the vast piazza could accommodate any overflow and also served as a fairground and, allegedly since the middle of the 16th century, as a playing field for no-holds-barred soccer games. A center of leatherworking since the Middle Ages, the neighborhood is still packed with leatherworkers and leather shops.

TOP ATTRACTIONS

Piazza Santa Croce. Originally outside the city's 12th-century walls, this piazza grew with the Franciscans, who used the large square for public preaching. During the Renaissance it was used for *giostre* (jousts), including one sponsored by Lorenzo de' Medici. "Bonfires of the vanities" occurred here, as well as soccer matches in the 16th century. Lined with many palazzi dating from the 15th and 16th centuries, the square remains one of Florence's loveliest piazze and is a great place to people-watch. ⊠ *Florence*.

5

Fodor'sChoice
★

Santa Croce. As a burial place, this Gothic church with a 19th-century facade probably contains more skeletons of Renaissance celebrities than any other in Italy. Besides Michelangelo, famous tombs include that of Galileo Galilei; Niccolò Machiavelli; Lorenzo Ghiberti, creator of the Baptistery doors; and composer Gioacchino Rossini. The collection of art within is by far the most important of any church in Florence. The most famous works are probably the Giotto frescoes in the two chapels immediately to the right of the high altar. They illustrate scenes from the lives of St. John the Evangelist and St. John the Baptist (in the right-hand chapel) and scenes from the life of St. Francis (in the left-hand chapel). Among the church's other highlights are Donatello's *Annunciation*; 14th-century frescoes by Taddeo Gaddi (circa 1300–66) illustrating scenes from the life of the Virgin Mary; and Donatello's *Crucifix*, criticized by Brunelleschi for making Christ look like a peasant. ⊠ *Piazza Santa Croce 16* ☎ *055/2466105* ⊕ *www.santacroceopera. it* ⊠ *Church and museum €8.*

Sinagoga. Jews were well settled in Florence by the end of the 14th century, but by 1570 they were required to live within the large "ghetto," at the north side of today's Piazza della Repubblica, by decree of Cosimo I, who had cut a deal with Pope Pius V (1504–72): in exchange for ghettoizing the Jews, he would receive the title Grand Duke of Tuscany.

Construction of the modern Moorish-style synagogue began in 1874 as a bequest of David Levi, who wished to endow a synagogue "worthy of the city." Falcini, Micheli, and Treves designed the building on a domed Greek cross plan with galleries in the transept and a roofline bearing three distinctive copper cupolas visible from all over Florence. The exterior has alternating bands of tan travertine and pink granite, reflecting an Islamic style repeated in Giovanni Panti's ornate interior. Of particular interest are the cast-iron gates by Pasquale Franci, the eternal light by Francesco Morini, and the Murano glass mosaics by

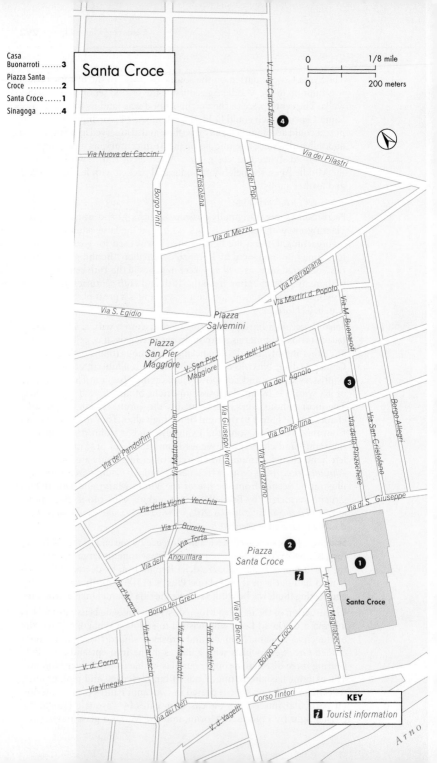

Santa Croce

0   1/8 mile

0   200 meters

4

Via Nuova dei Caccini

Via dei Pilastri

Via Fiesolana

Via dei Pepi

Borgo Pinti

V. Luigi Carlo Farini

Via di Mezzo

Via Pietrapiana

Via Martiri d. Popoto

Via S. Egidio

Piazza
Salvemini

Via M. Buonarrofi

Piazza
San Pier
Maggiore

Via dell' Ulivo

V. San Pier
Maggiore

Via dell' Agnolo

3

Via de' Pandolfini

Via Matteo Palmieri

Via Giuseppi Verdi

Via Ghibellina

Via delle Pinzochere

Via San Cristofano

Borgo Allegri

Via dei Pandolfini

Via Verrazzano

Via di S. Giuseppe

Via della Vigna Vecchia

Via d. Buretta

Via Torta

Piazza
Santa Croce

2

Via dell' Anguillara

Via d'Acqua

Borgo dei Greci

Via de' Benci

Borgo S. Croce

V. Antonio Magliabechi

1

Santa Croce

V. d. Corno

Via d. Parlascio

Via d. Magalotti

Via d. Rustici

Via dei Neri

Corso Tintori

Via Vinegia

V. d. Vagelli

Arno

Giacomo dal Medico. The gilded doors of the Moorish ark, which fronts the pulpit and is flanked by extravagant candelabra, are decorated with symbols of the ancient Temple of Jerusalem and bear bayonet marks from vandals. The synagogue was used as a garage by the Nazis, who failed to inflict much damage in spite of an attempt to blow up the place with dynamite. Only the columns on the left side were destroyed, and even then, the Women's Balcony above did not collapse. Note the Star of David in black and yellow marble inlay on the floor. The original capitals can be seen in the garden.

Some of the oldest and most beautiful Jewish ritual artifacts in all of Europe are displayed upstairs in the small **Museo Ebraico.** Exhibits document the Florentine Jewish community and the building of the synagogue. The donated objects all belonged to local families and date from as early as the late 16th century. Take special note of the exquisite needlework and silver pieces. A small but well-stocked gift shop is downstairs. ⊠ *Via Farini 4, Santa Croce* ☎ *055/2346654* ⊕ *www. coopculture.it* ✉ *Synagogue and museum €6.50.*

WORTH NOTING

Casa Buonarroti. If you really enjoy walking in the footsteps of the great genius, you may want to complete the picture by visiting the Buonarroti family home. Michelangelo lived here from 1516 to 1525, and later gave it to his nephew, whose son, called Michelangelo il Giovane (Michelangelo the Younger) turned it into a gallery dedicated to his great-uncle. The artist's descendants filled it with art treasures, some by Michelangelo himself. Two early marble works—the *Madonna of the Steps* and the *Battle of the Centaurs*—show the boy genius at work. ⊠ *Via Ghibellina 70, Santa Croce* ☎ *055/241752* ⊕ *www.casabuonarroti.it* ✉ *€6.50.*

THE OLTRARNO

A walk through the Oltrarno (literally "the other side of the Arno") takes in two very different aspects of Florence: the splendor of the Medici, manifest in the riches of the mammoth Palazzo Pitti and the gracious Giardino di Boboli; and the charm of the Oltrarno, a slightly gentrified but still fiercely proud working-class neighborhood with artisans' and antiques shops.

Farther east across the Arno, a series of ramps and stairs climb to Piazzale Michelangelo, where the city lies before you in all its glory (skip this trip if it's a hazy day). More stairs (behind La Loggia restaurant) lead to the church of San Miniato al Monte. You can avoid the long walk by taking Bus No. 12 or 13 at the west end of Ponte alle Grazie and getting off at Piazzale Michelangelo; you still have to climb the monumental stairs to and from San Miniato, but you can then take the bus from Piazzale Michelangelo back to the center of town. If you decide to take a bus, remember to buy your ticket before you board.

TOP ATTRACTIONS

Fodor's Choice ★ **Giardino Bardini.** Garden lovers, those who crave a view, and those who enjoy a nice hike should visit this lovely villa and garden, whose history spans centuries. The villa had a walled garden as early as the 14th century; the "Grand Stairs"—a zigzag ascent well worth scaling—have been around since the 16th. The garden is filled with irises, roses, and heirloom flowers, and includes a Japanese garden and statuary. A very pretty walk (all for the same admission ticket) takes you through the Giardino di Boboli and past the Forte Belvedere to the upper entrance to the giardino. ⊠ *Via de'Bardini, San Niccolò* ☎ *055/294883* ⌑ *€10 combined ticket, includes Galleria del Costume, Giardino di Boboli, Museo degli Argenti, Museo delle Porcellane.*

Giardino di Boboli (*Boboli Gardens*). The main entrance to these landscaped gardens is from the right side of the courtyard of **Palazzo Pitti.** The gardens began to take shape in 1549, when the Pitti family sold the palazzo to Eleanor of Toledo, wife of the Medici grand duke Cosimo I. Niccolò Tribolo (1500–50) laid out the first landscaping plans, and after his death, Ammannati, Giambologna, Bernardo Buontalenti (circa 1536–1608), and Giulio (1571–1635) and Alfonso Parigi (1606–56), among others, continued his work. Italian landscaping is less formal than French, but still full of sweeping drama. A copy of the famous *Morgante,* Cosimo I's favorite dwarf astride a particularly unhappy tortoise, is near the exit. Sculpted by Valerio Cioli (circa 1529–99), the work seems to illustrate the perils of culinary overindulgence. A visit here can be disappointing, because the gardens are somewhat underplanted and undercared for, but it's still a great walk with some terrific views. ⊠ *Enter through Palazzo Pitti* ☎ *055/294883* ⊕ *www.polomuseale.firenze.it* ⌑ *€10 combined ticket, includes Museo degli Argenti, Museo delle Porcellane, Villa Bardini, and Giardino Bardini.*

Palazzo Pitti. This enormous palace is one of Florence's largest architectural set pieces. The original palazzo, built for the Pitti family around 1460, comprised only the main entrance and the three windows on either side. In 1549 the property was sold to the Medici, and Bartolomeo Ammannati was called in to make substantial additions. Today the palace houses several museums. The **Museo degli Argenti** displays a vast collection of Medici treasures, including exquisite antique vases belonging to Lorenzo the Magnificent. The **Galleria del Costume** showcases fashions from the past 300 years. The **Galleria d'Arte Moderna** holds a collection of 19th- and 20th-century paintings, mostly Tuscan. Most famous of the Pitti galleries is the **Galleria Palatina,** which contains a broad collection of paintings from the 15th to 17th centuries. Though some consider the floor-to-ceiling paintings completely over-the-top, the collection possesses high points, including a number of portraits by Titian and an unparalleled collection of paintings by Raphael. ⊠ *Piazza Pitti* ☎ *055/210323* ⊕ *www.polomuseale.firenze.it* ⌑ *€13 combined ticket, includes Galleria Palatina and Galleria d'Arte Moderna; €13 combined ticket, includes Galleria del Costume, Giardino Bardini, Giardino di Boboli, Museo degli Argenti, and Museo Porcellane.*

The Oltrarno

0 | 1/4 mile
0 | 400 meters

Giardino Bardini **6**
Giardino di Boboli **5**
Museo Bardini **7**
Palazzo Pitti **4**
Piazzale
Michelangelo **8**

San Miniato al Monte **9**
Santa Felicita **3**
Santa Maria del Carmine ...**1**
Santo Spirito **2**

FAMILY **Piazzale Michelangelo.** From this lookout you have a marvelous view of Florence and the hills around it, rivaling the vista from the Forte di Belvedere. A copy of Michelangelo's *David* overlooks outdoor cafés packed with tourists during the day and with Florentines in the evening. In May the **Giardino dell'Iris** (Iris Garden) off the piazza is abloom with more than 2,500 varieties of the flower. The **Giardino delle Rose** (Rose Garden) on the terraces below the piazza is also in full bloom in May and June. ⊠ *Florence.*

San Miniato al Monte. This church, like the Baptistery, is a fine example of Romanesque architecture and is one of the oldest churches in Florence, dating from the 11th century. A 12th-century mosaic topped by a gilt bronze eagle, emblem of San Miniato's sponsors, the Calimala (cloth merchants' guild) crowns the lovely green-and-white marble facade. Inside are a 13th-century inlaid-marble floor and apse mosaic. Artist Spinello Aretino (1350–1410) covered the walls of the **Sagrestia** with frescoes depicting scenes from the life of St. Benedict. The **Cappella del Cardinale del Portogallo** (Chapel of the Portuguese Cardinal) is one of the richest 15th-century Renaissance works in Florence. It contains the tomb of a young Portuguese cardinal, Prince James of Lusitania, who died in Florence in 1459. Its glorious ceiling is by Luca della Robbia, and the sculpted tomb by Antonio Rossellino (1427–79). Every day at 6:30 pm, the monks fill the church with the sounds of Gregorian chanting. ⊠ *Viale Galileo Galilei, Piazzale Michelangelo, Oltrarno* ☎ *055/2342731* ⊕ *www.sanminiatoalmonte.it.*

Santa Maria del Carmine. The **Cappella Brancacci,** at the end of the right transept of this church, houses a masterpiece of Renaissance painting: a fresco cycle that changed the course of Western art. The cycle is the work of three artists: Masaccio and Masolino (1383–circa 1447), who began it around 1424, and Filippino Lippi, who finished it some 50 years later. It was Masaccio's work that opened a new frontier for painting, as he was among the first artists to employ single-point perspective. His style predominates in the *Tribute Money,* on the upper-left wall; *St. Peter Baptizing,* on the upper altar wall; the *Distribution of Goods,* on the lower altar wall; and the *Expulsion of Adam and Eve,* on the chapel's upper-left entrance pier. The figures of Adam and Eve possess a startling presence primarily thanks to the dramatic way in which their bodies seem to reflect light. In the faces of Adam and Eve, you see terrible shame and suffering depicted with a humanity rarely achieved in art. Reservations to see the chapel are mandatory; your time inside is limited to 15 minutes. ⊠ *Piazza del Carmine, Santo Spirito* ☎ *055/2768224 reservations* ⊕ *www.museocivicifiorentini.comune.fi.it* ⌑ €6.

Santo Spirito. The interior of this church is one of a pair designed in Florence by Filippo Brunelleschi in the early decades of the 15th century (the other is San Lorenzo). It was here that Brunelleschi supplied definitive solutions to the two major problems of interior Renaissance church design: how to build a cross-shape interior using classical architectural elements borrowed from antiquity, and how to reflect in that interior the order and regularity that Renaissance scientists were at the time discovering in the natural world around them.

Continued on page 305

WHO'S WHO IN RENAISSANCE ART

Michelangelo. Leonardo da Vinci. Raphael. This heady triumvirate of the Italian Renaissance is synonymous with artistic genius. Yet they are only three of the remarkable cast of characters whose work defines the Renaissance, that extraordinary flourishing of art and culture in Italy, especially in Florence, as the Middle Ages drew to a close. The artists were visionaries, who redefined painting, sculpture, architecture, and even what it means to be an artist.

THE PIONEER. In the mid-14th century, a few artists began to move away the flat, two-dimensional painting of the Middle Ages. **Giotto**, who painted seemingly three-dimensional figures who show emotion, had a major impact on the artists of the next century.

THE GROUNDBREAKERS. The generations of **Brunelleschi** and **Botticelli** took center stage in the 15th century. **Ghiberti, Masaccio, Donatello, Uccello, Fra Angelico**, and **Filippo Lippi** were other major players. Part of the Renaissance (or "re-birth") was a renewed interest in classical sources—the texts, monuments, and sculpture of Ancient Greece and Rome. Perspective and the illusion of three-dimensional space in painting was another discovery of this era, known as the Early Renaissance. Suddenly the art appearing on the walls looked real, or more realistic than it used to.

Roman ruins were not the only thing to inspire these artists. There was an incredible exchange of ideas going on. In Santa Maria del Carmine, Filippo Lippi was inspired by the work of Masaccio, who in turn was a friend of Brunelleschi. Young artists also learned from the masters via the apprentice system. Ghiberti's workshop (*bottega* in Italian) included, at one time or another, Donatello, Masaccio, and Uccello. Botticelli was apprenticed to Filippo Lippi.

THE BIG THREE. The mathematical rationality and precision of 15th-century art gave way to what is known as the High Renaissance. **Leonardo, Michelangelo**, and **Raphael** were much more concerned with portraying the body in all its glory and with achieving harmony and grandeur in their work. Oil paint, used infrequently up until this time, became more widely employed: as a result, Leonardo's colors are deeper, more sensual, more alive. For one brief period, all three were in Florence at the same time. Michelangelo and Leonardo surely knew one another, as they were simultaneously working on frescoes (never completed) inside Palazzo Vecchio.

When Michelangelo left Florence for Rome in 1508, he began the slow drain of artistic exodus from Florence, which never really recovered her previous glory.

A RENAISSANCE TIMELINE

IN THE WORLD

Black Death in Europe kills one third of the population, 1347-50.

Joan of Arc burned at the stake, 1431.

IN FLORENCE

Dante, a native of Florence, writes *The Divine Comedy*, 1302-21.

Founding of the Medici bank, 1397.

Medici family made official papal bankers.

1434, Cosimo il Vecchio becomes de facto ruler of Florence. The Medici family will dominate the city until 1494.

1300   1400

IN ART   EARLY RENAISSANCE

GIOTTO (ca. 1267-1337)

Masaccio and Masolino fresco Santa Maria del Carmine, 1424-28.

Giotto fresoes in Santa Croce, 1320-25.

BRUNELLESCHI (1377-1446)

LORENZO GHIBERTI (ca. 1381-1455)

DONATELLO (ca. 1386-1466)

PAOLO UCCELLO (1397-1475)

FRA ANGELICO (ca. 1400-1455)

MASACCIO (1401-1428)

FILIPPO LIPPI (ca. 1406-1469)

1334, 67-year-old Giotto is appointed chief architect of Santa Maria del Fiore, Florence's Duomo (below). He begins to work on the Campanile, which will be completed in 1359, after his death.

Donatello sculpts his bronze *David*, ca. 1440.

Fra Angelico frescoes friars' cells in San Marco, ca. 1438-45.

Uccello's *Sir John Hawkwood*, ca. 1436.

Ghiberti wins the competition for the Baptistery doors (above) in Florence, 1401.

Brunelleschi wins the competition for the Duomo's cupola (right), 1418.

Gutenberg Bible
is printed, 1455.

Columbus discovers
America, 1492.

Martin Luther posts his 95 theses on
the door at Wittenberg, kicking off the
Protestant Reformation, 1517.

Constantinople falls
to the Turks, 1453.

Machiavelli's *Prince*
appears, 1513.

Copernicus proves that
the earth is not the center
of the universe, 1530-43.

Lorenzo "il Magnifico"
(right), the Medici
patron of the arts, rules
in Florence, 1449-92.

Two Medici popes Leo X
(1513-21) and Clement
VII (1523-34) in Rome.

Catherine de'Medici
becomes Queen of
France, 1547.

1450   **1500**   **1550**

HIGH RENAISSANCE   MANNERISM

5

Fra Filippo Lippi's
*Madonna and
Child*, ca. 1452.

1508, Raphael begins
work on the chambers
in the Vatican, Rome.

Giorgio Vasari
publishes his first
edition of *Lives
of the Artists*,
1550.

1504, Michelangelo's
David is put on
display in Piazza
della Signoria,
where it remains
until 1873.

Michelangelo
begins to fresco
the Sistine Chapel
ceiling, 1508.

Botticelli paints the
Birth of Venus, ca.
1482.

BOTTICELLI (ca. 1444-1510)

LEONARDO DA VINCI (1452-1519)

RAPHAEL (1483-1520)

MICHELANGELO (1475-1564)

Leonardo paints *The Last Supper* in Milan,
1495-98.

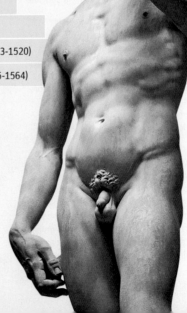

Giotto's *Nativity*

Donatello's *St. John the Baptist*

Ghiberti's *Gates of Paradise*

GIOTTO (CA. 1267-1337)
Painter/architect from a small town north of Florence.
He unequivocally set Italian painting on the course that led to the triumphs of the Renaissance masters. Unlike the rather flat, two-dimensional forms found in then prevailing Byzantine art, Giotto's figures have a fresh, life-like quality. The people in his paintings have bulk, and they show emotion, which you can see on their faces and in their gestures. This was something new in the late Middle Ages. Without Giotto, there wouldn't have been a Raphael.
In Florence: **Santa Croce; Uffizi; Campanile; Santa Maria Novella**
Elsewhere in Italy: **Scrovegni Chapel, Padua; Vatican Museums, Rome**

FILIPPO BRUNELLESCHI (1377-1446)
Architect/engineer from Florence.
If Brunelleschi had beaten Ghiberti in the Baptistery doors competition in Florence, the city's Duomo most likely would not have the striking appearance and authority that it has today. After his loss, he sulked off to Rome, where he studied the ancient Roman structures first-hand. Brunelleschi figured out how to vault the Duomo's dome, a structure unprecedented in its colossal size and great height. His Ospedale degli Innocenti employs classical elements in the creation of a stunning, new architectural statement; it is the first truly Renaissance structure.
In Florence: **Duomo; Ospedale degli Innocenti; San Lorenzo; Santo Spirito; Baptistery Doors Competition Entry, Bargello; Santa Croce**

LORENZO GHIBERTI (CA. 1381-1455)
Sculptor from Florence.
Ghiberti won a competition—besting his chief rival, Brunelleschi—to cast the gilded bronze North Doors of the Baptistery in Florence. These doors, and the East Doors that he subsequently executed, took up the next 50 years of his life. He created intricately worked figures that are more true-to-life than any since antiquity, and he was one of the first Renaissance sculptors to work in bronze. Ghiberti taught the next generation of artists; Donatello, Uccello, and Masaccio all passed through his studio.
In Florence: **Door Copies, Baptistery; Original Doors, Museo dell'Opera del Duomo; Baptistry Door Competition Entry, Bargello; Orsanmichele**

DONATELLO (CA. 1386-1466)
Sculptor from Florence.
Donatello was an innovator who, like his good friend Brunelleschi, spent most of his long life in Florence. Consumed with the science of optics, he used light and shadow to create the effects of nearness and distance. He made an essentially flat slab look like a three- dimensional scene. His bronze is probably the first free-standing male nude since antiquity. Not only technically brilliant, his work is also emotionally resonant; few sculptors are as expressive.
In Florence: *David*, **Bargello;** *St. Mark*, **Orsanmichele; Palazzo Vecchio; Museo dell'Opera del Duomo; San Lorenzo; Santa Croce**
Elsewhere in Italy: **Padua; Prato; Venice**

Fra Angelico's *The Deposition*   Masaccio's *Trinity*   Filippo Lippi's *Madonna and Child*

PAOLO UCCELLO (1397–1475)
Painter from Florence.

Renaissance chronicler Vasari once observed that had Uccello not been so obsessed with the mathematical problems posed by perspective, he would have been a very good painter. The struggle to master single-point perspective and to render motion in two dimensions is nowhere more apparent than in his battle scenes. His first major commission in Florence was the gargantuan fresco of the English mercenary Sir John Hawkwood (the Italians called him Giovanni Acuto) in Florence's Duomo.

In Florence: ***Sir John Hawkwood,*** Duomo; *Battle of San Romano,* Uffizi; Santa Maria Novella

Elsewhere in Italy: **Urbino, Prato**

FRA ANGELICO (CA. 1400–1455)
Painter from a small town north of Florence.

A Dominican friar, who eventually made his way to the convent of San Marco, Fra Angelico and his assistants painted frescoes for aid in prayer and meditation. He was known for his piety; Vasari wrote that Fra Angelico could never paint a crucifix without a tear running down his face. Perhaps no other painter so successfully translated the mysteries of faith and the sacred into painting. And yet his figures emote, his command of perspective is superb, and his use of color startles even today.

In Florence: **Museo di San Marco; Uffizi**

Elsewhere in Italy: **Vatican Museums, Rome; Fiesole; Cortona; Perugia; Orvieto**

MASACCIO (1401–1428)
Painter from San Giovanni Valdarno, southeast of Florence.

Masaccio and Masolino, a frequent collaborator, worked most famously together at Santa Maria del Carmine. Their frescoes of the life of St. Peter use light to mold figures in the painting by imitating the way light falls on figures in real life. Masaccio also pioneered the use of single-point perspective, masterfully rendered in his His friend Brunelleschi probably introduced him to the technique, yet another step forward in rendering things the way the eye sees them. Masaccio died young and under mysterious circumstances.

In Florence: **Santa Maria del Carmine;** *Trinity,* Santa Maria Novella

FILIPPO LIPPI (CA. 1406–1469)
Painter from Prato.

At a young age, Filippo Lippi entered the friary of Santa Maria del Carmine, where he was highly influenced by Masaccio and Masolino's frescoes. His religious vows appear to have made less of an impact; his affair with a young nun produced a son, Filippino (Little Philip, who later apprenticed with Botticelli), and a daughter. His religious paintings often have a playful, humorous note; some of his angels are downright impish and look directly out at the viewer. Lippi links the earlier painters of the 15th century with those who follow; Botticelli apprenticed with him.

In Florence: **Uffizi; Palazzo Medici Riccardi; San Lorenzo; Palazzo Pitti**

Elsewhere in Italy: **Prato**

Botticelli's *Primavera*

Leonardo's *Portrait of a Young Woman*

Raphael's *Madonna on the Meadow*

BOTTICELLI (CA. 1444-1510)
Painter from Florence.
Botticelli's work is characterized by stunning, elongated blondes, cherubic angels (something he undoubtedly learned from his time with Filippo Lippi), and tender Christs. Though he did many religious paintings, he also painted monumental, nonreligious panels—his *Birth of Venus* and *Primavera* being the two most famous of these. A brief sojourn took him to Rome, where he and a number of other artists frescoed the Sistine Chapel walls.
In Florence: **Birth of Venus, *Primavera*, Uffizi; Palazzo Pitti**
Elsewhere in Italy: **Vatican Museums, Rome**

LEONARDO DA VINCI (1452-1519)
Painter/sculptor/engineer from Anchiano, a small town outside Vinci.
Leonardo never lingered long in any place; his restless nature and his international reputation led to commissions throughout Italy, and took him to Milan, Vigevano, Pavia, Rome, and, ultimately, France. Though he is most famous for his mysterious *Mona Lisa* (at the Louvre in Paris), he painted other penetrating, psychological portraits in addition to his scientific experiments: his design for a flying machine (never built) predates Kitty Hawk by nearly 500 years. The greatest collection of Leonardo's work in Italy can be seen on one wall in the Uffizi.
In Florence: ***Adoration of the Magi*, Uffizi**
Elsewhere in Italy: ***Last Supper*, Santa Maria delle Grazie, Milan**

RAPHAEL (1483-1520)
Painter/architect from Urbino.
Raphael spent only four highly productive years of his short life in Florence, where he turned out made-to-order panel paintings of the Madonna and Child for a hungry public; he also executed a number of portraits of Florentine aristocrats. Perhaps no other artist had such a fine command of line and color, and could render it, seemingly effortlessly, in paint. His painting acquired new authority after he came up against Michelangelo toiling away on the Sistine ceiling. Raphael worked nearly next door in the Vatican, where his figures take on an epic, Michelangelesque scale.
In Florence: **Uffizi; Palazzo Pitti**
Elsewhere in Italy: **Vatican Museums, Rome**

MICHELANGELO (1475-1564)
Painter/sculptor/architect from Caprese.
Although Florentine and proud of it (he famously signed his St. Peter's *Pietà* to avoid confusion about where he was from), he spent most of his 89 years outside his native city. He painted and sculpted the male body on an epic scale and glorified it while doing so. Though he complained throughout the proceedings that he was really a sculptor, Michelangelo's Sistine Chapel ceiling is arguably the greatest fresco cycle ever painted (and the massive figures owe no small debt to Giotto).
In Florence: ***David*, Galleria dell'Accademia; Uffizi; Casa Buonarroti; Bargello**
Elsewhere in Italy: **St. Peter's Basilica, Vatican Museums, and Piazza del Campidoglio in Rome**

Brunelleschi's solution to the first problem was brilliantly simple: turn a Greek temple inside out. His solution to the second problem—making the entire interior orderly and regular—was mathematically precise: he designed the ground plan of the church so that all its parts were proportionally related. He believed that mathematical regularity and aesthetic beauty were flip sides of the same coin, that one was not possible without the other. ⊠ *Piazza Santo Spirito* ☎ *055/2382383* ⊕ *www.basilicasantospirito.it* 🎫 *Church free.*

WORTH NOTING

Museo Bardini. The 19th-century collector and antiquarian Stefano Bardini turned his palace into his own private museum. Upon his death, the collection was turned over to the state and includes an interesting assortment of Etruscan pieces, sculpture, paintings, and furniture that dates mostly from the Renaissance and the Baroque. ⊠ *Piazza de' Mozzi 1* ☎ *055/2342427* ⊕ *museicivicifiorentini. comune.fi.it* 🎫 *€6.*

Santa Felicita. This late Baroque church (its facade was remodeled between 1736 and 1739) contains the mannerist Jacopo Pontormo's *Deposition,* the centerpiece of the Cappella Capponi (executed 1525–28) and a masterpiece of 16th-century Florentine art. The remote figures, which transcend the realm of Renaissance classical form, are portrayed in tangled shapes and intense pastel colors (well preserved because of the low lights in the church), in a space and depth that defy reality. Note, too, the exquisitely frescoed *Annunciation,* also by Pontormo, at a right angle to the *Deposition.* The granite column in the piazza was erected in 1381 and marks a Christian cemetery. ⊠ *Piazza Santa Felicita, Via Guicciardini, Palazzo Pitti.*

WHERE TO EAT

Florence's popularity with tourists means that, unfortunately, there's a higher percentage of mediocre restaurants here than you'll find in most Italian towns (Venice, perhaps, might win that prize). Some restaurant owners cut corners and let standards slip, knowing that a customer today is unlikely to return tomorrow, regardless of the quality of the meal. So, if you're looking to eat well, it pays to do some research, starting with the recommendations here. Dining hours start at around 1 for lunch and 8 for dinner. Many of Florence's restaurants are small, so reservations are a must. You can sample such specialties as creamy *fegatini* (a chicken-liver spread) and *ribollita* (minestrone thickened with bread and beans and swirled with extra-virgin olive oil) in a bustling, convivial trattoria, where you share long wooden tables set with paper place mats, or in an upscale *ristorante* with linen tablecloths and napkins.

WHAT IT COSTS				
	$	$$	$$$	$$$$
At dinner	under €15	€15–€24	€25–€35	over €35

Restaurant prices are the average cost of a main course at dinner or, if dinner is not served, at lunch.

Use the coordinate (✢ B2) at the end of each listing to locate a site on the Where to Eat and Stay in Florence map.

AROUND THE DUOMO

$$ ITALIAN 🍴 **Coquinarius.** This rustically elegant space, which has served many purposes over the past 600 years, offers some of the tastiest food in town at great prices. It's the perfect place to come if you aren't sure what you're hungry for, as they offer a little bit of everything: salad-lovers will have a hard time choosing from among the lengthy list (the Scozzese, with poached chicken, avocado, and bacon, is a winner); those with a yen for pasta will face agonizing choices (the ravioli with pecorino and pears is particularly good). A revolving list of *piatti unici* (single dishes that can be ordered on their own, usually served only at lunch) can also whet the whistle, as well as terrific cheese and cured meat plates. The well-culled wine list has lots of great wines by the glass, and even more by the bottle. [$] *Average main: €15* ✉ *Via delle Oche 15/r, Duomo* ☎ *055/2302153* 🌐 *www.coquinarius.it* ✢ *E3.*

$ ITALIAN 🍴 **Gelateria Edoardo.** It's the latest, hottest gelateria on the block in part because the *gelati* is certified organic, and because it's right next to the Duomo. Their daring *sorbetto al Chianti Colli Fiorentini* (Chianti ice cream) is new, original, tasty, and contains 4% alcohol. [$] *Average main: €2* ✉ *Piazza del Duomo 45/r, Duomo* ☎ *055/281055* 🌐 *www.edoardobio.it* ✢ *F3.*

$ ITALIAN 🍴 **Grom.** Although the original Grom hails from Turin (and there's a Grom in New York City), this is still probably the best gelato in town. Flavors change frequently according to the season, so expect a fragrant gelato *di cannella* (cinnamon) in winter and lively fresh fruit flavors in summer. [$] *Average main: €3* ✉ *Via del Campanile, Duomo* ☎ *055/216158* 🌐 *www.grom.it* 💳 *No credit cards* ✢ *E3.*

$ ITALIAN 🍴 **'ino.** Serving arguably the best panini in town, proprietor Alessandro sources only the very best ingredients. Located right behind the Uffizi, 'ino is a perfect place to grab a tasty sandwich and glass of wine before forging on to the next museum. [$] *Average main: €8* ✉ *Via dei Georgofili 3/r–7/r, Piazza della Signoria* ☎ *055/219208* 🌐 *www.inofirenze.com* ✢ *E4.*

$$ ITALIAN 🍴 **Pegna.** Looking for some cheddar cheese to pile in your panino? Pegna has been selling both Italian and non-Italian food since 1860. It's closed Saturday afternoon in July and August, Wednesday afternoon September through June, and Sunday year-round. [$] *Average main: €24* ✉ *Via dello Studio 8, Duomo* ☎ *055/282701* 🌐 *www.pegnafirenze.com* ✢ *F3.*

$$ ITALIAN Fodor's Choice ★

🍴 **Rivoire.** One of the best spots in Florence for people-watching offers stellar service, light snacks, and terrific aperitivi. It's been around since the 1860s, and has been famous for its hot and cold chocolate (with or without cream) for more than a century. Though the food is mostly good (it's not a bad place for a light, but expensive, lunch), it's best to stick to drinks (both alcoholic and non-) and their terrific cakes, pies, and pastries. [$] *Average main: €15* ✉ *Via Vacchereccia 4/r, Piazza della Signoria* ☎ *055/214412* 🌐 *www.rivoire.it* ⊕ *E4.*

SAN LORENZO

$ INTERNATIONAL Fodor's Choice ★

🍴 **Baroni.** The cheese collection at Baroni may be the most comprehensive in Florence. They also have high-quality truffle products, vinegars, and other delicacies. [$] *Average main: €10* ✉ *Mercato Central, enter at Via Signa, San Lorenzo* ☎ *055/289576* 🌐 *www.baronialimentari.it* ⊕ *D1.*

$ TUSCAN Fodor's Choice ★

🍴 **da Nerbone.** This *tavola calda* in the middle of the covered Mercato Centrale has been serving up food to Florentines who like their tripe since 1872. Tasty primi and secondi are available every day, but cognoscenti come for the *panino con il lampredotto* (tripe sandwich). Less adventurous sorts might want to sample the *bollito* (boiled beef sandwich). Ask that the bread be *bagnato* (briefly dipped in the tripe cooking liquid), and have both the salsa verde and *salsa piccante* (a spicy cayenne sauce) slathered on top. And go early, as they inevitably sell out of them. [$] *Average main: €13* ✉ *Mercato San Lorenzo* ☎ *055/219949* 💳 *No credit cards* 🕒 *Closed Sun. No dinner* ⊕ *D1.*

$ TUSCAN Fodor's Choice ★

🍴 **da Sergio.** In 2015, this little eatery celebrated its centenary, and with good reason. It's been in the capable hands of the Gozzi family, who have ensured continuity and stuck to Tuscan tradition. The food's terrific, eminently affordable, and just across the way from the basilica of San Lorenzo, which means that you can imbibe well-prepared food while marveling at the Brunelleschi and Michelangelo you've just seen. The menu is short, and changes daily. Their *lombatina alla griglia* (a grilled veal T-bone steak) is almost always on, and meat eaters should not miss it. Pastas are equally terrific. Dessert, in true Florentine fashion is usually limited to biscotti with vin santo. [$] *Average main: €9* ✉ *Piazza San Lorenzo 8/r, San Lorenzo* 🕒 *Closed Sun.* ⊕ *E2.*

$ ITALIAN

🍴 **Gelateria Carabe.** Specializing in things Sicilian, this shop is known for its tart and flavorful *granità* (granular flavored ices), made only in the summer, which are great thirst-quenchers. [$] *Average main: €3* ✉ *Via Ricasoli 60/r, San Marco* ☎ *055/289476* 🌐 *www.parcocarabe.it* 💳 *No credit cards* ⊕ *F1.*

$ TUSCAN

🍴 **il Desco.** This tiny boîte, with a mere handful of tables, is an oasis in an area that is pretty much a culinary wasteland. It's owned by the Bargiacchi family, who are proprietors of the lovely hotel Guelfo Bianco just next door. Their organic farm in the Tuscan countryside provides much of what is on the frequently changing menu. The menu plays to all tastes—Tuscan classics such as *peposo* (a hearty, black pepper–filled beef stew) can be found, as well as vegetarian dishes. Even vegans have options: the seitan in *salsa fredda di ceci ai capperi e rosmarino* (seitan in a room-temperature pureed chickpea sauce flavored with capers and rosemary) is a winner. The wine list is well thought out, and artisanal beer is also on the menu. $ *Average main: €13* ⊠ *Via Cavour 55/r, San Lorenzo* ☎ *055/288330* ⊕ *www.ildescofirenze.it* ✚ *F1.*

$ ✕ **Mario.** Florentines flock to this narrow family-run trattoria near San
TUSCAN Lorenzo to feast on Tuscan favorites served at simple tables under a
Fodor's Choice wooden ceiling dating from 1536. A distinct cafeteria feel and genuine
★ Florentine hospitality prevail: you'll be seated wherever there's room, which often means with strangers. Yes, there's a bit of extra oil in most dishes, which imparts calories as well as taste, but aren't you on vacation in Italy? Worth the caloric splurge is *riso al ragù* (rice with ground beef and tomatoes). $ *Average main: €10* ⊠ *Via Rosina 2/r, corner of Piazza del Mercato Centrale, San Lorenzo* ☎ *055/218550* ⊕ *www. trattoria-mario.com* ⊗ *Closed Sun., and Aug. No dinner* ✚ *E1.*

$$ ✕ **Perini.** It's possible to break the bank here, as this might be the best
ITALIAN salumeria in Florence. Perini sells prosciutto, mixed meats, sauces for
Fodor's Choice pasta, and a wide assortment of antipasti, and is closed Sunday. $ *Av-*
★ *erage main: €20* ⊠ *Mercato Centrale, enter at Via dell'Aretino, San Lorenzo* ☎ *055/2398306* ⊕ *www.perinigastronomia.it* ✚ *E1.*

$$ ✕ **Taverna del Bronzino.** Want to have a sophisticated meal in a 16th-
TUSCAN century Renaissance artist's studio? The former studio of Santi di Tito,
Fodor's Choice a student of Bronzino's, has a simple, formal decor, with white table-
★ cloths and place settings. The classic, elegantly presented Tuscan food is superb, and the solid, affordable wine list rounds out the menu—especially because Stefano, the sommelier, really knows his stuff. Desserts shine at this place, so remember to save room, and conclude with a limoncello or mirtillo postprandial drink. Both are made in-house, and provide a perfect conclusion to the meal. Outstanding service makes a meal here heavenly. Reservations are advised, especially for eating at the wine cellar's only table. $ *Average main: €22* ⊠ *Via delle Ruote 25/r, San Marco* ☎ *055/495220* ⊕ *www.tavernadelbronzino.net* ⊗ *Closed Sun., and 3 wks in Aug.* ✚ *G1.*

SANTA MARIA NOVELLA

$$$ ✕ **Buca Lapi.** The Antinori family started selling wine from their palace's
TUSCAN basement in the 15th century. Six hundred years later, this *buca* (hole) is a lively, subterranean restaurant filled with Florentine aristocrats chowing down on what might be the best (and most expensive) bistecca fiorentina in town. The classical Tuscan menu has the usual suspects: *crostino di cavolo nero* (black cabbage on toasted garlic bread), along with ribollita and pappa al pomodoro, You might want to cut directly to the chase, however, and order the bistecca, an immense slab of Chianina beef impeccably grilled on the outside, just barely warmed on the inside. (If you're not into rare meat, order something else from the grill.) Roast potatoes and cannellini beans make perfect accompaniments. $ *Average main: €35* ⊠ *Via del Trebbio 1, Santa Maria Novella* ☎ *055/213768* ⊕ *www.bucalapi.com* ✚ *C3.*

$$$ ✕ **Cantinetta Antinori.** After a morning of shopping on Via Tornabuoni,
TUSCAN stop for lunch in this 15th-century palazzo in the company of Florentine ladies (and men) who come to see and be seen over lunch. The panache of the food matches its clientele: expect treats such as *tramezzino con*

pane di campagna al tartufo (country pâté with truffles served on bread) and the *insalata di gamberoni e gamberetti con carciofi freschi* (crayfish and prawn salad with shaved raw artichokes). $ *Average main: €25* ⊠ *Piazza Antinori 3, Santa Maria Novella* ☎ *055/292234* ⊕ *www. cantinetta-antinori.com* ⊘ *Closed weekends, 20 days in Aug., and Dec. 25–Jan. 6* ✛ *D3.*

$$
TUSCAN ✕ **Il Latini.** It may be the noisiest, most crowded trattoria in Florence, but it's also one of the most fun. The genial host, Torello ("little bull") Latini, presides over his four big dining rooms, and somehow it feels as if you're dining in his home. Ample portions of ribollita prepare the palate for the hearty meat dishes that follow. Both Florentines and tourists alike tuck into the *agnello fritto* (fried lamb) with aplomb. Their lombatina might be the best in town. Even with a reservation, there's always a wait. $ *Average main: €18* ⊠ *Via dei Palchetti 6/r, Santa Maria Novella* ☎ *055/210916* ⊕ *www.illatini.com* ⊘ *Closed Mon., and 15 days at Christmas* ✛ *C3.*

$ ✕ **Mangiafoco.** It's got brightly colored purple and orange walls, and a
TUSCAN warren of small rooms; it also has a large room along with a counter that sells terrific take-away options. Created by Francesco and Elisa in 2001, this little spot, nestled in the heart of the centro storico on a romantic medieval side street, serves Tuscan classics *con fantasia* (with fantasy) created by Luca, Elisa's brother. The menu changes daily, reflecting both what's in season and the whims of the chef. The wine list is long, as is the number of wines offered by the glass. You can tuck into a plate of *fettucine ragù toscana e carciofi* (flat noodes with a meat sauce and artichokes) or opt for any number of their *taglieri* (mixed meat and cheese plates). The last are served with various gelatins, made from such delicacies as Chianti, vin santo, and balsamic vinegar. They are justifiably proud of their desserts, made in-house. You can also just drop in for a glass of wine, perch on one of their steps, and watch the world go by. $ *Average main: €12* ⊠ *Borgo Santi Apostoli 26/r, Santa Maria Novella* ☎ *055/2658170* ⊕ *www. mangiafoco.com* ⊘ *Closed Sun.* ✛ *D4.*

$$
ITALIAN ✕ **Obicà.** Mozzarella takes center stage at this sleek eatery on Florence's swankiest street. The cheese, along with its culinary cousin *burrata* (a fresh cheese filled with cream), arrives daily from southern Italy to become the centerpiece for various salads and pastas. Four different kinds of *rotoli* (rolled, stuffed mozzarella) are available; the one with smoked salmon and arugula is particularly tasty. You can pair your cheese with a number of accompaniments, including *caponata* (a Sicilian eggplant mélange) and mortadella from nearby Prato. Efficient service (in a 16th-century palazzo courtyard when the weather's nice) and a well-priced wine list add to the pleasure of a meal here. Nightly happy hour, with an extensive selection of snacks, is fun and a bargain. $ *Average main: €16* ⊠ *Via Tornabuoni 16, Santa Maria Novella* ☎ *055/2773526* ⊕ *www.obica.com* ✛ *D3.*

$$
ITALIAN ✕ **Procacci.** At this classy Florentine institution dating to 1885, try one
Fodor's Choice of the panini tartufati and swish it down with a glass of prosecco. It's
★ closed Sunday. $ *Average main: €15* ⊠ *Via Tornabuoni 64/r, Santa Maria Novella* ☎ *055/211656* ⊕ *www.procacci1885.it* ⊘ *Closed Sun.* ✛ *D3.*

5

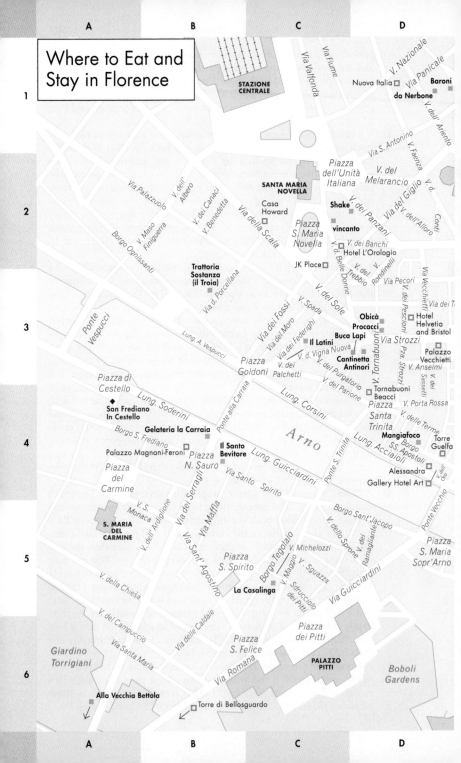

Where to Eat and Stay in Florence

A **B** **C** **D**

1

STAZIONE CENTRALE

Via Fiume

Via Valfonda

Nuova Italia □

Baroni

da Nerbone

V. Nazionale

Via Panicale

Via dell' Ariento

V. dei Faenza

Via S. Antonino

V. del Melarancio

Piazza dell'Unità Italiana

V. del Giglio

V. dell'Alloro

V. d.

Conti

2

Via Palazzuolo

V. dell' Albero

Via dei Canaci

v. Benedetta

Via della Scala

SANTA MARIA NOVELLA

Casa Howard

Piazza S. Maria Novella

Shake

V. dei Panzani

vincanto

V. dei Banchi

Hotel L'Orologio

V. d. Belle Donne

V. del Trebbio

V. dei Rondinelli

Via Pecori

Via Vecchietti

V. Maso Finiguerra

Borgo Ognissanti

Trattoria Sostanza (il Troia)

Via d. Porcellana

JK Place

V. del Sole

V. dei Fossi

V. Spada

V. del Moro

Via dei Federighi

Il Latini

V. d. Vigna Nuova

3

Ponte Vespucci

Lung. A. Vespucci

Piazza Goldoni

V. dei Palchetti

V. dei Purgatorio

V. del Parione

Obicà

Procacci

Buca Lapi

Cantinetta Antinori

V. dei Pesciori

V. Tornabuoni

Via Strozzi

Pza. Strozzi

Hotel Helvetia and Bristol

V. dei T.

Palazzo Vecchietti

V. Anselmi

V. dei Sassetti

4

Piazza di Cestello

Lung. Soderini

San Frediano In Cestello

Gelateria la Carraia

Borgo S. Frediano

Palazzo Magnani-Feroni

Piazza N. Sauro

Il Santo Bevitore

Ponte alla Carraia

Lung. Corsini

Arno

Lung. Guicciardini

Ponte S. Trinita

Lung. Acciaioli

Tornabuoni Beacci

Piazza Santa Trinita

V. Porta Rossa

V. delle Terme

Mangiafoco

Borgo SS. Apostoli

Torre Guelfa

Alessandra

Gallery Hotel Art

V. dei Or...

Ponte Vecchio

5

Piazza del Carmine

V. S. Monaca

V. dell' Ardiglione

Via Sant' Agostino

Via Serragli

Via Maffia

Via Santo Spirito

Piazza S. Spirito

Borgo Tegolaio

V. Michelozzi

V. Maggio

V. Squazza

V. Sdrucciolo dei Pitti

La Casalinga

Borgo Sant'Jacopo

V. dello Sprone

V. dei Ramaglianta

Borgo Sant'Jacopo

Borgo Guicciardini

Piazza S. Maria Sopr'Arno

6

Giardino Torrigiani

V. della Chiesa

V. del Campuccio

Via Santa Maria

Via delle Caldaie

Piazza S. Felice

Via Romana

Piazza dei Pitti

PALAZZO PITTI

Boboli Gardens

Alla Vecchia Bettola
↓

Torre di Bellosguardo □
↓

S. MARIA DEL CARMINE

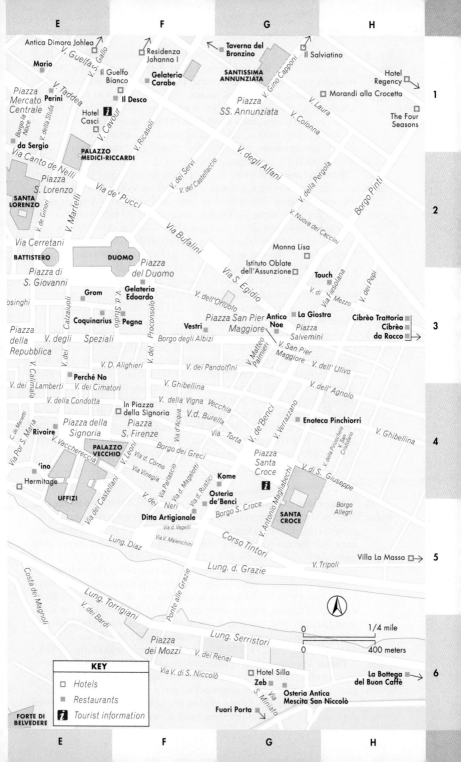

$ ITALIAN 🍴 **Shake.** If you're on your way to the train station, or arriving from the train station, this little juice bar at Piazza Santa Maria Novella provides a perfect place for a rest stop. They serve tasty croissants and panini all day, make wraps, salads, and sandwiches at lunch (all of which are available to go as they are handily packed). There's also ice cream and, of course, their juices. The "Shake" smoothie, comprised of avocado, apple, banana, and yogurt, provides a great way to start the day. [$] *Average main: €5* ✉ *Via degli Avelli 2/r, Santa Maria Novella* ☎ *055/295310* 🌐 *www.shakecafe.bio* ✥ *D2.*

$$ TUSCAN Fodor's Choice ★ 🍴 **Trattoria Sostanza (il Troia).** Since opening its doors in 1869, this trattoria has been serving top-notch, unpretentious food to Florentines who like their bistecca fiorentina very large and very rare. A single room with white tiles on the wall and paper mats on the tables provides the setting for delicious meals. Along with fine Tuscan classics, they have two signature dishes: the *tortino di carciofi* (artichoke tart) and the *pollo al burro* (chicken with butter). The latter is an amazing surprise, a succulent chicken breast cooked very quickly and served as soon as it leaves the grill. Leave room for dessert, as their *torta alla Meringa* (a semi-frozen dessert flecked with chocolate and topped with meringue) is scrumptious. [$] *Average main: €15* ✉ *Via della Porcellana 25, Santa Maria Novella* ☎ *055/212691* 💳 *No credit cards* ✥ *B3.*

$ ITALIAN 🍴 **vincanto.** It opens at 11 am, and closes at midnight: this is a rarity in Florentine dining. They do a little bit of everything here, including fine pastas (don't miss the ignudi), salads, and pizzas. You can come here for an American-style breakfast, or simply a cup of coffee, or a glass of wine. Because the kitchen stays open continuously, if you're hankering at 4 pm for a chicken burger with curried fried onions, or a pizza laden with Italian pork products, you're in luck. And all of this can be enjoyed with a splendid view of Piazza Santa Maria Novella. [$] *Average main: €12* ✉ *Piazza Santa Maria Novella 23/r, Santa Maria Novella* ☎ *055/2679300* 🌐 *www.ristorantevincanto.com* ✥ *C2.*

SANTA CROCE

$$ TUSCAN 🍴 **Antico Noe.** If Florence had diners (it doesn't), this would be the best diner in town. The short menu at the one-room eatery relies heavily on seasonal ingredients picked up daily at the market. Although the secondi are good, the antipasti and primi really shine. The menu comes alive particularly during truffle and artichoke season (don't miss the grilled artichokes if they're on the menu). Locals rave about the tagliatelle *ai porcini* (with mushrooms); the fried eggs liberally laced with truffle might be the greatest truffle bargain in town. Ask for the menu in Italian, as the English version is much more limited. The short wine list has some great bargains, and note that if you opt to order bistecca, you'll jump to a higher price category. [$] *Average main: €16* ✉ *Volta di San Piero 6/r, Santa Croce* ☎ *055/2340838* ⏲ *Closed Sun., and 2 wks in Aug.* ✥ *G3.*

$$$$ TUSCAN Fodor's Choice ★ 🍴 **Cibrèo.** The food at this upscale trattoria is fantastic, from the creamy crostini *di fegatini* (a savory chicken-liver spread) to the melt-in-your-mouth desserts. Many Florentines hail this as the city's best restaurant, and justifiably so. Chef-owner Fabio Picchi knows Tuscan food better than anyone, and although there's not a pasta dish to be seen on the

menu (he argues that Florence doesn't really have any native pasta dishes), his deep understanding of Tuscan food shines through. If you thought you'd never try tripe—let alone like it—this is the place to lay any doubts to rest: the *trippa in insalata* (cold tripe salad) with parsley and garlic is an epiphany. The food is impeccably served by a staff that's multilingual—which is a good thing, because there are no written menus. [$] *Average main: €40* ✉ *Via A. del Verrocchio 8/r, Santa Croce* ☎ *055/2341100* ⏲ *Closed Sun. and Mon., and July 25–Sept. 5* ✥ *H3.*

$$ TUSCAN 🍴 **Cibrèo Trattoria.** This intimate little trattoria, known to locals as Cibreino, shares its kitchen with the famed Florentine culinary institution from which it gets its name. They share the same menu, too, though Cibreino's is much shorter. Start with *il gelatina di pomodoro* (tomato gelatin) liberally laced with basil, garlic, and a pinch of hot pepper, and then sample the justifiably renowned *passato in zucca gialla* (pureed yellow-pepper soup) before moving on to any of the succulent secondi. Save room for dessert, as the pastry chef has a deft hand with chocolate tarts. To avoid sometimes agonizingly long waits, come early (7 pm) or late (after 9:30). [$] *Average main: €15* ✉ *Via dei Macci 118, Santa Croce* ☎ *055/2341100* 💳 *No credit cards* ⏲ *Closed Sun. and Mon., and July 25–Sept. 5* ✥ *H3.*

$ TUSCAN 🍴 **da Rocco.** At one of Florence's biggest markets you can grab lunch to go, or you could cram yourself into one of the booths and pour from the straw-cloaked flask (wine here is *da consumo,* which means they charge you for how much you drink). Food is abundant, Tuscan, and fast; locals pack in. The ample menu changes daily (nine secondi are the norm), and the prices are great. [$] *Average main: €7* ✉ *Mercato Sant'Ambrogio, Piazza Ghiberti, Santa Croce* 💳 *No credit cards* ⏲ *Closed Sun. No dinner* ✥ *H3.*

$ ITALIAN 🍴 **Ditta Artigianale.** Seattle has finally come to Florence, and coffee fans couldn't be happier. This place is always crowded with mostly young folk lingering over non-Italian cups of coffee. Light lunch and brunch are also on offer, and in between there's a steady supply of cakes, cookies, and croissants. Cocktail hour brings on the "Tapas" part of their menu. It opens at 8 in the morning, and stays open until at least 10 every night. [$] *Average main: €8* ✉ *Via de'Neri 32, Santa Croce* ☎ *055/274 1541* 🌐 *www.dittaartigianale.it* 💳 *No credit cards* ✥ *F5.*

$$$$ ITALIAN 🍴 **Enoteca Pinchiorri.** A sumptuous Renaissance palace with high frescoed ceilings and bouquets in silver vases provides the backdrop for this restaurant, one of the most expensive in Italy. Some consider it one of the best, and others consider it a non-Italian rip-off, as the kitchen is presided over by a Frenchwoman with sophisticated, yet internationalist, leanings. Prices are high (think $100 for a plate of spaghetti) and portions are small; the vast holdings of the wine cellar (undoubtedly the best in Florence), as well as stellar service, dull the pain, however, when the bill is presented. [$] *Average main: €100* ✉ *Via Ghibellina 87, Santa Croce* ☎ *055/242777* 🌐 *www.enotecapinchiorri.com* ⏲ *Closed Sun. and Mon., and Aug. No lunch* 👔 *Jacket required* ✥ *G4.*

$$ JAPANESE 🍴 **Kome.** If you're looking for a break from the ubiquitous ribollita, stop in at this eatery, which may be the only Japanese restaurant in the world to be housed in a 15th-century Renaissance palazzo. High, vaulted

arches frame the Kaiten sushi conveyor belt. It's Japanese food, cafeteria style: selections, priced according to the color of the plate, make their way around a bar, where diners pick whatever they find appealing. Those seeking a more substantial meal head to the second floor, where Japanese barbecue is prepared at your table. The minimalist basement provides a subtle but dramatic backdrop for a well-prepared cocktail. $ *Average main: €20* ⊠ *Via de' Benci 41/r, Santa Croce* ☎ *055/2008009* ⊕ *www.komefirenze.it* ✛ *G4.*

$$$ ✕ **La Giostra.** This clubby spot, whose name means "carousel" in Italian,
ITALIAN was created by the late Prince Dimitri Kunz d'Asburgo Lorena, and is
Fodor'sChoice now expertly run by Soldano and Dimitri, his handsome twin sons. In
★ perfect English they will describe favorite dishes, such as the *taglierini con tartufo bianco,* a decadently rich pasta with white truffles. The constantly changing menu has terrific vegetarian and vegan options, and any meal that does not include truffles is significantly less expensive than those that do. For dessert, this might be the only show in town with a sublime tiramisù *and* a wonderfully gooey Sacher torte. $ *Average main: €27* ⊠ *Borgo Pinti 12/r, Santa Croce* ☎ *055/241341* ⊕ *www.ristorantelagiostra.com* ☾ *No lunch weekends* ✛ *G3.*

$$ ✕ **Osteria de'Benci.** A few minutes from Santa Croce, this charming oste-
ITALIAN ria serves some of the most eclectic food in Florence. Try the spaghetti
Fodor'sChoice *degli eretici* (in tomato sauce with fresh herbs). The grilled meats are jus-
★ tifiably famous; the *carbonata* is a succulent piece of grilled beef served rare. Weekly specials complement what's happening in the market, and all of the food pairs beautifully with their wine list, which is heavy on things Tuscan. When it's warm, you can dine outside with a view of the 13th-century tower belonging to the prestigious Alberti family. $ *Average main: €15* ⊠ *Via de' Benci 11–13/r, Santa Croce* ☎ *055/2344923* ⊕ *www.osteriadeibenci.it* ☾ *Closed 2 wks in Aug.* ✛ *F5.*

$ ✕ **Perché No.** They've been making ice cream at this much-loved-by-
CAFÉ Florentines place since 1939. Such continuity might be the reason why
Fodor'sChoice this might be the best gelateria in the historic center. $ *Average main:*
★ *€3* ⊠ *Santa Croce* ☎ *055/239–8969* ⊕ *www.percheno.firenze.it* ▭ *No credit cards* ✛ *E3.*

$$ ✕ **Touch.** It's called "Touch" because it's the first restaurant in Florence
MODERN ITALIAN with the menu written on an iPad. Stefano, Matteo, and Max, whose combined ages hover at well less than 100, met at hotel school a few years ago. Their imaginative food plays with the classics in a marvelous way. Fortunately, they've done their homework. Redone is the classic bollito: the meats are combined, encased with a raviolo covering, and graced with an egg sauce. Then there's the Tuscan club sandwich featuring not turkey, but fegatini. Any fears of eating raw egg in the classic Roman carbonara may be assuaged by watching the egg cook, briefly, tableside. Desserts are as creative as what comes before. $ *Average main: €20* ⊠ *Via Fiesolana 18/r, Santa Croce* ☎ *055/2466150* ⊕ *www.touchflorence.com* ☾ *No lunch* ✛ *H3.*

$ ✕ **Vestri.** This shop is devoted to chocolate in all its guises. The small
ITALIAN but sublime selection of chocolate-based gelati includes one with hot peppers. $ *Average main: €3* ⊠ *Borgo Albizi 11/r, Santa Croce* ☎ *055/2340374* ⊕ *www.vestri.it* ▭ *No credit cards* ✛ *F3.*

THE OLTRARNO

$$ ✕**Alla Vecchia Bettola.** The name doesn't exactly mean "old dive," but
TUSCAN it comes pretty close. This lively trattoria has been around only since
1979, but it feels as if it's been a whole lot longer. Tile floors and simple
wood tables and chairs provide the interior decoration, such as it is. The
recipes come from "wise grandmothers" and celebrate Tuscan food in
its glorious simplicity. Here prosciutto is sliced with a knife, portions
of grilled meat are tender and ample, service is friendly, and the wine
list is well priced and good. This place is worth a taxi ride, even though
it's just outside the centro storico. $ *Average main: €16* ✉ *Viale Vasco
Pratolini, Oltrarno* ☎ *055/224158* ⊙ *Closed Sun. and Mon.* ✛ *A6.*

$ ✕**Fuori Porta.** One of the oldest and best wine bars in Florence, in busi-
WINE BAR ness since 1987, this place serves cured meats and cheeses, as well as
daily specials such as the sublime spaghetti *al curry. Crostini* and *cros-
toni*—grilled breads topped with a mélange of cheeses and meats—are
the house specialty; the *verdure sott'olio* (vegetables with oil) are divine.
If the *torta caprese* is on the menu, don't miss it: it's a chocolate bomb
with almonds, perhaps the best brownie in Florence. The lengthy wine
list offers great wines by the glass, and terrific bottles from all over
Italy and beyond. All this can be enjoyed at rustic wooden tables, and
outdoors when weather allows. $ *Average main: €10* ✉ *Via Monte alle
Croci 10/r, San Niccolò* ☎ *055/2342483* ⊕ *www.fuoriporta.it* ✛ *G6.*

$ ✕**Gelateria la Carraia.** Although it's a bit of a haul to get here (it's at
ITALIAN the foot of Ponte Carraia, two bridges down from the Ponte Vecchio),
you'll be well-rewarded for doing so. They do standard flavors, and then
creative ones such as *limone con biscotti* (lemon sorbet biscuits), and
they do both of these very well. $ *Average main: €3* ✉ *Piazza Nazario
Sauro 2, Santo Spirito* ☎ *055/280 695* ⊕ *www.lacarraiagroup.eu* ▭ *No
credit cards* ✛ *B4.*

$$ ✕**Il Santo Bevitore.** Florentines and other lovers of good food flock to
TUSCAN "The Holy Drinker" for tasty, well-priced dishes. Unpretentious white
walls, dark wood furniture, and paper placemats provide the simple
decor; start with the exceptional verdure sott'olio or the *terrina di
fegatini* (a creamy chicken-liver spread) before sampling any of the
divine pastas, such as the fragrant spaghetti with shrimp sauce. Count
yourself lucky if the extraordinary potato gratin, served in compact
triangular wedges, is on the menu. The extensive wine list is well priced,
and the well-informed staff are happy to explain it. $ *Average main:
€16* ✉ *Via Santo Spirito 64/66r, Santo Spirito* ☎ *055/211264* ⊕ *www.
ilsantobevitore.com* ⊙ *No lunch Sun.* ✛ *B4.*

$$$ ✕**La Bottega del Buon Caffè.** It translates to "The Shop of Good Cof-
MODERN ITALIAN fee," which may be the biggest understatement in the Florentine din-
ing scene. This recently relocated restaurant (it used to be outside the
centro storico) is a symphony in gustatory pleasures in a room with
exposed sandy brick walls and high, luminous windows. Executive chef
Antonello Sardi is young and gifted, as is his ace brigade. The restaurant
has an organic farm in the Tuscan countryside, and most of the fruit,
vegetables, herbs, and honey on the menu is sourced from there. À la
carte possibilities include *code ai scampi scottate, crudo di gamberi
rosso su crema di zucchine biologiche e salsa all'arancia* (two different

kinds of shrimp—one cooked, one raw—on a creamy organic zucchini and orange sauce) and terrific pastas. Two tasting menus, however, might be the way to go. Service is attentive and unobtrusive, making a meal here memorable. [$] *Average main: €27* ✉ *Lungarno, Cellini, 69/r, Oltrarno* ☎ *055/5535677* 🌐 *www.labottegadelbuoncaffe.com* ✣ *H6.*

$ TUSCAN Fodor's Choice ★ 🍴 **La Casalinga.** *Casalinga* means "housewife," and this place, which has been around since 1963, has the nostalgic charm of a midcentury kitchen with Tuscan comfort food to match. If you eat ribollita anywhere in Florence, eat it here—it couldn't be more authentic. Mediocre paintings clutter the semipaneled walls, tables are set close together, and the place is usually jammed. The menu is long, portions are plentiful, and service is prompt and friendly. For dessert, the lemon sorbet perfectly caps off the meal. [$] *Average main: €13* ✉ *Via Michelozzi 9/r, Santo Spirito* ☎ *055/218624* 🌐 *www.trattorialacasalinga.it* 🕓 *Closed Sun., and 1 wk at Christmas and 3 wks in Aug.* ✣ *C5.*

$ TUSCAN 🍴 **Osteria Antica Mescita San Niccolò.** It's always crowded, always good, and always inexpensive. The osteria is next to the church of San Niccolò, and if you sit in the lower part you'll find yourself in what was once a chapel dating from the 11th century. The subtle but dramatic background is a nice complement to the food, which is simple Tuscan at its best. The *pollo con limone* is tasty pieces of chicken in a lemon-scented broth. In winter, try the *spezzatino di cinghiale con aromi* (wild boar stew with herbs). Reservations are advised. [$] *Average main: €10* ✉ *Via San Niccolò 60/r, San Niccolò* ☎ *055/2342836* 🌐 *www.osteriasanniccolo.it* 🕓 *Closed Sun., and Aug.* ✣ *G6.*

$ TUSCAN 🍴 **Zeb.** The food is incredibly tasty at this well-priced *alimentari* (delicatessen). Zeb stands for *zuppa e bollito* (soup and boiled things), and nothing here disappoints. This is home-style Tuscan cuisine at its very best, served in unpretentious, intimate surroundings: there's room for only about 15 guests. In the kitchen are Giuseppina and Alberto, her son. They staunchly insist on cooking what's best that day; which means the menu changes daily, reflecting the season's best offerings. [$] *Average main: €10* ✉ *Via San Miniato 2, Oltrarno* ☎ *055/2342864* 🌐 *www.zebgastronomia.com* ✣ *G6.*

WHERE TO STAY

Florence is equipped with hotels for all budgets; for instance, you can find both budget and luxury hotels in the centro storico and along the Arno. Florence has so many famous landmarks that it's not hard to find lodging with a panoramic view. The equivalent of the genteel *pensioni* of yesteryear can still be found, though they are now officially classified as "hotels." Generally small and intimate, they often have a quaint appeal that usually doesn't preclude modern plumbing. Florence's importance not only as a tourist city but also as a convention center and the site of the Pitti fashion collections guarantees a variety of accommodations.

The high demand also means that, except in winter, reservations are a must. If you find yourself in Florence with no reservations, go to **Consorzio ITA** (Stazione Centrale, Santa Maria Novella ☎ *055/282893*). You must go there in person to make a booking.

WHAT IT COSTS			
$	**$$**	**$$$**	**$$$$**
For two people under €125	€125–€200	€201–€300	over €300

Exact prices listed are for a standard double room in high season.

Use the coordinate (✛ B2) at the end of each listing to locate a site on the Where to Eat and Stay in Florence map. Hotel reviews have been shortened. For full information, visit Fodors.com.

AROUND THE DUOMO

$$$
HOTEL
🖼 **Hermitage.** All rooms here are decorated with lively wallpaper, and some have views of Palazzo Vecchio and others of the Arno. **Pros:** views; friendly, English-speaking staff; enviable position a stone's throw from the Ponte Vecchio. **Cons:** short flight of stairs to reach elevator. $ *Rooms from: €245* ✉ *Vicolo Marzio 1, Piazza della Signoria* ☎ *055/287216* ⊕ *www.hermitagehotel.com* ↪ *27 rooms, 1 suite* ⍾ *Breakfast* ✛ *E4.*

$$$$
HOTEL
🖼 **Hotel Helvetia and Bristol.** From the cozy yet sophisticated lobby with its stone columns to the guest rooms decorated with prints, you might feel as if you're a guest in a sophisticated manor house. **Pros:** central location; superb staff. **Cons:** rooms facing the street get some noise. $ *Rooms from: €360* ✉ *Via dei Pescioni 2, Piazza della Repubblica* ☎ *055/26651* ⊕ *www.hotelhelvetiabristol.com* ↪ *54 rooms, 13 suites* ⍾ *No meals* ✛ *D3.*

$$$
B&B/INN
Fodor'sChoice
★
🖼 **In Piazza della Signoria.** A cozy feeling permeates these charming rooms, all of which are uniquely decorated and lovingly furnished; some have damask curtains, others fanciful frescoes in the bathroom. **Pros:** marvelous staff; tasty breakfast with a view of Piazza della Signoria; some rooms easily accommodate three. **Cons:** short flight of stairs to reach elevator. $ *Rooms from: €250* ✉ *Via dei Magazzini 2, Piazza della Signoria* ☎ *055/2399546* ⊕ *www.inpiazzadellasignoria.com* ↪ *10 rooms, 3 apartments* ⍾ *Breakfast* ✛ *F4.*

$$$$
HOTEL
🖼 **Palazzo Vecchietti.** If you're looking for a swank setting, and the possibility of staying in for a meal (each room has a tiny kitchenette), look no further than this hotel which, while thoroughly modern, dates to the 15th century. **Pros:** great service; central location; good-size rooms. **Cons:** no restaurant. $ *Rooms from: €500* ✉ *Via degli Strozzi 4, Duomo* ☎ *055/230–2802* ⊕ *www.palazzovecchietti.it* ↪ *12 rooms, 2 apartments* ⍾ *Breakfast* ✛ *D3.*

SAN LORENZO

$$
B&B/INN
Fodor'sChoice
★
🖼 **Antica Dimora Johlea.** Lively color runs rampant on the top floor of this 19th-century palazzo, with a charming flower-filled rooftop terrace where you can sip a glass of wine while taking in a view of Brunelleschi's cupola. **Pros:** great staff; cheerful rooms; honor bar. **Cons:** staff goes home at 7:30; narrow staircase to get to roof terrace; steps to breakfast room. $ *Rooms from: €149* ✉ *Via San Gallo 80, San Marco* ☎ *055/4633292* ⊕ *www.antichedimorefiorentine.it* ▭ *No credit cards* ↪ *6 rooms* ⍾ *Breakfast* ✛ *E1.*

$$ HOTEL 🏨 **Hotel Casci.** In this refurbished 14th-century palace, the home of Giacchino Rossini from 1851 to 1855, the friendly Lombardi family runs a hotel with spotless, functional rooms. **Pros:** helpful staff; good option for families; English-language DVD collection with good selections for kids. **Cons:** bit of a college-dorm atmosphere; small elevator. [$] *Rooms from: €150* ✉ *Via Cavour 13, San Marco* ☎ *055/211686* 🌐 *www.hotelcasci.com* 🛏 *25 rooms* 🍴 *Breakfast* ⊕ *E1.*

$$ HOTEL 🏨 **Il Guelfo Bianco.** The 15th-century building has all modern conveniences, but Renaissance charm still shines in the high-ceiling rooms. **Pros:** stellar multilingual staff. **Cons:** rooms facing the street can be noisy. [$] *Rooms from: €181* ✉ *Via Cavour 29, San Marco* ☎ *055/288330* 🌐 *www.ilguelfobianco.it* 🛏 *40 rooms* 🍴 *Breakfast* ⊕ *F1.*

$ B&B/INN 🏨 **Residenza Johanna I.** Savvy travelers and those on a budget should look no further, as this *residenza* is a tremendous value for quality and location. **Pros:** great value. **Cons:** staff go home at 7; no credit cards. [$] *Rooms from: €119* ✉ *Via Bonifacio Lupi 14, San Marco* ☎ *055/481896* 🌐 *www.antichedimorefiorentine.it* 💳 *No credit cards* 🛏 *11 rooms* 🍴 *No meals* ⊕ *F1.*

SANTA MARIA NOVELLA

$$ B&B/INN 🏨 **Alessandra.** An aura of grandeur pervades these clean, ample rooms a block from the Ponte Vecchio. **Pros:** several rooms have views of the Arno; the spacious suite is a bargain; tiny terrace allows for solitude while sipping a glass of wine. **Cons:** stairs to elevator; two rooms do not have en suite baths. [$] *Rooms from: €150* ✉ *Borgo Santi Apostoli 17, Santa Maria Novella* ☎ *055/283438* 🌐 *www.hotelalessandra.com* 🕓 *Closed Dec. 10–26* 🛏 *26 rooms, 1 suite, 1 apartment* 🍴 *Breakfast* ⊕ *D4.*

$$ HOTEL 🏨 **Casa Howard.** This unassuming little inn has no two rooms alike, and an aura of eclectic funk pervades: one room takes its inspiration from Japan; others are geared to families; others have access to a garden. **Pros:** great location near the basilica of Santa Maria Novella; good vibe; dogs allowed. **Cons:** limited concierge service; staff go home early in the evening; breakfast must be taken elsewhere. [$] *Rooms from: €164* ✉ *Via della Scala 18, Santa Maria Novella* ☎ *06/69924555* 🌐 *www.casahoward.com* 🛏 *13 rooms* 🍴 *No meals* ⊕ *C2.*

$$$$ HOTEL 🏨 **Gallery Hotel Art.** High design resides at this art showcase near the Ponte Vecchio, where sleek, uncluttered rooms are dressed mostly in neutrals and luxe touches, such as leather headboards and kimono robes, abound. **Pros:** cool atmosphere; beautiful people; the in-house Fusion Bar, which pours delightful cocktails. **Cons:** too cool for some. [$] *Rooms from: €320* ✉ *Vicolo dell'Oro 5, Santa Maria Novella* ☎ *055/27263* 🌐 *www.lungarnocollection.com* 🛏 *65 rooms, 9 suites* 🍴 *Breakfast* ⊕ *D4.*

$$$ HOTEL 🏨 **Hotel L'Orologio.** The owner of this quietly understated, elegant hotel has a real passion for watches, which is why he chose to name his hotel after them (and why you will see them in many places). **Pros:** location; great staff; stunning breakfast room; fantastic in-house bar. **Cons:** some folks think it's too close to the train station. [$] *Rooms from: €300* ✉ *Piazza Santa Maria Novella, 24, Santa Maria Novella* ☎ *055/277380* 🌐 *www.hotellorologioflorence.com* 🛏 *44 rooms, 8 suites* 🍴 *Breakfast* ⊕ *C2.*

$$$$ HOTEL Fodor's Choice ★ 🏨 **JK Place.** Hard to spot from the street, these sumptuous appointments provide all the comforts of a luxe home away from home—expect soothing earth tones in the guest rooms, free minibars, crisp linens, and a room service menu with organic dishes. **Pros:** private, intimate feel; stellar staff; free minibar; organic meal choices; small dogs allowed. **Cons:** breakfast at a shared table (which can be easily gotten around with room service); books up quickly. [$] *Rooms from: €500* ✉ *Piazza Santa Maria Novella 7* ☎ *055/2645181* 🌐 *www.jkplace.com* 🛏 *14 doubles, 6 suites* 🍴 *Breakfast* ✥ *C2.*

$ HOTEL 🏨 **Nuova Italia.** The genial English-speaking Viti family oversee these clean and simple rooms near the train station and well within walking distance of the sights. **Pros:** reasonable rates; close to everything. **Cons:** no elevator. [$] *Rooms from: €120* ✉ *Via Faenza 26, Santa Maria Novella* ☎ *055/268430* 🌐 *www.hotel-nuovaitalia.com* ⏲ *Closed Dec. 8–26* 🛏 *20 rooms* 🍴 *Breakfast* ✥ *D1.*

$$$ HOTEL 🏨 **Tornabuoni Beacci.** Florentine pensioni don't get any classier than this: old-fashioned style with enough modern comfort to keep you happy in a 14th-century palazzo. **Pros:** multilingual staff; flower-filled terrace. **Cons:** hall noise can sometimes be a problem. [$] *Rooms from: €219* ✉ *Via Tornabuoni 3, Santa Maria Novella* ☎ *055/212645* 🌐 *www.tornabuonihotels.com* 🛏 *37 rooms, 16 suites* 🍴 *Breakfast* ✥ *D4.*

$$ B&B/INN 🏨 **Torre Guelfa.** If you want a taste of medieval Florence, try one of these character-filled guest rooms—some with canopied beds, some with balconies—housed within a 13th-century tower. **Pros:** rooftop terrace with tremendous views; wonderful staff; some family-friendly triple and quadruple rooms. **Cons:** 72 steps to get to the terrace. [$] *Rooms from: €190* ✉ *Borgo Santi Apostoli 8, Santa Maria Novella* ☎ *055/2396338* 🌐 *www.hoteltorreguelfa.com* 🛏 *28 rooms, 3 suites* 🍴 *Breakfast* ✥ *D4.*

SANTA CROCE

$$$$ HOTEL 🏨 **The Four Seasons.** Seven years of restoration have turned this 15th-century palazzo in Florence's center into a luxury hotel where no two guest rooms are alike; many have original 17th-century frescoes, some face the garden, others quiet interior courtyards. **Pros:** a unique "city meets country" experience; the marvelous garden. **Cons:** for this price, breakfast really should be included; some feel it's a little too removed from the historic center. [$] *Rooms from: €675* ✉ *Borgo Pinti 99e, Santa Croce* ☎ *055/26261* 🌐 *www.fourseasons.com/florence* 🛏 *117 rooms* 🍴 *No meals* ✥ *H1.*

$$$$ HOTEL 🏨 **Hotel Regency.** Rooms dressed in richly colored fabrics and antique-style furniture remain faithful to the premises' 19th-century origins as a private mansion. **Pros:** faces one of the few green parks in the center of Florence. **Cons:** a small flight of stairs takes you to reception. [$] *Rooms from: €359* ✉ *Piazza d'Azeglio 3, Santa Croce* ☎ *055/245247* 🌐 *www.regency-hotel.com* 🛏 *30 rooms, 4 suites* 🍴 *Breakfast* ✥ *H1.*

$ B&B/INN 🏨 **Istituto Oblate dell'Assunzione.** Seven nuns run this convent, minutes from the Duomo, with spotlessly clean, simple rooms; some have views of the cupola, and others look out onto a carefully tended garden where you are welcome to relax. **Pros:** bargain price; great location; quiet rooms;

garden. **Cons:** curfew; no credit cards. $ *Rooms from: €40* ⊠ *Borgo Pinti 15, Santa Croce* ☎ *055/2480582, 055/2346291* ⊕ *www.monasterystays. com* ⊟ *No credit cards* ↗ *28 rooms, 22 with bath* ✛ *G3.*

$$$
HOTEL
Fodor'sChoice
★

🖫 **Monna Lisa.** Although some rooms are small, they are tastefully decorated, and best of all, housed in a 15th-century palazzo that retains some of its wood-coffered ceilings from the 1500s, as well as its original staircase. **Pros:** lavish buffet breakfast; cheerful staff; garden. **Cons:** rooms in annex are less charming than those in palazzo; street noise in some rooms. $ *Rooms from: €209* ⊠ *Borgo Pinti 27, Santa Croce* ☎ *055/2479751* ⊕ *www.monnalisa.it* ↗ *45 rooms* ⦿ *Breakfast* ✛ *G2.*

$$
B&B/INN
Fodor'sChoice
★

🖫 **Morandi alla Crocetta.** You're made to feel like privileged friends of the family at this charming and distinguished residence, furnished comfortably in the classic style of a gracious Florentine home. **Pros:** interesting, offbeat location near the sights; terrific staff; great value; courtesy tea/coffee tray in each room. **Cons:** two flights of stairs to reach reception and rooms. $ *Rooms from: €177* ⊠ *Via Laura 50, Santissima Annunziata* ☎ *055/2344747* ⊕ *www.hotelmorandi.it* ↗ *10 rooms* ✛ *H1.*

THE OLTRARNO

$$
HOTEL

🖫 **Hotel Silla.** Rooms in this 15th-century palazzo, entered through a courtyard lined with potted plants and sculpture-filled niches, are simply furnished and walls are papered; some have views of the Arno, others have stuccoed ceilings. **Pros:** in the middle of everything except the crowds. **Cons:** some readers complain of street noise and too-small rooms. $ *Rooms from: €150* ⊠ *Via de' Renai 5, San Niccolò* ☎ *055/2342888* ⊕ *www.hotelsilla.it* ↗ *35 rooms* ⦿ *Breakfast* ✛ *G6.*

$$$$
HOTEL

🖫 **Palazzo Magnani-Feroni.** The perfect place to play the part of a Florentine aristocrat is here at this 16th-century palazzo, which despite its massive halls and sweeping staircase, could almost feel like home. **Pros:** 24-hour room service; billiards room; generous buffet breakfast including prosecco; terrific staff. **Cons:** a few steps up to the elevator; many steps up to the rooftop terrace. $ *Rooms from: €650* ⊠ *Borgo San Frediano 5, Oltrarno* ☎ *055/2399544* ⊕ *www.florencepalace.it* ↗ *12 suites* ✛ *B4.*

BEYOND THE CITY CENTER

$$$$
HOTEL
Fodor'sChoice
★

🖫 **Il Salviatino.** The dramatic approach (via a curving private drive lined with cypresses) to this 14th-century villa sets the tone: it's all uphill from there, from the welcome glass of prosecco in the hall, to its remarkable rooms. **Pros:** great views; attentive staff; startlingly original breakfast; views; not in town. **Cons:** not in town; some hall noise. $ *Rooms from: €680* ⊠ *Via del Salviatino 21* ☎ *055/904111* ⊕ *www.salviatino.com* ↗ *23 rooms, 22 suites* ⦿ *Breakfast* ✛ *G1.*

$$$
B&B/INN
FAMILY
Fodor'sChoice
★

🖫 **Torre di Bellosguardo.** *Bellosguardo* means "beautiful view," and given the view of Florence you get here, the name is fitting. **Pros:** great for escaping heat of the city in summer; a villa experience with the city just minutes away; some rooms can accommodate three and four people. **Cons:** a car is a necessity; breakfast is not included during high season. $ *Rooms from: €300* ⊠ *Via Roti Michelozzi 2* ☎ *055/2298145* ⊕ *www. torrebellosguardo.com* ↗ *9 rooms, 7 suites* ⦿ *No meals* ✛ *B6.*

$$$$ HOTEL Fodor's Choice ★ **Villa La Massa.** In this tall and imposing villa, 15 minutes out of town, public rooms are outfitted in Renaissance style and guest rooms have high ceilings, plush carpeting, and deep bathtubs. **Pros:** pleasing mix of city and country life; sumptuous buffet breakfast; views of the Tuscan hills; the restaurant; phenomenal staff. **Cons:** not open year-round. [$] *Rooms from: €510* ✉ *Via della Massa 24, Candeli* ☎ *055/62611* 🌐 *www.villalamassa.com* ⏲ *Closed Dec.–Mar.* 🛏 *19 rooms, 18 suites* 🍴 *Breakfast* ✥ *H5.*

NIGHTLIFE AND PERFORMING ARTS

NIGHTLIFE

Florentines are rather proud of their nightlife options. Most bars now have some sort of happy hour, which usually lasts for many hours and often has snacks that can substitute for a light dinner. (Check, though, that the buffet is free or comes with the price of a drink.) Clubs typically don't open until very late in the evening, and don't get crowded until 1 or 2 in the morning.

5

AROUND THE DUOMO

Hard Rock Cafe. Hard Rock packs in young Florentines and travelers eager to sample the iconic chain's take on classic American grub. ✉ *Piazza della Repubblica, Piazza della Repubblica* ☎ *055/2670499* 🌐 *www.hardrock.com.*

Fodor's Choice ★ **il bar de l'O.** This swanky, American-style bar is attached to the Hotel l'Orologio. It's a good spot for a well-executed cocktail with tasty snacks; when it's warm, you can sit outside and gaze at the beautiful facade of Santa Maria Novella. ✉ *Via delle Belle Donne 34/r, Duomo* ☎ *055/277380* 🌐 *www.ilbardelo.com.*

Yab. Yab never seems to go out of style, though it increasingly becomes the haunt of Florentine high schoolers and university students intent on dancing and doing vodka shots. ✉ *Via Sassetti 5/r, Piazza della Repubblica* ☎ *055/215160* 🌐 *www.yab.it.*

SAN LORENZO

Kitsch. Choose from indoor or outdoor seating and take advantage of the great list of wines by the glass. At aperitivo time €10 will buy you a truly tasty cocktail and give you access to the tremendous buffet; it's so good, you won't need dinner afterward—in fact, they called it "Apericena." That means, roughly, drink and dinner. ✉ *Via San Gallo 22/r, San Marco* ☎ *055/2343890* 🌐 *www.kitschfirenze.com.*

SANTA CROCE

Jazz Club. Enjoy live music in this small basement club. ✉ *Via Nuova de' Caccini 3, corner of Borgo Pinti, Santa Croce* ☎ *339/4980752.*

Sant'Ambrogio Caffè. Come here in the summer for outdoor seating with a view of an 11th-century church (Sant'Ambrogio) directly across the street. Come here when it's not for perfectly mixed drinks and a lively atmosphere filled with (mostly) locals. ✉ *Piazza Sant'Ambrogio 7–8/r, Santa Croce* ☎ *055/2477277.*

THE OLTRARNO

Montecarla. People sip cocktails against a backdrop of exotic flowers, leopard-print chairs and chintz, and red walls on the two crowded floors at Montecarla. ⊠ *Via de' Bardi 2, San Niccolò* ☎ *055/2340259.*

Negroni. Well-dressed young Florentines flock to Negroni at happy hour. ⊠ *Via de' Renai 17/r, San Niccolò* ☎ *055/243647* ⊕ *www.negronibar.it.*

Zoe. Though it's called a *caffetteria,* and coffee is served (as well as terrific salads and burgers at lunchtime), Zoe's fine cocktails are the real draw for elegant, youngish Florentines who come here to see and be seen. Here's people-watching at its very best. ⊠ *Via de' Renai 13/r, San Niccolò* ☎ *055/243111* ⊕ *www.zoebar.it.*

PERFORMING ARTS

Florence has a lively classical music scene. The internationally famous annual Maggio Musicale lights up the musical calendar in early spring, and continues throughout most of the rest of the year. Fans of rock, pop, and hip-hop might be somewhat surprised by the absence of live acts that make it to town (for such offerings, travel to Rome or Milan is often a necessity). What it lacks in contemporary music, however, is more than made up for with its many theatrical offerings.

FESTIVALS AND SPECIAL EVENTS

Festa di San Giovanni (*Feast of St. John the Baptist*). On June 24 Florence grinds to a halt to celebrate the Festa di San Giovanni in honor of its patron saint. Many shops and bars close, and at night a fireworks display lights up the Arno and attracts thousands. ⊠ *Florence.*

Scoppio del Carro (*Explosion of the Cart*). On Easter Sunday Florentines and foreigners alike flock to the Piazza del Duomo to watch as the Scoppio del Carro, a monstrosity of a carriage, pulled by two huge oxen decorated for the occasion, makes its way through the city center and ends up in the piazza. Through an elaborate wiring system, an object representing a "dove" is sent from inside the cathedral to the Baptistery across the way. The dove sets off an explosion of fireworks that come streaming from the carriage. You have to see it to believe it. If you don't like crowds, don't worry: video replays figure prominently on the nightly newscasts afterward. ⊠ *Florence.*

MUSIC

Accademia Bartolomeo Cristofori. Also known as the Amici del Fortepiano (Friends of the Fortepiano), the Accademia Bartolomeo Cristofori sponsors fortepiano concerts throughout the year. ⊠ *Via di Camaldoli 7/r, Santo Spirito* ☎ *055/221646* ⊕ *www.accademiacristofori.it.*

Amici della Musica. This organization sponsors classical and contemporary concerts at the Teatro della Pergola (Box office, Via Alamanni 39, Lungarno North ☎ *055/210804* ⊕ *www.teatrodellapergola.com*). ⊠ *Via Pier Capponi 41* ⊕ *www.amicimusica.fi.it.*

Maggio Musicale Fiorentino. After some delay due to funding issues, a new music hall opened in spring 2014; the area is called the Parco della Musica (Music Park), and was designed by Paolo Desideri and associates. Three concert halls (two indoor, one outdoor) are planned, and only one has been completed. Maggio Musicale has taken up residence there, and continues to hold forth at the Teatro Comunale (Corso Italia 16, Lungarno North ☎ *055/287222* ⊕ *www.maggiofio-rentino.com*). Within Italy you can purchase tickets from late April through July directly at the box office or by phone (☎ *055/2779309*). You can also buy them online. ✉ *Via Alamanni 39* ☎ *055/210804* ⊕ *www.operadifirenze.it/it.*

OBIHALL. This large exhibition space, formerly Teatro Saschall, hosts many events throughout the year, including a large Christmas bazaar run by the Red Cross, visiting rock stars, and trendy bands from all over Europe. ✉ *Lungarno Aldo Moro 3, Santa Maria Novella* ☎ *055/6503068* ⊕ *www.obihall.it.*

Orchestra da Camera Fiorentina. This orchestra performs various concerts of classical music throughout the year at Orsanmichele, the grain market–turned–church. ✉ *Via Monferrato 2, Piazza della Signoria* ☎ *055/783374* ⊕ *www.orcafi.it.*

Orchestra della Toscana. The concert season of the Orchestra della Toscana runs from November to June. ✉ *Via Ghibellina 101, Santa Croce* ☎ *055/2340710* ⊕ *www.orchestradellatoscana.it.*

SHOPPING

Window-shopping in Florence is like visiting an enormous contemporary-art gallery. Many of today's greatest Italian artists are fashion designers, and most keep shops in Florence. Discerning shoppers may find bargains in the street markets. ■TIP→ **Do not buy any knockoff goods from any of the hawkers plying their fake Prada (or any other high-end designer) on the streets. It's illegal, and fines are astronomical if the police happen to catch you. (You pay the fine, not the vendor.)**

Shops are generally open 9–1 and 3:30–7:30, and are closed Sunday and Monday mornings most of the year. Summer (June to September) hours are usually 9–1 and 4–8, and some shops close Saturday afternoon instead of Monday morning. When looking for addresses, you'll see two color-coded numbering systems on each street. The red numbers are commercial addresses and are indicated, for example, as "31/r." The blue or black numbers are residential addresses. Most shops take major credit cards and ship purchases, but because of possible delays it's wise to take your purchases with you.

SHOPPING DISTRICTS

Florence's most fashionable shops are concentrated in the center of town. The fanciest designer shops are mainly on **Via Tornabuoni** and **Via della Vigna Nuova.** The city's largest concentrations of antiques shops are on **Borgo Ognissanti** and the Oltrarno's **Via Maggio.** The **Ponte Vecchio** houses reputable but very expensive jewelry shops, as it has since the 16th century. The area near **Santa Croce** is the heart of the leather merchants' district.

AROUND THE DUOMO

ART

Mandragora Art Store. This is one of the first attempts in Florence to cash in on the museum-store craze. It's a lovely store with reproductions of valued works of art and jewelry. ⊠ *Piazza del Duomo 50/r, Duomo* ☎ *055/292559* ⊕ *www.mandragora.it.*

CLOTHING

Fodor's Choice ★ **Bernardo.** Come here for men's trousers, cashmere sweaters, and shirts with details like mother-of-pearl buttons. ⊠ *Via Porta Rossa 87/r, Piazza della Repubblica* ☎ *055/283333* ⊕ *www.bernardofirenze.it.*

Cabó. Missoni knitwear is the main draw at Cabó. ⊠ *Via Porta Rossa 77–79/r, Piazza della Repubblica* ☎ *055/215774.*

Diesel. Trendy Diesel started in Vicenza; its gear is on the "must have" list of many self-respecting Italian teens. ⊠ *Via dei Lamberti 13/r, Piazza della Signoria* ☎ *055/2399963* ⊕ *www.diesel.com.*

Patrizia Pepe. The Florentine designer has body-conscious clothes perfect for all ages, especially for women with a tiny streak of rebelliousness. Women who are not size zero—or close to it—need not apply. ⊠ *Via Strozzi 11/19r, Duomo* ☎ *055/2302518* ⊕ *www.patriziapepe.com.*

Spazio A. For cutting-edge fashion, these fun and funky window displays merit a stop. The shop carries such well-known designers as Alberta Ferretti and Moschino, as well as lesser-known Italian, English, and French designers. ⊠ *Via Porta Rossa 109–115/r, Piazza della Repubblica* ☎ *055/212995* ⊕ *www.spazioafirenze.it.*

MARKETS

Mercato dei Fiori (*flower market*). Every Thursday morning from September through June the covered loggia in Piazza della Repubblica hosts a Mercato dei Fiori; it's awash in a lively riot of plants, flowers, and difficult-to-find herbs. ⊠ *Piazza della Repubblica.*

Mercato del Porcellino. If you're looking for cheery, inexpensive trinkets to take home, you might want to stop and roam through the stalls under the loggia of the Mercato del Porcellino. ⊠ *Via Por Santa Maria at Via Porta Rossa, Piazza della Repubblica.*

SHOES AND LEATHER ACCESSORIES

Furla. Internationally renowned Furla makes beautiful leather bags, shoes, and wallets in up-to-the-minute designs. ⊠ *Via Calzaiuoli 10/r, Piazza della Repubblica* ☎ *055/2382883* ⊕ *www.furla.com.*

SAN LORENZO

JEWELRY AND ACCESSORIES

Penko. Renaissance goldsmiths provide the inspiration for this dazzling jewelry with a contemporary feel. ⊠ *Via F. Zannetti 14/16r, Duomo* ☎ *055/211661* ⊕ *www.paolopenko.com.*

MARKETS

FAMILY

Fodor's Choice

★

Mercato Centrale. This huge indoor food market offers a staggering selection of all things edible. Downstairs is full of vendors hawking their wares—meat, fish, fruit, vegetables; upstairs (daily 10 am–midnight) is full of food stalls offering up the best of what Italy has to offer. ☒ *Piazza del Mercato Centrale, San Lorenzo* ⊕ *www.mercatocentrale.it* ⊙ *Closed Sun., and Mon.–Sat. after 2.*

FAMILY

Mercato di San Lorenzo. The clothing and leather-goods stalls of the Mercato di San Lorenzo in the streets next to the church of San Lorenzo have bargains for shoppers on a budget. Do please remember that you get what you pay for. ☒ *Florence.*

SANTA MARIA NOVELLA

BOOKS AND PAPER

Alberto Cozzi. You'll find an extensive line of Florentine papers and paper products here. The artisans in the shop rebind and restore books and works on paper. Their hours are tricky, so it's best to call first before stopping by. ☒ *Via del Parione 35/r, Santa Maria Novella* ☎ *055/294968.*

Pineider. Although it has shops throughout the world, Pineider started out in Florence and still does all its printing here. Stationery and business cards are the mainstay, but the stores also sell fine leather desk accessories as well as a less stuffy, more lighthearted line of products. ☒ *Piazza Rucellai, Santa Maria Novella* ☎ *055/284655* ⊕ *www.pineider.com.*

CLOTHING

Emilio Pucci. The aristocratic Marchese di Barsento, Emilio Pucci, became an international name in the late 1950s when the stretch ski clothes he designed for himself caught on with the *dolce vita* crowd—his pseudo-psychedelic prints and "palazzo pajamas" became all the rage. ☒ *Via Tornabuoni 20–22/r, Santa Maria Novella* ☎ *055/2658082* ⊕ *www. emiliopucci.com.*

Principe. This Florentine institution sells casual clothes for men, women, and children at far-from-casual prices. It also has a great housewares department. ☒ *Via del Sole 2, Santa Maria Novella* ☎ *055/292764* ⊕ *www.principedifirenze.com.*

FRAGRANCES

Antica Officina del Farmacista Dr. Vranjes. Dr. Vranjes elevates aromatherapy to an art form, with scents for the body and for the house. ☒ *Via della Spada 9* ☎ *055/288796* ⊕ *www.drvranjes.it.*

Fodor's Choice

★

Officina Profumo Farmaceutica di Santa Maria Novella. The essence of a Florentine holiday is captured in the sachets of this Art Nouveau emporium of herbal cosmetics and soaps that are made following centuries-old recipes created by friars. It celebrated its 400th birthday in 2012. ☒ *Via della Scala 16, Santa Maria Novella* ☎ *055/216276* ⊕ *www.smnovella.it.*

JEWELRY

Fodor's Choice ★

Angela Caputi. Angela Caputi wows Florentine cognoscenti with her highly creative, often outsize plastic jewelry. A small, but equally creative, collection of women's clothing made of fine fabrics is also on offer. ⊠ *Borgo Santi Apostoli 44/46* ☎ *055/292993* ⊕ *www.angelacaputi.com.*

Carlo Piccini. Still in operation after several generations, this Florentine institution sells antique jewelry and makes pieces to order; you can also get old jewelry reset here. ⊠ *Ponte Vecchio 31/r, Piazza della Signoria* ☎ *055/292030* ⊕ *www.carlopiccini.com.*

Cassetti. This jeweler combines precious and semiprecious stones and metals in contemporary settings. ⊠ *Ponte Vecchio 54/r, Piazza della Signoria* ☎ *055/2396028* ⊕ *www.cassetti.it.*

Gatto Bianco. This contemporary jeweler has breathtakingly beautiful pieces worked in semiprecious and precious stones. ⊠ *Borgo Santi Apostoli 12/r, Santa Maria Novella* ☎ *055/282989* ⊕ *www.gattobiancogioielli.com.*

Oro Due. Gold jewelry and other beauteous objects are priced according to the level of craftsmanship and the price of gold bullion that day. ⊠ *Via Lambertesca 12/r, Piazza della Signoria* ☎ *055/292143.*

Tiffany. One of Florence's oldest jewelers has supplied Italian (and other) royalty with finely crafted gems for centuries. Its selection of antique-looking classics has been updated with contemporary silver. ⊠ *Via Tornabuoni 25/r, Santa Maria Novella* ☎ *055/215506* ⊕ *www.tiffany.it.*

LINENS AND FABRICS

Fodor's Choice ★

Loretta Caponi. Synonymous with Florentine embroidery, the luxury lace, linens, and lingerie have earned the eponymous signora worldwide renown. There's also beautiful (and expensive) clothing for children. ⊠ *Piazza Antinori 4/r, Santa Maria Novella* ☎ *055/213668* ⊕ *www.lorettacaponi.com.*

SHOES AND LEATHER ACCESSORIES

Casadei. The ultimate fine leathers are crafted into classic shapes, winding up as women's shoes and bags. ⊠ *Via Tornabuoni 74/r, Santa Maria Novella* ☎ *055/287240* ⊕ *www.casadei.com.*

Cellerini. In a city where it seems just about everybody wears an expensive leather jacket, Cellerini is an institution. ⊠ *Via del Sole 37/r, Santa Maria Novella* ☎ *055/282533* ⊕ *www.cellerini.it.*

Ferragamo. This classy institution, in a 13th-century palazzo, displays designer clothing and accessories, though elegant footwear still underlies the Ferragamo success. ⊠ *Via Tornabuoni 2/r, Santa Maria Novella* ☎ *055/292123* ⊕ *www.ferragamo.com.*

Giotti. You'll find a full line of leather goods, including clothing. ⊠ *Piazza Ognissanti 3–4/r, Lungarno North* ☎ *055/294265* ⊕ *www.giotti.com.*

SANTA CROCE

MARKETS
Mercato di Sant'Ambrogio. It's possible to strike gold at this lively market, where clothing stalls abut the fruits and vegetables. ⊠ *Piazza Ghiberti, off Via dei Macci, Santa Croce.*

Piazza dei Ciompi flea market. You can find bargains here Monday through Saturday and on the last Sunday of the month. ⊠ *Sant'Ambrogio, Santa Croce.*

SHOES AND LEATHER ACCESSORIES
Paolo Carandini. Stop in here for exquisite leather objects such as picture frames, jewelry boxes, and desk accessories. ⊠ *Borgo Allegri 7/r, Santa Croce* ☎ *055/245397* ⊕ *www.paolocarandini.com.*

Fodor'sChoice ★ **Scuola del Cuoio.** A consortium of leatherworkers ply their trade at Scuola del Cuoio (Leather School), in the former dormitory of the convent of Santa Croce; high-quality, fairly priced jackets, belts, and purses are sold here. ⊠ *Piazza Santa Croce 16* ☎ *055/2445334* ⊕ *www. scuoladelcuoio.com.*

THE OLTRARNO

BOOKS AND PAPER
Giulio Giannini e Figlio. One of Florence's oldest paper-goods stores is *the* place to buy the marbleized stock, which comes in many shapes and sizes, from flat sheets to boxes and even pencils. ⊠ *Piazza Pitti 37/r, Oltrarno* ☎ *055/212621* ⊕ *www.giuliogiannini.it.*

Fodor'sChoice ★ **Il Torchio.** Photograph albums, frames, diaries, and other objects dressed in handmade paper are high-quality, and the prices lower than usual. ⊠ *Via dei Bardi 17, San Niccolò* ☎ *055/2342862* ⊕ *www.legatoriail-torchio.com.*

CLOTHING
Maçel. Browse collections by lesser-known Italian designers, many of whom use the same factories as the A-list, at this women's clothing shop. ⊠ *Via Guicciardini 128/r, Palazzo Pitti* ☎ *055/287355.*

Fodor'sChoice ★ **Madova.** Complete your winter wardrobe with a pair of high-quality leather gloves, available in a rainbow of colors and a choice of linings (silk, cashmere, and unlined), from Madova. ⊠ *Via Guicciardini 1/r, Palazzo Pitti* ☎ *055/2396526* ⊕ *www.madova.com.*

FRAGRANCES
Lorenzo Villoresi. Proprietor Lorenzo Villoresi makes one-of-a-kind fragrances, which he develops after meeting with you. Such personalized attention does not come cheap. ⊠ *Via de'Bardi 14, Oltrarno* ☎ *055/2341187* ⊕ *www.lorenzovilloresi.it.*

MARKETS
Santo Spirito flea market. The second Sunday of every month brings the Santo Spirito flea market. On the third Sunday of the month, vendors at the Fierucola organic fest sell such delectables as honeys, jams, spice mixes, and fresh vegetables. ⊠ *Florence.*

BEYOND THE CITY CENTER

For bargains on Italian designer clothing, you need to leave the city.

Barberino Designer Outlet. Prada, Pollini, Missoni, and Bruno Magli, among others, are all found at Barberino Designer Outlet. To get here, take the A1 to the Barberino di Mugello exit, and follow signs to the mall. ⊠ *Via Meucci snc* ☎ *055/842161* ⊕ *www.mcarthurglen.com.*

Mall. One-stop bargain shopping awaits at this collection of stores selling goods by such names as Bottega Veneta, Giorgio Armani, Loro Piana, Sergio Rossi, and Yves St. Laurent. ⊠ *Via Europa 8* ☎ *055/8657775* ⊕ *www.themall.it.*

Prada Outlet. Cognoscenti drive 45 minutes (or take the train to Montevarchi, and then a taxi) to find a bargain here. ⊠ *Levanella Spacceo, Estrada Statale 69, Montevarchi* ☎ *055/9196528* ⊕ *www.prada.com.*

FIESOLE: SIDE TRIP FROM FLORENCE

A half-day excursion to Fiesole, in the hills 8 km (5 miles) above Florence, gives you a pleasant respite from museums and a wonderful view of the city. From here the view of the Duomo gives you a new appreciation for what the Renaissance accomplished. Fiesole began life as an ancient Etruscan and later Roman village that held some power until it succumbed to barbarian invasions. Eventually it gave up its independence in exchange for Florence's protection. The medieval cathedral, ancient Roman amphitheater, and lovely old villas behind garden walls are clustered on a series of hilltops. A walk around Fiesole can take from one to two or three hours, depending on how far you stroll from the main piazza.

GETTING HERE AND AROUND

The trip from Florence by car takes 20–30 minutes. Drive to Piazza Liberta and cross the Ponte Rosso heading in the direction of the SS65/SR65. Turn right on to Via Salviati and continue on to Via Roccettini. Make a left turn to Via Vecchia Fiesolana, which will take you directly to the center of town. There are several possible routes for the two-hour walk from central Florence to Fiesole. One route begins in a residential area of Florence called Salviatino (Via Barbacane, near Piazza Edison, on the No. 7 bus route), and after a short time, offers peeks over garden walls of beautiful villas, as well as the view over your shoulder at the panorama of Florence in the valley.

VISITOR INFORMATION

Fiesole Tourism Office. ⊠ *Via Portigiani 3* ☎ *055/5961323* ⊕ *www.fiesoleforyou.it.*

EXPLORING

Anfiteatro Romano (*Roman Amphitheater*). The beautifully preserved 2,000-seat Anfiteatro Romano, near the Duomo, dates from the 1st century BC and is still used for summer concerts. To the right of the amphitheater are the remains of the **Terme Romani** (Roman Baths), where you can see the gymnasium, hot and cold baths, and rectangular chamber where the water was heated. A beautifully designed **Museo Archeologico**, its facade evoking an ancient Roman temple, is built amid the ruins and contains objects dating from as early as 2000 BC. The nearby **Museo Bandini** is filled with the private collection of Canon Angelo Maria Bandini (1726–1803); he fancied 13th- to 15th-century Florentine paintings, terra-cotta pieces, and wood sculpture, which he later bequeathed to the Diocese of Fiesole. ☒ *Via Portigiani 1* ☎ *055/5961293* ⊕ *www.museidifiesole.it* ✑ *€12, includes access to archaeological park and museums* ☉ *Closed Tues. in Nov.–Feb.*

Badia Fiesolana. From the church of San Domenico it's a five-minute walk northwest to the Badia Fiesolana, which was Fiesole's original cathedral. Dating to the 11th century, it was first the home of the Camaldolese monks. Thanks to Cosimo il Vecchio, the complex was substantially restructured. The facade, never completed owing to Cosimo's death, contains elements of its original Romanesque decoration. The attached convent once housed Cosimo's valued manuscripts. Its mid-15th-century cloister is well worth a look. ☒ *Via della Badia dei Roccettini 11* ⊕ *www.iue.it.*

Duomo. A stark medieval interior yields many masterpieces. In the raised presbytery, the **Cappella Salutati** was frescoed by 15th-century artist Cosimo Rosselli, but it was his contemporary, sculptor Mino da Fiesole (1430–84), who put the town on the artistic map. The Madonna on the altarpiece and the tomb of Bishop Salutati are fine examples of the artist's work. ☒ *Piazza Mino da Fiesole* ☎ *055/59400.*

San Domenico. If you really want to stretch your legs, walk 4 km (2½ miles) toward the center of Florence along Via Vecchia Fiesolana, a narrow lane in use since Etruscan times, to the church of San Domenico. Sheltered in the church is the *Madonna and Child with Saints* by Fra Angelico, who was a Dominican friar here. ☒ *Piazza San Domenico, off Via Giuseppe Mantellini* ☎ *055/59230.*

San Francesco. This lovely hilltop church has a good view of Florence and the plain below from its terrace and benches. Off the little cloister is a small, eclectic museum containing, among other things, two Egyptian mummies. Halfway up the hill you'll see sloping steps to the right; they lead to a fragrant wooded park with trails that loop out and back to the church. ☒ *Fiesole.*

WHERE TO EAT AND STAY

$$

ITALIAN

✗**La Reggia degli Etruschi.** If you want a breath of fresh air—literally—this lovely little eatery is worth a detour. Stamina is necessary to get here, as it's on a steep hill on the way up to the church of San Francesco. The rewards on arrival, in the form of inventive reworkings of Tuscan classics, are well worth it. The *mezzaluna di pera a pecorino* (little half moon pasta stuffed with pear and pecorino) is sauced with Roquefort and poppy seeds. Slivers of papaya—a rare commodity on restaurant menus in these parts—anoint the tasty *carpaccio di tonno affumicato* (smoked tuna carpaccio). The wine list and the attentive service help make this a terrific place to have a meal. When it's warm, you can sit on the little terrace outside. [$] *Average main: €21* ✉ *Via San Francesco* ☎ *055/59385* 🌐 *www.lareggiadeglietruschi.com.*

$$ HOTEL 🏨 **Villa Aurora.** The attractive, simply furnished hotel on the main piazza takes advantage of its hilltop spot, with beautiful views in many of the rooms, some of which are on two levels with beamed ceilings and balconies. **Pros:** some rooms have pretty views; air quality better than in Florence. **Cons:** no elevator; steps to breakfast room. [$] *Rooms from: €149* ✉ *Piazza Mino da Fiesole 39* ☎ *055/59363, 055/59587* 🌐 *www.villaurorafiesole.com* 🛏 *23 rooms, 2 suites* 🍴 *Breakfast.*

$$$$ HOTEL 🏨 **Villa San Michele.** The cypress-lined driveway provides an elegant preamble to this incredibly gorgeous (and very expensive) hotel nestled in the hills of Fiesole. **Pros:** exceptional convent conversion. **Cons:** money must be no object. [$] *Rooms from: €990* ✉ *Via Doccia 4* ☎ *055/5678200, 055/5678250* 🌐 *www.villasanmichele.com* 🕓 *Closed Nov.–Easter* 🛏 *21 rooms, 24 suites.*

NIGHTLIFE AND PERFORMING ARTS

Estate Fiesolana. From June through August, Estate Fiesolana, a festival of theater, music, dance, and film, takes place in Fiesole's churches and in the Roman amphitheater—demonstrating that the ancient Romans knew a thing or two about acoustics. ✉ *Teatro Romano* ☎ *055/59611* 🌐 *www.comune.fiesole.fi.it.*

6

TUSCANY AND
UMBRIA

WELCOME TO TUSCANY AND UMBRIA

TOP REASONS TO GO

★ **Leaning Tower of Pisa:** It may be touristy, but it's still a whole lot of fun to climb to the top and admire the view.

★ **Wine tasting in Chianti:** Sample the fruits of the region's gorgeous vineyards, either at the wineries themselves or in the wine bars found in the towns.

★ **Piazza del Campo, Siena:** Sip a cappuccino or enjoy some gelato as you take in this spectacular shell-shape piazza.

★ **Assisi, shrine to St. Francis:** Recharge your soul in this rose-color hill town with a visit to the gentle saint's majestic basilica, adorned with great frescoes.

★ **Spoleto, Umbria's musical Mecca:** Crowds may descend and prices ascend here during summer's Festival dei Due Mondi, but Spoleto's hushed charm enchants year-round.

★ **Orvieto's Duomo:** Arresting visions of heaven and hell on the facade and brilliant frescoes within make this Gothic cathedral a dazzler.

1 Tuscany. Nature outdid herself in Tuscany, the central Italian region that has Florence as its principal city. Descriptions and photographs can't do the landscape justice—the hills, draped with woods, vineyards, and olive groves, may not have the drama of mountain peaks or waves crashing on the shore, yet there's an undeniable magic about them. Aside from Florence, Tuscany has several midsize cities that are well worth visiting, but the greatest appeal lies in the smaller towns, often perched on hilltops and not significantly altered since the Middle Ages. Despite its popularity with fellow travelers, Tuscany remains a place you can escape to.

2 Umbria. This region is closer to the Apennines than Tuscany is, so the landscape is wilder, the valleys deeper, and the mountains higher. The greater isolation of Umbria's towns and, until the unification of Italy, their association with the Papal States, may have encouraged the development of a keen sense of spirituality. Several of Italy's major saints are from the region, including St. Benedict of Norcia, St. Rita of Cascia, St. Chiara of Assisi, and most famously St. Francis of Assisi. There's no city with the size or significance of Florence, but a number of the smaller towns, particularly Assisi, Perugia, Spoleto, and Orvieto, have lots to hold your interest. Umbria's Roman past is much in evidence—expect to see Roman villas, aqueducts, and temples.

GETTING ORIENTED

A mix of forests, vineyards, olive groves, and poppy fields, the hill regions of central Italy add up to Italian countryside at its most beautiful. The hillside towns, many dating from the days of ancient Rome, wear their history on their sleeves: you'll encounter towering Gothic cathedrals, glowing Renaissance frescoes, and cobblestone streets worn smooth by a thousand years of strollers. When people close their eyes and dream of Italy, Tuscany and Umbria is what they see.

6

EATING AND DRINKING WELL IN TUSCANY

The influence of the ancient Etruscans—who favored the use of fresh herbs—is still felt in Tuscan cuisine three millennia later. Simple and earthy, Tuscan food celebrates the seasons with fresh vegetable dishes, wonderful bread-based soups, and meats perfumed with sage, rosemary, and thyme.

Throughout Tuscany there are excellent upscale restaurants that serve elaborate dishes, but to get a real taste of the flavors of the region, head for the family-run trattorias found in every town. The service and setting are often basic, but the food can be memorable.

Few places serve lighter fare at midday, so expect substantial meals at lunch and dinner, especially in out-of-the-way towns. Dining hours are fairly standard: lunch between 12:30 and 2, dinner between 7:30 and 10.

HOLD THE SALT

Tuscan bread is famous for what it's missing: salt. That's because it's intended to pick up seasoning from the food it accompanies; it's not meant to be eaten alone or dipped in a bowl of oil (which is a custom developed by American restaurants—it's not standard practice in Italy).

That doesn't mean Tuscans don't like to start a meal with bread, but usually it's prepared in some way. It can be grilled and drizzled with olive oil (*fettunta*), covered with chicken liver spread (*crostino nero*), or toasted, rubbed with garlic, and topped with tomatoes (*bruschetta*).

AFFETTATI MISTI

The name, roughly translated, means "mixed cold cuts" and it's something Tuscans do exceptionally well. A platter of cured meats, served as an antipasto, is sure to include *prosciutto crudo* (ham, cut paper-thin) and *salame* (dry sausage, prepared in dozens of ways—some spicy, some sweet). The most distinctly Tuscan affettati are made from *cinta senese* (a once nearly extinct pig found only in the heart of the region) and *cinghiale* (wild boar, which roam all over central Italy). You can eat these delicious slices unadorned or layered on a piece of bread.

PASTA

Restaurants throughout Tuscany serve dishes similar to those in Florence, but they also have their own local specialties. Many recipes are from the *nonna* (grandmother) of the restaurant's owner, handed down over time but never written down.

Look in particular for pasta creations made with *pici* (a long, thick, hand-rolled spaghetti). *Pappardelle* (a long, ribbonlike pasta noodle) is frequently paired with sauces made with game, such as *lepre* (hare) or cinghiale. In the northwest, a specialty of Lucca is *tordelli di carne al ragù* (meat-stuffed pasta with a meat sauce).

MEAT

Bistecca fiorentina (a thick T-bone steak, grilled rare) is the classic meat dish of Tuscany, but there are other specialties as well. Many menus will include *tagliata di manzo* (thinly sliced, roasted beef, drizzled with olive oil), *arista di maiale* (roast pork with sage and rosemary), and *salsiccia e fagioli* (pork sausage and beans). In the southern part of the region, don't be surprised to find *piccione* (pigeon), which can be roasted, stuffed, or baked.

WINE

Grape cultivation here also dates from Etruscan times, and vineyards are abundant, particularly in Chianti. The resulting medium-body red wine is a staple on most tables; however, you can select from a multitude of other varieties, including such reds as Brunello di Montalcino and Vino Nobile di Montepulciano and such whites as vermentino and vernaccia.

Super Tuscans (a fanciful name given to a group of wines by American journalists) now command attention as some of the best produced in Italy; they have great depth and complexity. The dessert wine *vin santo* is made throughout the region, and is often sipped with *biscotti* (twice-baked almond cookies), perfect for dunking.

EATING AND DRINKING WELL IN UMBRIA AND THE MARCHES

Central Italy is mountainous, and its food is hearty and straightforward, with a stick-to-the-ribs quality that sees hardworking farmers and artisans through a long day's work and helps them make the steep climb home at night.

In restaurants here, as in much of Italy, you're rewarded for seeking out the local cuisines, and you'll often find better and cheaper food if you're willing to stray a few hundred yards from the main sights. Spoleto is noted for its good food and service, probably a result of high expectations from the international arts crowd. For gourmets, however, it's hard to beat Spello, which has both excellent restaurants and first-rate wine merchants.

A rule of thumb for eating well throughout Umbria is to order what's in season; the trick is to stroll through local markets to see what's for sale. A number of restaurants in the region offer *degustazione* (tasting) menus, which give you a chance to try different local specialties without breaking the bank.

TASTY TRUFFLES

More truffles are found in Umbria than anywhere else in Italy. Spoleto and Norcia are prime territory for the *tartufo nero* (reddish-black interior and fine white veins) prized for its extravagant flavor and intense aroma.

The mild summer truffle, *scorzone estivo* (black outside and beige inside), is in season from May through December. The *scorzone autunnale* (burnt brown color and visible veins inside) is found from October through December. Truffles can be shaved into omelets or over pasta, pounded into sauces, or chopped and mixed with oil.

OLIVE OIL

Nearly everywhere you look in Umbria, olive trees grace the hillsides. The soil of the Apennines allows the olives to ripen slowly, guaranteeing low acidity, a cardinal virtue of fine oil. Look for restaurants that proudly display their own oil, often a sign that they care about their food.

Umbria's finest oil is found in Trevi, where the local product is intensely green and fruity. You can sample it in the town's wine bars, which often do double duty, offering olive-oil tastings.

PORK PRODUCTS

Much of traditional Umbrian cuisine revolves around pork. It can be cooked in wood-fire stoves, sometimes basted with a rich sauce made from innards and red wine. The roasted pork known as *porchetta (pictured at left)* is grilled on a spit and flavored with fennel and herbs, leaving a crisp outer sheen.

The art of pork processing has been handed down through generations in Norcia, so much so that charcuterie producers throughout Italy are often known as *norcini*. Don't miss *prosciutto di Norcia*, which is aged for two years.

LENTILS AND SOUPS

The town of Castelluccio di Norcia is particularly known for its lentils and its farro (an ancient grain used by the Romans, similar to wheat), and a variety of beans used in soups. Throughout

Umbria, look for *imbrecciata*, a soup of beans and grains, delicately flavored with local herbs. Other ingredients that find their way into thick Umbrian soups are wild beet, sorrel, mushrooms, spelt, chickpeas, and the elusive, fragrant saffron, grown in nearby Cascia.

WINE

Sagrantino grapes are the star in Umbria's most notable red wines. For centuries they've been used in Sagrantino *passito*, a semisweet wine made by leaving the grapes to dry for a period after picking in order to intensify their sugar content. In recent decades, Montefalco Sagrantino *secco* (dry) has occupied the front stage. Both passito and secco have a deep red-ruby color, with a full body and rich flavor.

In the past few years the phenomenon of the *enoteca* (wineshop and wine bar) has taken off, making it easier to arrange wine tastings. Many also let you sample different olive oils on toasted bread, known as bruschetta. Some wine information centers, such as La Strada del Sagrantino in the town of Montefalco, will help set up appointments for tastings.

Updated by Peter Blackman and Patricia Rucidlo

No place better epitomizes the beauty and splendor of Italy than the central regions of Tuscany and Umbria. They are both characterized by midsize cities and small hilltop towns, each with its own rich history and art treasures. Highlights include the walled city of Lucca; Pisa and its Leaning Tower; Siena, home of the Palio; and Assisi, the city of St. Francis. In between, the gorgeous countryside produces some of Italy's finest wine.

PLANNER

WHEN TO GO

Throughout Tuscany and Umbria, the best times to visit are spring and fall. Days are warm, nights are cool, and though there are still tourists, the crowds are smaller. In the countryside the scenery is gorgeous, with abundant greenery and flowers in spring, and burnished leaves in autumn.

July and August are the most popular times to visit. Note, though, that the heat is often oppressive and mosquitoes are prevalent. Try to start your days early and visit major sights first to beat the crowds and the midday sun. For relief from the heat, head to the mountains of the Garfagnana, where hiking is spectacular, or hit the beach at resort towns such as Forte dei Marmi and Viareggio, along the Maremma coast, on the island of Elba, or on the long, flat stretches of sandy beach on the east coast of the Marches.

November through March you might wonder who invented the term "sunny Italy." The panoramas are still beautiful, even with overcast skies, frequent rain, and occasional snow. In winter Florence benefits from shorter museum lines and less competition for restaurant tables. Outside the cities, though, many hotels and restaurants close for the season.

MAKING THE MOST OF YOUR TIME

Central Italy isn't the place for a jam-packed itinerary. One of the greatest pleasures here is indulging in rustic hedonism, marked by long lunches and show-stopping sunsets. Whether by car, by bike, or on foot, you'll want to get out into the glorious landscape, but it's smart to keep your plans modest. Set a church or a hill town or an out-of-the-way restaurant as your destination, knowing that half the pleasure is in getting there—admiring as you go the stately palaces, the tidy geometry of row upon row of grapevines, the fields vibrant with red poppies, sunflowers, and yellow broom.

In Tuscany, you'll need to devise a strategy for seeing the sights. Take Siena: this beautiful, art-filled town simply can't be missed; it's compact enough that you can see the major sights on a day trip, and that's exactly what most people do. Spend the night, though, and you'll get to see the town breathe a sigh and relax on the day-trippers' departure. In Pisa, the famous tower and rest of the Camposanto are not only worth seeing but a must-see, a highlight of any trip to Italy. But nearby Lucca must not be overlooked either. In fact, this walled town has greater charms than Pisa does, making it a better choice for an overnight, so you should come up with a plan that takes in both places.

Umbria is a nicely compact collection of character-rich hill towns; you can settle in one, then explore the others, as well as the countryside and forest in between, on day trips. Perugia, Umbria's largest and liveliest city, is a logical choice for your base, particularly if you're arriving from the north. If you want something a little quieter, virtually any other town in the region will suit your purposes; even Assisi, which overflows with bus tours during the day, is delightfully quiet in the evening and early morning. Spoleto and Orvieto are the most developed towns to the south, but they're still of modest proportions.

GETTING HERE AND AROUND

Most flights to Tuscany originating in the United States stop either in Rome, London, Paris, or Frankfurt, and then connect to Florence's small **Aeroporto A. Vespucci** (commonly called Peretola), or to Pisa's **Aeroporto Galileo Galilei.** Delta currently has one seasonal direct flight from New York (JFK) to Pisa.

Alternatively, it's an hour by train or an hour and a half by car to reach the lovely town of Orvieto from Rome's **Aeroporto Leonardo da Vinci** (commonly called Fiumicino). Another option is to fly to Milan and pick up a connecting flight to Pisa, Florence, Perugia, or Ancona in the Marches.

Buses are a reliable but time-consuming means of getting around the region because they tend to stop in every town. Trains are a better option in virtually every respect when you're headed to Pisa, Lucca, Arezzo, and other cities with good rail service. But for most smaller towns, buses are the only option. Be aware that making arrangements for bus travel, particularly for a non-Italian speaker, can be a test of patience. Several direct daily trains run by the Italian state railway, **Trenitalia** (☎ *892021* ⊕ *www.trenitalia.com*), link Florence and Rome with Perugia and Assisi, and local service to the same area is available from Terontola (on the Rome–Florence line) and from Foligno (on the Rome–Ancona line). Intercity trains between Rome and Florence make stops in Orvieto, and the main Rome–Ancona line passes through Narni, Terni, Spoleto, and Foligno..

Driving is the only way (other than hiking or biking) to reach many of Central Italy's small towns and vineyards.

RESTAURANTS

A meal in Central Italy traditionally consists of five courses, and every menu you enounter will be organized along this plan of antipasto, primo, secondo, contorno, and dolce. The crucial rule of restaurant dining is that you should order at least two courses. Otherwise, you'll likely end up with a lonely piece of meat and no sides.

HOTELS

A visit to Central Italy is a trip into the country. There are plenty of good hotels in the larger towns, but the classic experience is to stay in one of the rural accommodations—often converted private homes, sometimes working farms or vineyards (known as *agriturismi*). Virtually every older town, no matter how small, has some kind of hotel. A trend, particularly around Gubbio, Orvieto, and Todi, is to convert old villas, farms, and monasteries into first-class hotels. The natural splendor of the countryside more than compensates for the distance from town—provided you have a car. Hotels in town tend to be simpler than their country cousins, with a few notable exceptions in Spoleto, Gubbio, and Perugia.

Although it's tempting to think you can stumble upon a little out-of-the-way hotel at the end of the day, you're better off not testing your luck. Make reservations before you go. If you don't have a reservation, you may be able to get help finding a room from the local tourist office. *Hotel reviews have been shortened. For full information, visit Fodors.com.*

WHAT IT COSTS				
	$	**$$**	**$$$**	**$$$$**
Restaurants	under €15	€15–€24	€25–€35	over €35
Hotels	under €125	€125–€200	€201–€300	over €300

Prices in the dining reviews are the average cost of a main course at dinner, or, if dinner is not served, at lunch. Prices in the reviews are the lowest cost of a standard double room in high season.

TUSCANY

Midway down the Italian peninsula, Tuscany (Toscana in Italian) is distinguished by rolling hills, snowcapped mountains, dramatic cypress trees, and miles of coastline on the Tyrrhenian Sea—which all adds up to gorgeous views at practically every turn. The beauty of the landscape proves a perfect foil for the region's abundance of superlative art and architecture. It also produces some of Italy's finest wines and olive oils. The combination of unforgettable art, sumptuous landscapes, and eminently drinkable wines that pair beautifully with its simple food makes a trip to Tuscany something beyond special.

Many of Tuscany's cities and towns have retained the same fundamental character over the past 500 years. Civic rivalries that led to bloody battles centuries ago have given way to soccer rivalries. Renaissance pomp lives on in the celebration of local feast days and centuries-old traditions such as the Palio in Siena and the Giostra del Saracino (Joust of the Saracen) in Arezzo. Often, present-day Tuscans look as though they might have served as models for paintings produced hundreds of years ago. In many ways, the Renaissance lives on in Tuscany.

LUCCA

Ramparts built in the 16th and 17th centuries enclose a charming fortress town filled with churches (99 of them), terra-cotta–roofed buildings, and narrow cobblestone streets, along which locals maneuver bikes to do their daily shopping. Here Caesar, Pompey, and Crassus agreed to rule Rome as a triumvirate in 56 BC; Lucca was later the first Tuscan town to accept Christianity. The town still has a mind of its own, and when most of Tuscany was voting communist as a matter of course, Lucca's citizens rarely followed suit. The famous composer Giacomo Puccini (1858–1924) was born here; he is celebrated during the summer Opera Theater and Music Festival of Lucca. The ramparts circling the centro storico are the perfect place to stroll, bicycle, or just admire the view.

GETTING HERE AND AROUND

You can reach Lucca easily by train from Florence; the centro storico is a short walk from the station. If you're driving, take the A11/E76.

VISITOR INFORMATION

Lucca Tourism Office. ✉ *Piazza Verdi, Lucca* ☎ *0583/91991* ⊕ *www.tur-ismo.provincia.lucca.it/en.*

EXPLORING

Traffic (including motorbikes) is restricted in the walled historic center of Lucca. Walking is the best, most enjoyable way to get around. Or you can rent a bicycle; getting around on bike is easy, as the center is quite flat.

TOP ATTRACTIONS

Duomo. The blind arches on the cathedral's facade are a fine example of the rigorously ordered Pisan Romanesque style, in this case happily enlivened by an extremely varied collection of small, carved columns. Take a closer look at the decoration of the facade and that of the portico below; they make this one of the most entertaining church exteriors in Tuscany. The Gothic interior contains a moving Byzantine crucifix—called the Volto Santo, or Holy Face—brought here, according to legend, in the 8th century (though it probably dates from between the

11th and early 13th centuries). The masterpiece of the Sienese sculptor Jacopo della Quercia (circa 1371–1438) is the marble *Tomb of Ilaria del Carretto* (1407–08). ⊠ *Piazza San Martino, Lucca* ☎ *0583/490530* ⊕ *www.museocattedralelucca.it* ✎ *Church free, tomb €3.*

FAMILY **Passeggiata delle Mura.** Any time of day when the weather is nice, you can find the citizens of Lucca cycling, jogging, strolling, or kicking a soccer ball in this green, beautiful, and very large park—neither inside nor outside the city but rather right atop and around the ring of ramparts that defines Lucca. Sunlight streams through two rows of tall plane trees to dapple the *passeggiata delle mura* (walk on the walls), which is 4.2 km (2½ miles) in length. Ten bulwarks are topped with lawns, many with picnic tables and some with play equipment for children. Be aware at all times of where the edge is—there are no railings, and the drop to the ground outside the city is a precipitous 40 feet. ⊠ *Lucca* ⊕ *www.lemuradilucca.it.*

FAMILY **Piazza dell'Anfiteatro Romano.** Here's where the ancient Roman amphitheater once stood; some of the medieval buildings built over the amphitheater retain its original oval shape and brick arches. ⊠ *Piazza Anfiteatro, Lucca.*

San Frediano. A 14th-century mosaic decorates the facade of this church just steps from the Anfiteatro. Inside are works by Jacopo della Quercia (circa 1371–1438) and Matteo Civitali (1436–1501), as well as the lace-clad mummy of St. Zita (circa 1218–78), the patron saint of household servants. ⊠ *Piazza San Frediano, Lucca* ☎ *No phone.*

San Michele in Foro. The facade here is even more fanciful than that of the Duomo. Its upper levels have nothing but air behind them (after the front of the church was built, there were no funds to raise the nave), and the winged Archangel Michael, who stands at the very top, seems precariously poised for flight. The facade, heavily restored in the 19th century, displays busts of such 19th-century Italian patriots as Garibaldi and Cavour. Check out the superb Filippino Lippi (1457/58–1504) panel painting of Saints Jerome, Sebastian, Rocco, and Helen in the right transept. ⊠ *Piazza San Michele, Lucca.*

FAMILY **Torre Guinigi.** The tower of the medieval Palazzo Guinigi contains one of the city's most curious sights: a grove of ilex trees has grown at the top of the tower, and their roots have pushed their way into the room below. From the top you have a magnificent view of the city and the surrounding countryside. (Only the tower is open to the public, not the palazzo.) ⊠ *Via Sant'Andrea, Lucca* ☎ *0583/583086* ✎ *€4.*

WORTH NOTING

Museo Nazionale di Villa Guinigi. On the eastern end of the historic center, this sadly overlooked museum has an extensive collection of local Etruscan, Roman, Romanesque, and Renaissance art. The museum represents an overview of Lucca's artistic traditions from Etruscan times until the 17th century, housed in the former 15th-century villa of the Guinigi family. ⊠ *Via della Quarquonia 4, Lucca* ☎ *0583/496033* ⊕ *www.luccamuseinazionali.it* ✎ *€4.*

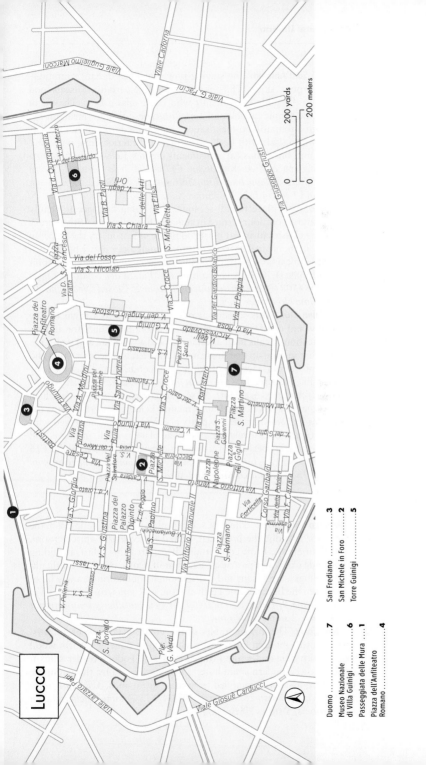

Lucca

Duomo **7**
Museo Nazionale
di Villa Guinigi **6**
Passeggiata delle Mura **1**
Piazza dell'Anfiteatro
Romano **4**

San Frediano **3**
San Michele in Foro **2**
Torre Guinigi **5**

0   200 yards
0   200 meters

WHERE TO EAT

$$ TUSCAN Fodor's Choice ★ 🍴 **Buca di Sant'Antonio.** The staying power of Buca di Sant'Antonio—it's been around since 1782—is the result of superlative Tuscan food brought to the table by waitstaff who don't miss a beat. The menu includes the simple but blissful *tortelli lucchesi al sugo* (meat-stuffed pasta with a tomato-and-meat sauce), and more daring dishes such as roast *capretto* (kid) with herbs. A white-wall interior hung with copper pots and brass musical instruments creates a classy but comfortable dining space. [$] *Average main: €17* ✉ *Via della Cervia 3, Lucca* ☎ *0583/55881* 🌐 *www.bucadisantantonio.com* ⏲ *Closed Mon., 1 wk in Jan., and 1 wk in July. No dinner Sun.*

$$ TUSCAN 🍴 **Il Giglio.** This place for all seasons, with a big fireplace for chilly weather and an outdoor terrace in summer, has quiet late-19th-century charm and classic cuisine. If mushrooms are in season, try the *tacchoni con funghi,* a homemade pasta with mushrooms and a native herb called *nepitella.* A local favorite during winter is the *coniglio con olive* (rabbit stew with olives). [$] *Average main: €16* ✉ *Piazza del Giglio 2, Lucca* ☎ *0583/494508* 🌐 *www.ristorantegiglio.com* ⏲ *Closed Wed., and 15 days in Nov. No dinner Tues.*

$$ TUSCAN Fodor's Choice ★ 🍴 **Port Ellen Clan.** This somewhat odd name refers to a town on the Scottish island of Islay, in the Hebrides, where the proprietor and his family vacation. It calls itself a restaurant and a wine bar, and it also is a whiskey bar serving up fine single malts and blends. The interesting and short menu offers a selection of primi and secondi, as well as some tasty antipasti like the *capesante tostato su purée di melanzane e olive* (grilled scallops with pureed eggplant). All secondi come with a side dish, which is somewhat of a novelty on Italian menus. Eclectic desserts such as the *pera cotta nel wine con gelato* (pears poached in red wine served with ice cream) provide a lovely end note. The place is small, intimate, and candlelit at night: perfect for a romantic meal. [$] *Average main: €16* ✉ *Via del Fosso 120, Lucca* ☎ *0583/493952* 🌐 *www.portellenclan.com* ⏲ *Closed Tues. No lunch Mon. and Wed.–Sat. No dinner Sun.*

WHERE TO STAY

$ B&B/INN FAMILY Fodor's Choice ★ 🏨 **Albergo San Martino.** The brocade bedspreads are fresh and crisp, the proprietor friendly, the breakfast, served in a cheerful apricot room, more than ample. **Pros:** comfortable beds; great breakfast, including homemade cakes and pastries; friendly staff. **Cons:** parking is difficult; surroundings are pleasant and stylish though not luxurious; a wee bit of noise when the Lucca Music Festival is on. [$] *Rooms from: €110* ✉ *Via della Dogana 9, Lucca* ☎ *0583/469181* 🌐 *www.albergosanmartino.it* 🛏 *6 rooms, 2 suites* 🍽 *No meals.*

$$ HOTEL 🏨 **Hotel Ilaria.** The former stables of the Villa Bottini have been transformed into a modern hotel with stylish rooms done in a warm wood veneer with blue-and-white fittings. **Pros:** one Fodor's reader sums it up as a "nice, modern small hotel"; free bicycles. **Cons:** though in the city center, it's a little removed from main attractions. [$] *Rooms from: €159* ✉ *Via del Fosso 26, Lucca* ☎ *0583/47615* 🌐 *www.hotelilaria.com* 🛏 *36 rooms, 5 suites* 🍽 *Breakfast.*

$$ 🏨 **Palazzo Alexander.** The building, dating from the 12th century, has
HOTEL been restructured to create the ease common to Lucchesi nobility: tim-
bered ceilings, warm yellow walls, and brocaded chairs adorn the public
rooms, and guest rooms have high ceilings and that same glorious dam-
ask. **Pros:** intimate feel; gracious staff; bacon and eggs included in the
buffet breakfast; a short walk from San Michele in Foro. **Cons:** some
Fodor's readers complain of too-thin walls. $ *Rooms from: €180* ✉ *Via
S. Giustina 48, Lucca* ☎ *0583/583571* ⊕ *www.hotelpalazzoalexander.
it* ↝ *9 rooms, 3 suites, 1 apartment* ⦿ *Breakfast.*

$ 🏨 **Piccolo Hotel Puccini.** Steps away from the busy square and church of
HOTEL San Michele, this little hotel is quiet and calm—and a great deal. **Pros:**
cheery, English-speaking staff. **Cons:** breakfast costs extra; some rooms
are on the dark side. $ *Rooms from: €100* ✉ *Via di Poggio 9, Lucca*
☎ *0583/55421* ⊕ *www.hotelpuccini.com* ↝ *14 rooms* ⦿ *No meals.*

SPORTS AND THE OUTDOORS

A good way to spend the afternoon is to go biking around the large
path atop the city's ramparts. There are two good spots right next to
each other where you can rent bikes. The prices are about the same
(about €12.50 per day and €2.50 per hour for city bikes) and they are
centrally located, just beside the town wall.

Berutto Nedo. The vendors at Berutto Nedo, who sell bikes near the
Piazza dell'Anfiteatro, are friendly and speak English. ✉ *Via dei Gas-
pari Alcide 83/r, Anfiteatro* ☎ *0583/517073* ⊕ *www.beruttonedo.com.*

Poli Antonio Biciclette. This is the best option for bicycle rental on the east
side of town. ✉ *Piazza Santa Maria 42, Lucca East* ☎ *0583/493787*
⊕ *www.biciclettepoli.com.*

SHOPPING

Lucca's justly famed olive oils are available throughout the city (and
exported around the world). Look for those made by Fattoria di Fub-
biano and Fattoria Fabbri—two of the best.

Caniparoli. Chocolate lovers will be pleased with the selection of arti-
sanal chocolates. This artisanal shop is so serious about their sweets
that they do not make any in August because of the heat. ✉ *Via San
Paolino 96, Lucca* ☎ *0583/53456* ⊕ *www.caniparolicioccolateria.it.*

Fodor's Choice **Enoteca Vanni.** A huge selection of wines, as well as an ancient cellar,
★ make this place worth a stop. For the cost of the wine only, tastings
can be organized through the shopkeepers and are held in the cellar or
outside in a lovely little piazza. All of this can be paired with affettati
misti and cheeses of the highest caliber. ✉ *Piazza del Salvatore 7, Lucca*
☎ *0583/491902* ⊕ *www.enotecavanni.com.*

Fodor's Choice **Pasticceria Taddeucci.** A particularly delicious version of *buccellato*—the
★ sweet, anise-flavored bread with raisins that is a Luccan specialty—
is baked at Pasticceria Taddeucci. ✉ *Piazza San Michele 34, Lucca*
☎ *0583/494933* ⊕ *www.buccellatotaddeucci.com.*

PISA

If you can get beyond the kitsch of the stalls hawking cheap souvenirs around the Leaning Tower, you'll find that Pisa has much to offer. Its treasures aren't as abundant as those of Florence, to which it is inevitably compared, but the cathedral-baptistery-tower complex of Piazza del Duomo, known collectively as the Campo dei Miracoli (Field of Miracles), is among the most dramatic settings in Italy.

Pisa may have been inhabited as early as the Bronze Age. It was certainly populated by the Etruscans and, in turn, became part of the Roman Empire. In the early Middle Ages it flourished as an economic powerhouse—along with Amalfi, Genoa, and Venice, it was one of the four maritime republics. The city's economic and political power ebbed in the early 15th century as it fell under Florence's domination, though it enjoyed a brief resurgence under Cosimo I in the mid-16th century. Pisa sustained heavy damage during World War II, but the Duomo and Tower were spared, along with some other grand Romanesque structures.

GETTING HERE AND AROUND

Pisa is an easy hour's train ride from Florence. By car it's a straight shot on the Firenze–Pisa–Livorno ("Fi-Pi-Li") autostrada. The Pisa–Lucca train runs frequently and takes about 30 minutes.

VISITOR INFORMATION

Pisa Tourism Office. ⊠ *Piazza Vittorio Emanuele II 16, Pisa* ☎ *050/42291* ⊕ *www.pisaunicaterra.it.*

EXPLORING

Pisa, like many Italian cities, is best explored on foot, and most of what you'll want to see is within walking distance. The views along the Arno River are particularly grand and shouldn't be missed—there's a feeling of spaciousness that isn't found along the Arno in Florence.

As you set out, note that there are various combination-ticket options for sights on the Piazza del Duomo.

TOP ATTRACTIONS

Battistero. This lovely Gothic baptistery, which stands across from the Duomo's facade, is best known for the pulpit carved by Nicola Pisano (circa 1220–84; father of Giovanni Pisano) in 1260. Every half hour, an employee will dramatically close the doors, then intone, thereby demonstrating how remarkable the acoustics are in the place. ⊠ *Piazza del Duomo, Pisa* ☎ *050/835011* ⊕ *www.opapisa.it* ☜ *€5, discounts available if bought in combination with tickets for other monuments.*

Duomo. Pisa's cathedral brilliantly utilizes the horizontal marble-stripe motif (borrowed from Moorish architecture) that became common to Tuscan cathedrals. It is famous for the Romanesque panels on the transept door facing the tower that depict scenes from the life of Christ. The beautifully carved 14th-century pulpit is by Giovanni Pisano. ⊠ *Piazza del Duomo, Pisa* ☎ *050/835011* ⊕ *www.opapisa.it* ☜ *€5.*

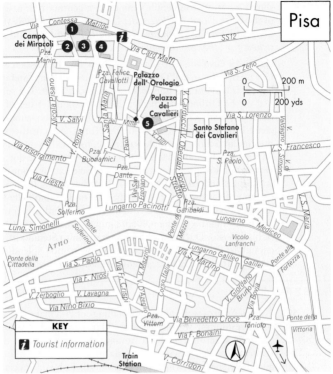

Leaning Tower (Torre Pendente). Legend holds that Galileo conducted an experiment on the nature of gravity by dropping metal balls from the top of the 187-foot-high Leaning Tower of Pisa (whether it's true is a matter of debate). Work on this tower, built as a campanile for the Duomo, started in 1173: the lopsided settling began when construction reached the third story. The tower's architects attempted to compensate by making the remaining floors slightly taller on the leaning side, but the extra weight made the problem worse. By the late 20th century, many feared the tower would simply topple over. The structure has since been firmly anchored to the earth, and by 2002, the tower was restored to its original tilt of 300 years ago. Reservations, which are essential, can be made online or by calling the Museo dell'Opera del Duomo; it's also possible to arrive at the ticket office and book for the same day. ⊠ *Piazza del Duomo, Pisa* ☎ *050/835011* ⊕ *www.opapisa.it* ☎ *€18.*

WORTH NOTING

Camposanto. According to legend, the cemetery—a walled structure on the western side of the Piazza dei Miracoli—is filled with earth that returning Crusaders brought back from the Holy Land. Contained within are numerous frescoes, notably *The Drunkenness of Noah,* by Renaissance artist Benozzo Gozzoli (1422–97), and the disturbing *Triumph of Death* (14th century; artist uncertain), whose subject matter shows what was on people's minds in a century that saw the ravages of the Black Death. ✉ *Piazza del Duomo, Pisa* ☎ *050/835011* 🌐 *www.opapisa.it* 🎟 *€5, discounts available if bought in combination with tickets for other monuments.*

Piazza dei Cavalieri. The piazza, with its fine Renaissance **Palazzo dei Cavalieri, Palazzo dell'Orologio,** and Chiesa di **Santo Stefano dei Cavalieri,** was laid out by Giorgio Vasari in about 1560. The square was the seat of the Ordine dei Cavalieri di San Stefano (Order of the Knights of St. Stephen), a military and religious institution meant to defend the coast from possible invasion by the Turks. Also in this square is the prestigious **Scuola Normale Superiore,** founded by Napoléon in 1810 on the French model. Here graduate students pursue doctorates in literature, philosophy, mathematics, and science. In front of the school is a large statue of Ferdinando I de' Medici dating from 1596. On the extreme left is the tower where the hapless Ugolino della Gherardesca (died 1289) was imprisoned with his two sons and two grandsons—legend holds that he ate them. Dante immortalized him in Canto XXXIII of his *Inferno*. Duck into the **Church of Santo Stefano** (if you're lucky enough to find it open) and check out Bronzino's splendid *Nativity of Christ* (1564–65). ✉ *Piazza dei Cavalieri, Pisa.*

WHERE TO EAT

$$$ TUSCAN Fodor's Choice ★ 🍴 **Beny.** Apricot walls hung with etchings of Pisa make this small, single-room restaurant warmly romantic. Husband and wife Damiano and Sandra Lazzerini have been running the place for two decades, and it shows in their obvious enthusiasm while talking about the menu and daily specials (which often astound). Fish is a specialty here: the *ripieno di polpa di pesce a pan grattato con salsa di seppie e pomodoro* (fish-stuffed ravioli with tomato-octopus sauce) delights. Seasonal ingredients are key throughout the menu; Sandra works wonders with *tartufi estivi* (summer truffles), artichokes, and market fish of the day. Remember to save room for desserts as they are scumptious. [$] *Average main: €27* ✉ *Piazza Gambacorti 22, Pisa* ☎ *050/25067* ⏲ *Closed Sun., and 2 wks in mid-Aug. No lunch Sat.*

$ ITALIAN 🍴 **Osteria dei Cavalieri.** This charming white-wall restaurant, a few steps from Piazza dei Cavalieri, is reason enough to come to Pisa. They can do it all here—serve up exquisitely grilled fish dishes, please vegetarians, and prepare tagliata for meat lovers. Three set menus, from the sea, garden, and earth, are available, or you can order à la carte. For dinner there's an early seating (around 7:30) and a later one (around 9); opt for the later one if you want time to linger over your meal. [$] *Average main: €14* ✉ *Via San Frediano 16, Pisa* ☎ *050/580858* 🌐 *www.osteriacavalieri.pisa.it* ⏲ *Closed Sun., 2 wks in Aug., and Dec. 29–Jan. 7. No lunch Sat.*

$ ITALIAN 🍴 **Trattoria la Faggiola.** It's only seconds away from the Leaning Tower, which probably explains the "No Pizza" sign written in big, bold letters on the blackboard outside. Inside, another blackboard lists two or three primi and secondi .The problem is deciding, because everything's good, from the *pasta pasticciata con speck e carciofi* (oven-baked penne with cured ham and artichokes) to the finishing touch of *castagnaccio con crema di ricotta* (a chestnut flan topped with ricotta cream). [$] *Average main: €10* ✉ *Via della Faggiola 1, Pisa* ☎ *050/556179* 🌐 *www.trattoriadellafaggiola.it* 💳 *No credit cards* 🕓 *Closed Tues.*

WHERE TO STAY

$ B&B/INN FAMILY Fodor's Choice ★ 🏨 **Fattoria di Migliarino.** Martino Salviati and his wife Giovanna have turned their working *fattoria* (farm)—on which they raise soybeans, corn, and sugar beets—into an inn. **Pros:** near Pisa airport, a good choice for a tranquil last night in Italy. **Cons:** mandatory one-week apartment stay during high season. [$] *Rooms from: €110* ✉ *Via dei Pini 289, 10 km (6 miles) northwest of Pisa, Migliarino* ☎ *050/803046, 335/6608411 mobile, 050/803170* 🌐 *www.fattoriadimigliarino.it* 🛏 *10 rooms in B&B, 13 apartments* 🍴 *Breakfast.*

$$ HOTEL 🏨 **Hotel Relais dell'Orologio.** What used to be a private family palace is now an intimate hideaway where 18th-century antiques fill the rooms and public spaces and some rooms have stenciled walls and wood-beam ceilings. **Pros:** location—in the center of town, but on a quiet side street. **Cons:** breakfast costs extra. [$] *Rooms from: €150* ✉ *Via della Faggiola 12/14, off Campo dei Miracoli, Pisa* ☎ *050/830361* 🌐 *www.hotelrelaisorologio.com* 🛏 *16 rooms, 5 suites* 🍴 *No meals.*

CHIANTI

This is the heartland: both sides of the Strada Chiantigiana (SR222) are embraced by glorious panoramic views of vineyards, olive groves, and castle towers. Traveling south from Florence, you first reach the aptly named one-street town of Strada in Chianti. Farther south, the number of vineyards on either side of the road dramatically increases—as do the signs inviting you in for a free tasting of wine. Beyond Strada lies Greve in Chianti, completely surrounded by wineries and filled with wineshops. There's art to be had as well: Passignano, west of Greve, has an abbey that shelters a 15th-century *Last Supper* by Domenico and Davide Ghirlandaio. Farther still, along the Strada Chiantigiana, are Panzano and Castellina in Chianti, both hill towns. It's from near Panzano and Castellina that branch roads head to the other main towns of eastern Chianti: Radda in Chianti, Gaiole in Chianti, and Castelnuovo Berardenga.

The Strada Chiantigiana gets crowded during the high season, but no one is in a hurry. The slow pace gives you time to soak up the beautiful scenery.

GREVE IN CHIANTI

27 km (17 miles) south of Florence, 40 km (25 miles) northeast of Colle Val d'Elsa.

If there is a capital of Chianti, it is Greve, a friendly market town with no shortage of cafés, enoteche, and crafts shops lining its streets.

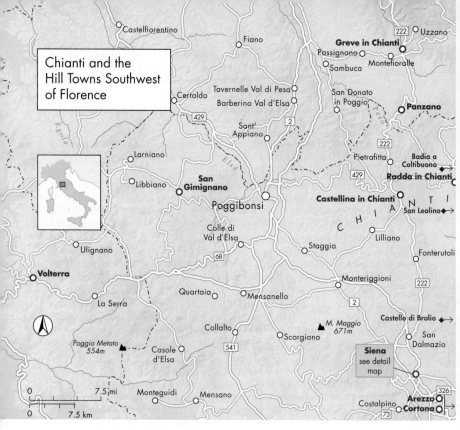

The map shows the following labeled locations:

Castelfiorentino, Fiano, Uzzano, 222, Greve in Chianti, Passignano, Montefioralle, Sambuca, Chianti and the Hill Towns Southwest of Florence, Certaldo, Tavernelle Val di Pesa, Barberino Val d'Elsa, San Donato in Poggio, Panzano, 429, 2, Sant' Appiano, Pietrafitta, Badia a Coltibuono, Larniano, 222, Radda in Chianti, 429, Libbiano, San Gimignano, Castellina in Chianti, Poggibonsi, San Leolino, Colle di Val d'Elsa, Staggia, Lilliano, Ulignano, 68, Fonterutoli, Volterra, Quartaia, Mensanello, Monteriggioni, 222, La Serra, 2, Collalto, M. Maggio 671m, Castello di Brolio, Poggio Metato 554m, Casole d'Elsa, Scorgiano, 541, San Dalmazio, Siena see detail map, Arezzo, 326, Monteguidi, Mensano, Costalpino, Cortona, 73, Egola, Elsa, Pesa, C H I A N T I

0 ——— 7.5 mi
0 ——— 7.5 km

GETTING HERE AND AROUND

Driving from Florence or Siena, Greve is easily reached via the Strada Chiantigiana (SR222). SITA buses travel frequently between Florence and Greve. Tra-In and SITA buses connect Siena and Greve, but a direct trip is virtually impossible. There is no train service.

VISITOR INFORMATION

Greve in Chianti tourism office. ⊠ *Piazza Matteotti 10* ☏ *055/8546299.*

EXPLORING

Montefioralle. A tiny hilltop hamlet, about 2 km (1 mile) west of Greve in Chianti, Montefioralle is the ancestral home of Amerigo Vespucci (1454–1512), the mapmaker, navigator, and explorer who named America. (His niece Simonetta may have been the inspiration for Sandro Botticelli's *Birth of Venus*, painted sometime in the 1480s.) ⊠ *Greve in Chianti.*

Piazza Matteotti. Greve's gently sloping and asymmetrical central piazza is surrounded by an attractive arcade with shops of all kinds. In the center stands a statue of the discoverer of New York harbor, Giovanni da Verrazano (circa 1480–1527). Check out the lively market held here on Saturday morning. ⊠ *Greve in Chianti.*

WHERE TO EAT

$$
TUSCAN
⨉**Da Padellina.** Locals don't flock to this restaurant on the outskirts of Strada in Chianti for the art on the walls, some of it questionable, most of it kitsch, but for the bistecca fiorentina. As big as a breadboard and served rare, one of these justly renowned steaks is enough to feed a family of four, with doggy bags willingly provided if required! First courses are typical, desserts are standard, but the wine list is a varied and extensive surprise. Outdoor seating on the upstairs terrace provides great views of the surrounding countryside. $ *Average main: €15* ⨉ *Via Corso del Popolo 54, 10 km (6 miles) north of Greve* ☎ *055/858388* ⊕ *www.ristorantedapadellina.com* ⊘ *Closed Tues.*

$
TUSCAN
⨉**Enoteca Fuoripiazza.** Detour off Greve's flower-strewn main square for food that relies heavily on local ingredients (like cheese and salami produced nearby). The lengthy wine list provides a bewildering array of choices to pair with affettati misti or one of their primi—the *pici* (a thick, short noodle) are deftly prepared here. All dishes are made with great care and outdoor seating makes summer dining particularly pleasant. $ *Average main: €14* ⨉ *Via I Maggio 2* ☎ *055/8546313* ⊕ *www. enotecafuoripiazza.it* ⊘ *Closed Mon.*

$$$
TUSCAN
⨉**Ristoro di Lamole.** Although off the beaten path up a winding road lined with olive trees and vineyards, this place is worth the effort to find. The view from the outdoor terrace is divine, as is the simple, exquisitely prepared Tuscan cuisine. Start with the bruschetta drizzled with olive oil or the sublime *verdure sott'olio* (marinated vegetables) before moving on to any of the fine secondi. The kitchen has a way with *coniglio* (rabbit); don't pass it up if it's on the menu. $ *Average main: €30* ⨉ *Via di Lamole 6, Località Lamole* ☎ *055/8547050* ⊕ *www.ristorodilamole. it* ⊘ *Closed Wed., and Nov.–Apr.*

WHERE TO STAY

$
B&B/INN
Albergo del Chianti. Simply but pleasantly decorated bedrooms with plain modern cabinets and wardrobes and wrought-iron beds have views of the town square or out over the tile rooftops toward the surrounding hills. **Pros:** central location; best value in Greve. **Cons:** rooms facing the piazza can be noisy; small bathrooms. $ *Rooms from: €100* ⨉ *Piazza Matteotti 86* ☎ *055/853763* ⊕ *www.albergodelchianti.it* ⊘ *Closed Jan.* ⬱ *16 rooms* ⫯◎⫯ *Breakfast.*

$$$
B&B/INN
Fodor'sChoice
★
Villa Bordoni. David and Catherine Gardner, Scottish expats, have transformed a ramshackle 16th-century villa into a stunning little retreat where no two rooms are alike—all have stenciled walls; some have four-poster beds, others small mezzanines. **Pros:** splendidly isolated in the hills above Greve; beautiful decor; wonderful hosts. **Cons:** on a long and bumpy dirt road; need a car to get around. $ *Rooms from: €245* ⨉ *Via San Cresci 31/32* ☎ *055/8546230* ⊕ *www.villabordoni.com* ⊘ *Closed 3 wks in Jan. and Feb.* ⬱ *8 rooms, 3 suites* ⫯◎⫯ *Breakfast.*

$$
B&B/INN
Fodor'sChoice
★
Villa Il Poggiale. Renaissance gardens, beautiful rooms with high ceilings and elegant furnishings, a panoramic pool, and expert staff are just a few of the things that make a stay at this 16th-century villa memorable. **Pros:** beautiful gardens and panoramic setting; elegant historical building; exceptionally professional staff. **Cons:** a little isolated, making private transportation necessary; some rooms face a country road and

may be noisy during the day. $ *Rooms from: €160* ✉ *Via Empolese 69, 20 km (12 miles) northwest of Greve, San Casciano Val di Pesa* ☎ *055/828311* ⊕ *www.villailpoggiale.it* ⊘ *Closed Jan. and Feb.* ⤳ *20 rooms, 4 suites* ⎺⎺⎺⎺ *Breakfast.*

SHOPPING

Enoteca del Gallo Nero. This is one of the best-stocked enoteche in the whole Chianti region, with a wide selection of labels. ✉ *Piazzetta S. Croce 8* ☎ *055/853297.*

PANZANO

7 km (4½ miles) south of Greve, 36 km (22 miles) south of Florence.

The magnificent views of the valleys of the Pesa and Greve rivers easily make Panzano one of the prettiest stops in Chianti. The triangular Piazza Bucciarelli is the heart of the new town. A short stroll along Via Giovanni da Verrazzano brings you up to the old town, Panzano Alto, which is still partly surrounded by medieval walls. The town's 13th-century castle is now almost completely absorbed by later buildings (its central tower is now a private home).

GETTING HERE AND AROUND

From Florence or Siena, Panzano is easily reached by car along the Strada Chiantigiana (SR222). SITA buses travel frequently between Florence and Panzano. From Siena, the journey by bus is extremely difficult because SITA and Tra-In do not coordinate their schedules. Train service is not available.

EXPLORING

San Leolino. Ancient even by Chianti standards, this hilltop church probably dates from the 10th century, but was completely rebuilt in the Romanesque style sometime in the 13th century. It has a 14th-century cloister worth seeing. The 16th-century terra-cotta tabernacles are attributed to Giovanni della Robbia, and there's also a remarkable triptych (attributed to the Master of Panzano) that was executed sometime in the mid-14th century. Open days and hours are unpredictable; check with the tourist office in Greve in Chianti for the latest. ✉ *Località San Leolino, 3 km (2 miles) south of Panzano* ☎ *055/8546299.*

WHERE TO EAT AND STAY

$$
INTERNATIONAL
FAMILY

✕ **Dario Doc.** Local butcher and restaurateur, Dario Cecchini, has extended his empire of meat to include this space located directly above his butcher's shop. Here, you'll find only four items on the menu: the Dario DOC ,a half-pound burger, without bun, served with roast potatoes and onions; the Super Dario, the former with salad and beans added; the Welcome, with four different dishes of beef and pork served with fresh garden vegetables; and a vegetarian dish. All offerings are a nice change from the more standard options found at restaurants throughout Chianti. Outdoor seating is available in summer, but get here early—it's enormously popular. Enter from the public parking area behind the restaurant. $ *Average main: €15* ✉ *Via XX Luglio 11* ☎ *055/852176* ⊕ *www.dariocecchini.com* ⊘ *Closed Sun.*

Continued on page 359

GRAPE ESCAPES
THE PLEASURES OF TUSCAN WINE

The vineyards stretching across the landscape of Tuscany may look like cinematic backdrops, but in fact they're working farms, and they produce some of Italy's best wines. No matter whether you're a wine novice or a connoisseur, there's great pleasure to be had from exploring this lush terrain, visiting the vineyards, and uncorking a bottle for yourself.

GETTING TO KNOW TUSCAN WINE

Most of the wine produced in Tuscany is red (though there are some notable whites as well), and most Tuscan reds are made primarily from one type of grape, sangiovese. That doesn't mean, however, that all wines here are the same. God (in this case Bacchus) is in the details: differences in climate, soil, and methods of production result in wines with several distinct personalities.

Chianti

Chianti is the most famous name in Tuscan wine, but what exactly the name means is a little tricky. It once identified wines produced in the region extending from just south of Florence to just north of Siena. In the mid-20th century, the official Chianti zone was expanded to include a large portion of central Tuscany. That area is divided into eight subregions. **Chianti Classico** is the name given to the original zone, which makes up 17,000 of the 42,000 acres of Chianti-producing vineyards.

Classico wines, which bear the *gallo nero* (black rooster) logo on their labels, are the most highly regarded Chiantis (with **Rùfina** running second), but that doesn't mean Classicos are always superior. All Chiantis are strictly regulated (they must be a minimum 75% to 80% sangiovese, with other varieties blended in to add nuance), and they share a strong, woodsy character that's well suited to Tuscan food. It's a good strategy to drink the local product—**Colli Senesi Chianti** when in Siena, for example. The most noticeable, and costly, difference comes when a Chianti is from *riserva* (reserve) stock, meaning it's been aged for at least two years.

WINE REGIONS OF CENTRAL TUSCANY

Prato
Carmignano
Florence
67
Chianti Rùfina e Pomino
Montelupo
E35
San Miniato
Colli Fiorentini (Chianti)
222
Greve
Arezzo
Vernaccia di San Gimignano
Chianti Classico
Poggibonsi
68
Colli Senesi (Chianti)
326
Siena
0 10 mi
0 10 km
2
E35
Nobile di Montepulcia
TUSCANY
223
Brunello di Montalcino

DOC & DOCG The designations "DOC" and "DOCG"—Denominazione di Origine Controllata (e Garantita)—mean a wine comes from an established region and adheres to rigorous standards of production. Ironically, the esteemed Super Tuscans are labeled *vini da tavola* (table wines), the least prestigious designation, because they don't use traditional grape blends.

Brunello di Montalcino

The area surrounding the hill town of Montalcino, to the south of Siena, is drier and warmer than the Chianti regions, and it produces the most powerful of the sangiovese-based wines. Regulations stipulate that Brunello di Montalcino be made entirely from sangiovese grapes (no blending) and aged at least four years. **Rosso di Montalcino** is a younger, less complex, less expensive Brunello.

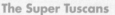

The Super Tuscans

Beginning in the 1970s, some winemakers, chafing at the regulations imposed on established Tuscan wine varieties, began blending and aging wines in innovative ways. Thus were born the so-called Super Tuscans. These pricey, French oak–aged wines are admired for their high quality, led by such star performers as **Sassicaia**, from the Maremma region, and **Tignanello**, produced at the Tenuta Marchesi Antinori near Badia a Passignano. Purists, however, lament the loss of local identity resulting from the Super Tuscans' use of nonnative grape varieties such as cabernet sauvignon and merlot.

Vino Nobile di Montepulciano

East of Montalcino is Montepulciano, the town at the heart of the third, and smallest, of Tuscany's top wine districts.

Blending regulations aren't as strict for Vino Nobile as for Chianti and Brunello, and as a result it has a wider range of characteristics. Broadly speaking, though, Vino Nobile is a cross between Chianti and Brunello—less acidic than the former and softer than the latter. It also has a less pricey sibling, **Rosso di Montepulciano.**

The Whites

Most whites from Tuscany are made from **trebbiano** grapes, which produce a wine that's light and refreshing but not particularly aromatic or flavorful—it may hit the spot on a hot afternoon, but it doesn't excite connoisseurs.

Golden-hewed **Vernaccia di San Gimignano** is a local variety with more limited production but greater personality—it's the star of Tuscan whites. Winemakers have also brought chardonnay and sauvignon grapes to the region, resulting in wines that, like some Super Tuscans, are pleasant to drink but short on local character.

TOURING & TASTING IN TUSCAN WINE COUNTRY

Strade del Vino di Toscana

Tuscany has visitor-friendly wineries, but the way you go about visiting is a bit different here from what it is in California or France. Many wineries welcome drop-ins for a tasting, but for a tour you usually need to make an appointment a few days in advance. There are several approaches you can take, depending on how much time you have and how serious you are about wine:

PLAN 1: FULL IMMERSION. Make an appointment to tour one of the top wineries (see our recommendations on the next page), and you'll get the complete experience: half a day of strolling through vineyards, talking grape varieties, and tasting wine, often accompanied by food. Groups are small; in spring and fall, it may be just you and the winemaker. The cost is usually €10 to €20 per person, but can go up to €40 if a meal is included. Remember to specify a tour in English.

PLAN 2: SEMI-ORGANIZED. If you want to spend a few hours going from vineyard to vineyard, make your first stop one of the local tourist information offices—they're great resources for maps, tasting itineraries, and personalized advice about where to visit. The offices in **Greve**, **Montalcino**, and **Montepulciano** are the best equipped. **Enoteche** (for more about them, turn the page) can also be good places to pick up tips about where to go for tastings.

PLAN 3: SPONTANEOUS. Along Tuscany's country roads you'll see signs for wineries offering **vendita diretta** (direct sales) and **degustazioni** (tastings). For a taste of the local product with some atmosphere thrown in, a spontaneous visit is a perfectly viable approach. You may wind up in a simple shop or an elaborate tasting room; either way, there's a fair chance you'll sample something good. Expect a small fee for a three-glass tasting.

THE PICK OF THE VINEYARDS

Within the Chianti Classico region, these wineries should be at the top of your to-visit list, whether you're dropping in for a taste or making a full tour. (Tours require reservations unless otherwise indicated.)

Badia a Coltibuono
(✉ Gaiole in Chianti ☎ 0577/749498 ⊕ www.coltibuono. com). Along with an extensive prelunch tour and tasting, there are shorter afternoon tours, no reservation required, starting on the hour from 2 to 5. (See "Radda in Chianti" in this chapter.)

Castello di Fonterutoli
(✉ Castellina in Chianti ☎ 0577/741385 ⊕ www. fonterutoli.it). Hour-long tours include a walk through the neighboring village.

Castello di Volpaia
(✉ Radda in Chianti ☎ 0577/738066 ⊕ www. volpaia.com). The tour here includes a visit to the olive oil press and a tour of the town.

Castello di Verrazzano
(✉ Via S. Martino in Valle 12, Greve in Chianti ☎ 055/854243 ⊕ www. verrazzano.com). Tours here take you down to the cellars, through the gardens, and into the woods in search of wild boar.

CHIANTI CLASSICO

TUSCANY

Villa Vignamaggio
(✉ Via Petriolo 5, Greve in Chianti ☎ 055/854661 ⊕ www. vignamaggio.com). Along with a wine tour, you can spend the night at this villa where Mona Lisa is believed to have been born. (See "Where to Stay" under "Greve in Chianti" in this chapter.)

Rocca delle Màcie

(✉ Località Le Macie 45, Castellina in Chianti ☎ 0577/732236 ⊕ www.rocca dellemacie.com). A full lunch or dinner can be incorporated into your tasting here.

Castello di Brolio
(✉ Gaiole in Chianti ☎ 0577/730220 ⊕ www.ricasoli.it). One of Tuscany's most impressive castles also has a centuries-old winemaking tradition. (See "Radda in Chianti" in this chapter.)

REMEMBER

Always have a designated driver when you're touring and tasting. Vineyards are usually located off narrow, curving roads. Full sobriety is a must behind the wheel.

6

IN FOCUS GRAPE ESCAPES

MORE TUSCAN WINE RESOURCES

Enoteche: Wine Shops

The word *enoteca* in Italian can mean "wine store," "wine bar," or both. In any event, *enoteche* (the plural, pronounced "ay-no-*tek*-ay") are excellent places to sample and buy Tuscan wines, and they're also good sources of information about local wineries. There are scores to choose from. These are a few of the best:

Enoteca Italiana, Siena (Fortezza Medicea, Viale Maccari ☎ 0577/288497 ⊕ www. enoteca-italiana.it). The only one of its kind, this *enoteca* represents all the producers of DOC and DOCG wines in Italy and stocks over 400 labels. Wine by the glass and snacks are available.

Enoteca Osticcio, Montalcino (✉ Via Matteotti 23 ☎ 0577/848271 ⊕ www. osticcio.com). There are more than one thousand labels in stock. With one of the best views in Montalcino, it is also a very pleasant place to sit and meditate over a glass of Brunello.

Enoteca del Gallo Nero, Greve in Chianti (✉ Piazzetta S. Croce 8 ☎ 055/853297). This is one of the best stocked *enoteche* in the Chianti region.

La Dolce Vita, Montepulciano (Via di Voltaia nel Corso 80/82 ☎ 0578/757872). An elegantly restored monastery is home to the excellent enoteca in the upper part of Montepulciano, which has a wide selction of wines by the glass.

Wine on the Web

Tuscan wine country is well represented on the Internet. A good place for an overview is ⊕ www.terreditoscana.regione. toscana.it. (Click on "Le Strade del Vino"; the page that opens next will give you the option of choosing an English-language version.) This site shows 14 *strade del vino* (wine roads) that have been mapped out by consortiums representing major wine districts (unfortunately, Chianti Classico isn't included), along with recommended itineraries. You'll also find links to the consortium Web sites, where you can dig up more detailed information on touring. The Chianti Classico consortium's site is ⊕ www.chianticlassico.com. The Vino Nobile di Montepulciano site is ⊕ www.vinonobiledimontepulciano.it, and Brunello di Montalcino is ⊕ www. consorziobrunellodimontalcino.it. All have English versions.

$$$ ✕ **Solociccia.** "Abandon all hope, ye who enter here," announces the
TUSCAN menu, "you're in the hands of a butcher." Indeed you are, for this res-
taurant is the creation of Dario Cecchini, Panzano's local merchant of
meat. Served at communal tables, there are three set meals to choose
from, all of which highlight meat dishes chosen at Dario's discretion.
All are accompanied by seasonal vegetables, white beans with olive oil,
focaccia bread, and a ¼ liter of wine. Although Cecchini emphasizes
that steak is never on the menu, this lively, crowded place is definitely
not for vegetarians. The entrance is on Via XX Luglio. $ *Average main:*
€30 ⊠ *Via Chiantigiana 5* ☎ *055/852727* ⊕ *www.dariocecchini.com*
⊘ *Closed Mon.–Wed. No dinner Sun.*

$$$ ⌂ **Villa Le Barone.** Once the home of the Viviani della Robbia fam-
B&B/INN ily, this 16th-century villa in a grove of ancient cypress trees retains
Fodor$Choice many aspects of a private country dwelling, complete with homey guest
★ quarters. **Pros:** beautiful location; wonderful restaurant; great base for
exploring the region. **Cons:** some rooms are a bit small; 15-minute
walk to nearest town. $ *Rooms from: €260* ⊠ *Via San Leolino 19*
☎ *055/852621* ⊕ *www.villalebarone.com* ⊘ *Closed Nov.–Easter* ⇥ *28*
rooms ⦿❘ *Breakfast.*

6

RADDA IN CHIANTI

*26 km (15 miles) southeast of Panzano, 55 km (34 miles) south of
Florence.*

Radda in Chianti sits on a ridge stretching between the Val di Pesa and Val
d'Arbia. It is easily reached by following the SR429 from Castellina. It's
another one of those tiny villages with steep streets for strolling; follow
the signs that point you toward the *camminamento medioevale,* a covered
14th-century walkway that circles part of the city inside the walls.

GETTING HERE AND AROUND
Radda can be reached by car from either Siena or Florence along the
SR222 (Strada Chiantigiana), and from the A1 autostrada. Three Tra-
In buses make their way from Siena to Radda. One morning SITA bus
travels from Florence to Radda. There is no train service convenient
to Radda.

VISITOR INFORMATION
Radda in Chianti Tourism Office. ⊠ *Piazza Castello 6* ☎ *0577/738494.*

EXPLORING
Badia a Coltibuono (*Abbey of the Good Harvest*). North of Gaiole a turn-
off leads to this Romanesque abbey that has been owned by Lorenza
de' Medici's family for more than a century and a half (the family isn't
closely related to the Renaissance-era Medici). Wine has been produced
here since the abbey was founded by Vallombrosan monks in the 11th
century. Today the family continues the tradition, making Chianti Classico and other wines, along with cold-pressed olive oil and various
flavored vinegars and floral honeys. A small church with campanile is
surrounded by 2,000 acres of oak, fir, and chestnut woods threaded
with walking paths—open to all—that pass two small lakes. Although
the abbey itself, built between the 11th and 18th centuries, serves as

the family's home, parts are open for tours (in English, German, or Italian). Visit the jasmine-draped main courtyard, the inner cloister with its antique well, the musty old aging cellars, and the Renaissance-style garden redolent of lavender, lemons, and roses. In the shop, **L'Osteria,** you can taste wine and honey, as well as pick up other items like homemade beeswax hand lotion in little ceramic dishes. The Badia is closed on public holidays. ✉ *Località Badia a Coltibuono, 4 km (2½ miles) north of Gaiole, Gaiole in Chianti* ☎ *0577/74481 for tours* ⊕ *www. coltibuono.com* 🖾 *Abbey €6.*

Fodor'sChoice
★
Castello di Brolio. If you have time for only one castle in Tuscany, this is it. At the end of the 12th century, when Florence conquered southern Chianti, Brolio became Florence's southernmost outpost. Brolio was built about AD 1000 and owned by the monks of the Badia Fiorentina; the "new" owners, the Ricasoli family, have been in possession since 1141. Bettino Ricasoli (1809–80), the so-called Iron Baron, was one of the founders of modern Italy, and is said to have invented the original formula for Chianti wine. Brolio, one of Chianti's best-known labels, is still justifiably famous. Its cellars may be toured by appointment. The grounds are worth visiting, even though the 19th-century manor house is not open to the public. A small museum, where the Ricasoli Collection is housed in a 12th-century tower, displays objects that relate the long history of the family and the origins of Chianti wine. ✉ *Località Brolio, 2 km (1 mile) southeast of Gaiole, Gaiole in Chianti* ☎ *0577/730280* ⊕ *www.ricasoli.it* 🖾 *€5 gardens, €8 gardens and museum, €10 guided tours.*

Palazzo del Podestà. Radda's town hall (aka Palazzo Comunale), in the middle of town, was built in the second half of the 14th century and has served the same function ever since. Fifty-one coats of arms (the largest is the Medici's) are imbedded in the facade, representing the past governors of the town, but unless you have official business, the building is closed to the public. ✉ *Piazza Ferrucci 1.*

WHERE TO EAT AND STAY

$$
TUSCAN
Fodor'sChoice
★
✕ **Osteria Le Panzanelle.** Silvia Bonechi's experience in the kitchen—with the help of a few precious recipes handed down from her grandmother—is one of the reasons for the success of this small restaurant in the tiny hamlet of Lucarelli. The other is the front-room hospitality of Nada Michelassi. These two *panzanelle* (women from Panzano) serve a short menu of tasty and authentic dishes at what the locals refer to as *il prezzo giusto* (the right price). Both the *pappa al pomodoro* (tomato soup) and the *peposo* (peppery beef stew) are exceptional. Whether you are eating inside or under large umbrellas on the terrace near a tiny stream, the experience is always congenial. "The best food we had in Tuscany," writes one user of Fodors.com. Reservations are essential in July and August. $ *Average main: €15* ✉ *Località Lucarelli 29, 8 km (5 miles) northwest of Radda on the road to Panzano* ☎ *0577/733511* ⊕ *www.lepanzanelle.it* ☉ *Closed Mon., and Jan. and Feb.*

$$$
B&B/INN
Fodor'sChoice
★
🛏 **La Locanda.** At an altitude of more than 1,800 feet, this converted farmhouse is probably the loftiest luxury inn in Chianti. **Pros:** idyllic setting; panoramic views; wonderful host. **Cons:** on a very rough gravel access road; isolated location; need a car to get around. $ *Rooms*

from: €220 ✉ Località Montanino di Volpaia, off Via della Volpaia, 13 km (8 miles) northwest of Radda ☎ 0577/738833 🌐 www.lalocanda.it ⏲ Closed mid-Oct.–mid-Apr. 🛏 6 rooms, 1 suite 🍴 Breakfast.

$ HOTEL 🏨 **Palazzo San Niccolò.** The wood-beam ceilings, terra-cotta floors, and some of the original frescoes of a 19th-century town palace remain, but the marble bathrooms have all been updated, some with Jacuzzi tubs. **Pros:** central location; friendly service. **Cons:** some rooms face a main street; room sizes vary. [$] *Rooms from: €120 ✉ Via Roma 16 ☎ 0577/735666 🌐 www.hotelsanniccolo.com ⏲ Closed Nov.–Mar. 🛏 17 rooms, 1 suite 🍴 Breakfast.*

$$ B&B/INN Fodor's Choice ★ 🏨 **Relais Fattoria Vignale.** A refined and comfortable country house offers numerous sitting rooms with terra-cotta floors and attractive stonework and wood-beamed guest rooms filled with simple wooden furnishings and handwoven rugs. **Pros:** intimate public spaces; excellent restaurant; helpful and friendly staff; nice grounds and pool. **Cons:** single rooms are small; annex across a busy road. [$] *Rooms from: €200 ✉ Via Pianigiani 9 ☎ 0577/738300 for hotel, 0577/738094 for restaurant 🌐 www.vignale.it ⏲ Closed Nov.–Mar. 15 🛏 42 rooms, 5 suites 🍴 Breakfast.*

6

CASTELLINA IN CHIANTI

14 km (8 miles) west of Radda, 59 km (35 miles) south of Florence.

Castellina in Chianti—or simply Castellina—is on a ridge above three valleys: the Val di Pesa, Val d'Arbia, and Val d'Elsa. No matter what direction you turn, the panorama is bucolic. The strong 15th-century medieval walls and fortified town gate give a hint of the history of this village, which was an outpost during the continuing wars between Florence and Siena. In the main square, the Piazza del Comune, there's a 15th-century palace and a 15th-century fort constructed around a 13th-century tower. It now serves as the town hall.

GETTING HERE AND AROUND

As with all the towns along the Strada Chiantigiana (SR222), Castellina is an easy drive from either Siena or Florence. From Siena, Castellina is well served by the local Tra-In bus company. However, only one bus a day travels here from Florence. The closest train station is at Castellina Scalo, some 15 km (9 miles) away.

VISITOR INFORMATION

Castellina in Chianti Tourism Office. ✉ *Via Ferruccio 40 ☎ 0577/741392.*

WHERE TO EAT AND STAY

$$$ TUSCAN 🍴 **Albergaccio.** The fact that the dining room can seat only 35 guests makes a meal here an intimate experience. The ever-changing menu mixes traditional and creative dishes. In late September and October *zuppa di funghi e castagne* (mushroom and chestnut soup) is a treat; grilled meats and seafood are on the list throughout the year. There's also an excellent wine list. When the weather is warm, make sure you dine on the terrace. [$] *Average main: €28 ✉ Via Fiorentina 63 ☎ 0577/741042 🌐 www.albergacciocast.com ⏲ Closed Sun.*

$$ TUSCAN 🍴 **Ristorante Le Tre Porte.** Grilled meat dishes are the specialty at this popular restaurant, with a bistecca fiorentina (served very rare) taking pride of place. Paired with grilled fresh porcini mushrooms when in season (spring and fall), it's a particularly heady dish. The panoramic terrace is a good choice for dining in summer. Inside, the upper floor offers an unmistakably Tuscan setting, while the downstairs is more modern and intimate. Reservations are essential in July and August. [$] *Average main: €16* ✉ *Via Trento e Trieste 4* ☎ *0577/741163* 🌐 *www.ristoranteinchianti.com* 🕒 *Closed Tues.*

$$ TUSCAN 🍴 **Sotto Le Volte.** As the name suggests, you'll find this small restaurant under the arches of Castellina's medieval walkway. The restaurant has vaulted ceilings, which make for a particularly romantic setting. The menu is short and eminently Tuscan, with typical soups and pasta dishes. The *costolette di agnello alle erbe* (herbed lamb chops) are especially tasty. [$] *Average main: €20* ✉ *Via delle Volte 14–16* ☎ *0577/056530* 🌐 *www.ristorantesottolevolte.it* 🕒 *Closed Wed.*

$$ B&B/INN Fodor's Choice ★ 🏨 **Palazzo Squarcialupi.** In this lovely 15th-century palace, rooms are spacious, with high ceilings, tile floors, and 18th-century furnishings, and many have views of the valley below. **Pros:** great location in town center; elegant public spaces; nice spa, pool, and grounds. **Cons:** on a street with no car access; across from a busy restaurant. [$] *Rooms from: €125* ✉ *Via Ferruccio 22* ☎ *0577/741186* 🌐 *www.squarcialupirelaxinchianti.com* 🕒 *Closed Nov.–Mar.* 🛏 *17 rooms* 🍽 *Breakfast.*

HILL TOWNS SOUTHWEST OF FLORENCE

Submit to the draw of Tuscany's enchanting fortified cities that crown the hills west of Siena, many dating to the Etruscan period. San Gimignano, known as the "medieval Manhattan" because of its forest of stout medieval towers built by rival families, is the most heavily visited. This onetime Roman outpost, with its tilted cobbled streets and ancient buildings, can make the days of Guelph-Ghibelline conflicts palpable. Rising from a series of bleak gullied hills and valleys, Volterra has always been popular for its minerals and stones, particularly alabaster, which was used by the Etruscans for many implements. Examples are now displayed in the exceptional (and exceptionally large) Museo Etrusco Guarnacci.

VOLTERRA

75 km (47 miles) southwest of Florence.

As you approach the town through bleak, rugged terrain, you can see that not all Tuscan hill towns rise above rolling green fields. Volterra stands mightily over Le Balze, a stunning series of gullied hills and valleys formed by erosion that has slowly eaten away at the foundation of the town—now considerably smaller than it was during its Etruscan glory days 25 centuries ago. The town began as the northernmost of the 12 cities that made up the Etruscan League, and excavations in the 18th century revealed a bounty of relics, which are on exhibit at the impressively overstocked Museo Etrusco Guarnacci. The Romans and later the Florentines laid siege to the town to secure its supply of minerals and stones, particularly alabaster, which is still worked into handicrafts on sale in many of the shops around town.

GETTING HERE AND AROUND

By car, the best route from San Gimignano follows the SP1 south to Castel San Gimignano and then the SS68 west to Volterra. Coming from the west, take the SS1, a coastal road to Cecina, then follow the SS68 east to Volterra. Either way, there's a long, winding climb at the end of your trip. Traveling to Volterra by bus or train is complicated; avoid it if possible, especially if you have lots of luggage. From Florence or Siena the journey by public transit is best made by bus and involves a change in Colle di Val d'Elsa. From Rome or Pisa, it is best to take the train to Cecina and then take a bus to Volterra or a train to the Volterra-Saline station. The latter is 10 km (6 miles) from town.

VISITOR INFORMATION

Volterra tourism office. ⊠ *Piazza dei Priori 10* ☎ *0588/86150* ⊕ *www. provolterra.it.*

EXPLORING

Duomo. Behind the textbook 13th-century Pisan–Romanesque facade is proof that Volterra counted for something during the Renaissance, when many important Tuscan artists came to decorate the church. Three-dimensional stucco portraits of local saints are on the gold, red, and blue ceiling (1580) designed by Francesco Capriani. The highlight of the Duomo is the brightly painted 13th-century wooden life-size *Deposition* in the chapel of the same name. The unusual Cappella dell'Addolorata (Chapel of the Grieved) has two terra-cotta Nativity scenes. The 16th-century pulpit in the middle of the nave is lined with fine 14th-century sculpted panels, attributed to a member of the Pisano family. Across from the Duomo in the center of the piazza is the **Battistero**, with stripes that match the Duomo. ⊠ *Piazza San Giovanni* ☎ *0588/88261.*

Fodor's Choice ★ **Museo Etrusco Guarnacci.** An extraordinarily large and unique collection of Etruscan relics is made all the more interesting by clear explanations in English. The bulk of the collection is comprised of roughly 700 carved funerary urns: the oldest, dating from the 7th century BC, were made from tufa (volcanic rock); a handful are made of terracotta; and the vast majority—from the 3rd to 1st century BC—are from alabaster. The urns are grouped by subject and taken together form a fascinating testimony about Etruscan life and death. Some illustrate domestic scenes, others the funeral procession of the deceased. Greek gods and mythology, adopted by the Etruscans, also figure prominently. The sculpted figures on many of the covers may have been made in the image of the deceased, reclining and often holding the cup of life overturned. Particularly well known is *Gli Sposi* (*Husband and Wife*), a haunting, elderly duo in terra-cotta. The *Ombra della Sera* (*Evening Shadow*)—an enigmatice bronze statue of an elongated, pencil-thin male nude—highlights the collection. Also on display are Attic vases, bucchero ceramics, jewelry, and household items. ⊠ *Via Don Minzoni 15* ☎ *0588/86347* 🏷 *€14, includes Pinacoteca and Teatro Romano.*

6

Pinacoteca. One of Volterra's best-looking Renaissance buildings contains an impressive collection of Tuscan paintings arranged chronologically on two floors. Head straight for Room 12, with Luca Signorelli's (circa 1445–1523) *Madonna and Child with Saints* and Rosso Fiorentino's *Deposition.* Though painted just 30 years apart, they serve to illustrate the shift in style from the early-16th-century Renaissance ideals to full-blown mannerism: the balance of Signorelli's composition becomes purposefully skewed in Fiorentino's painting, where the colors go from vivid but realistic to emotively bright. Other important paintings in the small museum include Ghirlandaio's *Apotheosis of Christ with Saints* and a polyptych of the *Madonna and Saints* by Taddeo di Bartolo, which once hung in the Palazzo dei Priori. ⊠ *Via dei Sarti 1* ☎ *0588/87580* 🎫 *€14, includes Museo Etrusco Guarnacci and Teatro Romano.*

Porta all'Arco Etrusco. Even if a good portion of the arch was rebuilt by the Romans, three dark and weather-beaten 4th-century-BC heads (thought to represent Etruscan gods) still face outward to greet those who enter here. A plaque on the outer wall recalls the efforts of the locals who saved the arch from destruction by filling it with stones during the German withdrawal at the end of World War II. ⊠ *Via Porta all'Arco.*

Teatro Romano. Just outside the walls past Porta Fiorentina are the ruins of the 1st-century-BC Roman theater, one of the best preserved in Italy, with adjacent remains of the Roman *terme* (baths). You can enjoy an excellent bird's-eye view of the theater from Via Lungo le Mura. ⊠ *Viale Francesco Ferrucci* 🎫 *€3.50; €14, includes Museo Etrusco Guarnacci and Pinacoteca.*

WHERE TO EAT AND STAY

$
TUSCAN
✕ **Da Badò.** This is the best place in town to eat traditional food elbow-to-elbow with the locals. Da Badò is family-run, with Lucia in the kitchen and her sons Giacomo and Michele waiting tables. Lucia likes to concentrate on just a few dishes, so it won't take long to decide between the standards, all prepared with a sure hand: *zuppa alla volterrana* (a soup made with vegetables and bread), *pappardelle alla lepre* (wide fettuccine with rabbit sauce), and a stew of either rabbit or wild boar. A slice of homemade almond tart is a must. $ *Average main: €14* ⊠ *Borgo San Lazzaro 9* ☎ *0588/86477* ⊕ *www.trattoriadabado. com* ⊘ *Closed Wed.*

$$
TUSCAN
✕ **Il Sacco Fiorentino.** Start with the *antipasti del Sacco Fiorentino*—a medley of sautéed chicken liver, porcini mushrooms, and polenta drizzled with balsamic vinegar. The meal just gets better when you move on to the *tagliatelle del Sacco Fiorentino,* a riot of curried spaghetti with chicken and roasted red peppers. The wine list is a marvel, as it's long and very well priced. White walls, tile floors, and red tablecloths create an understated tone that is unremarkable, but once the food starts arriving, it's easy to forgive the lack of decoration. $ *Average main: €18* ⊠ *Piazza XX Settembre 13* ☎ *0588/88537* ⊘ *Closed Tues.*

$
B&B/INN
▥ **Etruria.** The rooms are modest and there's no elevator, but the central location, the ample buffet breakfast, and the modest rates make this a good choice for those on a budget. **Pros:** great central location; friendly staff; tranquil garden with rooftop views. **Cons:** some rooms can be noisy during the day; no a/c; no elevator. $ *Rooms from:*

€100 ✉ *Via Matteotti 32* ☎ *0588/87377* 🌐 *www.albergoetruria.it* 🛏 *18 rooms* 🍴 *Breakfast.*

$ HOTEL 🏨 **San Lino.** Within the town's medieval walls, this convent-turned-hotel has wood-beam ceilings, graceful archways, and terra-cotta floors, with nice contemporary furnishings and ironwork in the rooms. **Pros:** steps away from center of town; friendly and helpful staff; convenient parking. **Cons:** rooms facing the street can be noisy; breakfast is adequate, but nothing to write home about. [$] *Rooms from: €100* ✉ *Via San Lino 26* ☎ *0588/85250* 🌐 *www.hotelsanlino.net* 🕒 *Closed Nov., Jan., and Feb.* 🛏 *43 rooms* 🍴 *Breakfast.*

SAN GIMIGNANO

27 km (17 miles) northeast of Volterra, 54 km (34 miles) southwest of Florence.

Fodor's Choice ★ When you're on a hilltop surrounded by soaring medieval towers silhouetted against the sky, it's difficult not to fall under the spell of San Gimignano. Its tall walls and narrow streets are typical of Tuscan hill towns, but it's the medieval "skyscrapers" that set the town apart from its neighbors. Today 14 towers remain, but at the height of the Guelph–Ghibelline conflict there was a forest of more than 70, and it was possible to cross the town by rooftop rather than by road. The towers were built partly for defensive purposes—they were a safe refuge and useful for pouring boiling oil on attacking enemies—and partly for bolstering the egos of their owners, who competed with deadly seriousness to build the highest tower in town.

Today San Gimignano isn't much more than a gentrified walled city, touristy but still very much worth exploring because, despite the profusion of cheesy souvenir shops lining the main drag, there's some serious Renaissance art to be seen here. Tour groups arrive early and clog the wine-tasting rooms—San Gimignano is famous for its light, white vernaccia—and art galleries for much of the day, but most sights stay open through late afternoon, when all the tour groups have long since departed.

San Gimignano is particularly beautiful in the early morning. Take time to walk up to the *rocca* (castle), at the highest point of town. Here you can enjoy 360-degree views of the surrounding countryside. Apart from when it's used for summer outdoor film festivals, it's always open.

GETTING HERE AND AROUND

You can reach San Gimignano by car from the Florence–Siena Superstrada. Exit at Poggibonsi Nord and follow signs for San Gimignano. Although it involves changing buses in Poggibonsi, getting to San Gimignano by bus from Florence is a relatively straightforward affair. SITA operates the service between Siena or Florence and Poggibonsi. From Siena, Tra-In offers direct service to San Gimignano several times daily. You cannot reach San Gimignano by train.

VISITOR INFORMATION

San Gimignano tourism office. ✉ *Piazza Duomo 1* ☎ *0577/940008* 🌐 *www.sangimignano.com.*

6

EXPLORING

Fodor'sChoice **Collegiata.** The town's main church is not officially a *duomo* (cathe-
★ dral), because San Gimignano has no bishop. But behind the simple
facade of the Romanesque Collegiata lies a treasure trove of fine frescoes, covering nearly every part of the interior. Bartolo di Fredi's
14th-century fresco cycle of Old Testament scenes extends along one
wall. Their distinctly medieval feel, with misshapen bodies, buckets of
spurting blood, and lack of perspective, contrasts with the much more
reserved scenes from the *Life of Christ* (attributed to 14th-century
artist Lippo Memmi), painted on the opposite wall just 14 years later.
Taddeo di Bartolo's otherworldly *Last Judgment* (late 14th century),
with its distorted and suffering nudes, reveals the great influence of
Dante's horrifying imagery in *Inferno* and was surely an inspiration
for later painters. Proof that the town had more than one protector,
Benozzo Gozzoli's arrow-riddled *St. Sebastian* was commissioned in
gratitude after the locals prayed to the saint for relief from plague. The
Renaissance **Cappella di Santa Fina** is decorated with a fresco cycle
by Domenico Ghirlandaio illustrating the life of St. Fina. A small girl
who suffered from a terminal disease, Fina repented her sins—among
them having accepted an orange from a boy—and in penance lived
out the rest of her short life on a wooden board, tormented by rats.
The scenes depict the arrival of St. Gregory, who appeared to assure
her that death was near; the flowers that miraculously grew from the
wooden plank; and the miracles that accompanied her funeral, including the healing of her nurse's paralyzed hand and the restoration of
a blind choirboy's vision. ⊠ *Piazza Pecori 1–2, entrance on left side
of church* ☎ *0577/286300* ⊕ *www.duomosangimignano.it* ⊠*€4; €6,
includes Museo d'Arte Sacra.*

Museo Civico. The impressive civic museum occupies what was the
"new" Palazzo del Popolo; the Torre Grossa is adjacent. Dante visited
San Gimignano for only one day as a Guelph ambassador from Florence
to ask the locals to join the Florentines in supporting the pope—just
long enough to get the main council chamber, which now holds a 14th-
century *Maestà* by Lippo Memmi, named after him. Off the stairway
is a small room containing the racy frescoes by Memmo di Filippuccio
(active 1288–1324), depicting the courtship, shared bath, and wedding of a young, androgynous-looking couple. That the space could
have been a private room for the commune's chief magistrate may have
something to do with the work's highly charged eroticism.

Upstairs, paintings by famous Renaissance artists Pinturicchio (*Madonna
Enthroned*), and Benozzo Gozzoli (*Madonna and Child*), and two large
tondi (circular paintings) by Filippino Lippi (circa 1457–1504) attest to
the importance and wealth of San Gimignano. Also worth seeing are
Taddeo di Bartolo's *Life of San Gimignano*, with the saint holding a
model of the town as it once appeared; Lorenzo di Niccolò's gruesome
martyrdom scene in the *Life of St. Bartholomew* (1401); and scenes
from the *Life of St. Fina* on a tabernacle that was designed to hold
her head. Admission includes the steep climb to the top of the **Torre
Grossa,** which on a clear day has spectacular views. ⊠ *Piazza Duomo
2* ☎ *0577/990312* ⊕ *www.sangimignanomusei.it* ⊠*€6.*

Sant'Agostino. Make a beeline for Benozzo Gozzoli's superlative 15th-century fresco cycle depicting scenes from the life of St. Augustine. The saint's work was essential to the early development of church doctrine. As thoroughly discussed in his autobiographical *Confessions* (an acute dialogue with God), Augustine, like many saints, sinned considerably in his youth before finding God. But unlike the lives of other saints, where the story continues through a litany of deprivations, penitence, and often martyrdom, Augustine's life and work focused on philosophy and the reconciliation of faith and thought. Benozzo's 17 scenes on the choir wall depict Augustine as a man who traveled and taught extensively in the 4th and 5th centuries. The 15th-century altarpiece by Piero del Pollaiolo (1443–96) depicts *The Coronation of the Virgin* and the various protectors of the city. On your way out of Sant'Agostino, stop in at the **Cappella di San Bartolo,** with a sumptuously elaborate tomb by Benedetto da Maiano (1442–97). ⊠ *Piazza Sant'Agostino 10* ☎ *0577/907012* ⊕ *www.sangimignano.com* ⊠ *Free.*

WHERE TO EAT

$ ✕ **Enoteca Gustavo.** There's no shortage of places to try Vernaccia di San TUSCAN Gimignano, the justifiably famous white wine with which San Gimignano would be singularly associated—if it weren't for all those towers. At this wine bar, run by energetic Maristella Becucci, you can buy a glass of Vernaccia di San Gimignano and sit down with a cheese plate or with one of the fine crostini. $ *Average main: €8* ⊠ *Via San Matteo 29* ☎ *0577/940057.*

$$ ✕ **Osteria del Carcere.** Although it calls itself an *osteria* (tavern), this ITALIAN place much more resembles a wine bar, with a bill of fare that includes several different types of pâtés and a short list of seasonal soups and salads. The sampler of goat cheeses, which can be paired with local wines, should not be missed. Operatic arias play softly in the background, and service is courteous. $ *Average main: €16* ⊠ *Via del Castello 13* ☎ *0577/941905* ☉ *Closed Wed., and early Jan.–Mar. No lunch Thurs.*

WHERE TO STAY

$$$ 🏨 **La Collegiata.** After serving as a Franciscan convent and then the HOTEL residence of the noble Strozzi family, the Collegiata has been converted into a fine hotel, with no expense spared in the process. **Pros:** gorgeous views from terrace; elegant rooms in main building. **Cons:** long walk into town; service can be impersonal; some rooms are dimly lit. $ *Rooms from: €220* ⊠ *Località Strada 27, 1 km (½ mile) north of San Gimignano town center* ☎ *0577/943201* ⊕ *www.lacollegiata.it* ☉ *Closed Nov.–Mar.* ⤴ *20 rooms, 1 suite* ⵐ *Breakfast.*

$ 🏨 **Pescille.** A rambling farmhouse has been transformed into a hand-B&B/INN some hotel with understated contemporary furniture in the bedrooms and country-classic motifs such as farm implements hanging on the walls in the bar. **Pros:** splendid views; quiet atmosphere; 10-minute walk to town. **Cons:** furnishings a bit austere; there's an elevator for luggage but not for guests. $ *Rooms from: €120* ⊠ *Località Pescille, 4 km (2½ miles) south of San Gimignano* ☎ *0577/940186* ⊕ *www.pescille.it* ☉ *Closed Nov.–Mar.* ⤴ *38 rooms, 12 suites* ⵐ *Breakfast.*

$$ 🏠 **Torraccia di Chiusi.** A perfect retreat for families, this tranquil hilltop
B&B/INN   *agriturismo* (farm stay) offers simple, comfortably decorated accom-
modations on extensive grounds 5 km (3 miles) from the hubbub of San
Gimignano. **Pros:** tranquil haven close to San Gimignano; great walking
possibilities; family-run hospitality; delightful countryside views. **Cons:**
30 minutes from the nearest town on a windy gravel road; need a car to
get here. 💲 *Rooms from: €140* ✉ *Località Montauto* ☎ *0577/941972*
🌐 *www.torracciadichiusi.it* 🛏 *8 rooms, 3 apartments* ⧖ *Breakfast.*

SIENA

With its narrow streets and steep alleys, a Gothic Duomo, a bounty of
early Renaissance art, and the glorious Palazzo Pubblico overlooking
its magnificent Campo, Siena is often described as Italy's best-preserved
medieval city. It is also remarkably modern: many shops sell clothes
by up-and-coming designers. Make a point of catching the *passeggiata*
(evening stroll), when locals throng the Via di Città, Banchi di Sopra,
and Banchi di Sotto, the city's three main streets.

Victory over Florence in 1260 at Montaperti marked the beginning
of Siena's golden age. Even though Florentines avenged the loss nine
years later, Siena continued to prosper. During the following decades
Siena erected its greatest buildings (including the Duomo); established
a model city government presided over by the Council of Nine; and
became a great art, textile, and trade center. All of these achievements
came together in the decoration of the Sala della Pace in Palazzo Pub-
blico. It makes you wonder what greatness the city might have gone
on to achieve had its fortunes been different, but in 1348 a plague
decimated the population, brought an end to the Council of Nine, and
left Siena economically vulnerable. Siena succumbed to Florentine rule
in the mid-16th century, when a yearlong siege virtually eliminated the
native population. Ironically, it was precisely this decline that, along
with Sienese pride, prevented further development, to which we owe
the city's marvelous medieval condition today.

But although much looks as it did in the early 14th century, Siena is no
museum. Walk through the streets and you can see that the medieval
contrade—17 neighborhoods into which the city has been historically
divided—are a vibrant part of modern life. You may see symbols of
the *contrada* emblazoned on banners and engraved on building walls:
Tartuca (turtle), Oca (goose), Istrice (porcupine), Torre (tower). The
Sienese still strongly identify themselves by the contrada where they
were born and raised; loyalty and rivalry run deep. At no time is this
more visible than during the centuries-old Palio, a twice-yearly horse
race held in the Piazza del Campo, but you need not visit then to come
to know the rich culture of Siena, evident at every step.

GETTING HERE AND AROUND

From Florence, the quickest way to Siena is via the Florence–Siena
superstrada. Otherwise, take the Via Cassia (SR2), for a scenic route.
Coming from Rome, leave the A1 at Valdichiana, and follow the
Siena–Bettole superstrada. SITA provides excellent bus service between

Florence and Siena. Because buses are direct and speedy, they are preferable to the train, which sometimes involves a change in Empoli.

If you come by car, you're better off leaving it in one of the parking lots around the perimeter of town. Driving is difficult or impossible in most parts of the city center. Practically unchanged since medieval times, Siena is laid out in a "Y" over the slopes of several hills, dividing the city into *terzi* (thirds).

Tra-In. City buses run frequently within and around Siena, including the centro storico. Tickets cost €1.30 and must be bought in advance at tobacconists or newsstands. Routes are marked with signposts. ⊠ *Siena* ☎ *0577/204111* ⊕ *www.trainspa.it.*

TIMING

It's a joy to walk in Siena—hills notwithstanding—as it's a rare opportunity to stroll through a medieval city rather than just a town. (There is quite a lot to explore, in contrast to tiny hill towns that can be crossed in minutes.) The walk can be done in as little as a day, with minimal stops at the sights. But stay longer and take time to tour the churches and museums, and to enjoy the streetscapes themselves. Many of the sites have reduced hours Sunday afternoon and Monday.

VISITOR INFORMATION

Siena tourism office. ⊠ *Piazza del Campo 56, Siena* ☎ *0577/280551* ⊕ *www.terresiena.it.*

6

EXPLORING

TOP ATTRACTIONS

Fodor'sChoice ★ **Cripta.** After it had lain unseen for possibly 700 years, a crypt was rediscovered under the grand *pavimento* (floor) of the Duomo during routine excavation work and was opened to the public in 2003. An unknown master executed the breathtaking frescoes here sometime between 1270 and 1280; they retain their original colors and pack an emotional punch even with sporadic damage. The *Deposition/Lamentation* gives strong evidence that the Sienese school could paint emotion just as well as the Florentine school—and did it some 20 years before Giotto. Guided tours in English take place more or less every half hour and are limited to no more than 35 persons. ⊠ *Scale di San Giovanni, Città* ⊹ *Down steps to right side of cathedral* ☎ *0577/286300* ⊕ *www.operaduomo. siena.it* ☑ *€6; €12 combined ticket, includes the Duomo, Battistero, and Museo dell'Opera Metropolitana.*

Fodor'sChoice ★ **Duomo.** Siena's cathedral, completed in two brief phases at the end of the 13th and 14th centuries, is beyond question one of the finest Gothic churches in Italy. The multicolored marbles and painted decoration are typical of the Italian approach to Gothic architecture, and the amazingly detailed facade has few rivals in the region. Highlights include the Duomo's striking interior, with its black-and-white striping and finely coffered and gilded dome; the oldest example of stained glass in Italy (from 1288) that fills the circular window; the carousel pulpit, carved around 1265; and the magnificent Renaissance frescoes in the Biblioteca Piccolomini. The Duomo is most famous for its unique and magnificent

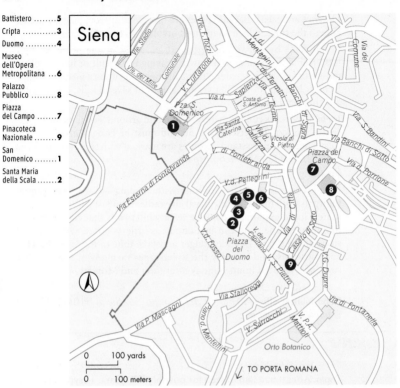

Siena

inlaid-marble floors, which took almost 200 years to complete; more than 40 artists contributed to the work, made up of 56 separate compositions depicting biblical scenes, allegories, religious symbols, and civic emblems. The floors are covered for most of the year, but are unveiled during September and October. ✉ *Piazza del Duomo, Città* ☎ *0577/286300* ⌧ *€4 Nov.–Aug., €7 Sept. and Oct.; €12 combined ticket, includes Cripta, Battistero, and Museo dell'Opera Metropolitana.*

Fodor'sChoice **Museo dell'Opera Metropolitana.** Part of the unfinished nave of what
★ was to have been a new cathedral, the museum contains the Duomo's treasury and some of the original decoration from its facade and interior. The first room on the ground floor displays weather-beaten 13th-century sculptures by Giovanni Pisano that were brought inside for protection and replaced by copies, as was a tondo of the *Madonna and Child* (now attributed to Donatello) that once hung on the door to the south transept. The masterpiece is unquestionably Duccio's *Maestà,* one side with 26 panels depicting episodes from the Passion, the other side with a *Madonna and Child Enthroned.* The second floor is divided between the treasury, with a crucifix by Giovanni Pisano, and La Sala della Madonna degli Occhi Grossi (the Room of the Madonna with the Big Eyes), named after the 13th-century painting. There is a fine view from the tower inside the museum. ✉ *Piazza del Duomo 8, Città*

☎ *0577/286300* ⊕ *www.operaduomo.siena.it* 🎫 *€7; €12 combined ticket, includes the Duomo, Cripta, and Battistero.*

Fodor'sChoice ★ **Palazzo Pubblico.** *(See the highlighted listing in this chapter)* ✉ *Piazza del Campo 1, Città* ☎ *0577/292232* 🎫 *Museum €9, tower €10*

Fodor'sChoice ★ **Piazza del Campo.** *(See the highlighted listing in this chapter)* ✉ *Città.*

Pinacoteca Nazionale. The superb collection of five centuries of local painting in Siena's national picture gallery can easily convince you that the Renaissance was by no means just a Florentine thing—Siena was arguably just as important a center of art and innovation as its rival to the north, especially in the mid-13th century. Accordingly, the most interesting section of the collection, chronologically arranged, has several important firsts. Room 1 contains a painting of the *Stories of the True Cross* (1215) by the so-called Master of Tressa, the earliest identified work by a painter of the Sienese school, and is followed in Room 2 by late-13th-century artist Guido da Siena's *Stories from the Life of Christ,* one of the first paintings ever made on canvas (earlier painters used wood panels). Rooms 3 and 4 are dedicated to Duccio, a student of Cimabue (circa 1240–1302) and considered to be the last of the proto-Renaissance painters. Ambrogio Lorenzetti's landscapes in Room 8 are the first truly secular paintings in Western art. Among later works in the rooms on the floor above, keep an eye out for the preparatory sketches used by Domenico Beccafumi (1486–1551) for the 35 etched marble panels he made for the floor of the Duomo. ✉ *Via San Pietro 29, Città* ☎ *0577/286143* ⊕ *www.pinacotecanazionale.siena.it* 🎫 *€4.*

Fodor'sChoice ★ **Santa Maria della Scala.** For more than 1,000 years, this complex across from the Duomo was home to Siena's hospital, but now it serves as a museum. Restored 15th-century frescoes in the Sala del Pellegrinaio tell the history of the hospital, which was created to give refuge to passing pilgrims and to those in need, and to distribute charity to the poor. Incorporated into the complex is the church of the Santissima Annunziata, with a celebrated *Risen Christ* by Vecchietta (also known as Lorenzo di Pietro, circa 1412–80). Down in the dark Cappella di Santa Caterina della Notte is where St. Catherine went to pray at night. The subterranean archaeological museum contained within the *ospedale* (hospital) is worth seeing even if you're not particularly taken with Etruscan objects. The displays are clearly marked and can serve as a good introduction to the history of regional excavations. Don't miss della Quercia's original sculpted reliefs from the Fonte Gaia. ✉ *Piazza del Duomo 1, Città* ☎ *0577/534511* ⊕ *www.santamariadellascala.com* 🎫 *€9.*

WORTH NOTING

Battistero. The Duomo's 14th-century Gothic Baptistery was built to prop up the apse of the cathedral. There are frescoes throughout, but the highlight is a large bronze 15th-century baptismal font designed by Jacopo della Quercia (1374–1438). It's adorned with bas-reliefs by various artists, including two by Renaissance masters: the *Baptism of Christ* by Lorenzo Ghiberti (1378–1455) and the *Feast of Herod* by Donatello. ✉ *Piazza San Giovanni, Siena* ☎ *0577/286300* ⊕ *www.operaduomo. siena.it* 🎫 *€4; €12 combined ticket, includes the Duomo, Cripta, and Museo dell'Opera del Duomo.*

Continued on page 376

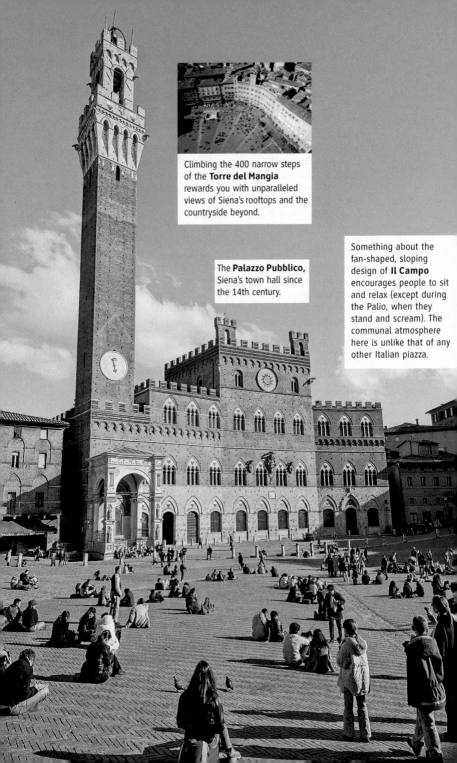

Climbing the 400 narrow steps of the **Torre del Mangia** rewards you with unparalleled views of Siena's rooftops and the countryside beyond.

The **Palazzo Pubblico,** Siena's town hall since the 14th century.

Something about the fan-shaped, sloping design of **Il Campo** encourages people to sit and relax (except during the Palio, when they stand and scream). The communal atmosphere here is unlike that of any other Italian piazza.

PIAZZA DEL CAMPO

Fodor'sChoice ★

The fan-shaped **Piazza del Campo**, known simply as il Campo (The Field), is one of the finest squares in Italy. Constructed toward the end of the 12th century on a market area unclaimed by any contrada, it's still the heart of town. The bricks of the Campo are patterned in nine different sections—representing each member of the medieval Government of Nine. At the top of the Campo is a copy of the **Fonte Gaia**, decorated in the early 15th century by Siena's greatest sculptor, Jacopo della Quercia, with 13 sculpted reliefs of biblical events and virtues. Those lining the rectangular fountain are 19th-century copies; the originals are in the Spedale di Santa Maria della Scala. On Palio horse race days (July 2 and August 16), the Campo and all its surrounding buildings are packed with cheering, frenzied locals and tourists craning their necks to take it all in.

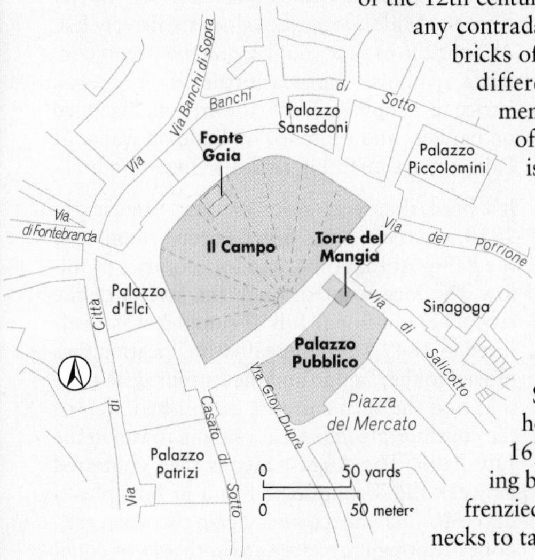

Map labels: Via Banchi di Sopra; Banchi; di; Sotto; Palazzo Sansedoni; Via; Fonte Gaia; Palazzo Piccolomini; Via; di Fontebranda; Il Campo; Torre del Mangia; Via del Porrione; Palazzo d'Elci; Via; Città; Palazzo Pubblico; Sinagoga; Via di Salicotto; Piazza del Mercato; Via Casato di Sotto; Via Giov. Duprè; Palazzo Patrizi; Via; 0 50 yards; 0 50 meters

The Gothic **Palazzo Pubblico**, the focal point of the Piazza del Campo, has served as Siena's town hall since the 1300s. It now also contains the **Museo Civico**, with walls covered in early Renaissance frescoes. The nine governors of Siena once met in the Sala della Pace, famous for Ambrogio Lorenzetti's frescoes called *Allegories of Good and Bad Government*, painted in the late 1330s to demonstrate the dangers of tyranny. The good government side depicts utopia, showing first the virtuous ruling council surrounded by angels and then scenes of a perfectly running city and countryside. Conversely, the bad government fresco tells a tale straight out of Dante. The evil ruler and his advisers have horns and fondle strange animals, and the town scene depicts the seven mortal sins in action. Interestingly, the bad government fresco is severely damaged, and the good government fresco is in terrific condition. The **Torre del Mangia**, the palazzo's famous bell tower, is named after one of its first bell ringers, Giovanni di Duccio (called Mangiaguadagni, or earnings eater). The climb up to the top is long and steep, but the view makes it worth every step. *For opening hours and prices, see the Exploring section.*

THE PALIO

The three laps around a makeshift racetrack in Piazza del Campo are over in less than two minutes, but the spirit of Siena's Palio—a horse race held every July 2 and August 16—lives all year long.

The Palio is contested between Siena's contrade, the 17 neighborhoods that have divided the city since the Middle Ages. Loyalties are fiercely felt. At any time of year you'll see on the streets contrada symbols—Tartuca (turtle), Oca (goose), Istrice (porcupine), Torre (tower)—emblazoned on banners and engraved on building walls. At Palio time, simmering rivalries come to a boil.

It's been that way since at least August 16, 1310, the date of the first recorded running of the Palio. At that time, and for centuries to follow, the race went through the streets of the city. The additional July 2 running was instituted in 1649; soon thereafter the location was moved to the Campo and the current system for selecting the race entrants established. Ten of the contrade are chosen at random to run in the July Palio. The August race is then contested between the 7 contrade left out in July, plus 3 of the 10 July participants, again chosen at random. Although the races are in theory of equal importance, Sienese will tell you that it's better to win the second and have bragging rights for the rest of the year.

The race itself has a raw and arbitrary character—it's no Kentucky Derby. There's barely room for the 10 horses on the makeshift Campo course, so falls and collisions are inevitable. Horses are chosen at random three days before the race, and jockeys (who ride bareback) are mercenaries hired from surrounding towns. Almost no tactic is considered too underhanded. Bribery, secret plots, and betrayal are commonplace—so much so that the word for "jockey," *fantino*, has come to mean "untrustworthy" in Siena. There have been incidents of drugging (the horses) and kidnapping (the jockeys); only sabotaging a horse's reins remains taboo.

Above: The tension of the starting line. Top left: The frenzy of the race. Bottom left: A solemn flag bearer follows in the footsteps of his ancestors.

AQUILA	BRUCO	CHIOCCIOLA

MEDIEVAL CONTRADE

Festivities kick off three days prior to the Palio, with the selection and blessing of the horses, trial runs, ceremonial banquets, betting, and late-night celebrations. Residents don their contrada's colors and march through the streets in medieval costumes. The Campo is transformed into a racetrack lined with a thick layer of sand. On race day, each horse is brought to the church of the contrada for which it will run, where it's blessed and told, "Go little horse and return a winner." The Campo fills through the afternoon, with spectators crowding into every available space until bells ring and the piazza is sealed off. Processions of flag wavers in traditional dress march to the beat of tambourines and drums and the roar of the crowds. The *palio* itself—a banner for which the race is named, dedicated to the Virgin Mary—makes an appearance, followed by the horses and their jockeys.

The race begins when one horse, chosen to ride up from behind the rest of the field, crosses the starting line. There are always false starts, adding to the frenzied mood. Once underway, the race is over in a matter of minutes. The victorious rider is carried off through the streets of the winning contrada (where in the past tradition dictated he was entitled to the local girl of his choice), while winning and losing sides use television replay to analyze the race from every possible angle. The winning contrada will celebrate into the night, at long tables piled high with food and drink. The champion horse is guest of honor.

CIVETTA — DRAGO
GIRAFFA — ISTRICE
LEOCORNO — LUPA
NICCHIO — OCA
ONDA — PANTERA
SELVA — TARTUCA
TORRE — VALDIMONTONE

San Domenico. Although the Duomo is celebrated as a triumph of 13th-century Gothic architecture, this church, built at about the same time, turned out to be an oversize, hulking brick box that never merited a finishing coat in marble, let alone a graceful facade. Named for the founder of the Dominican order, the church is now more closely associated with St. Catherine of Siena. Just to the right of the entrance is the chapel in which she received the stigmata. On the wall is the only known contemporary portrait of the saint, made in the late 14th century by Andrea Vanni (circa 1332–1414). Farther down is the famous **Cappella delle Santa Testa,** the church's official shrine. Catherine, or bits and pieces of her, was literally spread all over the country—a foot is in Venice, most of her body is in Rome, and only her head (kept in a reliquary on the chapel's altar) and her right thumb are here. She was revered throughout the country long before she was officially named a patron saint of Italy in 1939. On either side of the chapel are well-known frescoes by Sodoma (aka Giovanni Antonio Bazzi, 1477–1549) of *St. Catherine in Ecstasy.* Don't miss the view of the Duomo and town center from the apse-side terrace. ⊠ *Piazza San Domenico, Camollia* ☎ *0577/280893* ⊕ *www.basilicacateriniana.com.*

WHERE TO EAT

$$$
TUSCAN
Fodor'sChoice
★

✕ **Le Logge.** Bright flowers provide a dash of color at this classic Tuscan dining room, and stenciled designs on the ceilings add some whimsy. The wooden cupboards (now filled with wine bottles) lining the walls recall its past as a turn-of-the-19th-century grocery store. The menu, with four or five primi and secondi, changes regularly, but almost always includes their classic *malfatti all'osteria* (ricotta and spinach dumplings in a cream sauce). Desserts such as *coni con mousse al cioccolato e gelato allo zafferano* (two diminutive ice-cream cones with chocolate mousse and saffron ice cream) provide an inventive ending to the meal. When not vying for one of the outdoor tables, make sure to ask for one in the main downstairs room. Ⓢ *Average main: €25* ⊠ *Via del Porrione 33, San Martino* ☎ *0577/48013* ⊕ *www.giannibrunelli.it* ⊗ *Closed Sun., and 3 wks in Jan.*

$
TUSCAN

✕ **Osteria Il Grattacielo.** Wiped out from too much sightseeing? Consider a meal at this hole-in-the-wall restaurant where locals congregate for a simple lunch over a glass of wine. There's a collection of verdure sott'olio, a wide selection of affettati misti, and various types of frittatas. All of this can be washed down with the cheap, yet eminently drinkable, house red. A few bench tables provide outdoor seating in summer. Don't be put off by the absence of a written menu. All the food is displayed at the counter, so you can point if you need to. Ⓢ *Average main: €10* ⊠ *Via Pontani 8, Camollia* ☎ *0577/289326* ▭ *No credit cards.*

$
TUSCAN
Fodor'sChoice
★

✕ **Trattoria Papei.** The menu hasn't changed for years, and why should it? The pici *al cardinale* (with a duck and bacon sauce) is wonderful, and all the other typically Sienese dishes are equally delicious. Grilled meats are the true specialty; the *bistecca di vitello* (grilled veal steak) is melt-in-your-mouth wonderful. Tucked away behind the Palazzo

Pubblico in a square that serves as a parking lot for most of the day, the restaurant's location isn't great, but the food is. Thanks to portable heaters, there is outdoor seating all year-round. $ *Average main: €12* ⊠ *Piazza del Mercato 6, Città* ☎ *0577/280894* ⊕ *www. anticatrattoriapapei.com.*

WHERE TO STAY

$

B&B/INN

☖ **Antica Torre.** The cordial Landolfo family has carefully evoked a private home with their eight guest rooms inside a restored 16th-century tower. **Pros:** near the town center; charming atmosphere. **Cons:** narrow stairway up to the rooms; low ceilings; cramped bathrooms. $ *Rooms from: €100* ⊠ *Via Fieravecchia 7, San Martino* ☎ *0577/222255* ⊕ *www. anticatorresiena.it* ⤳ *8 rooms* ¶⊚¶ *Breakfast.*

$$

B&B/INN

☖ **Hotel Santa Caterina.** Manager Lorenza Capannelli and her fine staff are welcoming, hospitable, enthusiastic, and go out of their way to ensure a fine stay in rooms where dark, straight-lined wood furniture stands next to beds with floral spreads. **Pros:** friendly staff; a short walk to center of town; breakfast in the garden. **Cons:** on a busy intersection; outside city walls. $ *Rooms from: €195* ⊠ *Via Piccolomini 7, San Martino* ☎ *0577/221105* ⊕ *www.hscsiena.it* ⤳ *22 rooms* ¶⊚¶ *Breakfast.*

$$

HOTEL

Fodor's Choice

★

☖ **Palazzo Ravizza.** This romantic palazzo exudes a sense of genteel shabbiness, and lovely guest rooms have high ceilings, antique furnishings, and bathrooms decorated with hand-painted tiles. **Pros:** 10-minute walk to the center of town; pleasant garden with a view beyond the city walls; professional staff. **Cons:** not all rooms have views; some rooms are a little cramped. $ *Rooms from: €150* ⊠ *Pian dei Mantellini 34, Città* ☎ *0577/280462* ⊕ *www.palazzoravizza.it* ⤳ *38 rooms, 4 suites* ¶⊚¶ *Breakfast.*

SHOPPING

Enoteca Italiana. Italy's only state-sponsored enoteca has a vast selection of wines from all parts of the country. Housed in the fortress that the Florentines built to dominate Siena after they conquered the town in 1555, it's a must for any lover of Italian wines. ⊠ *Fortezza Medicea, Piazza Libertà 1, Camollìa* ☎ *0577/228811* ⊕ *www.enoteca-italiana.it* ⊙ *Closed Sun. and Mon.*

AREZZO AND CORTONA

The hill towns of Arezzo and Cortona are the main attractions of eastern Tuscany; despite their appeal, this part of the region gets less tourist traffic than its neighbors to the west. You'll truly escape the crowds if you venture north to the Casentino, which is backwoods Tuscany—tiny towns and abbeys are sprinkled through beautiful forestland, some of which is set aside as a national park.

AREZZO

63 km (39 miles) northeast of Siena, 81 km (50 miles) southeast of Florence.

Arezzo is best known for the magnificent Piero della Francesca frescoes in the church of San Francesco. It's also the birthplace of the poet Petrarch (1304–74), the Renaissance artist and art historian Giorgio Vasari, and Guido d'Arezzo (aka Guido Monaco), the inventor of contemporary musical notation. Arezzo dates from pre-Etruscan times, when around 1000 BC the first settlers erected a cluster of huts. Arezzo thrived as an Etruscan capital from the 7th to the 4th century BC, and was one of the most important cities in the Etruscans' anti-Roman 12-city federation, resisting Rome's rule to the last.

The city eventually fell and in turn flourished under the Romans. In 1248 Guglielmino degli Ubertini, a member of the powerful Ghibelline family, was elected bishop of Arezzo. This sent the city headlong into the enduring conflict between the Ghibellines (pro-emperor) and the Guelphs (pro-pope). In 1289 Florentine Guelphs defeated Arezzo in a famous battle at Campaldino. Among the Florentine soldiers was Dante Alighieri (1265–1321), who often referred to Arezzo in his *Divine Comedy*. Guelph–Ghibelline wars continued to plague Arezzo until the end of the 14th century, when Arezzo lost its independence to Florence.

GETTING HERE AND AROUND

Arezzo is easily reached by car from the A1, the main highway running between Florence and Rome. Direct trains connect Arezzo with Rome (2½ hours) and Florence (1 hour). Direct bus service is available from Florence, but not from Rome.

VISITOR INFORMATION

Arezzo Tourism Office. ⊠ *Emiciclo Giovanni Paolo II* ☎ *0575/1822770* ⊕ *www.arezzoturismo.it.*

EXPLORING

Fodor'sChoice ★ **Basilica di San Francesco.** The famous Piero della Francesca frescoes depicting *The Legend of the True Cross* (1452–66) were executed on the three walls of the Capella Bacci, the main apse of this 14th-century church. What Sir Kenneth Clark called "the most perfect morning light in all Renaissance painting" may be seen in the lowest section of the right wall, where the troops of Emperor Maxentius flee before the sign of the cross. The rest of the church is decorated with 14th-, 15th-, and 16th-century frescoes of mixed quality. Reservations are recommended June through September. ⊠ *Piazza San Francesco 2* ☎ *0575/352727* ⊕ *www.pierodellafrancesca-ticketoffice.it* ☜ *€8.*

Duomo. Arezzo's medieval cathedral at the top of the hill contains an eye-level fresco of a tender *Maria Maddalena* by Piero della Francesca (1420–92); look for it in the north aisle next to the large marble tomb near the organ. Construction of the Duomo began in 1278, but twice came to a halt, and the church wasn't completed until 1510. The ceiling decorations and the stained-glass windows date from the 16th century. The facade, designed by Arezzo's Dante Viviani, was added later (1901–14). ⊠ *Piazza del Duomo 1* ☎ *0575/23991.*

NEED A BREAK

🍴 Caffè dei Costanti. Outdoor seating on Arezzo's main pedestrian square and a tasty range of chef's salads (named after the waitresses that serve here) make this a very pleasant spot for a light lunch during a tour of town. In continuous operation since 1886, it's the oldest café in Arezzo, and the charming old-world interior served as backdrop to scenes in Roberto Benigni's 1997 film, *Life is Beautiful*. If you're here in the early evening, the dei Costanti serves up an ample buffet of snacks to accompany predinner aperitifs. ✉ *Piazza San Francesco 19* ☎ *0575/1824075* 🌐 *www.caffedeicostanti.it*.

Piazza Grande. With its irregular shape and sloping brick pavement, framed by buildings of assorted centuries, Arezzo's central piazza echoes Siena's Piazza del Campo. Though not quite so magnificent, it's lively enough during the outdoor antiques fair the first weekend of the month and when the **Giostra del Saracino** (Saracen Joust), featuring medieval costumes and competition, is held here on the third Saturday of June and on the first Sunday of September. ✉ *Piazza Grande*.

Santa Maria della Pieve (*Church of Saint Mary of the Parish*). The curving, tiered apse on Piazza Grande belongs to a fine Romanesque church that was originally an Early Christian structure, which had been constructed over the remains of a Roman temple. The church was rebuilt in Romanesque style in the 12th century. The splendid facade dates from the early 13th century, but includes granite Roman columns. A magnificent polyptych, depicting the Madonna and Child with four saints, by Pietro Lorenzetti (circa 1290–1348), embellishes the high altar. ✉ *Corso Italia 7* ☎ *0575/22629*.

WHERE TO EAT AND STAY

$$ SEAFOOD Fodor's Choice ★

🍴 **I Tre Bicchieri.** Chef Luigi Casotti hails from Amalfi and this shows through in his fine adaptations of dishes more commonly served near the Bay of Naples. The antipasti include a delicious *tonno scottato ai semi di papavero e agro di cipolla rossa* (lightly brazed tuna in a poppy seed crust with sweet and sour red onions) and an unusual but equally delightful *salmone selvaggio confit con julienne di zucchine, panna acida e polvere di liquirizia* (wild salmon carpaccio with sour cream, zucchini and liquorice). The *tagliolini alle rape, guanciale, seppie e bufala* (beet pasta with bacon and cuttlefish) makes for a particularly delightful first course. Two well-priced tasting menus are also available. [$] *Average main: €18* ✉ *Piazzetta Sopra i Ponti 3–5* ☎ *0575/26557* 🌐 *www.ristoranteitrebicchieri.com* 🕒 *Closed Sun. (except 1st weekend of the month)*.

$ ITALIAN

🍴 **La Torre di Gnicche.** Wine lovers shouldn't miss this wine bar/eatery, just off Piazza Grande, with more than 700 labels on the list. Seasonal dishes of traditional fare, such as *acquacotta del casentino* (porcini mushroom soup) and *baccalà in umido* (salt-cod stew), are served in the simply decorated, vaulted dining room. You can accompany your meal with one, or more, of the almost 30 wines that are available by the glass. Limited outdoor seating is available in warm weather. [$] *Average main: €14* ✉ *Piaggia San Martino 8* ☎ *0575/352035* 🌐 *www.latorredignicche.it* 🕒 *Closed Wed., Jan., and 2 wks in July*.

$$
B&B/INN
FAMILY
Fodor'sChoice
★

Calcione. The elegant Marchesa Olivella Lotteringhi della Stufa has turned her six-century-old family estate (circa 1483) into a top-notch agriturismo. **Pros:** houses sleep up to 10; large swimming pools; quiet, beautiful, remote setting. **Cons:** private transportation is a must; nearest village is 8 km (5 miles) away; no a/c. $ *Rooms from: €125* ⊠ *Località Il Calcione 102, 26 km (15 miles) southwest of Arezzo, Lucignano* ☎ *0575/837153* ⊕ *www.calcione.com* ⊙ *Closed Oct.–mid-Mar.* ⤳ *2 houses, 6 apartments* ❖ *No meals.*

$$$$
HOTEL
Fodor'sChoice
★

Il Borro. The location has been described as "heaven on earth," and a stay at this elegant Ferragamo estate is sure to bring similar descriptions to mind. **Pros:** superlative service; great location for exploring eastern Tuscany; unique setting and atmosphere. **Cons:** off the beaten track, making private transport a must; not all suites have country views. $ *Rooms from: €480* ⊠ *Località Il Borro 1, outside village of San Giustino Valdarno, 20 km (12 miles) northwest of Arezzo* ☎ *055/977053* ⊕ *www.ilborro. it* ⊙ *Closed Dec.–Mar.* ⤳ *3 villas, 7 farmhouses, 27 suites* ❖ *Breakfast.*

SHOPPING

Ever since Etruscan goldsmiths set up their shops here more than 2,000 years ago, Arezzo has been famous for its jewelry. Today the town lays claim to being one of the world's capitals of jewelry design and manufacture, and you can find an impressive display of big-time baubles in the town center's shops.

Arezzo is also famous, at least in Italy, for its antiques dealers. The first weekend of every month, between 8:30 and 5:30, a popular and colorful flea market selling antiques and not-so-antique items takes place in the town's main square, **Piazza Grande,** and in the streets and parks nearby.

CORTONA

29 km (18 miles) south of Arezzo, 79 km (44 miles) east of Siena, 117 km (73 miles) southeast of Florence.

Brought into the limelight by Frances Mayes's book *Under the Tuscan Sun* and a subsequent movie, Cortona is no longer the destination of just a few specialist art historians and those seeking reprieve from busier tourist venues. The main street, Via Nazionale, is now lined with souvenir shops and fills with crowds during summer. Although the main sights of Cortona make braving the bustling center worthwhile, much of the town's charm lies in its maze of quiet backstreets. It's here that you will see laundry hanging from windows, find children playing, and catch the smell of simmering pasta sauce. Wander off the beaten track and you won't be disappointed.

GETTING HERE AND AROUND

Cortona is easily reached by car from the A1 autostrada: take the Valdichiana exit toward Perugia, then follow signs for Cortona. Regular bus service, provided by Etruria Mobilità, is available between Arezzo and Cortona (one hour). Train service to Cortona is made inconvenient by the location of the train station, in the valley 3 km (2 miles) steeply below the town itself. From there, you have to rely on bus or taxi service to get up to Cortona.

VISITOR INFORMATION

Cortona Tourism Office. ✉ *Piazza Signorelli 9* ☎ *0575/637223* ⊕ *www. turismo.provincia.arezzo.it.*

EXPLORING

Museo Diocesano. Housed in part of the original cathedral structure, this nine-room museum houses an impressive number of large, splendid paintings by native son Luca Signorelli (1445–1523), as well as a beautiful *Annunciation* by Fra Angelico (1387/1400–55), which is a delightful surprise in this small town. The former oratory of the Compagnia del Gesù, reached by descending the 1633 staircase opposite the Duomo, is part of the museum. The church was built between 1498 and 1505 and restructured by Giorgio Vasari in 1543. Frescoes depicting sacrifices from the Old Testament by Doceno (1508–56), based on designs by Vasari, line the walls. ✉ *Piazza Duomo 1* ☎ *0575/62830* 🎫 *€5.*

Santa Maria al Calcinaio. Legend has it that the image of the Madonna appeared on a wall of a medieval *calcinaio* (lime pit used for curing leather), the site on which the church was then built between 1485 and 1513. The linear gray-and-white interior recalls Florence's Duomo. Sienese architect Francesco di Giorgio (1439–1502) most likely designed the sanctuary: the church is a terrific example of Renaissance architectural principles. ✉ *Località Il Calcinaio 227, 3 km (2 miles) southeast of Cortona's center* ☎ *0575/604830.*

WHERE TO EAT AND STAY

$$
TUSCAN

✕ **Osteria del Teatro.** Photographs from theatrical productions spanning many years line the walls of this tavern off Cortona's large Piazza del Teatro. The food is simply delicious—try the *filetto al lardo di colonnata e prugne* (beef cooked with bacon and prunes); service is warm and friendly. $ *Average main: €18* ✉ *Via Maffei 2* ☎ *0575/630556* ⊕ *www.osteria-del-teatro.it* ☉ *Closed Wed., and 2 wks in Nov. and Feb.*

$$$
B&B/INN

🏨 **Il Falconiere.** Accommodation options here include rooms in an 18th-century villa, suites in the *chiesetta* (chapel, or little church), or for more seclusion, Le Vigne del Falco suites at the far end of the property. **Pros:** attractive setting in the valley beneath Cortona; excellent service; elegant, but relaxed. **Cons:** a car is a must; some find rooms in main villa a little noisy. $ *Rooms from: €290* ✉ *Località San Martino 370, 3 km (2 miles) north of Cortona* ☎ *0575/612679* ⊕ *www.ilfalconiere.com* ☉ *Closed last 3 wks in Jan.–mid-Feb.* ⇥ *15 rooms, 8 suites* ⦿| *Breakfast.*

UMBRIA

Birthplace of saints and home to some of the country's greatest artistic treasures, central Italy is a collection of misty green valleys and picture-perfect hill towns laden with centuries of history.

Umbria and the Marches are the Italian countryside as you've imagined it: verdant farmland, steep hillsides topped with medieval fortresses, and winding country roads. No single town here has the extravagant wealth of art and architecture of Florence, Rome, or Venice, but this works in your favor; small jewels of towns feel knowable, not overwhelming. And the cultural cupboard is far from bare. Orvieto's cathedral and Assisi's basilica are two of the most important sights in Italy, while Perugia, Todi, Gubbio, and Spoleto are rich in art and architecture.

PERUGIA

Perugia is a majestic, handsome, wealthy city, and with its trendy boutiques, refined cafés, and grandiose architecture, it doesn't try to hide its affluence. A student population of more than 30,000 means that the city, with a permanent population of about 170,000, is abuzz with activity throughout the year. Umbria Jazz, one of the region's most important music festivals, attracts music lovers from around the world every July, and Eurochocolate, the international chocolate festival, is an irresistible draw each October for anyone with a sweet tooth.

GETTING HERE AND AROUND

The best approach to the city is by train. The area around the station doesn't attest to the rest of Perugia's elegance, but buses running from the station to Piazza d'Italia, the heart of the old town, are frequent. If you're in a hurry, take the *minimetro,* a one-line subway, to Stazione della Cupa. If you're driving to Perugia and your hotel doesn't have parking facilities, leave your car in one of the lots close to the center. Electronic displays indicate the location of lots and the number of spaces free. If you park in the Piazza Partigiani, take the escalators that pass through the fascinating subterranean excavations of the Roman foundations of the city and lead to the town center.

EXPLORING

TOP ATTRACTIONS

Collegio del Cambio (*Bankers' Guild Hall*). These elaborate rooms, on the ground floor of the **Palazzo dei Priori,** served as the meeting hall and chapel of the guild of bankers and moneychangers. Most of the frescoes were completed by the most important Perugian painter of the Renaissance, Pietro Vannucci, better known as Perugino. He included a remarkably honest self-portrait on one of the pilasters. The iconography includes common religious themes, such as the Nativity and the Transfiguration seen on the end walls. On the left wall are female figures representing the virtues, and beneath them are the heroes and sages of antiquity. On the right wall are figures presumed to have been painted in part by Perugino's most famous pupil, Raphael. (His hand, experts say, is most apparent in the figure of Fortitude.) The *cappella* (chapel) of San Giovanni Battista has frescoes painted by Giannicola di Paolo, another student of Perugino's. ⊠ *Corso Vannucci 25, Perugia* ☎ *075/5728599* ⊕ *www.collegiodelcambio.it* ⊠ *€4.50, includes Collegio della Mercanzia.*

Corso Vannucci. A string of elegantly connected palazzos expresses the artistic nature of this city center, the heart of which is concentrated

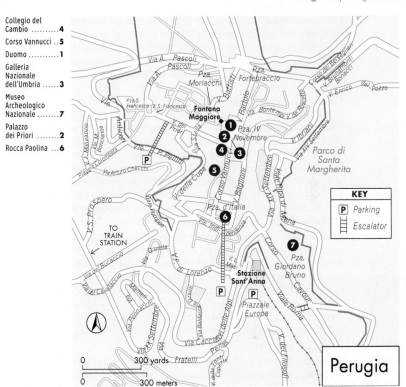

along Corso Vannucci. Stately and broad, this pedestrians-only street runs from Piazza Italia to Piazza IV Novembre. Along the way, the entrances to many of Perugia's side streets might tempt you to wander off and explore. But don't stray too far as evening falls, when Corso Vannucci fills with Perugians out for their evening *passeggiata,* a pleasant predinner stroll that may include a pause for an aperitif at one of the many bars that line the street. ⊠ *Perugia.*

Fodor'sChoice **Galleria Nazionale dell'Umbria.** The region's most comprehensive art gal-
★ lery is housed on the fourth floor of the **Palazzo dei Priori.** Enhanced by skillfully lit displays and computers that allow you to focus on the works' details and background information, the collection includes work by native artists—most notably Pintoricchio (1454–1513) and Perugino (circa 1450–1523)—and others of the Umbrian and Tuscan schools, among them Gentile da Fabriano (1370–1427), Duccio (circa 1255–1318), Fra Angelico (1387–1455), Fiorenzo di Lorenzo (1445–1525), and Piero della Francesca (1420–92). In addition to paintings, the gallery has frescoes, sculptures, and some superb examples of crucifixes from the 13th and 14th centuries. Some rooms are dedicated to Perugia itself, showing how the medieval city evolved. ⊠ *Corso Vannucci 19, Piazza IV Novembre, Perugia* ☎ *075/58668410* ⊕ *www. artiumbria.beniculturali.it* 🎟️ *€6.50.*

Palazzo dei Priori (*Palace of the Priors*). A series of elegant connected buildings, the palazzo serves as Perugia's city hall and houses three of the city's museums. The buildings string along Corso Vannucci and wrap around the Piazza IV Novembre, where the original entrance is located. The steps here lead to the **Sala dei Notari** (Notaries' Hall). Other entrances lead to the **Galleria Nazionale dell'Umbria**, the **Collegio del Cambio**, and the **Collegio della Mercanzia**. The Sala dei Notari, which dates back to the 13th century and was the original meeting place of the town merchants, had become the seat of the notaries by the second half of the 15th century. Wood beams and an interesting array of frescoes attributed to Maestro di Farneto embellish the room. Coats of arms and crests line the back and right lateral walls; you can spot some famous figures from Aesop's *Fables* on the left wall. The palazzo facade is adorned with symbols of Perugia's pride and past power: the griffin is the city symbol, and the lion denotes Perugia's allegiance to the Guelph (or papal) cause. ⊠ *Piazza IV Novembre 25, Perugia* ⌑ *Free.*

Rocca Paolina. A labyrinth of little streets, alleys, and arches, this underground city was originally part of a fortress built at the behest of Pope Paul III between 1540 and 1543 to confirm papal dominion over the city. Parts of it were destroyed after the end of papal rule, but much still remains. Begin your visit by taking the escalators that descend through the subterranean ruins from Piazza Italia down to Via Masi. In the summer this is the coolest place in the city. At time of writing, the site is closed indefinitely for extensive restoration. ⊠ *Piazza Italia, Perugia* ⌑ *€3.*

WORTH NOTING

Duomo. Severe yet mystical, the Cathedral of San Lorenzo is most famous for being the home of the wedding ring of the Virgin Mary, stolen by the Perugians in 1488 from the nearby town of Chiusi. The ring, kept high up in a red-curtained vault in the chapel immediately to the left of the entrance, is stored under lock—15 locks, to be precise—and key most of the year. It's shown to the public on July 30 (the day it was brought to Perugia) and the second-to-last Sunday in January (Mary's wedding anniversary). The cathedral itself dates from the Middle Ages, and has many additions from the 15th and 16th centuries. The most visually interesting element is the altar to the Madonna of Grace; an elegant fresco on a column at the right of the entrance of the altar depicts *La Madonna delle Grazie* and is surrounded by prayer benches decorated with handwritten notes to the Holy Mother. Around the column are small amulets—symbols of gratitude from those whose prayers were answered. There are also elaborately carved choir stalls, executed by Giovanni Battista Bastone in 1520. The altarpiece (1484), an early masterpiece by Luca Signorelli (circa 1441–1523), shows the Madonna with St. John the Baptist, St. Onophrius, and St. Lawrence. Sections of the church may be closed to visitors during religious services.

The **Museo Capitolare** displays a large array of precious objects associated with the cathedral, including vestments, vessels, and manuscripts. Outside the Duomo is the elaborate **Fontana Maggiore,** which dates from 1278. It's adorned with zodiac figures and symbols of the seven arts. ⊠ *Piazza IV Novembre, Perugia* ☎ *075/5723832* ⌑ *Museum €3.50.*

Museo Archeologico Nazionale. An excellent collection of Etruscan artifacts from throughout the region sheds light on Perugia as a flourishing Etruscan city long before it fell under Roman domination in 310 BC. Little else remains of Perugia's mysterious ancestors, although the Arco di Augusto, in Piazza Fortebraccio, the northern entrance to the city, is of Etruscan origin. ✉ *Piazza G. Bruno 10, Perugia* ☎ *075/5727141* 🌐 *www.archeopg.arti.beniculturali.it* 🎟 *€4.*

WHERE TO EAT

$$ UMBRIAN 🍴 **Antica Trattoria San Lorenzo.** Brick vaults are not the only distinguishing feature of this small, popular eatery next to the Duomo, as both the food and the service are outstanding. Particular attention is paid to adapting traditional Umbrian cuisine to the modern palate. There's also a nice variety of seafood dishes on the menu. The *trenette alla farina di noce con pesce di mare* (flat noodles made with walnut flour topped with fresh fish) is a real treat. [$] *Average main: €18* ✉ *Piazza Danti 19/a, Perugia* ☎ *075/5721956* 🌐 *www.anticatrattoriasanlorenzo.com* 🕒 *Closed Sun.*

$ UMBRIAN 🍴 **Dal Mi' Cocco.** A great favorite with Perugia's university students, it is fun, crowded, and inexpensive. You may find yourself seated at a long table with other diners, but some language help from your neighbors could come in handy—the menu is in pure Perugian dialect. Fixed-price meals change with the season, and each day of the week brings some new creation *dal cocco* (from the "coconut," or head) of the chef. Get here early, reservations are not accepted. [$] *Average main: €14* ✉ *Corso Garibaldi 12, Perugia* ☎ *075/5732511* 💳 *No credit cards* 🕒 *Closed late July–mid-Aug.*

$$ ITALIAN 🍴 **La Rosetta.** The dining room of the hotel of the same name is a peaceful, elegant spot. In winter you dine inside under medieval vaults; in summer, in the cool courtyard. The food is simple but reliable, and flawlessly served. The restaurant caters to travelers seeking to get away from the bustle of central Perugia. [$] *Average main: €17* ✉ *Piazza d'Italia 19, Perugia* ☎ *075/5720841* 🌐 *www.larosetta.eu.*

$$ UMBRIAN 🍴 **La Taverna.** Medieval steps lead to a rustic two-story space where wine bottles and artful clutter decorate the walls. Good choices from the regional menu include *caramelle al gorgonzola* (pasta rolls filled with red cabbage and mozzarella and topped with a Gorgonzola sauce) and grilled meat dishes, such as the *medaglioni di vitello al tartuffo* (grilled veal with truffles). [$] *Average main: €18* ✉ *Via delle Streghe 8, off Corso Vannucci, Perugia* ☎ *075/5724128* 🌐 *www.ristorantelataverna.com.*

WHERE TO STAY

$$ HOTEL 🏨 **Castello dell'Oscano.** A splendid neo-Gothic castle, a late 19th-century villa, and a converted farmhouse hidden in the tranquil hills north of Perugia offer a wide range of accommodations. **Pros:** quiet elegance; fine gardens; Umbrian wine list. **Cons:** distant from Perugia; not easy to find. [$] *Rooms from: €200* ✉ *Strada della Forcella 37, Cenerente* ☎ *075/584371* 🌐 *www.oscano.com* 🛏 *24 rooms, 8 suites, 13 apartments* 🍽 *Breakfast.*

6

$$ **Hotel Fortuna.** The elegant decor in the large rooms, some with bal-
HOTEL conies, complements the frescoes, which date from the 1700s. **Pros:**
central but quiet; cozy, friendly atmosphere; elevator. **Cons:** some
small rooms; no restaurant. $ *Rooms from: €128* ✉ *Via Bonazzi 19,
Perugia* ☎ *075/5722845* ⊕ *www.hotelfortunaperugia.com* ⤴ *51 rooms*
|O| *Breakfast.*

$$ **Locanda della Posta.** Renovations have left the lobby and other public
HOTEL areas rather bland, but the rooms in this converted 18th-century palazzo
are soothingly decorated in muted colors. **Pros:** some fine views; central
location. **Cons:** some street noise; some small rooms. $ *Rooms from:
€150* ✉ *Corso Vannucci 97, Perugia* ☎ *075/5728925* ⊕ *www.locand-
adellapostahotel.it* ⤴ *38 rooms, 1 suite* |O| *Breakfast.*

$$ **Posta dei Donini.** Beguilingly comfortable guest rooms are set on lovely
HOTEL grounds, where gardeners go quietly about their business. **Pros:** plush
atmosphere; a quiet and private getaway. **Cons:** outside Perugia; unin-
teresting village. $ *Rooms from: €150* ✉ *Via Deruta 43, 15 km (9
miles) south of Perugia, San Martino in Campo* ☎ *075/609132* ⊕ *www.
postadonini.it* ⤴ *33 rooms* |O| *No meals.*

$$ **Tre Vaselle.** Rooms spread throughout four stone buildings are spa-
HOTEL cious and graced with floors of typical red-clay Tuscan tiles. **Pros:** per-
fect for visiting Torgiano wine area and Deruta; friendly staff; nice
pool. **Cons:** somewhat far from Perugia; in center of uninspiring village.
$ *Rooms from: €150* ✉ *Via Garibaldi 48, Torgiano* ☎ *075/9880447*
⊕ *www.3vaselle.it* ⤴ *47 rooms* |O| *No meals.*

NIGHTLIFE AND PERFORMING ARTS

With its large student population, the city has plenty to offer in the way
of bars and clubs. The best ones are around the city center, off Corso
Vannucci. *Viva Perugia* is a good source of information about nightlife;
the monthly, sold at newsstands, has a section in English.

MUSIC FESTIVALS

Sagra Musicale Umbra. Held mid-September, the Sagra Musicale Umbra
celebrates sacred music in Perugia and in several towns throughout the
region. ✉ *Perugia* ☎ *338/8668820* ⊕ *www.perugiamusicaclassica.com.*

SHOPPING

Take a stroll down any of Perugia's main streets, including Corso Vannucci, Via dei Priori, Via Oberdan, and Via Sant'Ercolano, and you'll
see many well-known designer boutiques and specialty shops.

The most typical thing to buy in Perugia is some Perugina chocolate,
which you can find almost anywhere. The best-known chocolates made
by Perugina (now owned by Nestlé) are the chocolate-and-hazelnut-
filled nibbles called Baci (literally, "kisses"). They're wrapped in silver
foil that includes a sliver of paper, like the fortune in a fortune cookie,
with multilingual romantic sentiments or sayings.

ASSISI

The small town of Assisi is one of the Christian world's most important pilgrimage sites and home of the Basilica di San Francesco—built to honor St. Francis (1182–1226) and erected in swift order after his death. The peace and serenity of the town is a welcome respite after the hustle and bustle of some of Italy's major cities.

Like most other towns in the region, Assisi began as an Umbri settlement in the 7th century BC and was conquered by the Romans 400 years later. The town was Christianized by St. Rufino, its patron saint, in the 3rd century, but it's the spirit of St. Francis, a patron saint of Italy and founder of the Franciscan monastic order, that's felt throughout its narrow medieval streets. The famous 13th-century basilica was decorated by the greatest artists of the period.

GETTING HERE AND AROUND

Assisi lies on the Terontola–Foligno rail line, with almost hourly connections to Perugia and direct trains to Rome and Florence several times a day. The Stazione Centrale is 4 km (2½ miles) from town, with a bus service about every half hour. Assisi is easily reached from the A1 autostrada (Rome–Florence) and the S75b highway. The walled town is closed to traffic, so cars must be left in the parking lots at Porta San Pietro, near Porta Nuova, or beneath Piazza Matteotti. Pay your parking fee at the *cassa* (ticket booth) before you return to your car to get a ticket to insert in the machine that will allow you to exit. It's a short but sometimes steep walk into the center of town; frequent minibuses (buy tickets from a newsstand or tobacco shop near where you park your car) make the rounds for weary pilgrims.

EXPLORING

Assisi is pristinely medieval in architecture and appearance, owing in large part to relative neglect from the 16th century until 1926, when the celebration of the 700th anniversary of St. Francis's death brought more than 2 million visitors. Since then, pilgrims have flocked here in droves, and today several million arrive each year to pay homage. But not even the constant flood of visitors to this town of just 3,000 residents can spoil the singular beauty of this significant religious center, the home of some of the Western tradition's most important works of art. The hill on which Assisi sits rises dramatically from the flat plain, and the town is dominated by a medieval castle at the very top.

Even though Assisi is sometimes besieged by busloads of sightseers who clamor to visit the famous basilica, it's difficult not to be charmed by the tranquillity of the town and its medieval architecture. Once you've seen the basilica, stroll through the town's narrow winding streets to see beautiful vistas of the nearby hills and valleys peeking through openings between the buildings.

TOP ATTRACTIONS

Fodor's Choice **Basilica di San Fransisco.** *See the highlighted feature in this chapter for more information.* ⊠ *Piazza di San Francesco* ☎ *075/819001* ⊕ *www.sanfrancescoassisi.org.*

Basilica di Santa Chiara. The lovely, wide piazza in front of this church is reason enough to visit. The red-and-white-striped facade frames the piazza's panoramic view over the Umbrian plains. Santa Chiara is dedicated to St. Clare, one of the earliest and most fervent of St. Francis's followers and the founder of the order of the Poor Ladies—or Poor Clares—which was based on the Franciscan monastic order. The church contains Clare's body, and in the **Cappella del Crocifisso** (on the right) is the cross that spoke to St. Francis. A heavily veiled nun of the Poor Clares order is usually stationed before the cross in adoration of the image. ✉ *Piazza Santa Chiara, Assisi* ☎ *075/812282* 🌐 *www.assisisantachiara.it.*

Cattedrale di San Rufino. St. Francis and St. Clare were among those baptized in Assisi's Cattedrale, which was the principal church in town until the 12th century. The baptismal font has since been redecorated, but it's possible to see the crypt of St. Rufino, the bishop who brought Christianity to Assisi and was martyred on August 11, 238 (or 236 by some accounts). Admission to the crypt includes the small **Museo Capitolare,** with its detached frescoes and artifacts. ✉ *Piazza San Rufino, Assisi* ☎ *075/812712* 🌐 *www.assisiinforma.it* 🎟 *Church free, Crypt and Museo Capitolare €3.50.*

WORTH NOTING

OFF THE BEATEN PATH

Eremo delle Carceri. About 4 km (2½ miles) east of Assisi is a monastery set in a dense wood against Monte Subasio: the Hermitage of Prisons. This was the place where St. Francis and his followers went to "imprison" themselves in prayer. The only site in Assisi that remains essentially unchanged since St. Francis's time, the church and monastery are the kinds of tranquil places that St. Francis would have appreciated. The walk out from town is very pleasant, and many trails lead from here across the wooded hillside of Monte Subasio (now a protected forest), with beautiful vistas across the Umbrian countryside. True to their Franciscan heritage, the friars here are entirely dependent on alms from visitors. ✉ *Via Santuario delle Carceri, 4 km (2½ miles) east of Assisi, Assisi* ☎ *075/812301* 🎟 *Donations accepted.*

Santa Maria Sopra Minerva. Dating from the time of the Emperor Augustus (27 BC–AD 14), this structure was originally dedicated to the Roman goddess of wisdom, in later times used as a monastery and prison before being converted into a church in the 16th century. The expectations raised by the perfect classical facade are not met by the interior, which was subjected to a thorough Baroque transformation in the 17th century. ✉ *Piazza del Comune, Assisi* ☎ *075/812361.*

WHERE TO EAT

$$ UMBRIAN

🍴 **Buca di San Francesco.** In summer, dine in a cool green garden; in winter, under the low brick arches of the cozy cellars. The unique settings and the first-rate fare make this central restaurant Assisi's busiest. Try homemade spaghetti *alla buca,* served with a roasted mushroom sauce. [$] *Average main: €18* ✉ *Via Eugenio Brizi 1, Assisi* ☎ *075/812204* 🌐 *www.bucadisanfrancesco.it* 🕒 *Closed Mon., and 10 days in late July.*

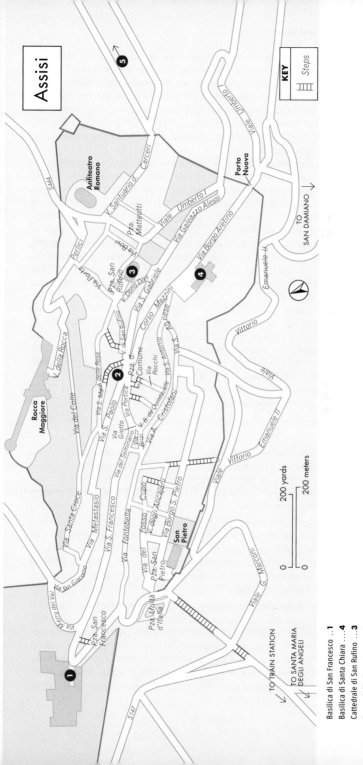

Assisi

Anfiteatro Romano

Rocca Maggiore

Porto Nuova

San Pietro

KEY

▦ Steps

TO SAN MARIA DEGLI ANGELI

TO TRAIN STATION

TO SAN DAMIANO

0 — 200 yards
0 — 200 meters

Basilica di San Francesco ...**1**
Basilica di Santa Chiara **4**
Cattedrale di San Rufino ...**3**
Eremo delle Carceri **5**
Santa Maria
Sopra Minerva **2**

S.444 · Perlici · V. della Rocca · V. Santa Croce · Via del Colle · Via San Giacomo · Via Merry del Val · Pza. San Francesco · Via S. Croce · Via Metastasio · Via S. Francesco · Via Fontebella · Via del Fosso · V. degli Ancajani · Via Borgo S. Pietro · Pza. San Pietro · Pza. Unità d'Italia · Viale G. Marconi · Viale Vittorio Emanuele II · Via A. Cristofani · Via del Seminario · Via Giotto · Via S. Paolo · Via Portica · Via S. Maria delle Rose · V. B. del Comitamore · Via Fortini · Pza. del Comune · Via Rocchi · Via S. Antonio · Via S. · Corso Mazzini · Via S. Gabriele · V. Dono Doni · Via di San Rufino · Pza. San Rufino · Via Borgo · V. Santuario d. Carceri · Pza. Mattegotti · Viale Umberto I · Viale Umberto · Via Galeazzo Alessi · Via Borgo Aretino · Vittorio · Viale S.

$ ✕ **La Pallotta.** At this homey, family-run trattoria with a crackling
UMBRIAN   fireplace and stone walls, the women do the cooking and the men
Fodor'sChoice   serve the food. Try the *stringozzi alla pallotta* (thick spaghetti with
★   a pesto of olives and mushrooms). Connected to the restaurant is
an inn whose eight rooms have firm beds and some views across the
rooftops of town. $ *Average main: €12* ⊠ *Vicolo della Volta Pinta 3,
Assisi* ☏ *075/812649* ⊕ *www.trattoriapallotta.it* ⊘ *Closed Tues., and
2 wks in Jan. or Feb.*

$$ ✕ **Osteria Piazzetta dell'Erba.** Hip service and sophisticated presentations
UMBRIAN   attract locals, who enjoy a wide selection of appetizers, including
smoked goose breast, and four or five types of pasta, plus various
salads and a good selection of *torta al testo* (dense flatbread stuffed
with vegetables or cheese). For dessert, try the homemade biscuits,
which you dunk in sweet wine. The owners carefully select wine at
local vineyards, buy it in bulk, and then bottle it themselves, resulting
in high quality and reasonable prices. Outdoor seating is available.
$ *Average main: €16* ⊠ *Via San Gabriele dell'Addolorata 15/b, Assisi*
☏ *075/815352* ⊕ *www.osterialapiazzetta.it* ⊘ *Closed Mon., and a few
wks in Jan. or Feb.*

$$ ✕ **San Francesco.** An excellent view of the Basilica di San Francesco from
UMBRIAN   the covered terrace is just one reason to enjoy the best restaurant in
town, where creative Umbrian dishes are made with aromatic locally
grown herbs. The seasonal menu might include gnocchi topped with
a sauce of wild herbs and *oca stufata di finocchio selvaggio* (goose
stuffed with wild fennel). Appetizers and desserts are especially good.
$ *Average main: €20* ⊠ *Via di San Francesco 52, Assisi* ☏ *075/813302*
⊕ *www.ristorantesanfrancesco.com* ⊘ *Closed Wed., and July 15–30.*

WHERE TO STAY

Advance reservations are essential at Assisi's hotels between Easter and
October and over Christmas. Latecomers are often forced to stay in
the modern town of Santa Maria degli Angeli, 8 km (5 miles) away.
As a last-minute option, you can always inquire at restaurants to see if
they're renting out rooms.

Until the early 1980s, pilgrim hostels outnumbered ordinary hotels in
Assisi, and they present an intriguing and economical alternative to
conventional lodgings. They're usually called *conventi* or *ostelli* ("convents" or "hostels") because they're run by convents, churches, or other
Catholic organizations. Rooms are spartan but peaceful. Check with
the tourist office for a list.

$$ ⊞ **Castello di Petrata.** Wood beams and sections of exposed medieval
HOTEL   stonework add a lot of character to this fortress built in the 14th cen-
Fodor'sChoice   tury, while comfortable couches turn each individually decorated room
★   into a delightful retreat. **Pros:** great views of town and countryside;
medieval character; pool. **Cons:** slightly isolated; far from Assisi town
center. $ *Rooms from: €140* ⊠ *Via Petrata 25, Località Petrata, Assisi*
☏ *075/815451* ⊕ *www.castellopetrata.it* ⊘ *Closed Jan.–Mar.* ⌿ *16
rooms, 7 suites* ⦿ *Breakfast.*

Continued on page 394

ASSISI'S BASILICA DI SAN FRANCESCO

The legacy of St. Francis, founder of the Franciscan monastic order, pervades Assisi. Each year the town hosts several million pilgrims, but the steady flow of visitors does nothing to diminish the singular beauty of one of Italy's most important religious centers. The pilgrims' ultimate destination is the massive Basilica di San Francesco, which sits halfway up Assisi's hill, supported by graceful arches.

The basilica is not one church but two. The Romanesque **Lower Church** came first; construction began in 1228, just two years after St. Francis's death, and was completed within a few years. The low ceilings and candlelit interior make an appropriately solemn setting for St. Francis's tomb, found in the crypt below the main altar. The Gothic **Upper Church**, built only half a century later, sits on top of the lower one, and is strikingly different, with soaring arches and tall stained-glass windows (the first in Italy). Inside, both churches are covered floor to ceiling with some of Europe's finest frescoes: the Lower Church is dim and full of candlelit shadows, and the Upper Church is bright and airy.

VISITING THE BASILICA

THE LOWER CHURCH

The most evocative way to experience the basilica is to begin with the dark Lower Church. As you enter, give your eyes a moment to adjust. Keep in mind that the artists at work here were conscious of the shadowy environment—they knew this was how their frescoes would be seen.

In the first chapel to the left, a superb fresco cycle by Simone Martini depicts scenes from the life of St. Martin. As you approach the main altar, the vaulting above you is decorated with the *Three Virtues of St. Francis* (poverty, chastity, and obedience) and *St. Francis's Triumph*, frescoes attributed to Giotto's followers. In the transept to your left, Pietro Lorenzetti's *Madonna and Child with St. Francis and St. John* sparkles when the sun hits it. Notice Mary's thumb; legend has it Jesus is asking which saint to bless, and Mary is pointing to Francis. Across the way in the right transept, Cimabue's *Madonna Enthroned Among Angels and St. Francis* is a famous portrait of the saint. Surrounding the portrait are painted scenes from the childhood of Christ, done by the assistants of Giotto. Nearby is a painting of the crucifixion attributed to Giotto himself.

You reach the crypt via stairs midway along the nave—on the crypt's altar, a stone coffin holds the saint's body. Steps up from the transepts lead to the cloister, where there's a gift shop, and the treasury, which contains holy objects.

THE UPPER CHURCH

The St. Francis fresco cycle is the highlight of the Upper Church. (See facing page.) Also worth special note is the 16th-century choir, with its remarkably delicate inlaid wood. When a 1997 earthquake rocked the basilica, the St. Francis cycle sustained little damage, but portions of the ceiling above the entrance and altar collapsed, reducing their frescoes (attributed to Cimabue and Giotto) to rubble. The painstaking restoration is ongoing. ⚠ The dress code is strictly enforced—no bare shoulders or bare knees.

FRANCIS, ITALY'S PATRON SAINT

St. Francis was born in Assisi in 1181, the son of a noblewoman and a well-to-do merchant. His troubled youth included a year in prison. He planned a military career, but after a long illness Francis heard the voice of God, renounced his father's wealth, and began a life of austerity. His mystical embrace of poverty, asceticism, and the beauty of man and nature struck a responsive chord in the medieval mind; he quickly attracted a vast number of followers. Francis was the first saint to receive the stigmata (wounds in his hands, feet, and side corresponding to those of Christ on the cross). He died on October 4, 1226, in the Porziuncola, the secluded chapel in the woods where he had first preached the virtue of poverty to his disciples. St. Francis was declared patron saint of Italy in 1939, and today the Franciscans make up the largest of the Catholic orders.

THE UPPER CHURCH'S ST. FRANCIS FRESCO CYCLE

The 28 frescoes in the Upper Church depicting the life of St. Francis are the most admired works in the entire basilica. They're also the subject of one of art history's biggest controversies. For centuries they thought to be by Giotto (1267-1337), the great early Renaissance innovator, but inconsistencies in style, both within this series and in comparison to later Giotto works, have thrown their origin into question. Some scholars now say Giotto was the brains behind the cycle, but that assistants helped with the execution; others claim he couldn't have been involved at all.

Two things are certain. First, the style is revolutionary—

which argues for Giotto's involvement. The tangible weight of the figures, the emotion they show, and the use of perspective all look familiar to modern eyes, but in the art of the time there was nothing like it. Second, these images have played a major part in shaping how the world sees St. Francis. In that respect, who painted them hardly matters.

Starting in the transept, the frescoes circle the church, showing events in the saint's life (and afterlife). Some of the best are grouped near the church's entrance—look for the nativity at Greccio, the miracle of the spring, the death of the knight at Celano, and, most famously, the sermon to the birds.

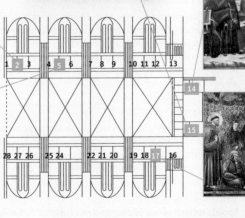

The St. Francis fresco cycle
1. Homage of a simple man
2. Giving cloak to a poor man
3. Dream of the palace
4. Hearing the voice of God
5. Rejection of worldly goods
6. Dream of Innocent III
7. Confirmation of the rules
8. Vision of flaming chariot
9. Vision of celestial thrones
10. Chasing devils from Arezzo
11. Before the sultan
12. Ecstasy of St. Francis
13. Nativity at Greccio
14. Miracle of the spring
15. Sermon to the birds
16. Death of knight at Celano
17. Preaching to Honorius III
18. Apparition at Arles
19. Receiving the stigmata
20. Death of St. Francis
21. Apparition before Bishop Guido and Fra Agostino
22. Verification of the stigmata
23. Mourning of St. Clare
24. Canonization
25. Apparition before Gregory IX
26. Healing of a devotee
27. Confession of a woman
28. Repentant heretic freed

$$ HOTEL **Hotel Subasio.** The converted monastery was well past its prime when Marlene Dietrich and Charlie Chaplin were guests, but such vestiges of glamour as Venetian chandeliers remain, as do the splendid views. **Pros:** perfect location next to the basilica; views of the Assisi plain. **Cons:** lobby a bit drab; some small rooms; service can be spotty. [$] *Rooms from: €130* ✉ *Via Frate Elia 2, Assisi* ☎ *075/812206* 🌐 *www.hotelsubasioassisi.it* 🛏 *54 rooms, 8 suites* 🍴 *Breakfast.*

$ HOTEL **Hotel Umbra.** Rooms on the upper floors of this charming 16th-century town house near Piazza del Comune look out over the Assisi rooftops to the valley below, as does a sunny terrace. **Pros:** friendly welcome; pleasant small garden. **Cons:** difficult parking; some small rooms. [$] *Rooms from: €110* ✉ *Via degli Archi 6, Assisi* ☎ *075/812240* 🌐 *www.hotelumbra.it* ⏲ *Closed Dec. and Jan.* 🛏 *25 rooms* 🍴 *Breakfast.*

SPOLETO

For most of the year, Spoleto is one more in a pleasant succession of sleepy hill towns, resting regally atop a mountain. But for three weeks every summer the town shifts into high gear for a turn in the international spotlight during the Festival dei Due Mondi (Festival of Two Worlds), an extravaganza of theater, opera, music, painting, and sculpture. As the world's top artists vie for honors, throngs of art aficionados vie for hotel rooms. If you plan to spend the night in Spoleto during the festival, make sure you have confirmed reservations, or you may find yourself scrambling at sunset.

Spoleto has plenty to lure you during the rest of the year as well: the final frescoes of Filippo Lippi, beautiful piazzas and streets with Roman and medieval attractions, and superb natural surroundings with rolling hills and a dramatic gorge. Spoleto makes a good base for exploring all of southern Umbria, as Assisi, Orvieto, and the towns in between are all within easy reach.

GETTING HERE AND AROUND

Spoleto is an hour's drive from Perugia. From the E45 highway, take the exit toward Assisi and Foligno, then merge onto the SS75 until you reach the Foligno Est exit. Merge onto the SS3, which leads to Spoleto. There are regular trains on the Perugia–Foligno line. From the train station it's a 15-minute uphill walk to the center, so you'll probably want to take a taxi.

VISITOR INFORMATION

Spoleto tourism office. ✉ *Piazza della Libertà 7, Spoleto* ☎ *0743/220773* 🌐 *www.comune.spoleto.gov.it.*

EXPLORING

The walled city is set on a slanting hillside, with the most interesting sections clustered toward the upper portion. Parking options inside the walls include Piazza Campello (just below the Rocca) on the southeast end, Via del Trivio to the north, and Piazza San Domenico on the west end. You can also park at Piazza della Vittoria farther north, just outside the walls. There are also several well-marked lots near the train station.

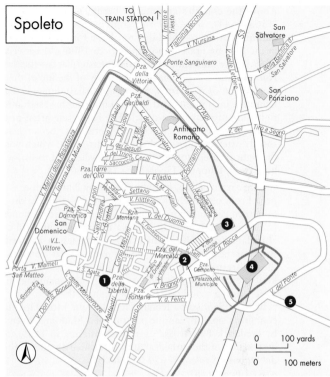

If you arrive by train, you can walk 1 km (½ mile) from the station to the entrance to the lower town. Regular bus connections are every 15–30 minutes. You can also use the *trenino,* as locals call the shuttle service, from the train station to Piazza della Libertà, near the upper part of the old town, where you'll find the tourist office.

Like most other towns with narrow, winding streets, Spoleto is best explored on foot. Bear in mind that much of the city is on a steep slope, so there are lots of stairs and steep inclines. The well-worn stones can be slippery even when dry; wear rubber-sole shoes for good traction. Several pedestrian walkways cut across Corso Mazzini, which zigzags up the hill. A €12 combination ticket purchased at the tourist office allows you entry to all the town's museums and galleries.

TOP ATTRACTIONS

Duomo. The 12th-century Romanesque facade received a Renaissance face-lift with the addition of a loggia in a rosy pink stone, creating a stunning contrast in styles. One of the finest cathedrals in the region is lit by eight rose windows that are especially dazzling in the late afternoon sun. The original floor tiles remain from an earlier church destroyed by Frederick I (circa 1123–90).

Above the church's entrance is Bernini's bust of Pope Urban VIII (1568–1644), who had the church redecorated in 17th-century Baroque; fortunately he didn't touch the 15th-century frescoes painted in the apse by Fra Filippo Lippi (circa 1406–69) between 1466 and 1469. These immaculately restored masterpieces—the *Annunciation, Nativity,* and *Dormition*—tell the story of the life of the Virgin. The *Coronation of the Virgin,* adorning the half dome, is the literal and figurative high point. Portraits of Lippi and his assistants are on the right side of the central panel. The Florentine artist-priest, "whose colors expressed God's voice" (the words inscribed on his tomb), died shortly after completing the work. His tomb, which you can see in the right transept (note the artist's brushes and tools), was designed by his son, Filippino Lippi (circa 1457–1504).

Another fresco cycle, including work by Pinturicchio, is in the Cappella Eroli, off the right aisle. Note the grotesques in the ornamentation, then very much in vogue with the rediscovery of ancient Roman paintings. The bounty of Umbria is displayed in vivid colors in the abundance of leaves, fruits, and vegetables that adorn the center seams of the cross vault. In the left nave, not far from the entrance, is the well-restored 12th-century crucifix by Alberto Sozio, the earliest known example of this kind of work, with a painting on parchment attached to a wood cross. To the right of the presbytery is the Cappella della Santissima Icona (Chapel of the Most Holy Icon), which contains a small Byzantine painting of a Madonna given to the town by Frederick Barbarossa as a peace offering in 1185, following his destruction of the cathedral and town three decades earlier. ⊠ *Piazza del Duomo, Spoleto* ☎ *0743/231063.*

Fodor'sChoice
★
Ponte delle Torri (*Bridge of the Towers*). Standing massive and graceful through the deep gorge that separates Spoleto from Monteluco, this 14th-century bridge is one of Umbria's most photographed monuments, and justifiably so. Built over the foundations of a Roman-era aqueduct, it soars 262 feet above the forested gorge—higher than the dome of St. Peter's in Rome. Sweeping views over the valley and a pleasant sense of vertigo make a walk across the bridge a must, particularly on a starry night. ⊠ *Via del Ponte, Spoleto.*

WORTH NOTING

Casa Romana. Spoleto became a Roman colony in the 3rd century BC, but the best excavated remains date from the 1st century AD. Best preserved among them is the Casa Romana. According to an inscription, it belonged to Vespasia Polla, the mother of Emperor Vespasian (one of the builders of the Colosseum and perhaps better known by the Romans for taxing them to install public toilets, later called "Vespasians"). The rooms, arranged around a large central atrium built over an *impluvium* (rain cistern), are decorated with black-and-white geometric mosaics. ⊠ *Palazzo del Municipio, Via Visiale 9, Spoleto* ☎ *0743/234350* ⊕ *www.spoletocard.it* ⊠ *€3; €6 combination ticket, includes Pinacoteca Comunale and Galleria d'Arte Moderna.*

La Rocca. Built in the mid-14th century for Cardinal Egidio Albornoz, this massive fortress served as a seat for the local pontifical governors, a tangible sign of the restoration of the Church's power in the area when the pope was ruling from Avignon. Several popes spent time here, and one of them, Alexander VI, in 1499 sent his capable teenage daughter Lucrezia Borgia (1480–1519) to serve as governor for three months. The Gubbio-born architect Gattapone (14th century) used the ruins of a Roman acropolis as a foundation and took materials from many Roman-era sites, including the Teatro Romano. La Rocca's plan is long and rectangular, with six towers and two grand courtyards, an upper loggia, and inside some grand reception rooms. In the largest tower, Torre Maestà, you can visit an apartment with some interesting frescoes. A small shuttle bus gives you that last boost up the hill from the ticket booth to the entrance of the fortress. If you phone in advance, you may be able to secure an English-speaking guide. ✉ *Piazza Campello, Spoleto* ☎ *0743/224952* 🎫 *€7.50* 🕒 *Closed Mon.*

Teatro Romano. The Romans who colonized the city in 241 BC constructed this small theater in the 1st century AD; for centuries afterward it was used as a quarry for building materials. The most intact portion is the hallway that passes under the *cavea* (stands). The rest was heavily restored in the early 1950s and serves as a venue for Spoleto's Festival dei Due Mondi. The theater was the site of a gruesome episode in Spoleto's history: during the medieval struggle between Guelph (papal) and Ghibelline (imperial) forces, Spoleto took the side of the Holy Roman Emperor. Afterward, 400 Guelph supporters were massacred in the theater, their bodies burned in an enormous pyre. In the end, the Guelphs were triumphant, and Spoleto was incorporated into the states of the Church in 1354. Through a door in the west portico of the adjoining building is the **Museo Archeologico,** with assorted artifacts found in excavations primarily around Spoleto and Norcia. The collection contains Bronze Age and Iron Age artifacts from Umbrian and pre-Roman eras. Another section contains black-glaze vases from the Hellenistic period excavated from the necropolis of St. Scolastica in Norcia. The highlight is the stone tablet inscribed on both sides with the Lex Spoletina (Spoleto Law). Dating from 315 BC, this legal document prohibited the desecration of the woods on the slopes of nearby Monteluco. ✉ *Piazza della Libertà, Spoleto* ☎ *0743/223277* 🌐 *www.spoletocard.it* 🎫 *€4.*

6

WHERE TO EAT

$$ UMBRIAN 🍴 **Apollinare.** Low wooden ceilings and flickering candlelight make this monastery from the 10th and 11th centuries Spoleto's most romantic spot. The kitchen serves sophisticated, innovative variations on local dishes. Sauces of cherry tomatoes, mint, and a touch of red pepper, or of porcini mushrooms, top the long, slender strangozzi. The *caramella* (light puff-pastry cylinders filled with local cheese and served with a creamy Parmesan sauce) is popular. In warm weather you can dine under a canopy on the piazza across from the archaeological museum. [$] *Average main: €20* ✉ *Via Sant'Agata 14, Spoleto* ☎ *0743/223256* 🌐 *www.ristoranteapollinare.it* 🕒 *Closed Tues.*

A Taste of Truffles

Umbria is rich with truffles—more are found here than anywhere else in Italy—and those not consumed fresh are processed into pastes or flavored oils. The primary truffle areas are around the tiny town of Norcia, which holds a truffle festival every February, and near Spoleto, where signs warn against unlicensed truffle hunting at the base of the Ponte delle Torri.

Although grown locally, the rare delicacy can cost a small fortune, up to $200 for a quarter pound—fortunately, a little goes a long way. At such a price there's great competition among the nearly 10,000 registered truffle hunters in the province, who use specially trained dogs to sniff them out among the roots of several types of trees, including oak and ilex. Despite a few incidents involving inferior tubers imported from China, you can be reasonably assured that the truffle shaved onto your pasta has been unearthed locally. Don't pass up the opportunity to try this delectable treat. The intense aroma of a dish perfumed with truffles is unmistakable and the flavor memorable.

$$ ✕ **Il Tartufo.** As the name indicates, dishes prepared with truffles are the
UMBRIAN specialty here—don't miss the risotto al tartufo. Incorporating the ruins of a Roman villa, the surroundings are rustic on the ground floor and more modern upstairs. In summer, tables appear outdoors and the traditional fare is spiced up to appeal to the cosmopolitan crowd attending (or performing in) the Festival dei Due Mondi. $ *Average main: €21* ⊠ *Piazza Garibaldi 24, Spoleto* ☎ *0743/40236* ⊕ *www.ristoranteiltartufo.it* ⊘ *Closed Mon., and last 2 wks in July. No dinner Sun.*

$$ ✕ **Osteria del Trivio.** Everything is made on the premises and the seasonal
UMBRIAN menu changes daily. Dishes might include stuffed artichokes, pasta with local mushrooms, or chicken with artichokes. For dessert, try the homemade biscotti, made for dunking in sweet wine. There's a printed menu, but the owner can explain the dishes in a number of languages. $ *Average main: €17* ⊠ *Via del Trivio 16, Spoleto* ☎ *0743/44349* ⊘ *Closed Tues., and 3 wks in Jan.*

$$ ✕ **Ristorante Panciolle.** A small garden filled with lemon trees in the heart
UMBRIAN of Spoleto's medieval quarter provides one of the most appealing settings you could wish for. Dishes change throughout the year, and may include pastas served with asparagus or mushrooms, as well as grilled meats. More expensive dishes prepared with fresh truffles are also available in season. $ *Average main: €18* ⊠ *Via Duomo 3/5, Spoleto* ☎ *0743/45677* ⊕ *www.ilpanciolle.it* ⊘ *Closed Wed.*

WHERE TO STAY

$ ▦ **Hotel Clitunno.** Cozy guest rooms and intimate public rooms, some
HOTEL with timbered ceilings, give the sense of a traditional Umbrian home—albeit one with a good restaurant. **Pros:** friendly staff; good restaurant. **Cons:** difficult to find a parking space; some small rooms. $ *Rooms from: €80* ⊠ *Piazza Sordini 6, Spoleto* ☎ *0743/223340* ⊕ *www.hotelclitunno.com* ⇔ *45 rooms* ⍩ *Breakfast.*

$$ HOTEL Fodor's Choice ★ **Hotel San Luca.** Hand-painted friezes decorate the walls of the spacious guest rooms, and elegant comfort is the gracenote throughout—you can sip afternoon tea in oversize armchairs by the fireplace, or take a walk in the sweet-smelling rose garden. **Pros:** very helpful staff; peaceful location. **Cons:** outside the town center; a long walk to the main sights. [$] *Rooms from: €150* ✉ *Via Interna delle Mura 19, Spoleto* ☎ *0743/223399* 🌐 *www.hotelsanluca.com* 🛏 *33 rooms, 2 suites* 🍴 *Breakfast.*

PERFORMING ARTS

Fodor's Choice ★ **Festival dei Due Mondi** (*Festival of Two Worlds*). In 1958, composer Gian Carlo Menotti chose Spoleto for the first Festival dei Due Mondi, a gathering of artists, performers, and musicians intending to bring together the "new" and "old" worlds of America and Europe. (The famed, corresponding festival in Charleston, South Carolina is no longer connected to this festival.) The annual event, held in late June and early July, is one of the most important cultural happenings in Europe, attracting big names in all branches of the arts, particularly music, opera, and theater. ✉ *Piazza del Comune 1, Spoleto* ☎ *0743/221689* 🌐 *www.festivaldispoleto.com.*

6

ORVIETO

30 km (19 miles) southwest of Todi, 81 km (51 miles) west of Spoleto.

Carved out of an enormous plateau of volcanic rock high above a green valley, Orvieto has natural defenses that made the high walls seen in many Umbrian towns unnecessary. The Etruscans were the first to settle here, digging a honeycombed network of more than 1,200 wells and storage caves out of the soft stone. The Romans attacked, sacked, and destroyed the city in 283 BC; since then, it has grown up out of the rock into an enchanting maze of alleys and squares. Orvieto was solidly Guelph in the Middle Ages, and for several hundred years popes sought refuge in the city, at times needing protection from their enemies, at times seeking respite from the summer heat of Rome.

When painting his frescoes inside the Duomo, Luca Signorelli asked that part of his contract be paid in Orvietan wine, and he was neither the first nor the last to appreciate the region's popular white. In past times the caves carved underneath the town were used to ferment the Trebbiano grapes used in making Orvieto Classico; now local wine production has moved out to more traditional vineyards, but you can still while away the afternoon in tastings at any number of shops in town.

GETTING HERE AND AROUND

Orvieto is well connected by train to Rome, Florence, and Perugia. It's also adjacent to the A1 autostrada that runs between Florence and Rome. Parking areas in the upper town tend to be crowded. A better idea is to follow the signs for the Porta Orvetiana parking lot, then take the funicular that carries people up the hill.

VISITOR INFORMATION

The Carta Orvieto Unica (single ticket) is expensive but a great deal if you want to visit everything. For €18 you get admission to the three major sights in town—Cappella di San Brizio (at the Duomo), Museo Archeologico Claudio Faina, and Orvieto Underground—along with entry to the Torre del Moro, with views of Orvieto, plus a combination bus-funicular pass or five hours of free parking.

Orvieto tourism office. ⊠ *Piazza del Duomo 24, Orvieto* ☏ *0763/341772* ⊕ *www.orvietoviva.com.*

EXPLORING

Fodor's Choice **Duomo.** Orvieto's stunning cathedral was built to commemorate the
★ Miracle at Bolsena. In 1263 a young priest who questioned the miracle of transubstantiation (in which the Communion bread and wine become the flesh and blood of Christ) was saying Mass at nearby Lago di Bolsena. His doubts were put to rest, however, when a wafer he had just blessed suddenly started to drip blood, staining the linen covering the altar. The cloth and the host were taken to the pope, who proclaimed a miracle and a year later provided for a new religious holiday—the Feast of Corpus Domini. Thirty years later, construction began on a duomo in Orvieto to celebrate the miracle and house the stained altar cloth.

It's thought that Arnolfo di Cambio (circa 1245–1302), the famous builder of the Duomo in Florence, was given the initial commission, but the project was soon taken over by Lorenzo Maitani (circa 1275–1330), who consolidated the structure and designed the monumental facade. Maitani also made the bas-relief panels between the doorways, which graphically tell the story of the Creation (on the left) and the Last Judgment (on the right). The lower registers, now protected by Plexiglas, succeed in conveying the horrors of hell as few other works of art manage to do, an effect made all the more powerful by the worn gray marble. Above, gold mosaics are framed by finely detailed Gothic decoration.

Inside, the cathedral is rather vast and empty; the major works are in the transepts. To the left is the **Cappella del Corporale,** where the square linen cloth (*corporale*) is kept in a golden reliquary that's modeled on the cathedral and inlaid with enamel scenes of the miracle. The cloth is removed for public viewing on Easter and on Corpus Domini (the ninth Sunday after Easter). In the right transept is the **Cappella di San Brizio,** or Cappella Nuova. In this chapel is one of Italy's greatest fresco cycles, notable for its influence on Michelangelo's *Last Judgment,* as well as for the extraordinary beauty of the figuration. In these works, a few by Fra Angelico and the majority by Luca Signorelli, the damned fall to hell, demons breathe fire and blood, and Christians are martyred. Some scenes are heavily influenced by the imagery in Dante's (1265–1321) *Divine Comedy.* ⊠ *Piazza del Duomo, Orvieto* ☏ *0763/342477* ⊕ *www. opsm.it* ✉ *Cappella di San Brizio €3.*

Museo Archeologico Claudio Faina. This superb private collection, beautifully arranged and presented, goes far beyond the usual museum offerings of a scattering of local remains. The collection is particularly rich

CLOSE UP

Hiking the Umbrian Hills

Magnificent scenery makes the heart of Italy excellent walking, hiking, and mountaineering country. In Umbria, the area around Spoleto is particularly good; several pleasant, easy, and well-signed trails begin at the far end of the Ponte alle Torri bridge over Monteluco. From Cannara, an easy half-hour walk leads to the fields of Pian d'Arca, the site of St. Francis's sermon to the birds. For slightly more arduous walks, you can follow the saint's path, uphill from Assisi to the Eremo delle Carceri, and then continue along the trails that crisscross Monte Subasio. At 4,250 feet, the Subasio's treeless summit affords views of Assisi, Perugia, far-off Gubbio, and the distant mountain ranges of Abruzzo.

For even more challenging hiking, the northern reaches of the Valnerina are exceptional; the mountains around Norcia should not be missed. Throughout Umbria and the Marches, you'll find that most recognized walking and hiking trails are marked with the distinctive red-and-white blazes of the Club Alpino Italiano. Tourist offices are a good source for walking and climbing itineraries to suit all ages and levels of ability, while bookstores, *tabacchi* (tobacconists), and *edicole* (newsstands) often have maps and hiking guides that detail the best routes in their area. Depending on the length and location of your walk, it can be important that you have comfortable walking shoes or boots, appropriate attire, and plenty of water to drink.

in Greek- and Etruscan-era pottery, from large Attic amphorae (6th–4th centuries BC) to Attic black- and red-figure pieces to Etruscan *bucchero* (dark-reddish clay) vases. Other interesting pieces in the collection include a 6th-century sarcophagus and a substantial display of Roman-era coins. ⊠ *Piazza del Duomo 29, Orvieto* ☎ *0763/341216* ⊕ *www.museofaina.it* 🎫 *€4.*

Pozzo della Cava. If you're short on time but want a quick look at the cisterns and caves beneath the city, head for the Pozzo della Cava, an Etruscan well for spring water. ⊠ *Via della Cava 28, Orvieto* ☎ *0763/342373* ⊕ *www.pozzodellacava.it* 🎫 *€3.*

Orvieto Underground. More than just about any other town, Orvieto has grown from its own foundations. The Etruscans, the Romans, and those who followed dug into the tufa (the same soft volcanic rock from which catacombs were made) to create more than 1,000 separate cisterns, caves, secret passages, storage areas, and production areas for wine and olive oil. Much of the tufa removed was used as building blocks for the city that exists today, and some was partly ground into *pozzolana*, which was made into mortar. You can see the labyrinth of dugout chambers beneath the city on the **Orvieto Underground tour** (*Orvieto tourism office, Piazza del Duomo 24*) run daily at 11, 12:15, 4, and 5:15. Admission for the hour-long English tour is €6. Tours start from Piazza Duomo 23. ⊠ *Orvieto* ☎ *0763/341772 for tourism office* ⊕ *www.orvietounderground.it.*

WHERE TO EAT

$$ ✕ **Il Giglio D'Oro.** A great view of the Duomo is coupled with superb
UMBRIAN food. Eggplant is transformed into an elegant custard with black truffles
Fodor'sChoice in the *sformatino di melenzane con vellutata al tartuffo nero*. Pastas,
★ like *ombrichelli al pesto umbro*, are traditional, but perhaps with a
new twist like fresh coriander leaves instead of the usual basil. Lamb
roasted in a crust of bread is delicately seasoned with a tomato cream
sauce. The wine cellar includes some rare vintages. $ *Average main:*
€19 ✉ *Piazza Duomo 8, Orvieto* ☎ *0763/341903* ⊕ *www.ilgigliodoro.*
it ⊘ *Closed Wed.*

$$ ✕ **Le Grotte del Funaro.** Dine inside tufa caves under central Orvieto,
UMBRIAN where the two windows afford splendid views of the hilly countryside.
The traditional Umbrian food is reliably good, with simple grilled meats
and vegetables and pizzas. Oddly, though, the food is outclassed by an
extensive wine list, with top local and Italian labels and quite a few
rare vintages. $ *Average main: €18* ✉ *Via Ripa Serancia 41, Orvieto*
☎ *0763/343276* ⊘ *Closed 1 wk in July.*

$ ✕ **Trattoria La Grotta.** Franco, the owner, has been in this location for
UMBRIAN more than 20 years and has attracted a steady American clientele without losing his local following—or his touch with homemade pasta,
perhaps with a duck or wild-boar sauce. Roast lamb, veal, and pork
are all good, and the desserts are homemade. Franco knows the local
wines well and has a carefully selected list, including some from smaller
but excellent wineries, so ask about them. $ *Average main: €15* ✉ *Via*
Luca Signorelli 5, Orvieto ☎ *0763/341348* ⊕ *www.trattorialagrotta.*
eu ⊘ *Closed Tues.*

WHERE TO STAY

$$ ▦ **Hotel La Badia.** In a 12th-century monastery, vaulted ceilings and
HOTEL exposed stone walls, along with wood-beam ceilings and polished
terra-cotta floors covered with rugs, establish rustic elegance in guest
rooms. **Pros:** elegant atmosphere; fine views. **Cons:** slightly overpriced;
need a car to get around. $ *Rooms from: €170* ✉ *Località La Badia,*
4 km (2½ miles) south of Orvieto, Orvieto Scalo ☎ *0763/301959*
⊕ *www.labadiahotel.it* ⊘ *Closed Nov.–Feb.* ⬳ *18 rooms, 9 suites*
⧉ *Breakfast.*

$$ ▦ **Hotel Palazzo Piccolomini.** This 16th-century family palazzo has been
HOTEL beautifully restored, with inviting public spaces and handsome guest
quarters where contemporary surroundings are accented with old
beams, vaulted ceilings, and other distinctive touches. **Pros:** peaceful
atmosphere; efficient staff; good location. **Cons:** slightly overpriced.
$ *Rooms from: €154* ✉ *Piazza Ranieri 36, Orvieto* ☎ *0763/341743*
⊕ *www.palazzopiccolomini.it* ⬳ *28 rooms, 3 suites* ⧉ *Breakfast.*

UNDERSTANDING ITALY

ITALIAN VOCABULARY

ITALIAN VOCABULARY

	ENGLISH	ITALIAN	PRONUNCIATION
BASICS			
	Yes/no	Sí/No	see/no
	Please	Per favore	pear fa- **vo**-ray
	Yes, please	Sí grazie	see **grah**-tsee-ay
	Thank you	Grazie	**grah**-tsee-ay
	You're welcome	Prego	**pray**-go
	Excuse me, sorry	Scusi	**skoo**-zee
	Sorry!	Mi dispiace!	mee dis-spee- **ah**-chay
	Good morning/ afternoon	Buongiorno	bwohn- **jor**-no
	Good evening	Buona sera	**bwoh**-na **say**-ra
	Good-bye	Arrivederci	a-ree-vah- **dare**-chee
	Mr. (Sir)	Signore	see- **nyo**-ray
	Mrs. (Ma'am)	Signora	see- **nyo**-ra
	Miss	Signorina	see-nyo- **ree**-na
	Pleased to meet you	Piacere	pee-ah- **chair**-ray
	How are you?	Come sta?	**ko**-may **stah**
	Very well, thanks	Bene, grazie	**ben**-ay **grah**-tsee-ay
	Hello (phone)	Pronto?	**proan**-to
NUMBERS			
	one	uno	**oo**-no
	two	due	**doo**-ay
	three	tre	Tray
	four	quattro	**kwah**-tro
	five	cinque	**cheen**-kway
	six	sei	Say
	seven	sette	**set**-ay
	eight	otto	**oh**-to
	nine	nove	**no**-vay
	ten	dieci	dee- **eh**-chee
	twenty	venti	**vain**-tee
	thirty	trenta	**train**-ta
	forty	quaranta	kwa- **rahn**-ta

ENGLISH	ITALIAN	PRONUNCIATION
fifty	cinquanta	cheen- **kwahn**-ta
sixty	sessanta	seh- **sahn**-ta
seventy	settanta	seh- **tahn**-ta
eighty	ottanta	o- **tahn**-ta
ninety	novanta	no- **vahn**-ta
one hundred	cento	**chen**-to
one thousand	mille	**mee**-lay
ten thousand	diecimila	dee-eh-chee- **mee**-la

USEFUL PHRASES

Do you speak English?	Parla inglese?	**par**-la een- **glay**-zay
I don't speak Italian	Non parlo italiano	non **par**-lo ee-tal- **yah**-no
I don't understand	Non capisco	non ka- **peess**-ko
Can you please repeat?	Può ripetere?	pwo ree- **pet**-ay-ray
Slowly!	Lentamente!	**len**-ta-men-tay
I don't know	Non lo so	non lo **so**
I'm American	Sono americano(a)	**so**-no a-may-ree- **kah**-no(a)
I'm British	Sono inglese	so-no een- **glay**-zay
What's your name?	Come si chiama?	**ko**-may see kee- **ah**-ma
My name is ...	Mi chiamo ...	mee kee- **ah**-mo
What time is it?	Che ore sono?	kay **o**-ray **so**-no
How?	Come?	**ko**-may
When?	Quando?	**kwan**-doe
Yesterday/today/tomorrow	Ieri/oggi/domani	**yer**-ee/ **o**-jee/ do- **mah**-nee
This morning	Stamattina/Oggi	sta-ma- **tee**-na/ **o**-jee
afternoon	pomeriggio	po-mer- **ee**-jo
Tonight	Stasera	sta- **ser**-a
What?	Che cosa?	kay **ko**-za
Why?	Perché?	pear- **kay**
Who?	Chi?	Kee

ENGLISH	ITALIAN	PRONUNCIATION
Where is ...	Dov'è ...	doe- **veh**
the bus stop?	la fermata dell'autobus?	la fer- **mah**-tadel ow-toe- **booss**
the train station?	la stazione?	la sta-tsee- **oh**-nay
the subway	la metropolitana?	la may-tro-po-lee- **tah**-na
the terminal?	il terminale?	eel ter-mee- **nah**-lay
the post office?	l'ufficio postale?	loo- **fee**-cho po- **stah**-lay
the bank?	la banca?	la **bahn**-ka
the ... hotel?	l'hotel ...?	lo- **tel**
the store?	il negozio?	eel nay- **go**-tsee-o
the cashier?	la cassa?	la **kah**-sa
the ... museum?	il museo ...?	eel moo- **zay**-o
the hospital?	l'ospedale?	lo-spay- **dah**-lay
the elevator?	l'ascensore?	la-shen- **so**-ray
the restrooms?	il bagno?	do- **vay** eel **bahn**-yo
Here/there	Qui/là	kwee/la
Left/right	A sinistra/a destra	a see- **neess**-tra/a **des**-tra
Straight ahead	Avanti dritto	a- **vahn**-tee **dree**-to
Is it near/far?	È vicino/lontano?	ay vee- **chee**-no/ lon- **tah**-no
I'd like ...	Vorrei ...	vo- **ray**
a room	una camera	**oo**-na **kah**-may-ra
the key	la chiave	la kee- **ah**-vay
a newspaper	un giornale	oon jor- **nah**-lay
a stamp	un francobollo	oon frahn-ko- **bo**-lo
I'd like to buy ...	Vorrei comprare ...	vo- **ray** kom- **prah**-ray
How much is it?	Quanto costa?	**kwahn**-toe **coast**-a
It's expensive/cheap	È caro/economico	ay **car**-o/ ay-ko- **no**-mee-ko
A little/a lot	Poco/tanto	**po**-ko/ **tahn**-to
More/less	Più/meno	pee- **oo** / **may**-no
Enough/too (much)	Abbastanza/troppo	a-bas- **tahn**-sa/tro-po

ENGLISH	ITALIAN	PRONUNCIATION
I am sick	Sto male	sto **mah**-lay
Call a doctor	Chiama un dottore	kee- **ah**-mah oondoe- **toe**-ray
Help!	Aiuto!	a- **yoo**-toe
Stop!	Alt!	ahlt
Fire!	Al fuoco!	ahl **fwo**-ko
Caution/Look out!	Attenzione!	a-ten- **syon**-ay

DINING OUT

A bottle of ...	Una bottiglia di ...	**oo**-na bo- **tee**-lee-ahdee
A cup of ...	Una tazza di ...	**oo**-na **tah**-tsa dee
A glass of ...	Un bicchiere di ...	oon bee-key- **air**-ay dee
Bill/check	Il conto	eel **cone**-toe
Bread	Il pane	eel **pah**-nay
Breakfast	La prima colazione	la **pree**-ma ko-la- **tsee**-oh-nay
Cocktail/aperitif	L'aperitivo	la-pay-ree- **tee**-vo
Dinner	La cena	la **chen**-a
Fixed price menu	Menù a prezzo fisso	may- **noo** a **pret**-so **fee**-so
Fork	La forchetta	la for- **ket**-a
I am diabetic	Ho il diabete	o eel dee-a- **bay**-tay
I am vegetarian	Sono vegetariano(a)	**so**-no vay-jay-ta-ree- **ah**-no/a
I'd like ...	Vorrei ...	vo- **ray**
I'd like to order	Vorrei ordinare	vo- **ray** or-dee- **nah**-ray
Is service included?	Il servizio è incluso?	eel ser- **vee**-tzee-o ay een- **kloo**-zo
It's good/bad	È buono/cattivo	ay **bwo**-no/ka- **tee**-vo
It's hot/cold	È caldo/freddo	ay **kahl**-doe/ **fred**-o
Knife	Il coltello	eel kol- **tel**-o
Lunch	Il pranzo	eel **prahnt**-so
Menu	Il menù	eel may- **noo**
Napkin	Il tovagliolo	eel toe-va-lee- **oh**-lo

ENGLISH	ITALIAN	PRONUNCIATION
Please give me ...	Mi dia ...	mee **dee**-a
Salt	Il sale	eel **sah**-lay
Spoon	Il cucchiaio	eel koo-kee- **ah**-yo
Sugar	Lo zucchero	lo **tsoo**-ker-o
Waiter/waitress	Cameriere/cameriera	ka-mare- **yer**-ay/ ka-mare- **yer**-a
Wine list	La lista dei vini	la **lee**-sta **day**-ee **vee**-nee

TRAVEL SMART
ITALY

GETTING HERE AND AROUND

■ AIR TRAVEL

Most nonstop flights between North America and Italy serve Rome and Milan, though the airports in Venice and Pisa also accommodate nonstop flights from the United States. Many travelers find it more convenient to connect via a European hub to Florence, Bologna, or another smaller Italian airport.

Flying time to Milan or Rome is approximately 8–8½ hours from New York, 10–11 hours from Chicago, and 11½ hours from Los Angeles.

Labor strikes are not as frequent in Italy as they were some years ago, but when they do occur they can affect not only air travel, but also local public transit that serves airports. Your airline will usually have details about strikes affecting its flight schedules.

A helpful website for information (location, phone numbers, local transportation, etc.) about all of the airports in Italy is ⊕ *www.italianairportguide.com*.

Airline Security Issues Transportation Security Administration (*TSA*). ☏ 866/289-9673 ⊕ *www.tsa.gov*.

AIRPORTS

The major gateways to Italy include Rome's Aeroporto Leonardo da Vinci (FCO), better known as Fiumicino, and Milan's Aeroporto Malpensa (MXP). Most flights to Venice, Florence, and Pisa make connections at Fiumicino and Malpensa or another European airport hub. You can take the Ferrovie dello Stato (FS) airport train or bus to Rome's Termini station or to Cadorna or Centrale in Milan; from the latter you can then catch a train to any other location in Italy. It'll take about 40 minutes to get from Fiumicino to Roma Termini, less than an hour to Milano Centrale.

Many carriers fly into the smaller airports. Milan also has Linate airport (LIN) and Rome has Ciampino (CIA). Venice is served by Aeroporto di Venezia Marco Polo (VCE), Naples by Aeroporto Internazionale di Napoli Capodichino (NAP), Palermo by Aeroporto di Palermo (PMO) and Cagliari by Aeroporto Elmas (CAG). Florence is serviced by Aeroporto di Firenze (FLR) and by Aeroporto di Pisa (PSA), which is about 2 km (1 mile) outside the center of Pisa and about one hour from Florence. Aeroporto de Bologna (BLQ) is a 20-minute direct Aerobus ride away from Bologna Centrale, which is 35 minutes from Florence by high-speed train.

Many Italian airports have undergone renovations in recent years and have been ramping up security measures, which include random baggage inspection and bomb-detection dogs. All airports have restaurants, snack bars, shopping, and Wi-Fi access. Each also has at least one nearby hotel. In the cases of Milan Linate, Florence, Pisa, Naples, and Bologna, the city centers are less than a 15-minute taxi or bus ride away—so if you encounter a long delay, spend it in town.

When you take a connecting flight from a European airline hub (Frankfurt or Paris, for example) to a local Italian airport (Florence or Venice), be aware that your luggage might not make it onto the second plane with you. The airlines' lost-luggage service is efficient, however, and your delayed luggage is usually delivered to your hotel or holiday rental within 12–24 hours.

Airport Information Aeroporto di Bologna (*BLQ, aka Guglielmo Marconi*). ✉ 6 km (4 miles) northwest of Bologna ☏ 051/6479615 5 am–midnight ⊕ *www.bologna-airport.it*. **Aeroporto di Cagliari.** ✉ 7 km (4½ miles) from Cagliari, Via dei Trasvolatori, Elmas, Cagliari ☏ 070/211211 ⊕ *www.cagliari-airport.com*. **Aeroporto di Firenze** (*FLR, aka Amerigo Vespucci or Peretola*). ✉ 6 km (4 miles) northwest of Florence ☏ 055/3061300 ⊕ *www.aeroporto.firenze.it*. **Aeroporto di Milan Linate** (*LIN*). ✉ 8 km (5 miles) southeast

of Milan ☎ 02/232323 ⊕ www.milanolinate.
eu. **Aeroporto di Palermo** (PMO, aka Falcone
e Borsellino or Punta Raisi). ✉ 32 km (19
miles) northwest of Palermo ☎ 091/7020111,
800/541880 in Italy, toll-free ⊕ www.gesap.it.
Aeroporto di Pisa (PSA, aka Aeroporto Galileo
Galilei). ✉ 2 km (1 mile) south of Pisa, 80 km
(50 miles) west of Florence ☎ 050/849300
⊕ www.pisa-airport.com. **Aeroporto di Roma
Ciampino** (CIA). ✉ 15 km (9 miles) southwest
of Rome ☎ 06/65951 ⊕ www.adr.it. **Aeroporto
di Venezia** (VCE, aka Marco Polo). ✉ 6 km (4
miles) north of Venice ☎ 041/2609260 ⊕ www.
veniceairport.com. **Aeroporto Fiumicino** (FCO,
aka Leonardo da Vinci). ✉ 35 km (20 miles)
southwest of Rome ☎ 06/65951 ⊕ www.adr.
it. **Aeroporto Internazionale di Napoli** (NAP,
aka Capodichino). ✉ 7 km (4 miles) northeast
of Naples ☎ 081/7896111 weekdays 8 am–4
pm, 848/888777 flight info ⊕ www.aeroporto-
dinapoli.it. **Aeroporto Malpensa** (MPX). ✉ 45
km (28 miles) north of Milan ☎ 02/232323
⊕ www.airportmalpensa.com.

FLIGHTS
From the United States, Alitalia and Delta
Air Lines serve Rome, Milan, Pisa, and
Venice. The major international hubs in
Italy (Milan and Rome) are also served
by United Airlines and American Airlines.
From June through October, the Italy-
based Meridiana has nonstop flights from
New York to Naples and Palermo.

Alitalia has direct flights from London to
Milan and Rome, while British Airways
and smaller budget carriers provide services between Great Britain and other
locations in Italy. EasyJet connects London's Gatwick and Stansted airports with
13 Italian destinations. Ryanair, departing
from Stansted, flies to 18 airports. Meridiana has flights between Gatwick and
Olbia on Sardinia in summer. For flights
within Italy, check Alitalia and smaller
airlines, such as blu-express and Meridiana. Since tickets are frequently sold at
discounted prices, it's wise to investigate
the cost of flying—even one way—as an
alternative to train travel.

Airline Contacts Aer Lingus.
☎ 02/43458326 in Italy, 516/6224222 in U.S.
⊕ www.aerlingus.com. **Alitalia.** ☎ 800/223–
5730 in U.S., 892/010 in Italy, 06/65640
Rome office ⊕ www.alitalia.it. **American
Airlines.** ☎ 800/433–7300, 199/257300
in Italy ⊕ www.aa.com. **British Airways.**
☎ 800/247–9297 in U.S., 02/69633602 in
Italy ⊕ www.britishairways.com. **Delta Air
Lines.** ☎ 888/750–3284 for international
reservations, 02/38591451 in Italy ⊕ www.
delta.com. **EasyJet.** ☎ +44330/3655454
from outside U.K., 199/201840 in Italy,
0330/3655000 in U.K. ⊕ www.easyjet.
com. **Ryanair.** ☎ 0871/2460000 in U.K., toll
number, 895/8958989 in Italy, toll number
⊕ www.ryanair.com. **United Airlines.**
☎ 800/864–8331 in U.S., 02/69633256
in Italy ⊕ www.united.com. **Volotea.**
☎ 895/8954404 in Italy, 0034/931220717
outside Italy ⊕ www.volotea.com.

Domestic Carriers blu-express.
☎ 06/98956666 ⊕ www.blu-express.
com. **Meridiana.** ☎ 866/387–6359 in U.S.,
0789/52682 in Italy, 0844/4822360 U.K. call
center ⊕ www.euroflyusa.com. **Transavia.**
☎ 899/009901 ⊕ www.transavia.com.

▌ BUS TRAVEL

Italy's far-reaching regional bus network,
often operated by private companies, is
not as attractive an option as in other
European countries, partly due to convenient train travel. Schedules are often
drawn up with commuters and students
in mind and may be sketchy on weekends.
But, car travel aside, regional bus companies often provide the only means of getting to out-of-the-way places. Even when
this isn't the case, buses can be faster and
more direct than local trains, so it's a good
idea to compare bus and train schedules.
Lazzi operates in Tuscany and central
Italy, while BusItalia–Sita Nord covers
Tuscany and Veneto. SitaSud caters to
travelers in Puglia, Foggia, Matera, Basil-
icata, and Campania. Flix Bus offers a
low-cost long-distance service.

All major cities in Italy have urban bus services. It's inexpensive, and tickets should be purchased from newsstands or tobacconists and validated on board (some city buses have ticket machines on the buses themselves). Buses can become jammed during busy travel periods and rush hours.

Smoking is not permitted on Italian buses. All, even those on long-distance routes, offer a single class of service. Cleanliness and comfort levels are high on private motor coaches, which have plenty of legroom, sizable seats, and luggage storage, but often do not have toilets. Private bus lines usually have a ticket office in town or allow you to pay when you board.

Bus Information ANM. ✉ *Via G. Marino 1, Naples* 🕾 *800/639525 toll-free in Italy* ⊕ *www. anm.it.* **ATAC.** 🕾 *06/46951* ⊕ *www.atac.roma. it.* **ATAF.** ✉ *Stazione Centrale di Santa Maria Novella, Florence* 🕾 *800/424500, 199/104245 from mobile phone (toll)* ⊕ *www.ataf.net.* **BusItalia-Sita Nord.** ✉ *Viale dei Cadorna, 105, Florence* 🕾 *800/373760 toll-free* ⊕ *www. fsbusitalia.it.* **Flix Bus.** 🕾 *30/300–137–300 German landline* ⊕ *www.flixbus.com.* **SitaSud.** ✉ *Via S. Francesco D'Assisi 1, Putignano* 🕾 *080/4052245* ⊕ *www.sitasudtrasporti.it.* **Trasporti Toscani.** ✉ *Via Bellatalla, 1, Pisa* 🕾 *050/884111* ⊕ *www.cttnord.it.*

▌ CAR TRAVEL

Italy has an extensive network of *autostrade* (toll highways), complemented by equally well-maintained but free *superstrade* (expressways). Save the ticket you're issued at an autostrada entrance, as you'll need it to exit; on some shorter autostrade, you pay the toll when you enter. Tollbooths also accept Visa and MasterCard, allowing you to exit at special lanes where you simply slip the card into a designated slot.

An *uscita* is an exit. A *raccordo annulare* is a ring road surrounding a city; a *tangenziale* generally bypasses a city entirely. *Strade, strade statale, strade regionale,* and *strade provinciale* (regional and provincial highways, denoted by *S, SS, SR,* or

SP numbers) may be two lanes, as are all secondary roads; directions and turnoffs aren't always clearly marked.

GASOLINE

You'll find gas stations on most main highways. Those on autostrade are open 24 hours. Otherwise, gas stations are generally open Monday through Saturday 7–7, with a break at lunchtime. At self-service stations the pumps are operated by a central machine for payment, which often doesn't take credit cards: it accepts bills in denominations of €5, €10, €20, and €50, and doesn't give change. Stations with attendants accept cash and credit cards. It's not customary to tip the attendant.

At this writing, gasoline (*benzina*) costs about €1.47 per liter and is available in unleaded (*verde*) and superunleaded (*super*). Many rental cars in Italy use diesel (*gasolio*), which costs about €1.31 per liter (remember to confirm the fuel type your car requires before leaving the agency).

DRIVING IN CENTRI STORICI (HISTORIC CENTERS)

To avoid hefty fines (which you may not be notified of until months after your departure from Italy), make sure you know the rules governing where you can and can't drive in historic city centers. You must have a permit to enter many towns, and this rule is very strictly enforced. Check with your lodging or car-rental company to find out about acquiring permits for access.

PARKING

Parking is at a premium in most towns, especially in historic centers. Fines for parking violations are high, and towing is common. Don't think about tearing up a ticket, as car-rental companies can use your credit card to be reimbursed for any fines incurred. It's a good idea to park in a designated (and preferably attended) lot; even small towns often have a large lot at the edge of historic centers.

In congested cities, indoor parking costs €25–€30 for 12–24 hours; outdoor parking costs about €10–€20. Parking in an area signposted *zona disco* (disk zone) is allowed for short periods (from 30 minutes to two hours or more—the time is posted); if you don't have an appropriate cardboard disk (check in the glove box of your rental car) to show what time you parked, you can write your arrival time on a piece of paper. In most metropolitan areas you can find curbside parking spaces, marked by blue lines; once you insert coins into the nearby *parcometro* machine, it prints a ticket that you then leave on your dashboard.

RENTALS

Fiats, Fords, and Alfa Romeos in a variety of sizes are the most typical rental cars. Note that most Italian cars have standard transmission—if you need an automatic, specify one when you make your reservation. Significantly higher rates will apply.

Most American chains have affiliates in Italy, but costs are usually lower if you book a car before leaving home. Rentals at airports usually cost less than city pickups (and airport offices are open later). An auto broker such as ⊕ *www.rent.it* lets you compare rates among companies while guaranteeing the lowest price.

Most rental companies won't rent to someone under age 21. Most also refuse to rent any model larger than an economy or subcompact to anyone under 23, and, further, require customers under that age to pay by credit card. There are no special restrictions on senior citizen drivers. Any additional drivers must be identified in the contract and qualify with the age limits. There's also a supplementary daily fee for additional drivers. Expect to pay extra for add-on features, too. A car seat (required for children under age three) will cost about €36 for the duration of the rental and should be booked in advance. In some areas, snow chains are compulsory in winter months and can be rented for €30–€60—it may be cheaper to buy your own at the first open garage. Upon rental, all companies require credit cards as a warranty; to rent bigger cars (2,000 cc or more), you may be required to show two credit cards.

Hiring a car with a driver can simplify matters, particularly if you plan to indulge in wine tastings or explore the distractingly scenic Amalfi Coast. Search online (the travel forums at ⊕ *Fodors. com* are a good resource) or ask at your hotel for recommendations. Drivers are paid by the day, and are usually rewarded with a tip of about 15% upon completion of the journey.

All rental agencies operating in Italy require you to buy a collision-damage waiver (CDW) and a theft-protection policy, but those costs should already be included in the rates you're quoted. Verify this, along with any deductible, which can vary greatly depending on the company and type of car. Be aware that coverage may be denied if the named driver on the rental contract isn't the driver at the time of an accident. Ask your rental company about other included coverage when you reserve the car or pick it up. Finally, try not to leave valuables in your car, because thieves often target rental vehicles. If you can't avoid doing so—for instance, if you want to stop to see a sight while traveling between cities—park in an attended lot.

ROAD CONDITIONS

Autostrade are well maintained, as are most interregional highways. Typically, autostrade have two or three lanes in both directions; the left lane should be used only for passing. Italians drive fast and are impatient with those who don't. Tailgating (and flashing with bright beams to signal intent to pass) is the norm if you dawdle in the left lane—the only way to avoid it is to stay to the right.

The condition of provincial (county) roads varies, but road maintenance at this level is generally good in Italy. In many small hill towns the streets are winding and extremely narrow, so try to park at the edge of town and explore on foot.

Driving on back roads isn't difficult as long as you're on the alert for bicycles and passing cars. In addition, street and road signs are often missing or placed in awkward spots; a good map or GPS is essential. If you feel pressure from a string of cars in your rearview mirror but don't feel comfortable speeding up, pull off to the right, and let them pass.

Be aware that some maps may not use the SR or SP (strade regionale and strade provinciale) highway designations, which took the place of the old SS designations in 2004. They may use the old SS designation or no numbering at all.

ROADSIDE EMERGENCIES
Automobile Club Italiano offers 24-hour road service; English-speaking operators are available. Your rental-car company may also have an emergency tow service with a toll-free phone number: keep it handy. Be prepared to report which road you're on, the *verso* (direction) you're headed, and your *targa* (license plate number). Also, in an emergency, call the police (☎ *113*).

When you're on the road, always carry a good road map and a flashlight—a reflective vest should be provided with the car. A mobile phone is highly recommended, though there are emergency phones on the autostrade and superstrade. To locate them, look on the pavement for painted arrows and the term "SOS."

Emergency Services American Automobile Association (AAA). ☎ *800/2224357* ⊕ *www.aaa.com.* **Automobile Club Italiano (ACI).** ☎ *803/116 for emergency service* ⊕ *www.aci.it.*

Rentals Sicily By Car. ☎ *091/6390111* ⊕ *www.autoeuropa.it.*

RULES OF THE ROAD
Driving is on the right. Speed limits are 130 kph (80 mph) on autostrade, reduced to 110 kph (70 mph) when it rains, and 90 kph (55 mph) on state and provincial roads, unless otherwise marked. In towns, the speed limit is 50 kph (30 mph), which may drop as low as 10 kph (6 mph) near schools, hospitals, and other designated areas. Note that right turns on red lights

are forbidden. Headlights are required to be on while driving on all roads (large or small) outside municipalities. You must wear seat belts and strap young children under 4 feet 11 inches into car seats at all times. Using handheld mobile phones while driving is illegal—and fines can exceed €100. In most Italian towns the use of the horn is forbidden in many areas. A large sign, *"zona di silenzio,"* indicates a "no honking" zone.

In Italy you must be 18 years old to drive a car. A U.S. driver's license is acceptable to rent a car, but by law Italy also requires non-Europeans to carry an International Driver's Permit (IDP), which essentially translates your license into Italian (and a dozen other languages). In practice, it depends on the police officer who pulls you over whether you'll be penalized for not carrying it. The IDP costs only $15, and obtaining one is easy: see the AAA website (⊕ *www.aaa.com*) for more information.

The blood-alcohol content limit for driving is 0.05% (stricter than in the United States). Surpass it and you'll face fines up to €6,000 and the possibility of one year's imprisonment. Although enforcement of laws varies depending on the region, fines for speeding are uniformly stiff: 10 kph over the speed limit can warrant a fine of up to €500; greater than 10 kph (6 mph), and your license could be taken away. The police have the power to levy on-the-spot fines.

❚ ITALY TRAIN TRAVEL

Traveling by train in Italy is simple and efficient. Service between major cities is frequent, and trains usually arrive on schedule. The fastest trains on the Trenitalia Ferrovie dello Stato (FS)—the Italian State Railways—are Freccie Rosse Alta Velocità. Ferrari mogul Montezemolo launched the competing NTV Italo high-speed service in 2012. Bullet trains on both services run between all major cities from Venice, Milan, and Turin down through Florence and Rome to Naples and Salerno. Seat reservations are mandatory, and you'll be assigned a specific seat; to avoid having to squeeze through narrow aisles, board only at your designated coach (the number on your ticket matches the one near the door of each coach). Reservations are also required for Eurostar and the slower Intercity (IC) trains; tickets for the latter are about half the price they are for the faster trains. If you miss your reserved train, go to the ticket counter within the hour and you may be able to move your reservation to a later one (this depends on the type of reservation, so check the rules when booking). Note that you'll still need to reserve seats in advance if you're using a rail pass.

There are often significant discounts when you book well in advance. On websites, you'll be presented with available promotional fares, such as Trenitalia's "Super Economy" (up to 60% off), "Famiglia" (a 20% discount for one adult and at least one child), and "A/R" (same-day round trip). Italo offers "Low Cost" and "Economy." The caveat is that the discounts come with restrictions on changes and cancellations; make sure you understand them before booking.

Reservations are not available on Interregionale trains, which are slower, make more stops, and are less expensive than high-speed and Intercity trains. Regionale and Espresso trains stop most frequently and are the most economical (many serve commuters). There are refreshments on long-distance trains, purchased from a mobile cart or a dining car, but not on the commuter trains.

All but commuter trains have first and second classes. On local trains, first-class fare ensures you a little more space; on long-distance trains, you also get wider seats (three across as opposed to four) and a bit more legroom, but the difference is minimal. At peak travel times a first-class fare may be worth the additional cost, as the coaches may be less crowded. In Italian, *prima classe* is first class; second is *seconda classe*.

Many cities—Milan, Turin, Genoa, Naples, Florence, Rome, and even Verona included—have more than one train station, so be sure you get off at the right station. When buying tickets, be particularly aware that in Rome and Florence some trains don't stop at all of the cities' stations and may not stop at the main, central station. When scheduling train travel online or through a travel agent, request to arrive at the station closest to your destination in Rome and Florence.

Except for Pisa, Milan, and Rome, none of the major cities have trains that go directly to the airports, but airport shuttle buses connect train stations and airports.

You can purchase train tickets and review schedules online, at travel agencies, at train station ticket counters, and at automatic ticketing machines located in all but the smallest stations. If you'd like to board a train and don't have a ticket, seek out the conductor prior to getting on; he or she will tell you whether you may buy a ticket on board and what the surcharge will be (usually €5). Fines for attempting to ride a train without a ticket are €100 (€50 if paid on the spot) plus the price of the ticket.

For trains without a reservation you must validate your ticket before boarding by punching it at wall- or pillar-mounted yellow or green boxes in train stations or at the track entrances of larger stations. If you forget, find a conductor immediately to avoid a hefty fine.

Train strikes of various kinds are not uncommon, so it's wise to ensure that your train is actually running. During a strike minimum service is guaranteed (especially for distance trains); ask at the station or search online to find out about your particular reservation.

Traveling by night can be a good deal—and somewhat of an adventure—because you'll pass a night without having to have a hotel room. Comfortable trains run on the longer routes (Sicily–Rome,

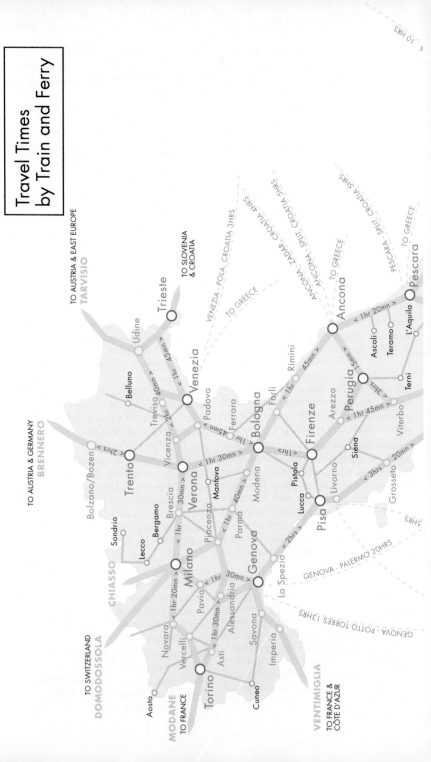

Travel Times by Train and Ferry

TO AUSTRIA & EAST EUROPE
TARVISIO

TO AUSTRIA & GERMANY
BRENNERO

TO SWITZERLAND
DOMODOSSOLA

CHIASSO

MODANE
TO FRANCE

VENTIMIGLIA
TO FRANCE &
CÔTE D'AZUR

TO SLOVENIA
& CROATIA

Trieste

Udine

Belluno

Bolzano/Bozen

Sondrio

Trento < 2hrs >

Bergamo

Lecco

Milano

Novara < 1hr 20mn >

Vercelli

Aosta

Torino

Cuneo

Asti

Pavia < 1hr >

< 1hr 30mn >

Alessandria

Savona

Imperia

Genova

La Spezia

< 30mn >

Verona

Brescia

< 1hr >

Piacenza

Parma

Mantova

Modena

< 40mn >

1hr 30mn >

Vicenza < 2hr >

Treviso < 40mn >

< 1hr 45mn >

Venezia

Padova

< 45mn >

Ferrara

< 1hr >

Bologna

Forlì

Rimini

< 45mn >

< 1hr >

Firenze

Pistoia

Lucca

Pisa

< 2hrs >

Livorno

Arezzo

Siena

Grosseto

< 3hrs >

20mn >

Viterbo

Perugia

< 1hr 45mn >

< 3hrs >

Terni

Ascoli

Teramo

L'Aquila

< 1hr 20mn >

Ancona

< 15mn >

Pescara

TO GREECE

VENEZIA - POLA- CROATIA 3HRS

TO GREECE

ANCONA - SPLIT, CROATIA 5HRS

ANCONA - ZADAR, CROATIA 4HRS

TO GREECE

PESCARA- SPLIT, CROATIA 3HRS

TO GREECE

5HRS

GENOVA - PALERMO 20HRS

GENOVA - POTTO TORRES 13HRS

4 10 HRS

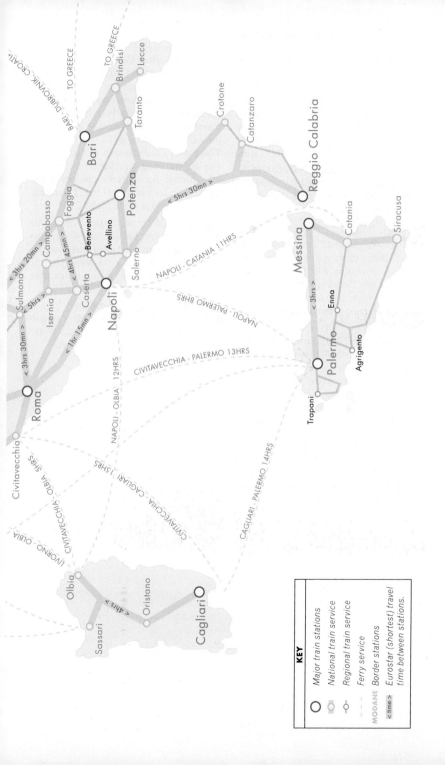

KEY

Major train stations

National train service

Regional train service

Ferry service

MODANE Border stations

< time > Eurostar (shortest) travel time between stations.

Sicily–Milan, Rome–Turin, Lecce–Milan); request the good-value T3 (three single beds), Intercity Notte, and Carrozza Comfort. The Vagone Letto has private bathrooms and single-, double-, or twin-bed suites. Overnight trains also travel to international destinations like Paris, Vienna, Munich, and other cities.

Information FS-Trenitalia. ☎ *06/68475475 from outside Italy (English), 892021 inside Italy* ⊕ *www.trenitalia.com.* **NTV Italo.** ☎ *06/0708* ⊕ *www.italotreno.it.*

TRAIN PASSES

Rail passes promise savings on train travel. But compare prices with actual fares to determine whether a pass will truly pay off. Generally, the more often you plan to travel long distances on high-speed trains, the more sense a rail pass makes.

Italy is one of 27 countries that accept the Eurail Pass, which provides unlimited first- and second-class travel. If you plan to rack up miles across the Continent, get a Global Eurail Pass (covering all participating nations). The Eurail Select Pass allows for travel in two to four contiguous countries. Other options are the Eurail Youth Pass (for those under 26), the Eurail Flexipass (valid for a certain number of travel days within a set period), and the Eurail Saver (aimed at two to five people traveling together).

The Eurail Two Country Select Pass, available for non-European residents, allows a certain number of travel days within two contiguous countries over the course of two months. Four to 10 days of travel in Italy and France cost $317–$518 (first class) or $255–$416 (second class). There is a 15% discount if two or more of you are traveling together; family passes offer further discounts for children under 12; kids under four travel free. Discounts are also given for those under 26.

Passes should be purchased before you leave for Europe, but can be delivered to your hotel for an additional cost. Keep in mind that even with a rail pass you still need to reserve seats on the trains that require them.

Contacts Eurail. ⊕ *www.eurail.com.* **Italia Rail.** ☎ *877/375-7245 in U.S.* ⊕ *www. italiarail.com.* **Rail Europe.** ☎ *800/622-8600 in U.S.* ⊕ *www.raileurope.com.* **RailPass.** ⊕ *www.railpass.com.*

ESSENTIALS

▌ACCOMMODATIONS

Hotels in Italy are becoming increasingly distinctive. Palazzi, villas, and monasteries have been restored as luxurious lodgings, while retaining their original atmosphere, and small hotels are revamping historic buildings with contemporary decor. Famed Italian wineries are offering rooms and apartments for three-day to weeklong stays.

The lodgings we list are the cream of the crop in each price category. Properties are assigned price categories based on the rate for two people sharing a standard double room in high season, including tax and service.

APARTMENT AND HOUSE RENTALS

Renting a vacation property can be economical depending on your budget and the number of people in your group. Most are owned by individuals and managed by rental agents who advertise online; and because many properties are represented by multiple agents, one may appear on different sites under different names (hence "Chianti Bella Vista," "Tuscan Sun Home," and "Casa Toscana Sole" could all refer to the same villa). In some cases rental agents handle only the online reservation and financial arrangements; in others, the agent or owner may meet you at the property for the initial check-in.

Issues to keep in mind when renting an apartment in a city or town are the neighborhood (street noise and ambience), the availability of an elevator or number of stairs, the furnishings (including pots and linens), what's supplied on arrival (dishwashing liquid, coffee or tea), and the cost of utilities (are all covered by the rental rate?). Inquiries about countryside properties should also include how isolated the property is (do you have to drive 45 minutes to reach the nearest town?). If you're arriving too late in the day to grocery shop, request that provisions for the next day's breakfast be supplied.

Contacts Airbnb. ⊕ *www.aribnb.com.* **Doorways Villa Vacations.** ☎ *610/520–0806, 800/261–4460* ⊕ *www.villavacations.com.* **HomeAway.** ☎ *512/493–0382* ⊕ *www. homeaway.com.* **Hosted Villas.** ☎ *800/374–6637, 416/920–1873* ⊕ *www.hostedvillas. com.* **Interhome.** ☎ *800/882–6864* ⊕ *www. interhome.com.* **Italy Rents.** ☎ *202/821–4273, 06/99268007 in Italy* ⊕ *www.italyrents.com.* **Parker Villas.** ☎ *800/280–2811* ⊕ *www. parkervillas.com.* **Rent A Villa.** ☎ *877/250–4366, 206/417–3444* ⊕ *www.rentavilla.com.* **Summer In Italy.** ☎ *800/509–8194 in U.S., 089/8426126 in Italy* ⊕ *www.summerini-taly.com.* **Tuscan House.** ☎ *800/844–6939* ⊕ *www.tuscanhouse.com.* **Villas & Apartments Abroad.** ☎ *212/213–6435* ⊕ *www. vaanyc.com.* **Villas International.** ☎ *800/221–2260, 415/499–9490* ⊕ *www. villasintl.com.* **Villas of Distinction.** ☎ *800/289–0900* ⊕ *www.villasofdistinction. com.* **WIMCO.** ☎ *800/449–1553, 401/849–8012* ⊕ *www.wimco.com.*

CONVENTS AND MONASTERIES

Throughout Italy tourists can find reasonably priced lodging at convents, monasteries, and religious houses. Religious orders commonly charge about €30–€60 per person per night for rooms that are clean, comfortable, and convenient. Many have private bathrooms; spacious lounge areas and secluded gardens or terraces are standard features. A continental breakfast ordinarily comes with the room, but be sure to ask. Sometimes, for an extra fee, family-style lunches and dinners are provided, too.

Be aware of three issues when considering a convent or monastery stay: many have a curfew of 11 pm or midnight; you need to book in advance because they fill up quickly; and your best means of booking is usually email or fax—the person answering the phone may not speak English.

Contact **Hospites.it**. ⊕ *www.hospites.it.*

FARM HOLIDAYS AND AGRITOURISM

Rural accommodations in the *agriturismo* category are growing in popularity among both Italians and visitors; you may have to look a little harder, though, to find an actual working farm or vineyard. Accommodations vary in size and range from luxury apartments, farmhouses, and villas to basic facilities. Agriturist has compiled *Agriturism,* which is available only in Italian, but includes more than 1,450 farms in Italy; pictures and the use of international symbols to describe facilities make the guide a good tool. Local APT tourist offices also have information.

Information **Agriturismo.com.**
☎ *800/911856 toll-free* ⊕ *www.agriturismo. com.* **Agriturismo.net.** ☎ *050/8665377* ⊕ *www.agriturismo.net.* **Agriturist-Farm Holidays.** ☎ *0564/417418* ⊕ *www.byfarm-holidays.com.* **Turismo Verde.** ☎ *06/3240111* ⊕ *www.turismoverde.it.*

HOME EXCHANGES

With a direct home exchange you stay in someone else's home while they stay in yours. Some outfits also deal with vacation homes, so you're not really occupying someone's full-time residence, just their vacant weekend place.

Italians have historically not been as enthusiastic about home exchanges as others; however, there are many great villas and apartments in Italy owned by foreigners (Americans, English, and others) who use home-exchange services.

Exchange Clubs **Home Exchange. com.** ☎ *800/877–8723, 310/798–3864, 02/94752664 in Italy* ⊕ *www.homeexchange. com.* **HomeLink International.** ☎ *800/638– 3841, 954/328–1643, 0422/815575 in Italy* ⊕ *www.homelink.org.* **Intervac Home Exchange.** ☎ *800/756–4663* ⊕ *www.intervac-homeexchange.com.*

▮ COMMUNICATIONS

INTERNET

Getting online in Italian cities isn't difficult: public Internet stations and Internet cafés are fairly common, and Wi-Fi is widely available. Most hotels have Wi-Fi or a computer for guests to use. Many business-oriented hotels also offer in-room broadband, though some (ironically, often the more expensive ones) charge for broadband and Wi-Fi access. Note that chargers and power supplies may need plug adapters to fit European-style electric sockets (a converter probably won't be necessary).

Italy is also looking to improve city Wi-Fi access; Rome, Venice, and Turin are continuing to develop and expand services, some free for now, some at a daily or weekly rate for temporary access.

Paid and free Wi-Fi hot spots can be found in major airports and train stations, and shopping centers; they're most likely to be free in bars or cafés that want your business.

Contact **Provincia Wi-Fi.** ☎ *06/40409434* ⊕ *www.cittametropolitanaroma.gov.it/ wifimetropolitano.*

PHONES

With the advent of mobile phones, public pay phones are becoming increasingly scarce in Italy, but they can be found at train and subway stations, main post offices, and in some bars. In rural areas, town squares usually have a pay phone. These require a *scheda telefonica.*

CALLING ITALY FROM ABROAD

When telephoning Italy from North America, dial 011 (to get an international line), followed by Italy's country code, 39, and the phone number, including any leading 0. Note that Italian mobile numbers have 10 digits and always begin with a 3; Italian landline numbers will contain from 4 to 10 digits and always begin with a 0. So, for example, when calling Rome, where local numbers start with 06, dial 011 + 39 + 06 + phone number; for a mobile phone, dial 011 + 39 + cell number.

LOCAL DO'S AND TABOOS

GREETINGS

Upon meeting and leave-taking, both friends and strangers wish each other good day or good evening (*buongiorno, buona sera*); *ciao* isn't used between strangers. Italians who are friends greet each other with a kiss, usually first on the left cheek, then on the right. When you meet a new person, shake hands and give your name.

SIGHTSEEING

Italy's churches house significant works of art, but they're also places of worship, so remember to dress appropriately.

Shorts, tank tops, and sleeveless garments are taboo in most churches throughout the country. To avoid being denied entrance, carry a shawl or other item of clothing to cover bare shoulders.

You should never bring food into a church, and don't sip from your water bottle inside. If you have a mobile phone, turn it off before entering. Ask whether photographs are allowed—and *never use a flash*. Never enter a church when a service is in progress either, especially if it's a private affair such as a wedding, funeral, or baptism.

OUT ON THE TOWN

Table manners in Italy are quite formal. In a restaurant, be reserved and polite with your waiter—no calling across the room for attention.

When you've finished your meal and are ready to go, ask for the check (*il conto*); unless it's well past closing time, it is unlikely a waiter will put a bill on your table until you've requested it.

Italians don't have a culture of sipping cocktails or chugging pitchers of beer. Wine, beer, and other alcoholic drinks are usually consumed only as part of a meal. Public drunkenness is abhorred.

Smoking has been banned in all public establishments, much as in the United States.

DOING BUSINESS

Showing up on time for business appointments is the norm and expected in Italy. There are more business lunches than business dinners, and even business lunches aren't common, as Italians view mealtimes as periods of pleasure and relaxation.

Business cards (*biglietti da visita*) are used throughout Italy, and business attire is the norm for both men and women. To be on the safe side, it's best not to use first names or a familiar form of address until invited to do so.

Business gifts aren't the norm, but if one is given it's usually small and symbolic of your home location or type of business.

LANGUAGE

One of the best ways to connect with Italians is to learn a little of the local language. You need not strive for fluency; just mastering a few basic words and terms is bound to make interactions more rewarding.

"Please" is *per favore*, "thank you" is *grazie*, "you're welcome" is *prego*, and "excuse me" is *scusi* (or *permesso* when you need to move past someone, as on a bus).

In larger cities like Venice, Rome, and Florence, language isn't a big problem. Most hotels have English-speakers at their reception desks, and if not, they can always find someone who speaks at least a little English. You may have trouble communicating in the countryside, but expressive gestures and a good phrase book—like *Fodor's Italian for Travelers* (available at bookstores everywhere)—will go a long way. Need audio assistance? Visit ⊕ *www.fodors.com/language/italian* to hear more than 150 essential phrases.

CALLING WITHIN ITALY

For all calls within Italy, whether local or long-distance, you'll dial the entire phone number that starts with 0 or 3 for mobile phone numbers. Calling a mobile phone will cost significantly more than calling a landline, depending on the calling plan. Italy uses the prefix "800" for toll-free or *numero verde* (green) numbers.

MAKING INTERNATIONAL CALLS

The country code for the United States and Canada is 1 (dial 00 + 1 + area code and number).

Because of the high rates charged by most hotels for long-distance and international calls, you're better off making such calls from public phones or your mobile phone or by using an international calling card.

Although not advised because of the exorbitant cost, you can place international calls or collect calls through an operator by dialing 170.

CALLING CARDS

Prepaid *schede telefoniche* (phone cards) are available throughout Italy for use in pay phones. Cards in different denominations are sold at post offices, newsstands, tobacco shops, and some bars. Before the first use, break off the corner of the card; then, to make a call, insert it into the phone's slot and dial. The card's credit will be displayed in the window as you chat. After you hang up, be sure not to walk off without retrieving the card.

International calling cards are different; you call a toll-free number from any phone, entering the access code found on the back of the card followed by the destination number. With calling cards offered by AT&T and MCI instructions and operator assistance are in English, avoiding language difficulties, and the charges appear on your phone bill. A reliable prepaid card for calling North America and elsewhere in Europe is the TIM Welcome card, offering 500 minutes to the United States for €5. A €10 card is also available. Cards can be purchased from TIM stores, tobacconists, and newsagents.

Calling Cards AT&T Direct. ☎ 800/172444 ⊕ www.shop.att.com. **Sprint International Access.** ☎ 866/275–1411 ⊕ shop.sprint.com. **TIM New Welcome.** ☎ 800/874874 toll-free in Italy ⊕ www.tim.it. **World Access.** ☎ 800/905825 ⊕ www.worldaccessnumbers.com.

MOBILE PHONES

Most mobile phones are now multiband (Europe and North America use different calling frequencies), so if your service provider uses the world-standard GSM network (as do T-Mobile, AT&T, and Verizon), you can use your own phone and provider abroad. But roaming fees can be steep—€0.99 per minute is considered quite low—and overseas you'll normally pay toll charges for incoming calls, too.

■TIP→ If you're carrying a laptop, tablet, or smartphone, investigate apps and services such as Skype, Viber, and Whatsapp, which offer free or low-cost calling and texting services.

To keep calling expenses to a minimum, consider purchasing an Italian SIM card—these can be purchased for as little as €5, depending on the provider (make sure your home service provider first unlocks your phone for use with a different SIM) and choose a prepaid service plan, topping off the credit as you go. You then have a local number and can make calls at local rates (about €0.15 per minute, and only for those made, not received), or send text messages for a reasonable fee (€0.12 per message or less). Have the service provider enable international calling; use an international calling card with your cell for even more savings.

■TIP→ If you're a frequent international traveler, save your old mobile phone (ask your service provider to unlock it for you) or buy an unlocked, multiband phone online. Use it as a travel phone, buying a new SIM card with pay-as-you-go service in each destination.

The cost of mobile phones is dropping: you can purchase a dual-band (Europe only) phone in Italy with a prepaid calling credit for as little as €20. Alternatively, you can buy a multiband phone that will also function in North America (European phones aren't usually "locked" to their provider's SIM, which is why they cost more). That means you can use it with your own service provider once you return home. You'll find dedicated mobile phone stores in all but the smallest towns. Service providers include TIM, Tre, Vodafone, and Wind; stop by a multivendor shop to compare offers, or check their websites. Note that you'll need to present your passport to purchase any SIM card.

Rental phones are available online prior to departure and in Italy's cities and larger towns. Shop around for the best deal. Most contracts require a refundable deposit that covers the cost of the mobile phone ($75–$300) and then set up a monthly service plan that's automatically charged to your credit card. Frequently, rental phones will be triple band with a plan that allows you to call North America. You should check the rate schedule, however, to avoid a nasty surprise on your credit card bill two or three months later. Often the local purchase with a prepaid plan will be the more cost-effective one.

■TIP→ Beware of mobile phone (and PDA) thieves. Use your device's security code option. Keep your phone or PDA in a secure pocket or purse. Don't lay it on the bar when you stop for an espresso. Don't zip it into the outside pocket of your backpack in crowded cities. Don't leave it in your hotel room. Notify your provider immediately if it's lost or stolen; providers can disable your SIM and give you a new one, copying the original's number and contents.

Contacts **Cellular Abroad.** ☎ 800/287–5072 ⊕ www.cellularabroad.com. **Mobal.** ☎ 888/888–9162, 212/785–5800 for support ⊕ www.mobal.com. **Planet Fone.** ☎ 888/988–4777 ⊕ www.planetfone.com.

■ CUSTOMS AND DUTIES

Travelers from the United States should experience little difficulty clearing customs at any Italian airport. It may be more difficult to clear customs when returning to the United States, where residents are normally entitled to a duty-free exemption of $800 on items accompanying them. You'll have to pay a tax (most often a flat percentage) on the value of everything beyond that limit. When you shop in Italy, keep all your receipts handy, as customs inspectors may ask to see them as well as the items you purchased.

Although there's no problem with aged cheese (vacuum-sealed works best), you cannot bring back any of that delicious prosciutto, salami, or any other meat product. Fresh mushrooms, truffles, or fresh fruits and vegetables are also forbidden. There are restrictions on the amount of alcohol allowed in duty-free, too. Generally, you can bring in one liter of wine, beer, or other alcohol without paying a customs duty; visit the travel area of the Customs and Border Patrol Travel website for complete information.

Italy requires documentation regarding the background of all antiques and antiquities before these items are taken out of the country. Under Italian law, all antiquities found on Italian soil are considered state property, and there are other restrictions on antique artwork. Even if purchased from a business in Italy, legal ownership of artifacts may be in question if brought into the United States. Therefore, although they don't necessarily confer ownership, documents such as export permits and receipts are required when importing such items into the United States.

Information in Italy **Dogana Sezione Viaggiatori.** ☎ 06/50241, 800/257428 toll-free ⊕ www.agenziadogane.it.

U.S. Information **U.S. Customs and Border Protection.** ☎ 877/227–5511, 202/325-8000 from abroad ⊕ www.cbp.gov.

▌EATING OUT

Italian cuisine is still largely regional. Ask what the specialties are—and, by all means, try spaghetti *alla carbonara* (with bacon and egg) in Rome, pizza in Naples, *bistecca alla fiorentina* (steak) in Florence, *cinghiale* (wild boar) in Tuscany, truffles in Piedmont, *la frittura* (fish fry) in Venice, and *risotto alla milanese* in Milan. Although most restaurants in Italy serve local dishes, you can find Asian and Middle Eastern alternatives in Rome, Venice, and other cities. The restaurants we list are the cream of the crop in each price category.

MEALS AND MEALTIMES

What's the difference between a *ristorante* and a *trattoria*? Can you order food at an *enoteca*? Can you go to a restaurant just for a snack or order only salad at a pizzeria? The following definitions should help.

Not long ago, *ristoranti* tended to be more elegant and expensive than *trattorie,* which serve traditional, home-style fare in an atmosphere to match, or *osterie,* which serve local wines and simple, regional dishes. But the distinction has blurred considerably, and an osteria in the center of town might now be far fancier (and pricier) than a ristorante across the street. In any sit-down establishment, however, you're generally expected to order at least a two-course meal, such as: a *primo* (first course) and a *secondo* (main course) or a *contorno* (vegetable side dish); an *antipasto* (starter) followed by either a primo or secondo; or a secondo and a *dolce* (dessert).

There is no problem if you'd prefer to eat less, but consider an enoteca or pizzeria as an alternative, where it's more common to order a single dish. An enoteca menu is often limited to a selection of cheese, cured meats, salads, and desserts, but if there's a kitchen you can also find soups, pastas, and main courses. The typical pizzeria serves *affettati misti* (a selection of cured pork), simple salads, various kinds of bruschetta, *crostini* (similar to bruschetta, with a variety of toppings) and, in Rome and Naples, *fritti* (deep-fried finger food) such as *olive ascolane* (green olives with a meat stuffing) and *supplì* or *arancini* (rice balls stuffed with mozzarella or minced meat).

The most convenient and least expensive places for a quick snack between sights are probably bars, cafés, and pizza *al taglio* (by the slice) spots. Pizza al taglio shops are easy to negotiate, but few have seats. They sell pizza by weight: just point out which kind you want and how much. Kebab stores are also omnipresent in every Italian city.

Note that Italians do not usually walk and eat.

Bars in Italy resemble what we think of as cafés, and are primarily places to get a coffee and a bite to eat, rather than drinking establishments. Expect a selection of panini warmed up on the griddle (*piastra*) and *tramezzini* (sandwiches made of untoasted white bread triangles). In larger cities, bars also serve vegetable and fruit salads, cold pasta dishes, and gelato. Most offer beer and a variety of alcohol, as well as wines by the glass (sometimes good but more often mediocre). A café is like a bar but typically has more tables. Pizza at a café should be avoided—it's usually heated in a microwave.

If you place your order at the counter, ask whether you can sit down. Some places charge for table service (especially in tourist centers); others don't. In self-service bars and cafés, it's good manners to clean your table before you leave. Be aware that in certain spots (such as train stations and stops along the highway) you first pay a cashier; then show your *scontrino* (receipt) at the counter to place your order. Menus are posted outside most restaurants (in English in tourist areas). If not, you might step inside and ask to take a look at the menu, but don't ask for a table unless you intend to stay.

Italians take their food as it's listed on the menu, seldom making special requests such as "dressing on the side" or "hold the olive oil." If you have special dietary needs, however, make them known; they can usually be accommodated. Vegetarians should be firm, as bacon and ham can slip into some dishes. Although mineral water makes its way to almost every table, you can order a carafe of tap water (*acqua di rubinetto* or *acqua semplice*) instead—just keep in mind that such water can be highly chlorinated.

An Italian would never ask for olive oil to dip bread in, and don't be surprised if there's no butter to spread on it either. Wiping your bowl clean with a (small) piece of bread, known locally as *la scarpetta*, is usually considered a sign of appreciation, not bad manners. Spaghetti should be eaten with a fork only, although a little help from a spoon won't horrify locals the way cutting spaghetti into little pieces might. Order your caffè (Italians drink cappuccino only in the morning) after dessert, not with it. As for doggy bags, Italians would never ask for one, though eateries popular with tourists are becoming more accustomed to travelers who do.

Breakfast (*la colazione*) is usually served from 7 to 10:30, lunch (*il pranzo*) from 12:30 to 2, and dinner (*la cena*) from 7:30 to 10, later in the south; outside those hours, best head for a bar. Peak times are usually 1:30 for lunch and 9 for dinner. Enoteche and Venetian *bacari* (wine bars) are also open in the morning and late afternoon for *cicheti* (finger foods) at the counter. Bars and cafés are open from 7 am until 8 or 9 pm; a few stay open until midnight.

Unless otherwise noted, the restaurants listed here are open for lunch and dinner, closing one or two days a week.

PAYING

Most restaurants have a cover charge per person, usually listed at the top of the check as *coperto* or *pane e coperto*. It should be modest (€1–€2.50 per person) except at the most expensive restaurants. Whenever in doubt, ask before you order to avoid unpleasant discussions later.

It's customary to leave a small cash tip (between 5% and 10%) in appreciation of good service: you will usually see a *servizio* charge included at the bottom of the check, but the server will not likely receive it.

The price of fish dishes is often given by weight (before cooking), so the price quoted on the menu is for 100 grams of fish, not for the whole dish. (An average fish portion is about 350 grams.) In Tuscany, bistecca alla fiorentina is also often priced by weight (about €4 for 100 grams, or $18 per pound).

Major credit cards are widely accepted in Italy; however, cash is always preferred. More restaurants take Visa and MasterCard than American Express or Diners Club.

When you leave a dining establishment, take your meal bill or receipt with you. Although not a common experience, the Italian finance (tax) police can approach you within 100 yards of the establishment at which you've eaten and ask for a receipt; if you don't have one, they can fine you and will fine the business owner for not providing it. The practice is intended to prevent tax evasion; it's not necessary to show receipts when leaving Italy.

RESERVATIONS AND DRESS

It's always safest to make a reservation for dinner. For popular restaurants, book as far ahead as you can (two to three weeks), and reconfirm as soon as you arrive. Large parties should always call ahead to check the reservations policy. If you change your mind, be sure to cancel, even at the last minute.

Unless they're dining outside or at a seafront resort, Italian men never wear shorts or running shoes in a restaurant. The same applies to women: no casual shorts, running shoes, or rubber sandals when going out to dinner. Shorts are acceptable in pizzerias and cafés.

WINES, BEER, AND SPIRITS

The grape has been cultivated in Italy since the time of the Etruscans, and Italians justifiably take pride in their local varieties, which are numerous. Although almost every region produces good-quality wine, Tuscany, Piedmont, the Veneto, Puglia, Calabria, and Sicily are some of the more renowned areas, with Le Marche and Umbria being well reputed, too. Italian wine is less expensive in Italy than almost anywhere else, so it's often affordable to order a bottle of wine at a restaurant rather than sticking with the house wine (which is usually good but quite simple). Many bars have their own *aperitivo della casa* (house aperitif); Italians are imaginative with their mixed drinks, so you may want to try one.

You can purchase beer, wine, and spirits in any bar, grocery store, or enoteca, any day of the week, any time of the day. Italian and German beer is readily available, but it can be more expensive than wine. Some excellent microbreweries are beginning to dot the Italian beer horizon, so ask if there's a local brew available to sample.

There's no minimum drinking age in Italy. Italian children begin drinking wine mixed with water at mealtimes when they're teens (or thereabouts). Italians are rarely seen drunk in public, and public drinking, except in a bar or eating establishment, isn't considered acceptable behavior. Bars usually close by 9 pm; hotel and restaurant bars stay open until midnight. Pubs and discos serve until about 2 am.

▌ELECTRICITY

The electrical current in Italy is 220 volts, 50 cycles alternating current (AC); wall outlets accept continental-type plugs, with two or three round prongs.

You may purchase a universal adapter, which has several types of plugs in one lightweight, compact unit, at travel specialty stores, electronics stores, and online. You can also pick up plug adapters in Italy in any electric supply store for about €2 each. You'll likely not need a voltage converter, though. Most portable devices are dual voltage (i.e., they operate equally well on 110 and 220 volts)—just check label specifications and manufacturer instructions to be sure. Don't use 110-volt outlets marked "for shavers only" for high-wattage appliances such as hair dryers.

Contacts Walkabout Travel Gear.
☎ 800/852–7085 ⊕ *www.walkabouttravel-gear.com.*

▌EMERGENCIES

No matter where you are in the European Union, you can dial ☎ *112* in case of an emergency: the call will be directed to the local police. Not all 112 operators speak English, so you may want to ask a local person to place the call. Asking the operator for *"pronto soccorso"* (first aid and also the emergency room of a hospital) should get you an *ambulanza* (ambulance). If you just need a doctor, ask for *"un medico."*

Italy has the *carabinieri* (national police force; their emergency number is ☎ *113* from anywhere in Italy) as well as the *polizia* (local police force). Both are armed and have the power to arrest and investigate crimes. Always report the loss of your passport to the carabinieri as well as to your embassy. When reporting a crime, you'll be asked to fill out *una denuncia* (official report)—keep a copy for your insurance company. You should also contact the police any time you have a car accident of any sort.

Local traffic officers, known as *vigili,* are responsible for, among other things, giving out parking tickets. They wear white (in summer), navy, or black uniforms. Should you find yourself involved in a minor car accident in town, contact the vigili.

Pharmacies are generally open weekdays 8:30–1 and 4–8, and Saturday 9–1. Local pharmacies rotate covering the off-hours in shifts: on the door of every pharmacy is a list of which pharmacies in the vicinity will be open late.

Foreign Embassies U.S. Consulate Florence. ✉ *Lungarno Vespucci 38, Florence* ☎ *055/266951* ⊕ *florence.usconsulate.gov.* **U.S. Consulate Milan.** ✉ *Via Principe Amedeo 2/10, Milan* ☎ *02/290351* ⊕ *milan.usconsulate. gov.* **U.S. Consulate Naples.** ✉ *Piazza della Repubblica, Naples* ☎ *081/5838111* ⊕ *naples. usconsulate.gov.* **U.S. Embassy.** ✉ *Via Vittorio Veneto 121, Rome* ☎ *06/46741* ⊕ *italy. usembassy.gov.*

General Emergency Contacts Emergencies. ☎ *115 for fire, 118 for ambulance.* **National and State Police.** ☎ *112 for Polizia (National Police), 113 for Carabinieri (State Police)* ⊕ *www.poliziadistato.it* ⊕ *www.carabinieri.it.*

▌ HOURS OF OPERATION

Religious and civic holidays are frequent in Italy. Depending on the holiday's local importance, businesses may close for the day. Businesses don't close Friday or Monday when the holiday falls on the weekend, though the Monday following Easter is a holiday.

Banks are open weekdays 8:30–1:30 and for one or two hours in the afternoon, depending on the bank. Most post offices are open Monday–Saturday 9–1:30, some until 2; central post offices are open weekdays 9–6:30, Saturday 9–12:30 or 9–6:30.

Most churches are open from early morning until noon or 12:30, when they close for three hours or more; they open again in the afternoon, closing at about 6. A few major churches, such as St. Peter's in Rome and San Marco in Venice, remain open all day. Walking around during services is discouraged. Many museums are closed one day a week, often Monday or Tuesday. During low season museums often close early; during high season many stay open until late at night.

Most shops are open Monday through Saturday 9–1 and 3:30 or 4–7:30. Clothing shops are generally closed Monday

mornings. Barbers and hairdressers, with certain exceptions, are closed Sunday and Monday. Some bookstores and fashion- or tourist-oriented shops in places such as Rome and Venice are open all day, as well as Sunday. Many branches of large chain supermarkets such as Standa, COOP, and Esselunga don't close for lunch and are usually open Sunday; smaller *alimentari* (delicatessens) and other food shops are usually closed one evening during the week (it varies according to the town) and are almost always closed Sunday.

HOLIDAYS

Traveling through Italy in July and August can be an odd experience. Although there are some deals to be had, the heat can be oppressive, and in August much of the population is on vacation. Most cities are deserted (except for foreign tourists) and privately run restaurants and shops are closed. National holidays in 2018 include January 1 (New Year's Day); January 6 (Epiphany); April 1 and 2 (Easter Sunday and Monday); April 25 (Liberation Day); May 1 (Labor Day or May Day); June 2 (Festival of the Republic); August 15 (Ferragosto); November 1 (All Saints' Day); December 8 (Immaculate Conception); and December 25 and 26 (Christmas Day and the Feast of St. Stephen).

In addition, feast days of patron saints are observed locally. Many businesses and shops may be closed in Florence, Genoa, and Turin on June 24 (St. John the Baptist); in Rome on June 29 (Sts. Peter and Paul); in Palermo on July 15 (Santa Rosalia); in Naples on September 19 (San Gennaro); in Bologna on October 4 (San Petronio); in Trieste on November 3 (San Giusto); and in Milan on December 7 (St. Ambrose). Venice's feast of St. Mark is April 25, the same as Liberation Day, so the Madonna della Salute on November 21 makes up for the lost holiday.

▌MAIL

The Italian mail system has a bad reputation but has become noticeably more efficient in recent times with some privatization. Allow 7–15 days for mail to get to the United States. Receiving mail in Italy, especially packages, can take weeks, usually due to customs (not postal) delays.

You can buy stamps at tobacco shops as well as post offices.

"Posta Prioritaria" (for regular letters and packages) is the name for standard postage. It guarantees delivery within Italy in three to five business days and abroad in five to six working days. The more expensive express delivery, "Postacelere" (for larger letters and packages), guarantees one-day delivery to most places in Italy and three- to five-day delivery abroad. Note that the postal service has no control over customs, however, which makes international delivery estimates meaningless. Mail sent as "Postamail Internazionale" to the United States costs €2.20 for up to 20 grams, €3.70 for 21–50 grams, and €4.60 for 51–100 grams. Mail sent as "Paccocelere" to the United States costs €40 for up to 500 grams.

Reliable two-day international mail is generally available during the week in all major cities and at popular resorts via UPS and Federal Express—but again, customs delays can slow down "express" service.

SHIPPING SERVICES

Sending a letter or small package to the United States via Federal Express takes at least two days and costs about €45. Other package services to check are Quick Pack Europe (for delivery within Europe) and Express Mail Service (a global three- to five-day service for letters and packages). Compare prices with those of Paccocelere to determine the cheapest option.

If your hotel can't assist you with shipping, try an Internet café; many offer two-day mail services using major carriers.

If you've purchased antiques, ceramics, or other fragile objects, ask if the vendor will do the shipping for you. In most cases this is possible, and preferable, because many merchants have experience with these kinds of shipments. If so, ask whether the article will be insured against breakage.

▌MONEY

Prices vary from region to region and are substantially lower in the country than in urban centers. Of Italy's major cities, Milan is by far the most expensive. Resort areas such as Capri, Portofino, and Cortina d'Ampezzo cater to wealthy vacationers and charge top prices. Good value can be had in the scenic Trentino–Alto Adige region of the Dolomites and in Umbria and Marche. With a few exceptions, southern Italy and Sicily also offer bargains for those who do their homework before they leave home.

ITEM	AVERAGE COST
Cup of Coffee	€0.80–€1.50
Soft Drink (glass/can/bottle)	€2–€3
Glass of Beer	€2–€5
Sandwich	€3–€4.50
2-km (1-mile) Taxi Ride in Rome	€8.50

Prices here are given for adults. Substantially reduced fees are almost always available for children, students, and senior citizens from the EU; citizens of non-EU countries rarely get discounts, but inquire before you purchase tickets, as this situation is constantly changing.

▌TIP➔ U.S. banks do not keep every foreign currency on hand, and it may take as long as a week to order. If you're planning to exchange funds before leaving home, don't wait until the last minute.

ATMS AND BANKS

An ATM (*bancomat* in Italian) is the easiest way to get euros in Italy. There are numerous ATMs in large cities and small towns, as well as in airports and train stations. Be sure to memorize your PIN in numbers, as ATM keypads in Italy won't always display letters. Check with your bank to confirm that you have an international PIN (*codice segreto*) that will be recognized in the countries you're visiting; to raise your maximum daily withdrawal allowance; and to learn what your bank's fee is for withdrawing money (Italian banks don't charge withdrawal fees). ■TIP→ Be aware that PINs beginning with a 0 (zero) tend to be rejected in Italy.

Your own bank may charge a fee for using ATMs abroad and for the cost of conversion from euros to dollars. Nevertheless, you can usually get a better rate of exchange at an ATM than you will at a currency-exchange office or even when changing money inside a bank with a teller, the next-best option. Whatever the method, extracting funds as you need them is safer than carrying around a large amount of cash. Finally, it's advisable to carry more than one card that can be used for cash withdrawal, in case something happens to your main one.

CREDIT CARDS

It's a good idea to inform your credit card company before you travel, especially if you're going abroad and don't travel internationally often. Otherwise, the credit card company might put a hold on your card owing to unusual activity—not a welcome occurrence halfway through your trip. Record all your credit card numbers—as well as the phone numbers to call if your cards are lost or stolen. Keep these in a safe place, so you're prepared should something go wrong. MasterCard and Visa have general numbers you can call (collect if you're abroad) if your card is lost. But you're better off calling the number of your issuing bank, because MasterCard and Visa generally just transfer you there; your bank's number is usually printed on your card.

■TIP→ North American toll-free numbers aren't available from abroad, so be sure to obtain a local number with area code for any business you may need to contact.

Although it's usually cheaper (and safer) to use a credit card abroad for large purchases (so you can cancel payments or be reimbursed if there's a problem), note that some credit card companies *and* the banks that issue them add substantial percentages to all foreign transactions, whether they're in a foreign currency or not. Check on these fees before leaving home, so there won't be any surprises when you get the bill. Because of these fees, avoid using your credit card for ATM withdrawals or cash advances (use a debit or cash card instead).

■TIP→ Before you charge something, ask the merchant whether he or she plans to do a dynamic currency conversion (DCC). In such a transaction the credit card processor (shop, restaurant, or hotel, not Visa or MasterCard) converts the currency and charges you in dollars. In most cases you'll pay the merchant a 3% fee for this service in addition to any credit card company and issuing-bank foreign-transaction surcharges.

Merchants who participate in dynamic currency conversion programs are supposed to ask whether you want to be charged in dollars or the local currency, but they don't always do so. And even if they do offer you a choice, they may well avoid mentioning the additional surcharges. The good news is that you *do* have a choice—you can simply say no. If this practice really gets your goat, you can avoid it entirely by using American Express; with its cards, DCC simply isn't an option.

Italian merchants prefer MasterCard and Visa (look for the CartaSi sign), but American Express is usually accepted in popular tourist destinations. Credit cards aren't accepted everywhere, though; if you want to pay with a credit card in a small shop, hotel, or restaurant, it's a good idea to make your intentions known early on.

Reporting Lost Cards American Express.
☎ 800/528–4800 in U.S., 905/474–0870 collect from abroad ⊕ www.americanexpress.com. **Diners Club.** ☎ 800/234–6377 in U.S., 514/877–1577 collect from abroad, 800/393939 in Italy ⊕ www.dinersclub.com. **MasterCard.** ☎ 800/307–7309 in U.S., 636/722–7111 collect from abroad, 800/870866 in Italy ⊕ www.mastercard.us. **Visa.** ☎ 800/847–2911 in U.S., 303/967–1096 from abroad, 800/819014 in Italy ⊕ usa.visa.com.

CURRENCY AND EXCHANGE

The euro is the main unit of currency in Italy. Under the euro system there are 100 *centesimi* (cents) to the euro. There are coins valued at 1, 2, 5, 10, 20, and 50 centesimi as well as 1 and 2 euros. There are seven notes: 5, 10, 20, 50, 100, 200, and 500 euros. At this writing, €1 was worth was about $1.12.

Post offices exchange currency at good rates, but employees speak limited English, so be prepared. (Writing your request can help in these cases.)

■TIP→ Even if a currency-exchange booth has a sign promising no commission, rest assured that there's some kind of huge, hidden fee. You're almost always better off getting foreign currency at an ATM or exchanging money at a bank or post office.

■ PASSPORTS AND VISAS

PASSPORTS

Although somewhat costly, a U.S. passport is relatively simple to obtain and is valid for 10 years. You must apply in person if you're getting a passport for the first time; if your previous passport was lost, stolen, or damaged; or if it has expired and was issued more than 15 years ago or when you were under 16. All children under 18 must appear in person to apply for or renew a passport. Both parents

must accompany any child under 14 (or send a notarized statement with their permission) and provide proof of their relationship to the child.

There are 25 regional passport offices as well as 7,000 passport acceptance facilities in post offices, public libraries, and other governmental offices. If you're renewing a passport, you may do so by mail; forms are available at passport acceptance facilities and online, where you trace the application's progress.

The cost of a new passport is $135 for adults, $105 for children under 16; renewals are $110 for adults, $105 for children under 16. Allow four to six weeks for processing, both for first-time passports and renewals. For an expediting fee of $60 you can reduce this time to two to three weeks. If your trip is less than two weeks away, you can get a passport even more rapidly by going to a passport office with the necessary documentation. Private expediters can get things done in as little as 48 hours, but charge hefty fees for their services.

■TIP→ Before your trip, make two copies of your passport's data page (one for someone at home and another for you to carry separately). Or scan the page and email it to someone at home and/or yourself.

GENERAL REQUIREMENTS FOR ITALY	
Passport	Must be valid for 6 months after date of arrival
Visa	Tourist visas aren't needed for stays of 90 days or less by U.S. citizens.
Vaccinations	None
Driving	International driver's license required. CDW is compulsory on car rentals and will be included in the quoted price.

VISAS

When staying for 90 days or less, U.S. citizens aren't required to obtain a visa prior to traveling to Italy. A recent law requires that you fill in a declaration of presence within eight days of your arrival—the stamp on your passport at airport arrivals substitutes for this. If you plan to travel or live in Italy or the European Union for longer than 90 days, you must acquire a valid visa from the Italian consulate serving your state *before you leave the United States.* Plan ahead, because the process of obtaining a visa will take at least 30 days, and the Italian government doesn't accept visa applications submitted by visa expediters.

U.S. Passport Information U.S. Department of State. ☎ 877/487–2778 ⊕ travel.state.gov.

U.S. Passport Expediters American Passport Express. ☎ 800/455–5166 ⊕ www.americanpassport.com. **Travel Document Systems.** ☎ 800/874–5100 ⊕ www.traveldocs.com. **Travel the World Visas.** ☎ 202/223–8822 ⊕ www.world-visa.com.

∎ TAXES

A 10% V.A.T. (value-added tax) is included in the rate at all hotels except those at the upper end of the range. You'll often have to pay a supplementary City Tax (in cash) at your hotel, varying from €1 per night to Rome's exorbitant €5 per night, as well.

No tax is added to the bill in restaurants. A service charge of approximately 10%–15% is often added to your check; in some cases a service charge is included in the prices.

The V.A.T. is 22% on clothing, wine, and luxury goods. On consumer goods it's already included in the amount shown on the price tag (look for the phrase *"IVA inclusa"*), whereas on services it may not be. If you're not a European citizen and if your purchases in a single day total more than €154.94, you may be entitled to a refund of the V.A.T.

When making a purchase, ask whether the merchant gives refunds—not all do, nor are they required to. If they do, they'll help you fill out the V.A.T. refund form, which you then submit to a company that will issue you the refund in the form of cash, check, or credit card adjustment.

Alternatively, as you leave the country (or, if you're visiting several European Union countries, on leaving the EU), present your merchandise and the form to customs officials, who will stamp it. Once through passport control, take the stamped form to a refund-service counter for an on-the-spot refund (the quickest and easiest option). You may also mail it to the address on the form (or on the envelope with it) after you arrive home, but processing time can be long, especially if you request a credit card adjustment. Note that in larger cities the cash refund can be obtained at in-town offices prior to departure; just ask the merchant or check the envelope for local office addresses.

Global Blue is the largest V.A.T.-refund service with 270,000 affiliated stores and more than 700 refund counters at major airports and border crossings. Premier Tax Free is another company that represents more than 150,000 merchants worldwide; look for their logos in store windows.

V.A.T. Refunds Global Blue. ☎ 866/706–6090 in North America, 421232/111111 from abroad, 00800/32111111 from Italy ⊕ www.global-blue.com. **Premier Tax Free.** ☎ 905/542–1710 from U.S., 06/69923383 from Italy ⊕ www.premiertaxfree.com.

∎ TIME

Italy is in the Central European Time Zone (CET). From March to October it institutes Daylight Saving Time. Italy is six hours ahead of U.S. Eastern Standard Time, one hour ahead of Great Britain, 10 hours behind Sydney, and 12 hours behind Auckland. Like the rest of Europe, Italy uses the 24-hour (or "military") clock, which means that after noon you continue counting forward: 13:00 is 1 pm, 23:30 is 11:30 pm.

▮ TIPPING

In restaurants a service charge of 10%–15% may appear on your check, but it's not a given that your server will receive this; so you may want to consider leaving a tip of 5%–10% (in cash) for good service. Tip checkroom attendants €1 per person and restroom attendants €0.50 (more in expensive hotels and restaurants). In major cities, tip €0.50 or more for table service in cafés. At a hotel bar, tip €1 and up for a round or two of drinks.

Italians rarely tip taxi drivers, which isn't to say that you shouldn't. A euro or two is appreciated, particularly if the driver helps with luggage. Service-station attendants are tipped only for special services; give them €1 for checking your tires. Railway and airport porters charge a fixed rate per bag. Tip an additional €0.25 per person, more if the porter is helpful. Give a barber €1–€1.50 and a hairdresser's assistant €1.50–€4 for a shampoo or cut, depending on the type of establishment.

On sightseeing tours, tip guides about €1.50 per person for a half-day group tour, more if they're especially knowledgeable. In monasteries and other sights where admission is free, a contribution (€0.50–€1) is expected.

In hotels, give the *portiere* (concierge) about 10% of the bill for services, or €2.50–€5 for help with dinner reservations and such. Leave the chambermaid about €0.75 per day, or about €4.50–€5 a week in a moderately priced hotel; tip a minimum of €1 for valet or room service. In an expensive hotel, double these amounts; tip doormen €0.50 for calling a cab and €1.50 for carrying bags to the check-in desk, and tip bellhops €1.50–€2.50 for carrying your bags to the room.

▮ TOURS

Guided tours are a good option when you don't want to do it all yourself. You travel along with a group (sometimes large, sometimes small), stay in pre-booked hotels, often eat with your fellow travelers (the cost of meals may or may not be included in the price of your tour), and follow a set schedule. Not all guided tours are an "if it's Tuesday this must be Belgium" experience, however. A knowledgeable guide can take you places that you might never discover on your own, give you a richer context, and lead you to a more in-depth experience than you would have otherwise. They may be just the thing if you don't have the time or inclination to make travel arrangements on your own.

Whenever you book a guided tour, find out what's included and what isn't. A "land-only" tour includes all your travel (by bus, in most cases) in the destination, but not necessarily your flights to and from or even within it. Also, in most cases prices in tour promotions don't include fees and taxes. You'll also want to review how much free time you'll have, and see if that meets with your personal preferences. Remember, too, that you'll be expected to tip your guide (in cash) at the end of the tour.

Even when planning independent travel, keep in mind that every province and city in Italy has tour guides licensed by the government. Some are eminently qualified in relevant fields such as architecture and art history and are a pleasure to spend time with. Lots of private guides have websites, and you can check the travel forums at ⊕ *Fodors.com* for recommendations (it's best to book before you leave home, especially for major destinations, as popular guides and tours are in demand). Once in Italy, tourist offices and hotel concierges can also provide the names of knowledgeable local guides and the rates for certain services. When hiring on the spot, ask about their background and qualifications—and make sure you can understand each other. Tipping is always appreciated, but never obligatory, for local guides.

Recommended Generalists Abercrombie & Kent. ☎ *800/554-7016, 630/725-3400* ⊕ *www.abercrombiekent.com.* **Andante.** ☎ *888/331-3476* ⊕ *www.andantetravels.com.* **Maupin Tour.** ☎ *800/255-4266, 954/653-3820* ⊕ *www.maupintour.com.* **Perillo Tours.** ☎ *800/431-1515* ⊕ *www.perillotours.com.* **Tauck.** ☎ *800/788-7885* ⊕ *www.tauck.com.* **Travcoa.** ☎ *888/979-2806, 310/730-1263* ⊕ *www.travcoa.com.*

Biking and Hiking Tour Contacts Backroads. ☎ *800/462-2848, 510/527-1555* ⊕ *www.backroads.com.* **Butterfield & Robinson.** ☎ *866/551-9090, 416/864-1354* ⊕ *www.butterfield.com.* **Genius Loci Travel.** ☎ *089/791896* ⊕ *www.genius-loci.it.* **Italian Connection.** ☎ *0932/231816 in Italy, 335/8016115 Italy mobile* ⊕ *www.italian-connection.com.*

Educational Programs Road Scholar. ☎ *800/454-5768, 877/426-8056* ⊕ *www.roadscholar.org.*

Golf Tour Contact Italy Vacations. ☎ *800/482-5925* ⊕ *www.italyvacations.com/vacations#Golf Packages.*

Wine Tour Contacts Cellar Tours. ☎ *310/496-8061, 030/8370783 Italy* ⊕ *www.cellartours.com.* **Food & Wine Trails.** ☎ *800/367-5348* ⊕ *www.foodandwinetrails.com.*

▌ TRIP INSURANCE

Comprehensive trip insurance is valuable if you're booking an expensive or complicated trip (particularly to an isolated region) or if you're booking far in advance. Comprehensive policies typically cover trip cancellation and interruption, letting you cancel or cut your trip short because of illness (yours or that of someone back home), or, in some cases, acts of terrorism in your destination. Such policies usually also cover evacuation and medical care.

(For trips abroad you should have at least medical and medical evacuation coverage. With a few exceptions, Medicare doesn't provide coverage abroad, nor does regular health insurance.) Some also cover you for trip delays because of bad weather or mechanical problems as well as for lost or delayed luggage.

Another type of coverage to consider is financial default—that is, when your trip is disrupted because a tour operator, airline, or cruise line goes out of business. Generally you must buy this when you book your trip or shortly thereafter, and it's available to you only if your operator isn't on a list of excluded companies.

Many travel insurance policies have exclusions for preexisting conditions as a cause for cancellation. Most companies waive those exclusions, however, if you take out your policy within a short period (which varies by company) after the first payment toward your trip.

Always read the fine print of your policy to make sure that you're covered for the risks that most concern you. Compare several policies to be sure you're getting the best price and range of coverage available.

Comprehensive Insurers Allianz. ☎ *866/884-3556* ⊕ *www.allianztravelinsurance.com.* **CSA Travel Protection.** ☎ *877/243-4135, 240/330-1529 collect* ⊕ *www.csatravelprotection.com.* **HTH Worldwide.** ☎ *610/254-8700, 888/243-2358 toll-free* ⊕ *www.hthworldwide.com.* **Travel Guard.** ☎ *800/826-4919, 800/3450505 toll-free from Italy* ⊕ *www.travelguard.com.* **Travel Insured International.** ☎ *800/243-3174, 603/328-1707 collect* ⊕ *www.travelinsured.com.* **Travelex Insurance.** ☎ *800/228-9792, 603/328-1739 collect* ⊕ *www.travelexinsurance.com.*

Insurance Comparison Info Insure My Trip. ☎ *800/487-4722, 401/773-9300* ⊕ *www.insuremytrip.com.* **Square Mouth.** ☎ *800/240-0369, 727/564-9203* ⊕ *www.squaremouth.com.*

INDEX

PHOTO CREDITS

Front cover: Olgacov I Dreamstime.com [Description: Gondolas on narrow canal, Venice, Italy.]. 1, Freesurf69 I Dreamstime.com. 2-3, Shaiith I Dreamstime.com. 5, Javier Larrea/age fotostock. **Chapter 1: Experience Italy:** 8-9, minnystock I Dreamstime.com. 16 (left), Ronald Sumners/Shutterstock. 16 (top center), Victoria German/Shutterstock. 16 (top right), Knud Nielsen/Shutterstock. 16 (bottom right), pxlar8/Shutterstock. 17 (left), Public domain. 17 (top center), Thomas M Perkins/Shutterstock. 17 (top right), Ivonne Wierink/Shutterstock. 17 (bottom right), Rostislav Glinsky/Shutterstock. 20, Eric Gevaert/Shutterstock. 21, Stefano Cellai/age footstock. **Chapter 2: Rome:** 25, Angelo Campus. 26, Paul D'Innocenzo. 28, Jono Pandolfi. 29 (top), Angelo Campus. 29 (bottom), Lisay/iStockphoto. 30, Vitalyedush I Dreamstime.com. 37 (left), Justin D. Paola. 37 (right), Edis Jurcys/age fotostock. 38-39 (bottom), Justin D. Paola. 39 (top left), Renata Sedmakova/ Shutterstock. 39 (top right), Mrallen I Dreamstime.com. 40-41 (bottom), Justin D. Paola. 41 (top left), Rome Tourist Board. 41 (top right), Atlantide S.N.C./age fotostock. 43 (left), Chie Ushio. 43 (right), Dan Radmacher/iStockphoto/Think-stock. 45 (left), Chie Ushio. 45 (right), Corbis. 70-71, Cezary Wojtkowski/age fotostock. 70 (bottom), public domain. 72, Russell Mountford/ age fotostock. 74-77, Dave Drapak. **Chapter 3: Venice:** 117, Paul D'Innocenzo. 118, Kevin Galvin/age fotostock. 120, Paul D'Innocenzo. 121 (right), Bon Appetit/ Alamy. 121 (left), Robert Milek/ Shutterstock. 122, S. Greg Panosian/iStockphoto. 127, Mapics I Dreamstime.com. 128, Alexey Arkhipov/Shutterstock. 129 (left), Agiampiccolo I Dreamstime.com. 129 (right), Paul D'Innocenzo. 130, Javier Larrea/age fotostock. 131 (left), Steve Allen/Brand X Pictures. 131 (right), Doug Scott/age fotostock. 132, Bruno Morandi/age fotostock. 133 (left), Corbis. 133 (right), Sergio Pitamitz/age fotostock. **Chapter 4: Northern Italy:** 183, Wojtek Buss/age fotostock. 184 (top), Atlantide S.N.C./age fotostock. 185, Vito Arcomano/Fototeca ENIT. 186, Francesco Majo/ age fotostock. 187 (top), Danilo Donadoni/age fotostock. 187 (bottom), Michele Bella/age fotostock. 188 and 189 (top), Matz Sjöberg/age fotostock. 189 (bottom), Franco Pizzochero/age fotostock. 190, vesilvio/iStockphoto. 239, Oana Dragan/iStockphoto. 240 (top left), Peter Phipp/age fotostock. 240 (top center), Borut Trdina/iStockphoto. 240 (top right), Loren Irving/age fotostock. 240 (bottom), Carson Ganci/age fotostock. 241 (top left), Angelo Cavalli/age fotostock. 241 (top center), Cornelia Doerr/age fotostock. 241 (top right), Bruno Morandi/age fotostock. **Chapter 5: Florence:** 265, alysta/ Shutterstock. 266, Ronald Sumners/Shutterstock. 267, Bertrand Collet/Shutterstock. 268, CuboImag-es srl/Alamy. 269 (top), Paolo Gallo/ Alamy. 269 (bottom), Sue Wilson/Alamy. 270, Luboslav Tiles/ Shutterstock. 278-79, Wojtek Buss/age fotostock. 280 (all), Public domain. 281 (top), eye35.com/ Alamy. 281 (inset), Jessmine/Shutterstock. 281 (bottom), Rough Guides/Alamy. 282 (top left), Mary Evans Picture Library/Alamy. 282 (top right), Library of Congress Prints and Photographs Division (LC-USZ62-10534). 282 (bottom), Bruno Morandi/age fotostock. 299 (left and right), Classic Vision/ age fotostock. 299 (center), SuperStock/age fotostock. 300 (left), Chie Ushio. 300 (right), Planet Art. 301 (top), Classic Vision/age fotostock. 301 (center), SuperStock/age fotostock. 301 (bottom left), Paola Ghirotti/Fototeca ENIT. 301 (bottom right), Corbis. 302 (left), Fototeca ENIT. 302 (center), SuperStock/age fotostock. 302 (right), Bruno Morandi/age fotostock. 303 (left), SuperStock/age fotostock. 303 (center), Art Collection 2 / Alamy. 303 (right), PTE/age fotostock. 304 (all), Planet Art. **Chapter 6: Tuscany and Umbria:** 331, Atlantide S.N.C./age fotostock. 333, Danilo Donadon/age fotostock. 334, Bon Appetit/Alamy. 335 (top), Marco Scataglini/age fotostock. 335 (bottom), Nico Tondini/age fotostock. 336, B&Y Photography/Alamy. 337 (top), 5 second Studio / Shutterstock. 337 (bottom), Doco Dalfi ano/age fotostock. 338, Ale_s/Shutterstock. 353 (left), Black Rooster Consor-tium. 353 (top right), Cephas Picture Library/Alamy. 353 (center right), Juergen Richter / age fotos-tock. 353 (bottom right), Cephas Picture Library/Alamy. 354, Cephas Picture Library/Alamy. 355 (top left), Chuck Pefley/Alamy. 355 (top right), Jon Arnold Images/Alamy. 356 (top left), CuboImages srl/ Alamy. 356 (middle right), Cephas Picture Library/Alamy. 356 (bottom), Black Rooster Consortium. 358 (left), Steve Dunwell/age fotostock. 358 (top right), IML Image Group Ltd/Alamy. 358 (bottom right), www.stradavinonobile.it. 372, Javier Larrea/age fotostock. 372 (inset), Photodisc. 374 (top and center), M Rohana/Shuterstock. 374 (bottom), Bruno Morandi/ age fotostock. Back cover, from left to right: vichie81/Shutterstock; javarman / Shutterstock; Andre Goncalves / Shutterstock. Spine: carolgaranda/Shutterstock. About Our Writers: All photos are courtesy of the writers except for the following: Nicole Arriaga, courtesy of Danielle Arriaga; Sofia Celeste, courtesy of Andrea Conzatti.

NOTES

NOTES

NOTES

NOTES

NOTES

ABOUT OUR WRITERS

Writer Ariston Anderson contributed to the Rome chapter.

After her first Italian coffee and her first Italian *bacio* in 1999, Nicole Arriaga just knew she'd have to find a way to make it back to Rome, and she moved to the Eternal City in 2003 to earn her master's in political science. Nicole's freelance work has appeared in various travel publications, including *Romeing, 10Best,* Eurocheapo, and *The American.* When not writing, Nicole works as a programs coordinator for an American Study Abroad organization based in Rome. She contributed to the Rome chapter this edition.

After completing his master's degree in art history, Peter Blackman settled permanently in Italy in 1986. Since then he's worked as a biking and walking tour guide, managing to see more of Italy than most of his Italian friends. When he's not leading a trip, you'll find Peter at home in Chianti, listening to opera and planning his next journey. He contributed to the Tuscany and Umbria chapter this edition.

Writer Agnes Crawford contributed to the Rome chapter.

Liz Humphreys is a recent transplant to Europe from New York City, where she spent a decade in editorial positions for media companies including Condé Nast, Time Inc., and *USA Today.* She has worked on several guidebooks for Fodor's, including Amsterdam, Germany, and Portugal, and currently writes and edits for ⊕ *Fodors.com* and *Forbes Travel Guide* on locales across Europe. Liz has an advanced certificate in wine studies from the WSET (Wine & Spirit Education Trust), and Italy is a favorite destination to indulge her obsessions

with food and wine, which she also chronicles on her blog, (⊕ *www.winderlust.com*). She updated the Milan section.

Specializing in the Neapolitan art of *arrangiarsi* (getting by), updater Fergal Kavanagh has dabbled in teacher training, DJ-ing, writing guidebooks, translating, and organizing cultural exchanges. He currently teaches at the University of Naples and through his website (⊕ *www.tuneintoenglish.com*) demonstrates how pop music can help students learn English. He updated the Travel Smart chapter.

Bruce Leimsidor studied Renaissance literature and art history at Swarthmore College and Princeton University, and in addition to his scholarly works, he has published articles on political and social issues in the *International Herald Tribune* and the *Frankfurter Allgemeine Zeitung.* He lives in Venice, where he teaches at the university, collects 17th- and 18th-century drawings, and is rumored to make the best *pasta e fagioli* in town. He updated the Venice chapter and contributed to the Northern Italy chapter.

After a dozen trips to and a two-decade love affair with Liguria, Cinque Terre updater Megan McCaffrey-Guerrera moved to the seaside village of Lerici in 2004. Soon after, she started a personal travel concierge service. When not organizing tailor-made vacations of the area, Megan can be found hiking the trails of the Cinque Terre, sailing the Gulf of Poets, or searching for the freshest anchovies in the Mediterranean.

Writer Maria Pasquale contributed to the Rome chapter.

Florence resident Patricia Rucidlo holds master's degrees in Italian Renaissance history and art history. When she's not extolling the virtues of a Pontormo masterpiece or angrily defending the Medici, she's leading wine tours in Chianti and catering private dinner parties. For this edition she updated the Experience Italy chapter and Emilia-Romagna section, and contributed to the Tuscany and Umbria chapter.